I0824254

THE ART OF

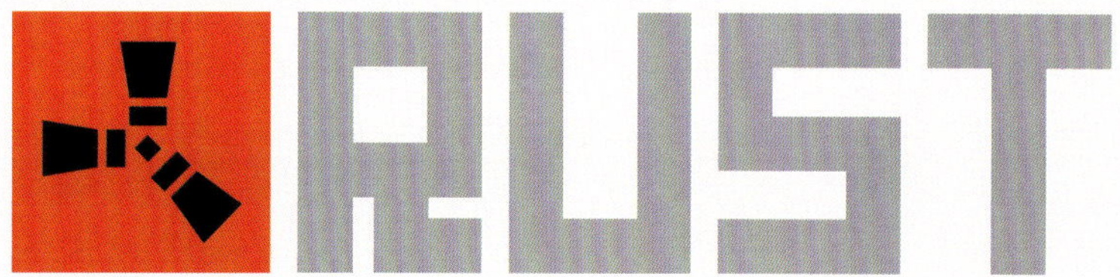

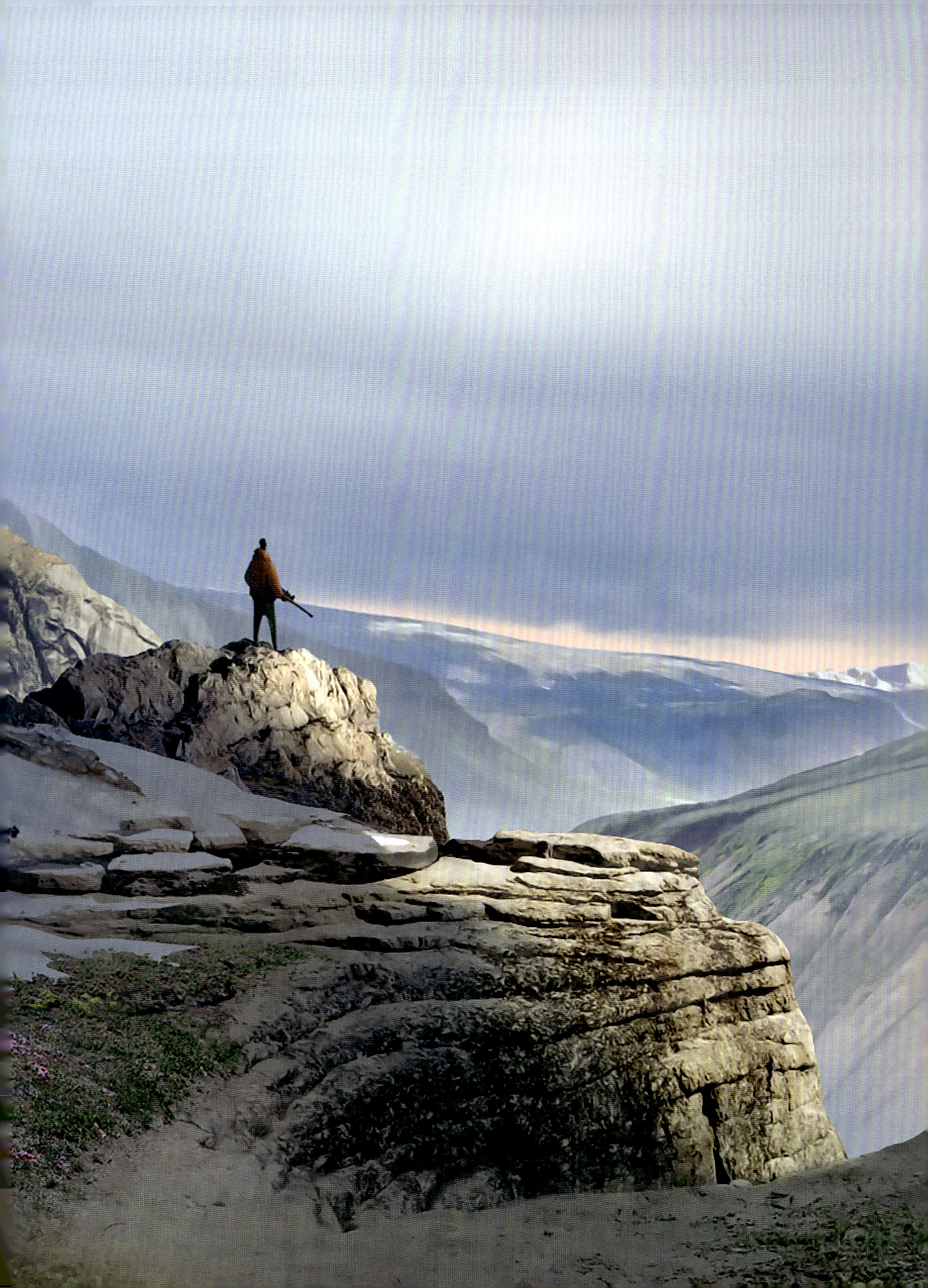

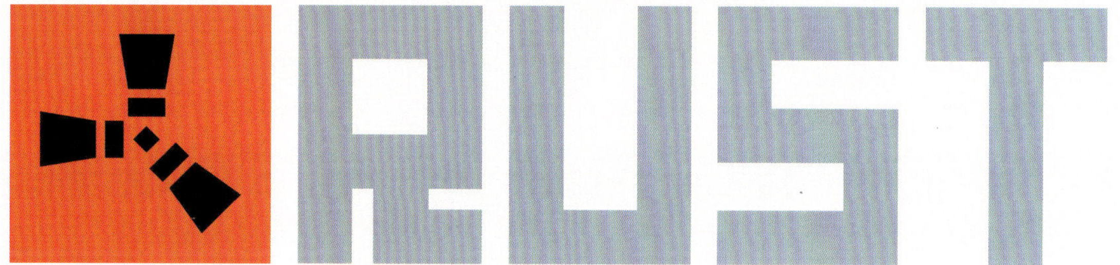
THE ART OF
RUST

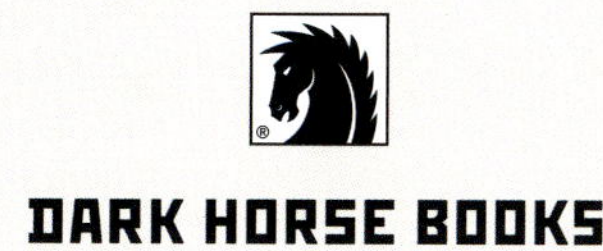
DARK HORSE BOOKS

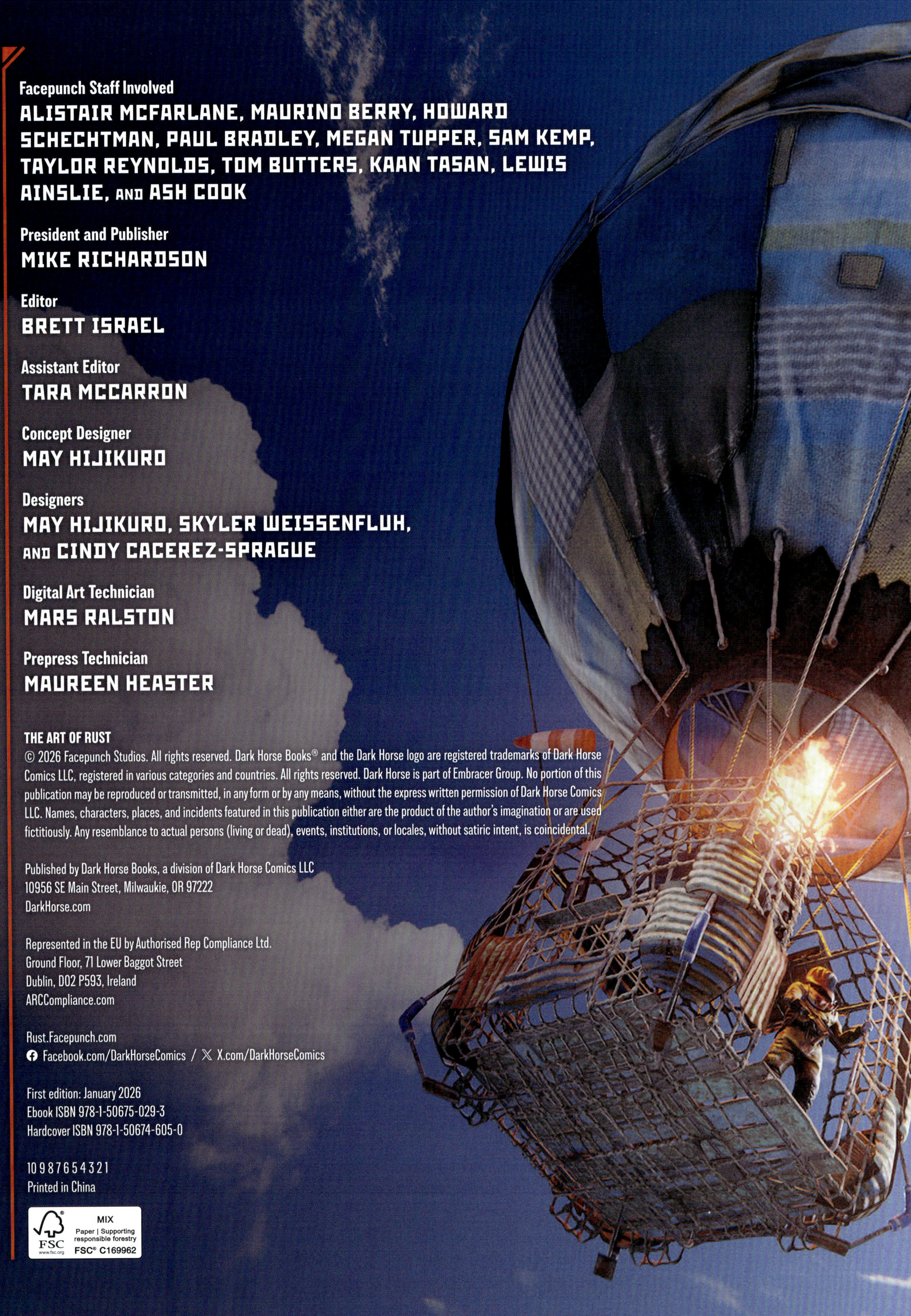

Facepunch Staff Involved
ALISTAIR MCFARLANE, MAURINO BERRY, HOWARD SCHECHTMAN, PAUL BRADLEY, MEGAN TUPPER, SAM KEMP, TAYLOR REYNOLDS, TOM BUTTERS, KAAN TASAN, LEWIS AINSLIE, AND ASH COOK

President and Publisher
MIKE RICHARDSON

Editor
BRETT ISRAEL

Assistant Editor
TARA MCCARRON

Concept Designer
MAY HIJIKURO

Designers
MAY HIJIKURO, SKYLER WEISSENFLUH, AND CINDY CACEREZ-SPRAGUE

Digital Art Technician
MARS RALSTON

Prepress Technician
MAUREEN HEASTER

THE ART OF RUST
© 2026 Facepunch Studios. All rights reserved. Dark Horse Books® and the Dark Horse logo are registered trademarks of Dark Horse Comics LLC, registered in various categories and countries. All rights reserved. Dark Horse is part of Embracer Group. No portion of this publication may be reproduced or transmitted, in any form or by any means, without the express written permission of Dark Horse Comics LLC. Names, characters, places, and incidents featured in this publication either are the product of the author's imagination or are used fictitiously. Any resemblance to actual persons (living or dead), events, institutions, or locales, without satiric intent, is coincidental.

Published by Dark Horse Books, a division of Dark Horse Comics LLC
10956 SE Main Street, Milwaukie, OR 97222
DarkHorse.com

Represented in the EU by Authorised Rep Compliance Ltd.
Ground Floor, 71 Lower Baggot Street
Dublin, D02 P593, Ireland
ARCCompliance.com

Rust.Facepunch.com
Facebook.com/DarkHorseComics / X.com/DarkHorseComics

First edition: January 2026
Ebook ISBN 978-1-50675-029-3
Hardcover ISBN 978-1-50674-605-0

10 9 8 7 6 5 4 3 2 1
Printed in China

MIX
Paper | Supporting responsible forestry
FSC® C169962
FSC www.fsc.org

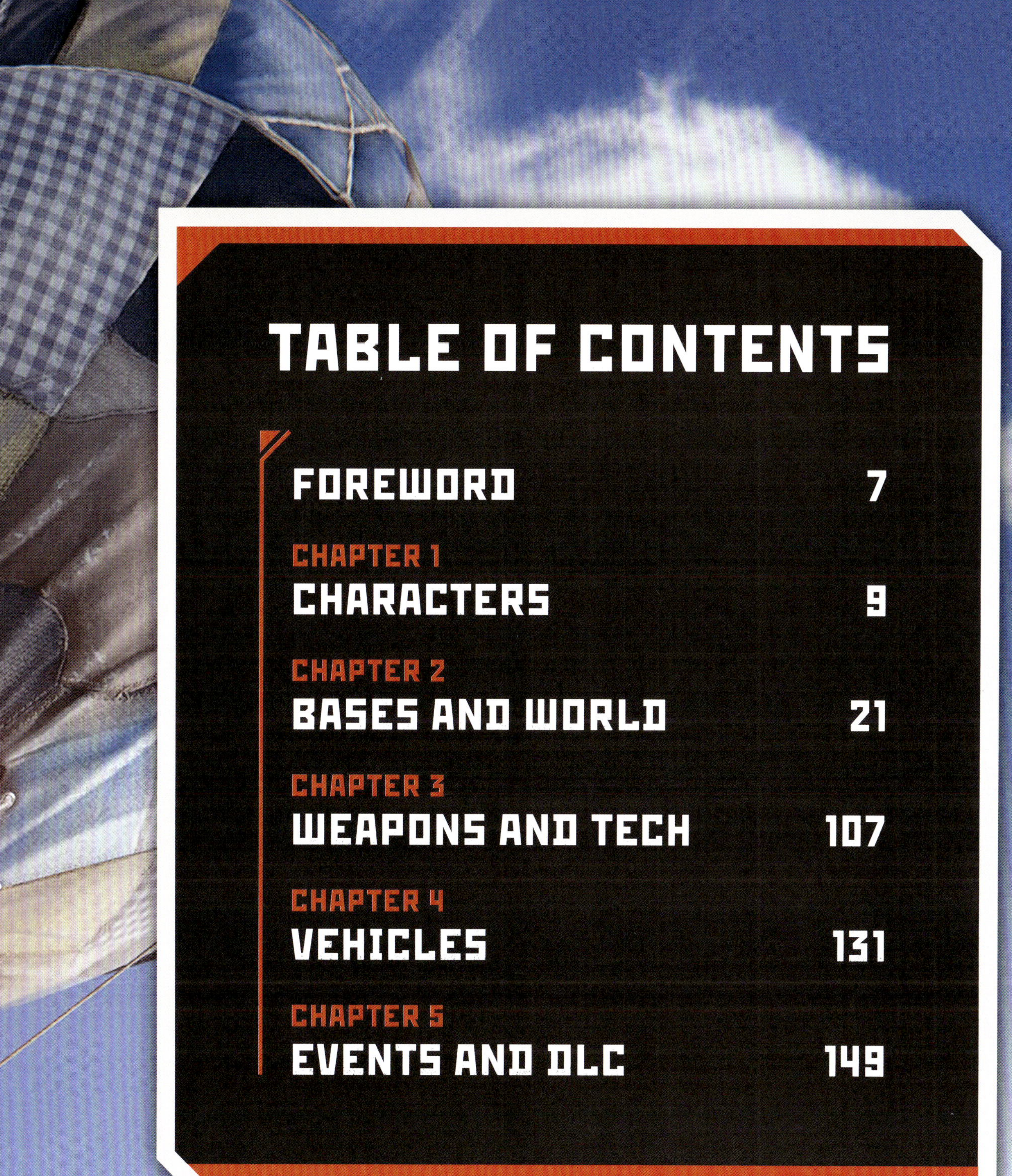

TABLE OF CONTENTS

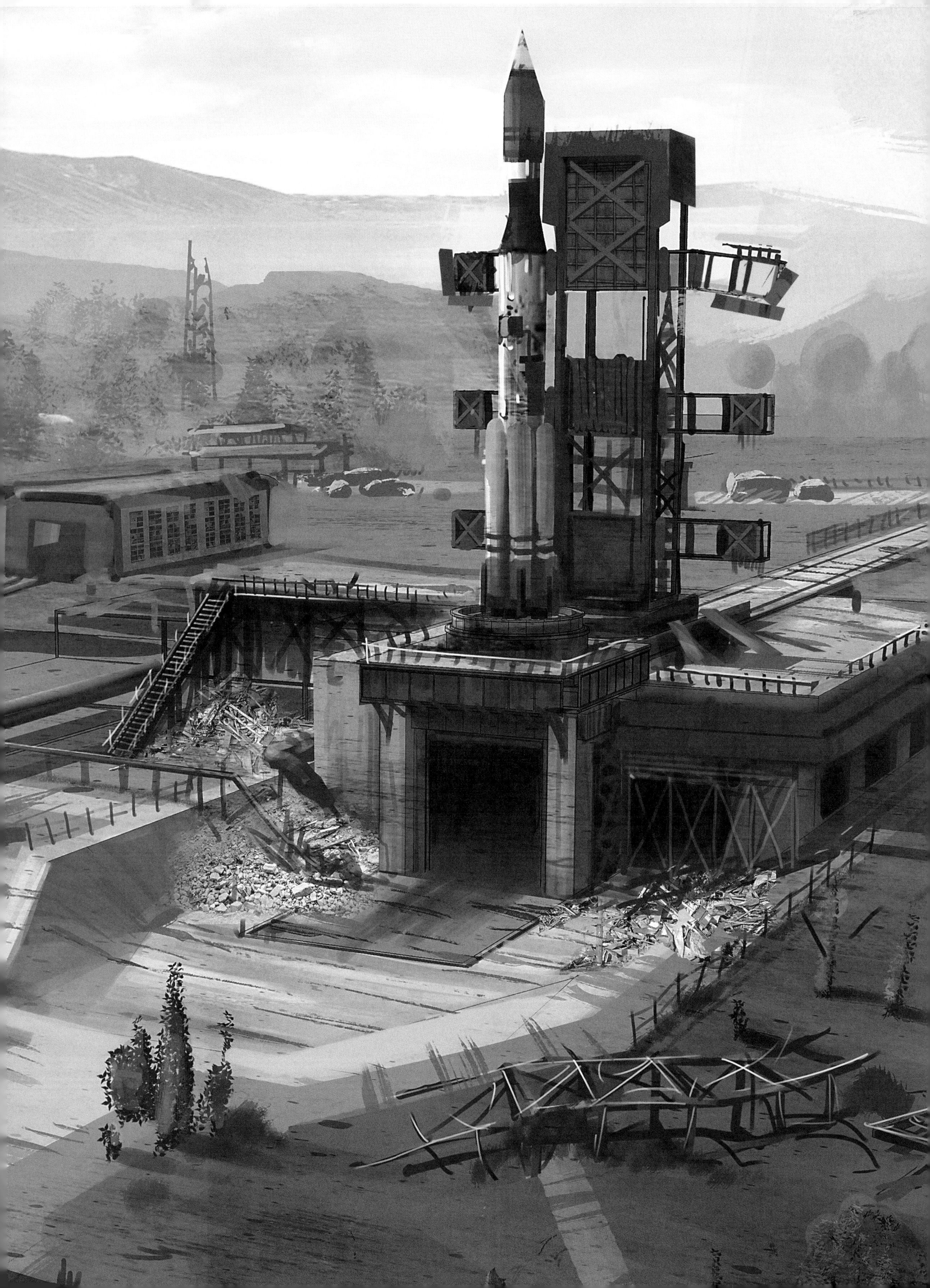

FOREWORD
BY MAURINO BERRY

The visual evolution of *Rust* is a testament to the game's journey from a janky prototype to one of the most defining survival games of the modern era. What started as a raw, experimental game has grown into a visually striking world that balances realism with a distinct handcrafted aesthetic.

Rust's art has always been shaped by necessity, innovation, and the unique demands of its survival-driven gameplay. In its earliest days, the game's look was crude, functional, and deliberately rough around the edges, a reflection of both its indie origins and the brutal, unfiltered nature of the world it had created. The environments were sparse, the character models simple. The game wasn't trying to be pretty—it was trying to be raw, immersive, and ruthless.

Over the years, as *Rust* gained momentum, the team at Facepunch continued refining its vision, resulting in the game's art style finding its identity. It evolved into something that wasn't just technically impressive but also deeply atmospheric. The introduction of procedural terrain generation, improved lighting, and reworked environmental assets turned the game world into something more believable and immersive. *Rust*'s landscapes became more than just a backdrop; they became an integral part of the player's journey, influencing strategy, movement, and ultimately survival.

Character and NPC design followed a similar route. The addition of detailed models, advanced clothing physics, and improved animations gave players a stronger sense of identity and presence.

The introduction of the Scientist NPCs brought an entirely new layer to the game. Their dystopian, militaristic look contrasted sharply with the scavenger-like player characters. Their design, inspired by HAZMAT suits and tactical gear, helped shape *Rust*'s evolving lore without ever needing explicit storytelling.

The game's art direction has always walked a fine line between realism and fiction. While *Rust* embraces a gritty, grounded aesthetic, it never veers into hyperrealism. The textures are worn, the materials feel tangible, but there's always a sense of handcrafted design.

Beyond environments and characters, *Rust*'s artistic identity is also reflected in its items, weapons, and base building elements. The makeshift aesthetic of crafted weapons, the Brutalist charm of player-made bases, and the scavenged look of armor sets all reinforce the game's themes of survival and adaptation. Nothing in *Rust* looks too perfect or clean, because nothing in its world should.

Looking back at *Rust*'s evolution, it's impossible not to appreciate the journey its art has taken. What began as a rough utilitarian experiment has become a visually rich world, one that tells a story without needing words. The game's art has never been about achieving photorealism; it has always been about atmosphere, immersion, and reinforcing the raw, unforgiving nature of *Rust* itself.

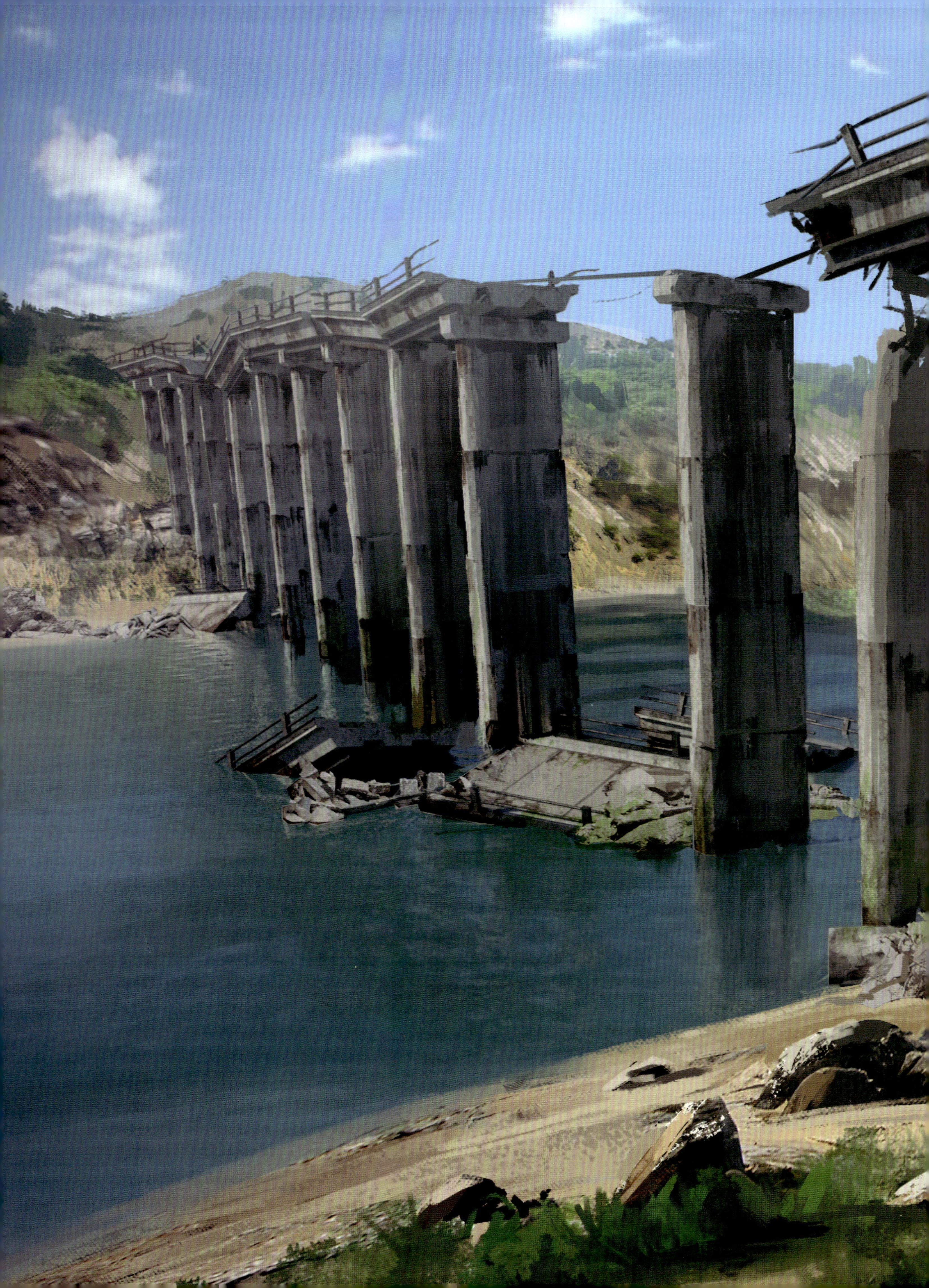

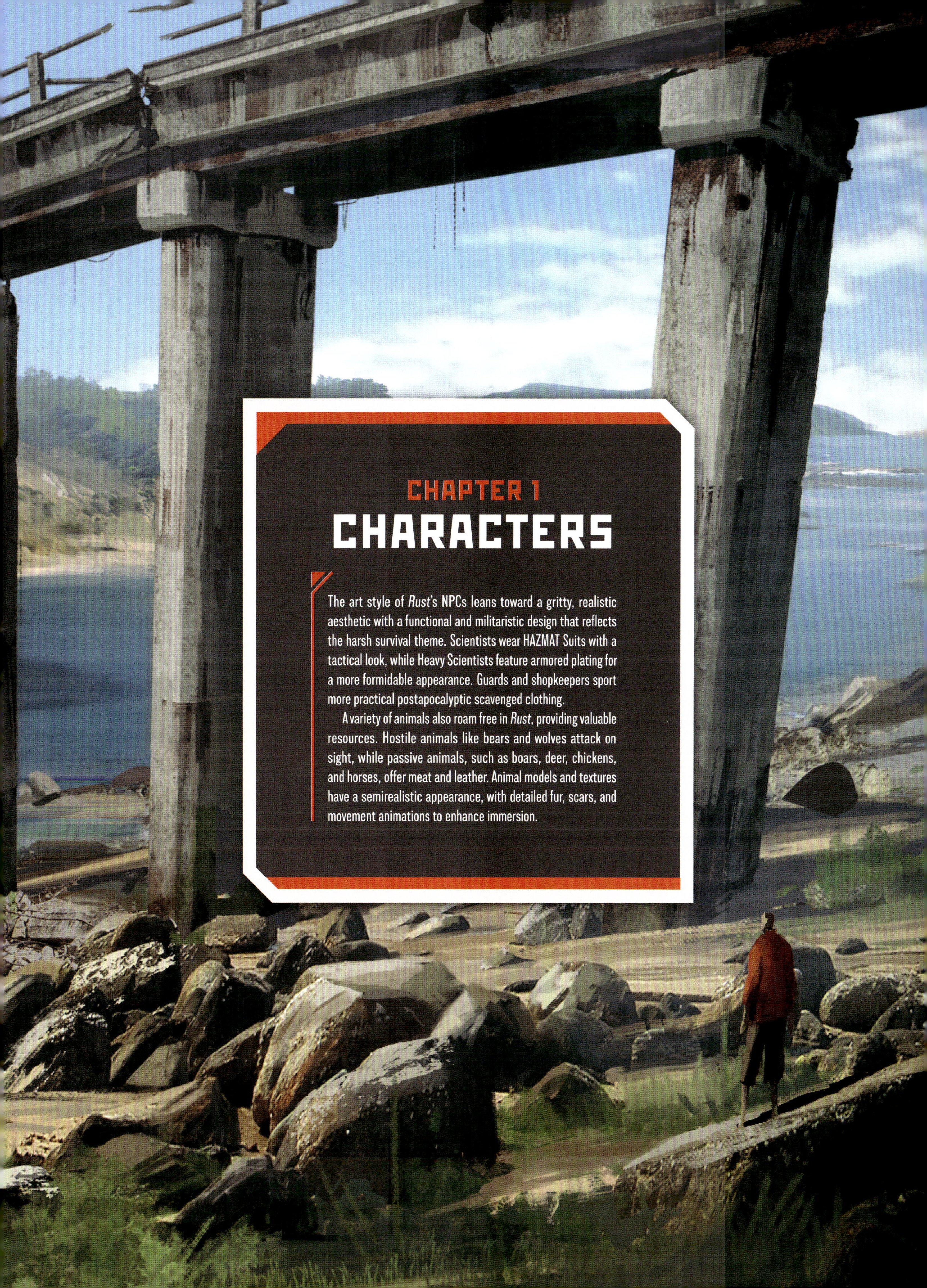

CHAPTER 1

CHARACTERS

The art style of *Rust*'s NPCs leans toward a gritty, realistic aesthetic with a functional and militaristic design that reflects the harsh survival theme. Scientists wear HAZMAT Suits with a tactical look, while Heavy Scientists feature armored plating for a more formidable appearance. Guards and shopkeepers sport more practical postapocalyptic scavenged clothing.

A variety of animals also roam free in *Rust*, providing valuable resources. Hostile animals like bears and wolves attack on sight, while passive animals, such as boars, deer, chickens, and horses, offer meat and leather. Animal models and textures have a semirealistic appearance, with detailed fur, scars, and movement animations to enhance immersion.

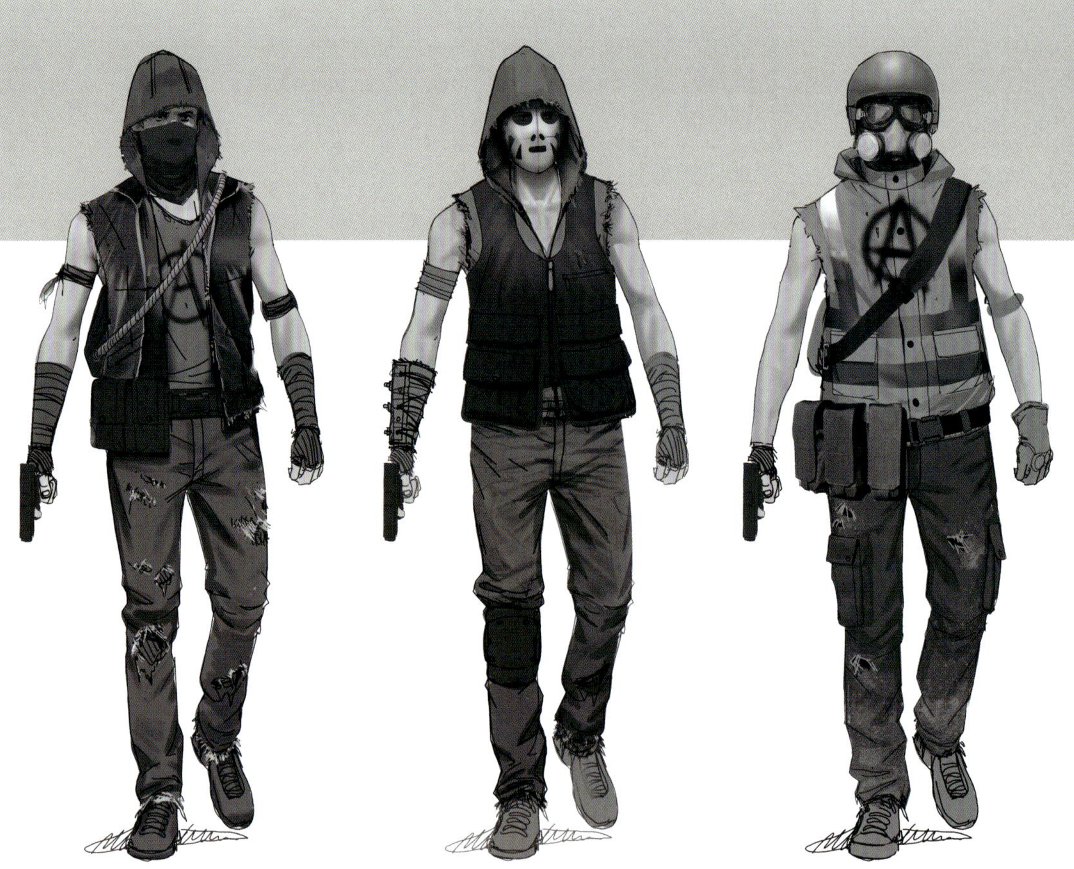

BANDITS

Bandits are NPCs that patrol and enforce the Bandit Camp. Early concept sketches kept their faces covered while experimenting with different ideas for their origins, such as militia groups, abandoned laborers, or black-market arms dealers using the island for business.

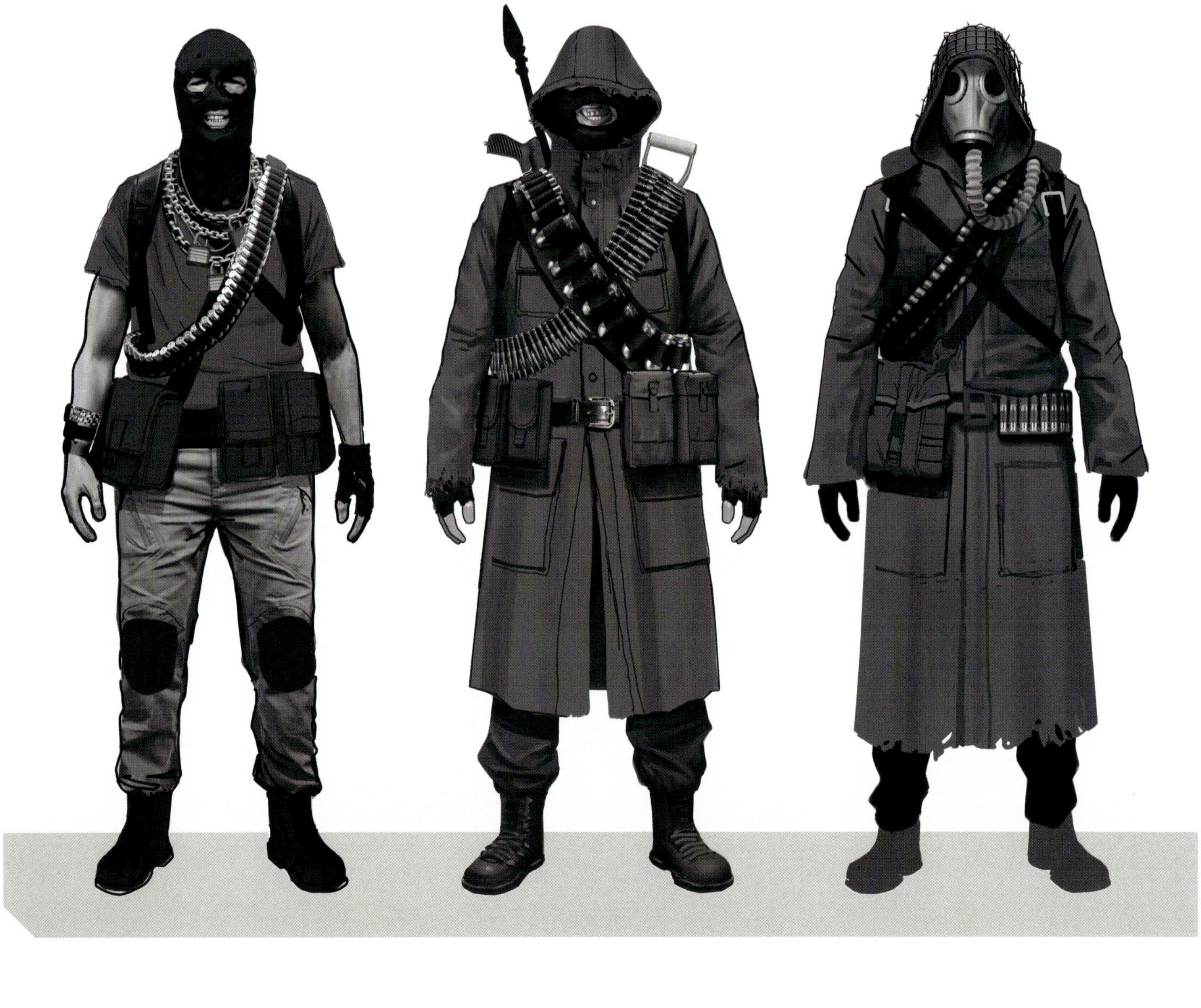

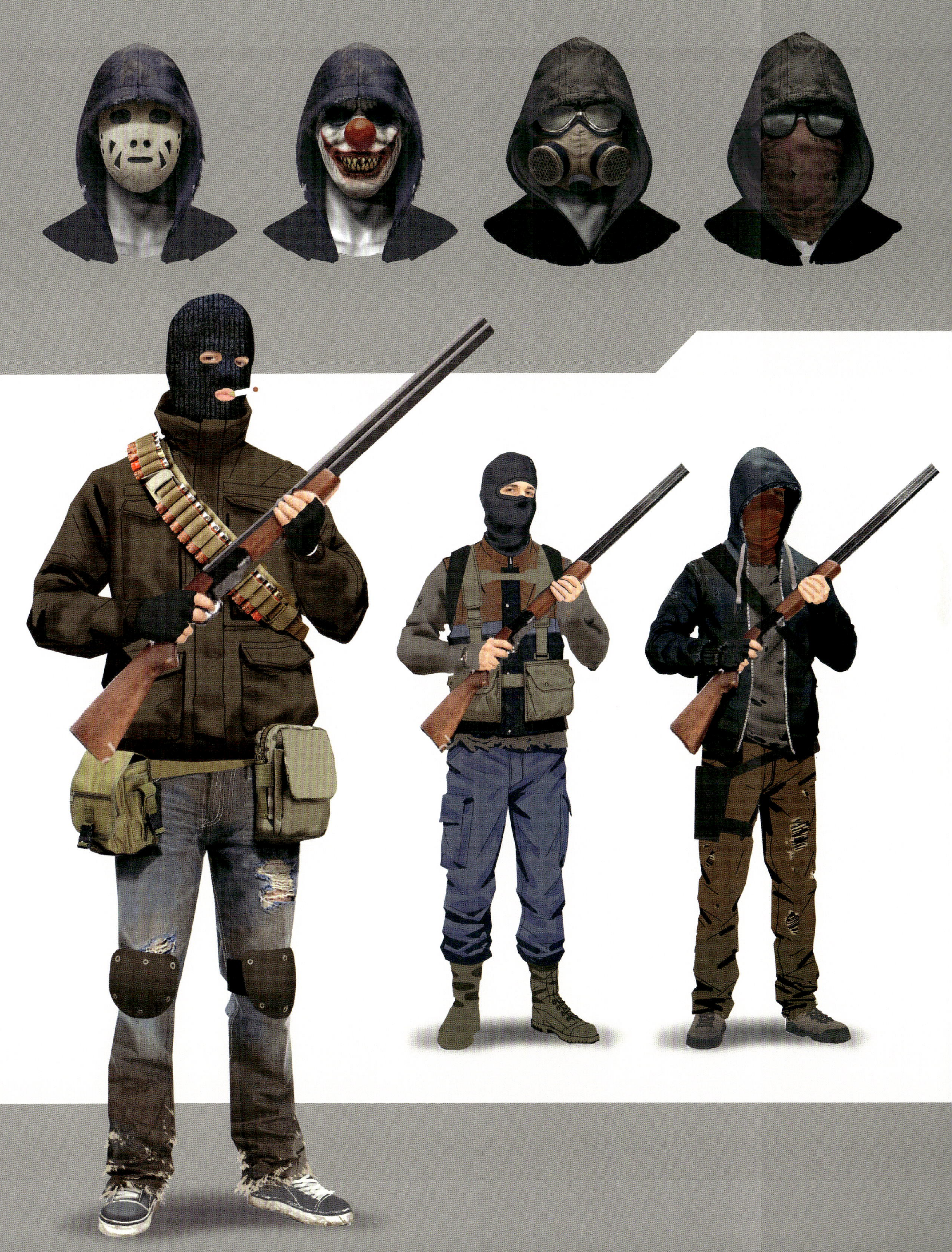

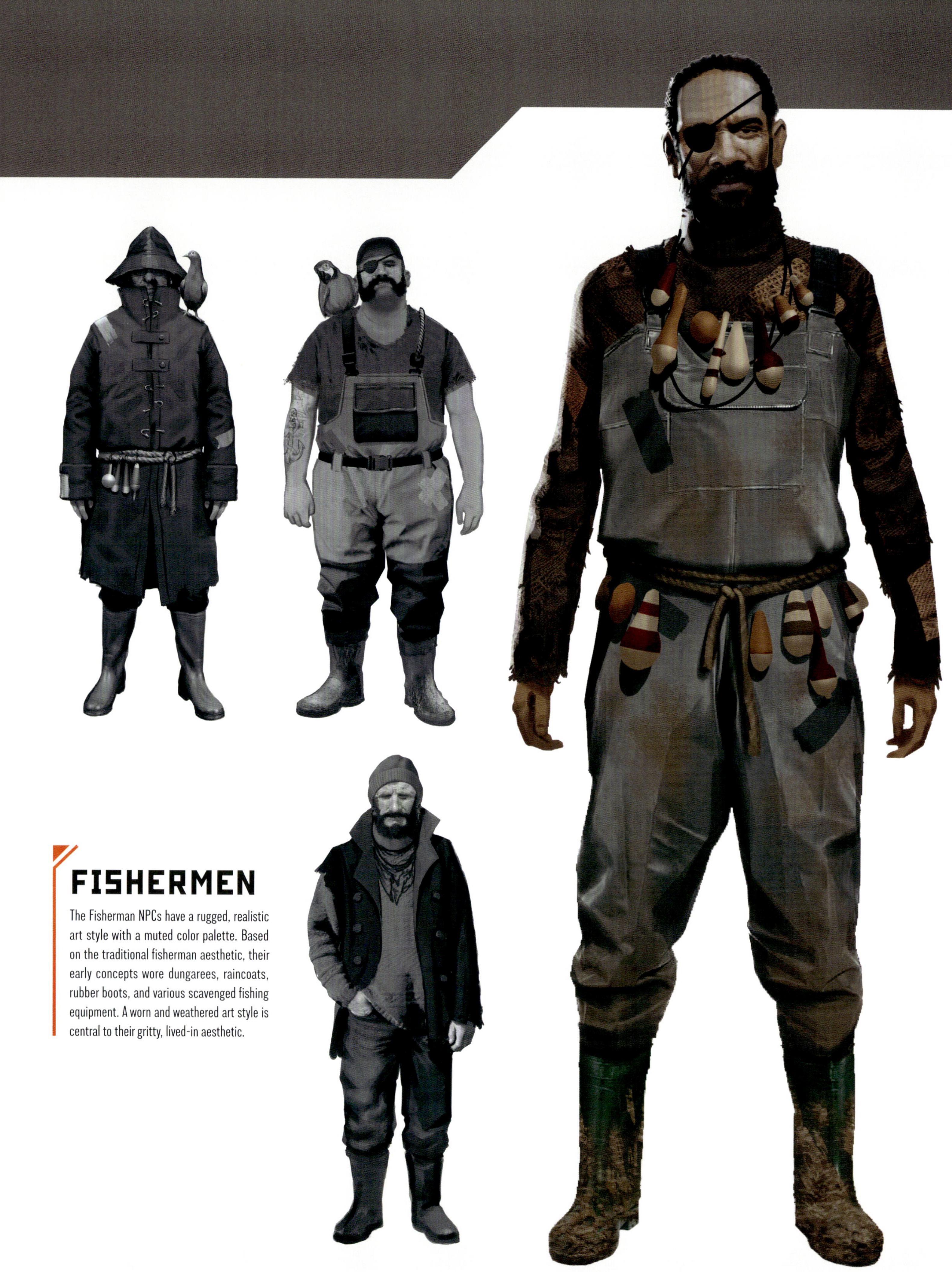

FISHERMEN

The Fisherman NPCs have a rugged, realistic art style with a muted color palette. Based on the traditional fisherman aesthetic, their early concepts wore dungarees, raincoats, rubber boots, and various scavenged fishing equipment. A worn and weathered art style is central to their gritty, lived-in aesthetic.

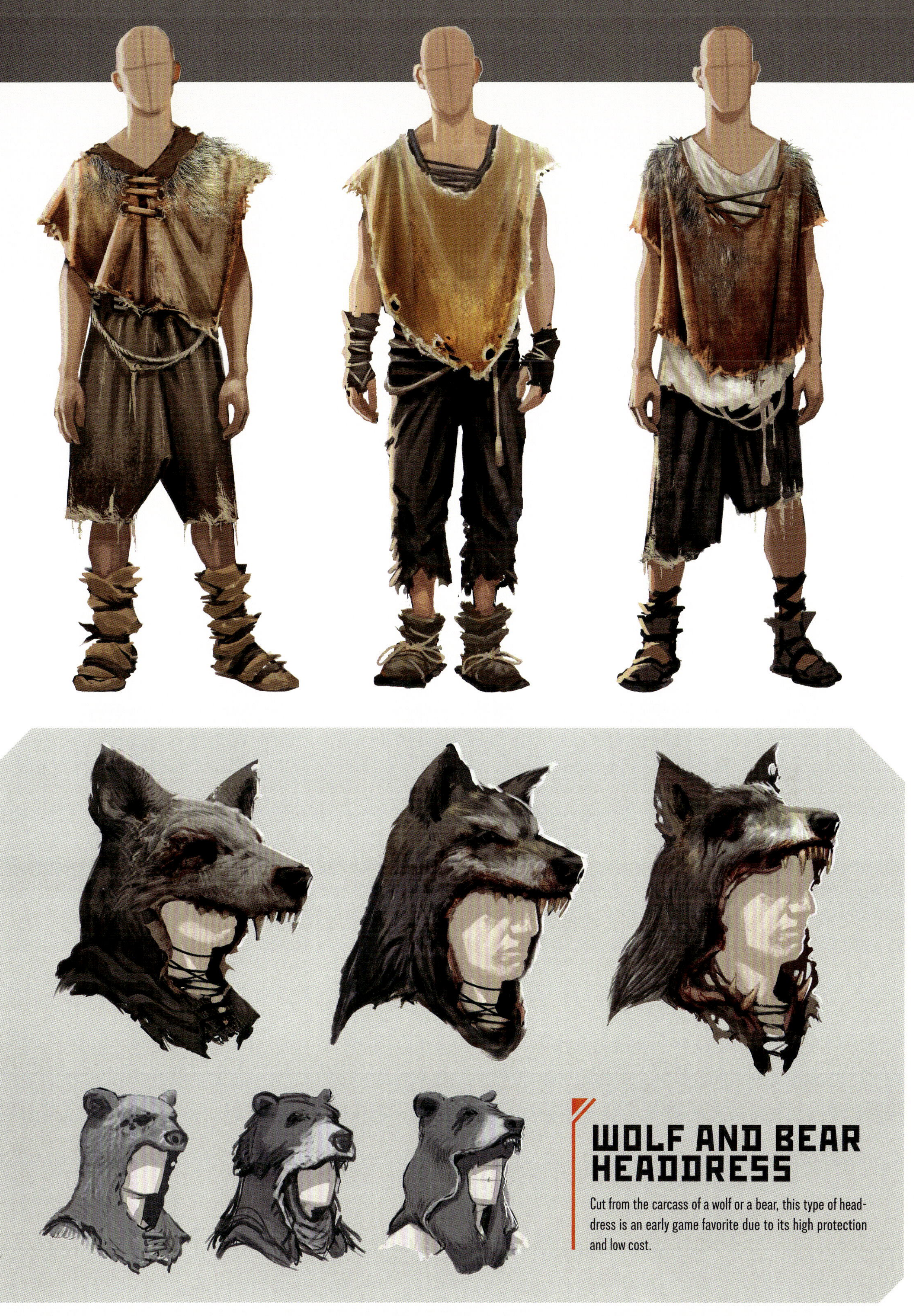

WOLF AND BEAR HEADDRESS

Cut from the carcass of a wolf or a bear, this type of headdress is an early game favorite due to its high protection and low cost.

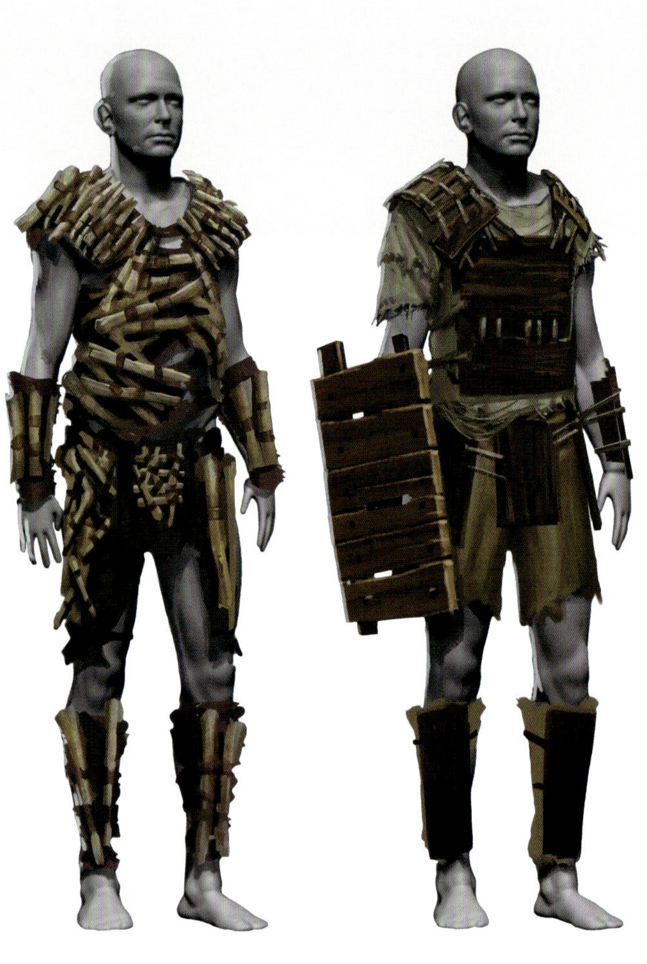

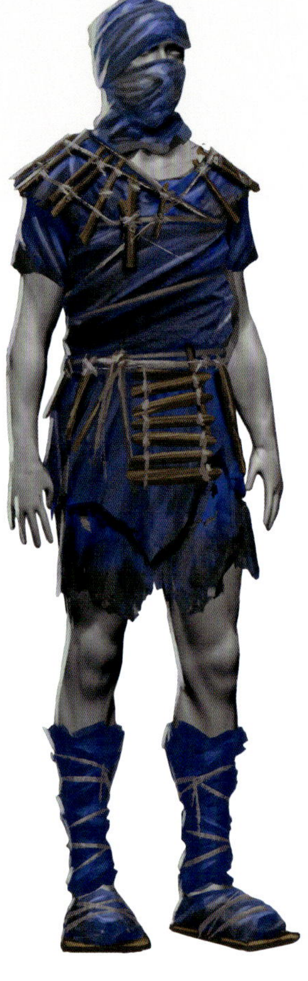

ARMOR EXPLORATION

Rust's armor follows a makeshift scavenged aesthetic depicted through rough, functional designs. Concept drawings emphasize this with worn textures and repurposed materials like bones, wood, scrap metal, and leather. The sketchy, semirealistic drawing style helps capture the game's brutal survival theme while balancing practicality, protection, and handcrafted ingenuity.

CRAFTED CLOTHING

The crafted clothing within *Rust* follows a primitive, minimalist, and almost crude art style. Early sketches show an anything-goes approach to using a variety of items to create clothing. Rough, textured lines, frayed edges, loose stitching, and coarse fabric create an almost medieval or caveman-like aesthetic.

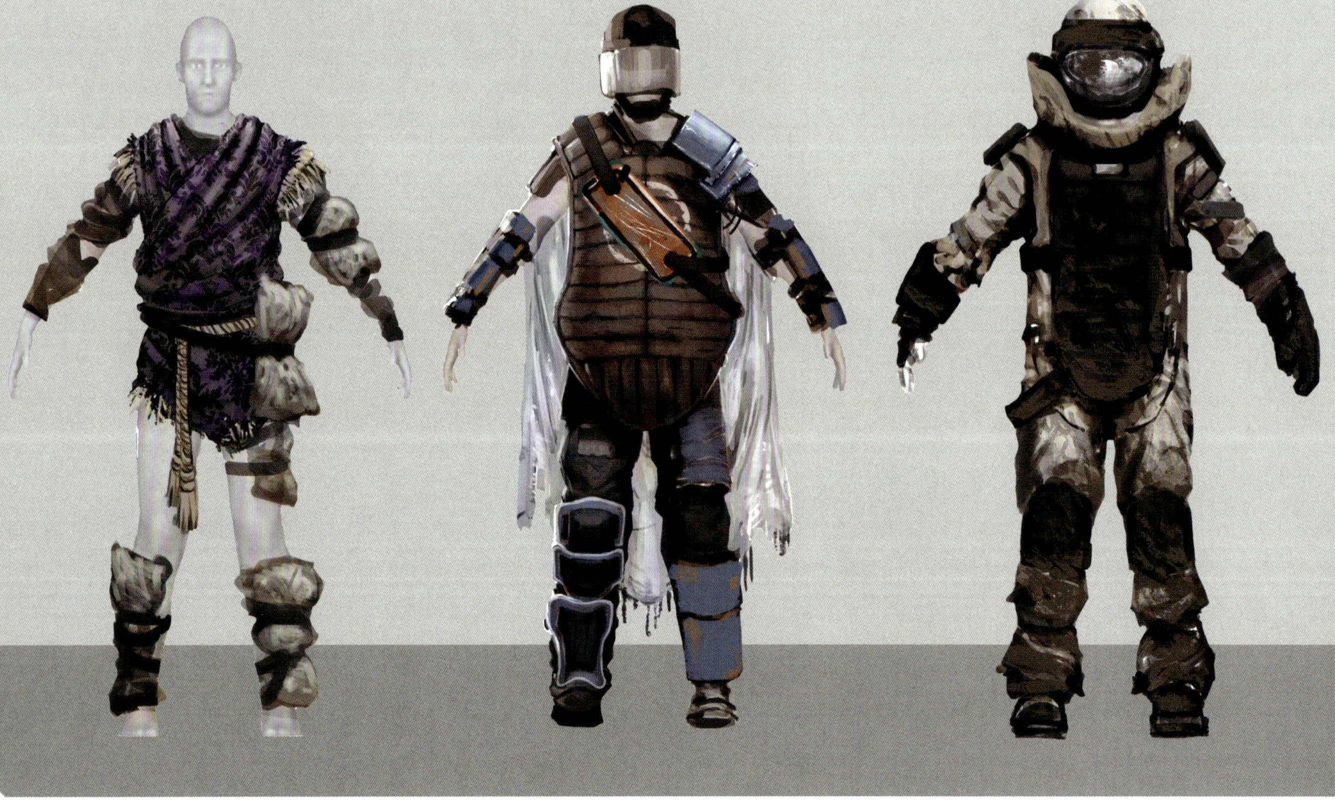

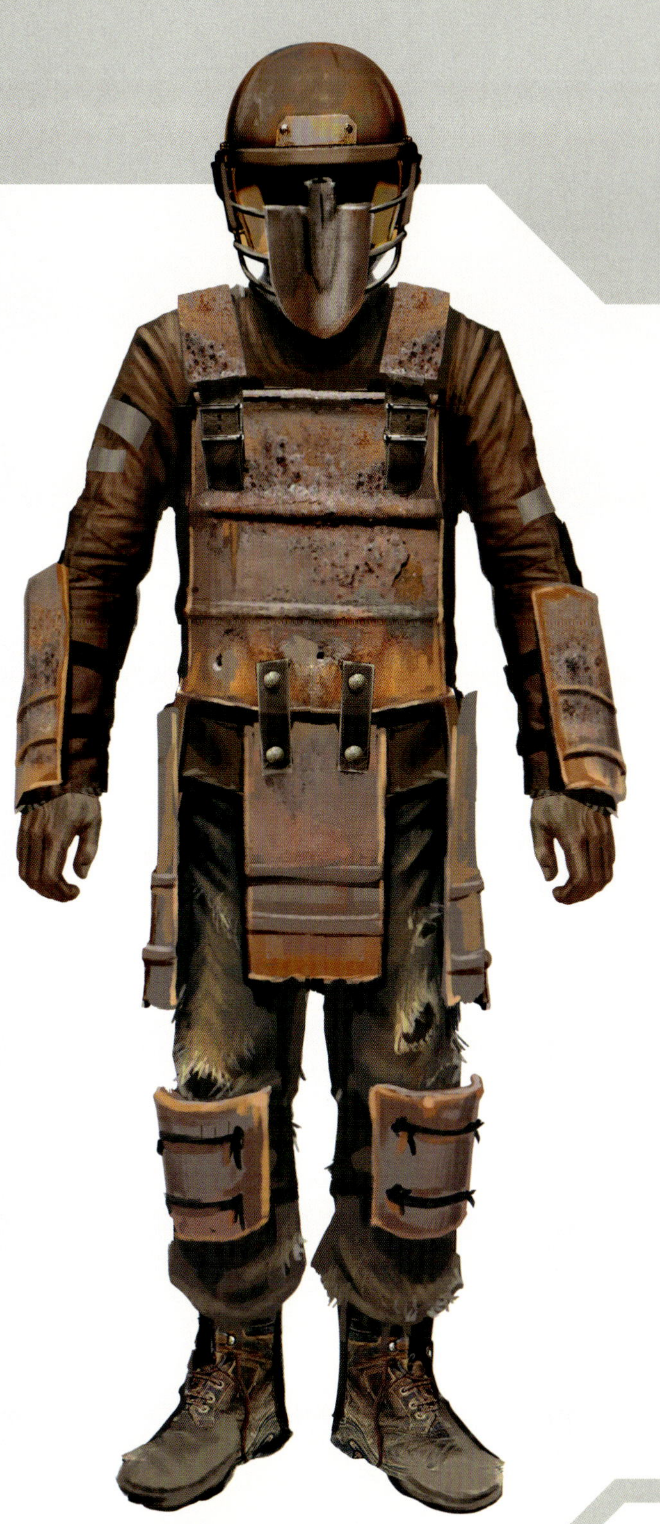

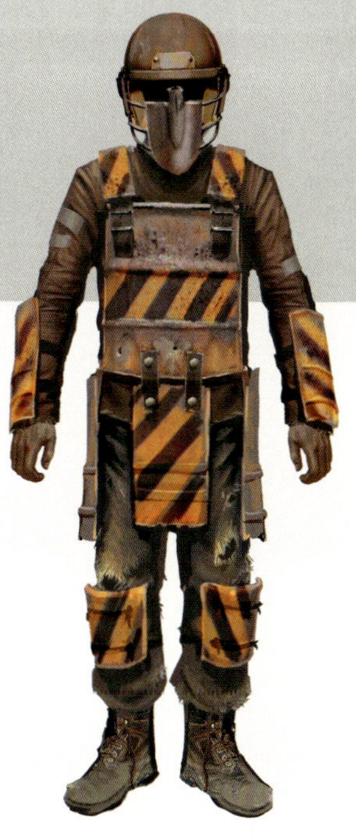

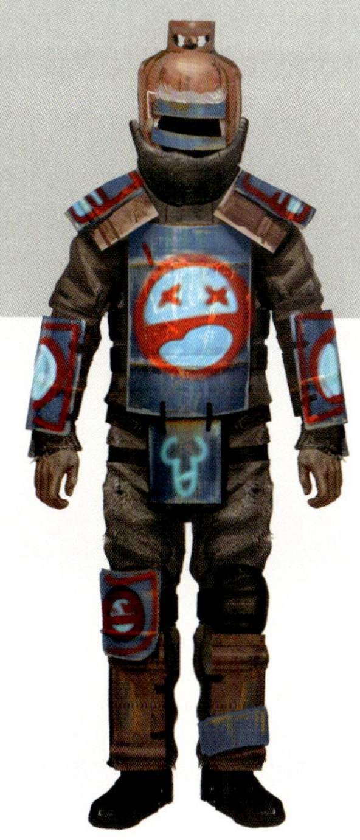

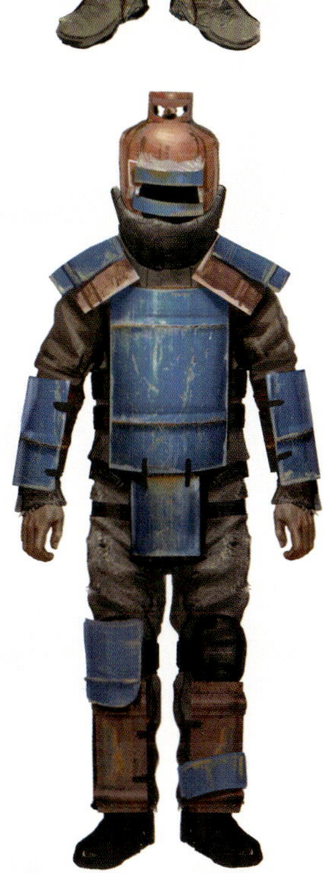

BARREL HEAVY ARMOR

Scavenged armor is integral to *Rust*. It follows a rough, improvised aesthetic, using repurposed materials like road signs, sheet metal, and bone. These concept sketches explored the idea of using Oil Barrels and Gas Canisters, which are readily available throughout the game, as a type of heavy armor.

CLIMBING BOOTS

Although the climbing boot never made it into *Rust*, early concepts were based around a primitive crampon and boot. Here are some of those early sketches.

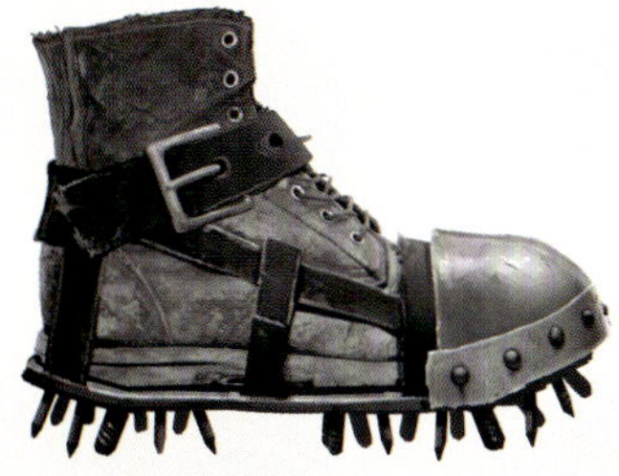

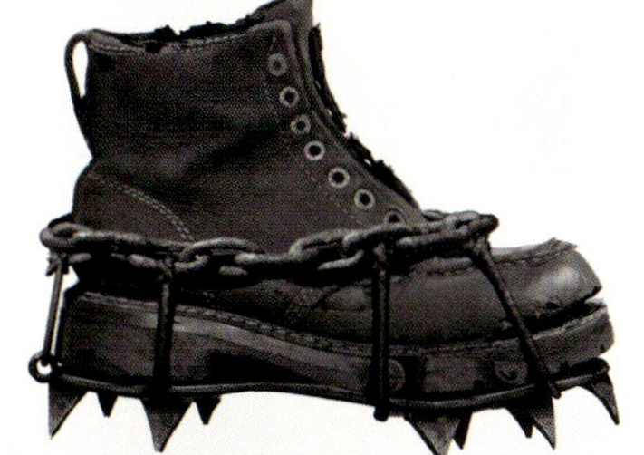

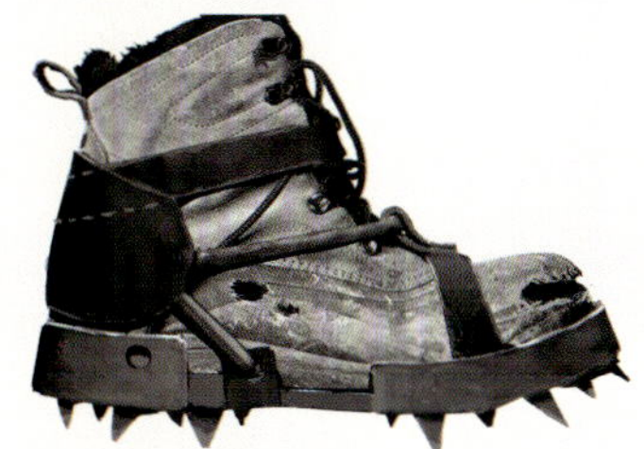

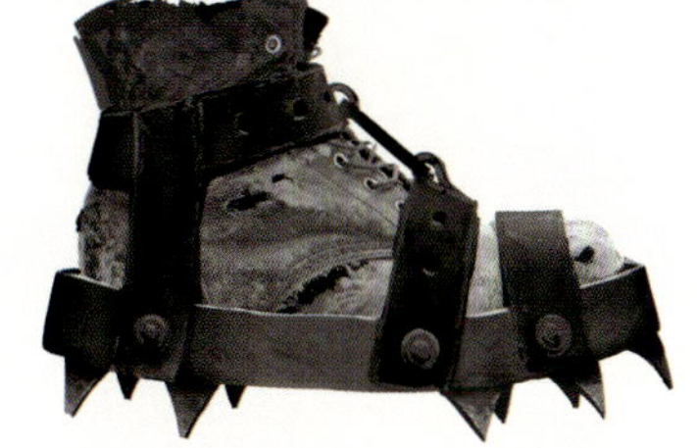

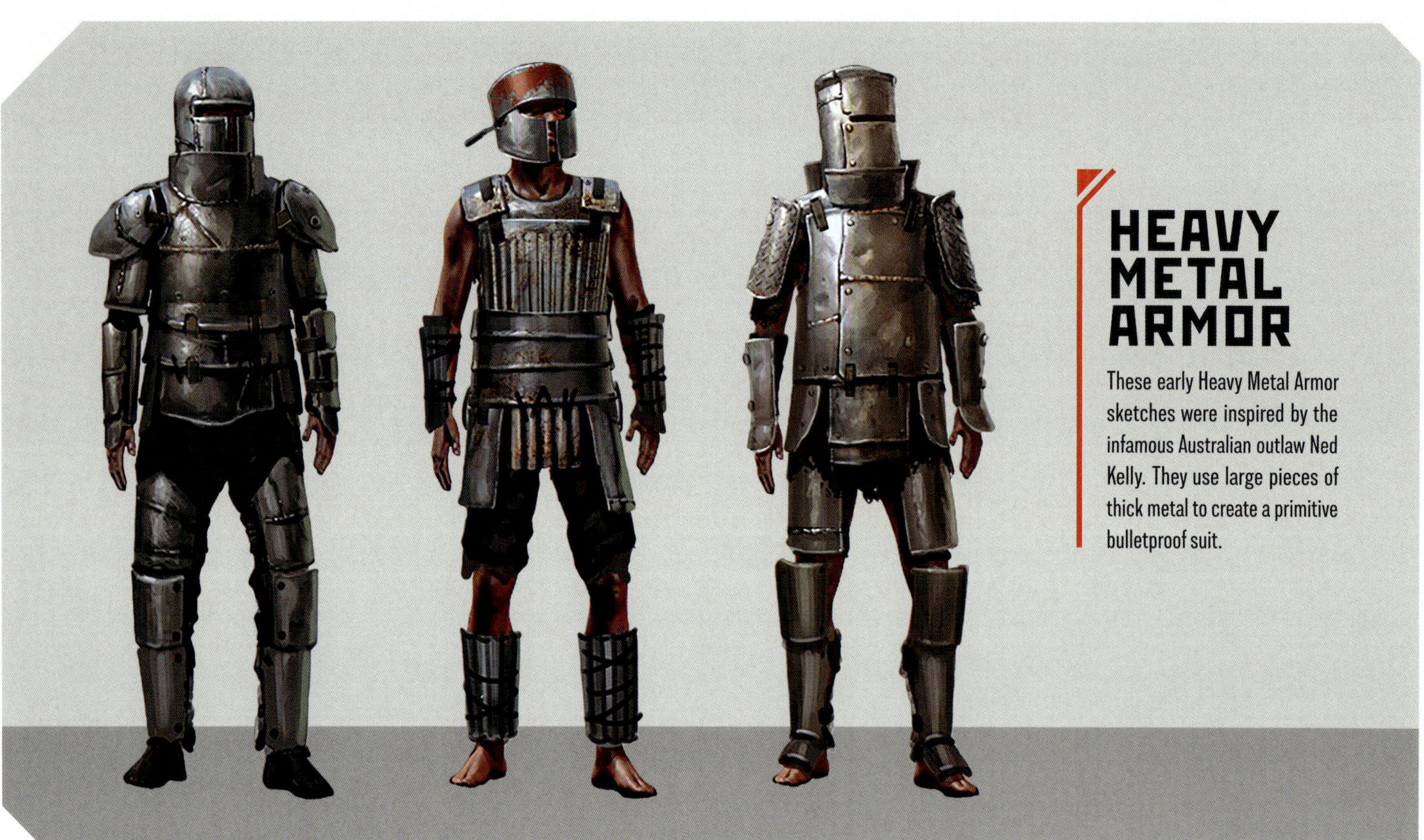

HEAVY METAL ARMOR

These early Heavy Metal Armor sketches were inspired by the infamous Australian outlaw Ned Kelly. They use large pieces of thick metal to create a primitive bulletproof suit.

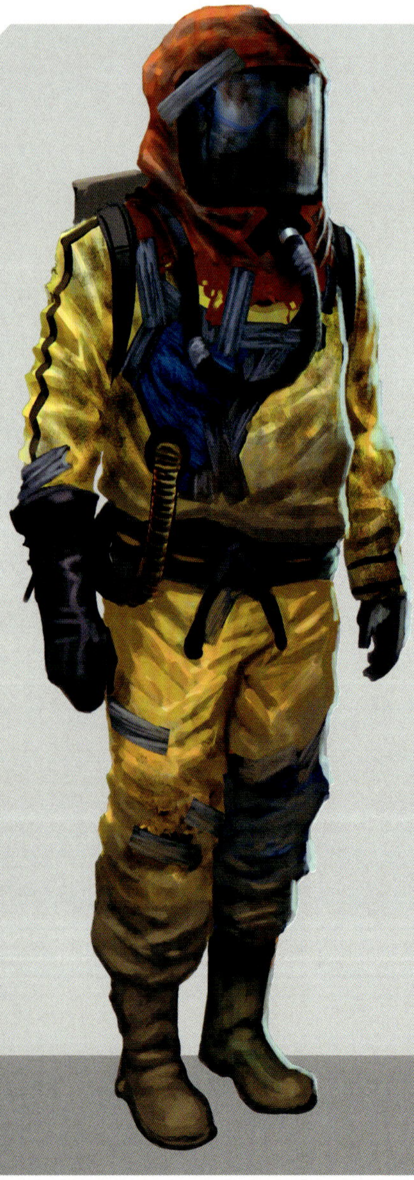

RAD SUITS

The iconic *Rust* HAZMAT Suit features a sleek synthetic and industrial design, grounded in *Rust*'s scavenged aesthetic. Here are some of the early variants of the concept drawings.

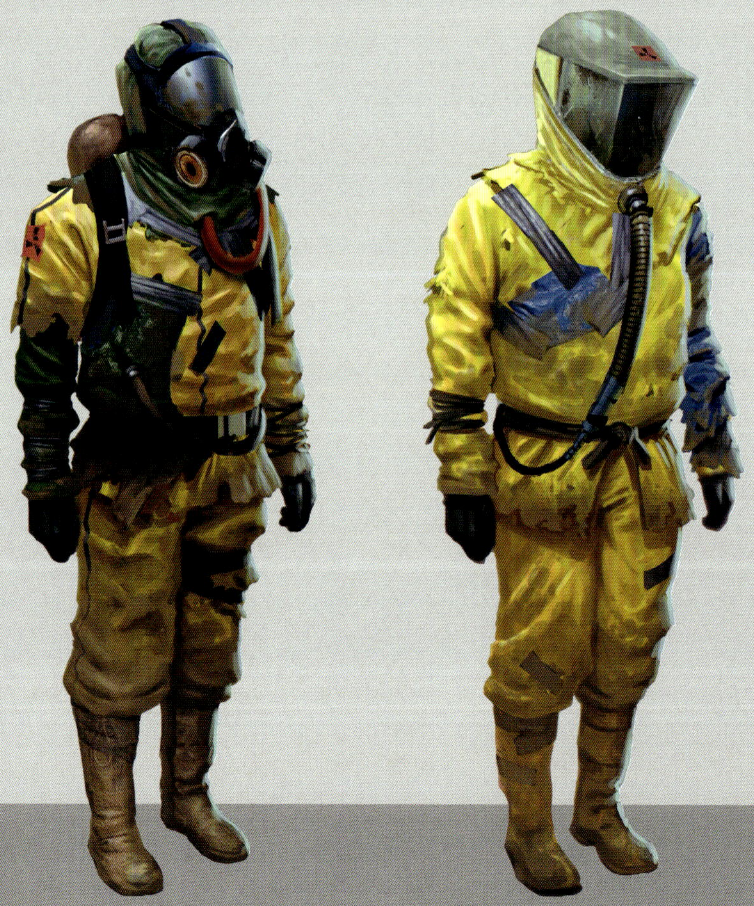

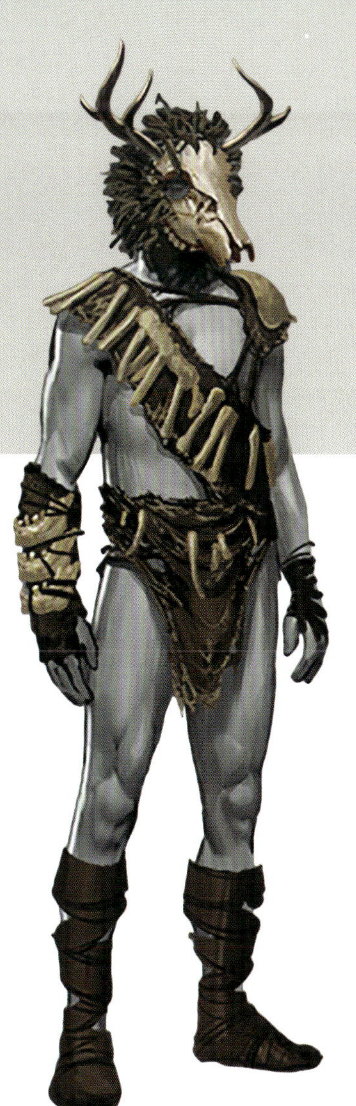
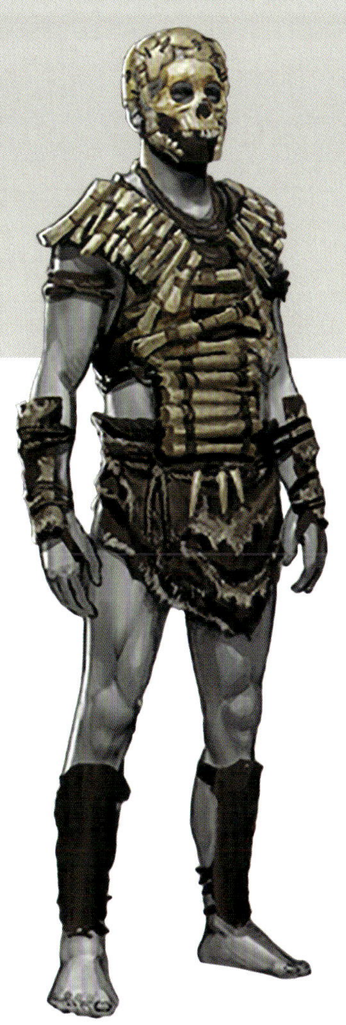
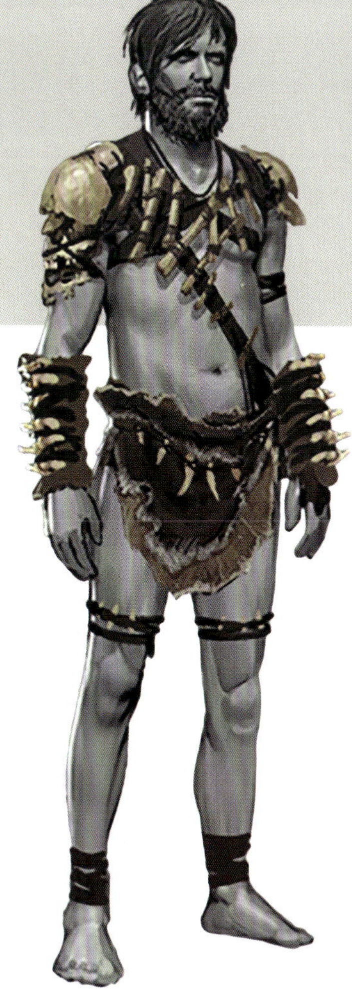

BONE ARMOR

Initial sketches of Bone Armor were inspired by Native American bone breastplates and pagan cultist headdresses. A primitive, raw survivalist look is crafted from bones, leather, and rope.

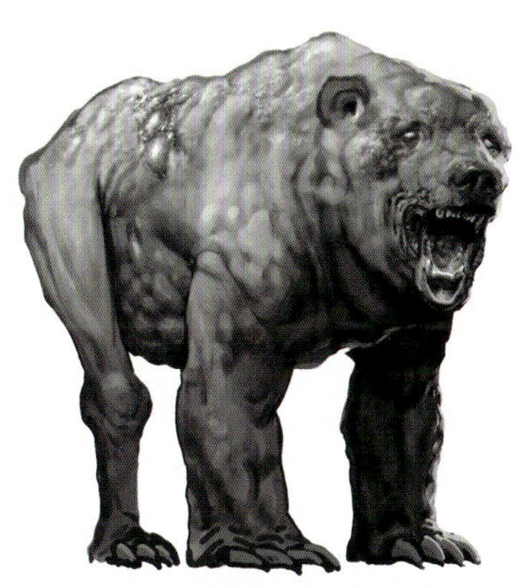
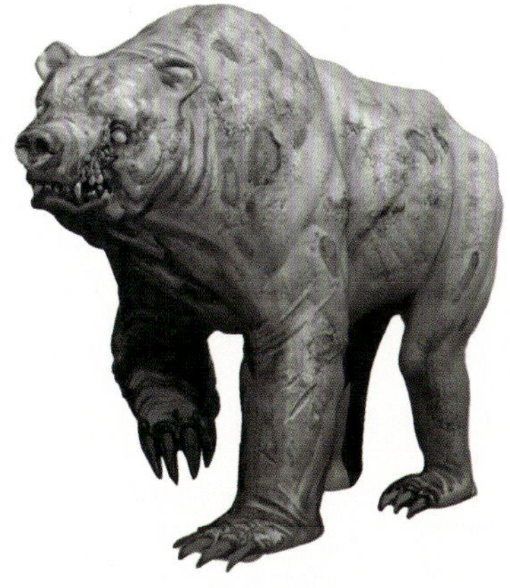
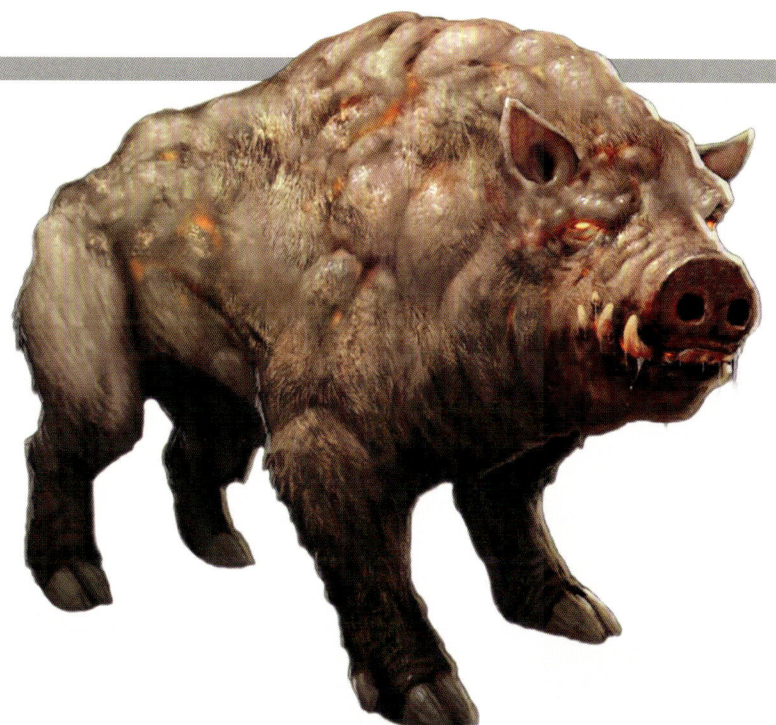

RAD ANIMALS

In an older version of *Rust*, there were irradiated animals roaming the island. These concepts were created by exaggerating the natural effects of radiation on animals while keeping them grounded in reality.

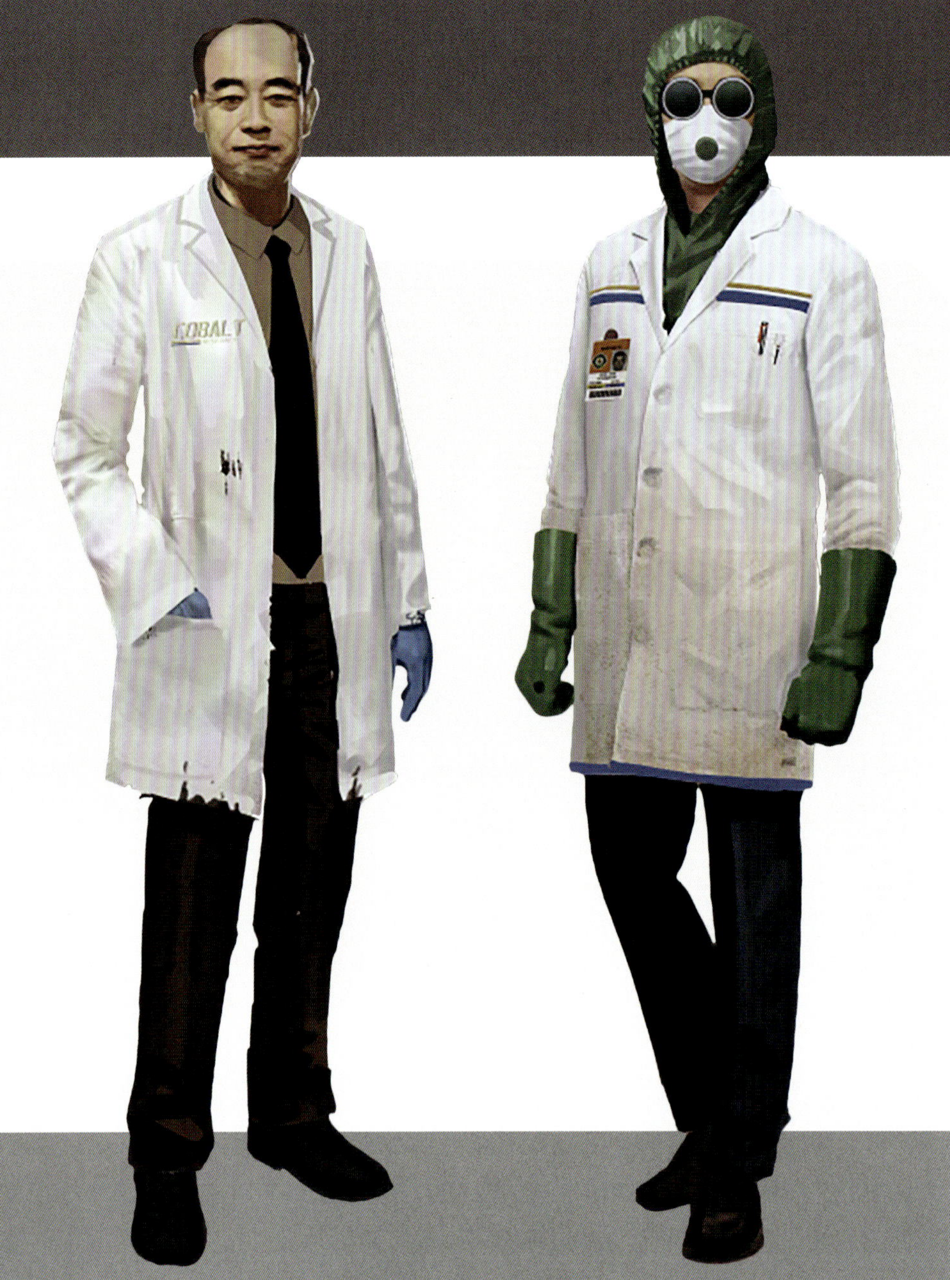

SCIENTISTS

Early concept art for the Scientists explored the idea of what the research team behind the scenes at Cobalt would look like. The hint of wear and tear on their clothing suggests they might be stretched thin and working with limited resources. Their designs evolved from basic lab coats to more sophisticated tactical suits with gas masks.

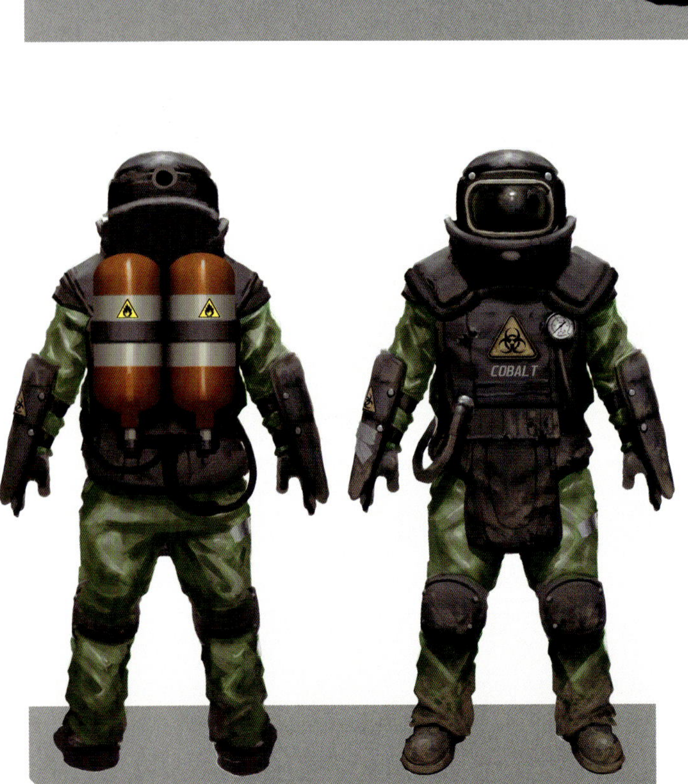

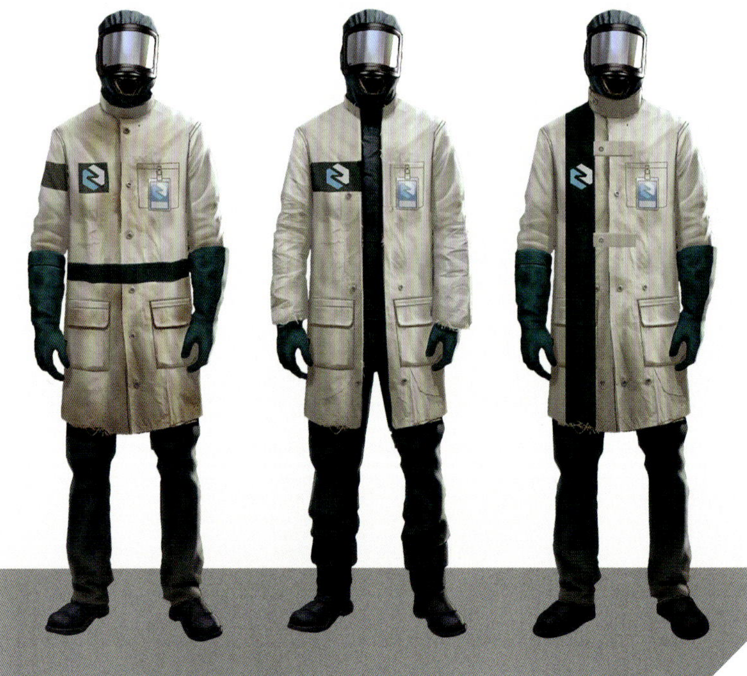

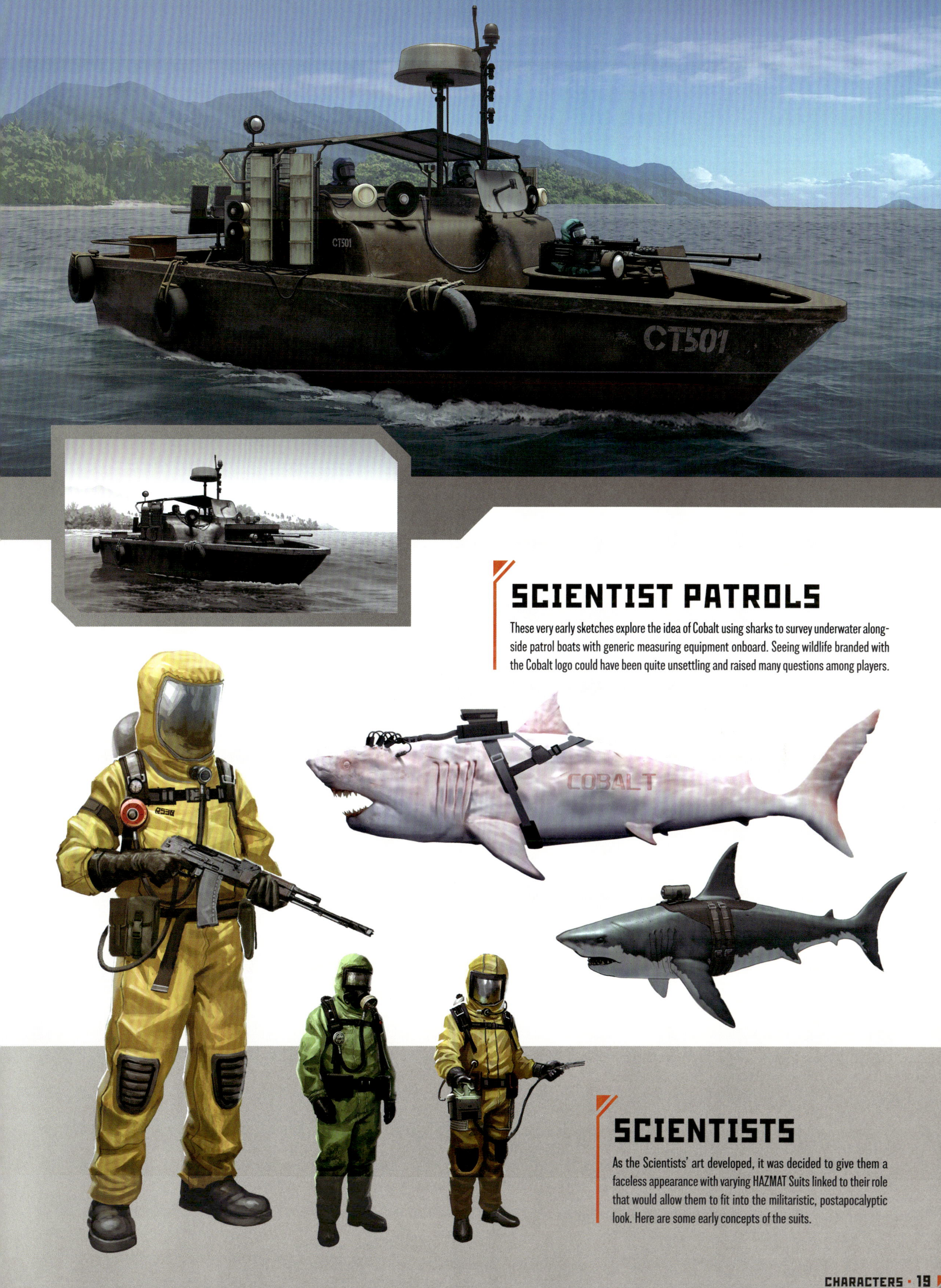

SCIENTIST PATROLS

These very early sketches explore the idea of Cobalt using sharks to survey underwater alongside patrol boats with generic measuring equipment onboard. Seeing wildlife branded with the Cobalt logo could have been quite unsettling and raised many questions among players.

SCIENTISTS

As the Scientists' art developed, it was decided to give them a faceless appearance with varying HAZMAT Suits linked to their role that would allow them to fit into the militaristic, postapocalyptic look. Here are some early concepts of the suits.

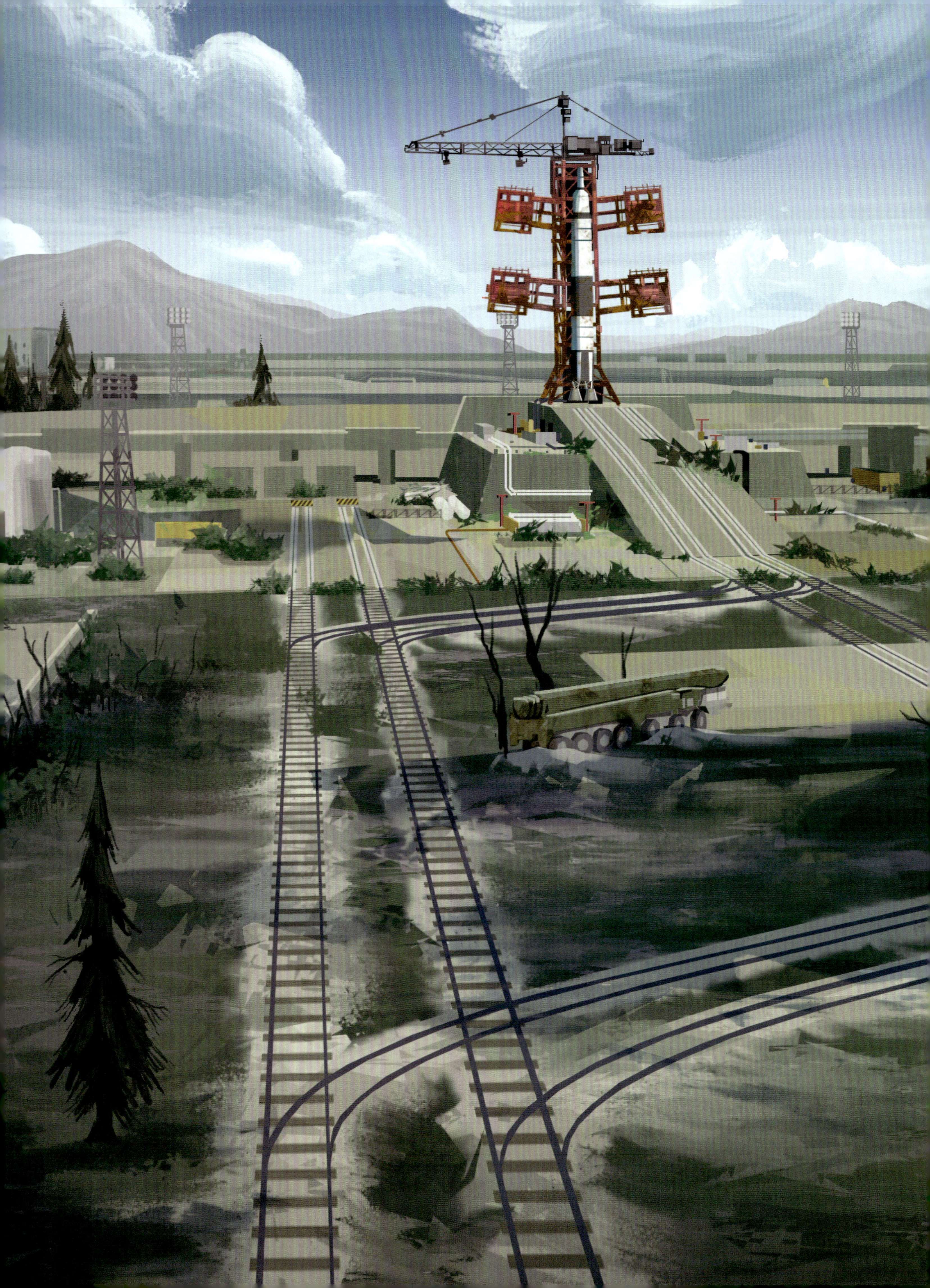

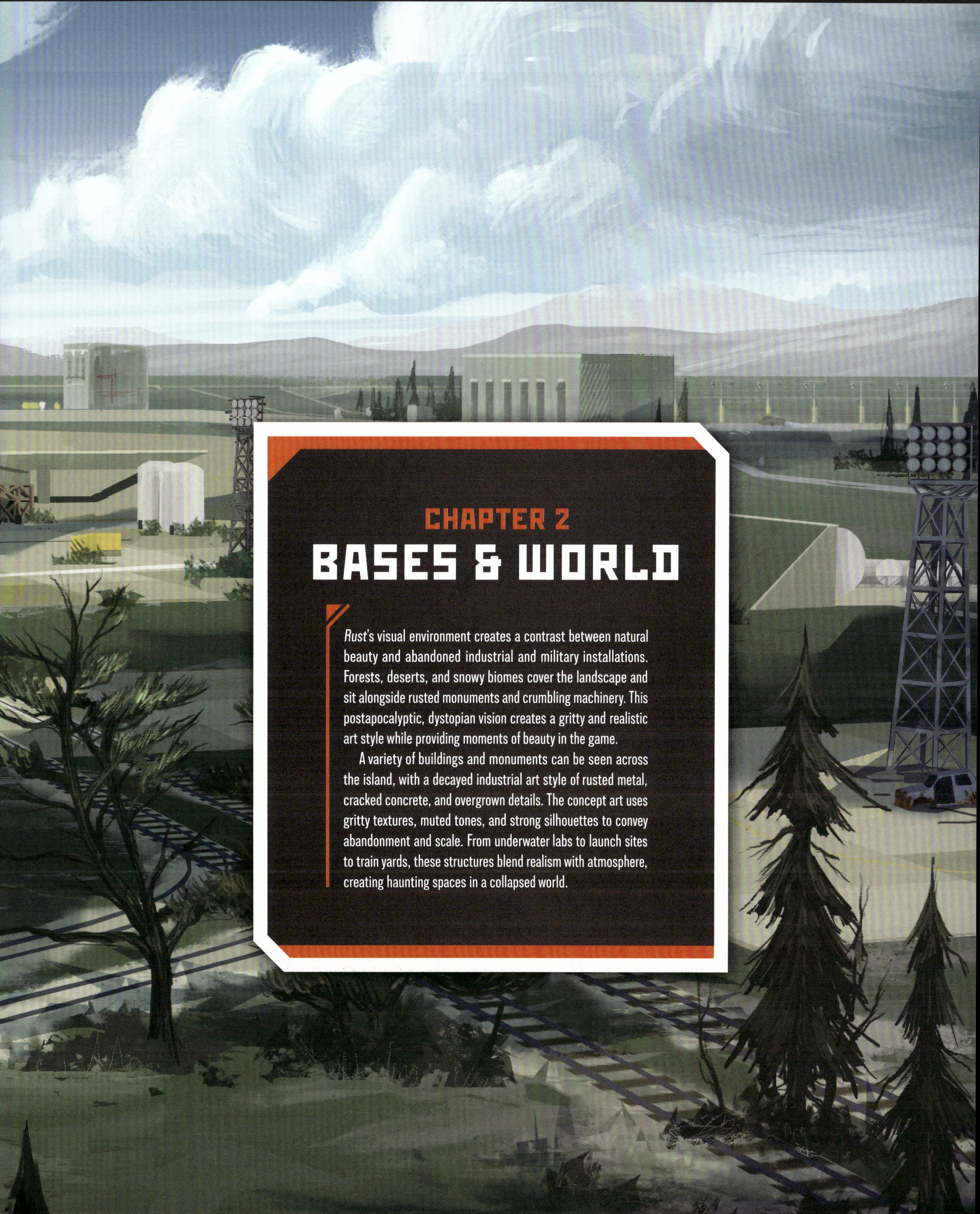

CHAPTER 2

BASES & WORLD

Rust's visual environment creates a contrast between natural beauty and abandoned industrial and military installations. Forests, deserts, and snowy biomes cover the landscape and sit alongside rusted monuments and crumbling machinery. This postapocalyptic, dystopian vision creates a gritty and realistic art style while providing moments of beauty in the game.

A variety of buildings and monuments can be seen across the island, with a decayed industrial art style of rusted metal, cracked concrete, and overgrown details. The concept art uses gritty textures, muted tones, and strong silhouettes to convey abandonment and scale. From underwater labs to launch sites to train yards, these structures blend realism with atmosphere, creating haunting spaces in a collapsed world.

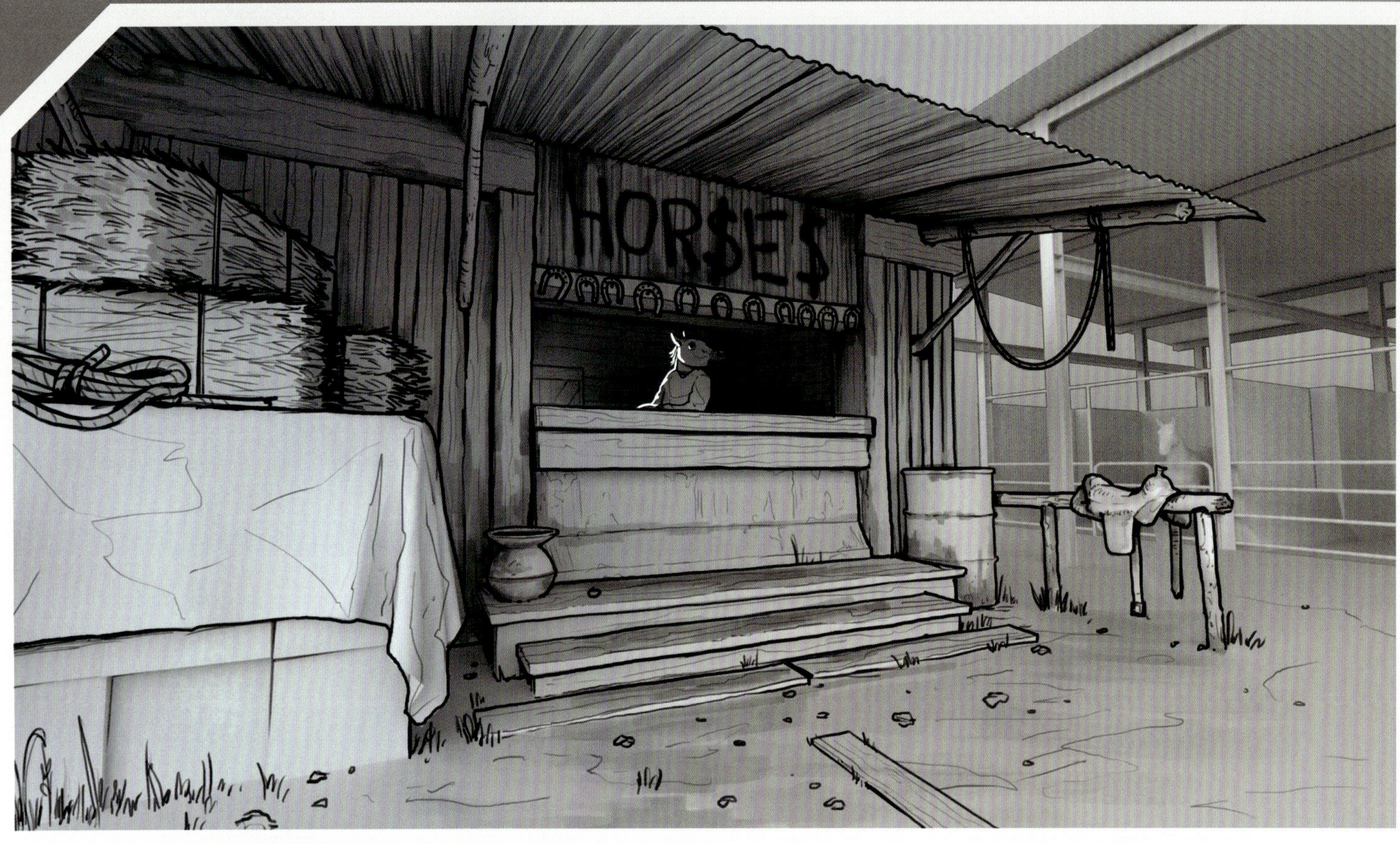

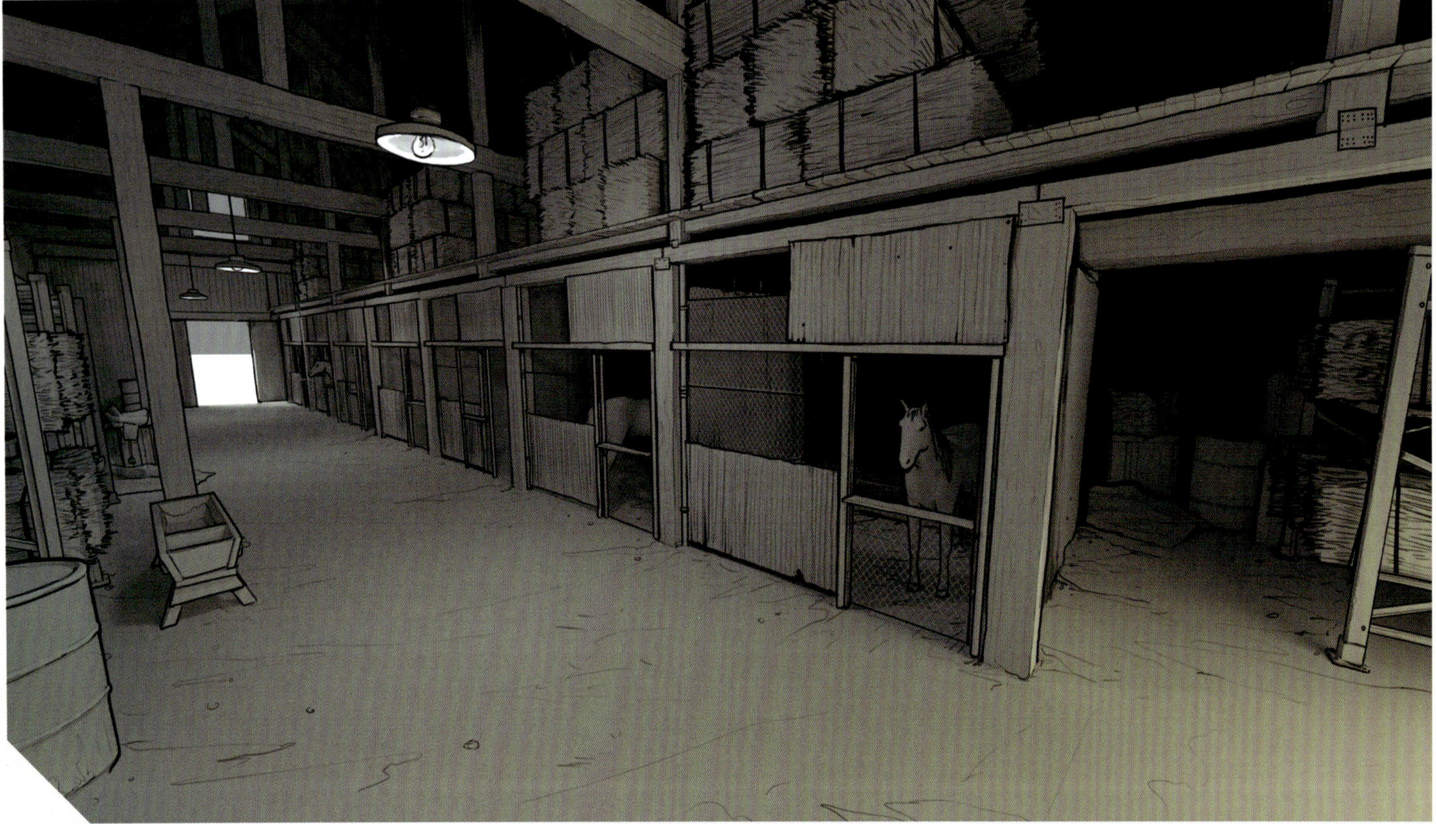

HORSE SHOP

Early renders of the Horse Shop were based on the idea of fixing up an old barn with scrap materials. The artists wanted to make it clear this was a place to purchase horses by showing plenty of horse-related equipment and supplies.

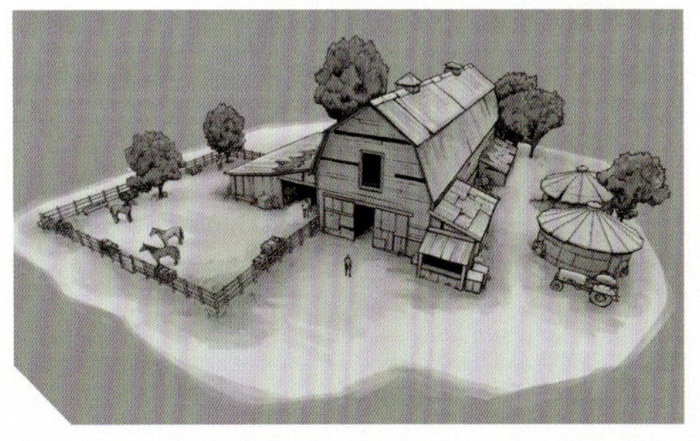

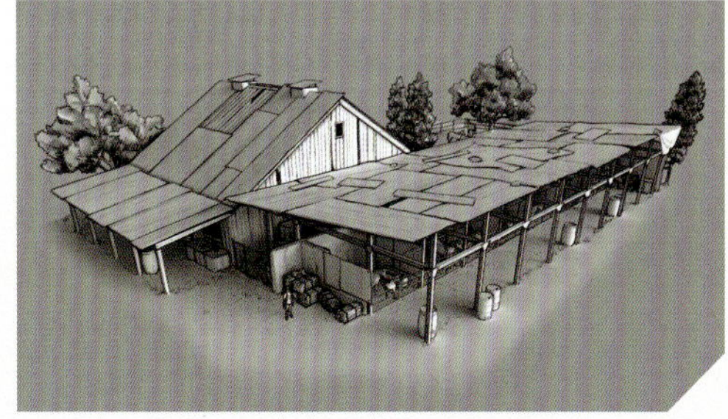

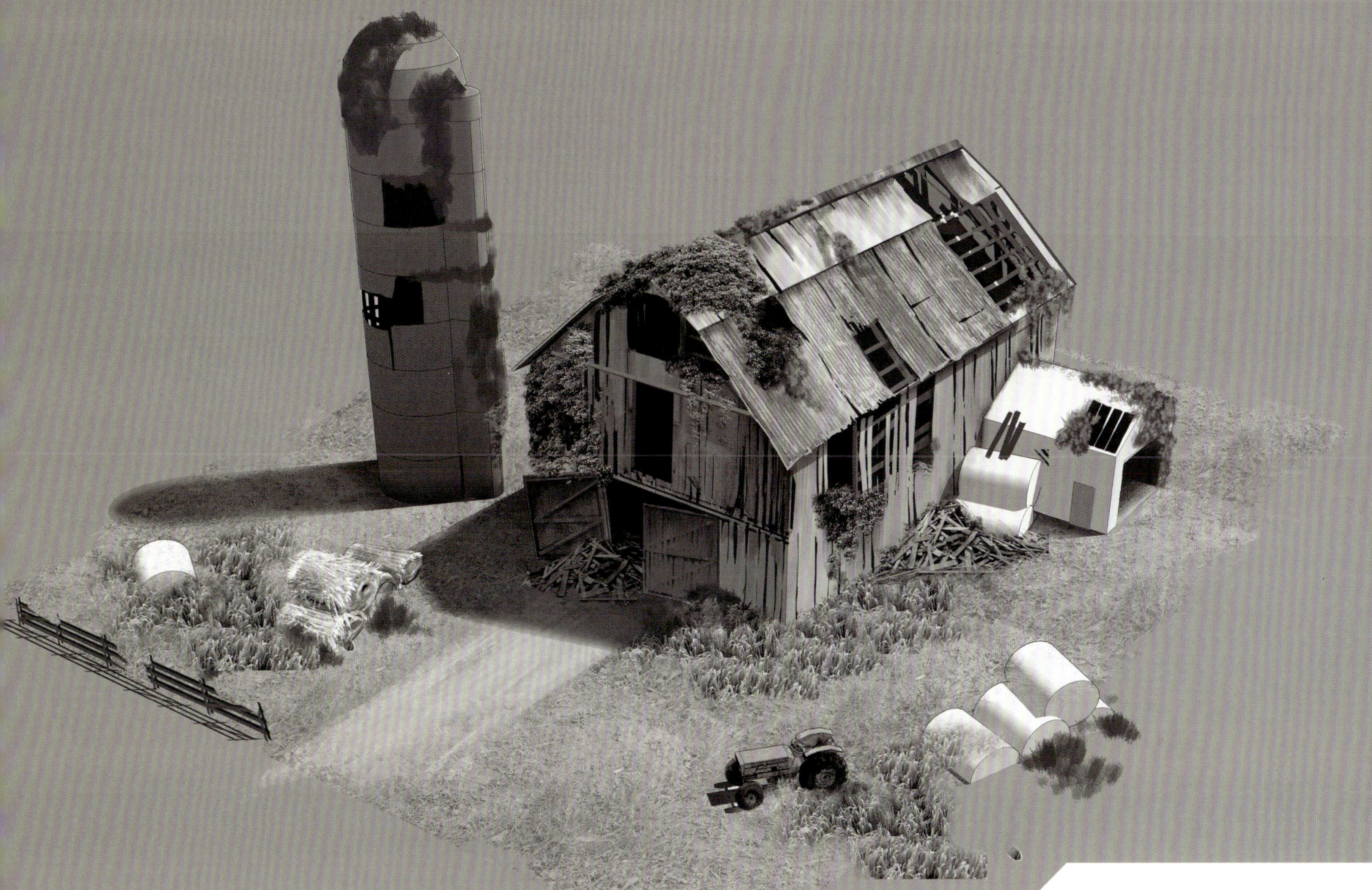

BARN

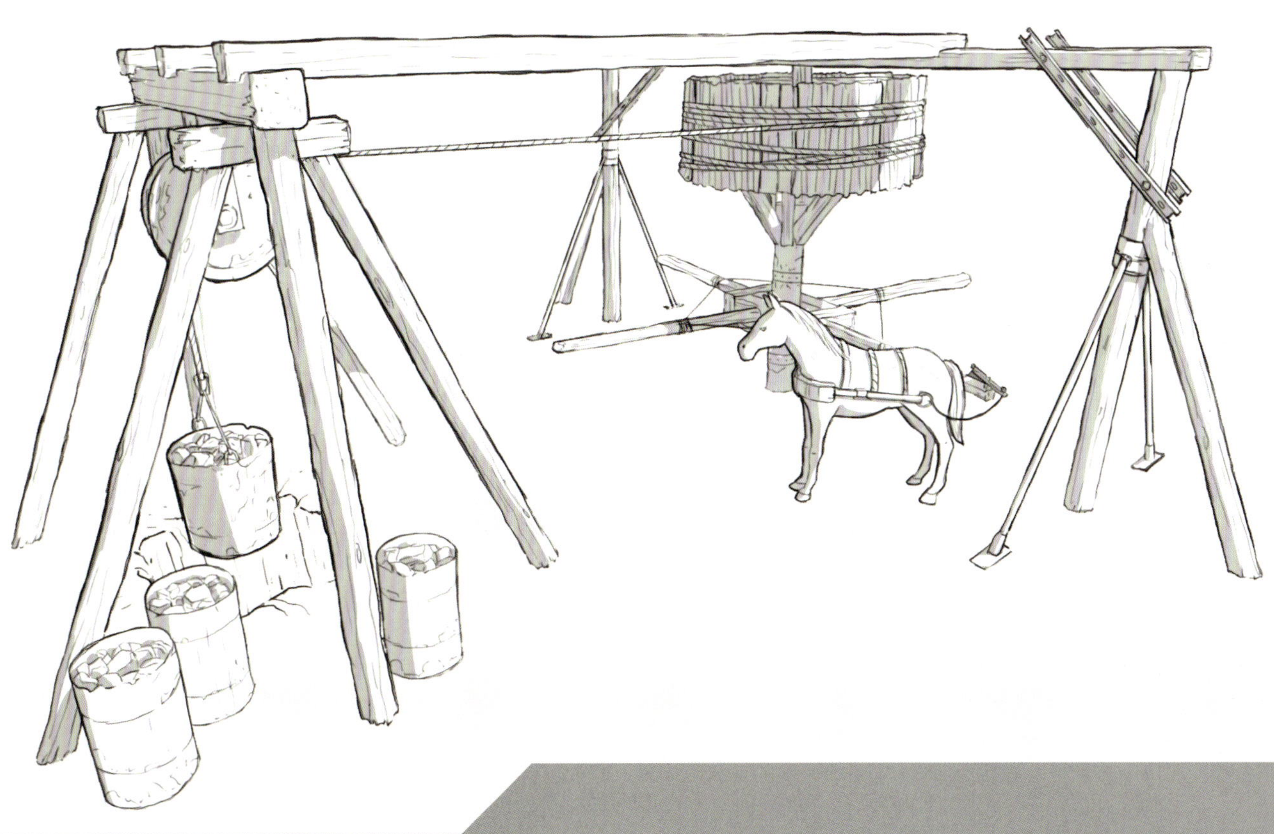

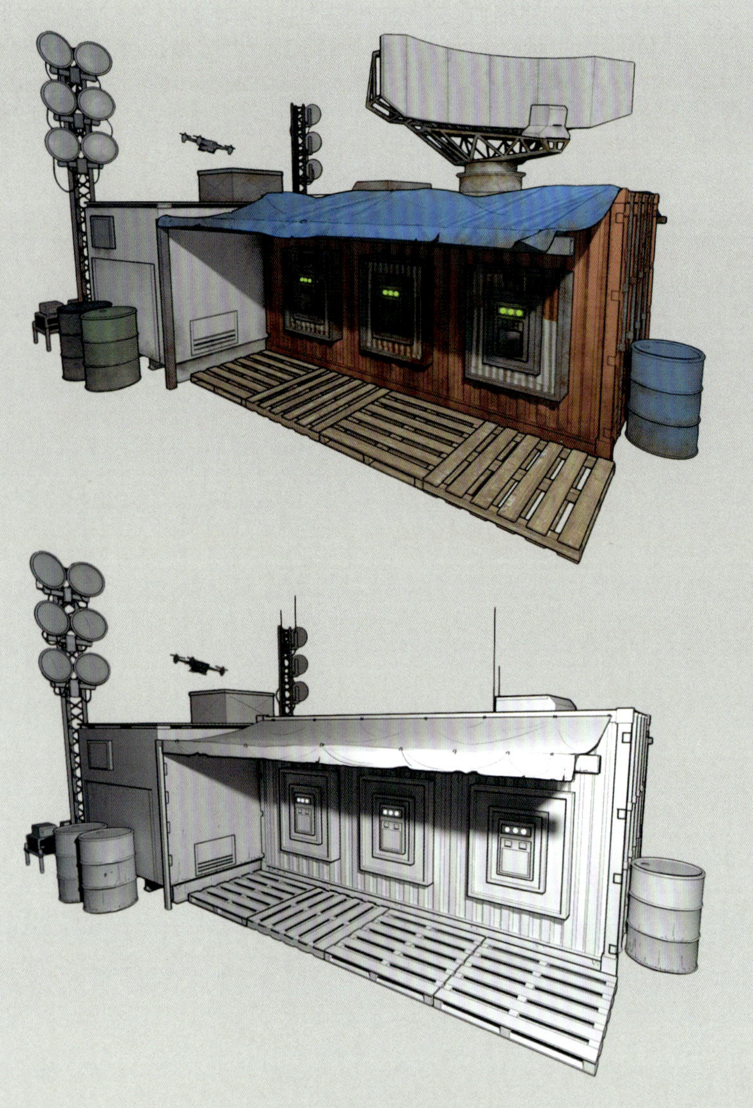

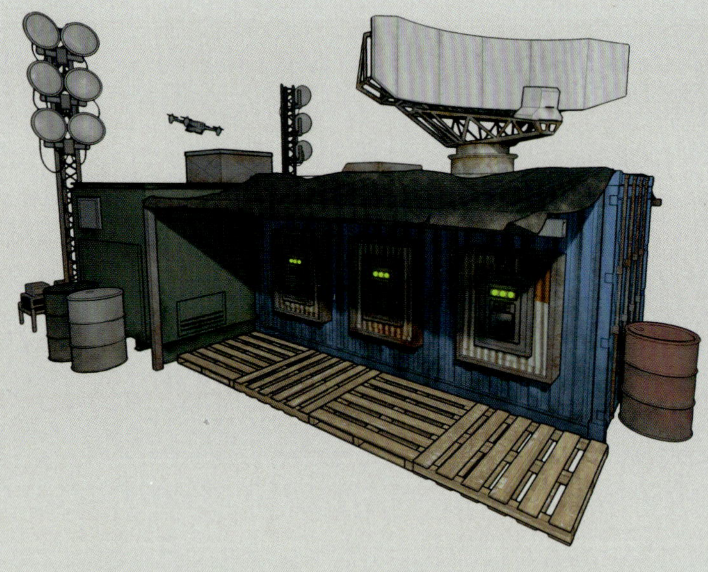

MARKETPLACE TERMINAL

The Marketplace Terminal is based on a repurposed shipping container. It looks weathered yet functional, with the addition of selling terminals, salvaged wood, rusted metal, and tarps. Players use these terminals to buy and sell goods, and drones deliver packages. Various satellite dishes and communication devices were experimented with to show how the drones were controlled.

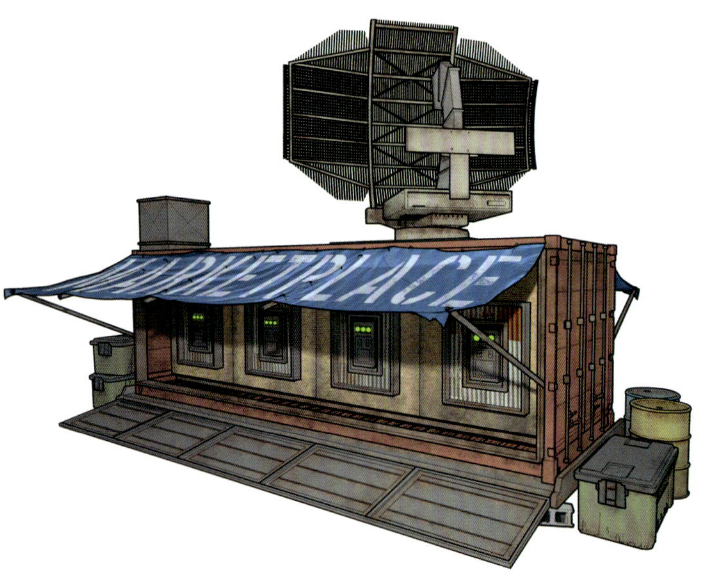

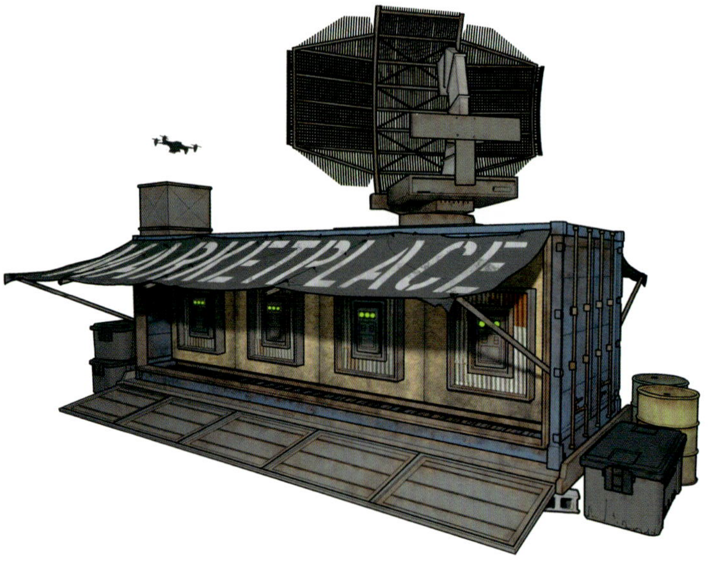

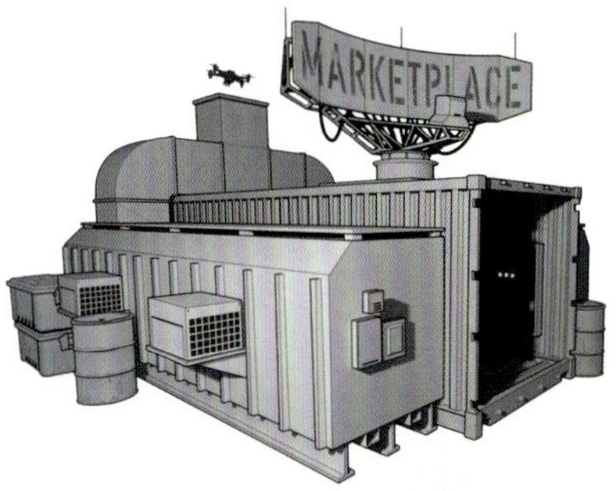

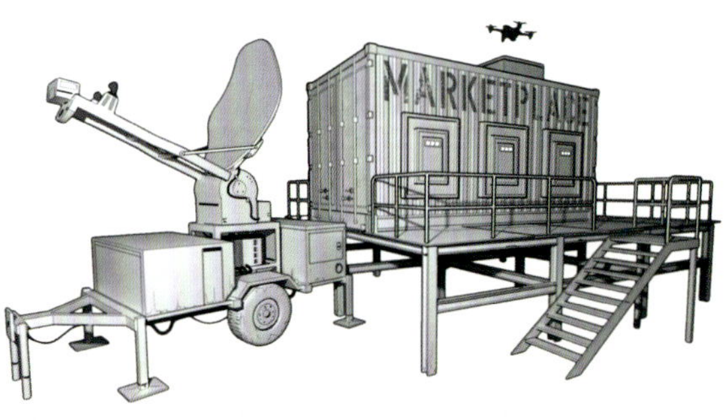

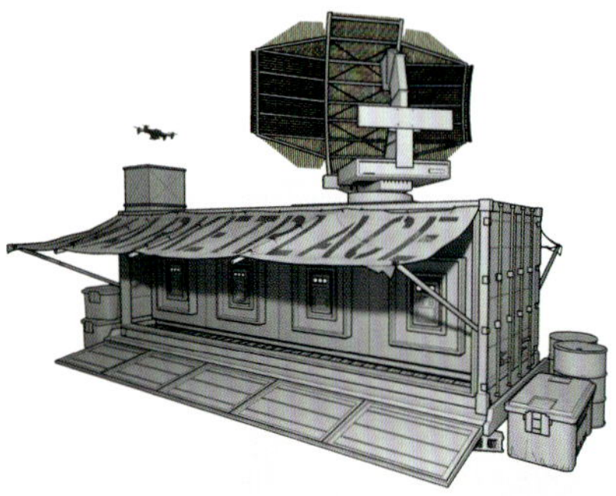

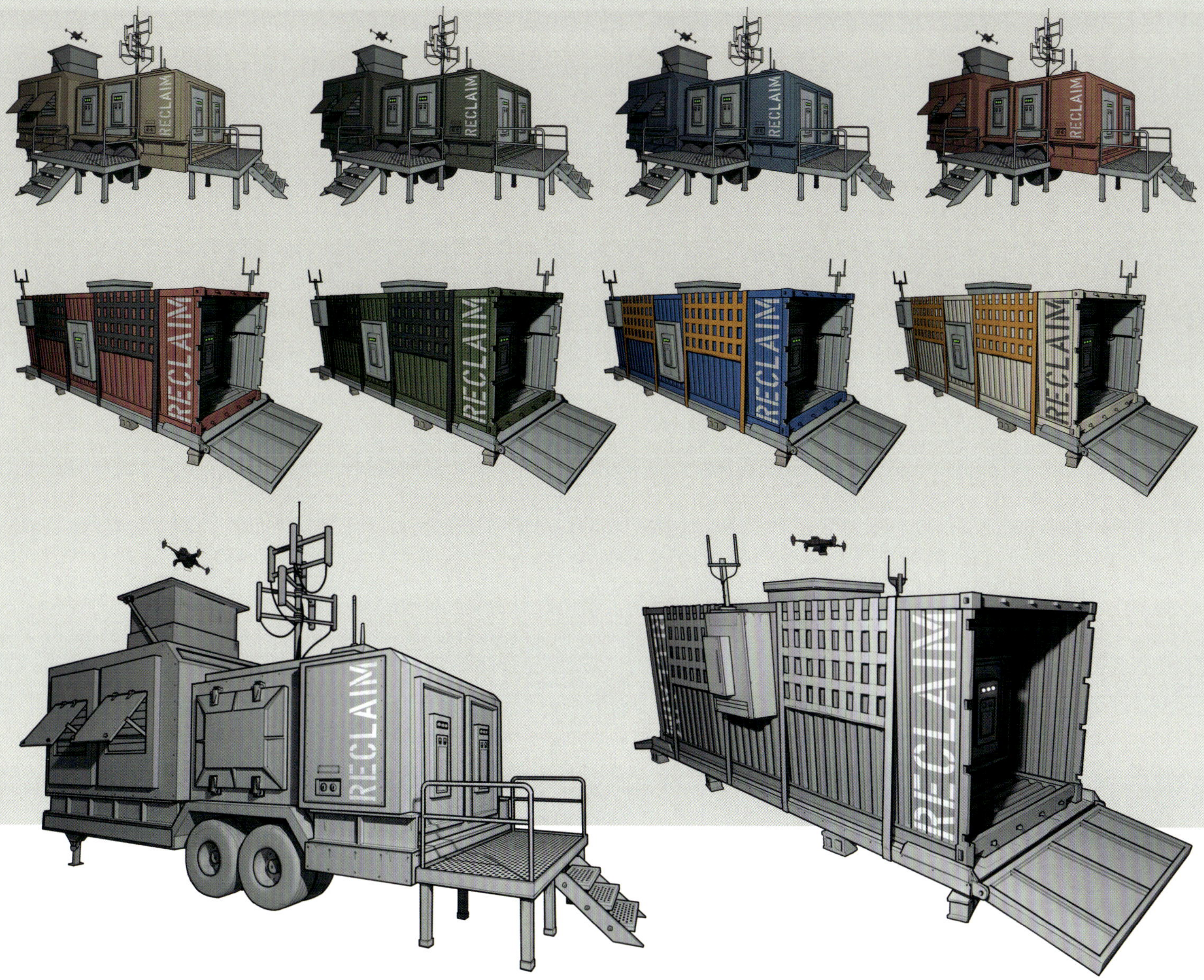

RECLAIM TERMINAL

Preliminary sketches of the Reclaim Terminal were inspired by military mobile base trailers. These terminals are hubs where players can visit and reclaim lost items from their inventory after they die.

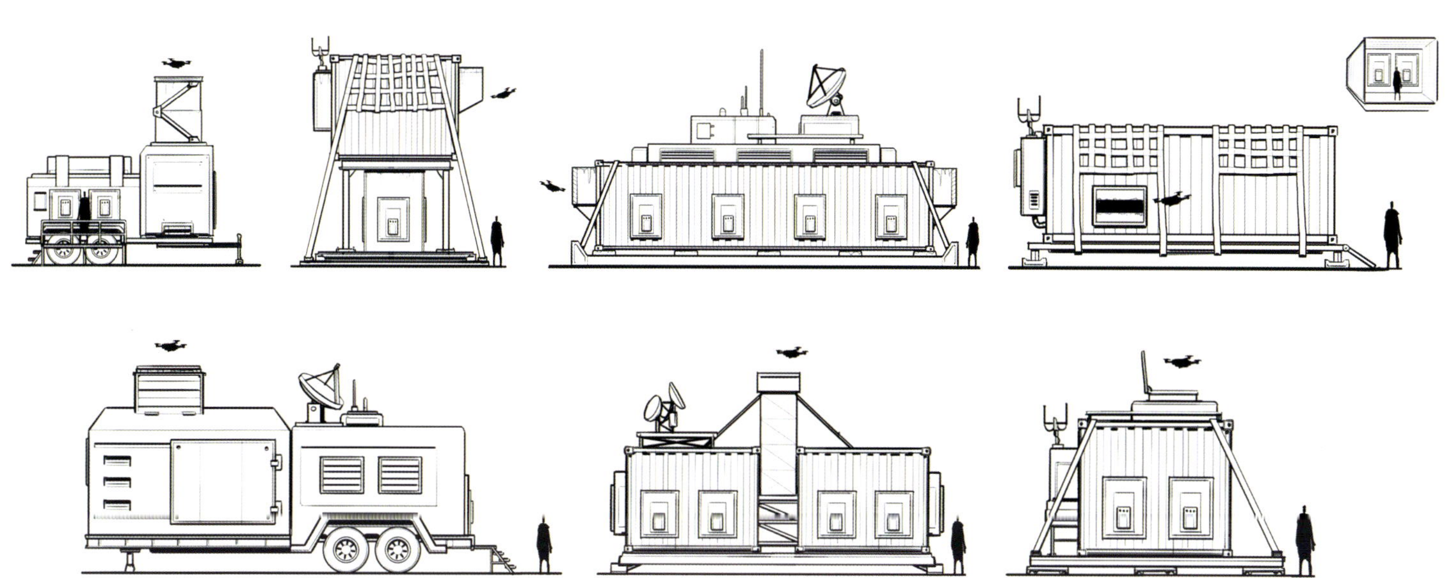

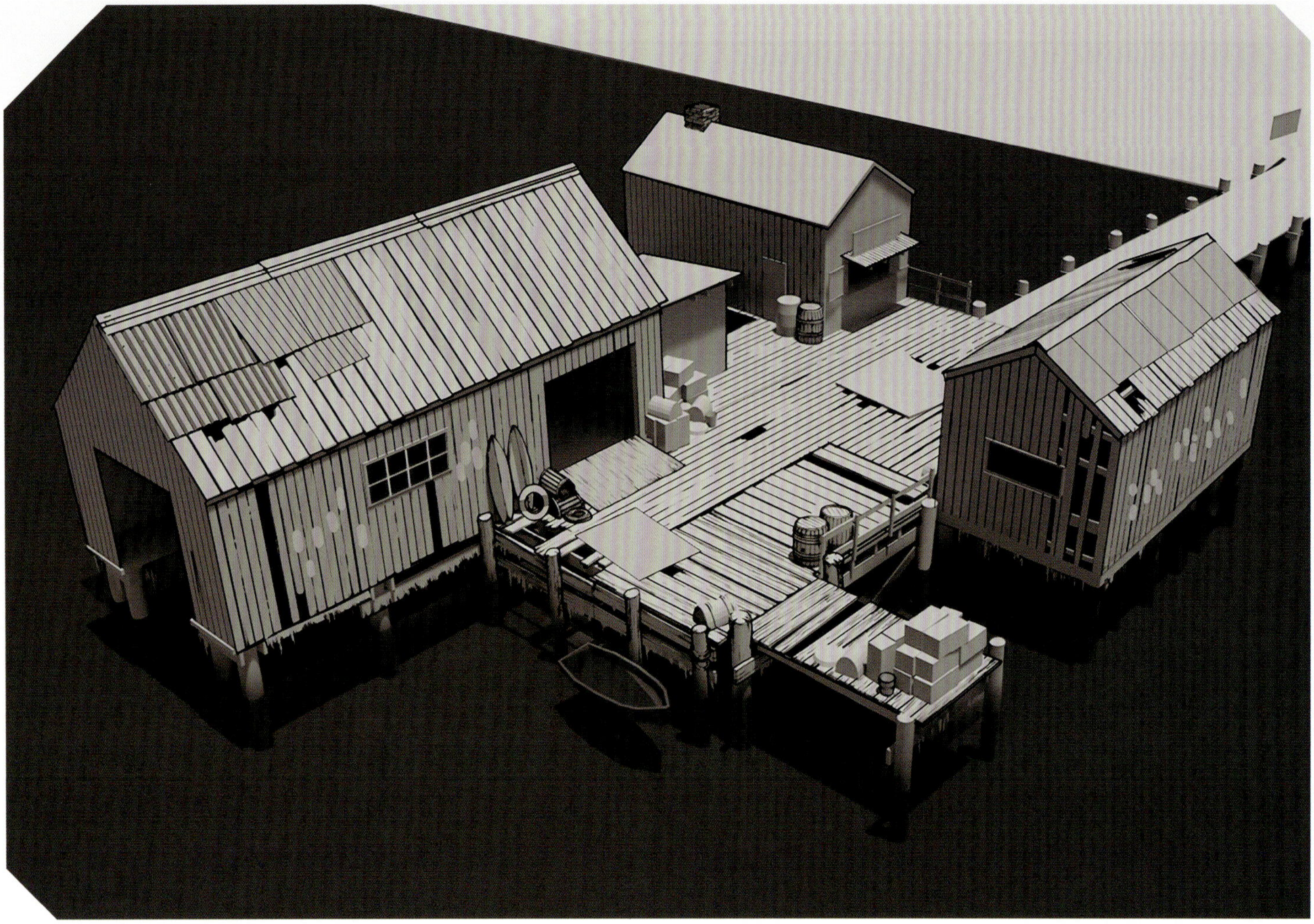

BOAT SHOP

The Boat Shop was based on the concept of the owner finding the structure in a dilapidated state, scavenging what they could to repair it, and then creating a sign to advertise the shop to the island inhabitants.

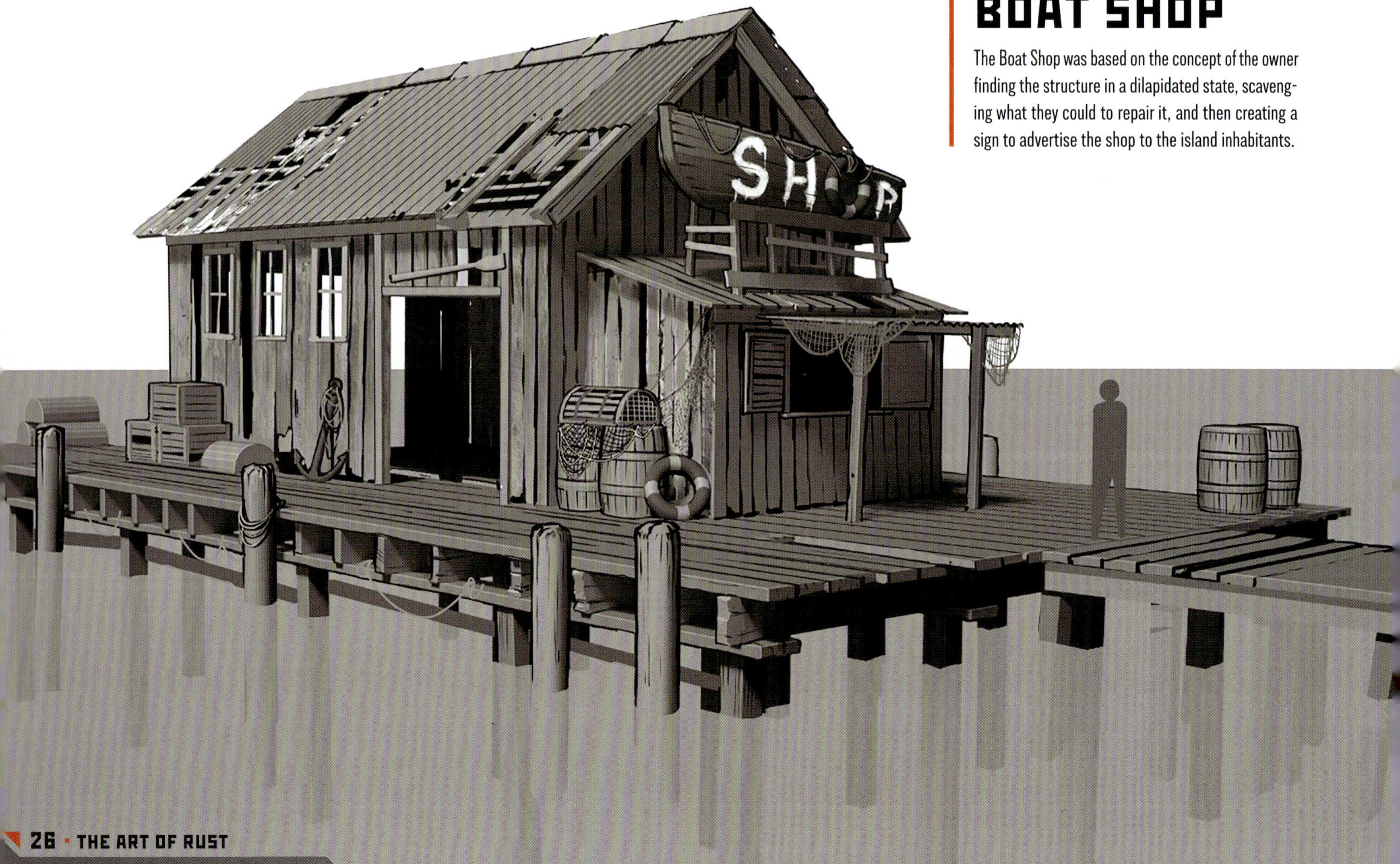

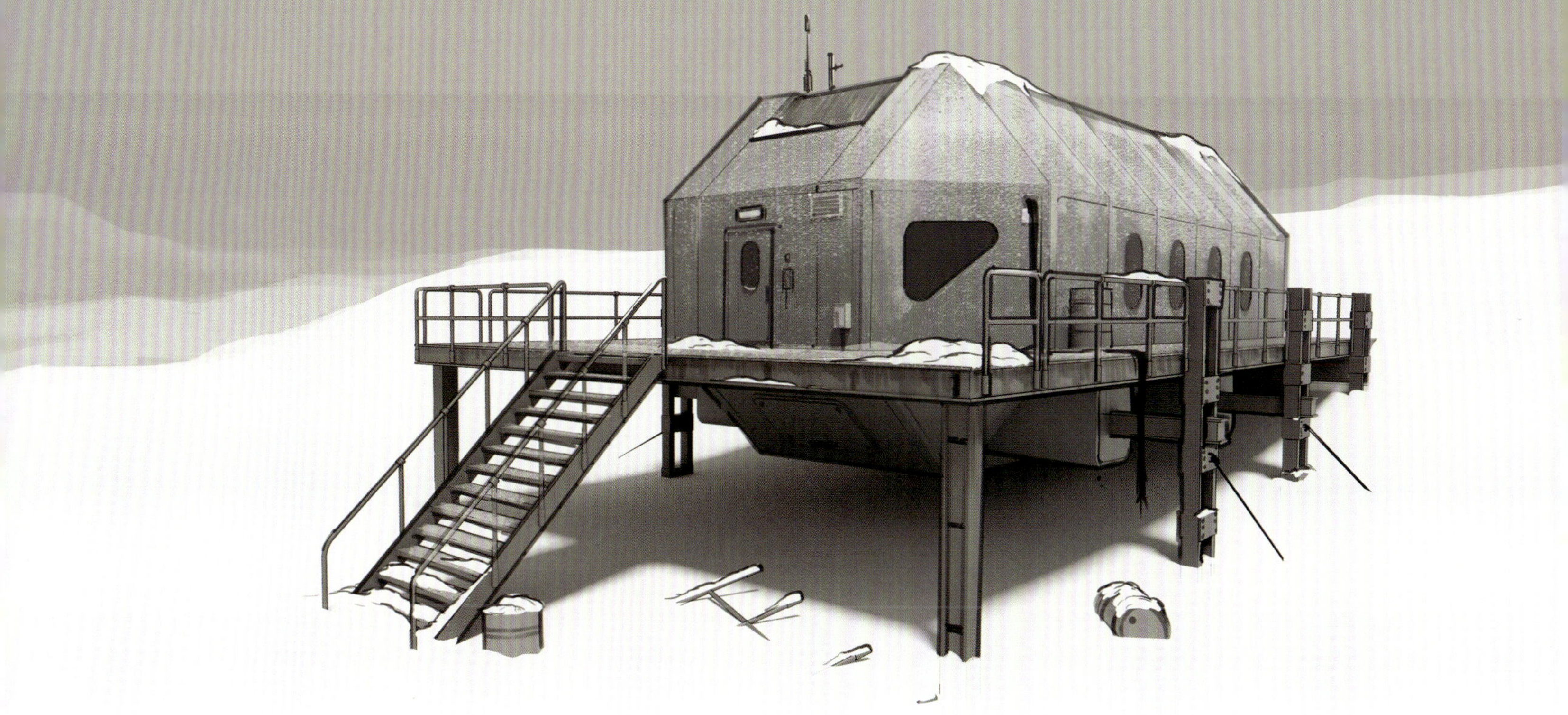

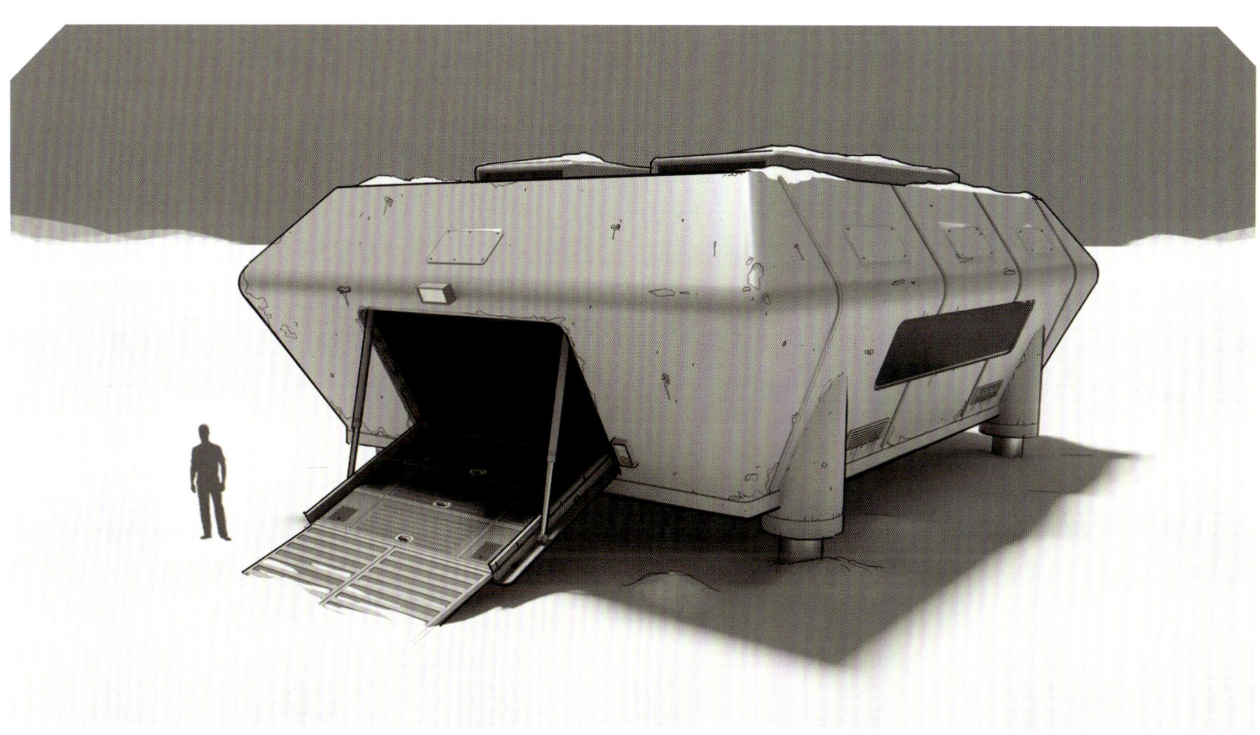

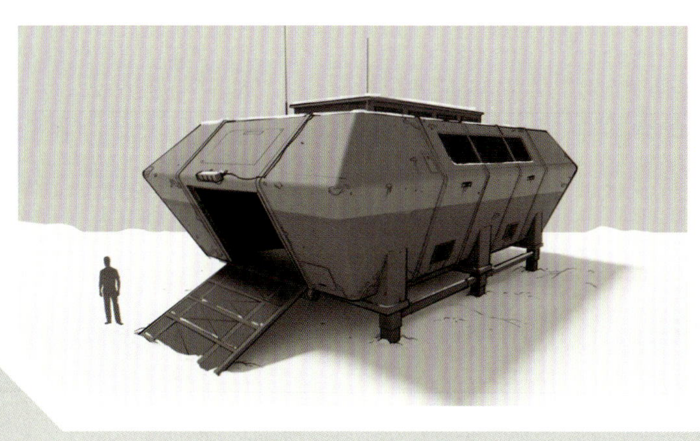

SNOWMOBILE GARAGE

Antarctic research pods were the main inspiration for these sketches, as they're used to set up bases of operations in cold-weather environments.

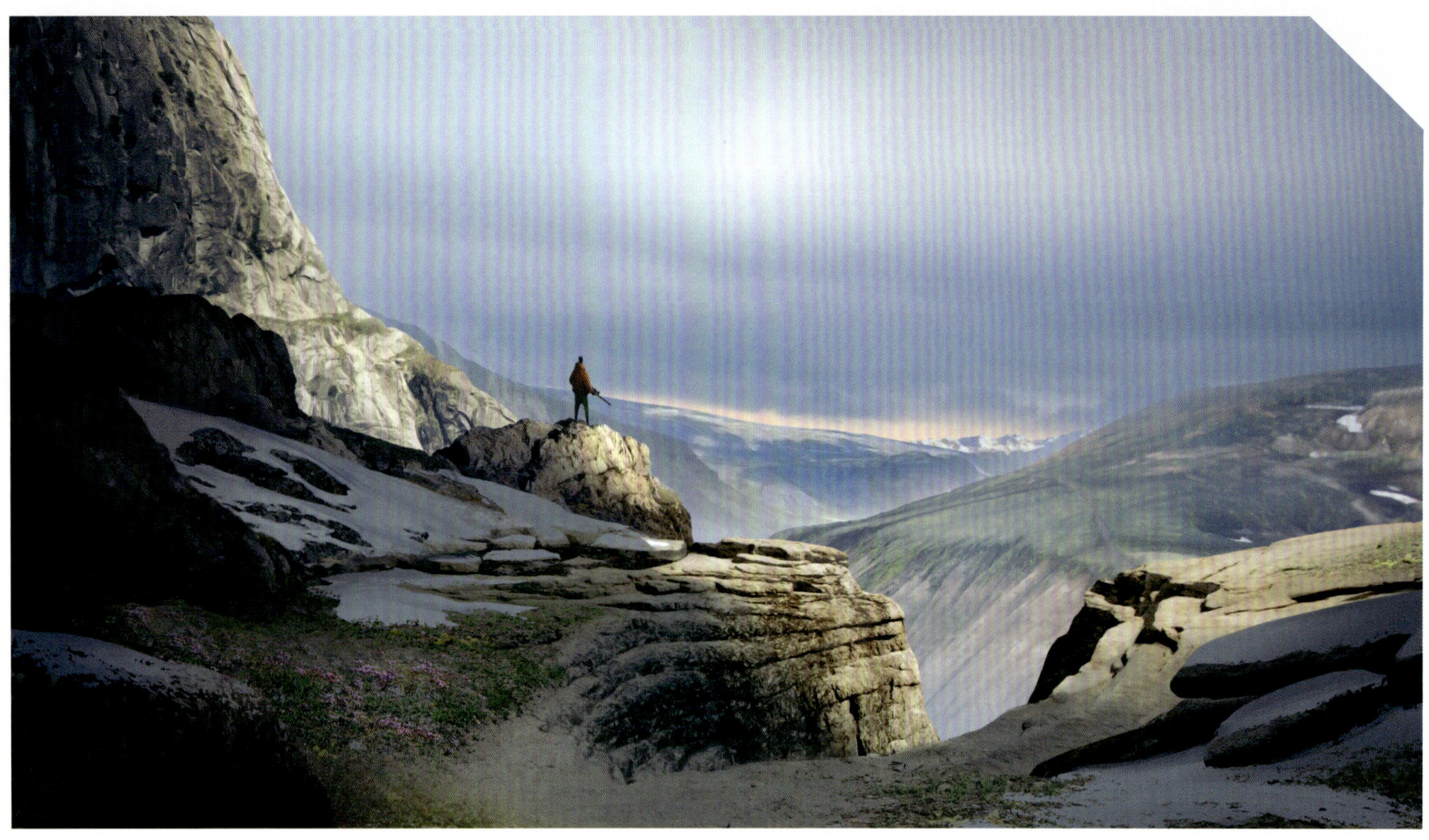

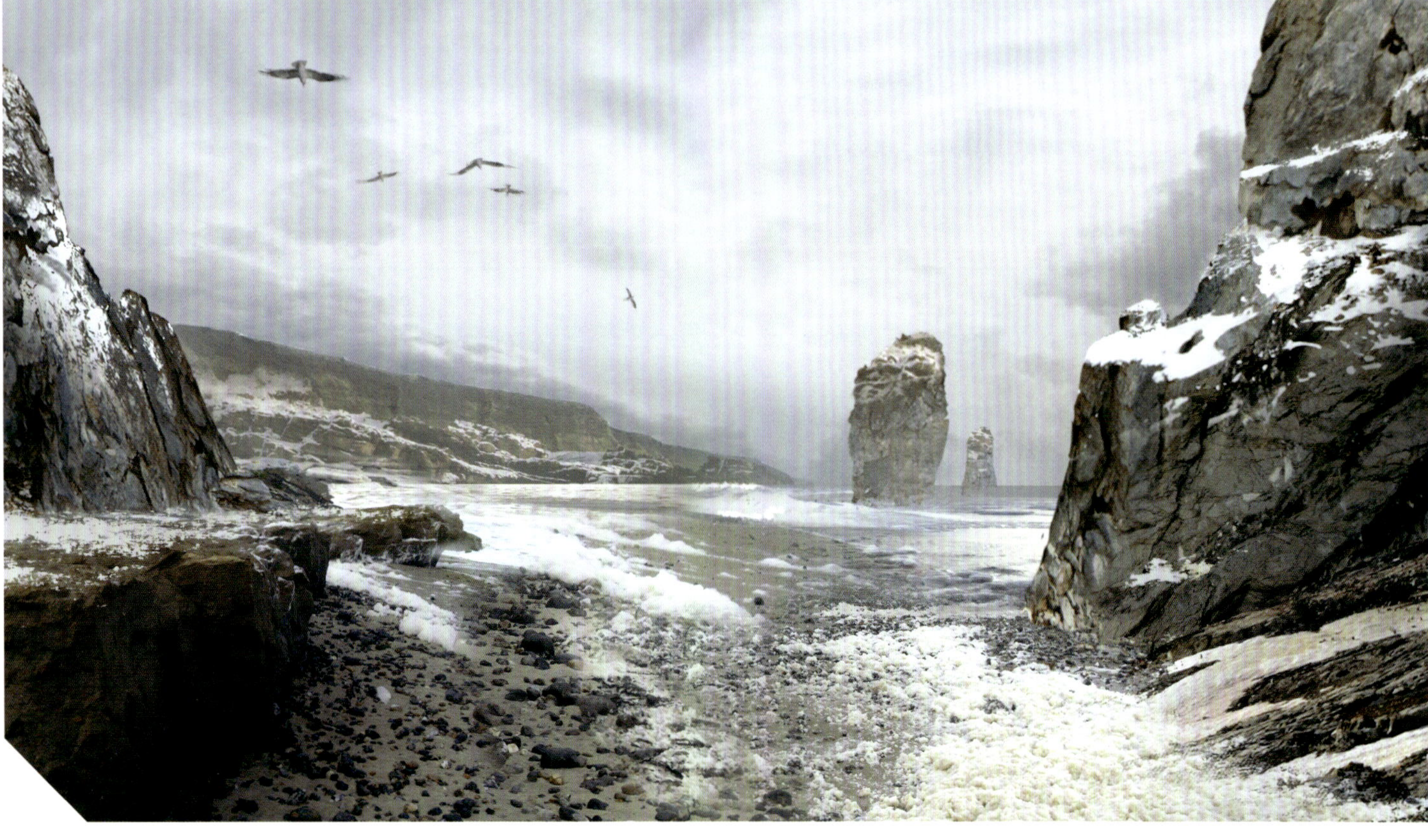

EXPLORATION

Tense and immersive, exploration in *Rust* blends survival with discovery. Players navigate expansive, diverse biomes, search decaying monuments, and seek loot while avoiding threats and surviving the elements. These early concept sketches show the desolate and dangerous beauty of *Rust*.

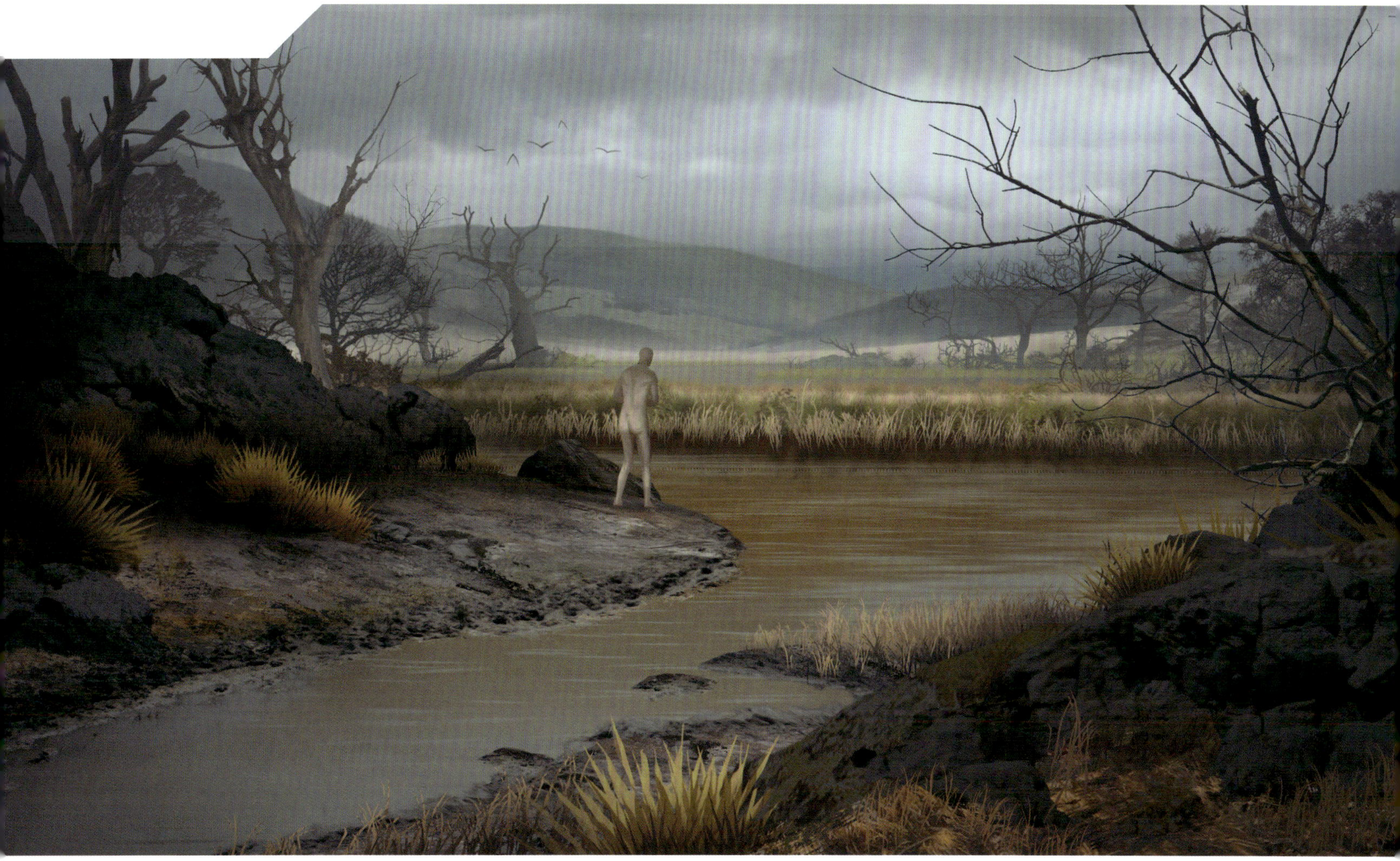

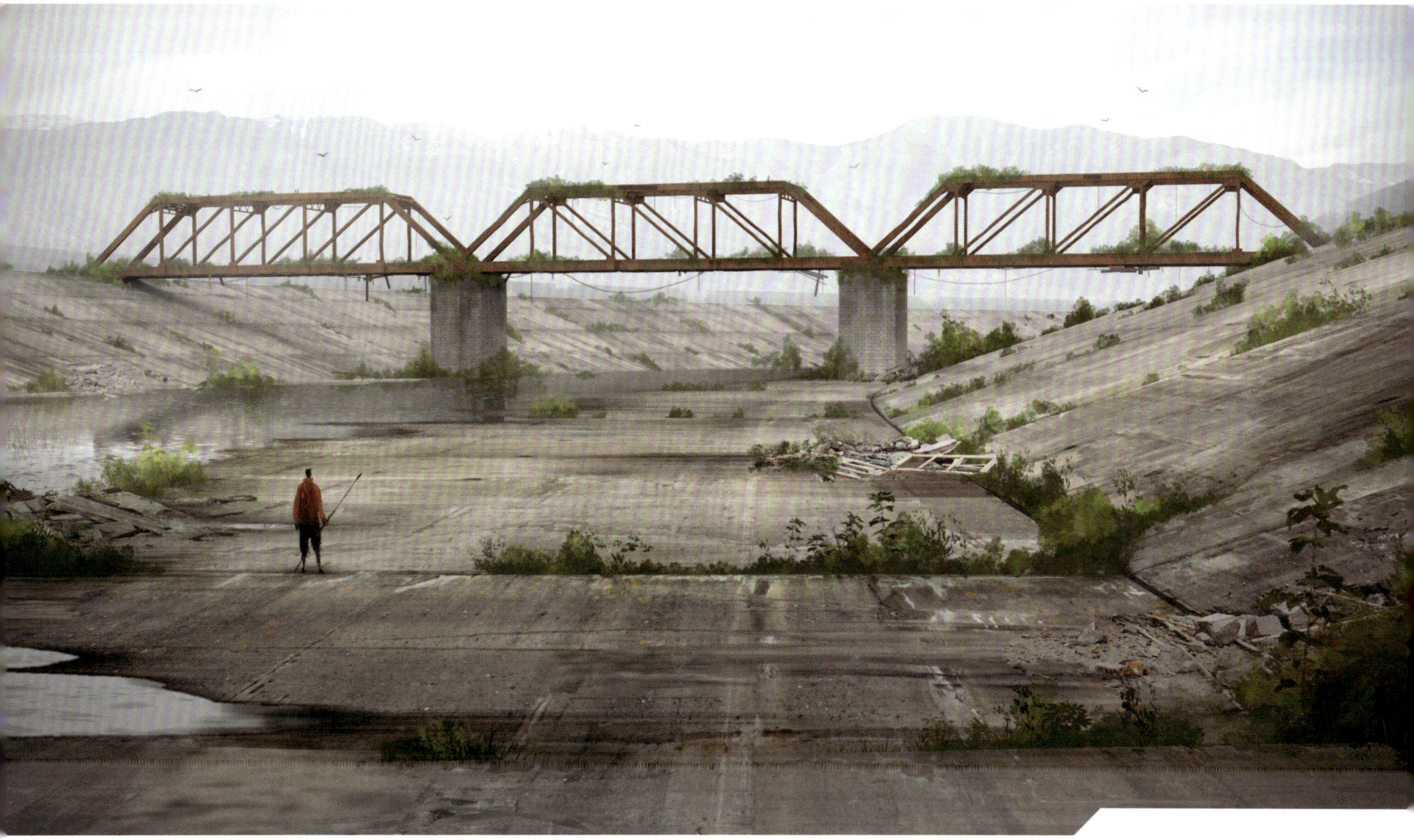

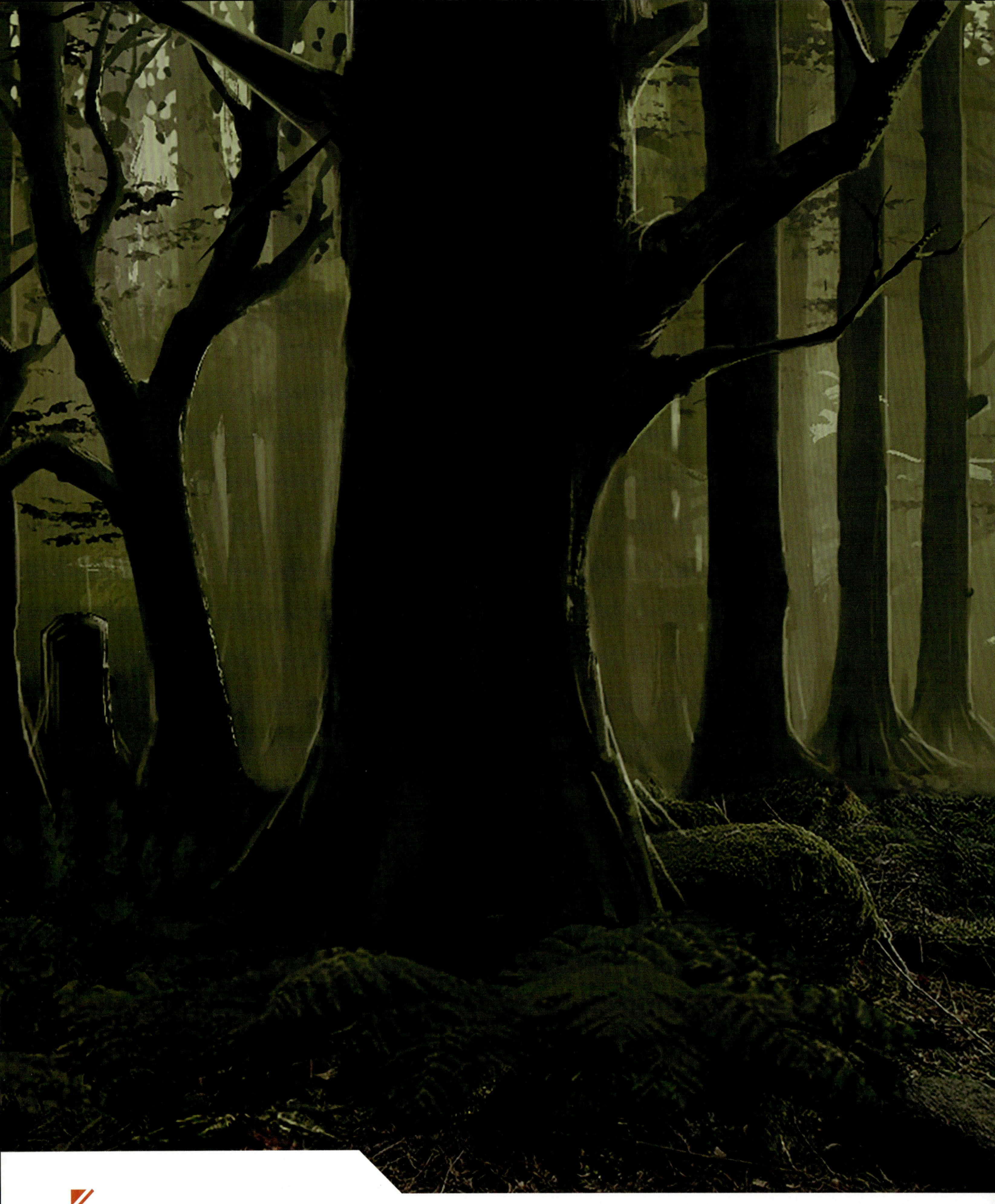

FORESTS

Rust's forests use a naturalistic, moody art style with dense, weathered trees and layered foliage. Soft lighting, mist, and environmental detail are at the core of creating these atmospheric concept sketches.

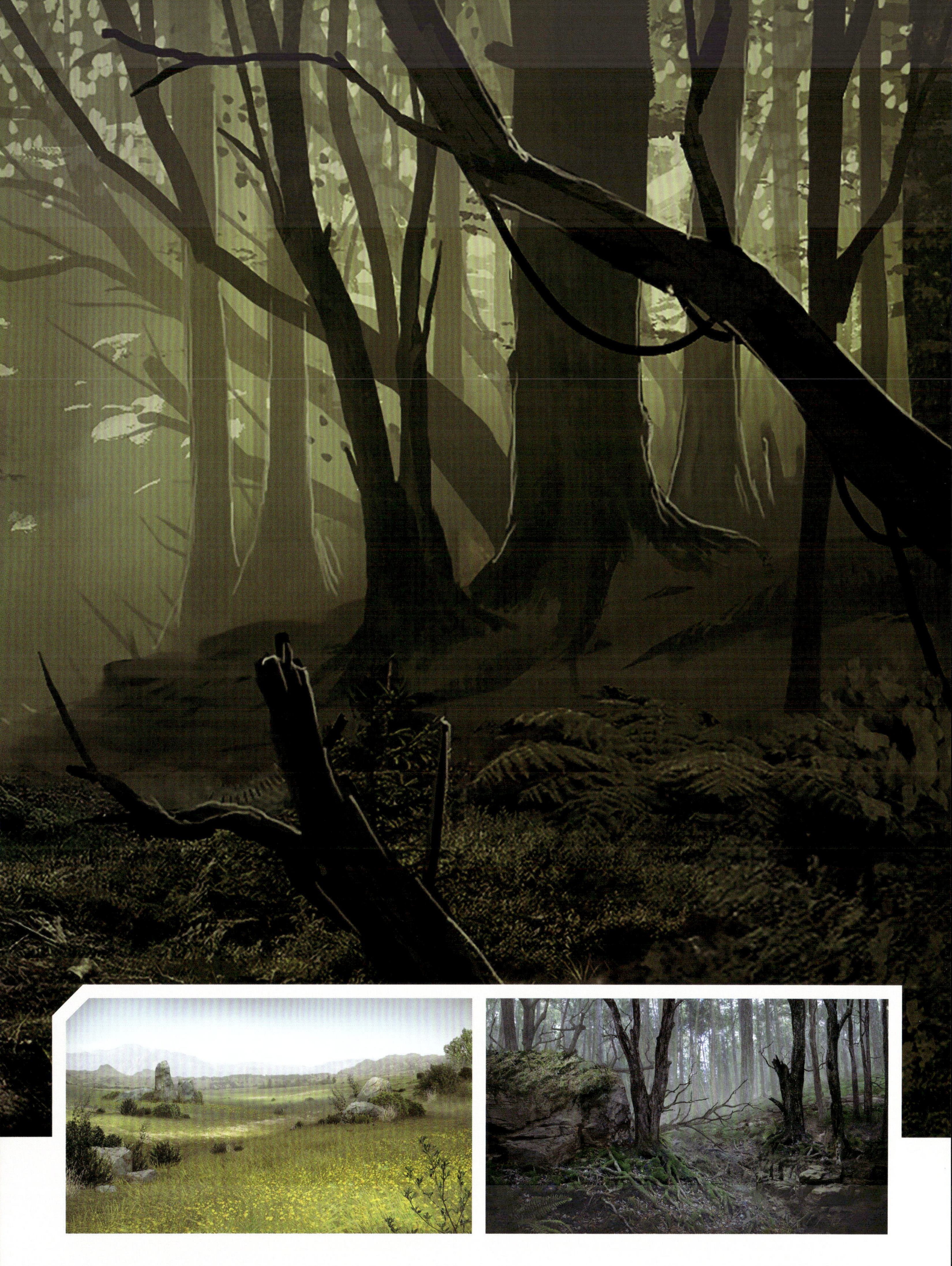

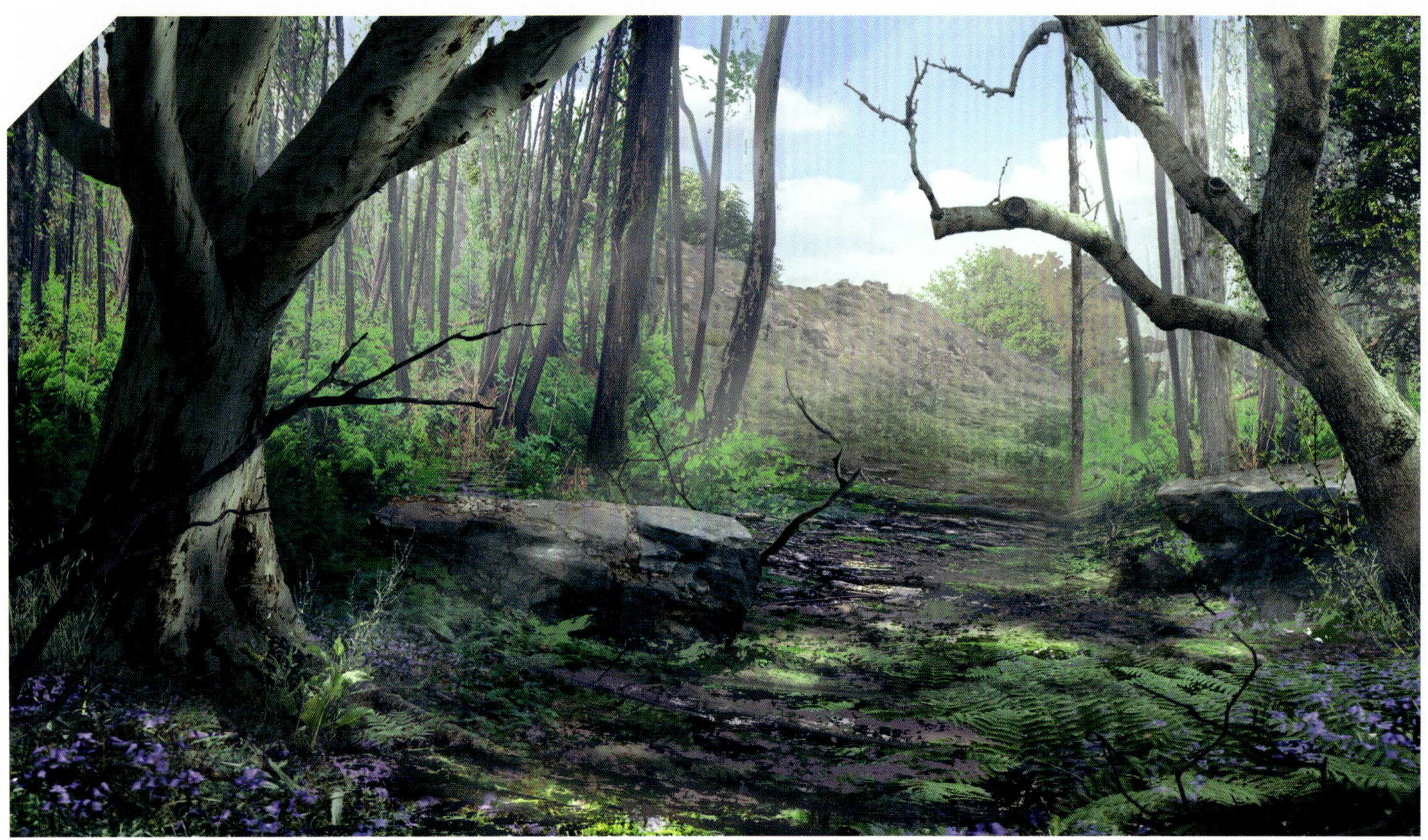

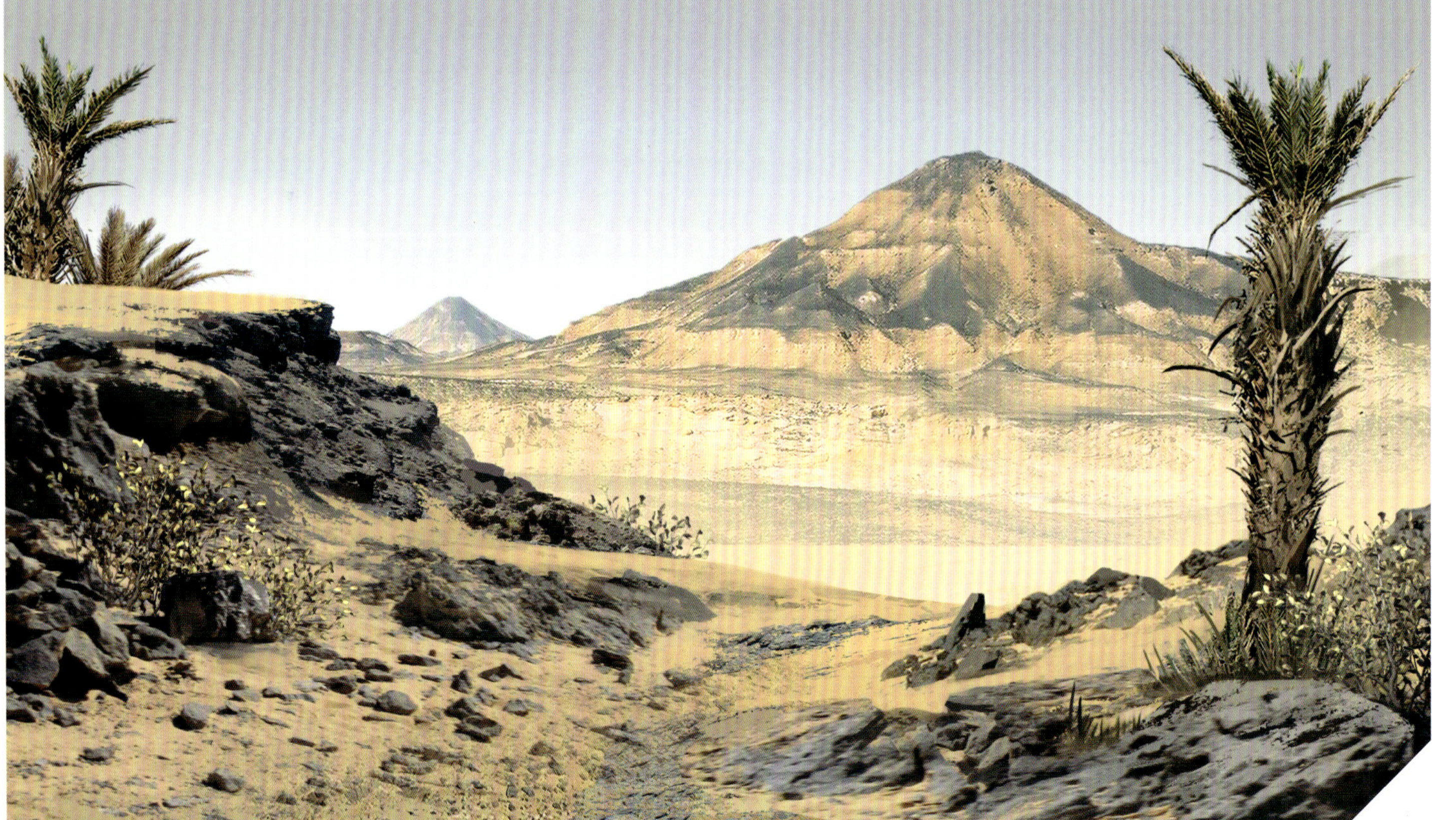

BIOMES

Rust's biomes use a realistic, atmospheric art style. Each has distinct tones, from lush forests to sun-bleached deserts to stark snowfields. The original concept art explored a wide variety of landscapes, making each biome feel unique while providing a different set of challenges to players.

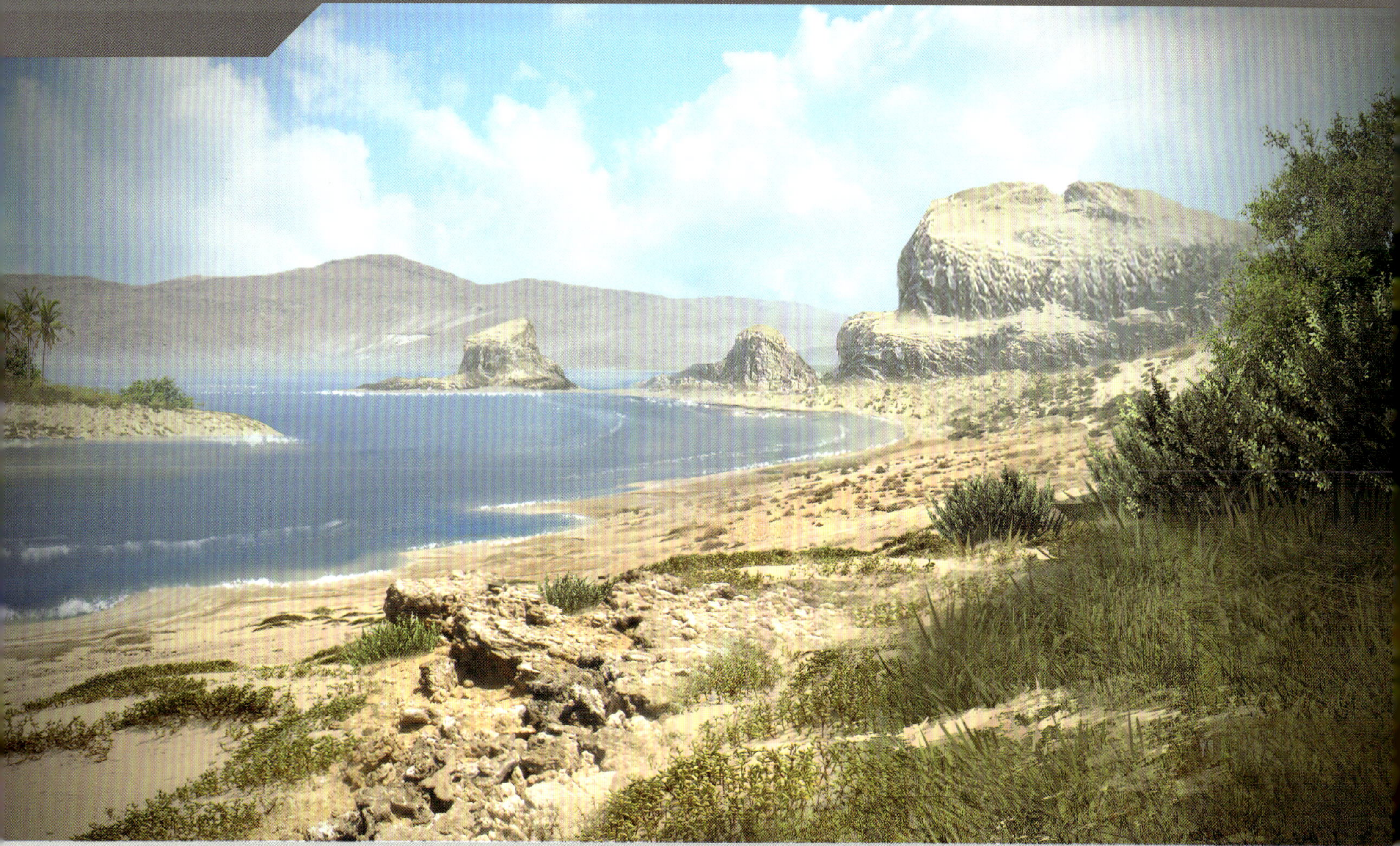

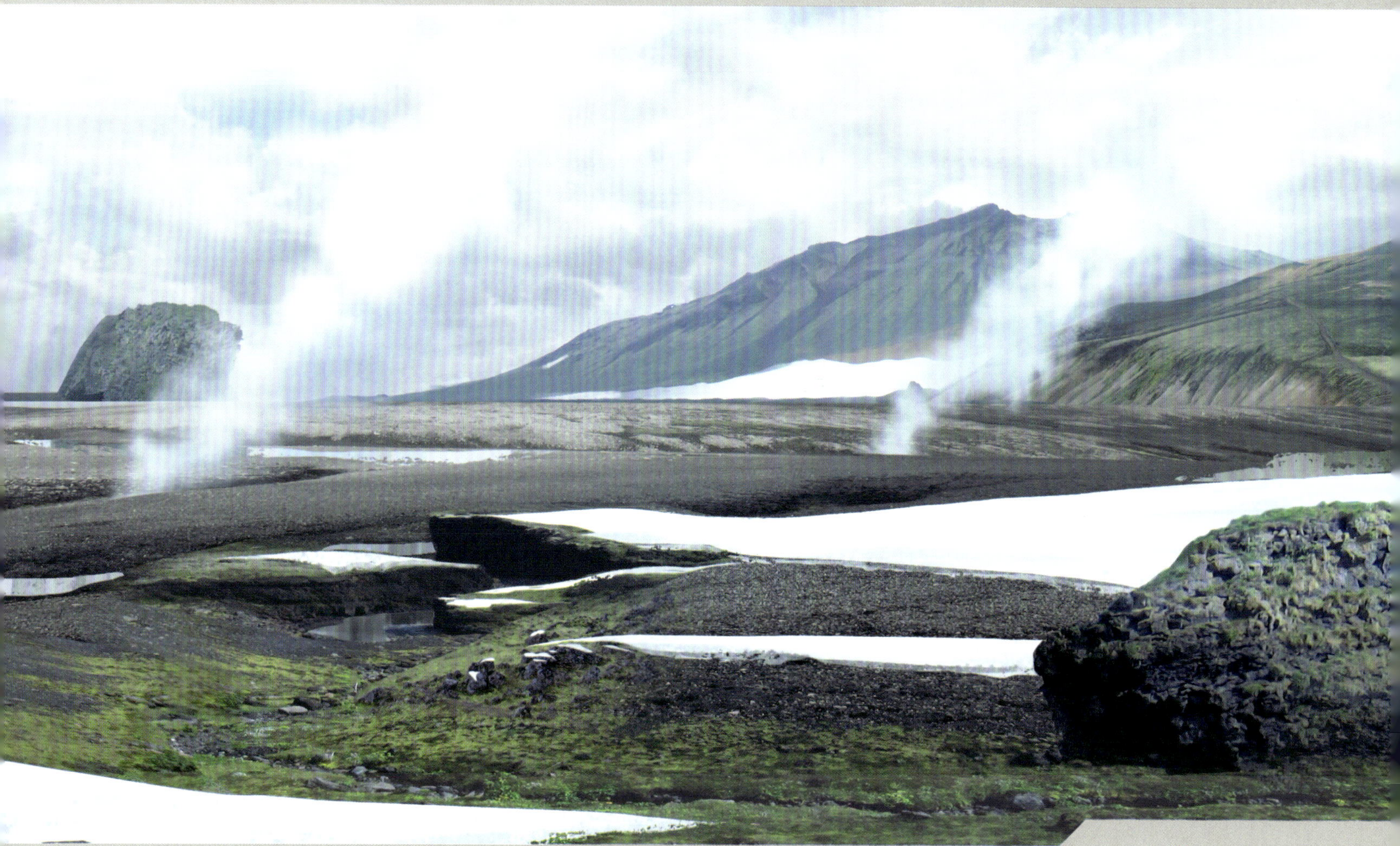

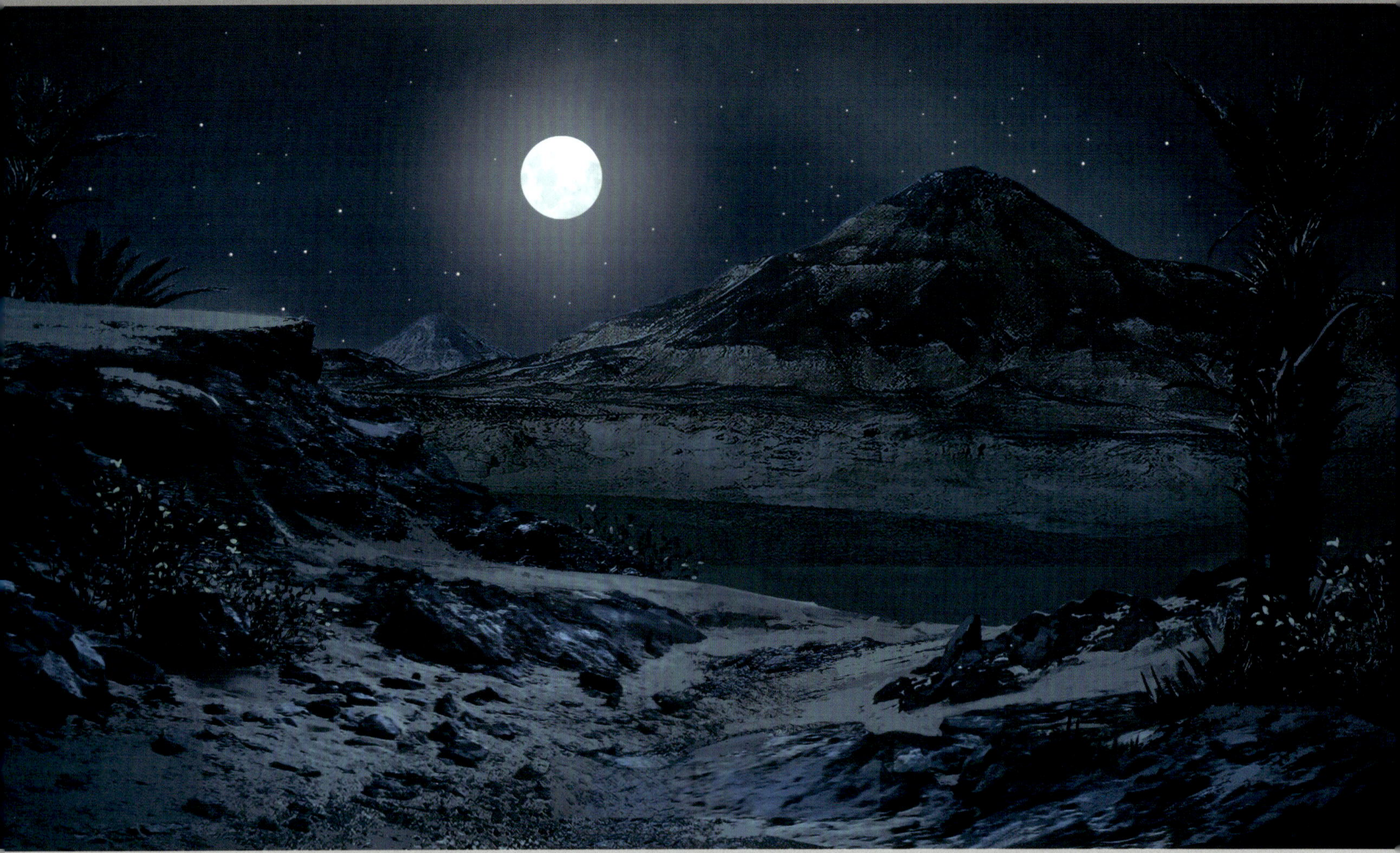

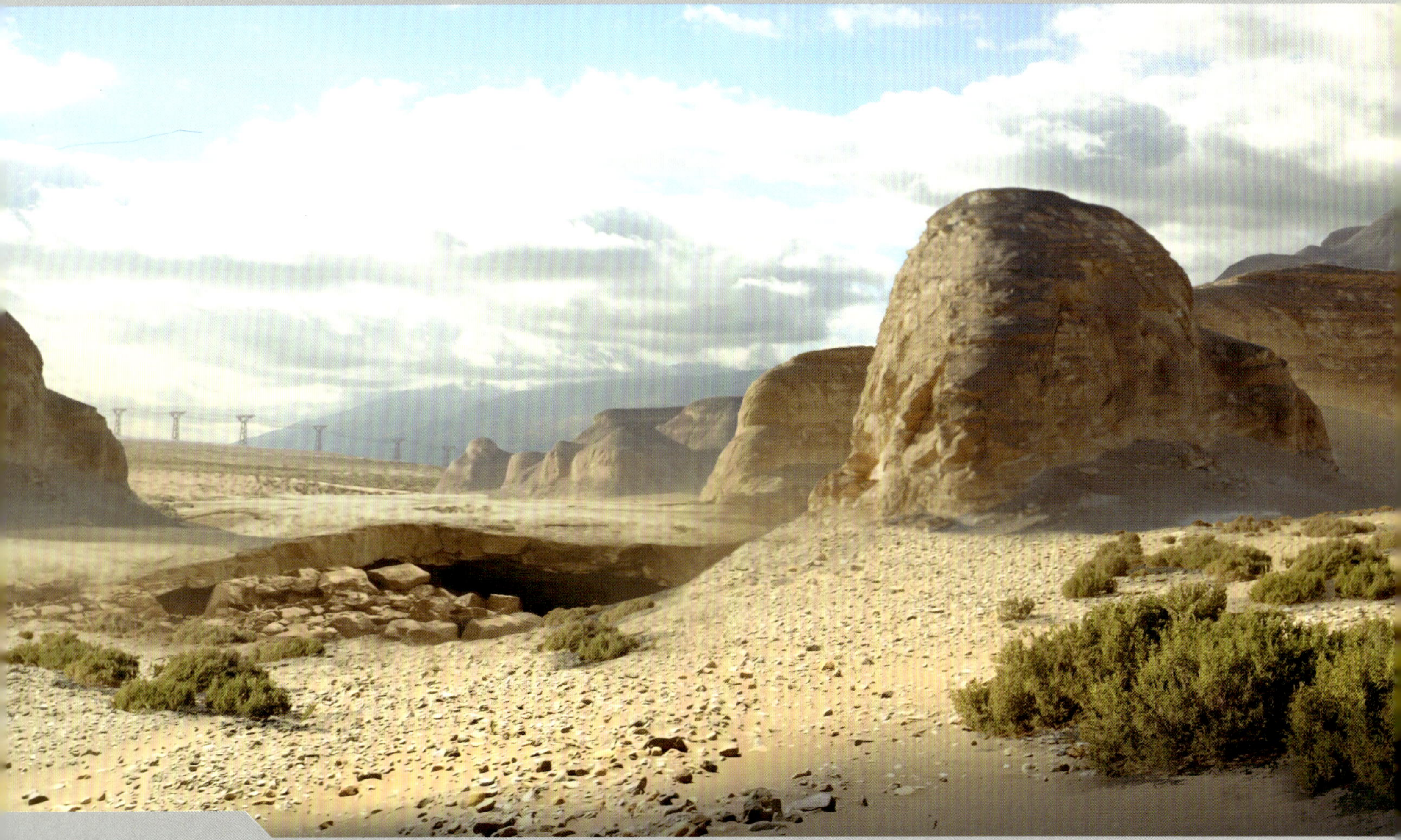

BASE DECAY

These early concepts of Base Decay explore the natural effects of what would happen to an abandoned base. Each sketch shows the progression of how natural elements would decay a building and leave it in ruins.

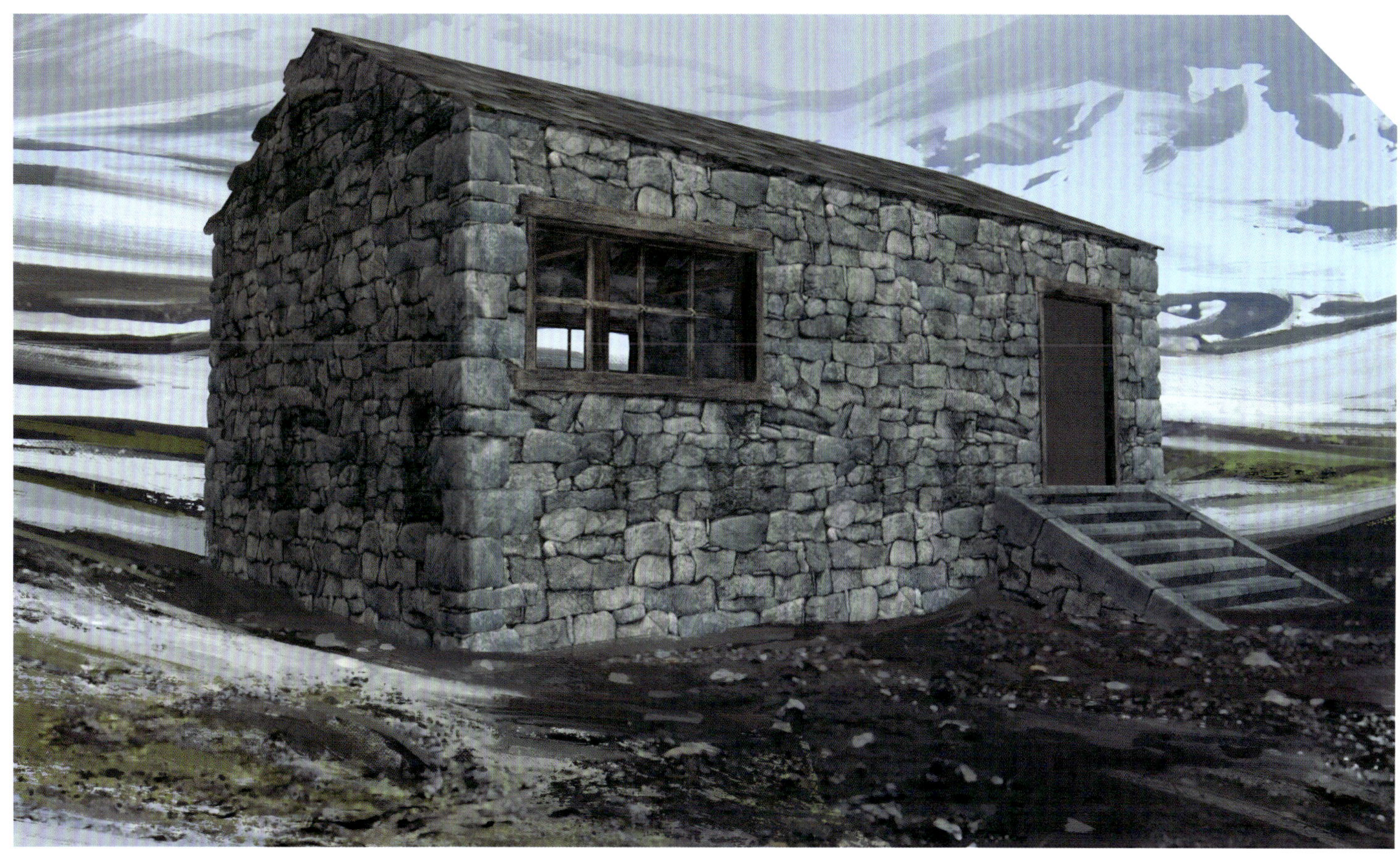

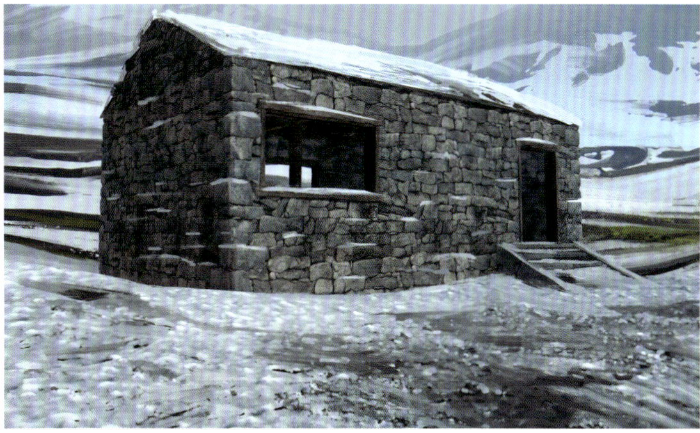

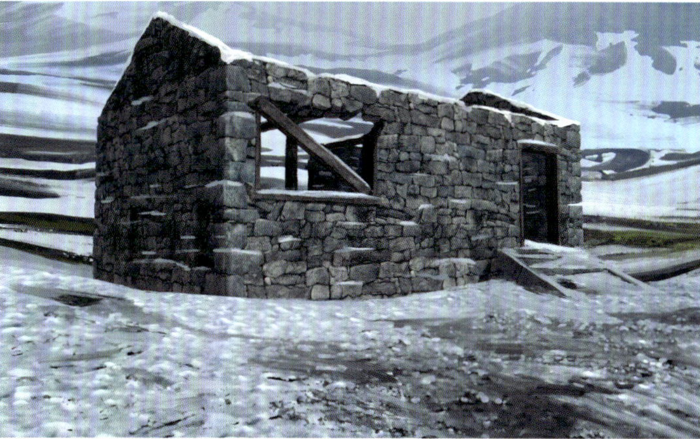

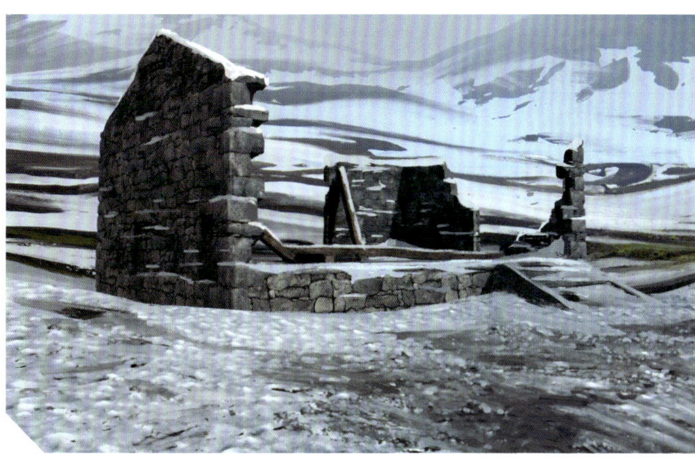

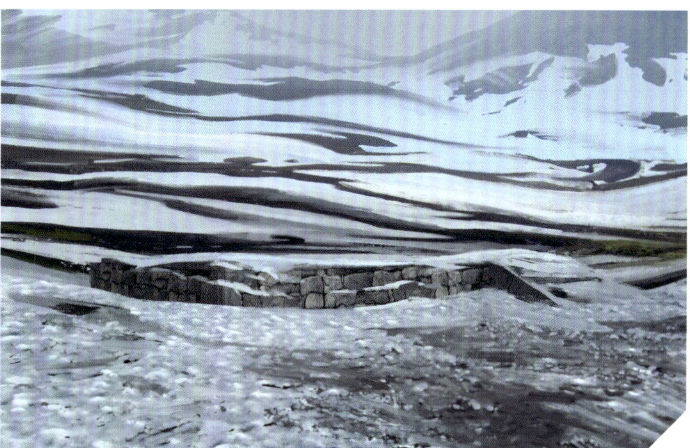

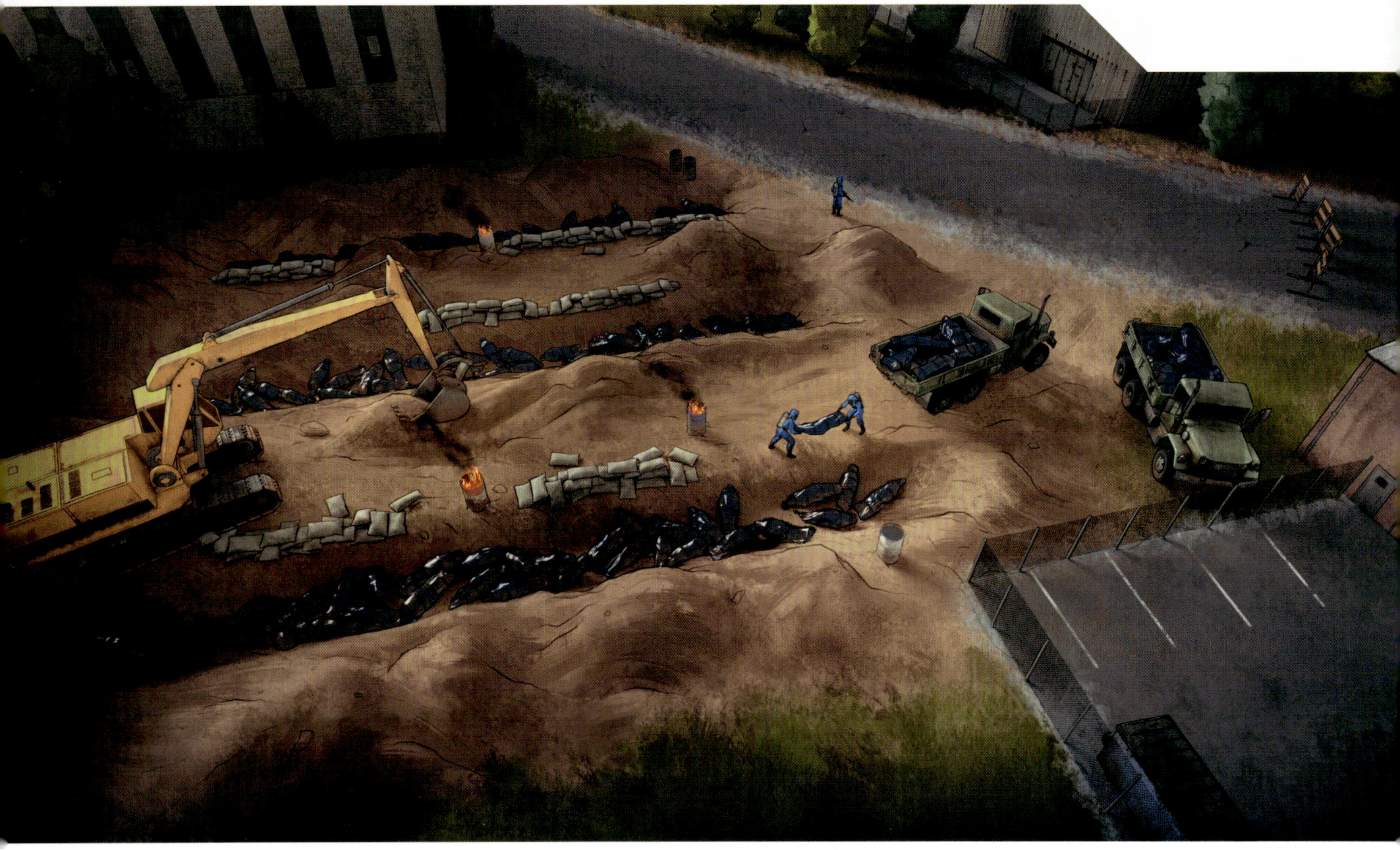

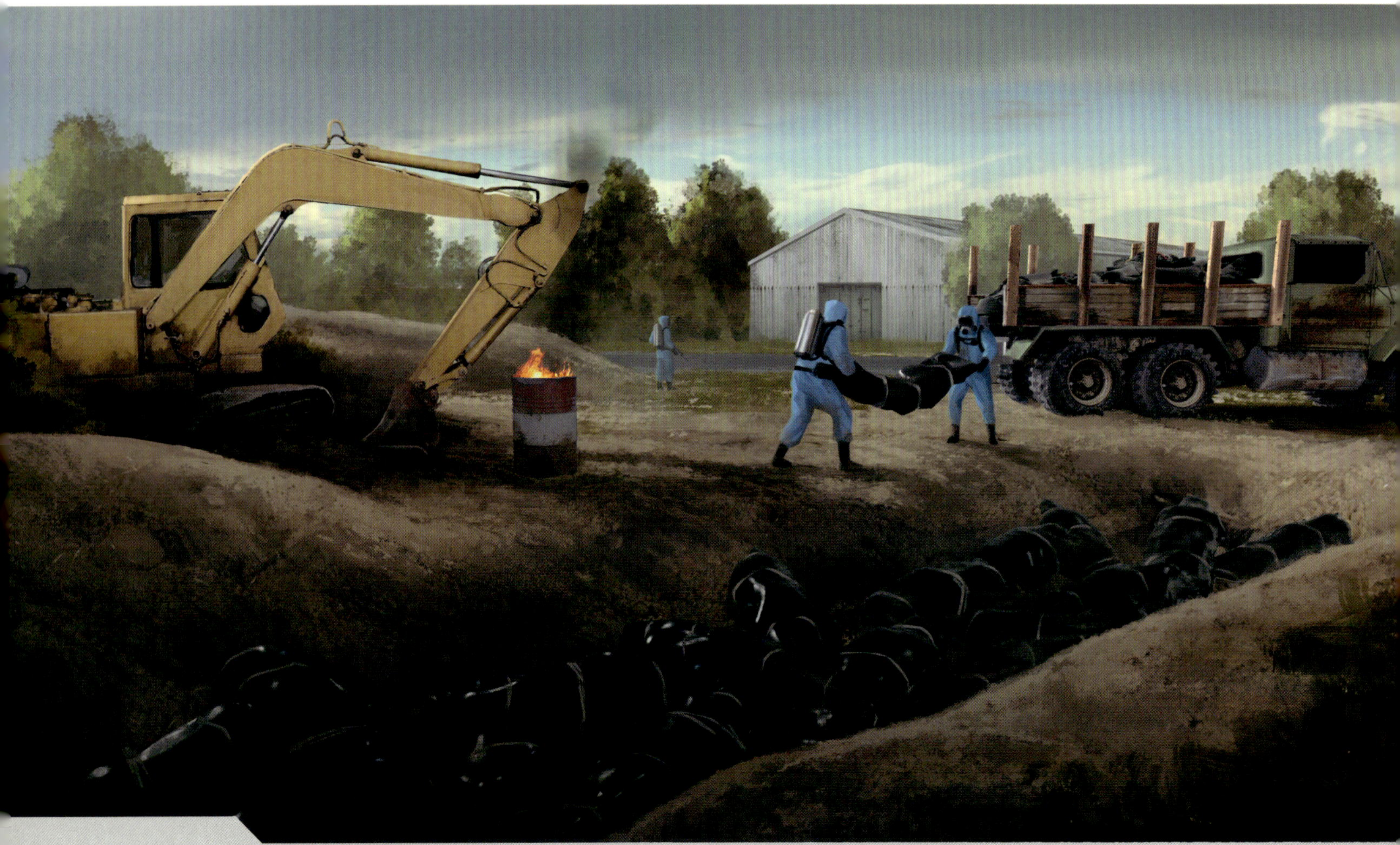

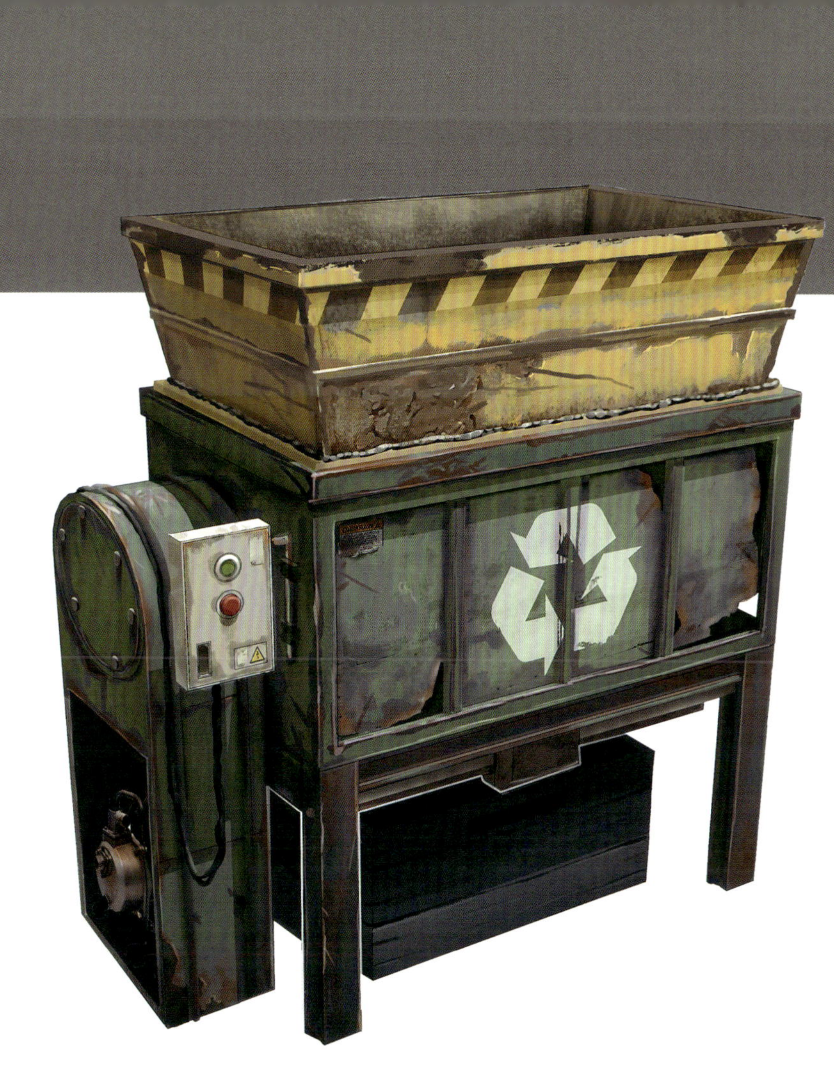

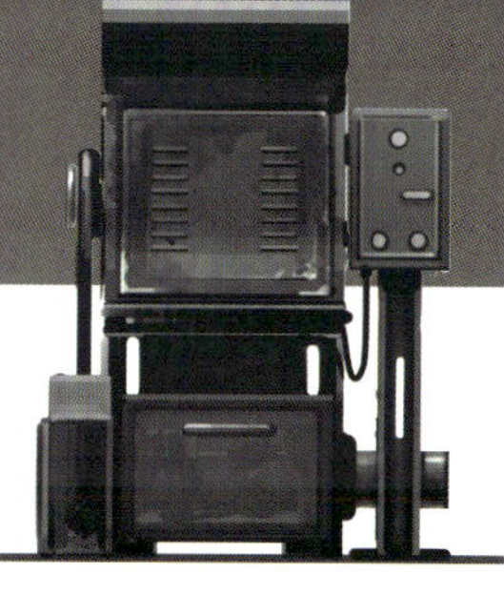

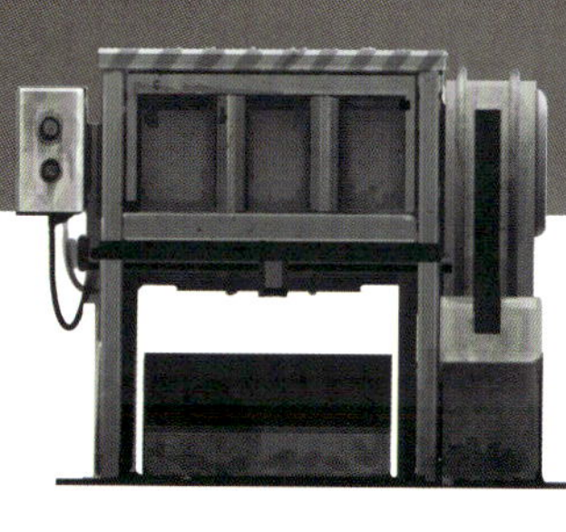

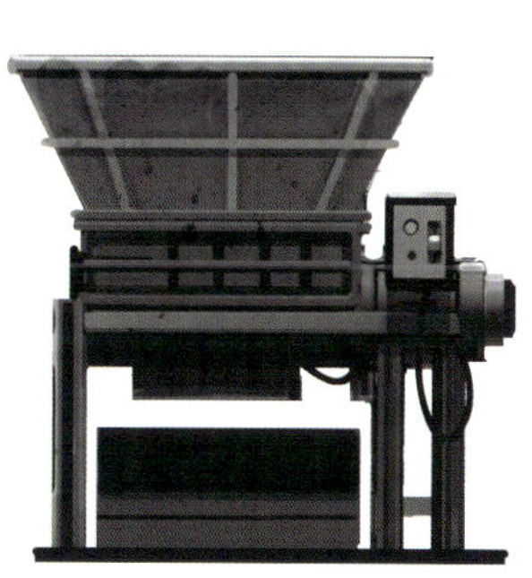

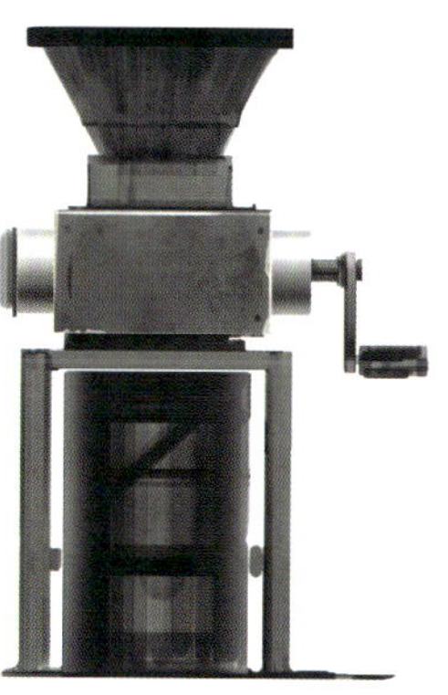

RECYCLERS

Rust's Recyclers feature a grimy industrial design with rusted metal, exposed gears, and chipped paint. Their concept art was inspired by large industrial machinery; their worn, mechanical look blends seamlessly into the monuments, reinforcing *Rust*'s decayed and abandoned aesthetic.

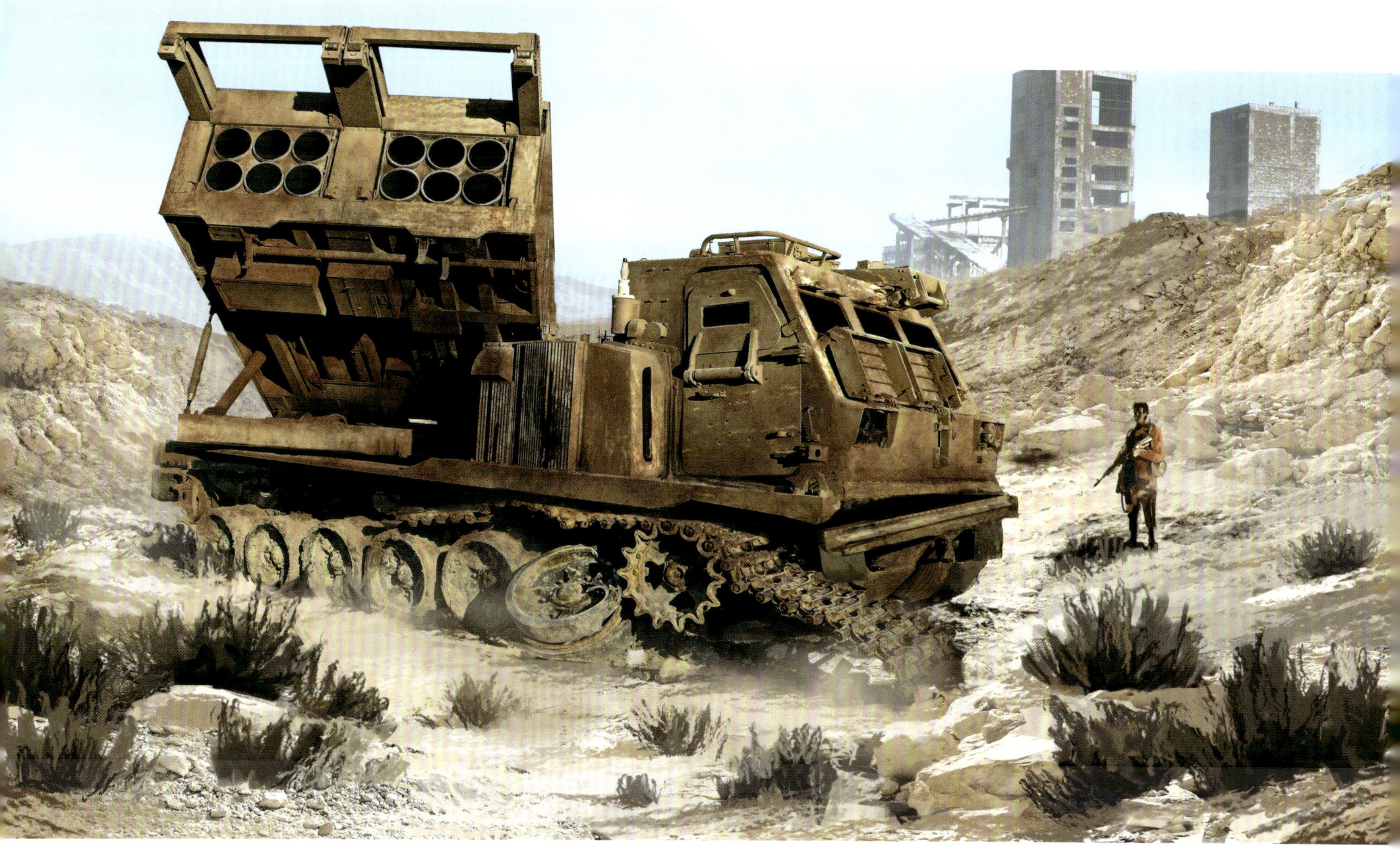

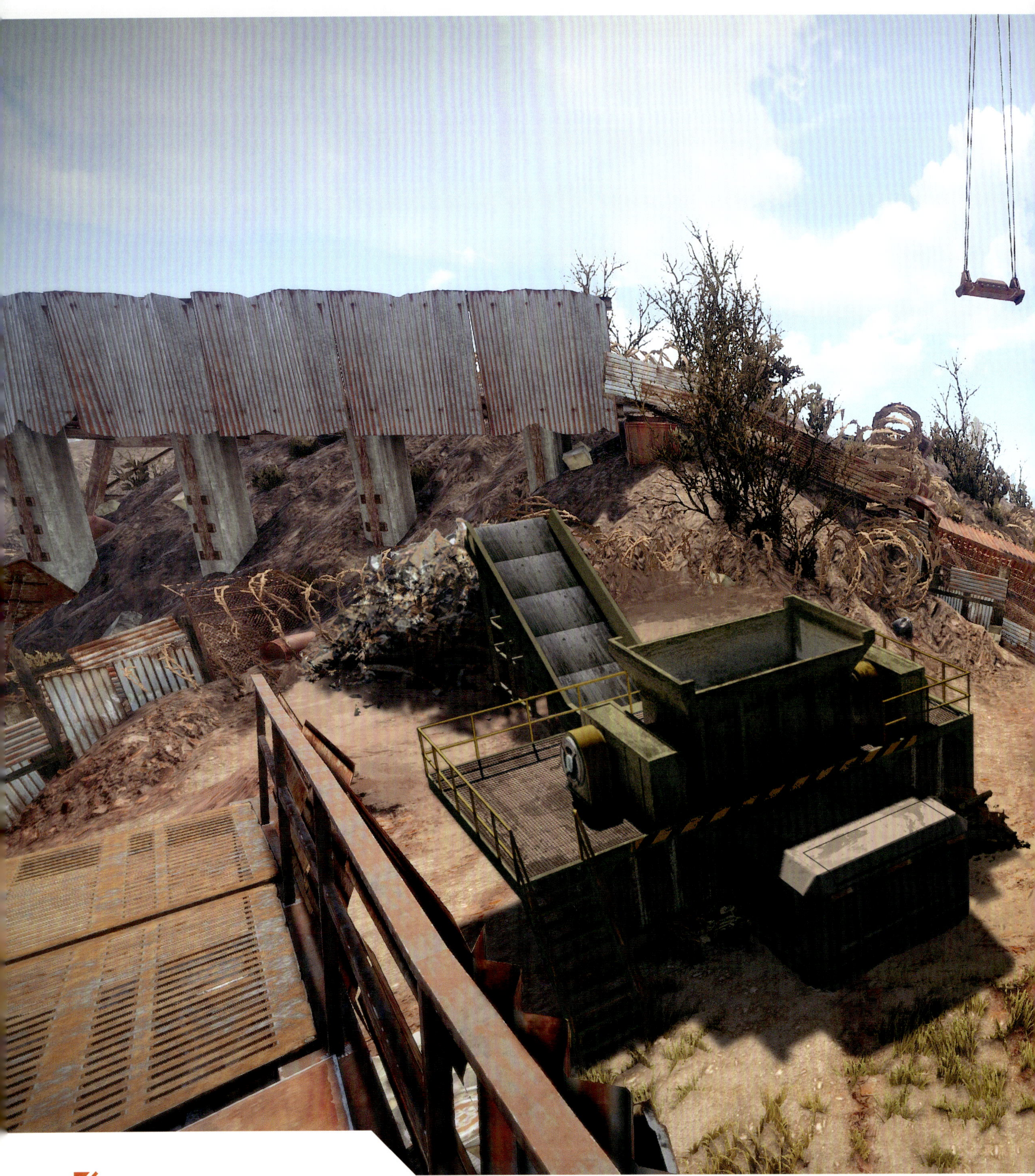

CAR SHREDDER

The *Rust* Car Shredder features a brutal industrial design inspired by scrap yard and car-lifting machinery. With sharp teeth, reinforced metal, and a large conveyor belt, the concept art pulls together a selection of shredding options based on real-life industrial machinery.

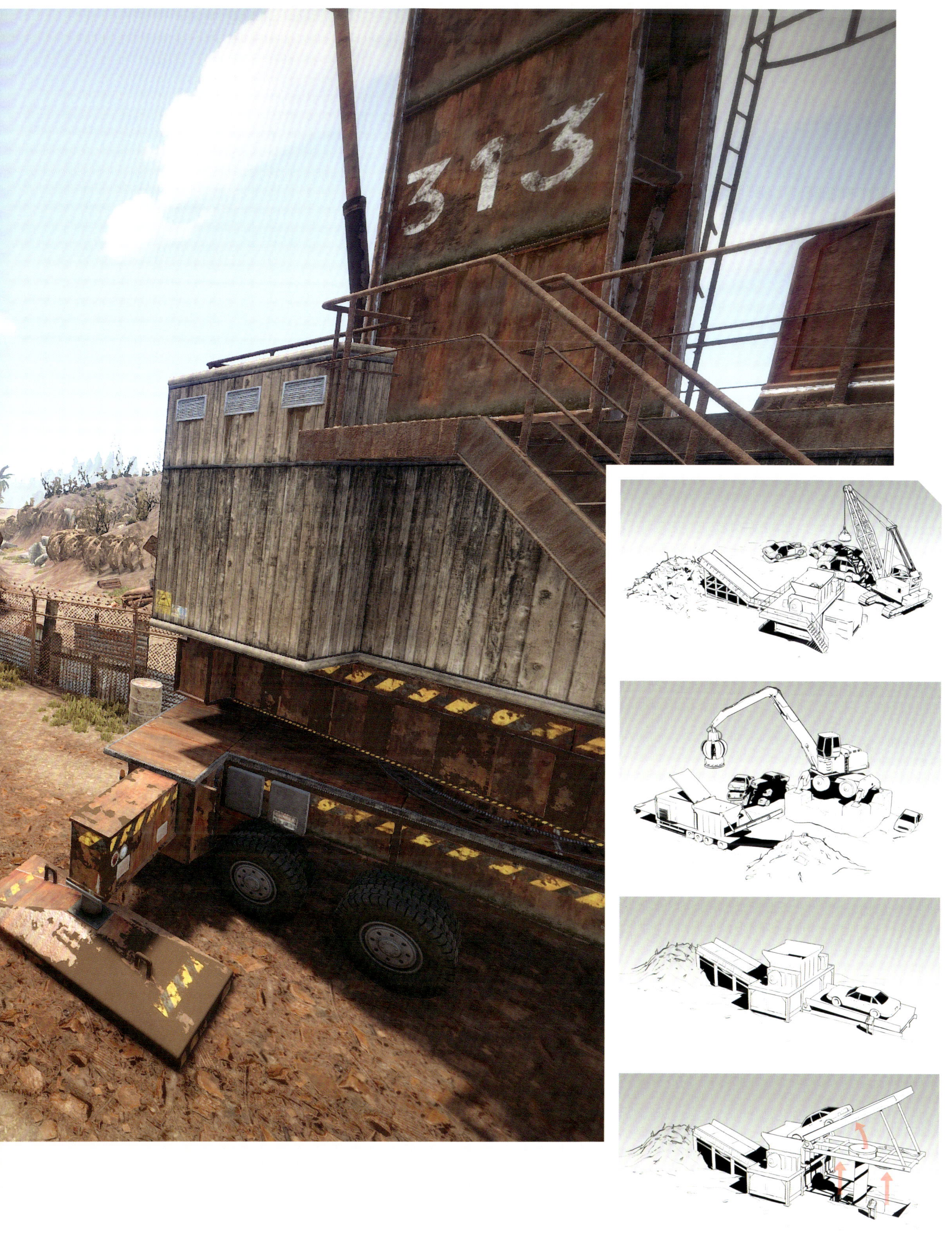
313

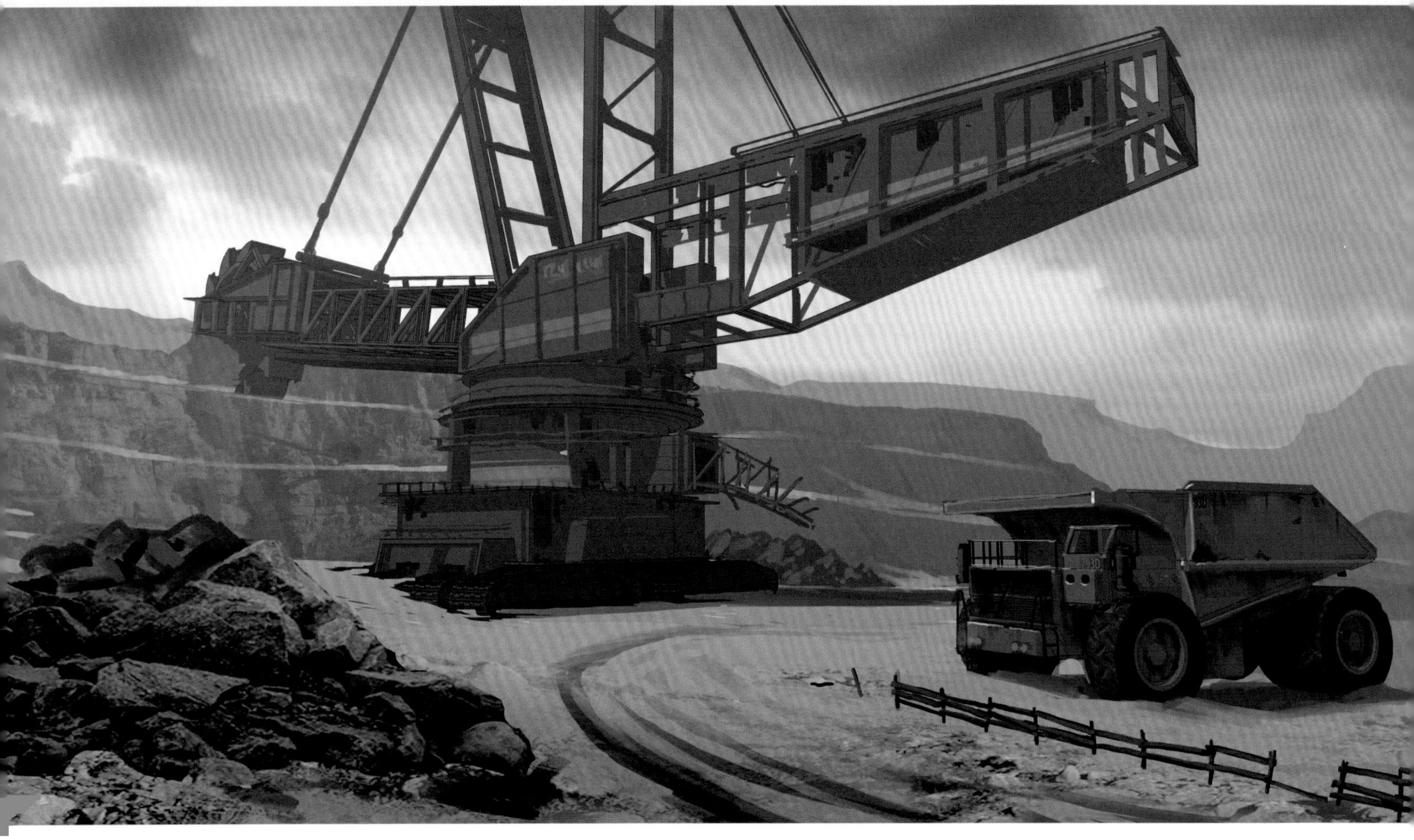

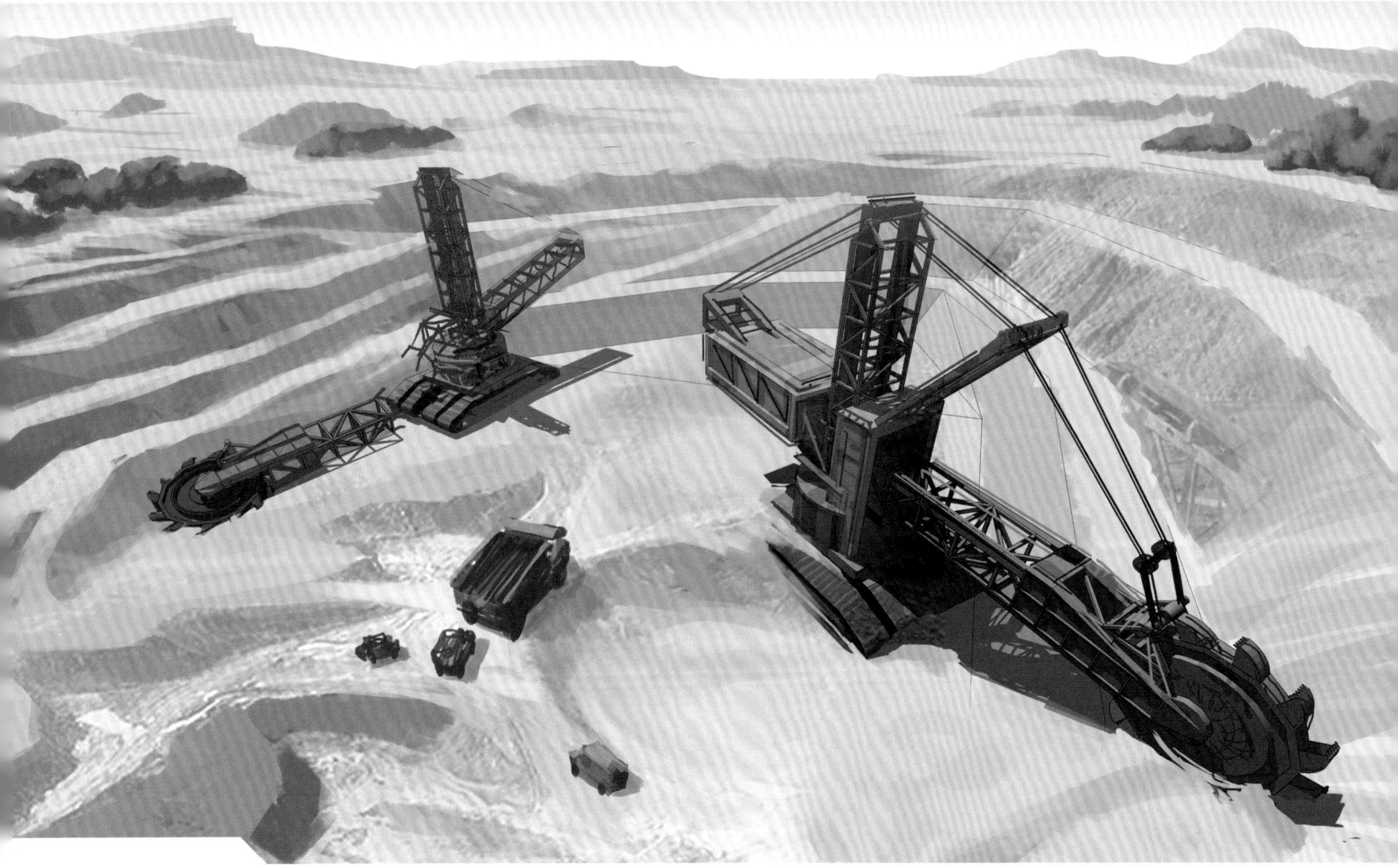

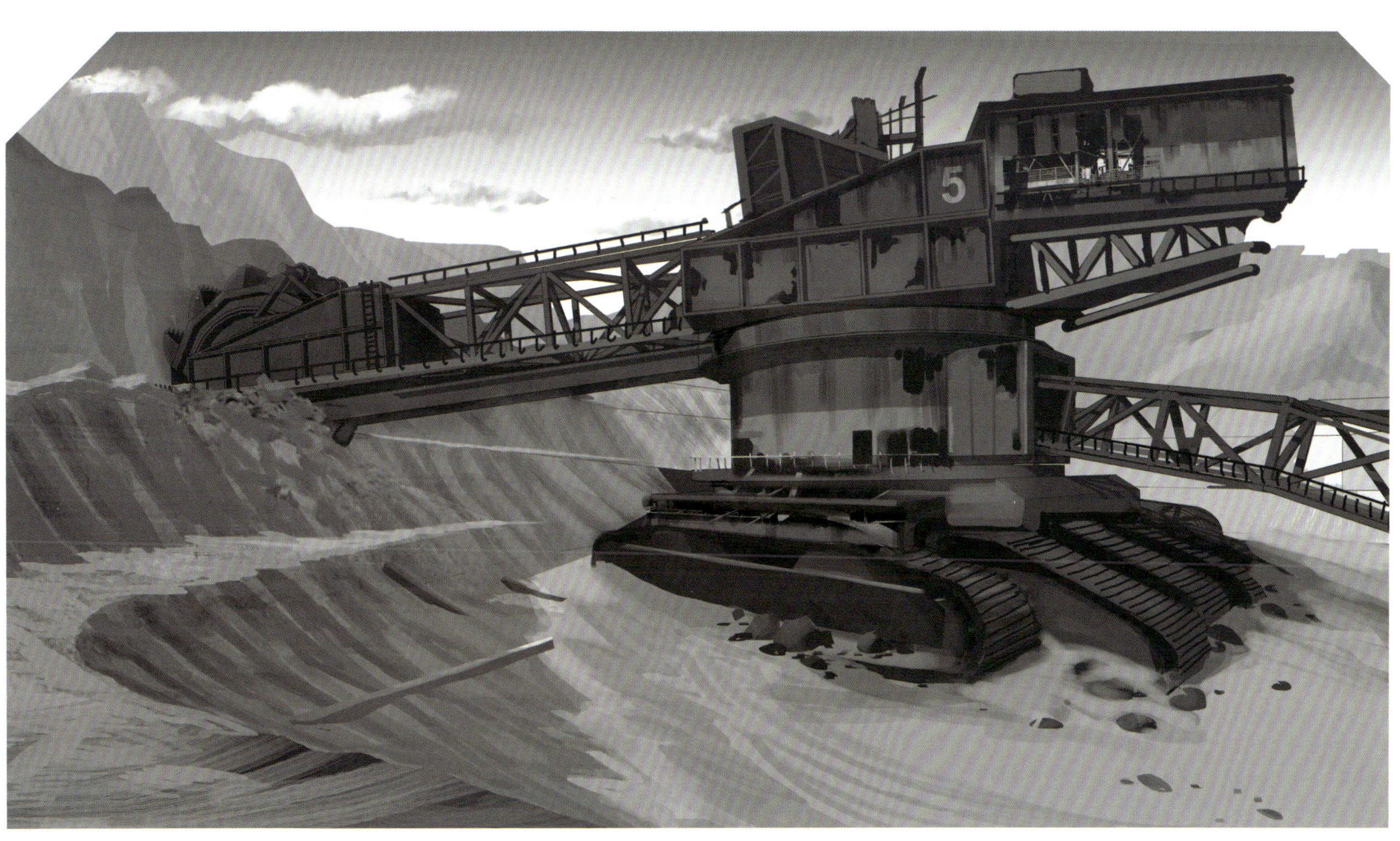

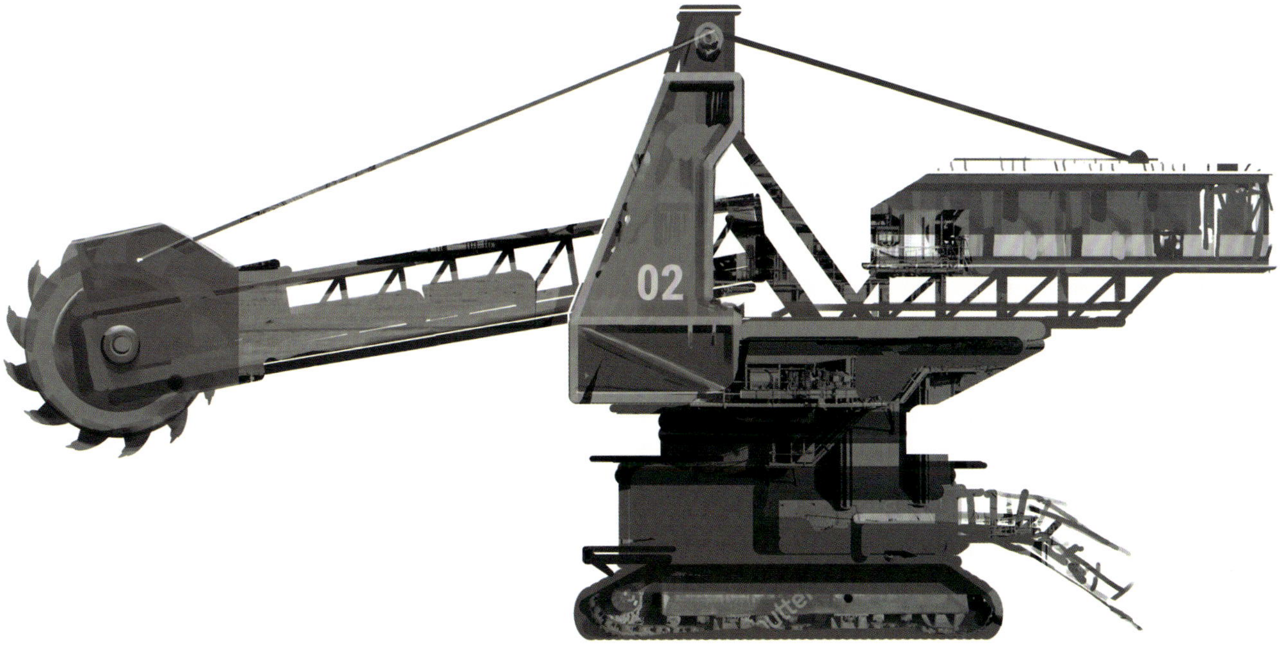

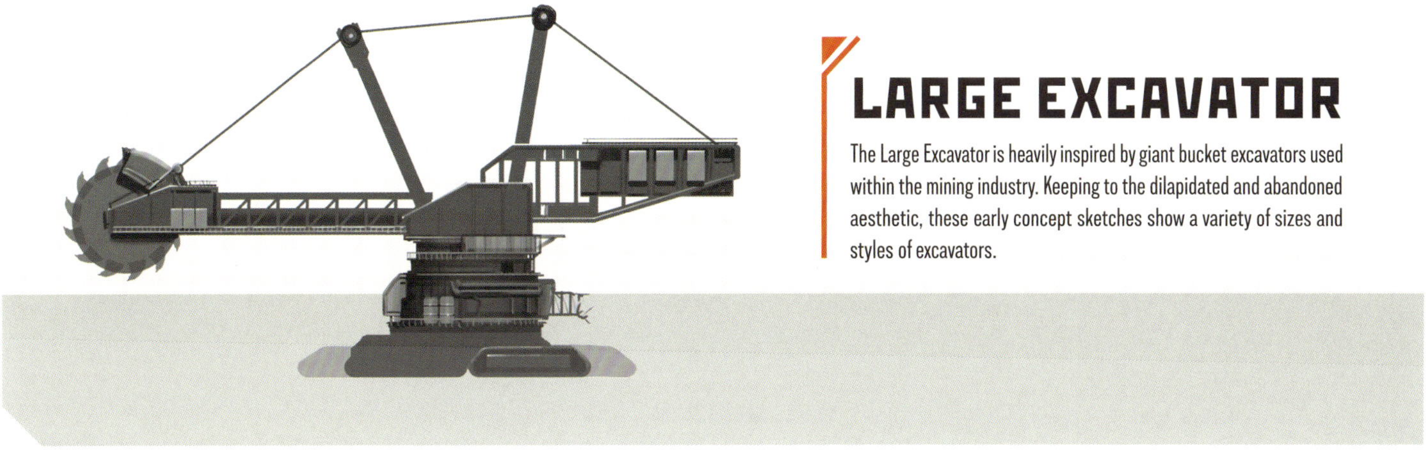

LARGE EXCAVATOR

The Large Excavator is heavily inspired by giant bucket excavators used within the mining industry. Keeping to the dilapidated and abandoned aesthetic, these early concept sketches show a variety of sizes and styles of excavators.

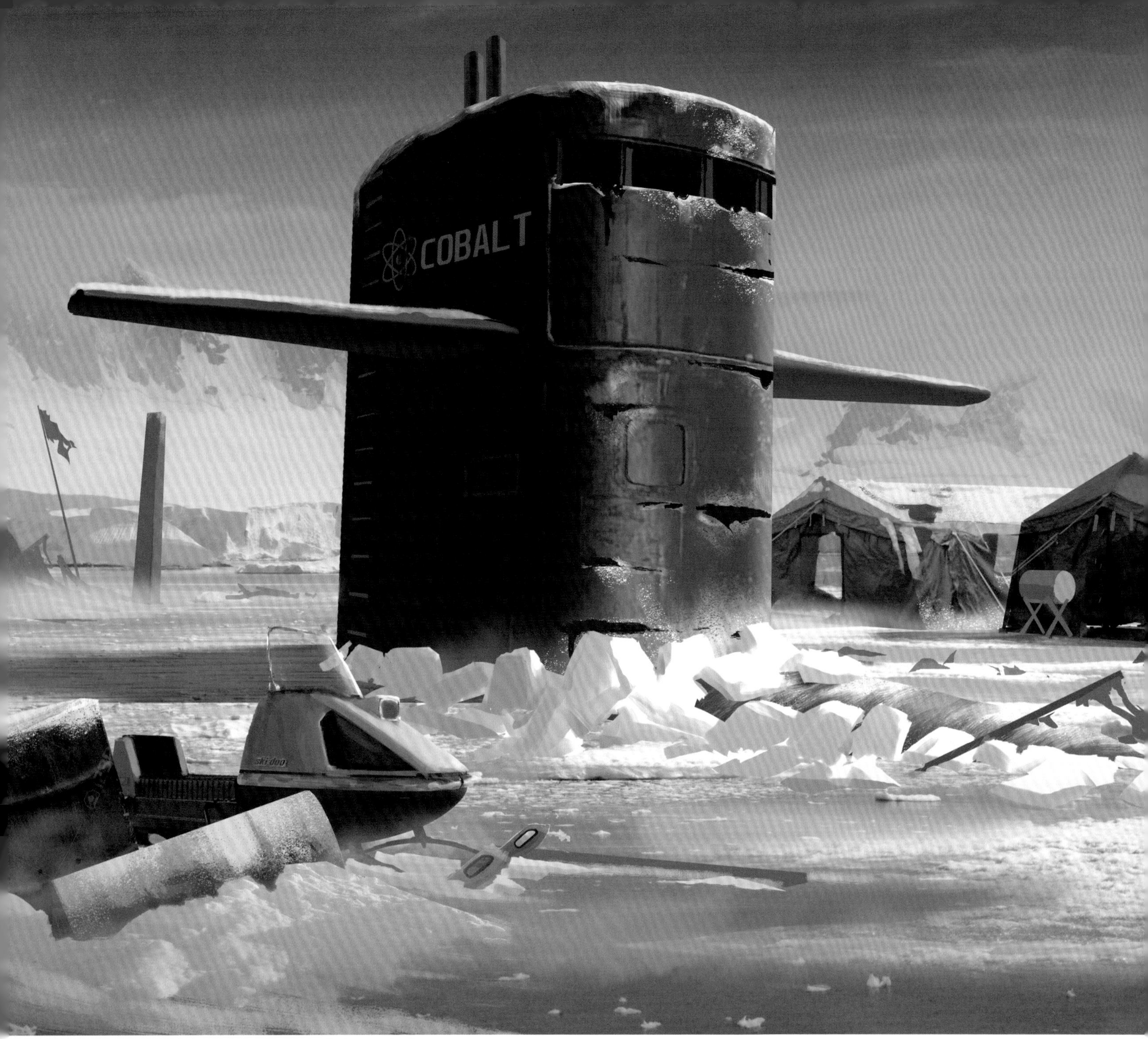

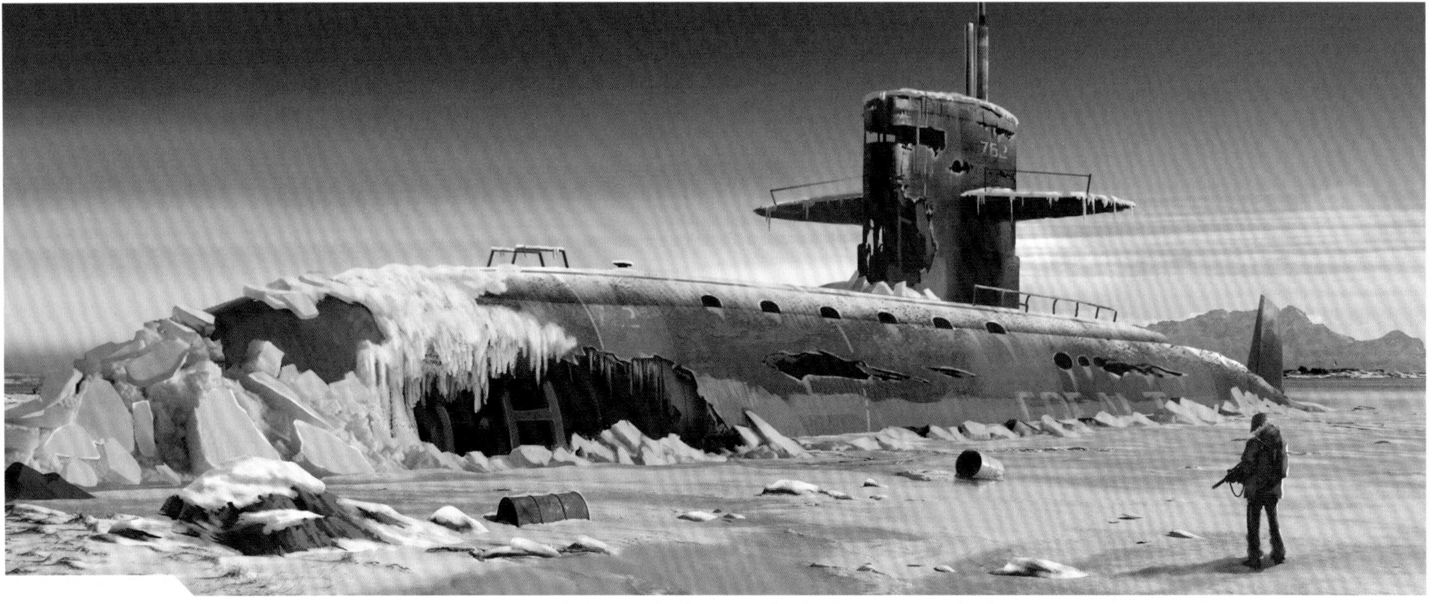
762

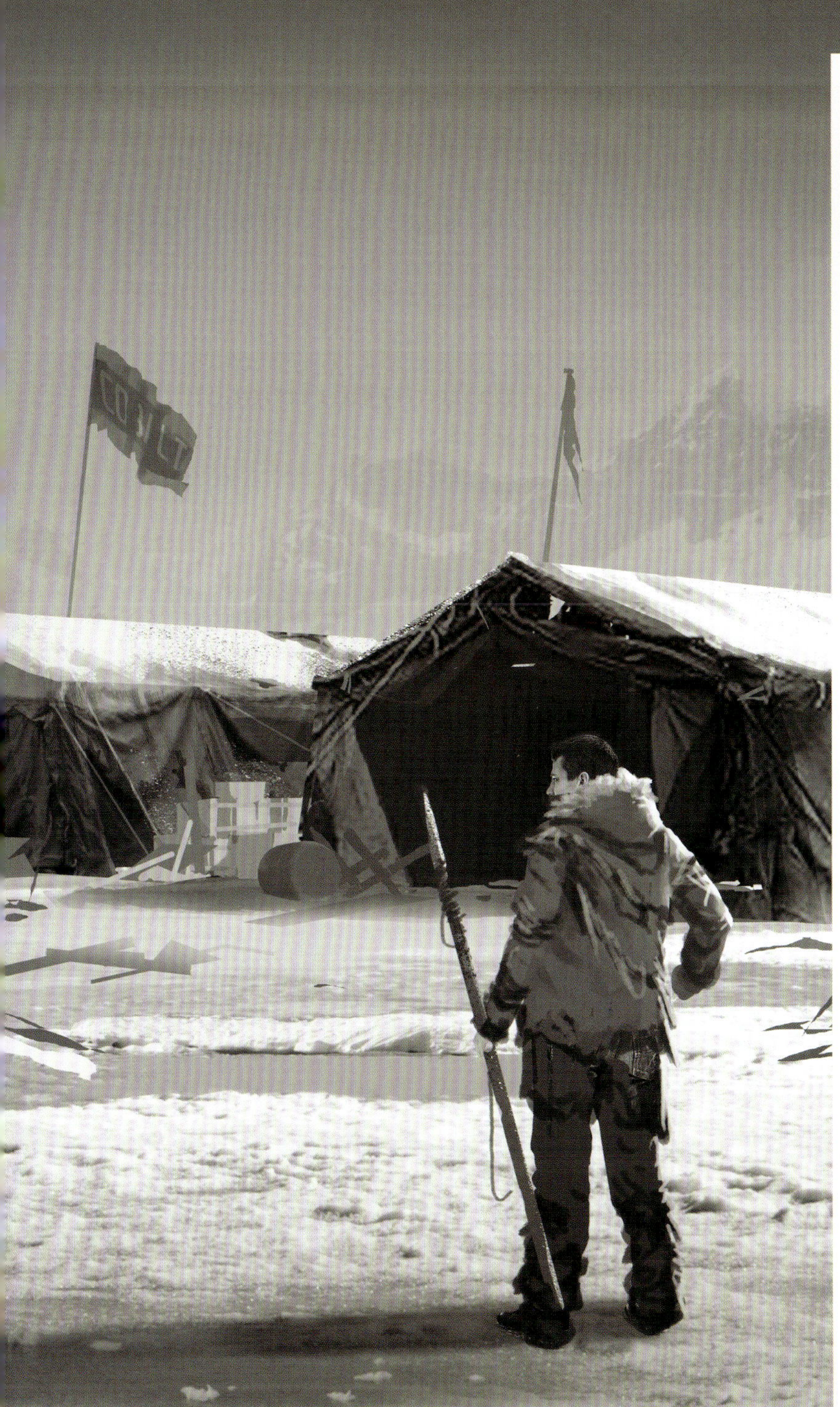

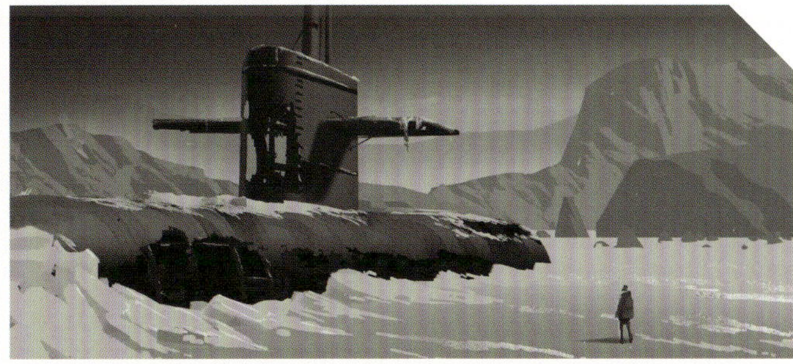

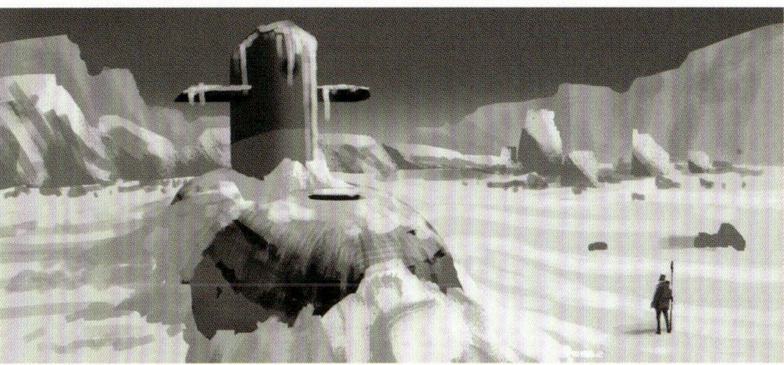

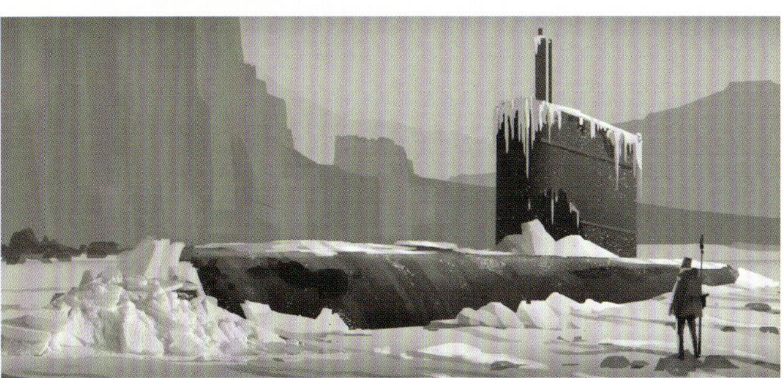

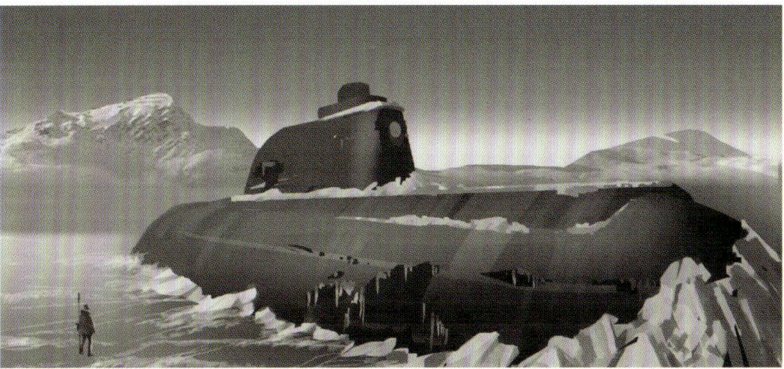

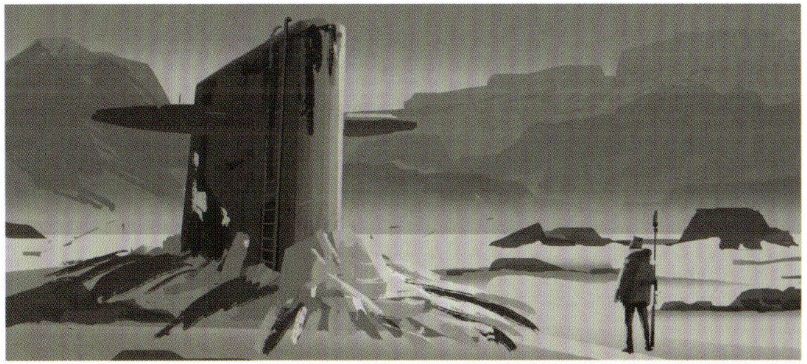

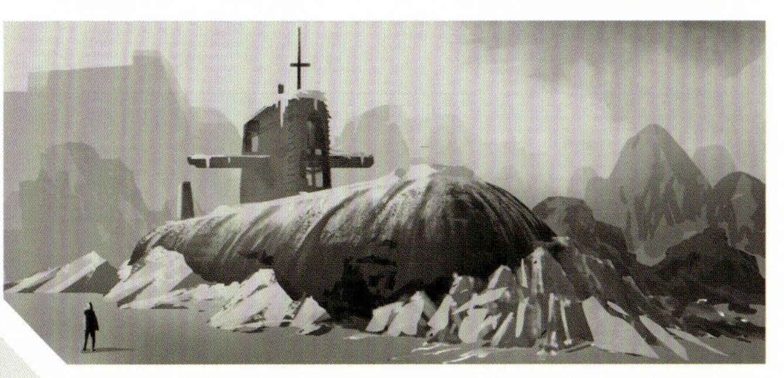

FROZEN SUBMARINE

The initial concepts for the frozen submarine monument were based on Soviet nuclear submarines. Even though this idea didn't make it into *Rust*, these sketches create an eerie atmosphere, blending harsh survival elements and the breached, battered submarine with the frozen biome's cold.

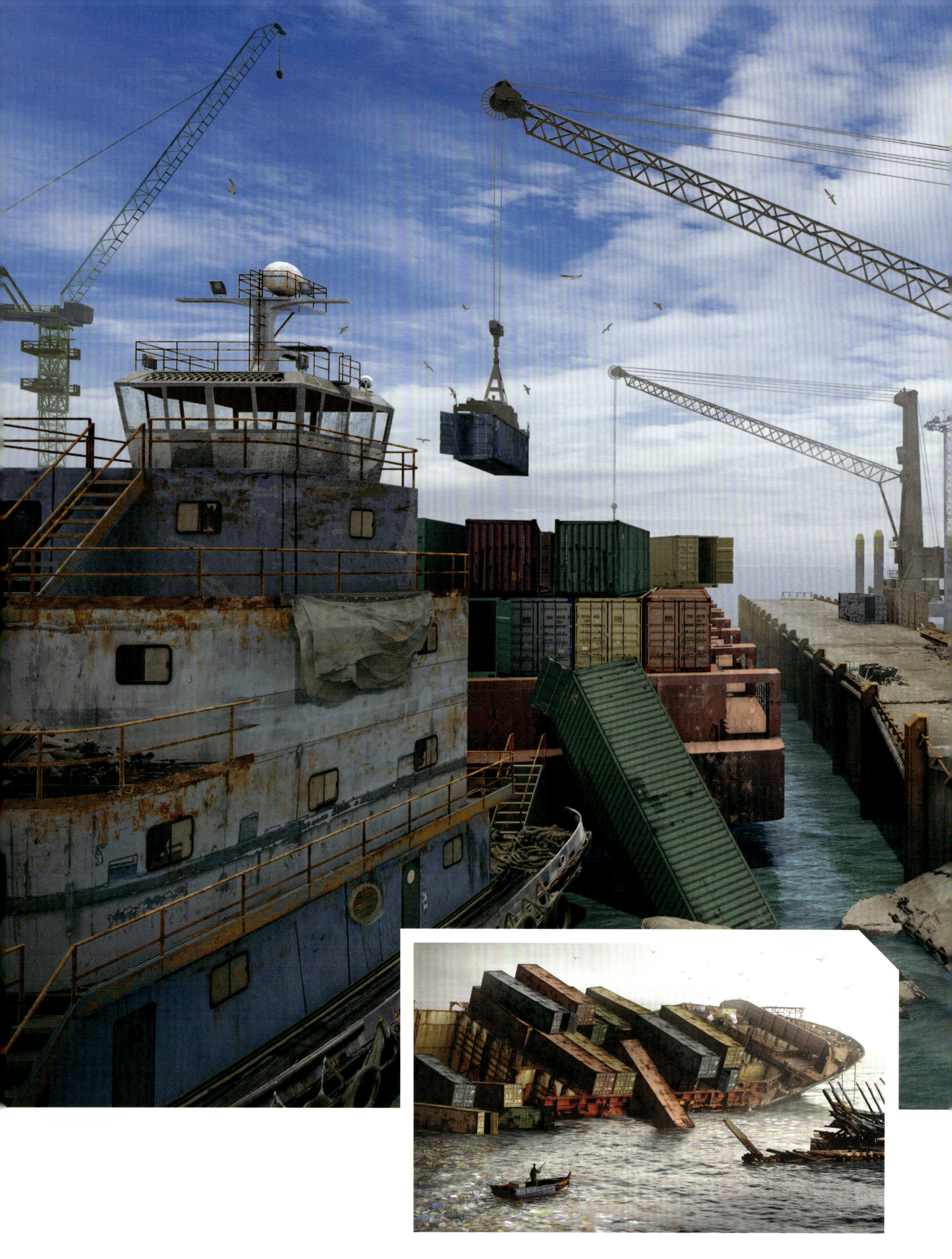

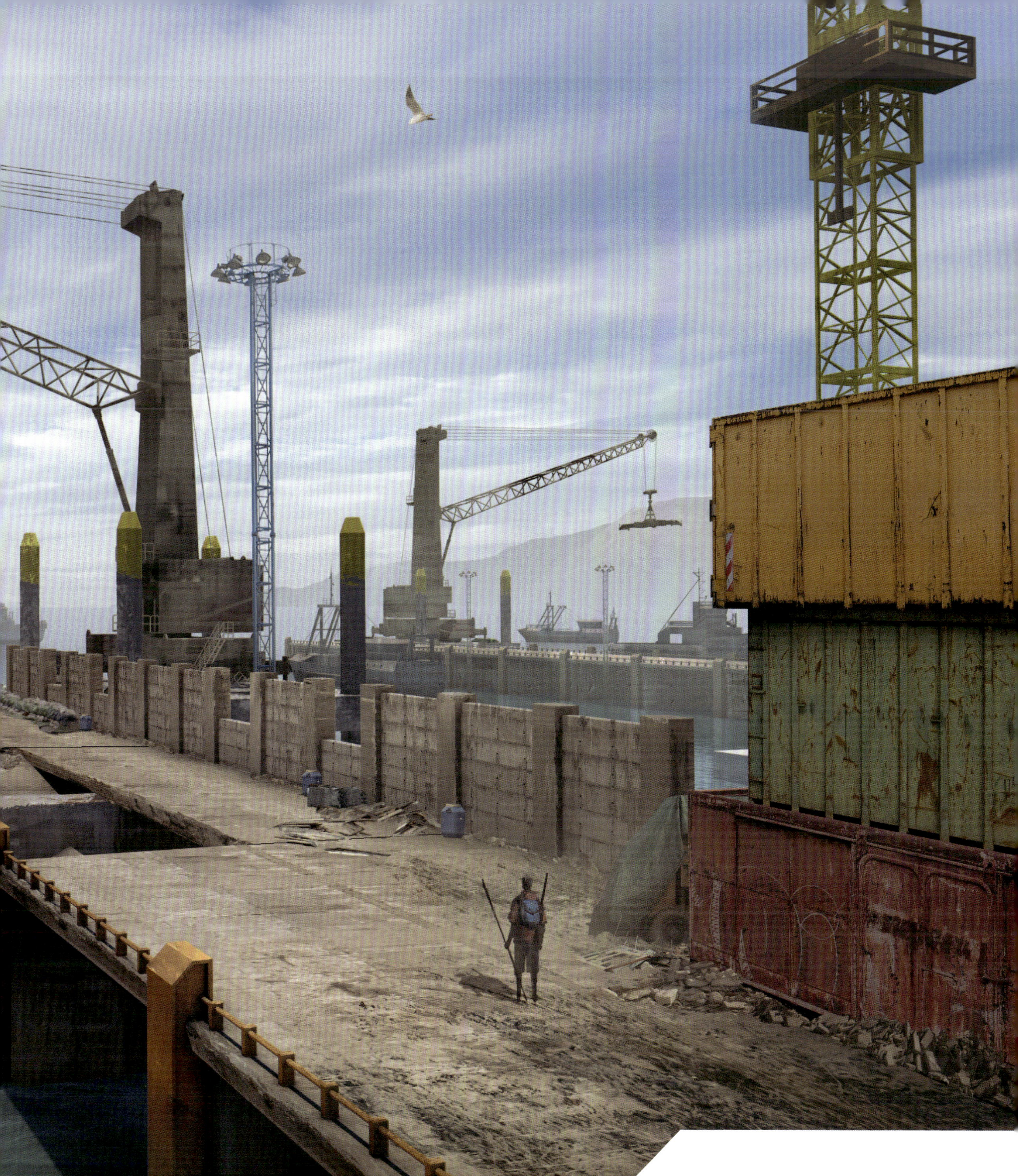

HARBOR

Rust's Harbor was designed to give an epic first impression while inspiring the player to explore their surroundings. Its early concepts show a vast decaying, abandoned space based on a functional harbor with rusted containers, worn cranes, and stranded ships. This provides a great monument where the player can explore, loot, and battle it out in PvP.

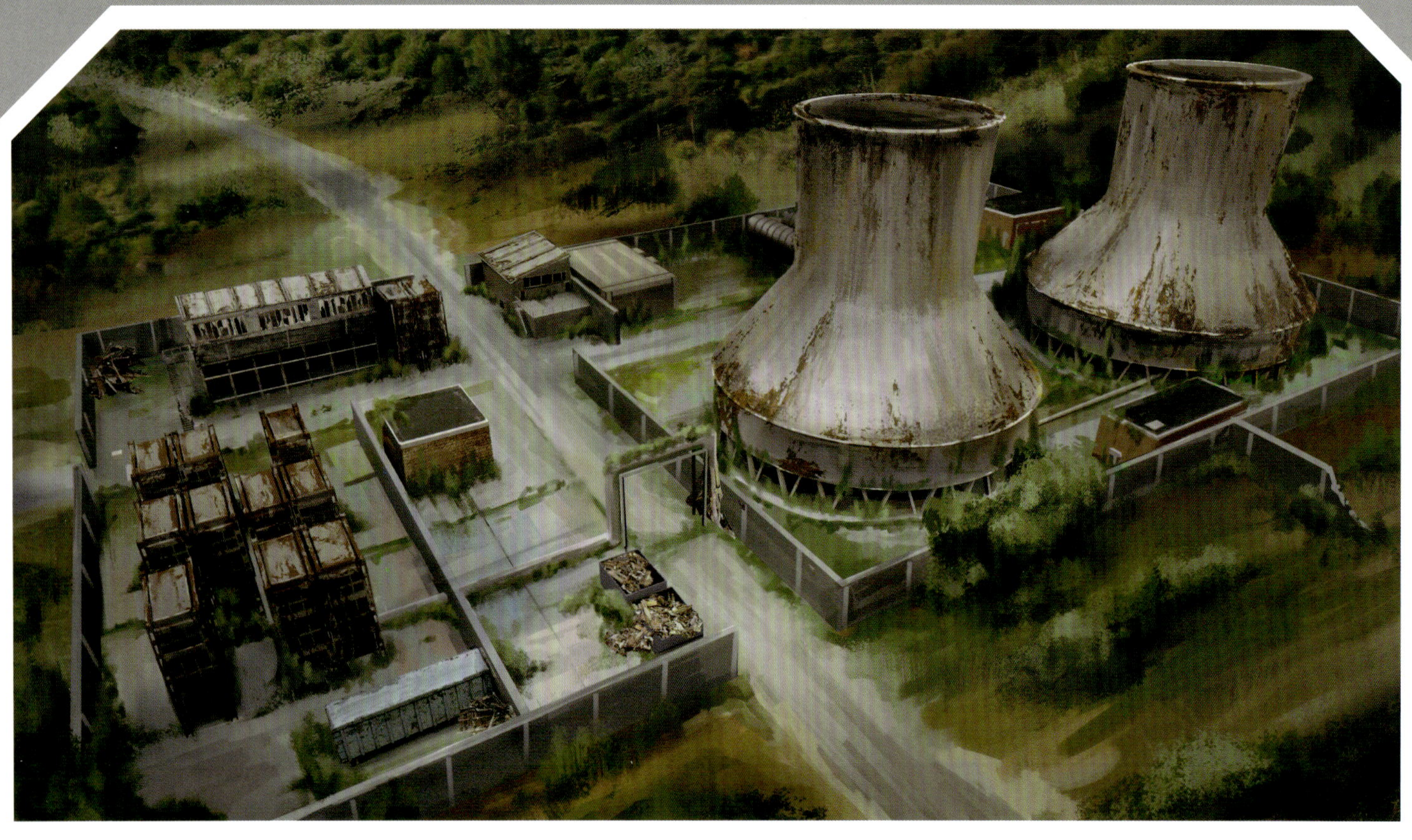

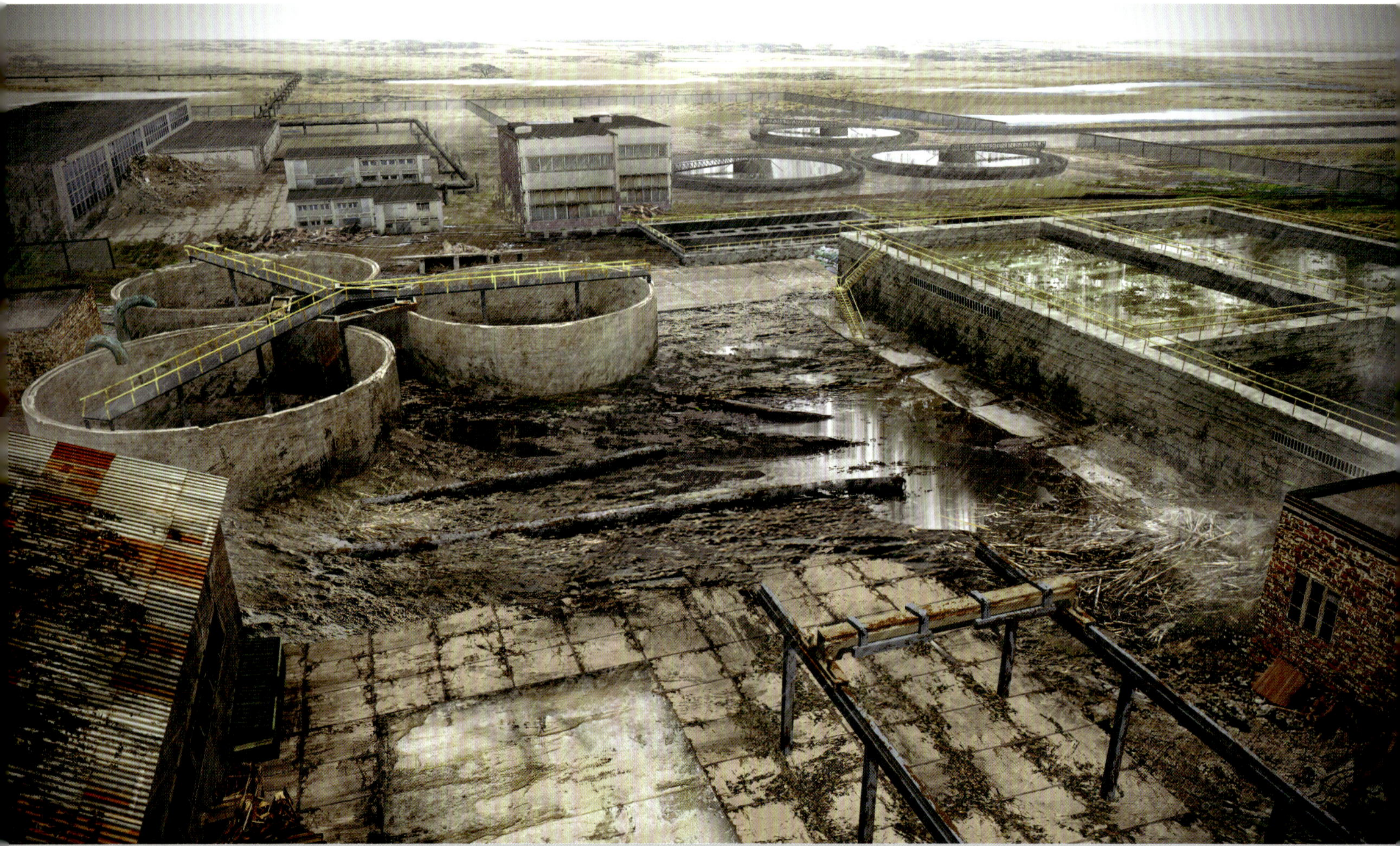

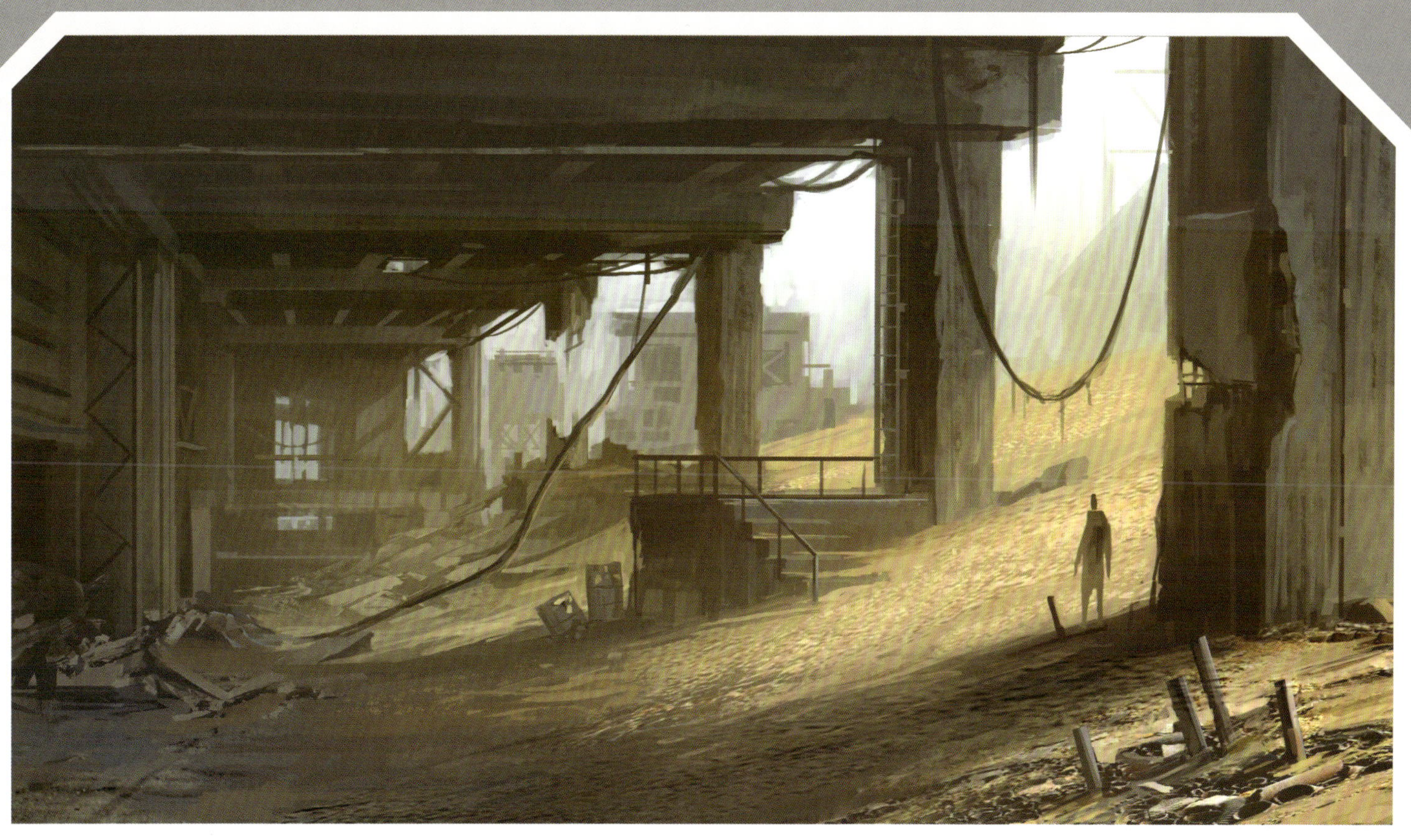

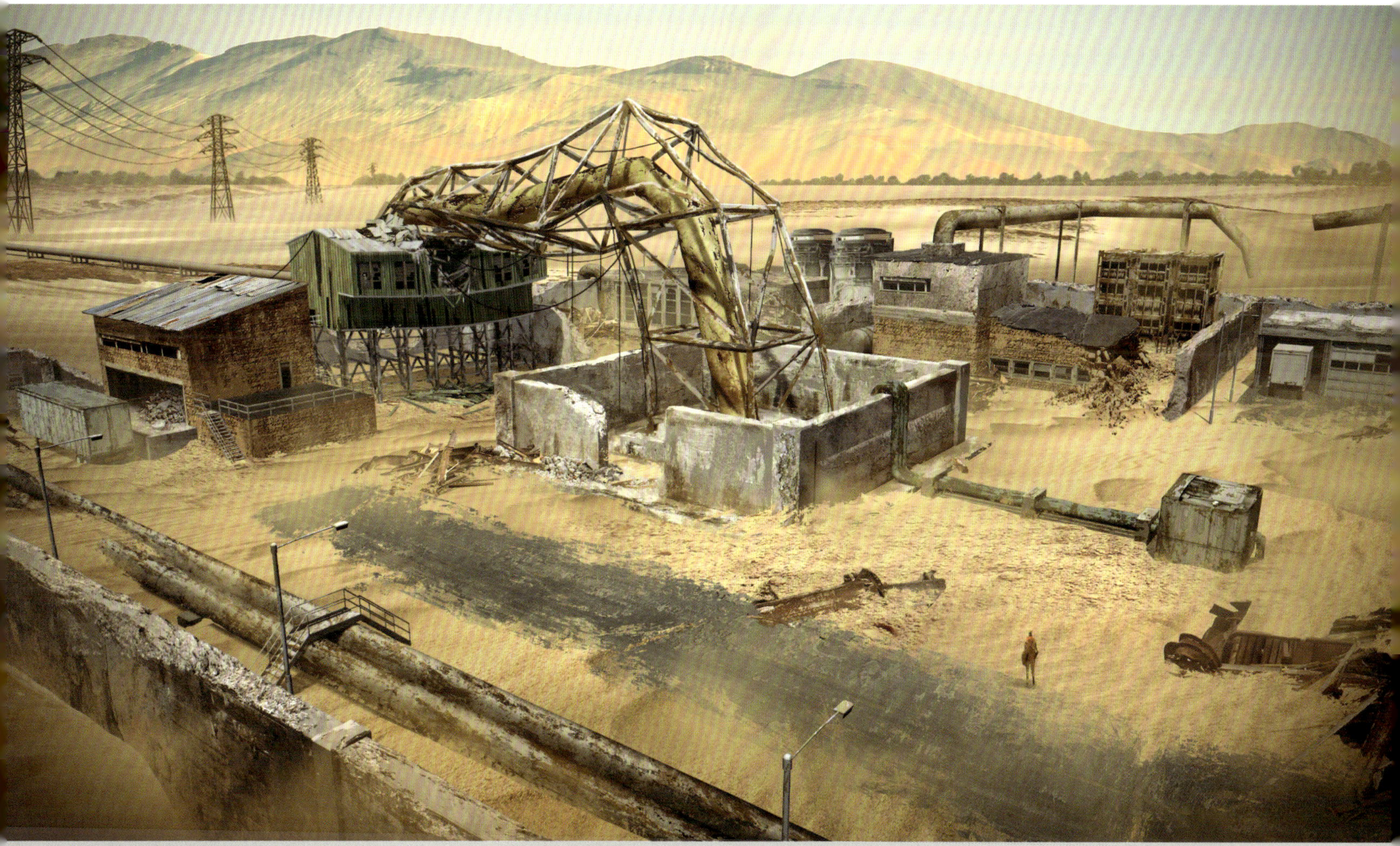

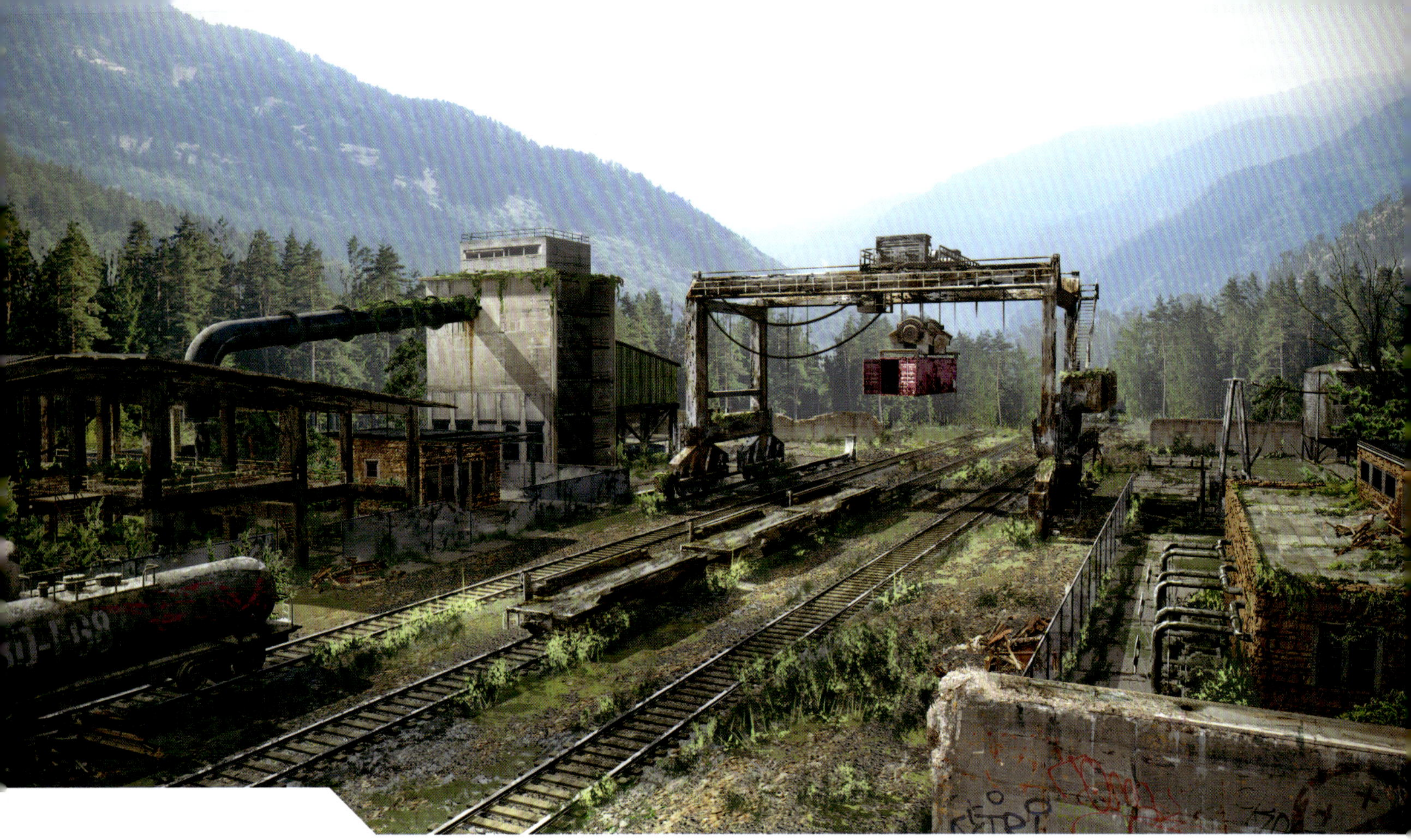

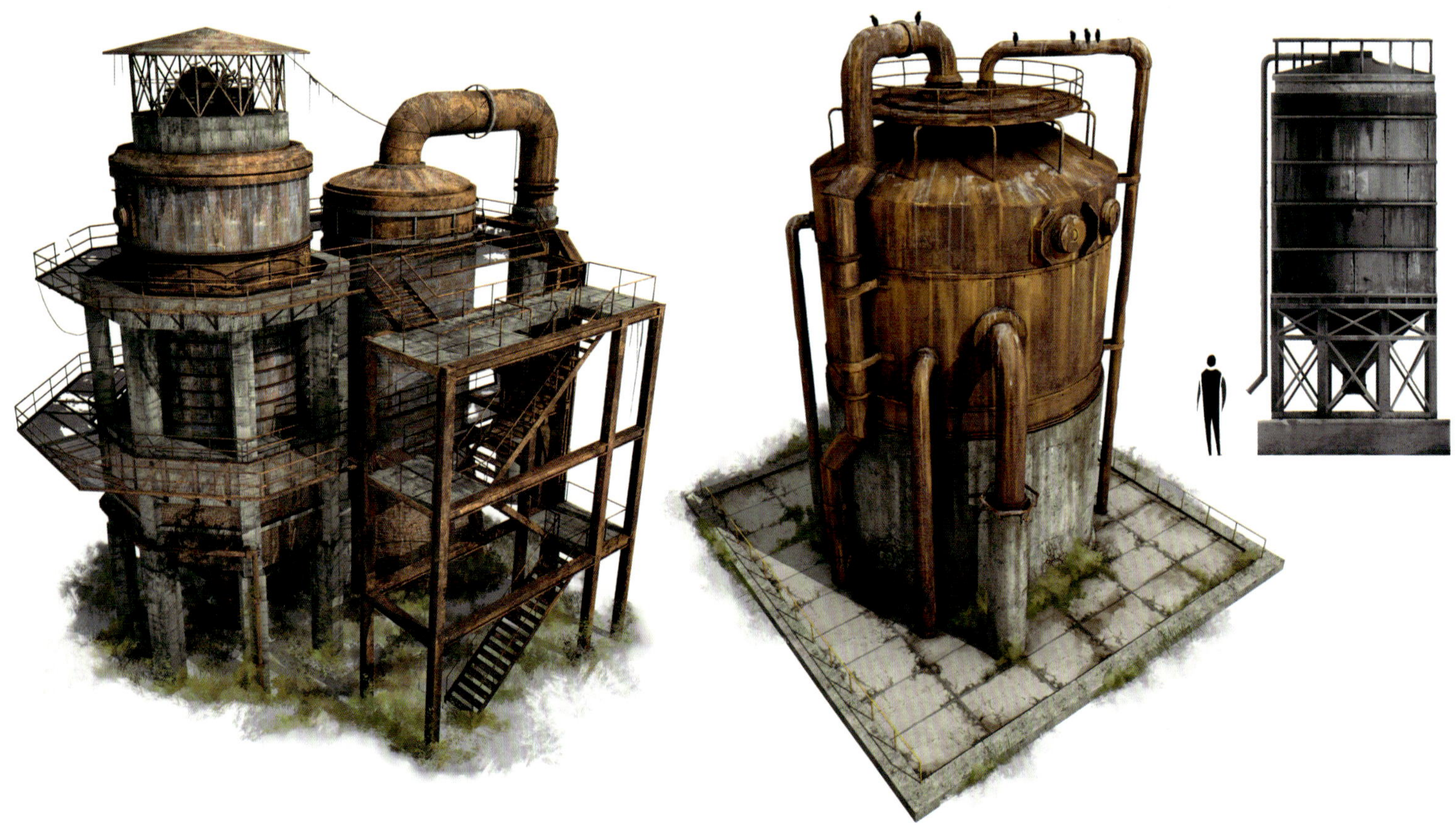

RADTOWN BUILDINGS

The Radtown monument is one of the game's early iconic locations, designed to provide close-quarter PvP scenarios within a decayed and irradiated setting. Its original concepts were based on a large factory or milling site featuring weathered silos, exposed rusted metal, and crumbling structures partially covered in overgrowth.

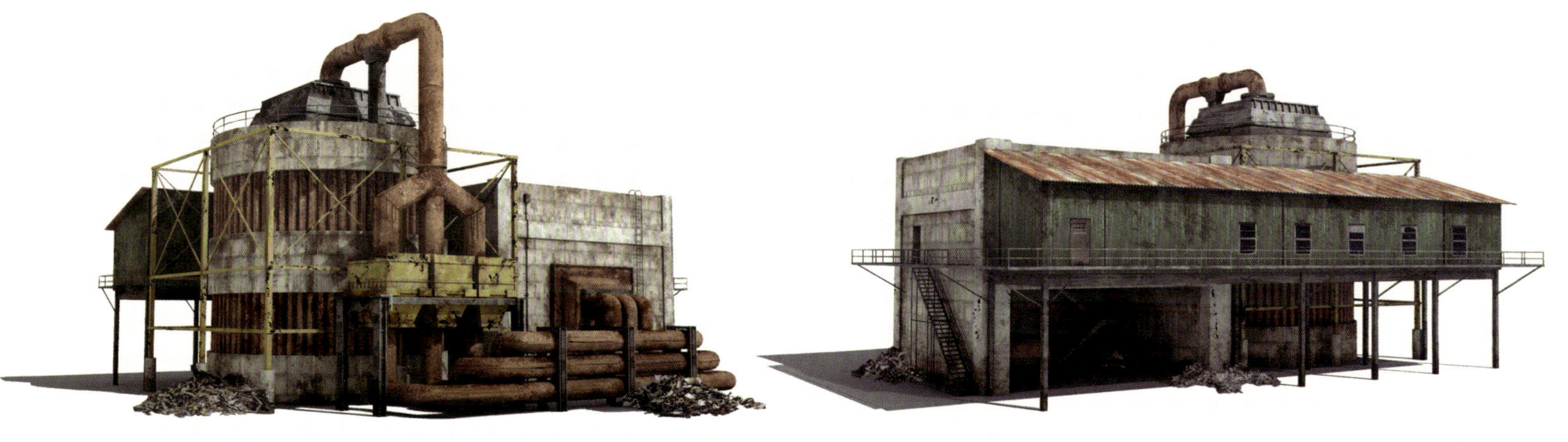

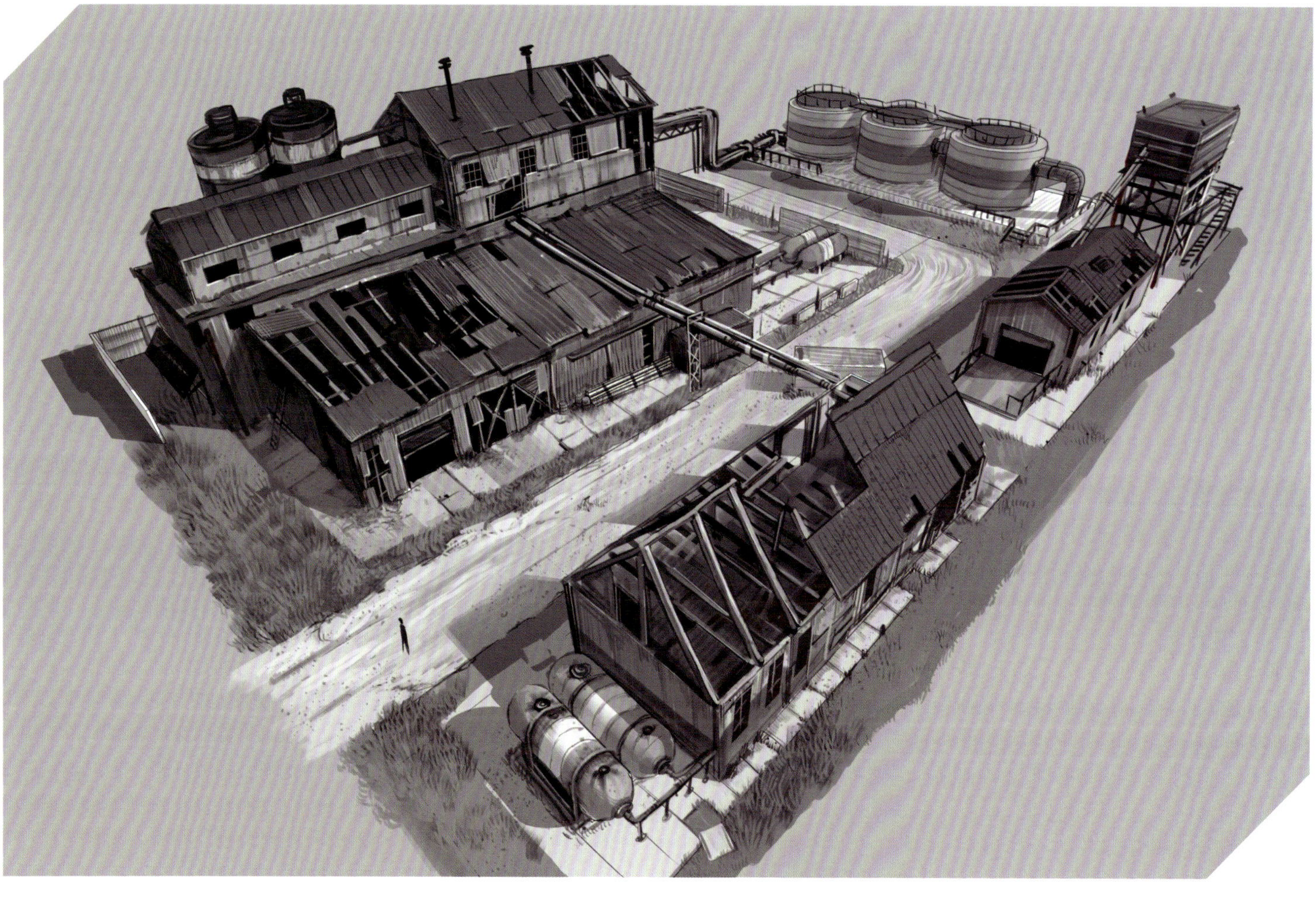

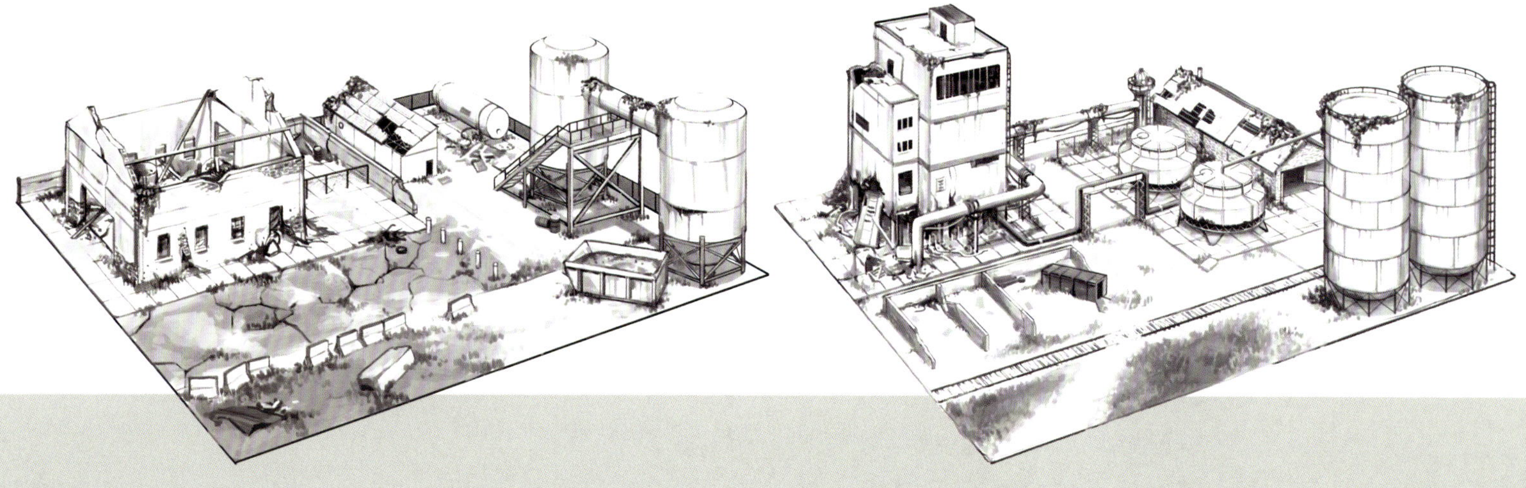

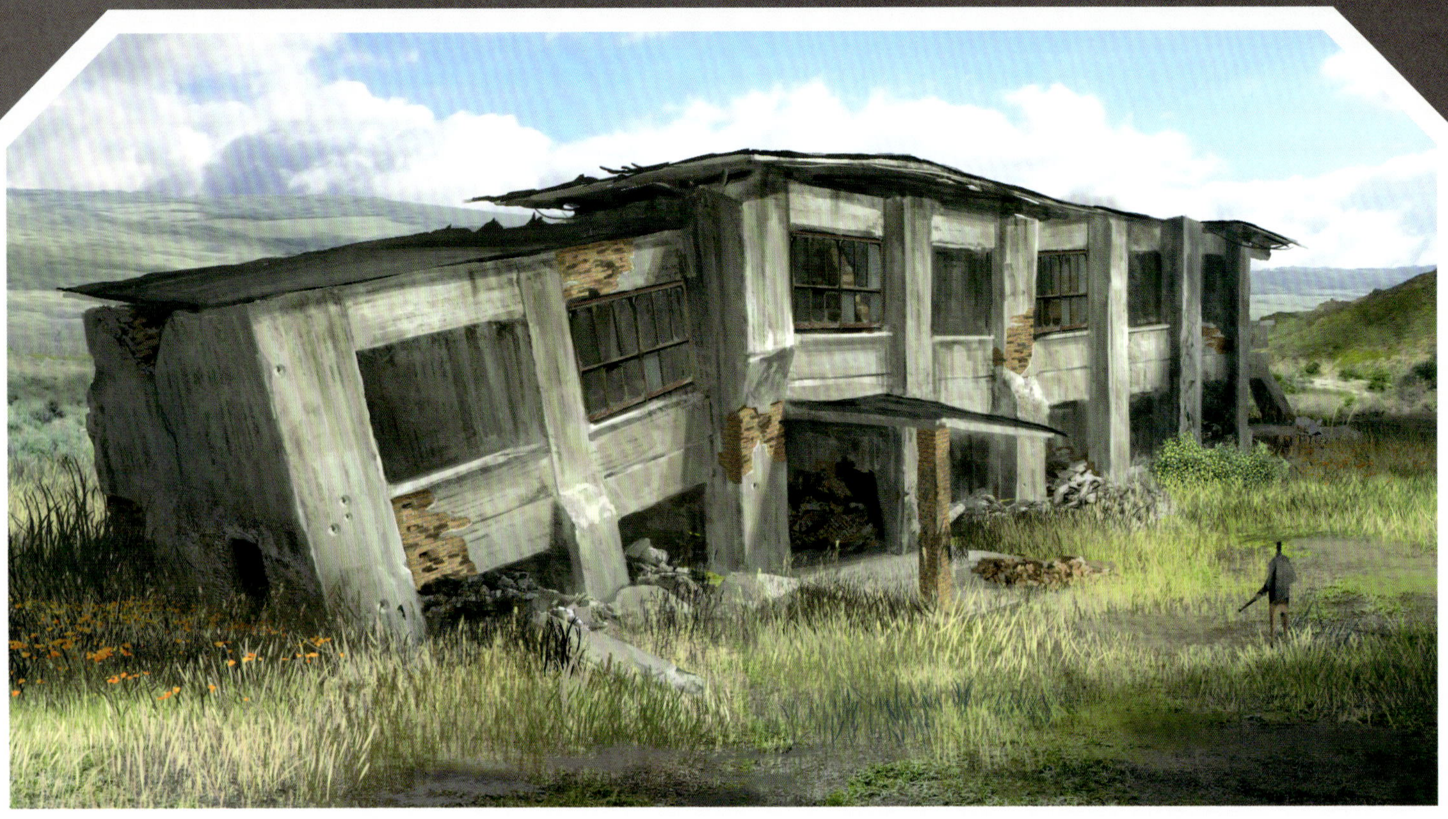

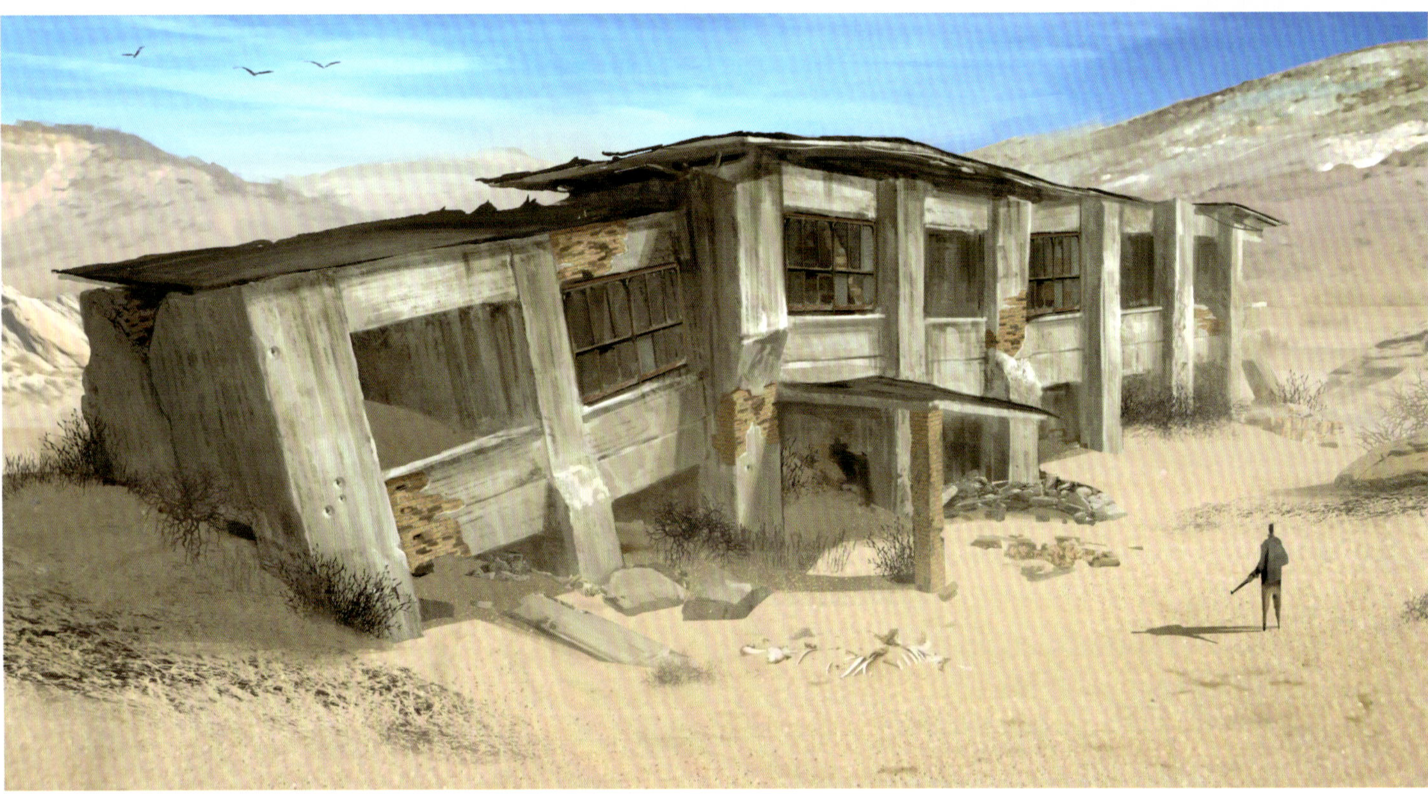

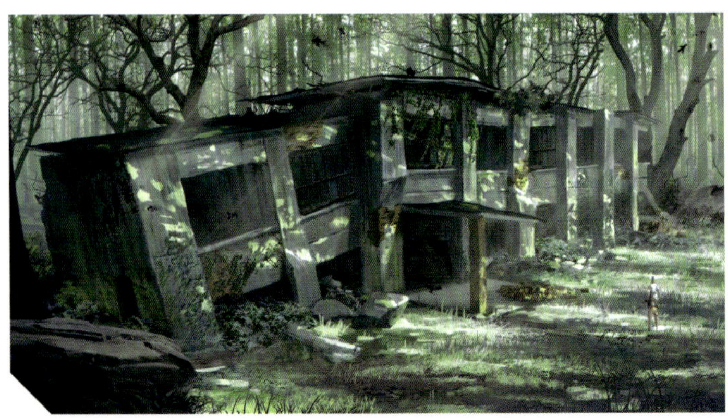

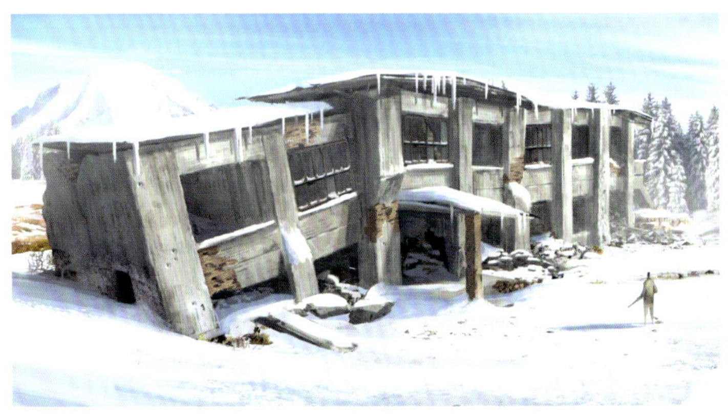

RESOURCE EXTRACTION

Designed to feel mechanically believable, the Quarry structures look like something a survivor could realistically create using scavenged materials. Taking inspiration from nodding donkeys and other prospector mining tools, their animation and movement were carefully considered to provide the impression of actively pulling resources straight out of the ground.

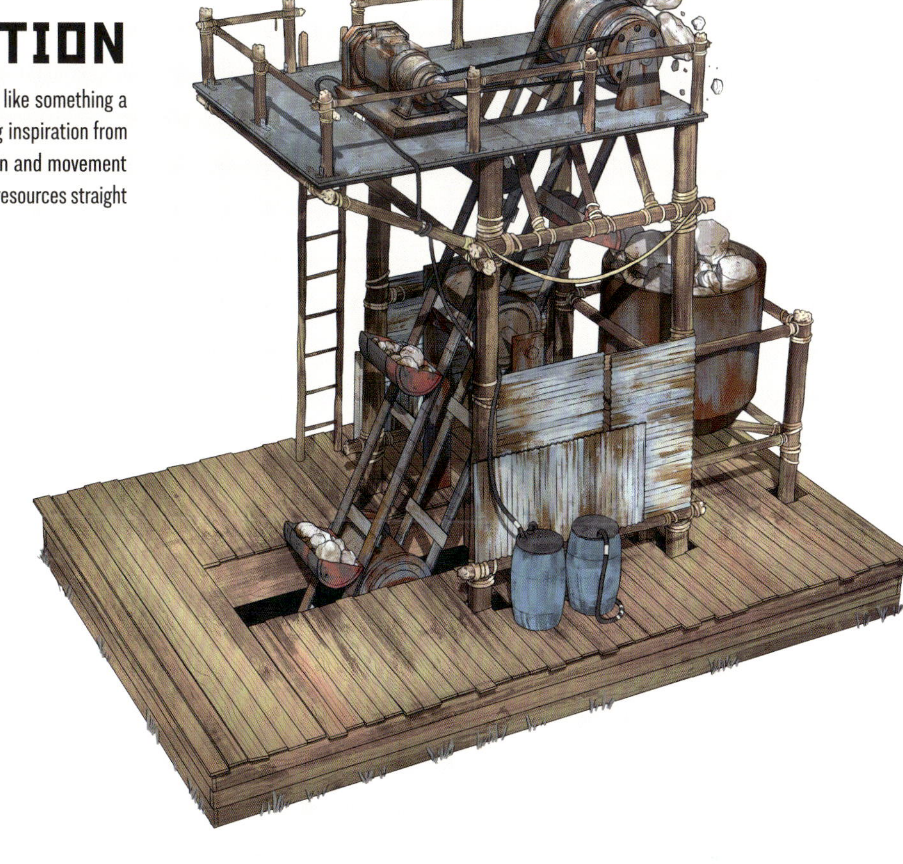

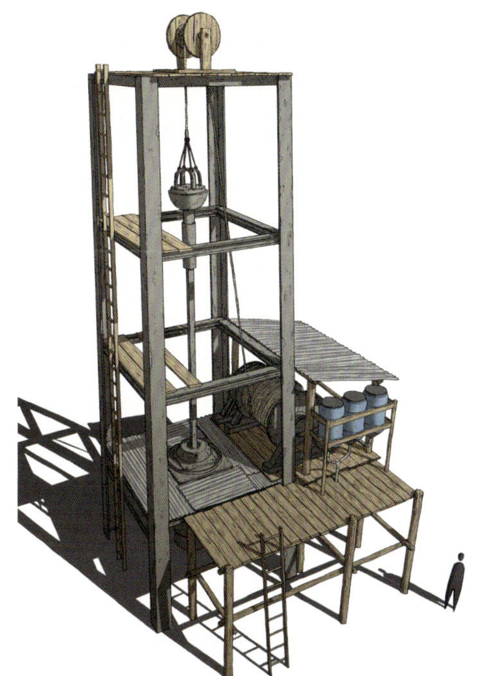

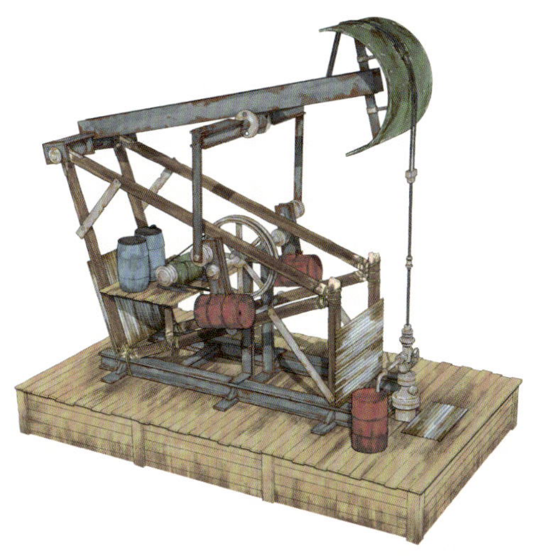

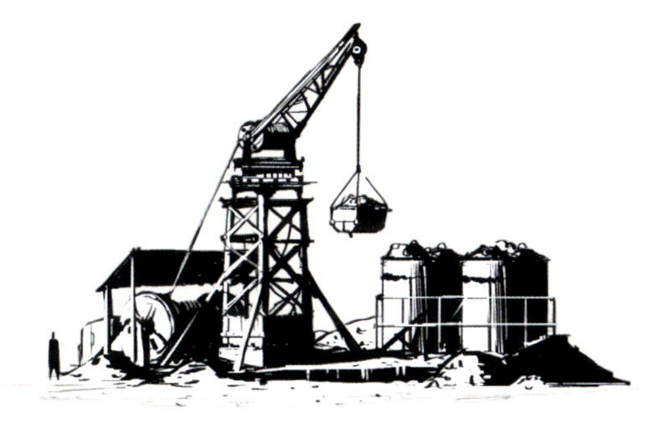

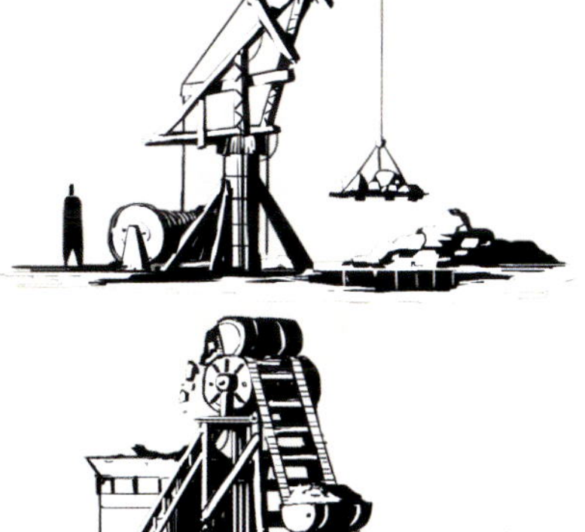

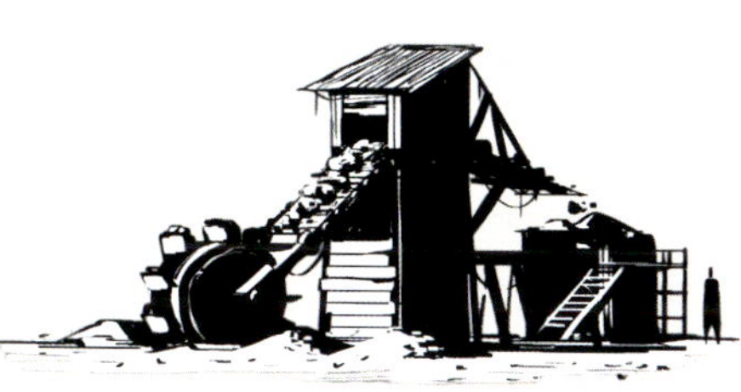

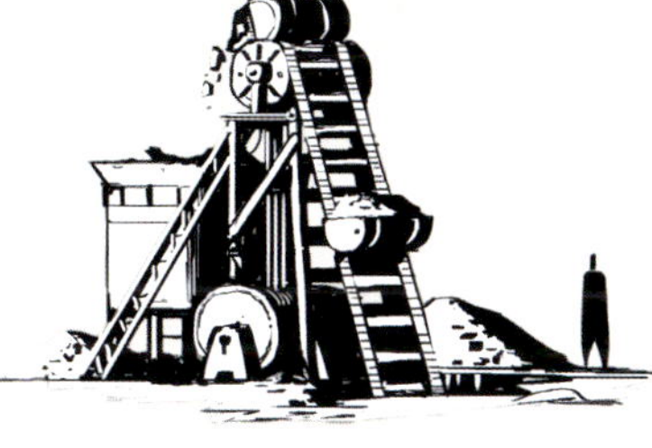

ABANDONED SUPERMARKETS

Rust's abandoned supermarkets blend believability with decay. Cracked floors, rusted shelves, and looted aisles tell a story of sudden collapse; faded signs, broken lights, and overgrowth reinforce the atmosphere. Designed for exploration and scavenging, they feel like real places where survivors might search for scraps and loot.

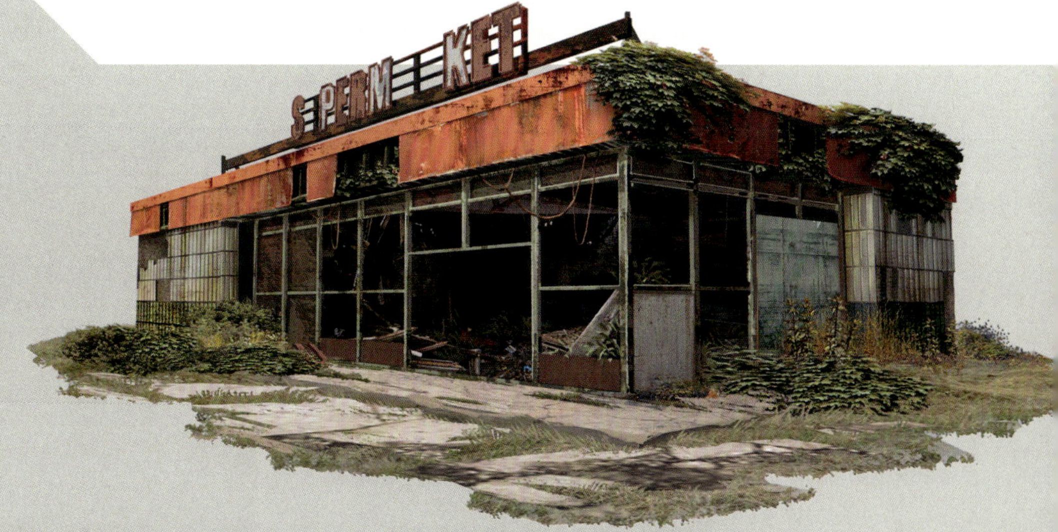

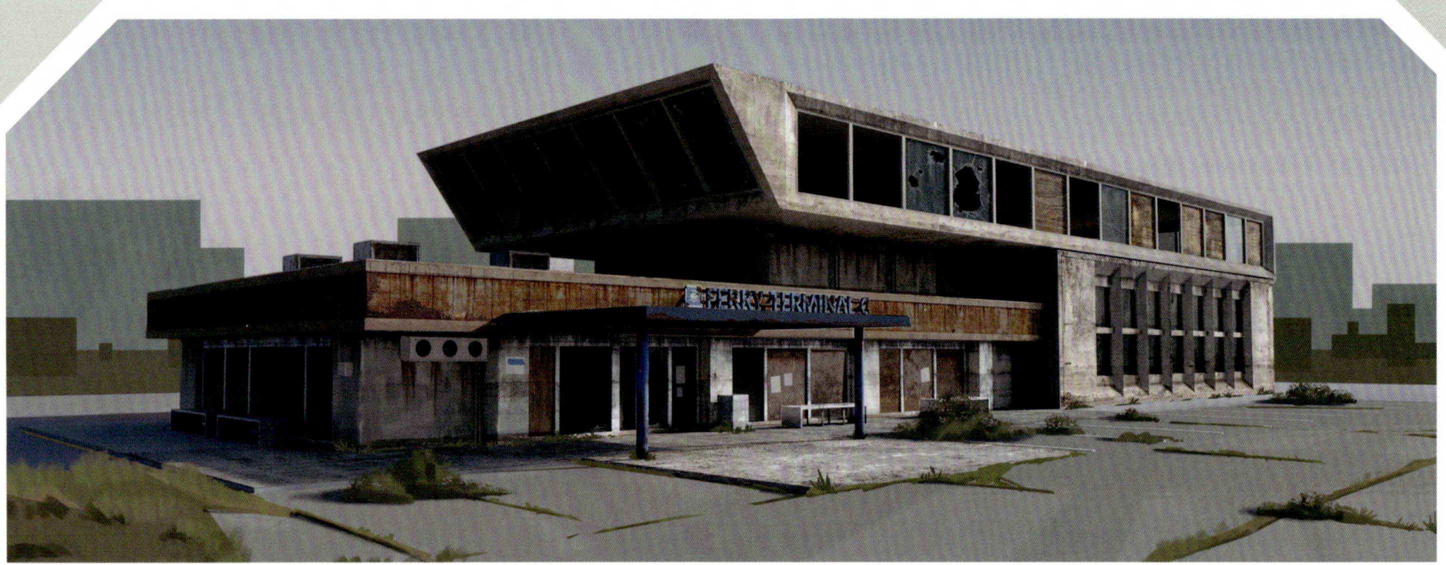

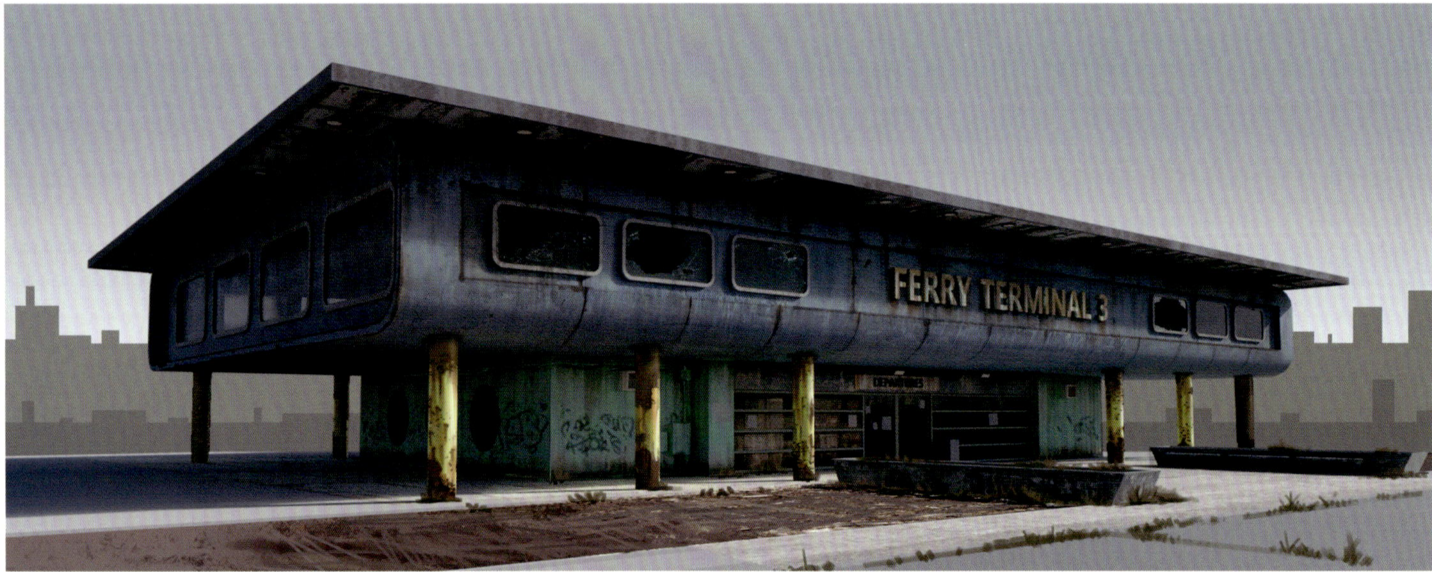

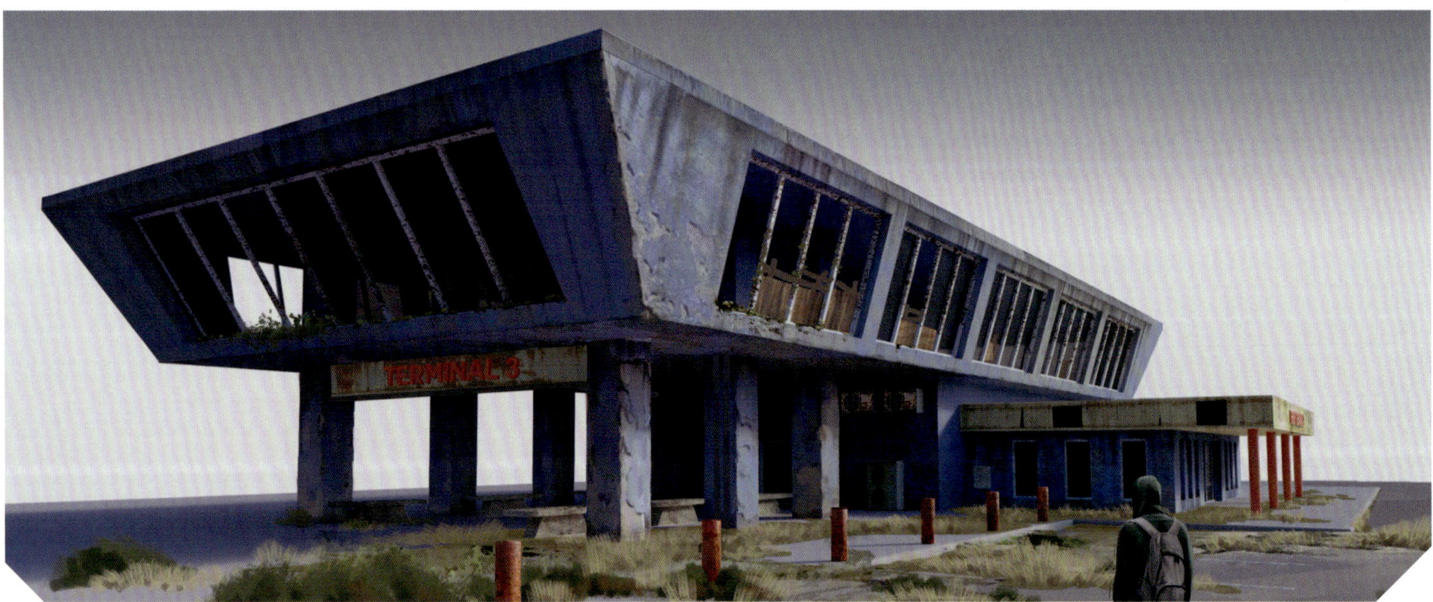

FERRY TERMINAL

The Ferry Terminal in *Rust* was designed with a Brutalist feel, reflecting a derelict, deteriorated public space. With corroded platforms, salt-stained walls, and broken fencing, it suggests a long-abandoned transit point.

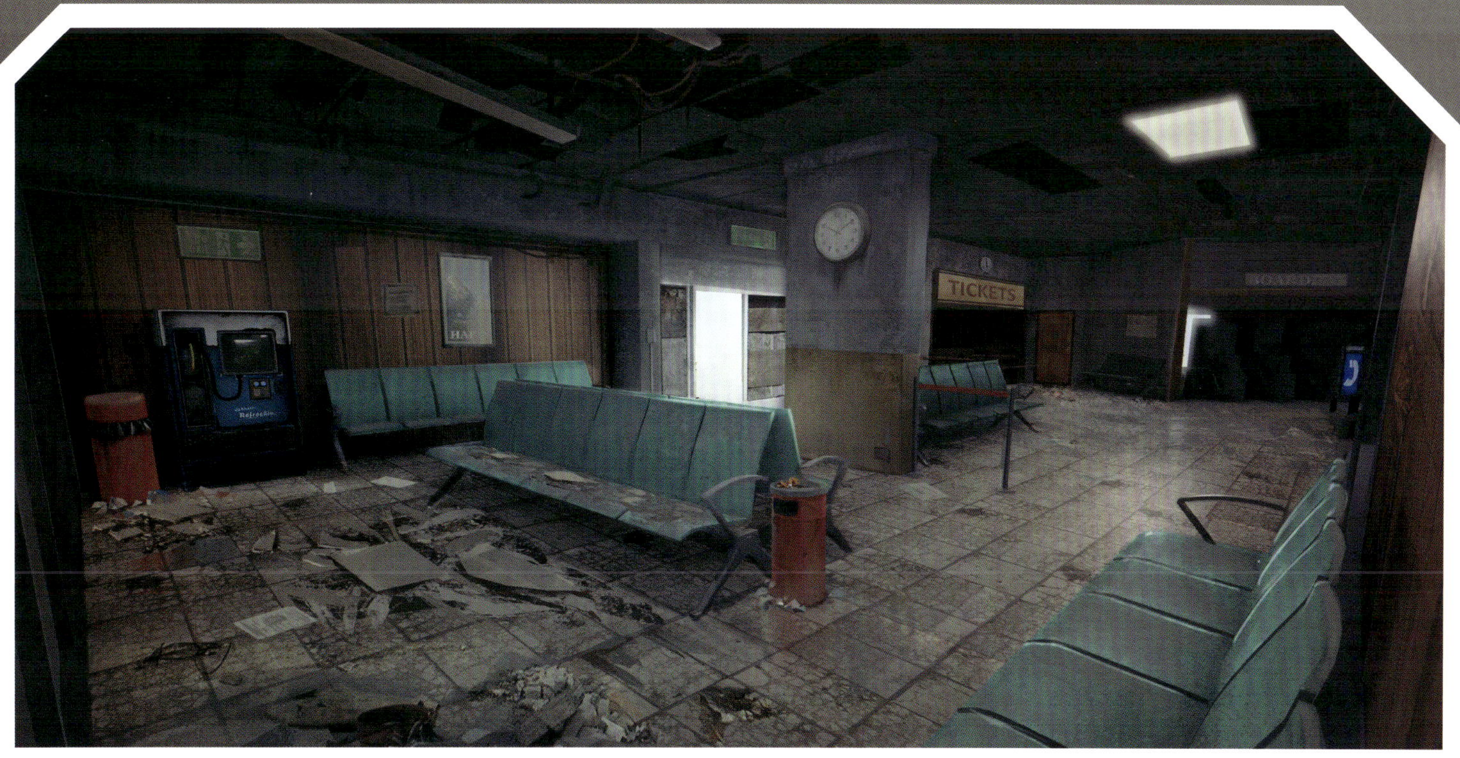
TICKETS

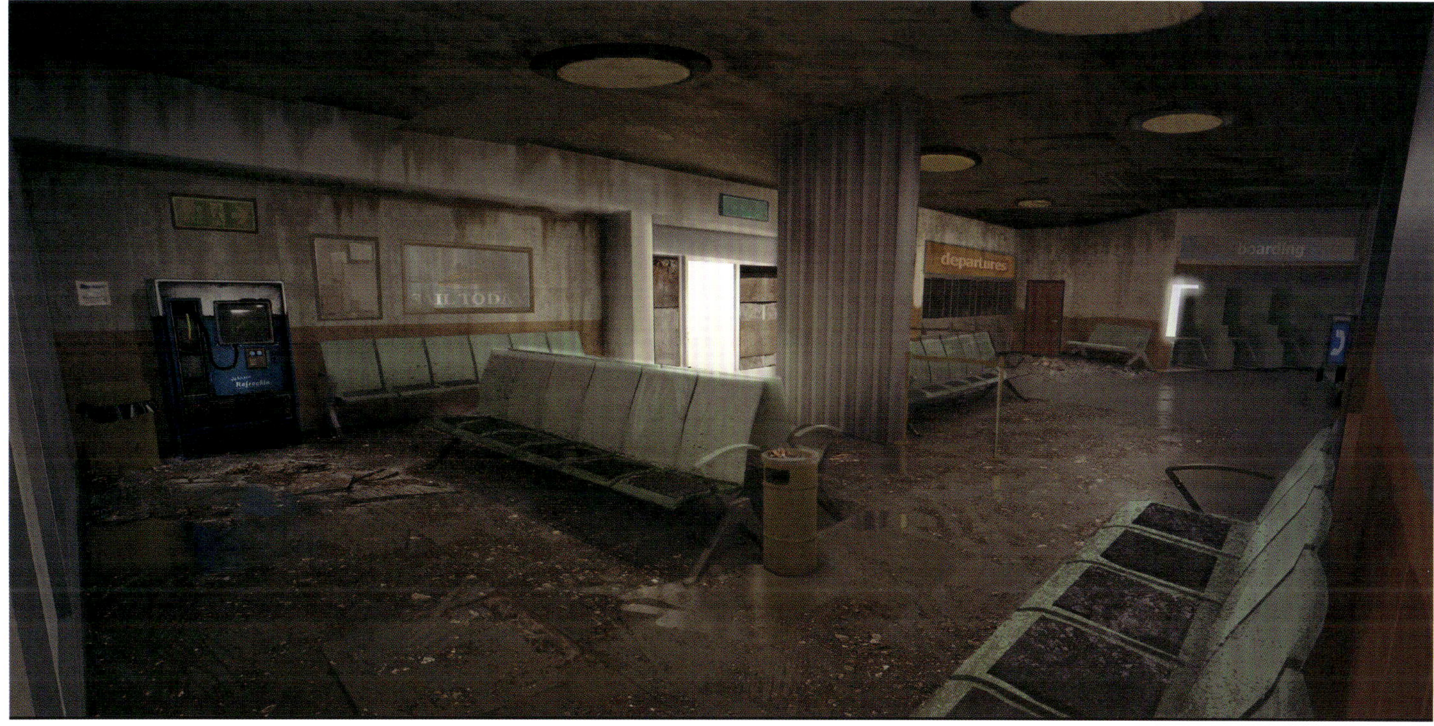
departures
boarding

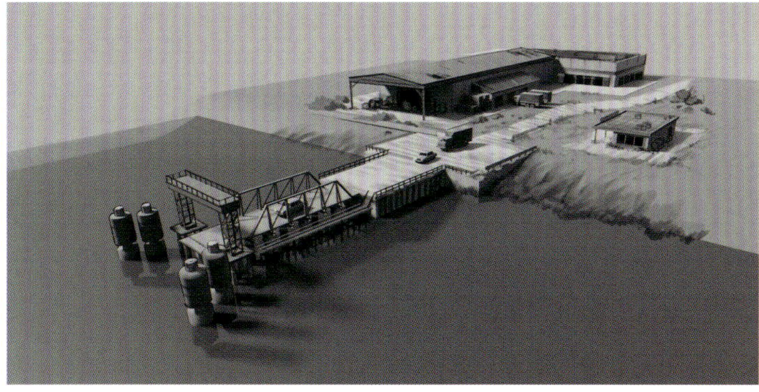

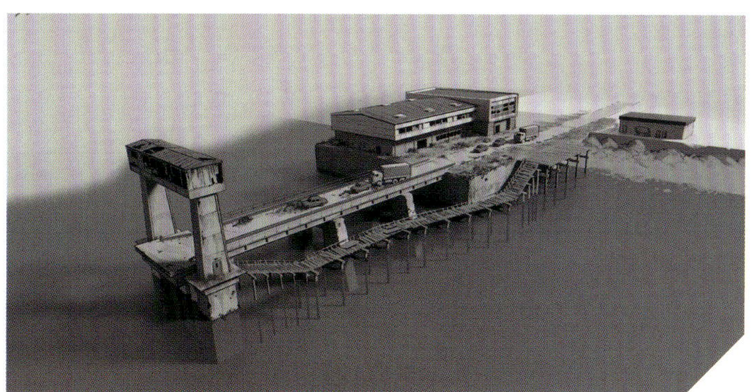

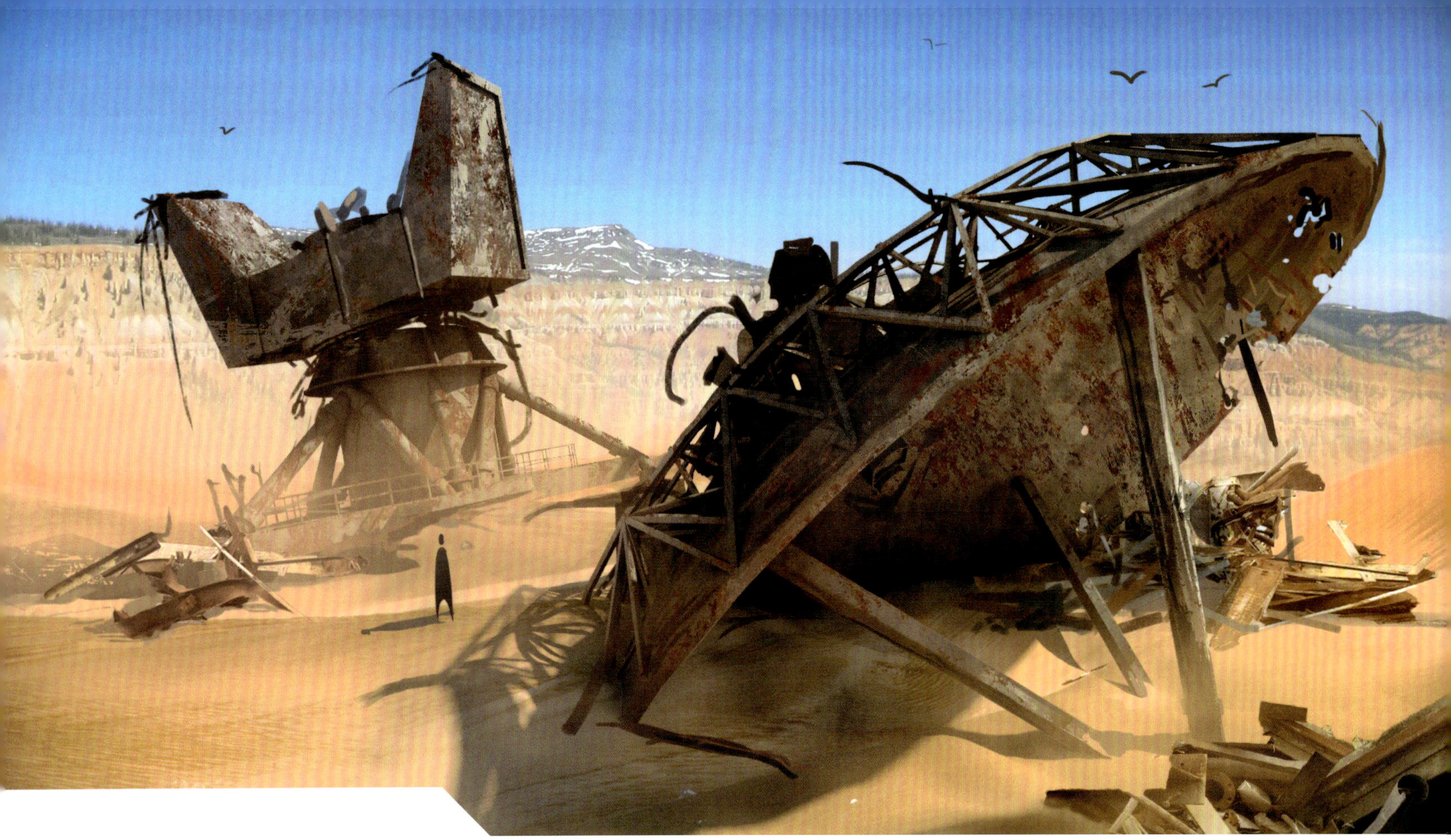

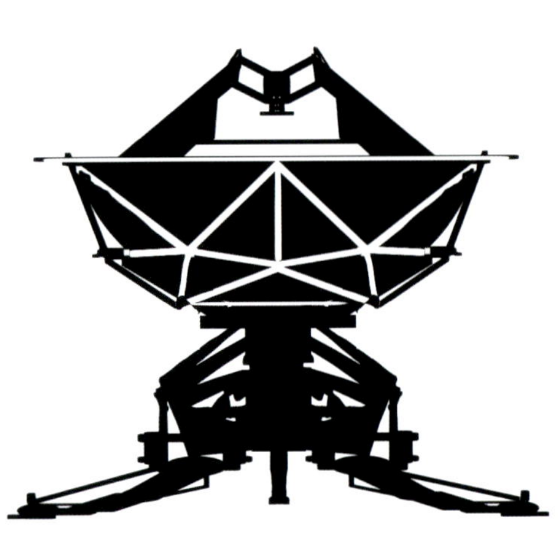
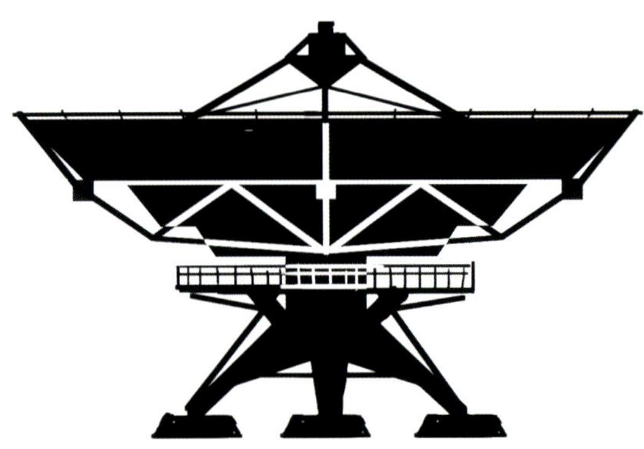
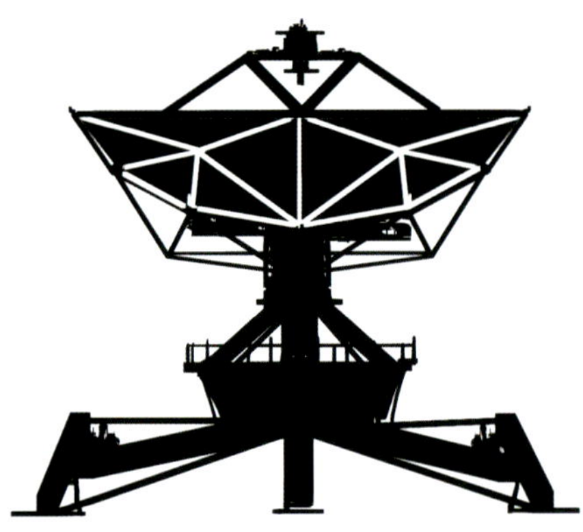
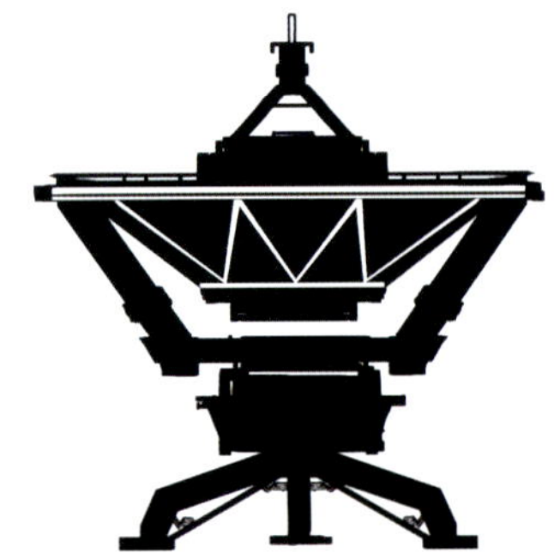
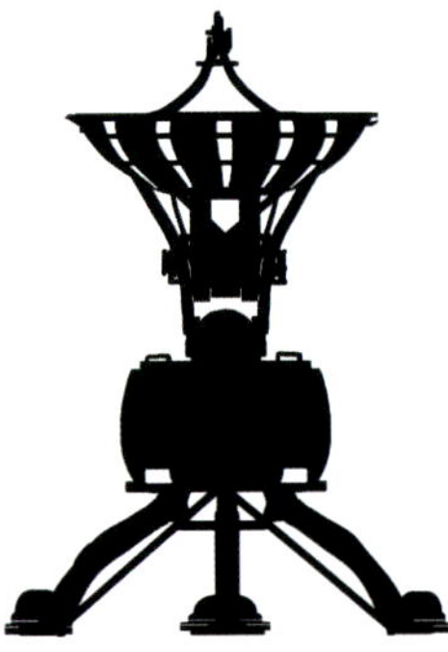
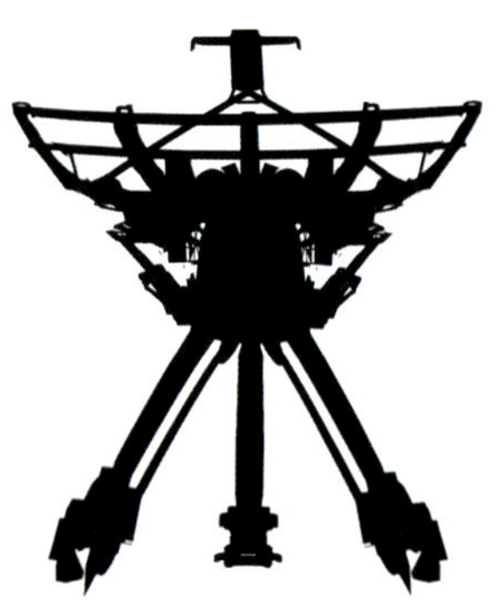
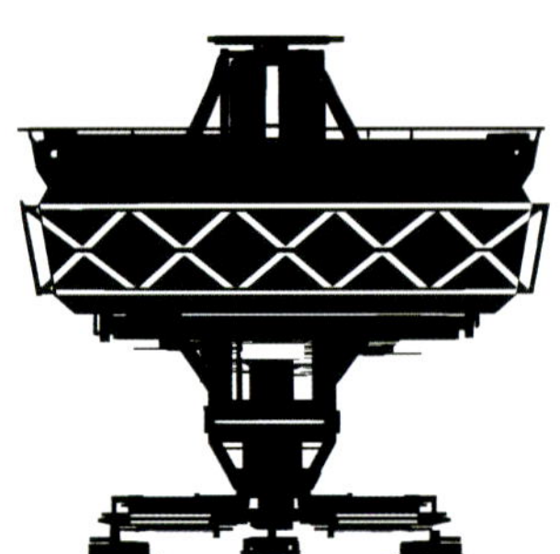

SATELLITES

The Satellite monuments showcase a cold, functional design rooted in abandoned technology. Towering dishes, exposed wiring, and rusted support frames create a space that feels weathered, isolated, and long forgotten. Materials like faded metal, cracked concrete, and tangled cables highlight its technical decay.

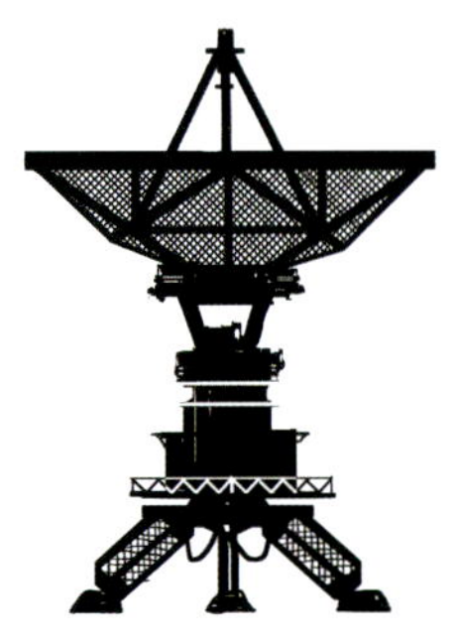
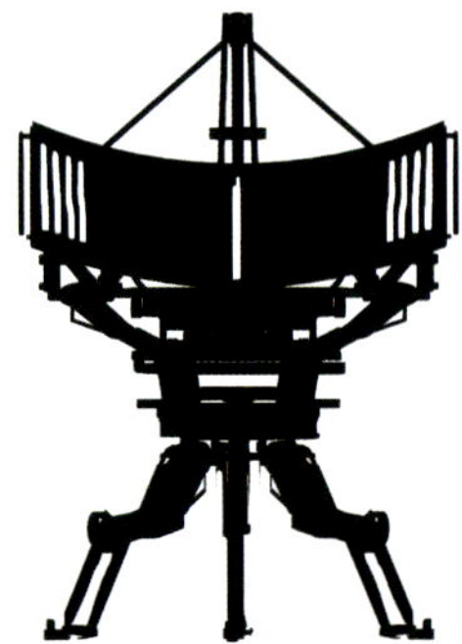

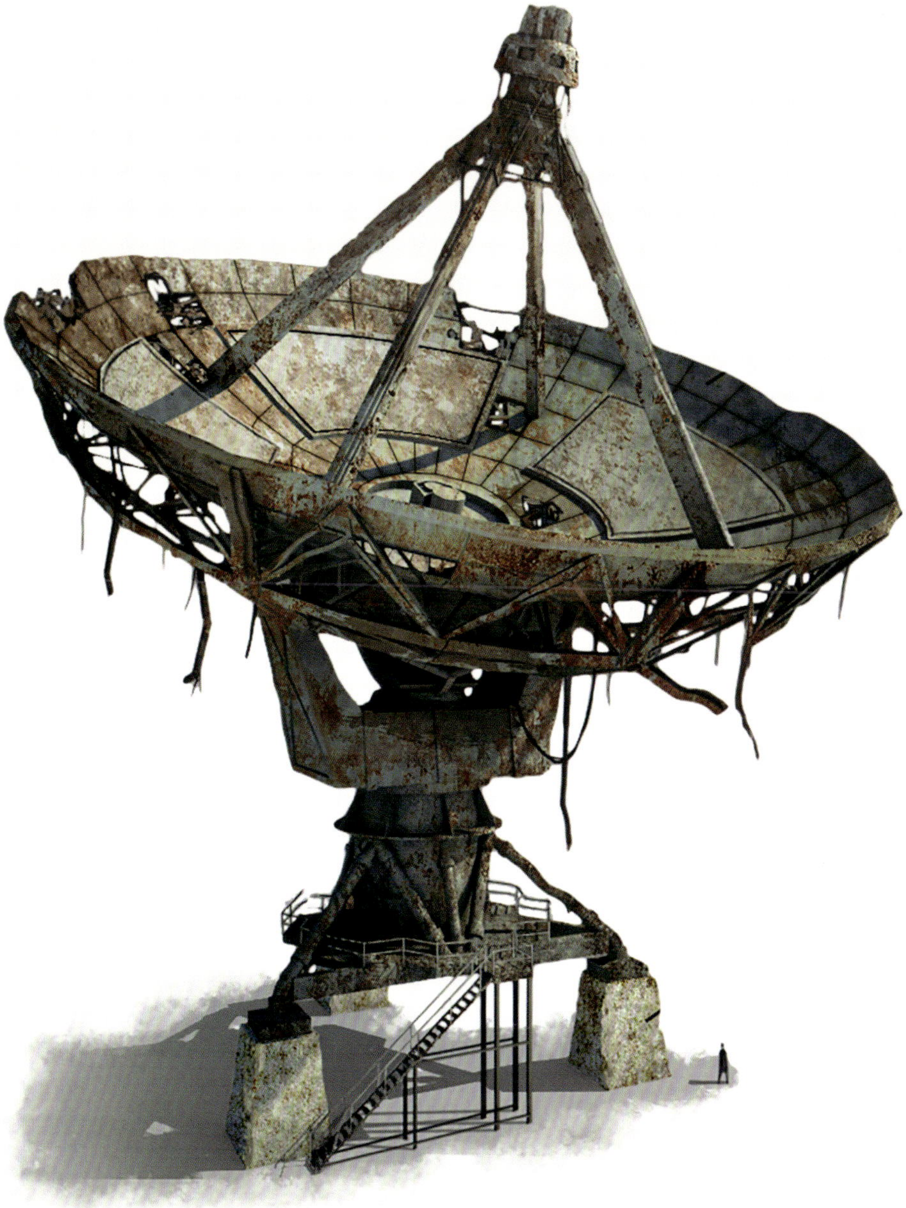

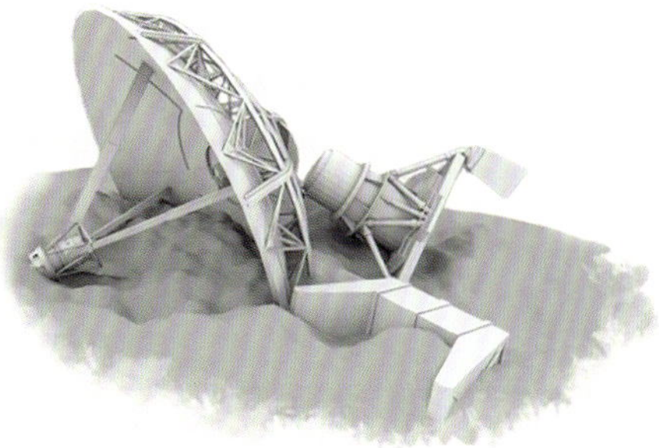

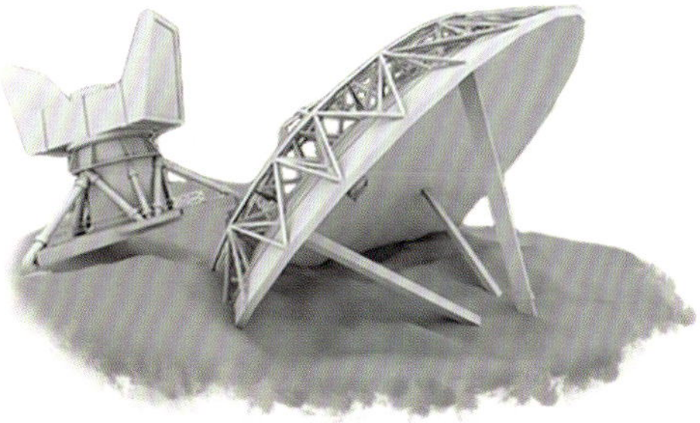

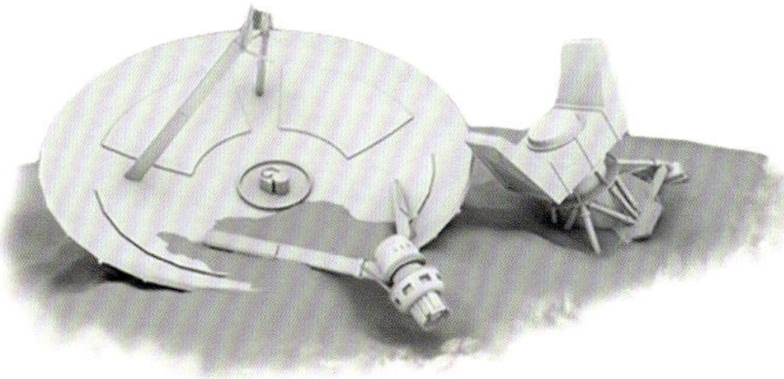

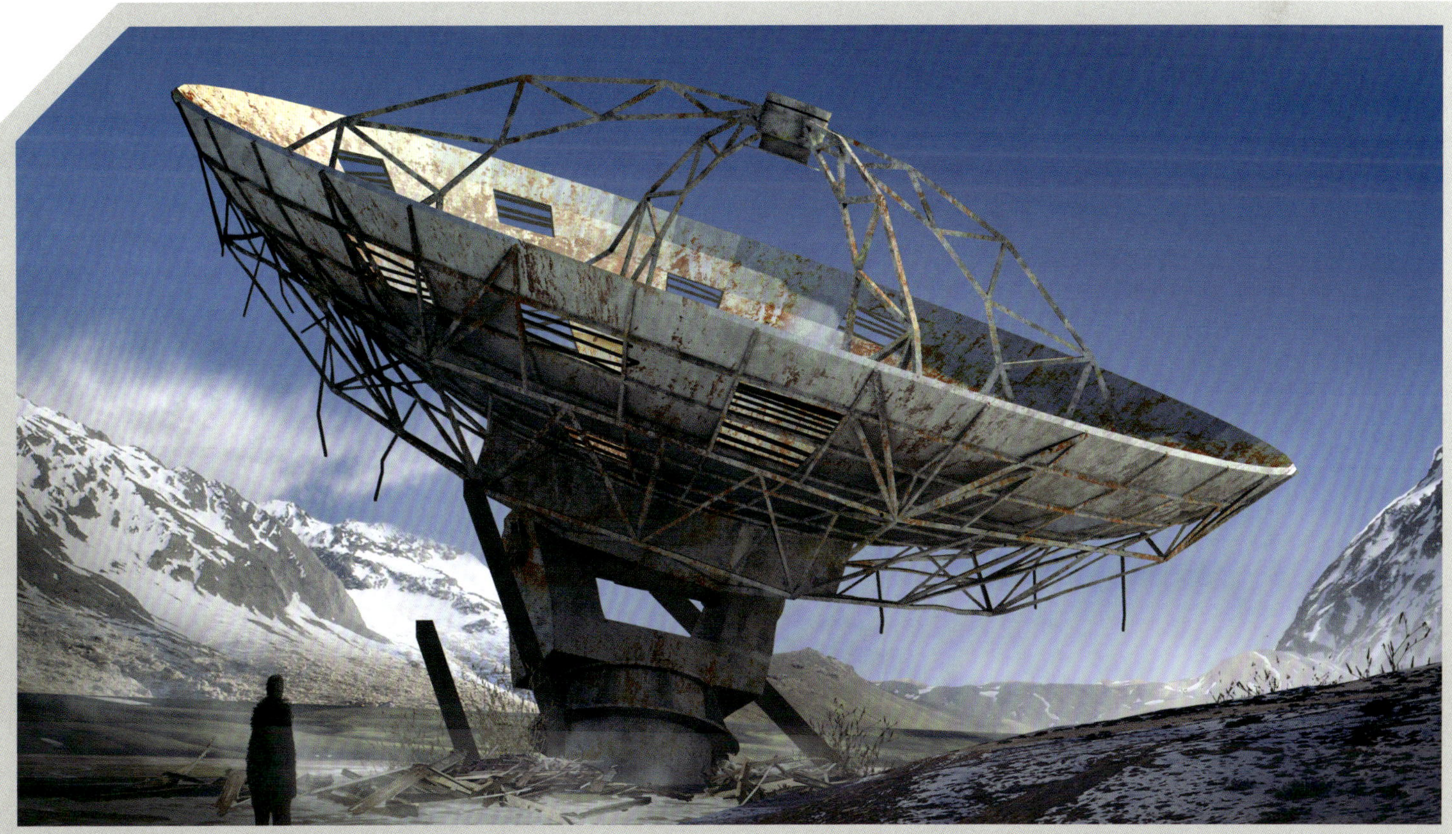

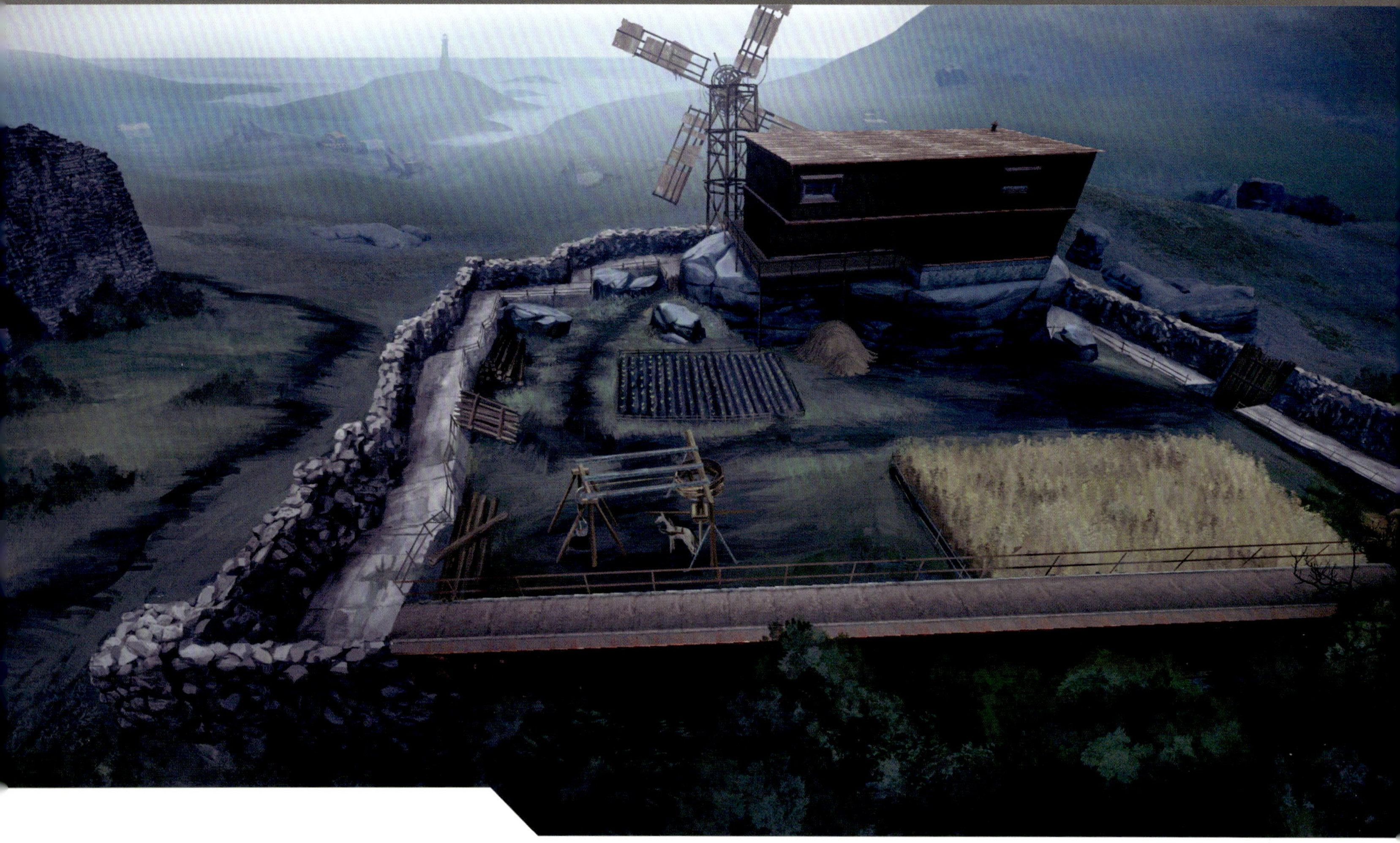

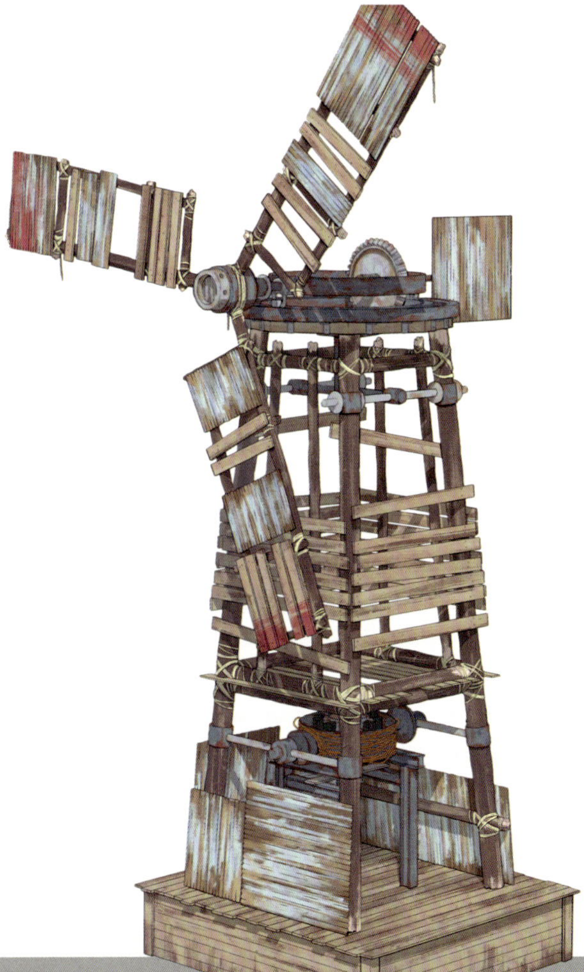

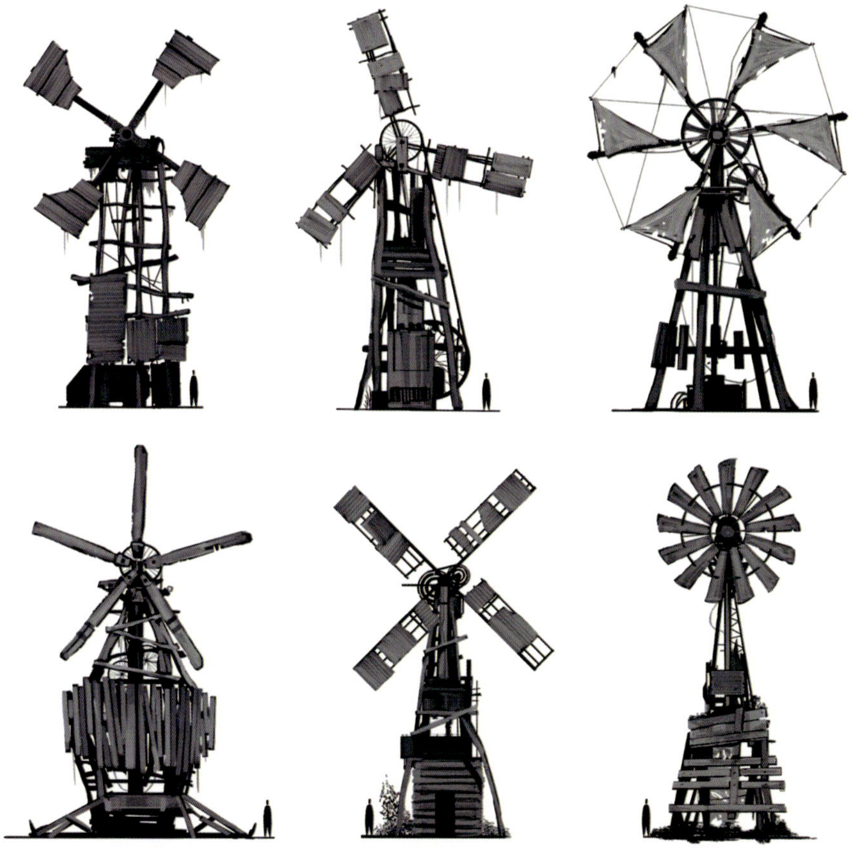

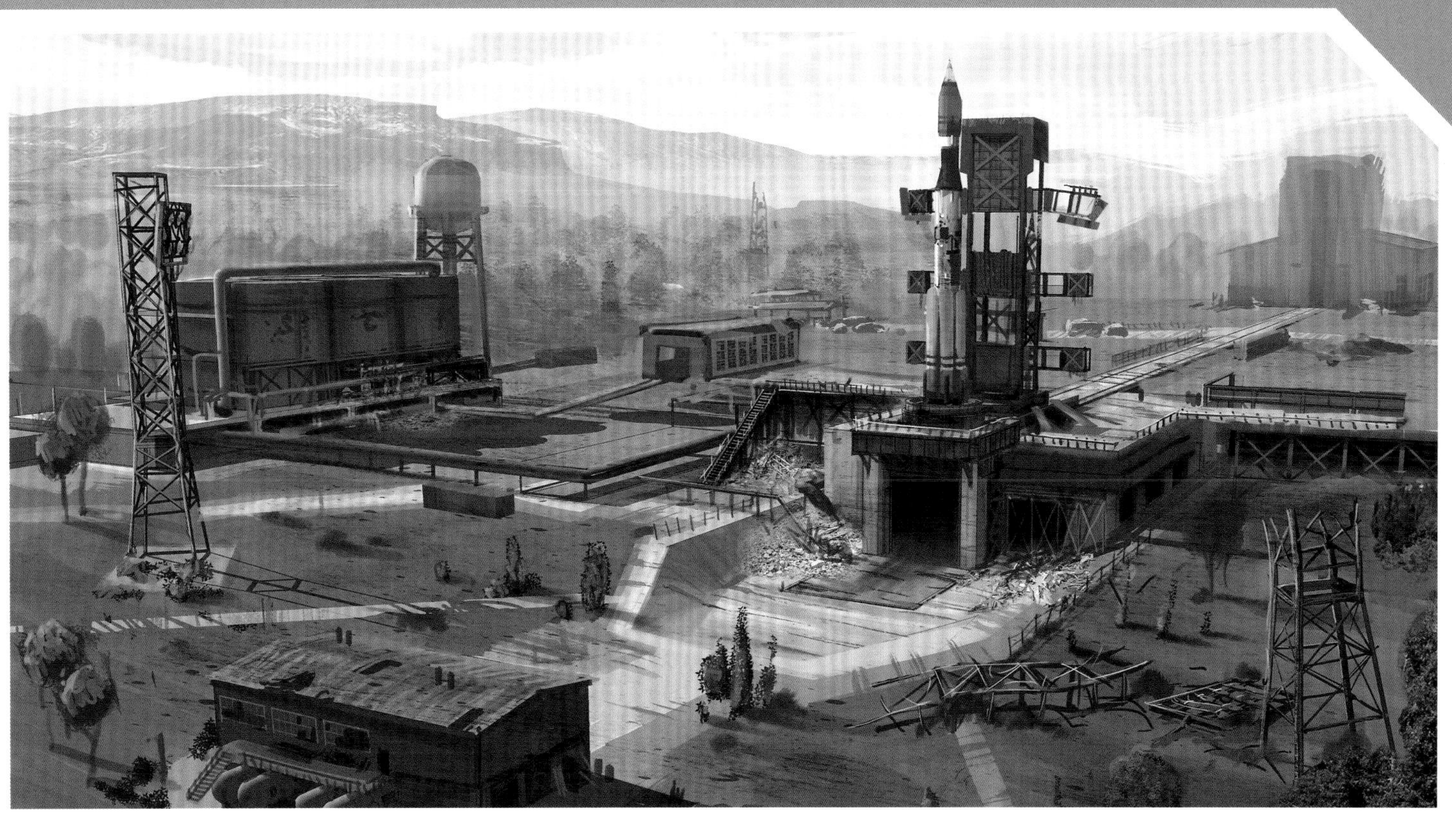

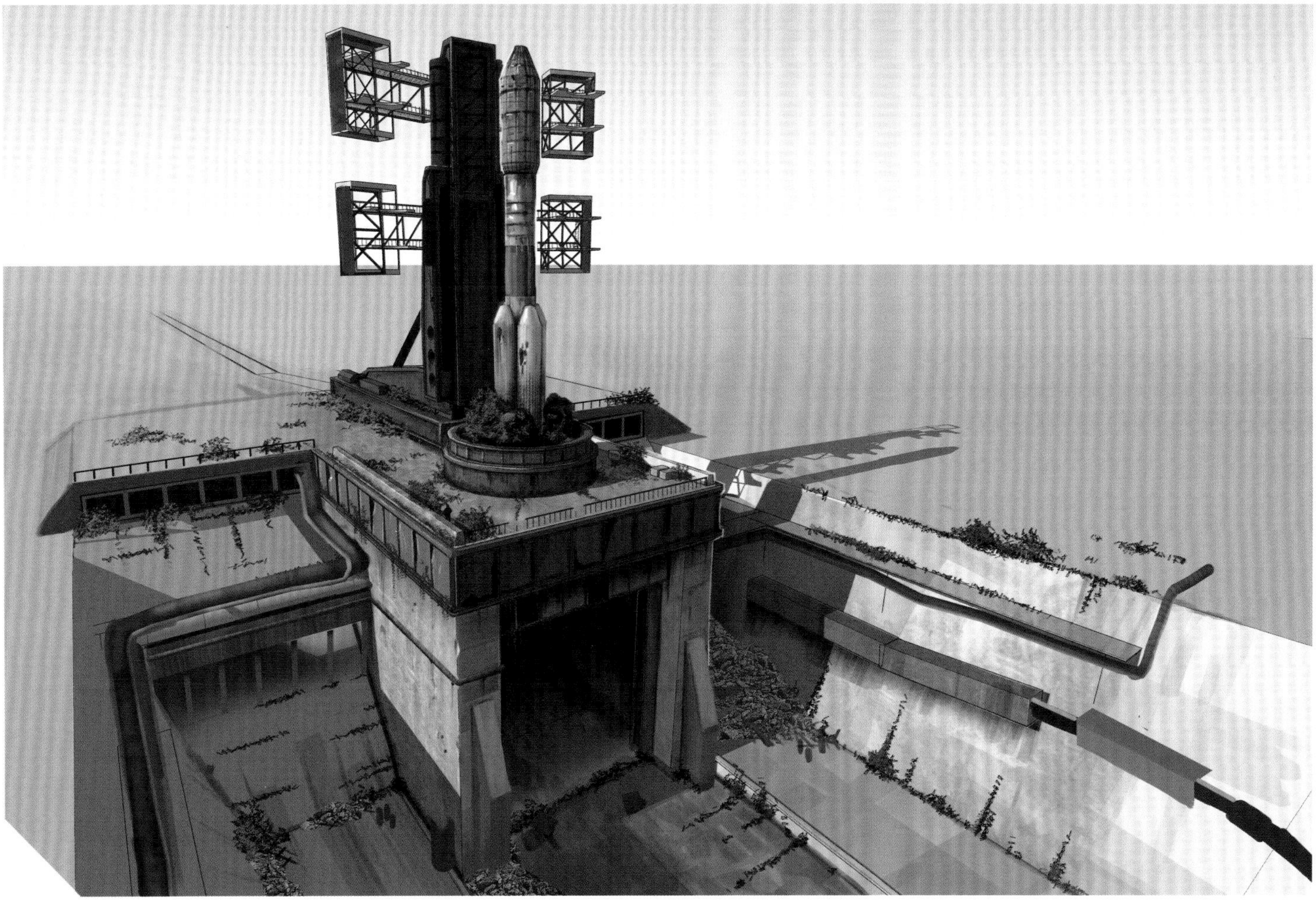

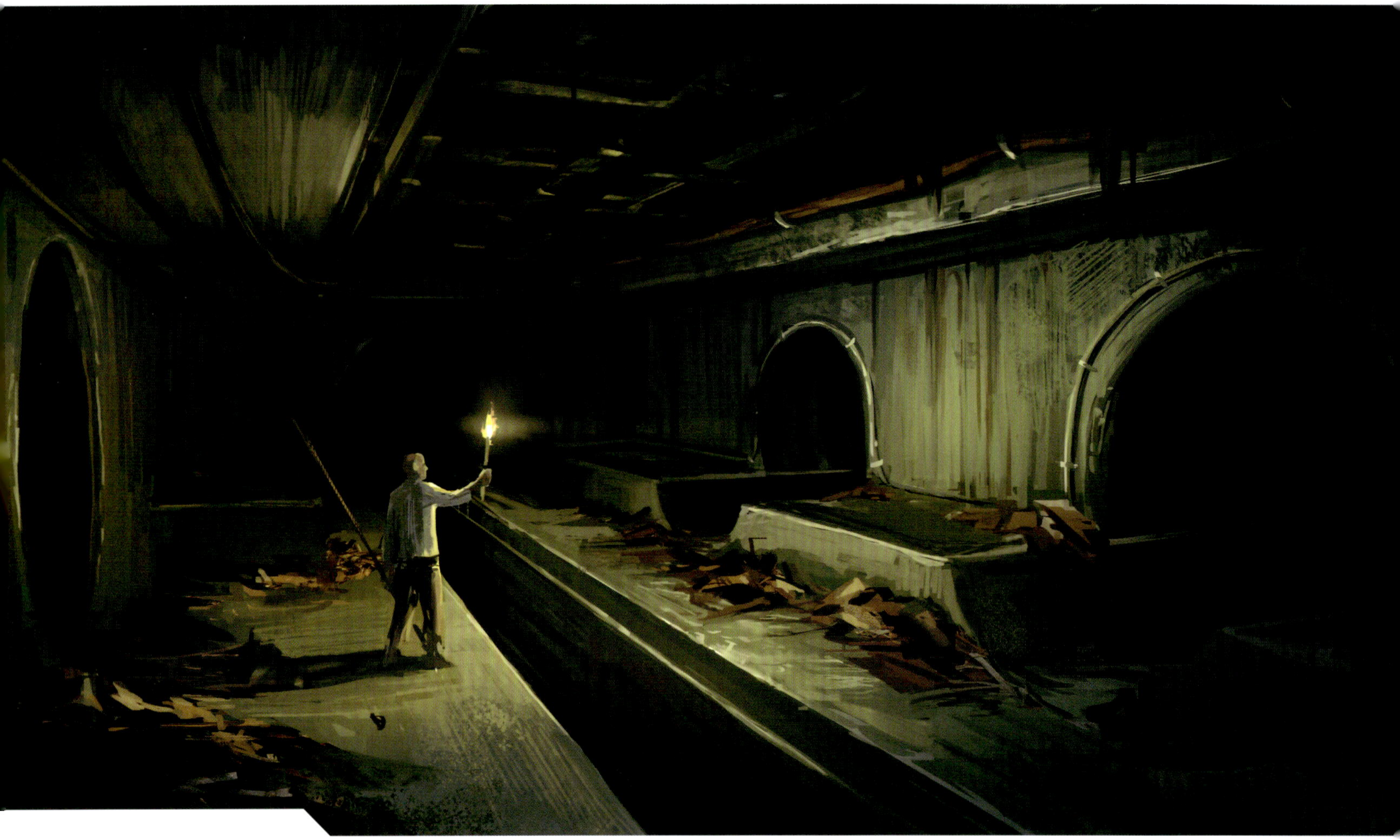

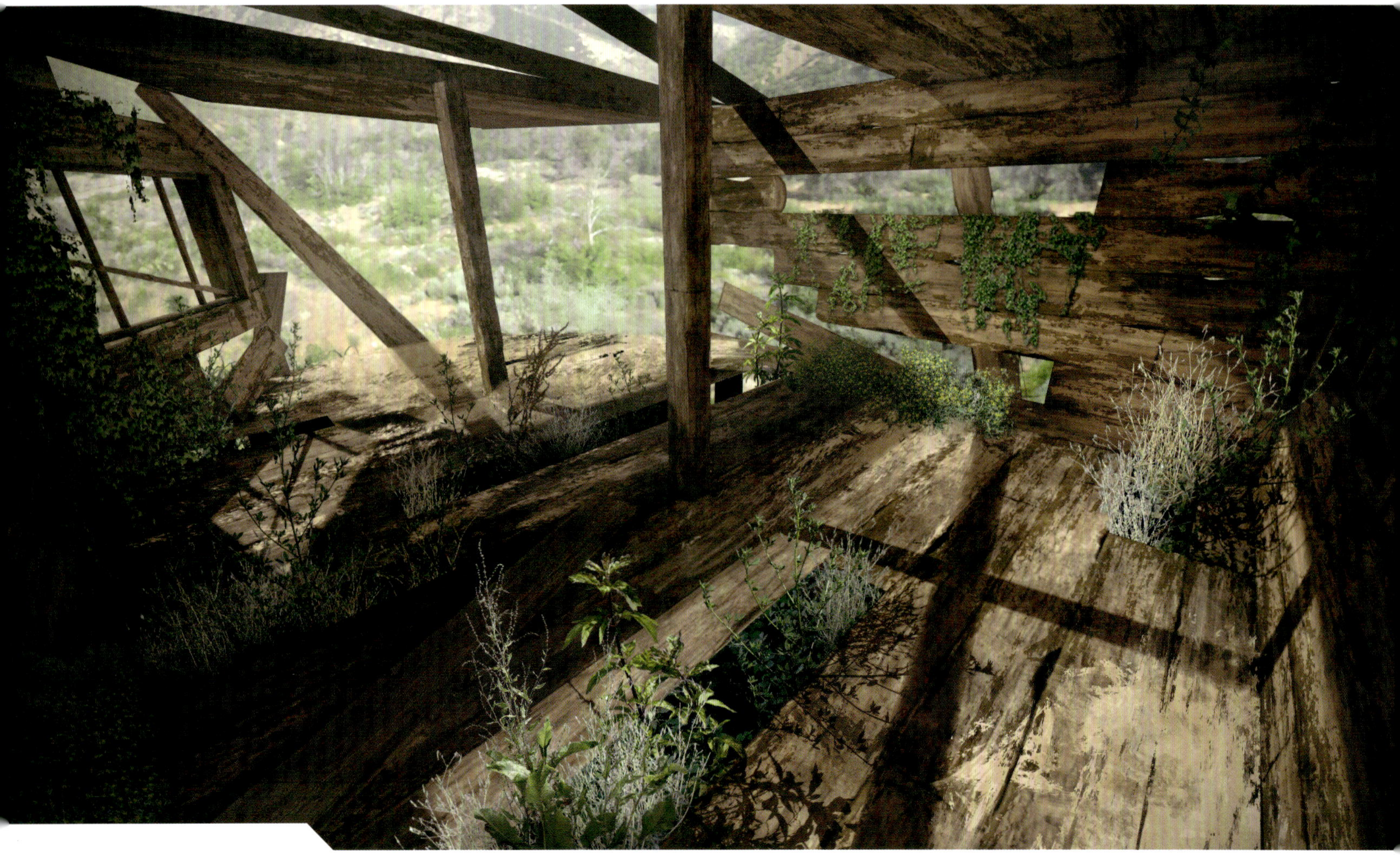

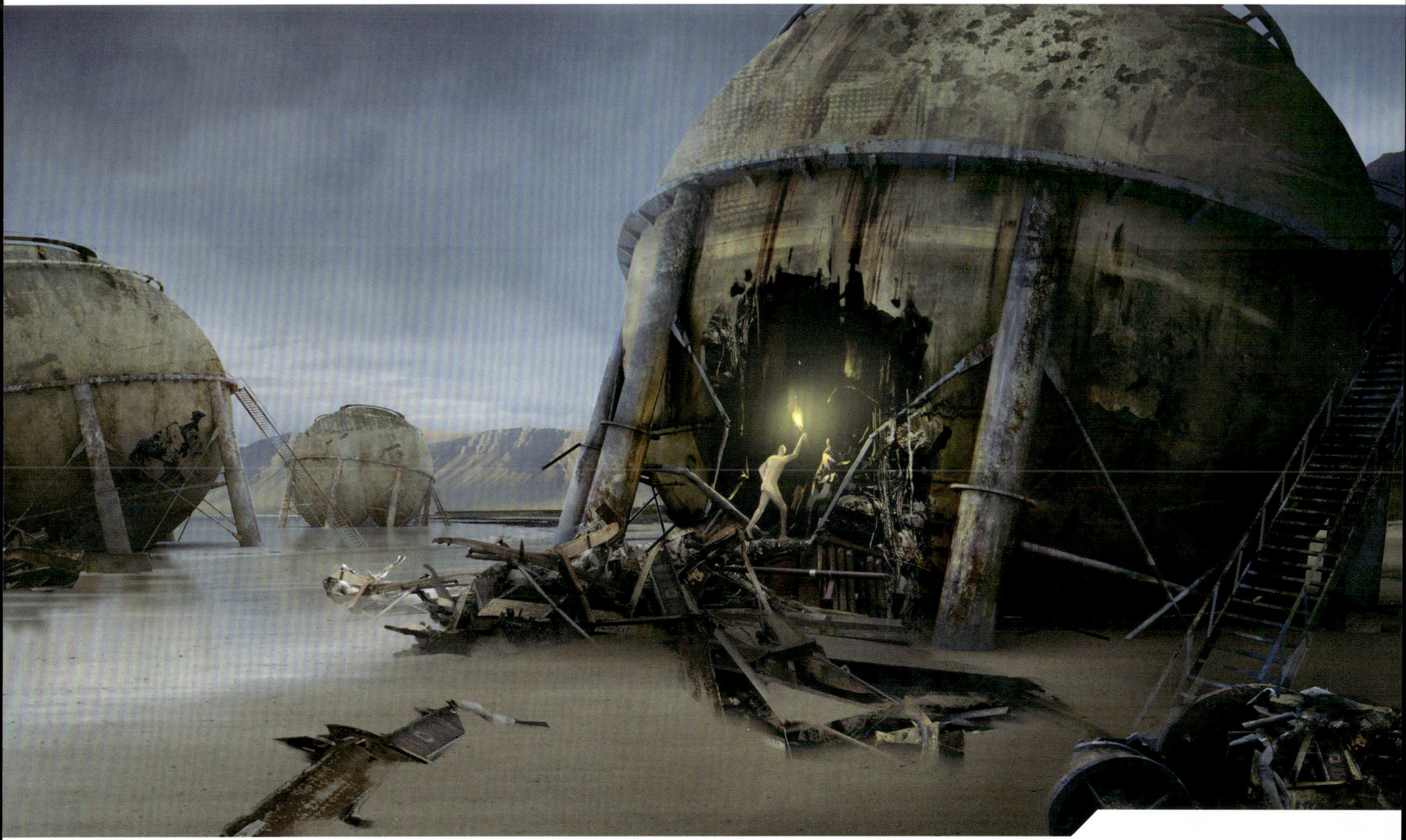

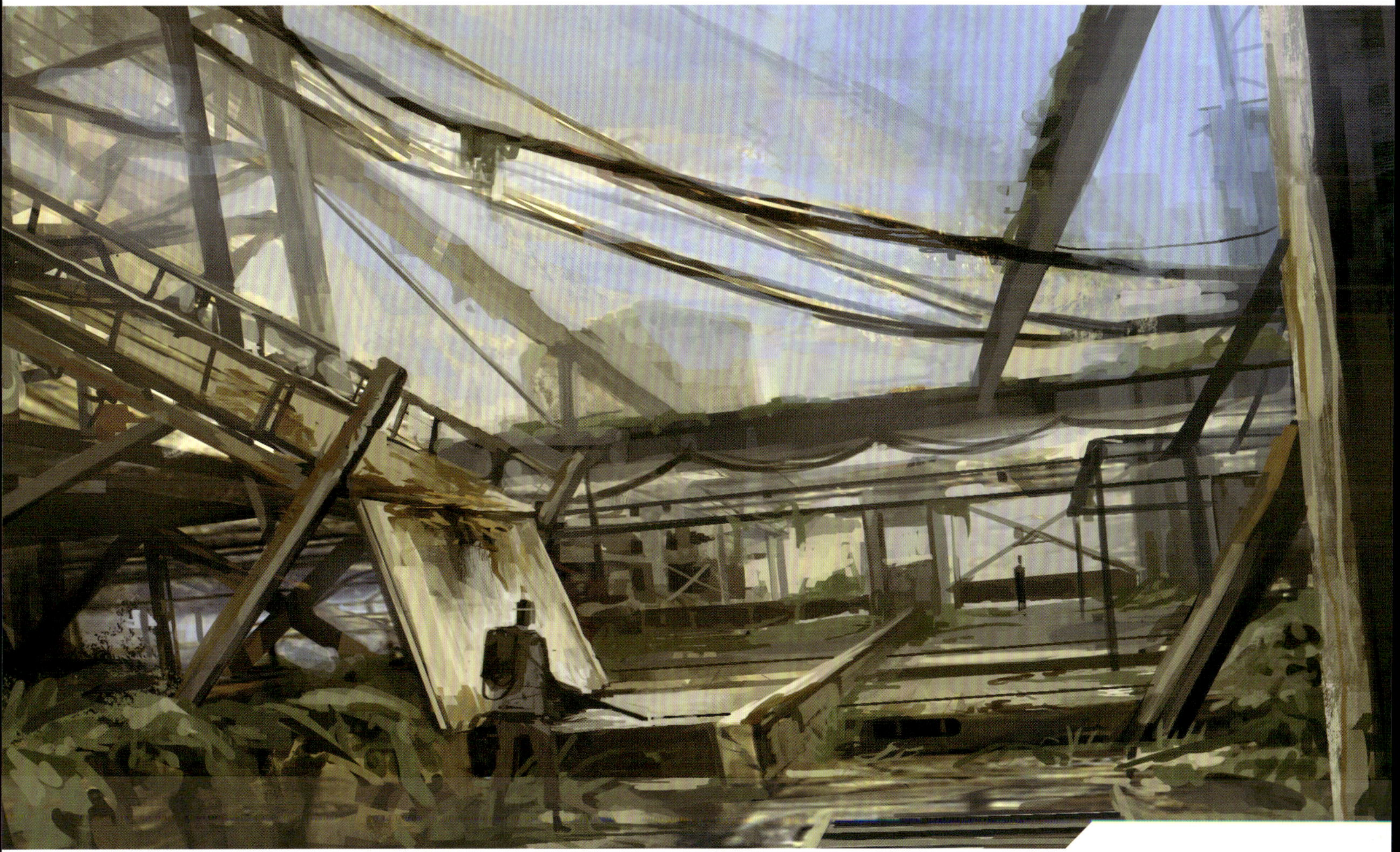

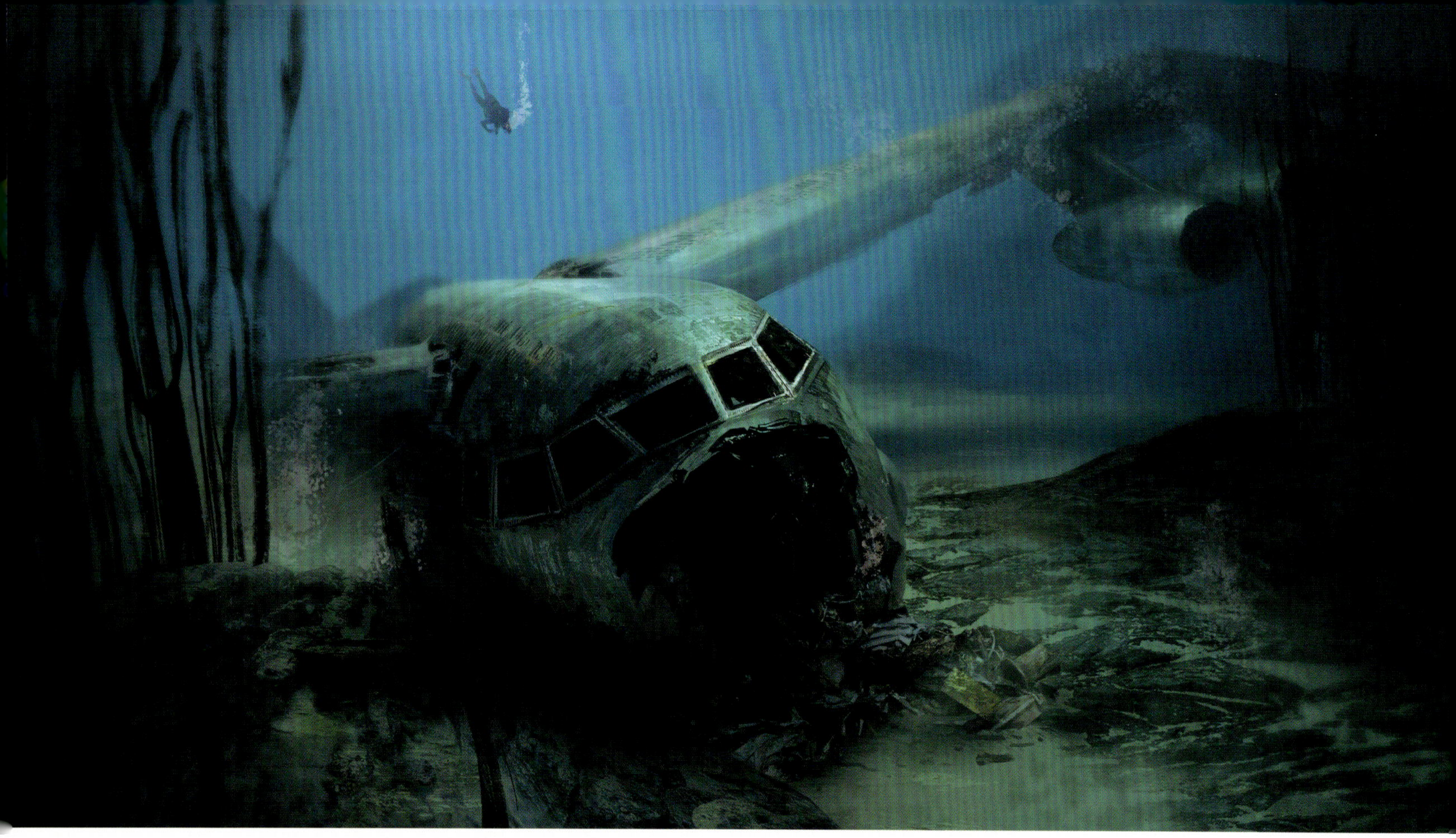

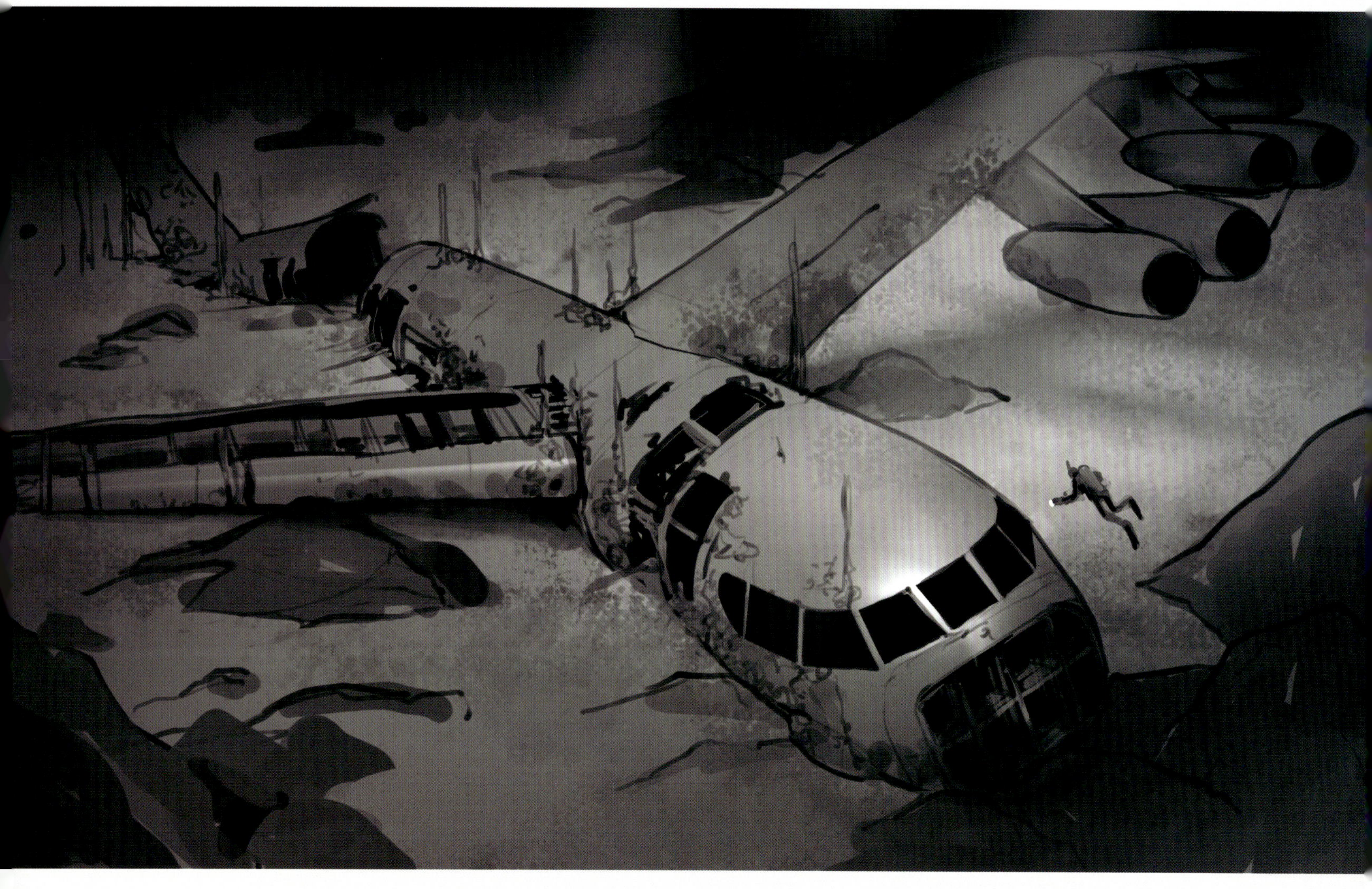

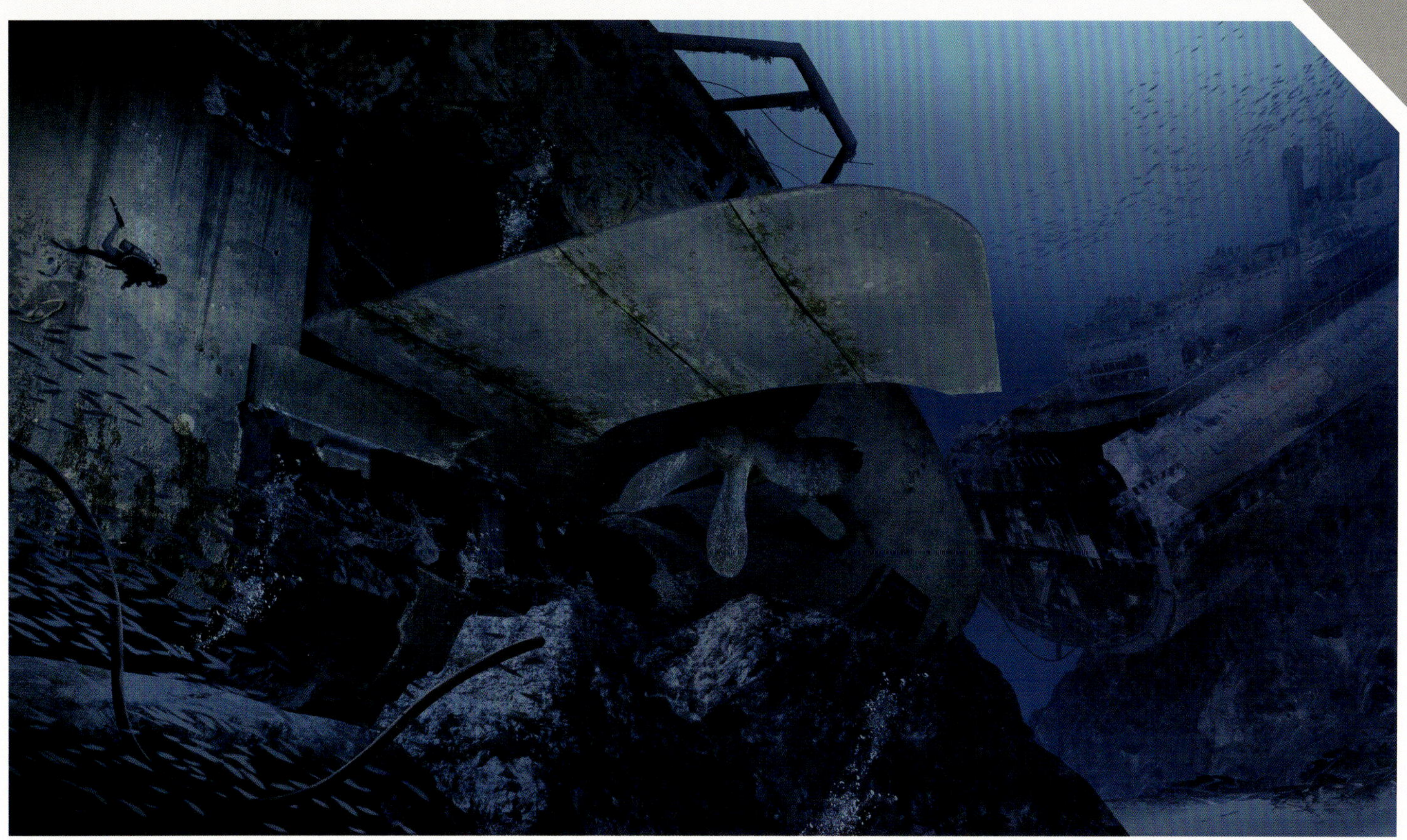

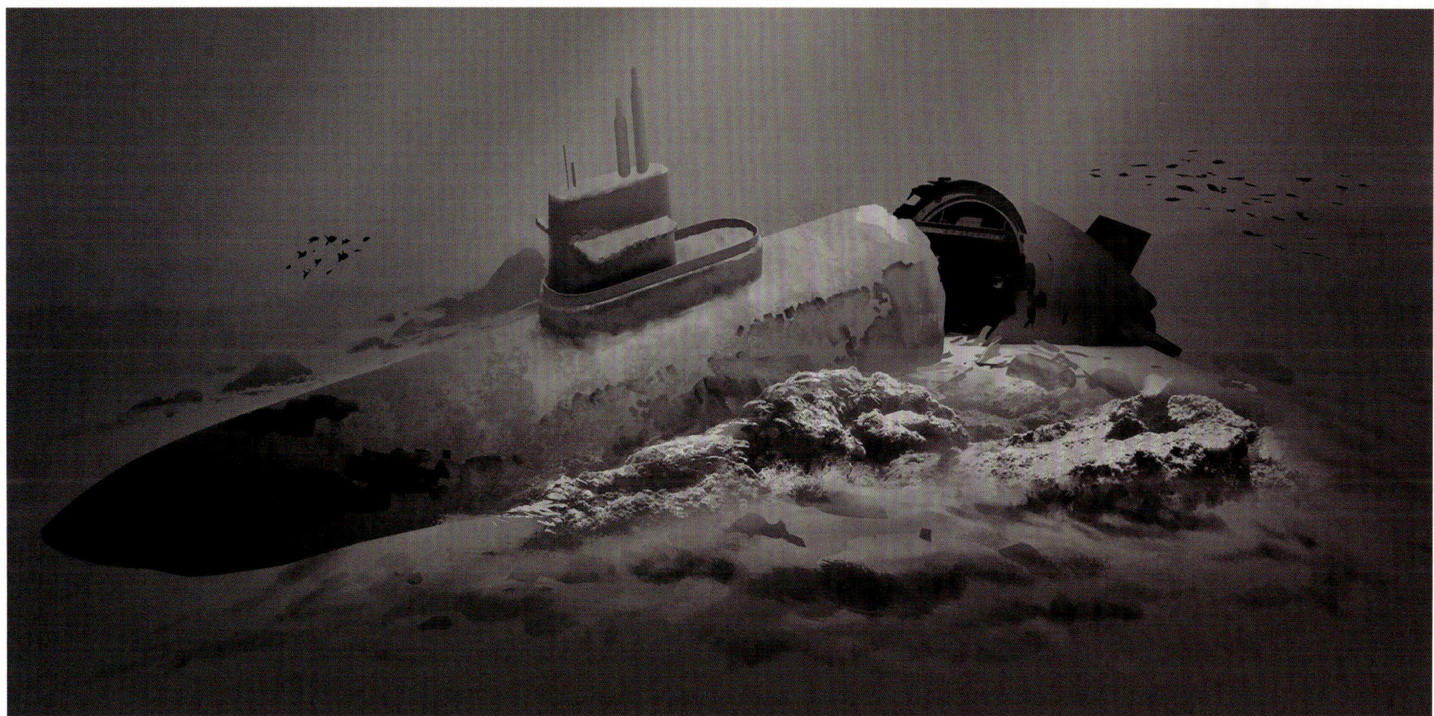

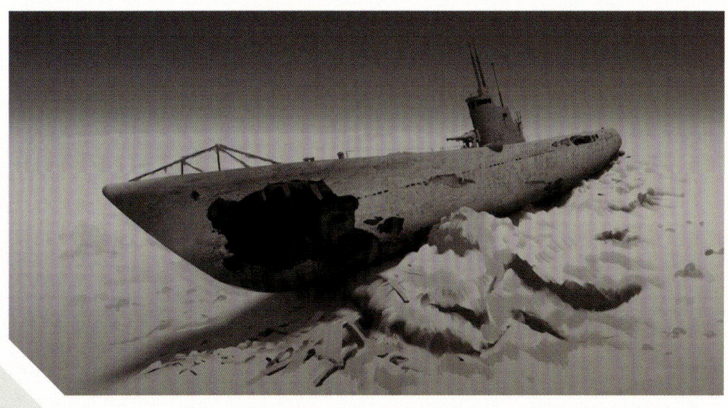

SUNKEN PLANES AND SHIPS

The sunken planes and ships in *Rust* serve as eerie, submerged reminders of past disasters. Their twisted metal, barnacle-covered hulls, and corroded frames reflect years of neglect beneath the waves. Often broken apart or half-buried, they blend seamlessly into the seabed, adding mystery and narrative depth.

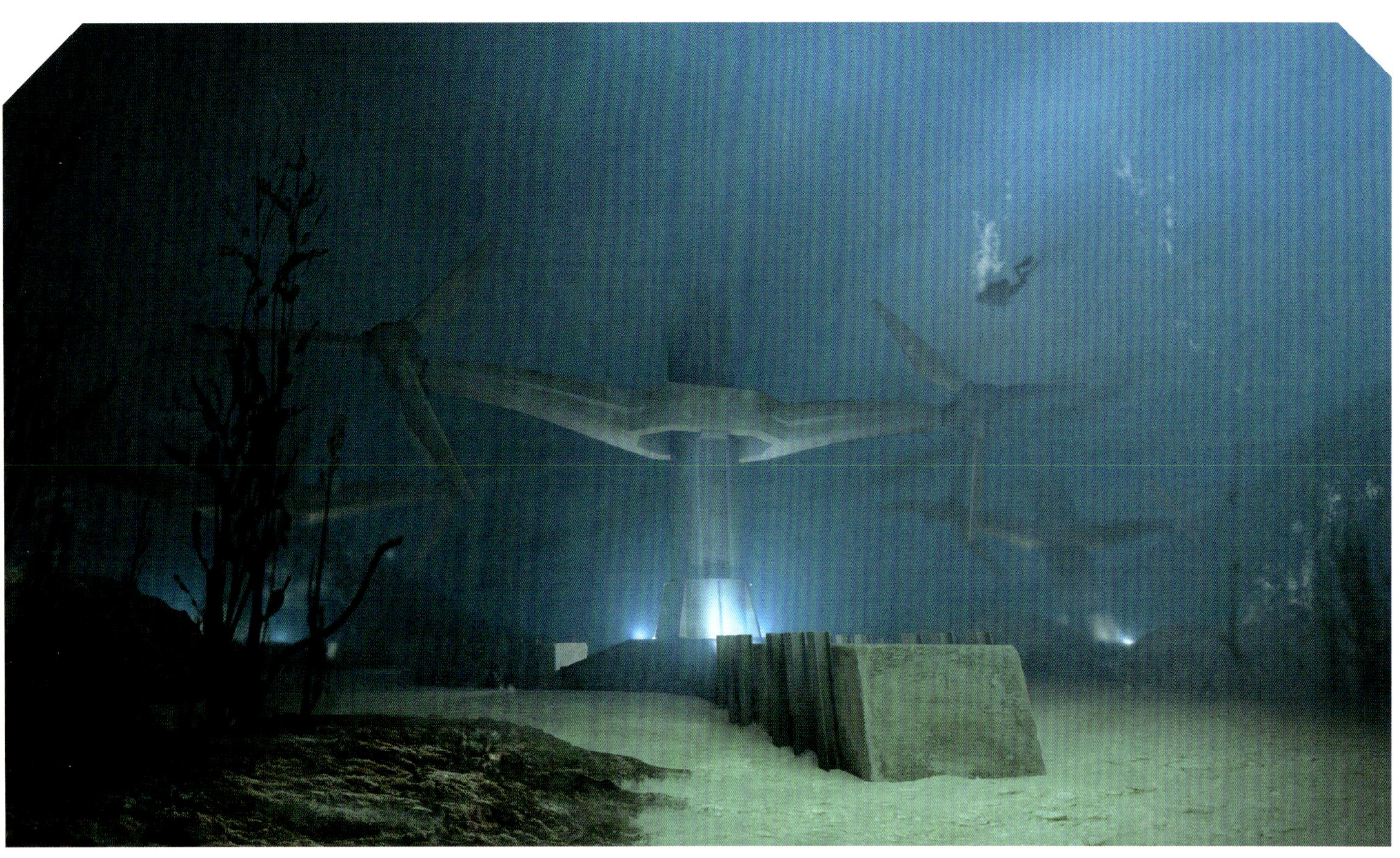

TURBINES

These first sketches of Underwater Turbines were aimed at creating an eerie submerged landmark for players to explore in the ocean, with the idea of players being able to hook up to and generate power from them. Ultimately, the landmark didn't make it into the game, but the artwork still provides a haunting depiction of what players could have encountered.

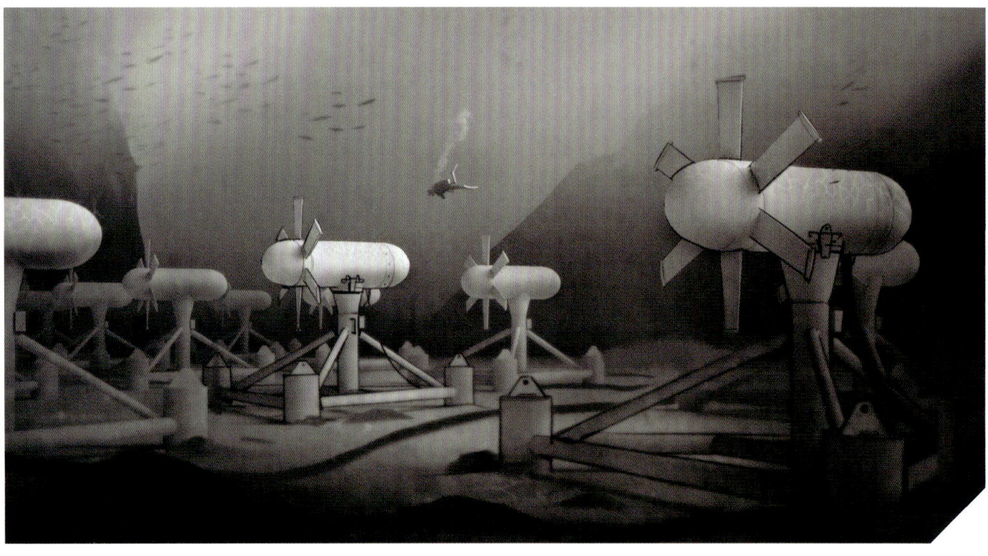

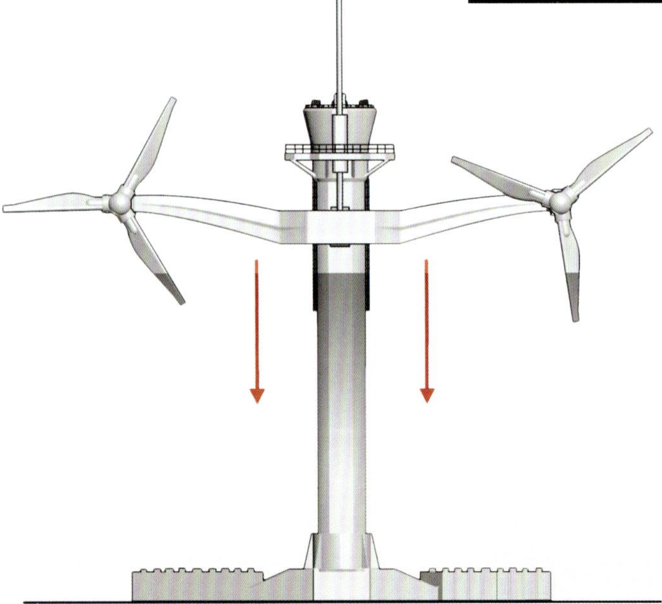

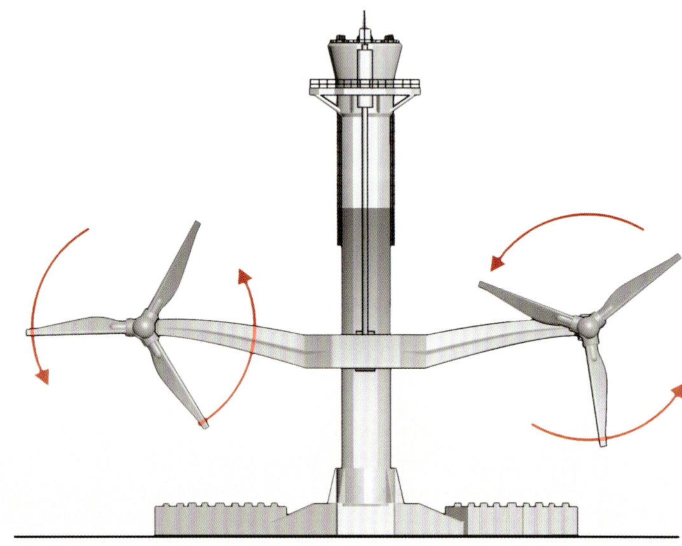

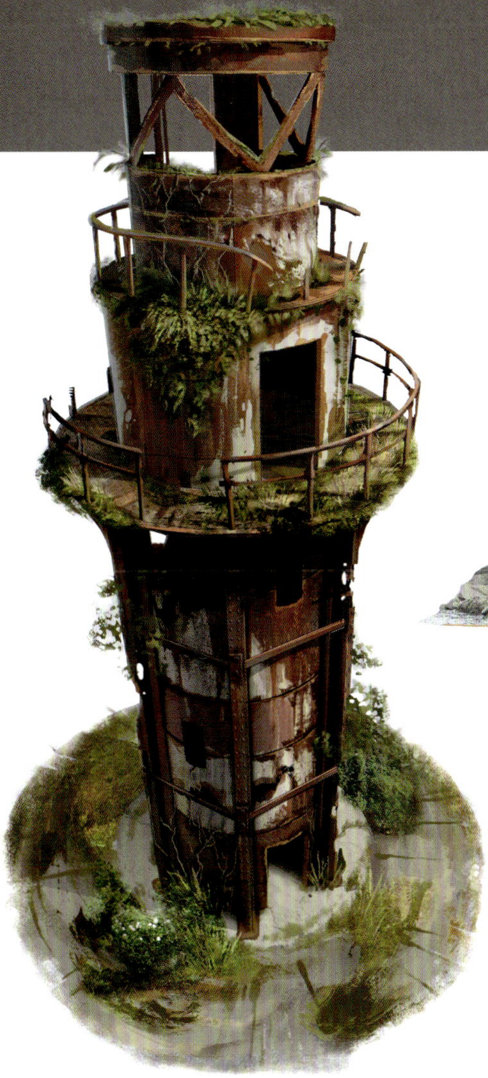

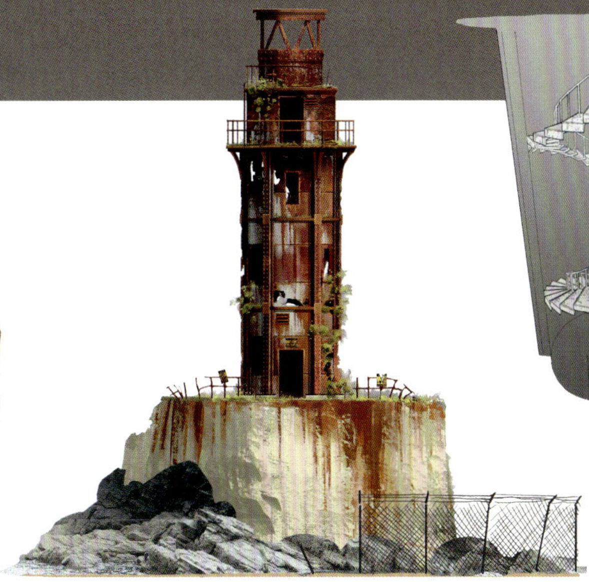

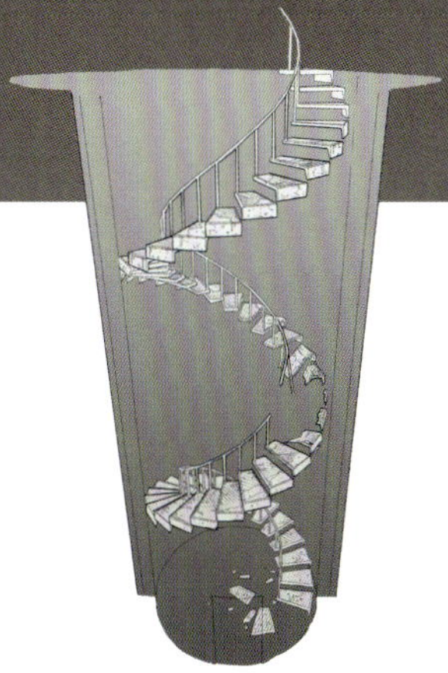

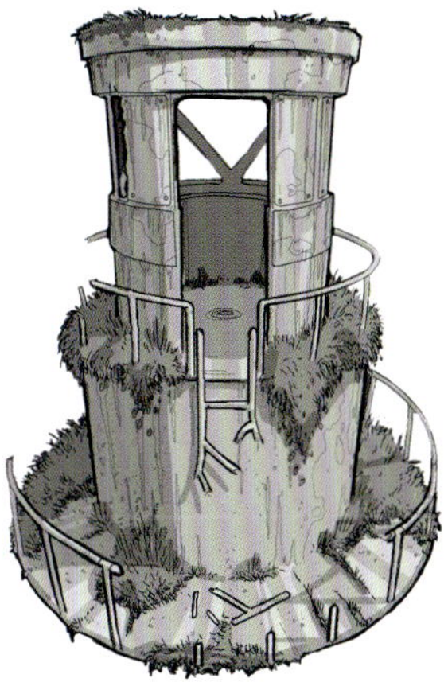

LIGHTHOUSE

The Lighthouse was one of the first monuments to be added to *Rust*. Its primary focus was to provide a point of reference to help players navigate the island before the map feature was added to the game.

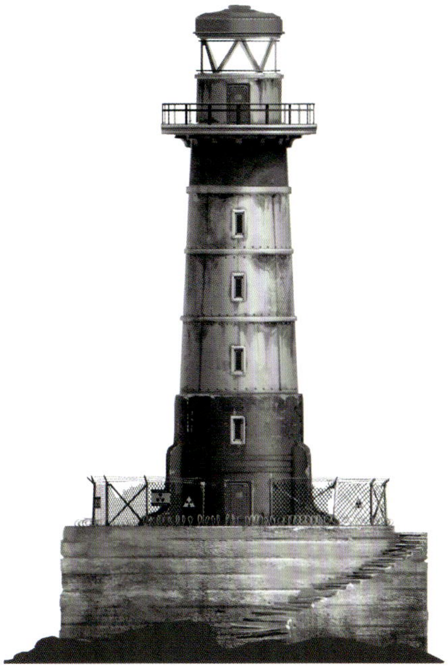

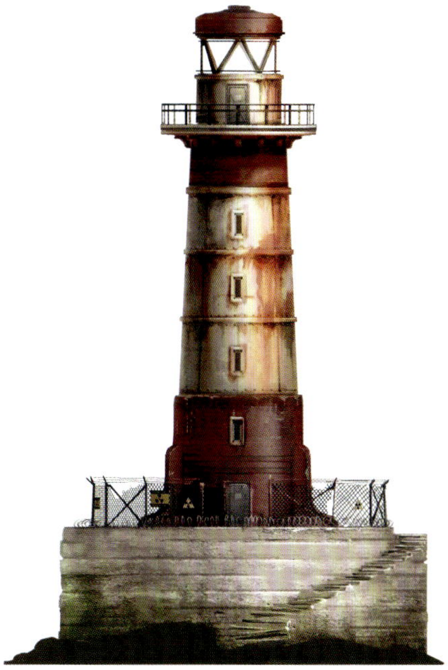

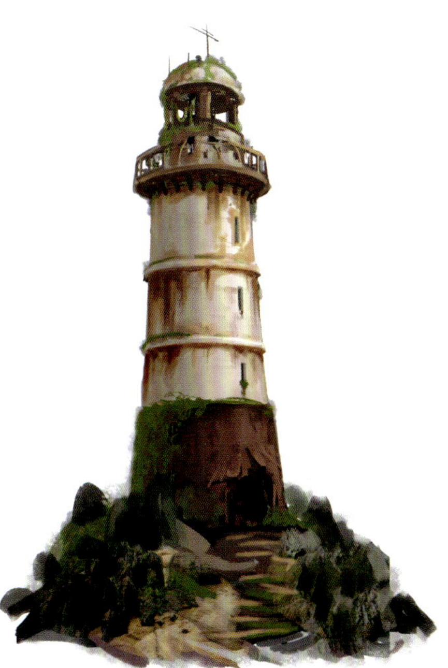

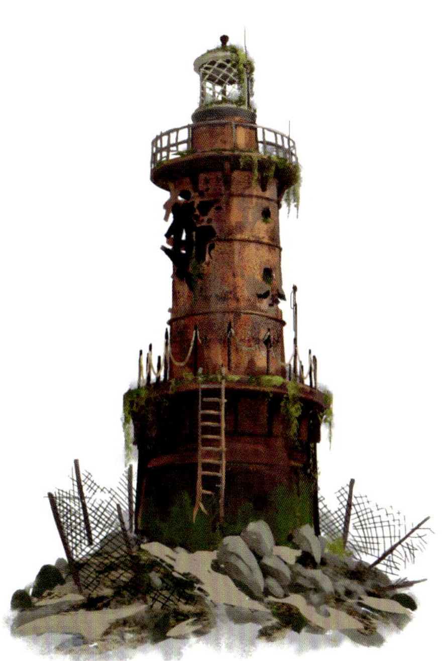

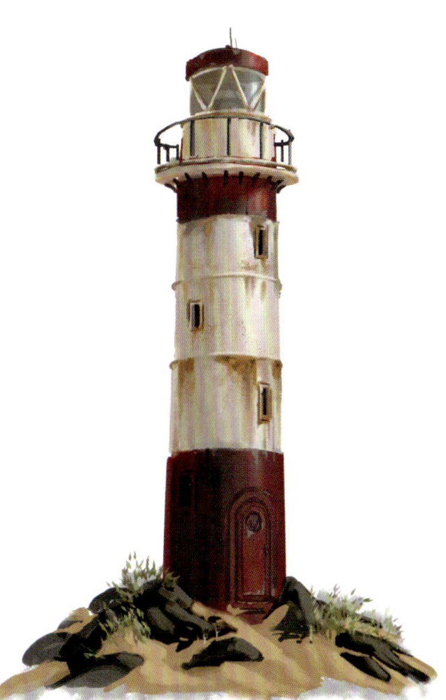

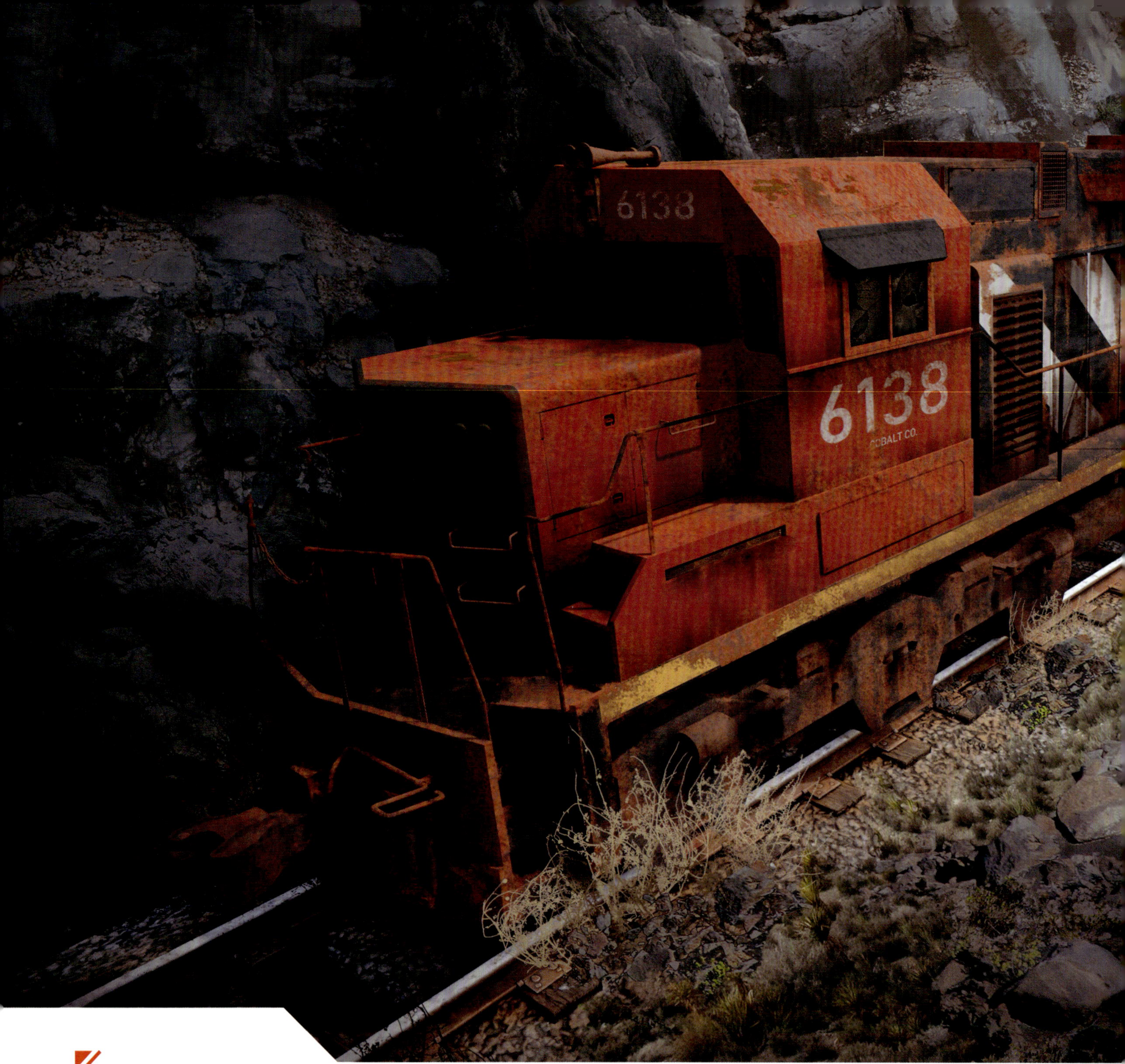

TRAINS

Trains are an integral part of *Rust*'s travel mechanics; these early concept drawings not only explored what the trains would look like but also how and where the tracks could be placed in the *Rust* world. Some cars were designed for players to build their bases on, creating rolling reinforced fortresses through the network of tracks.

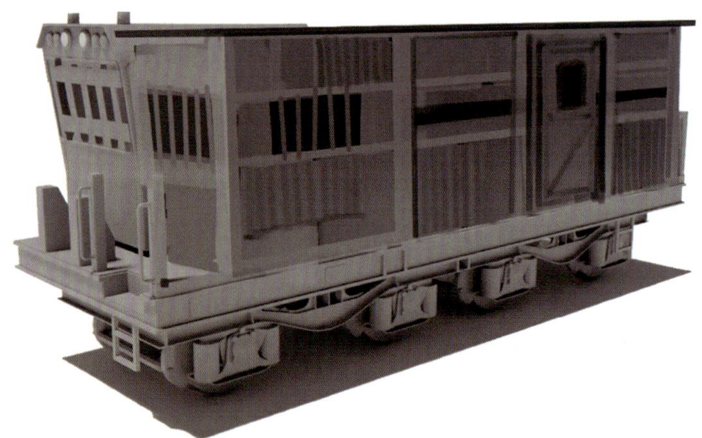

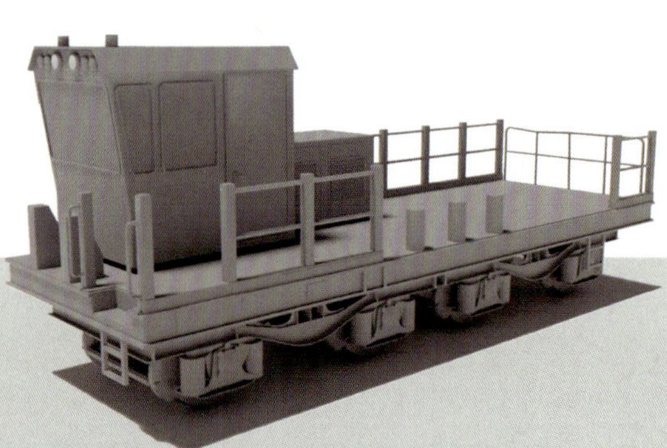

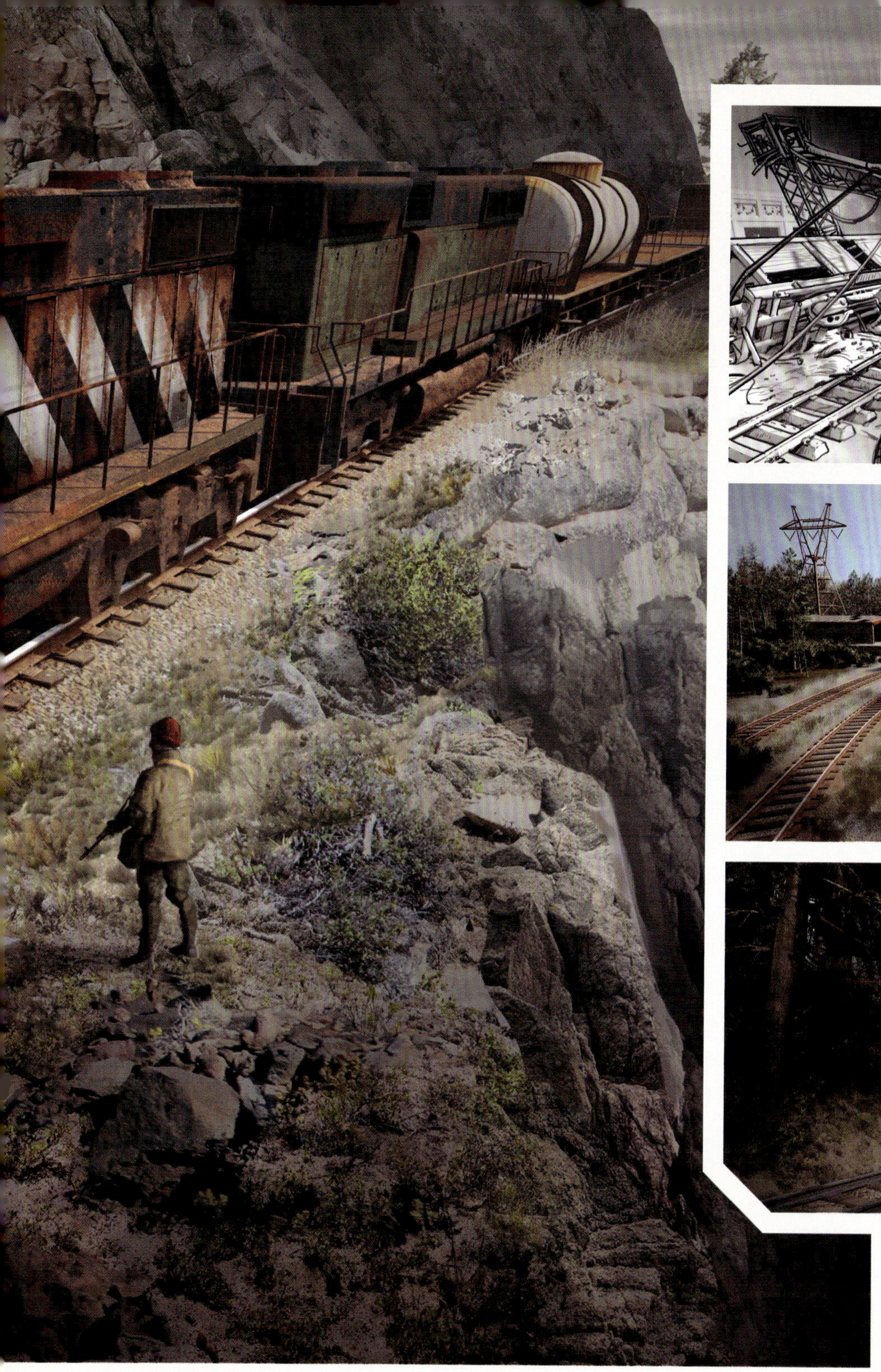

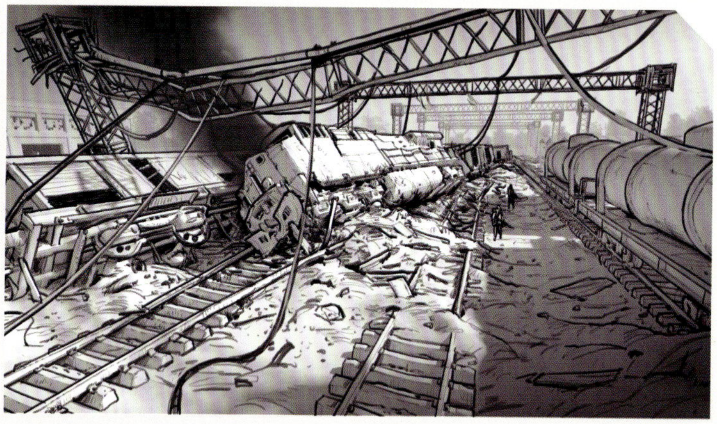

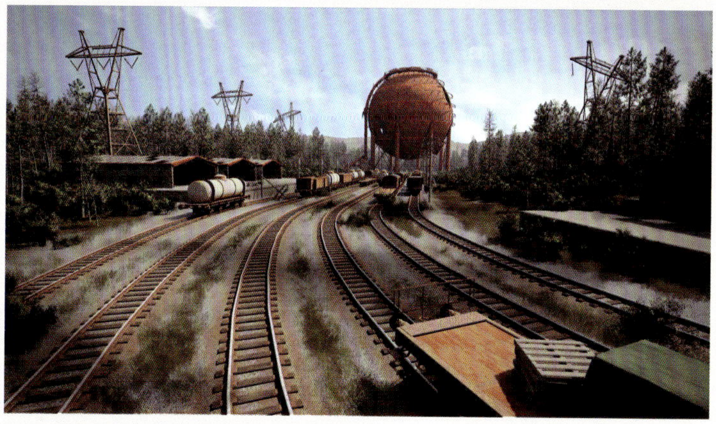

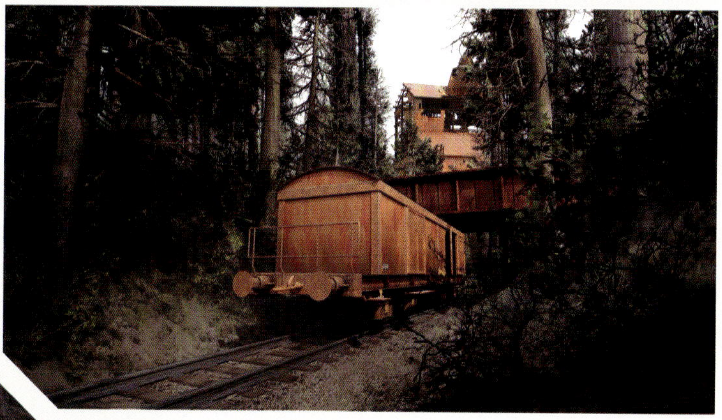

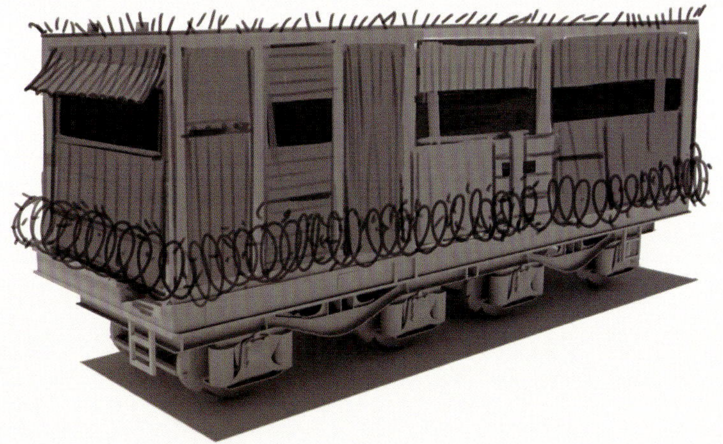

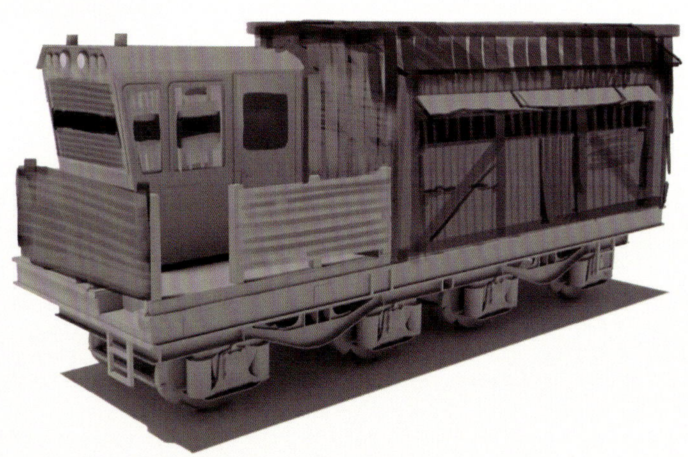

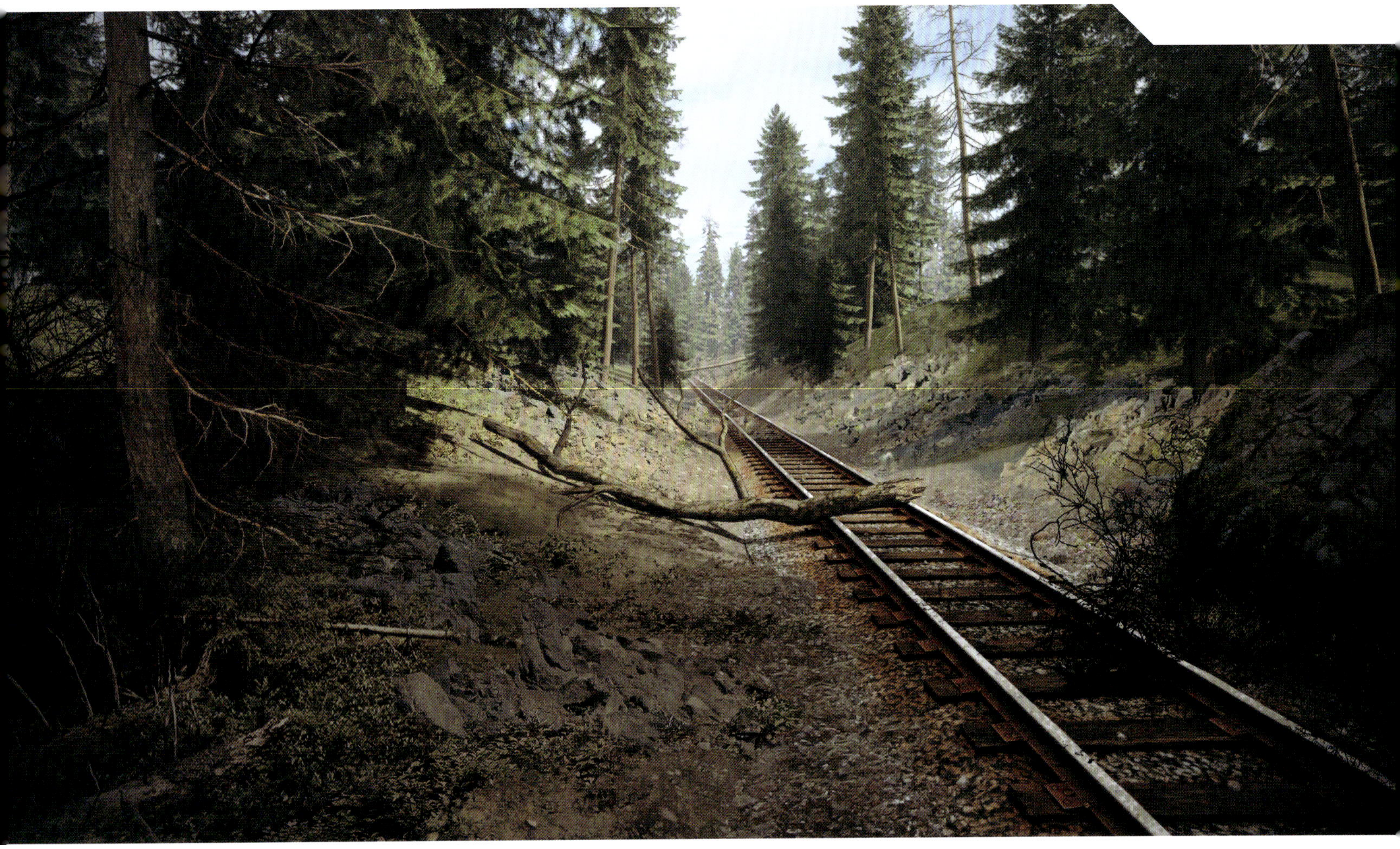

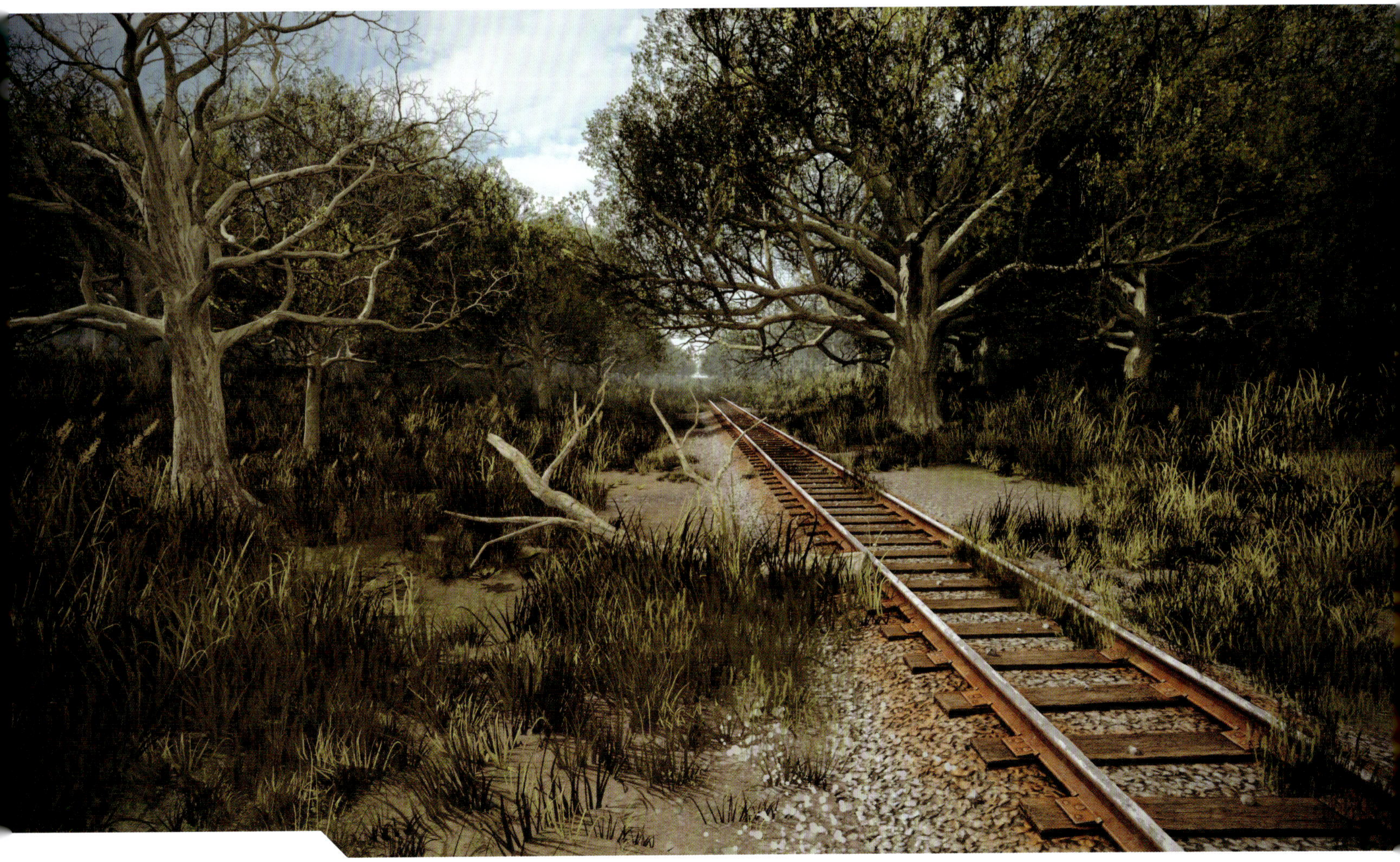

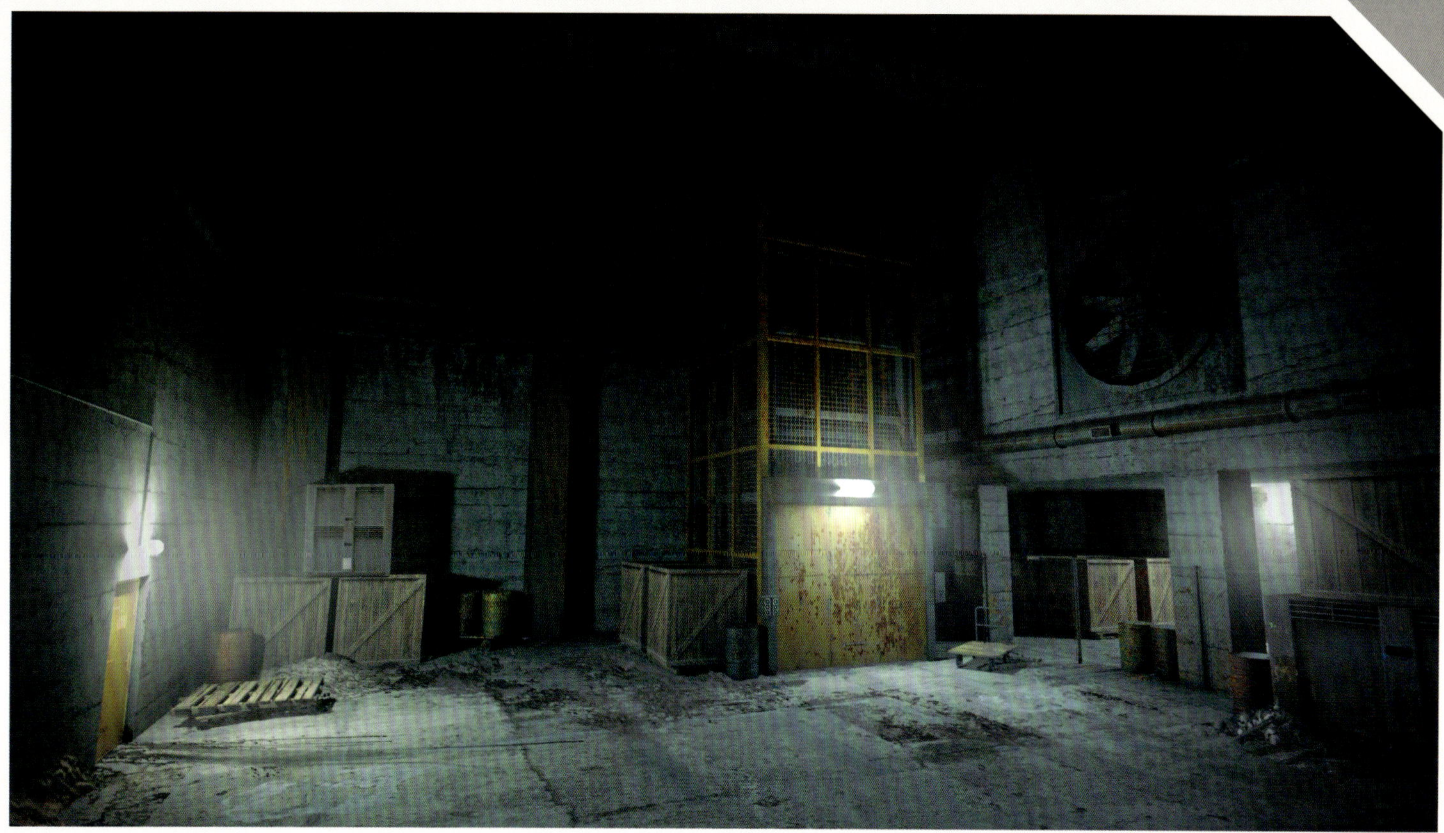

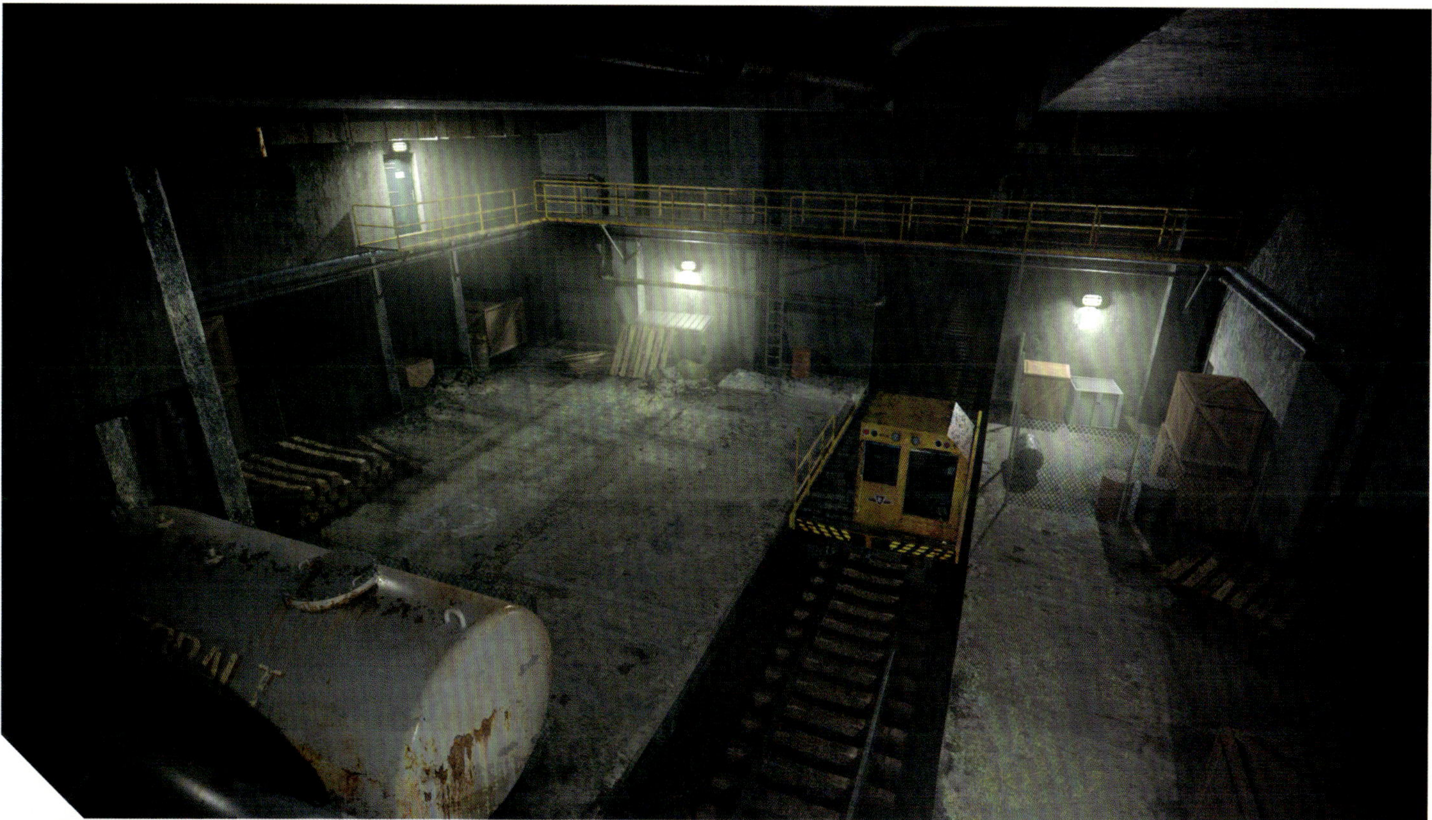

TUNNELS

The Tunnels are dark, claustrophobic spaces designed with a functional utilitarian aesthetic. Carved deep underground, they serve as both transport routes and combat zones. The reinforced concrete lining and steel supports suggest a once-operational transport infrastructure.

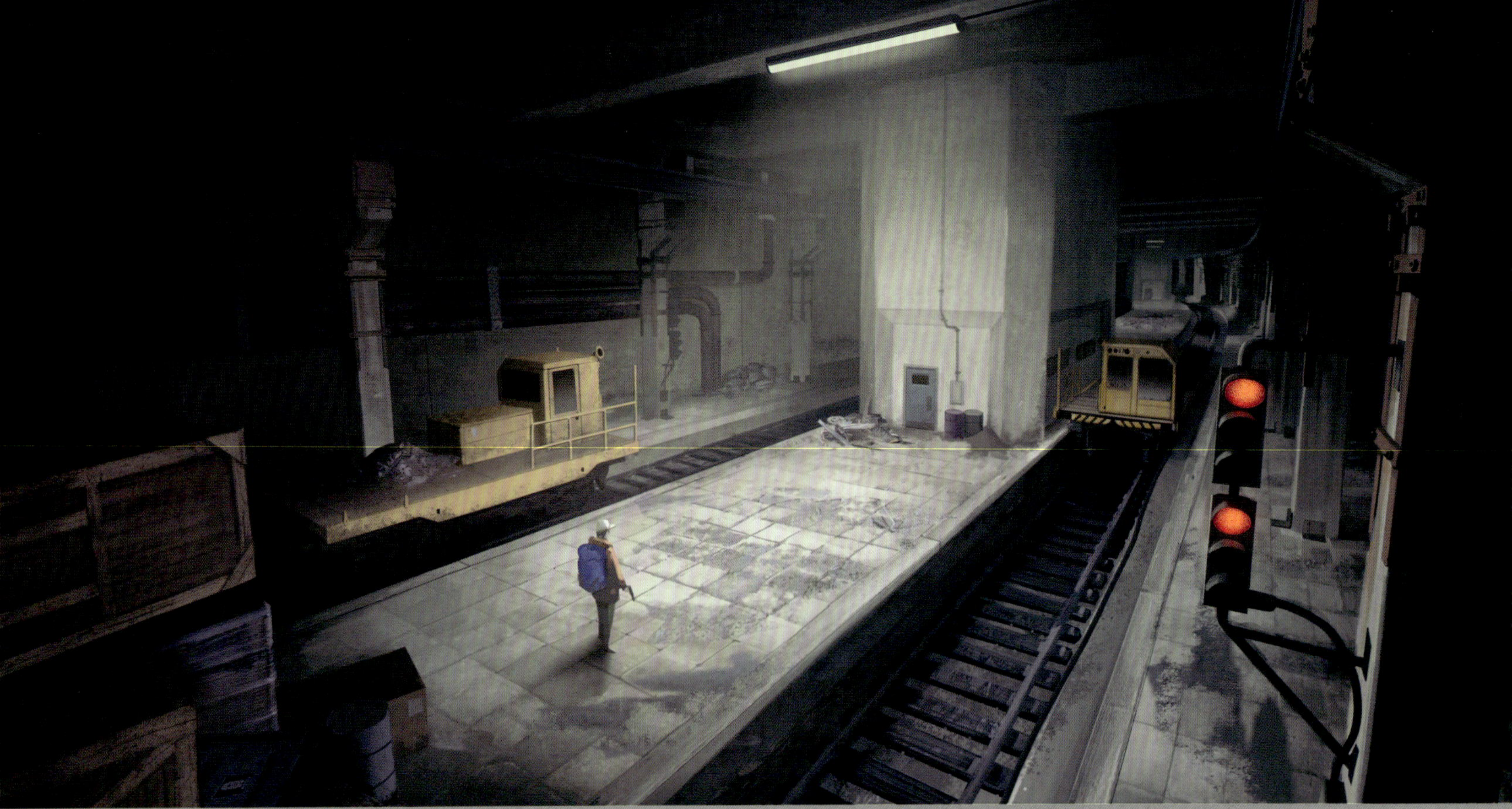

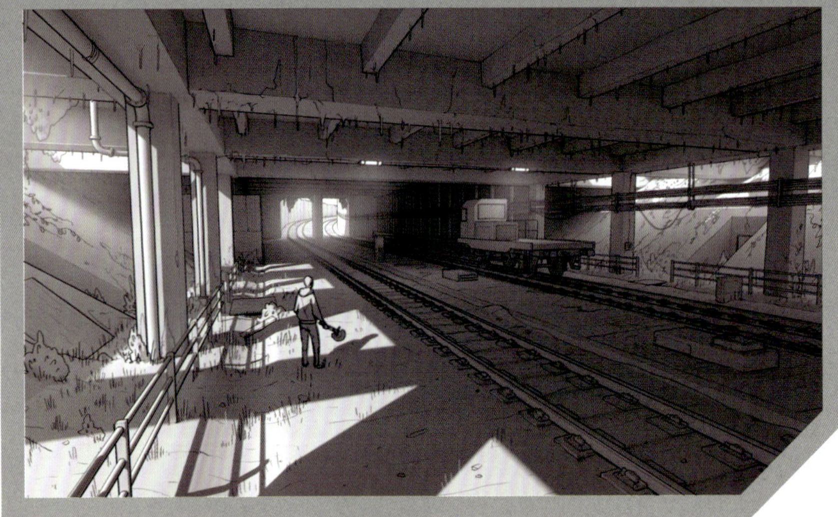

RAIL CARTS

Rail Carts are compact, rugged transport vehicles based on real-world flatbed train cars. Visually, they look worn and battered, with broken windows and bent safety rails, as if they were misused and then abandoned. Their design is meant to suggest function over form; their low-profile, open-frame structure allows visibility and fast movement along underground rail systems.

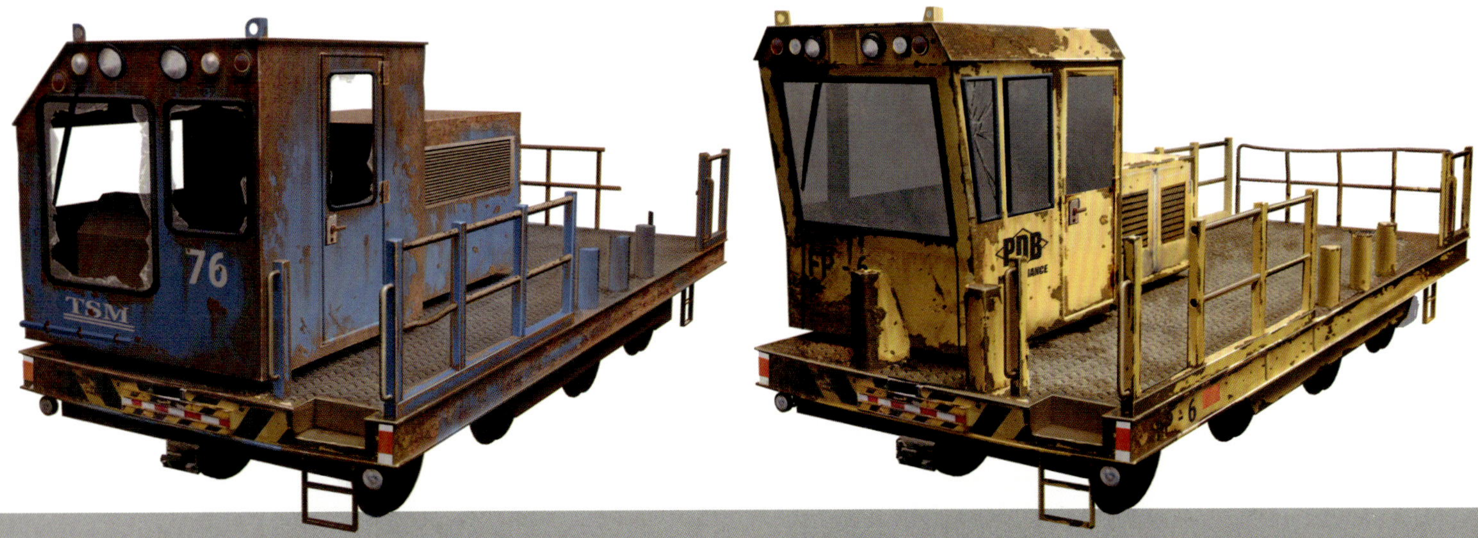

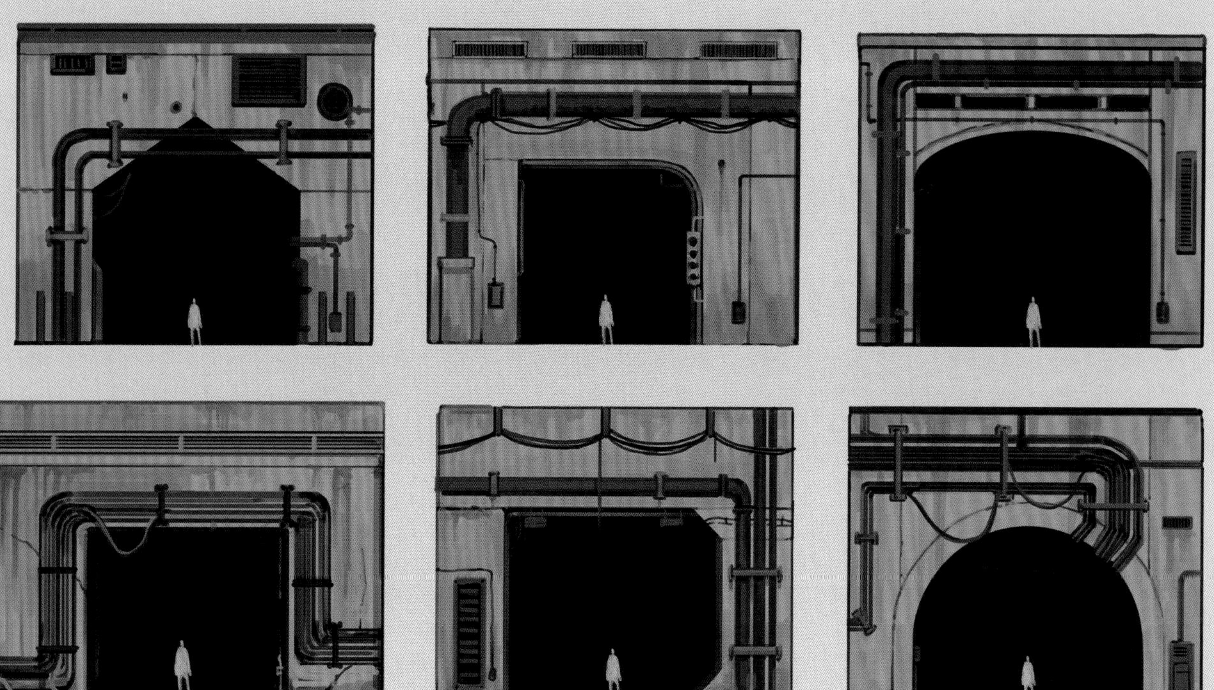

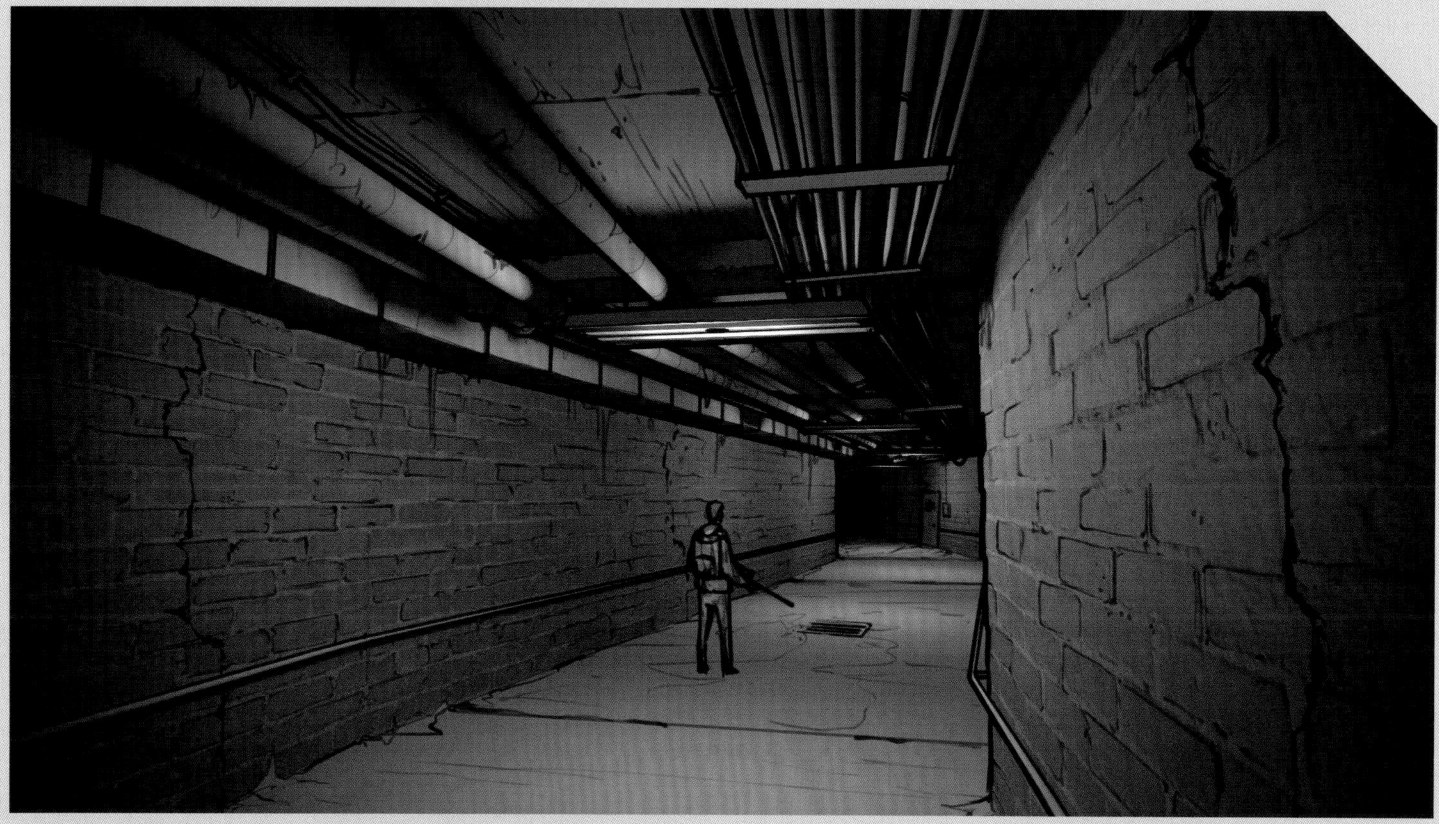

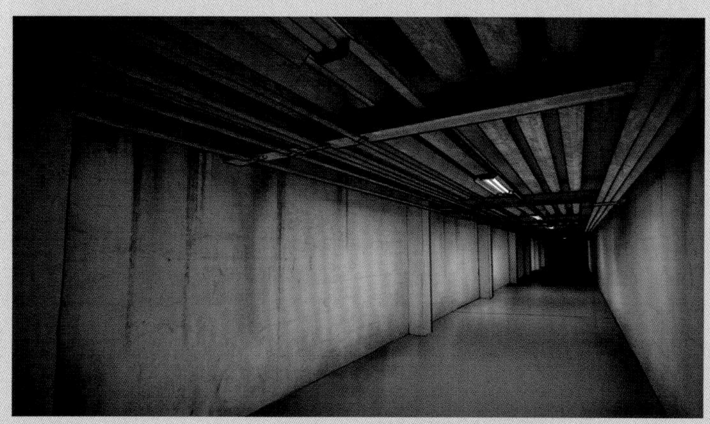

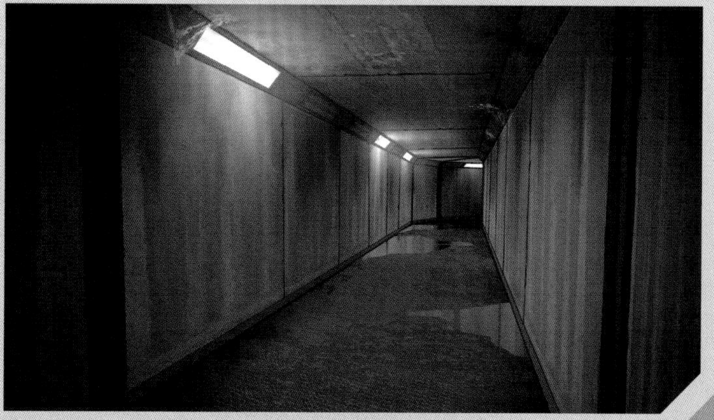

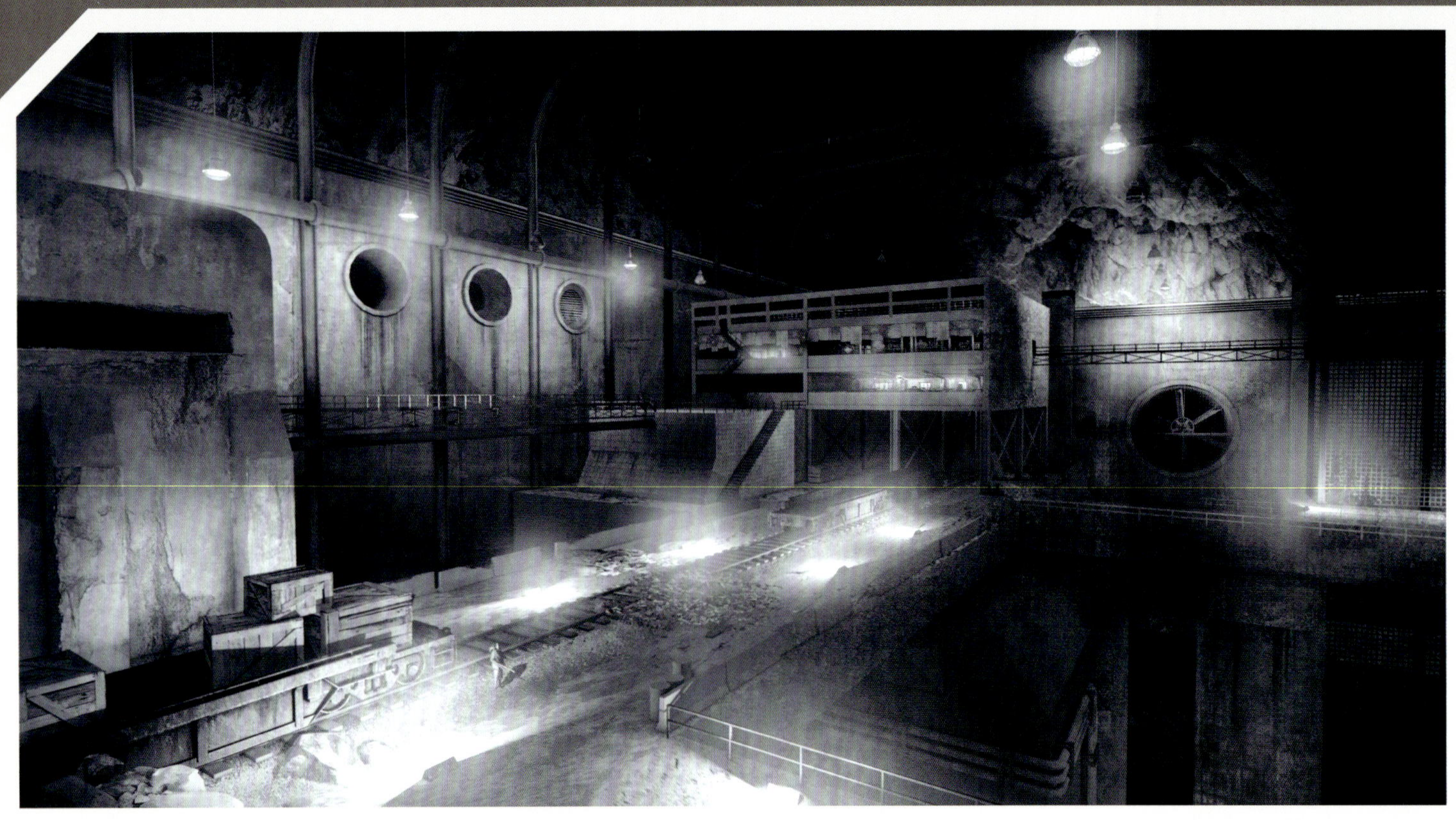

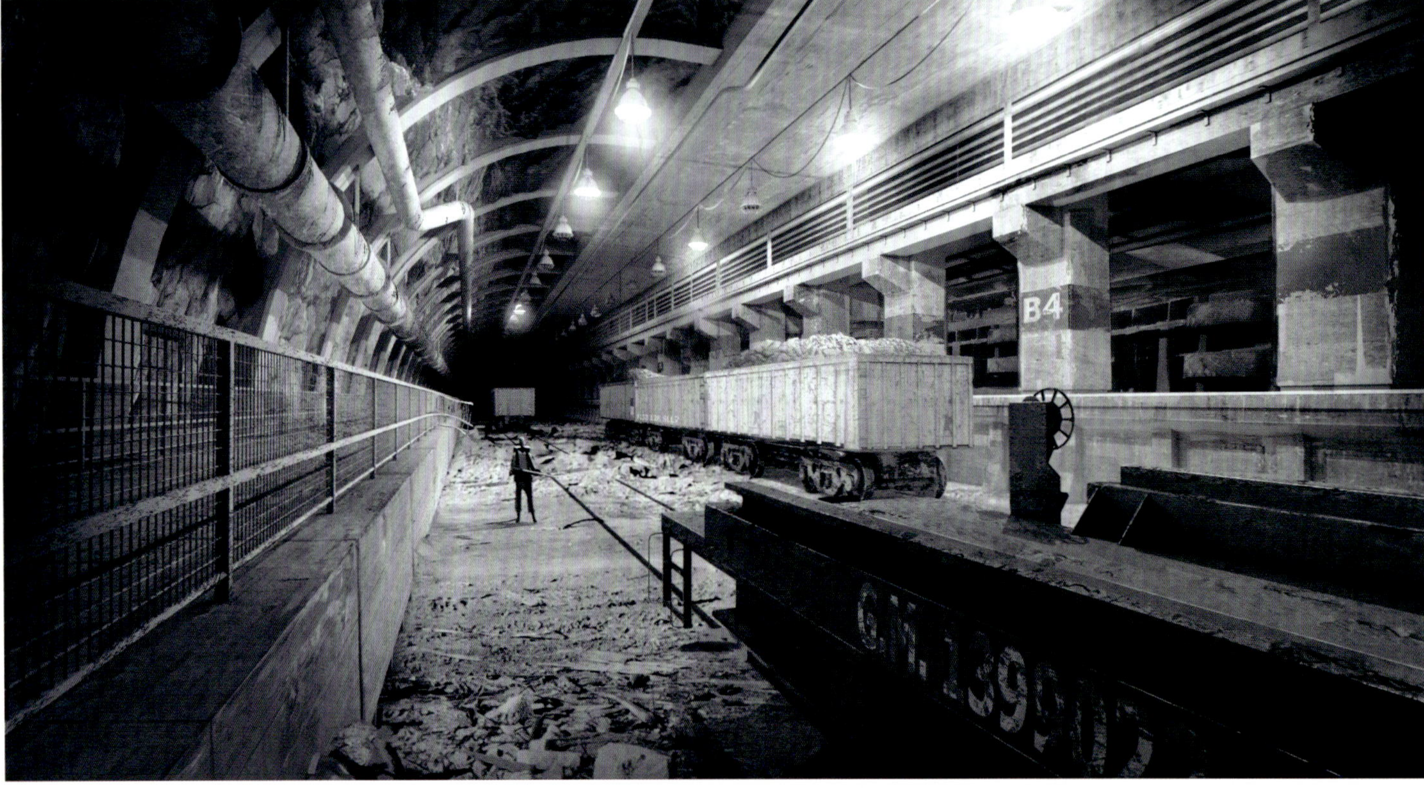

UNDERGROUND

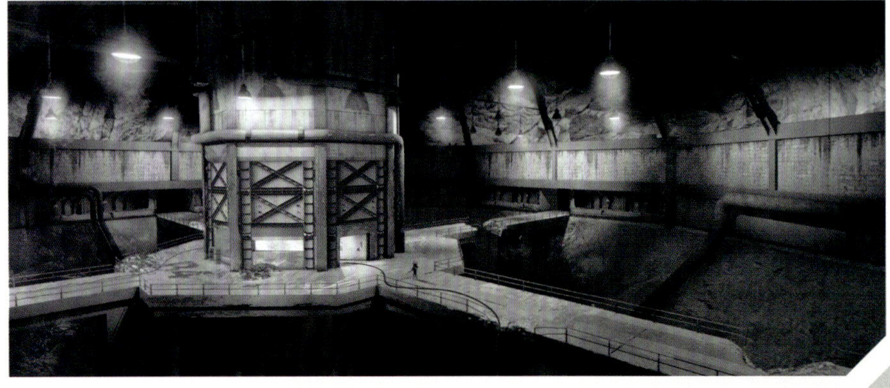

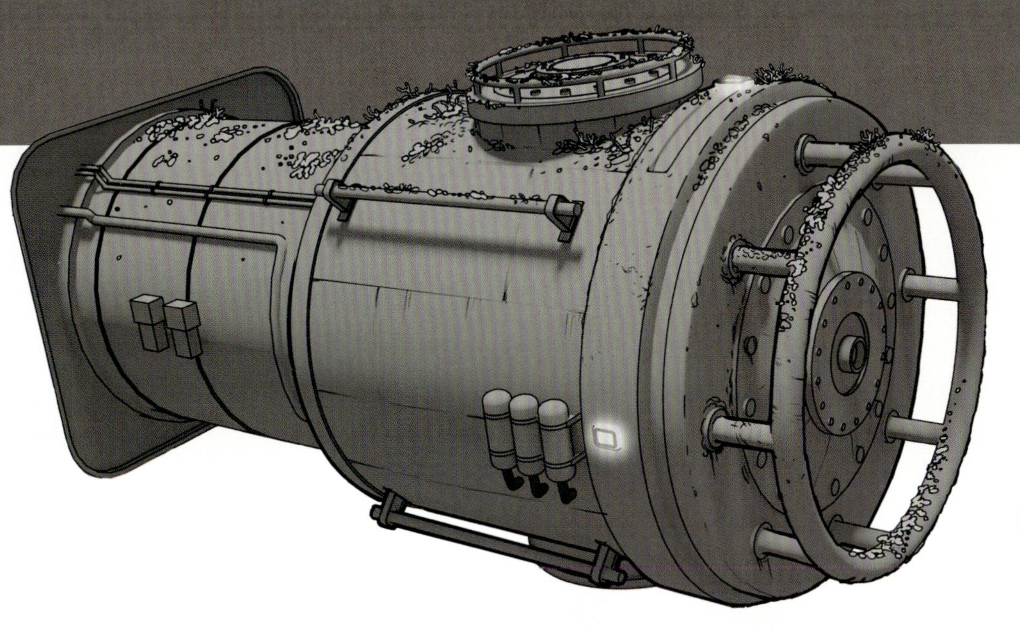

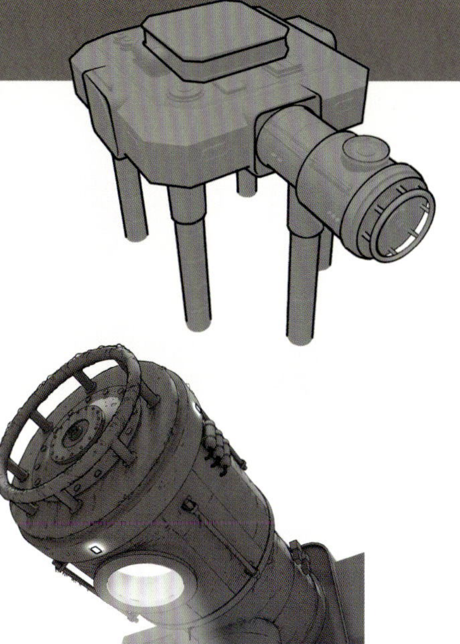

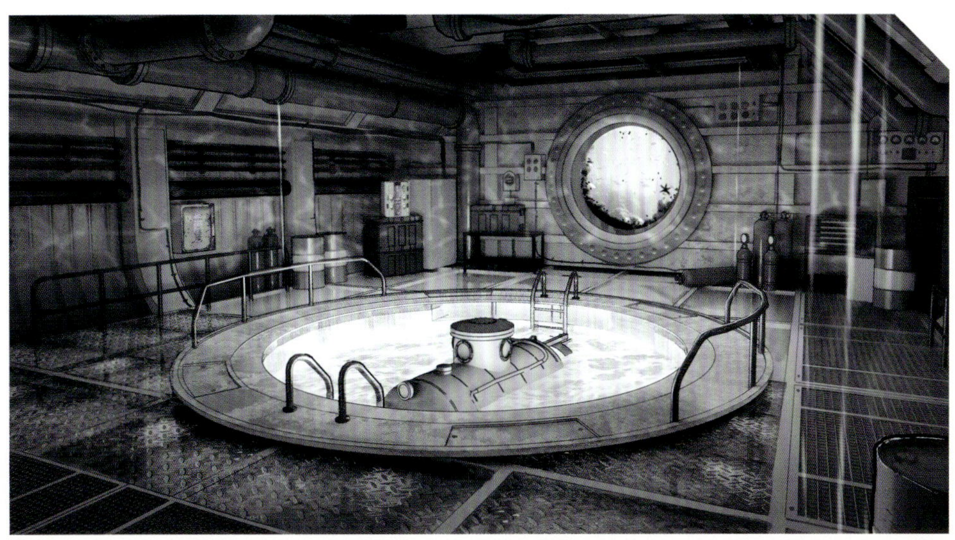

UNDERWATER LABS

The Underwater Labs are part of a sci-fi-inspired, pod-based underwater research facility with a clinical, high-tech, corroded aesthetic. Built with bulkhead corridors, reinforced glass, and a submarine bay, the labs resemble a once-advanced facility now succumbed to time and water damage. Dim lighting and echoing chambers create a cold, sunken atmosphere.

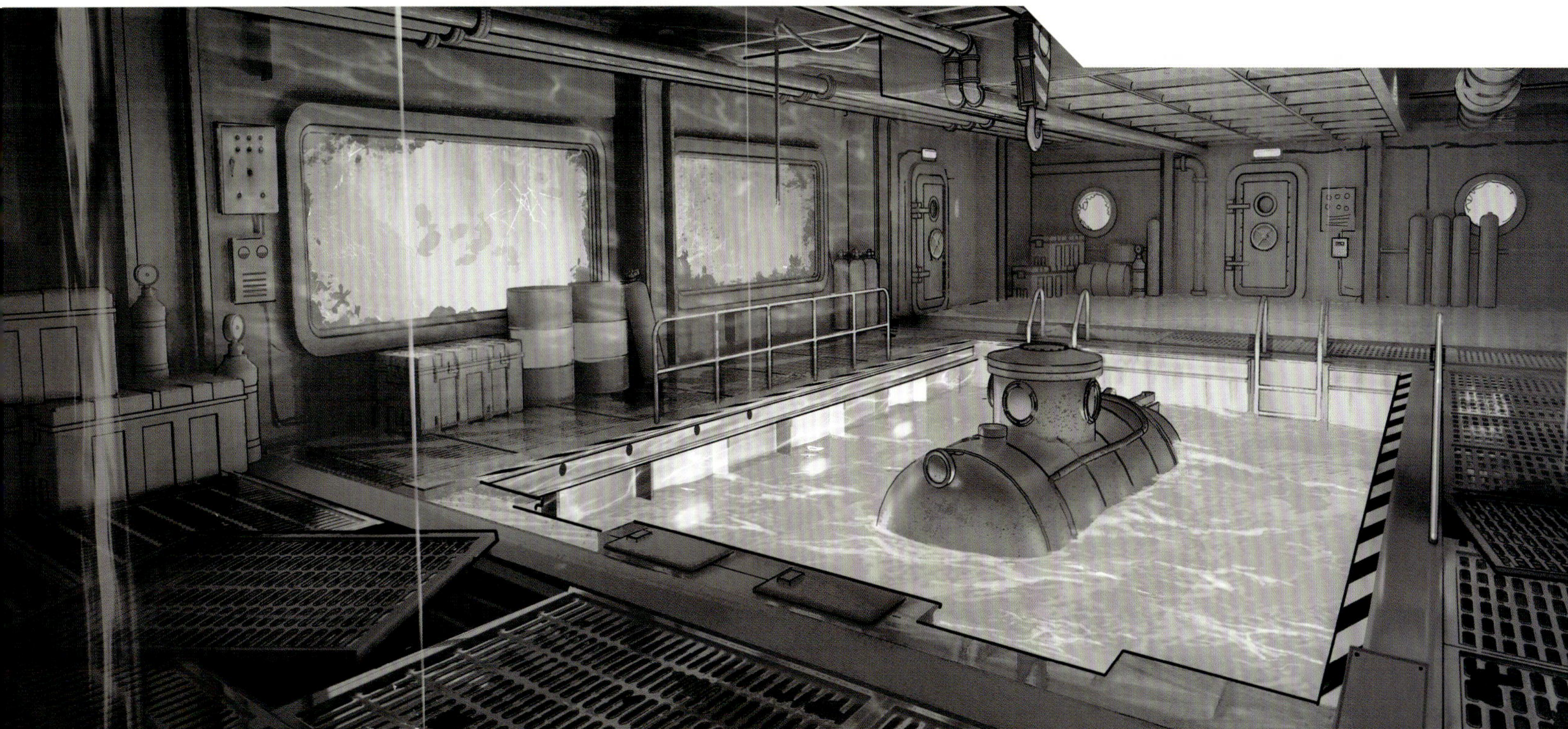

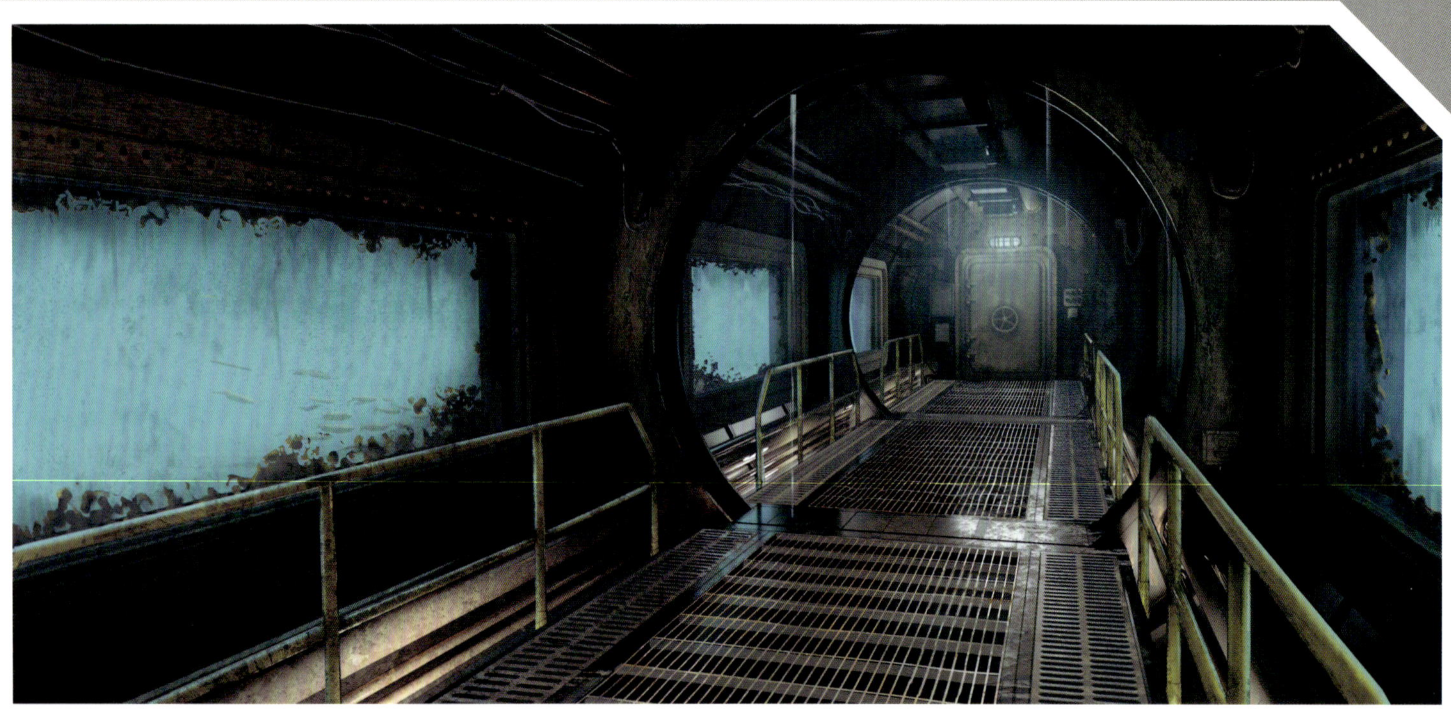

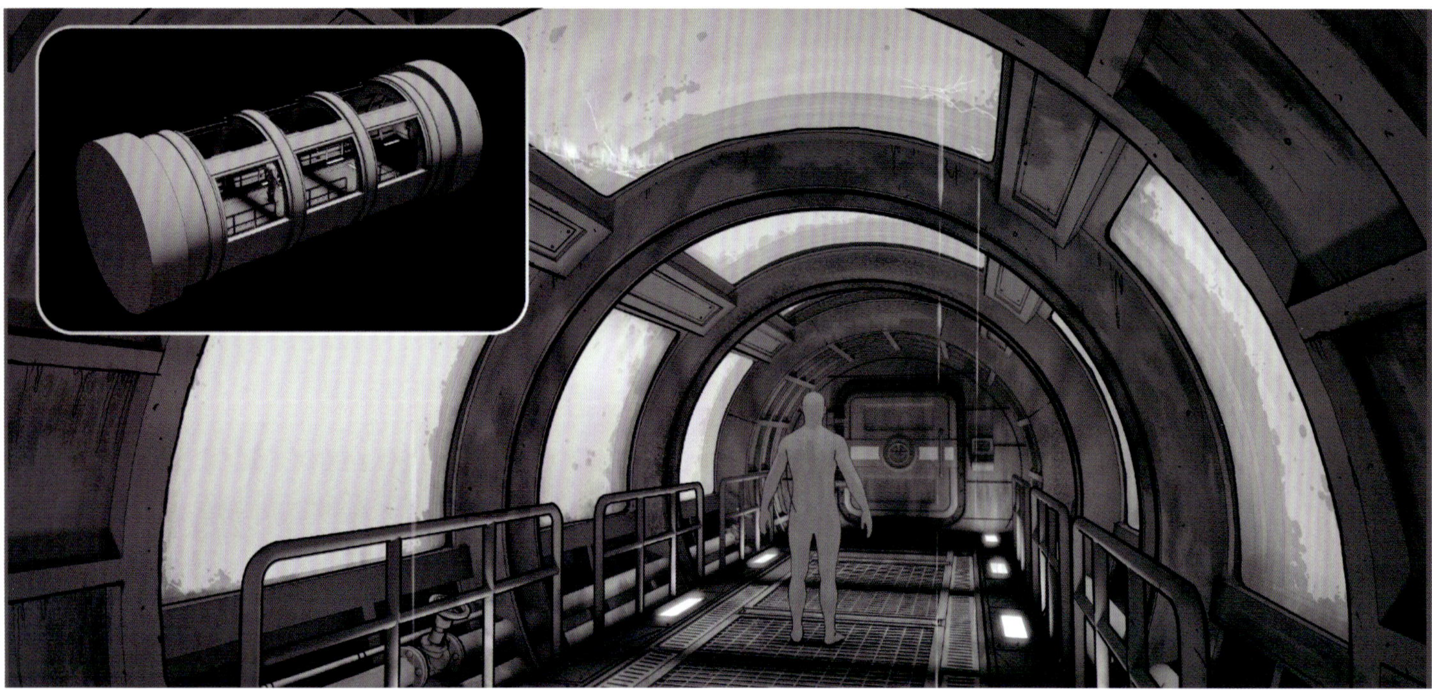

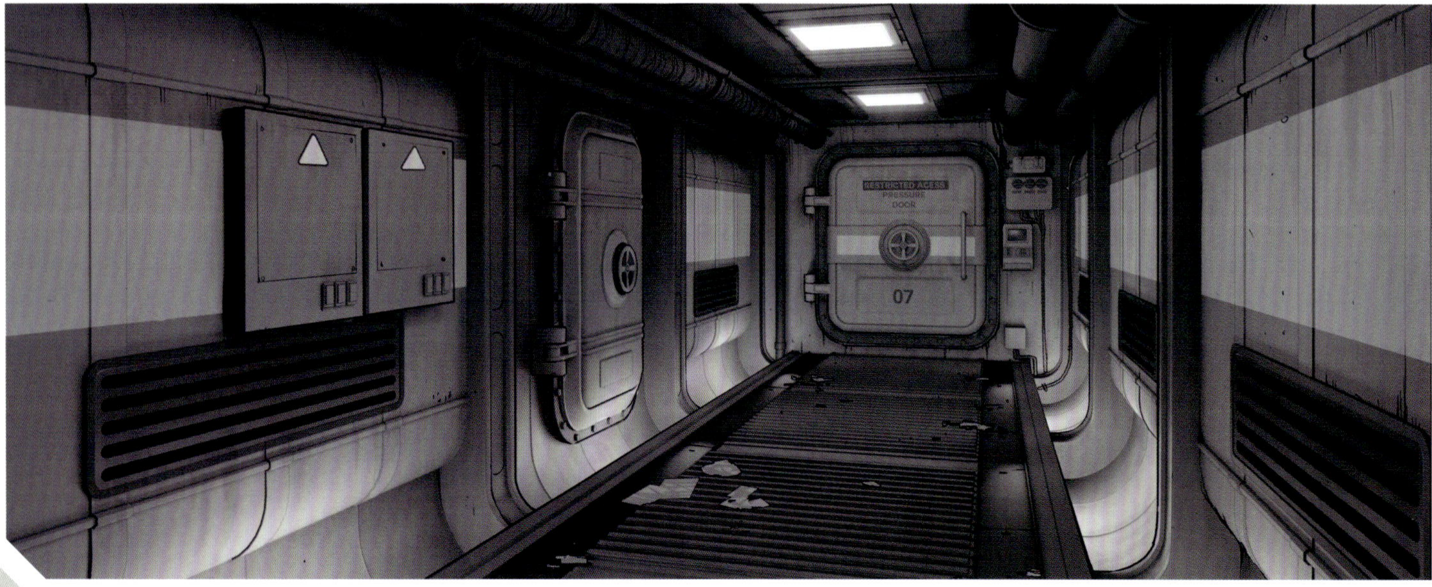
PRESSURE
DOOR
07

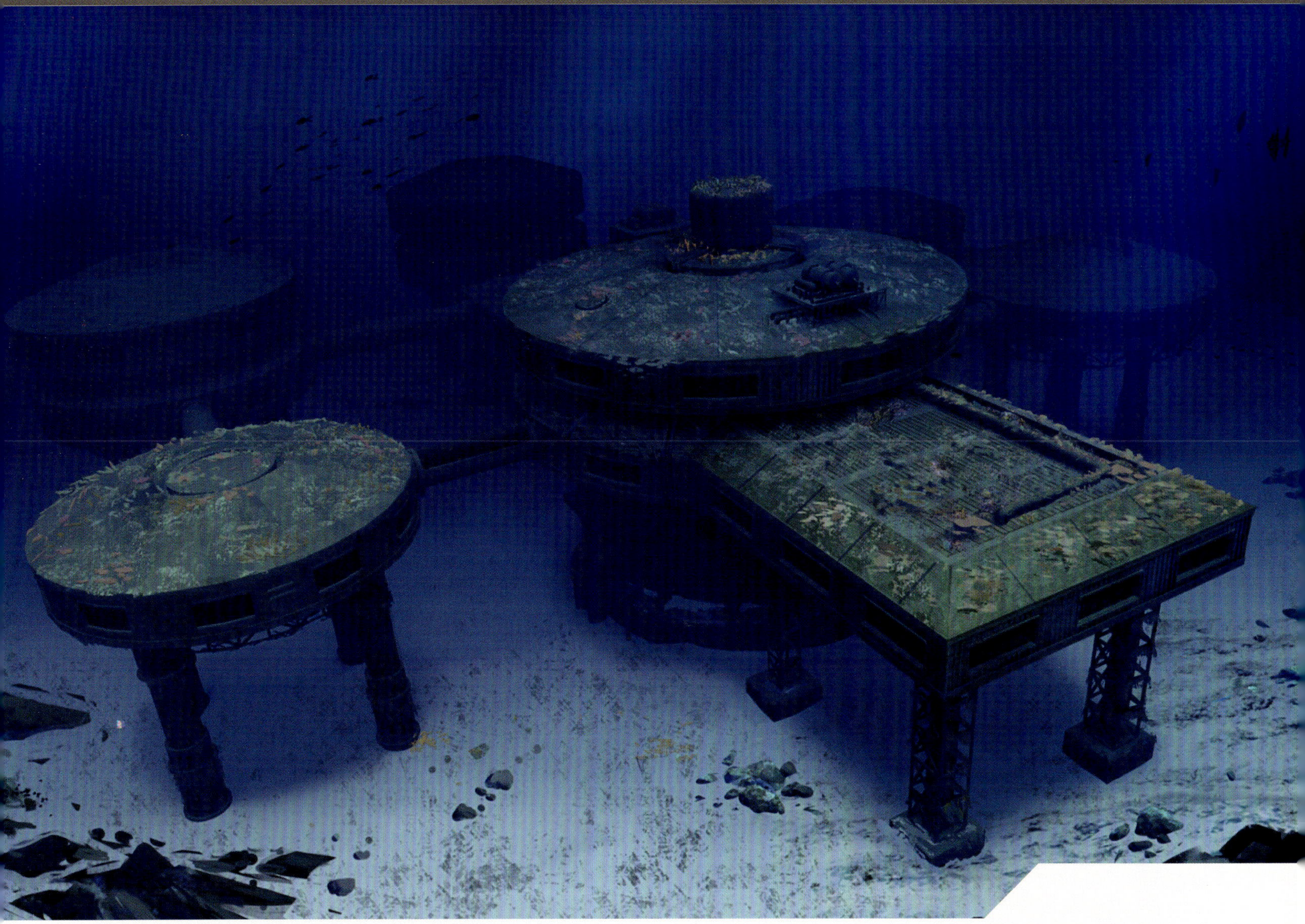

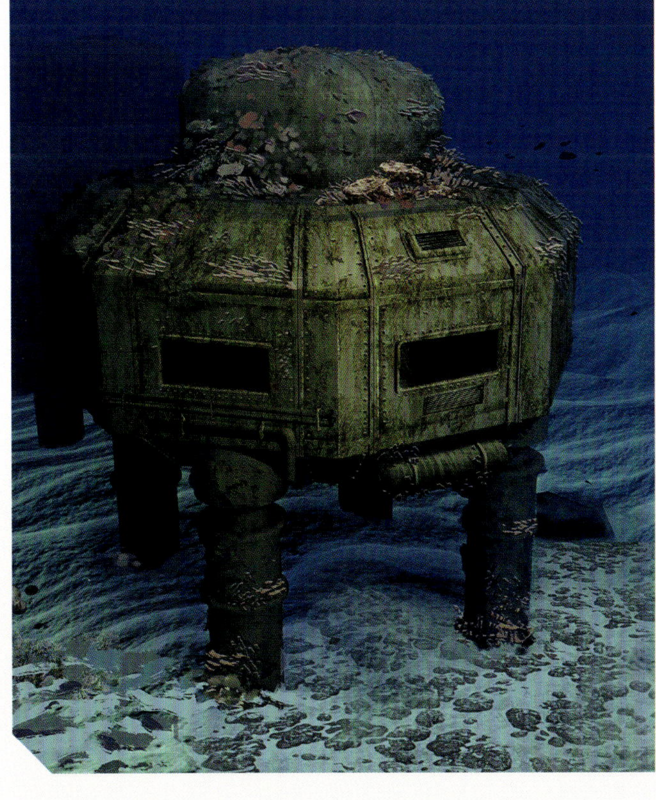

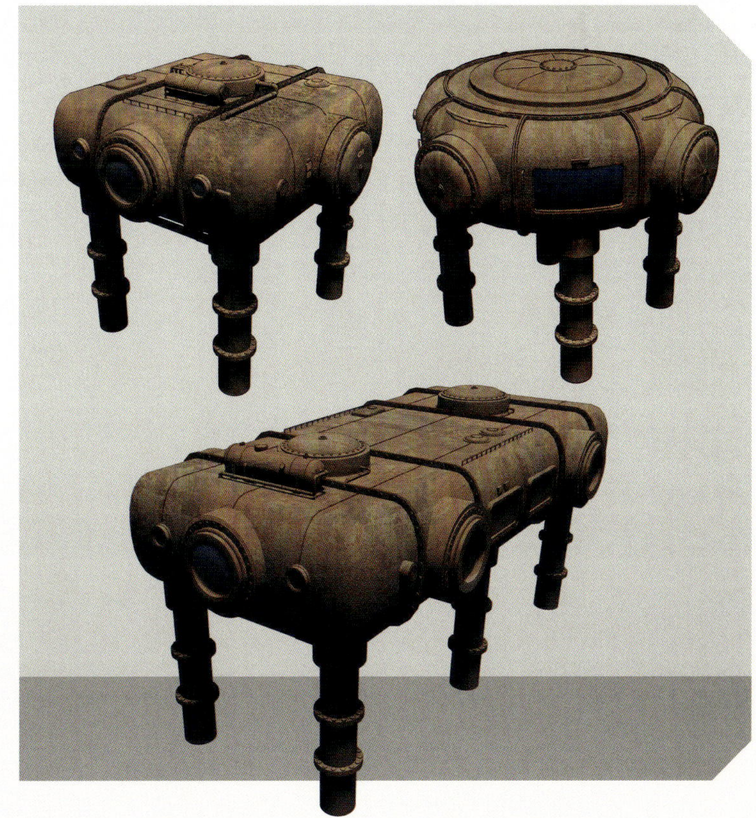

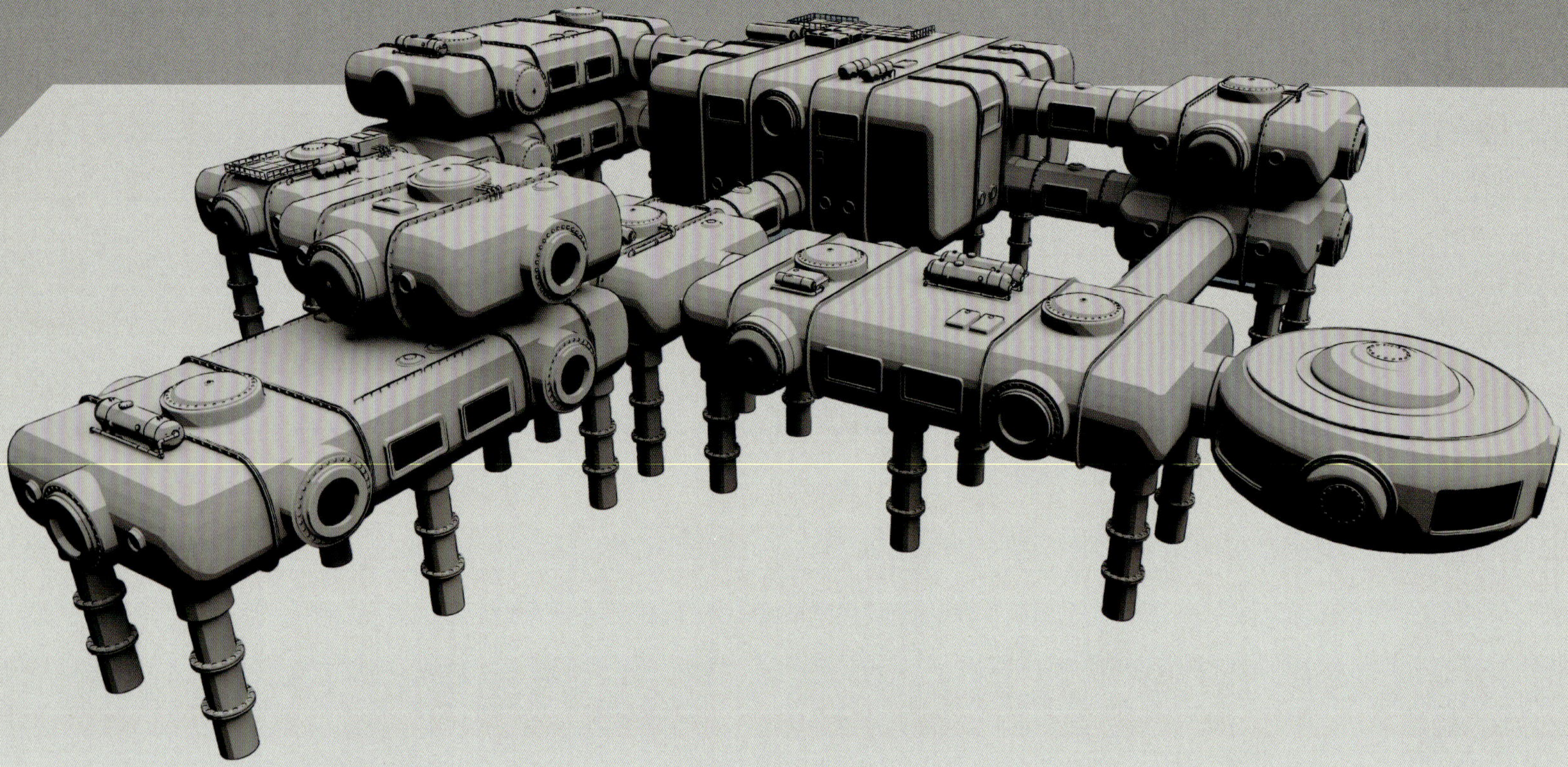

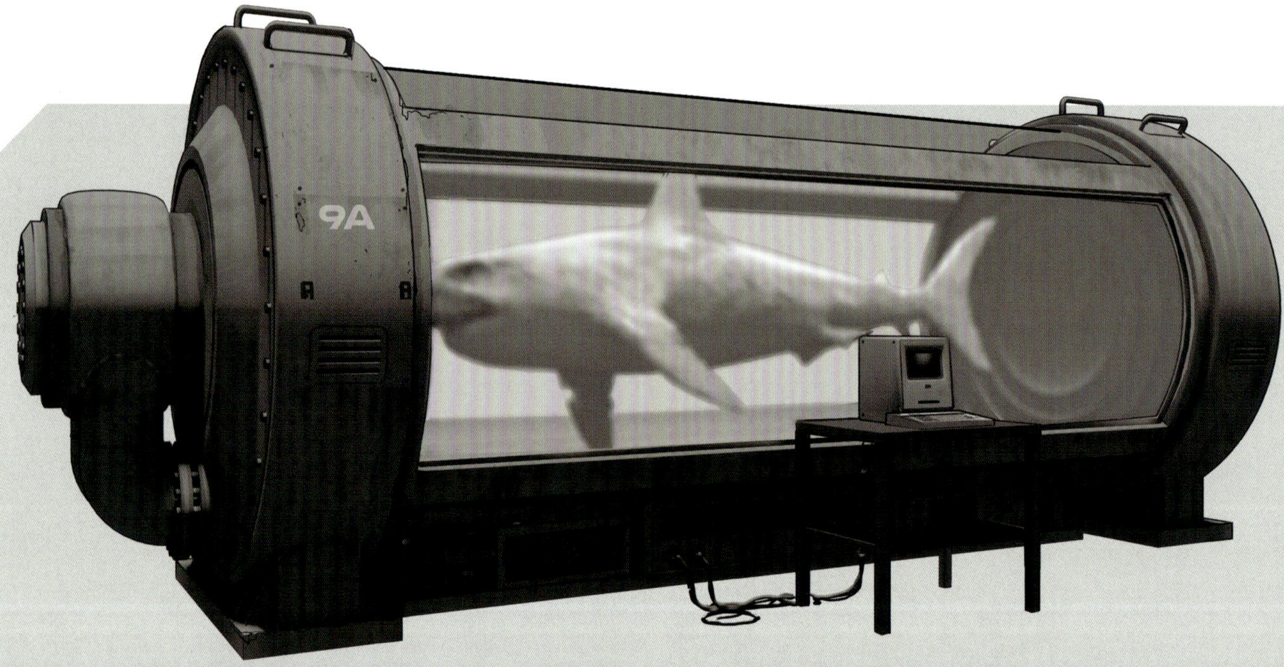

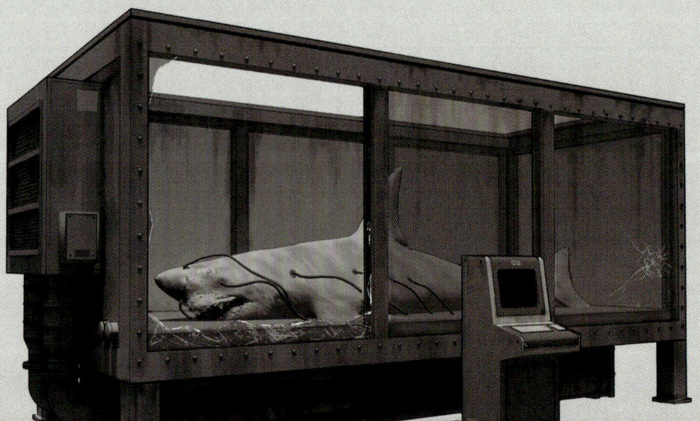

SHARK EXPERIMENTS

This concept art was created as part of the Underwater Labs to show the unsettling lengths to which Cobalt were willing to go with their scientific research. The research tanks didn't make it into the game, but the two sketches suggest a dark, ethically gray area of experimentation on sharks.

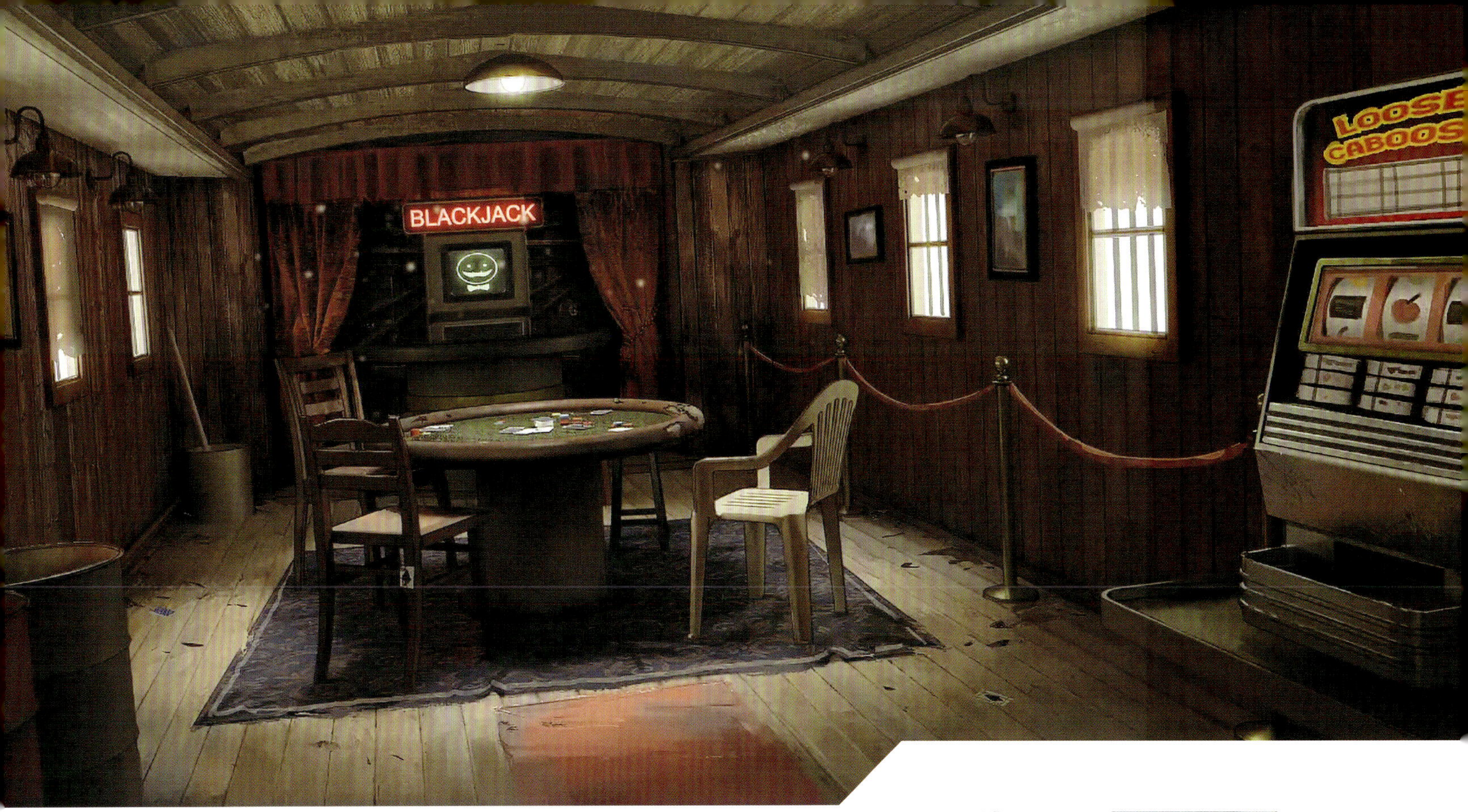

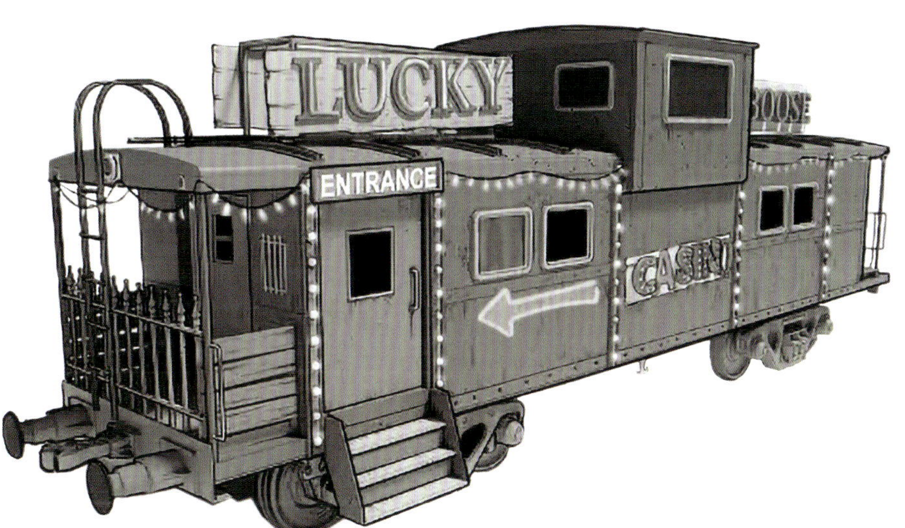

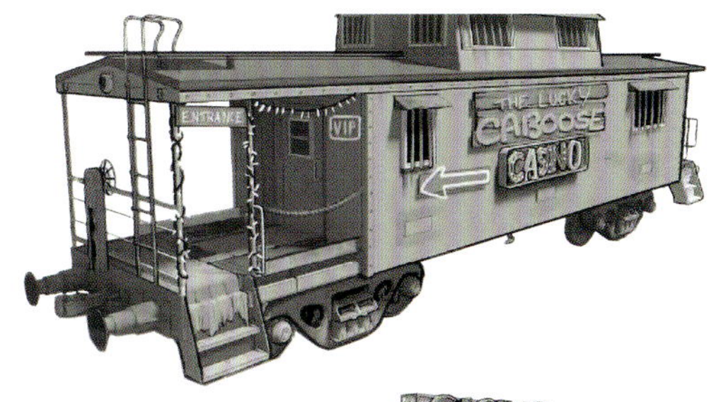

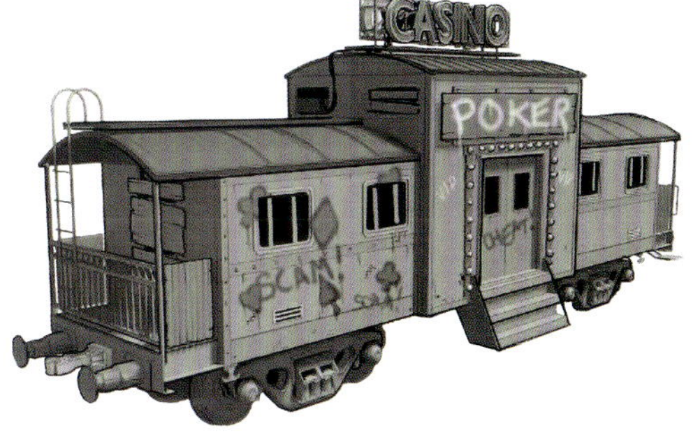

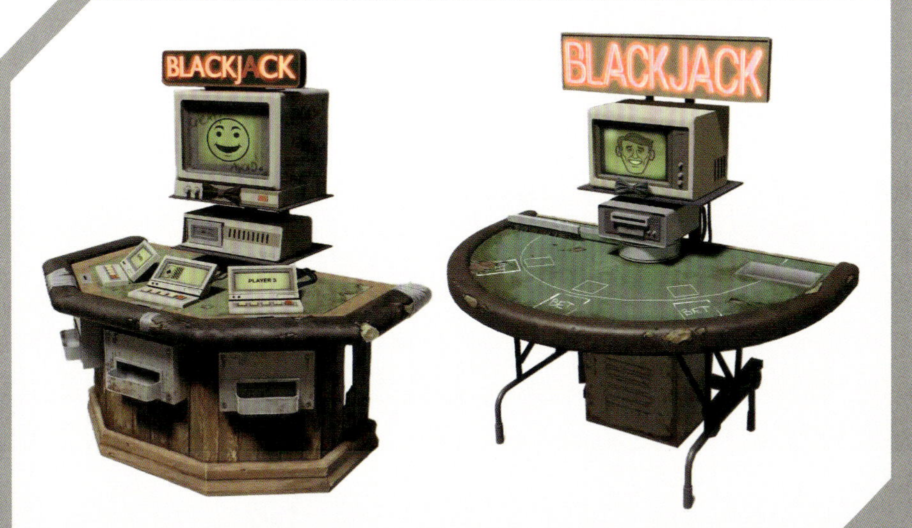

CASINO CART

The Casino Cart is a retrofitted train car made into a mobile casino. Early sketches show a fairground-style aesthetic with scavenged fairy lights and handmade signs. Inside, the car is outfitted with tattered curtains, worn-out poker tables, and faded slot machines. An unmanned automated blackjack machine was also drawn up, made ad hoc from scavenged 1980s tech.

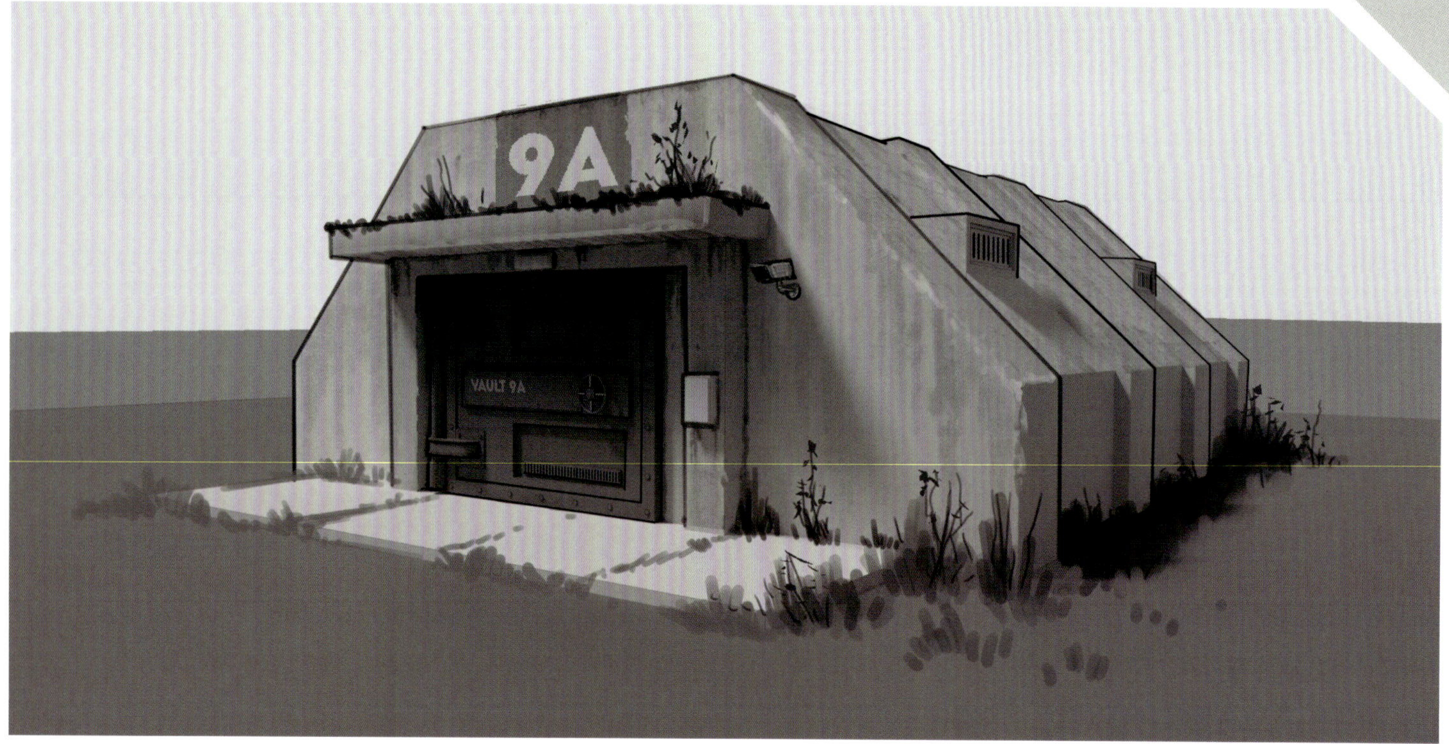

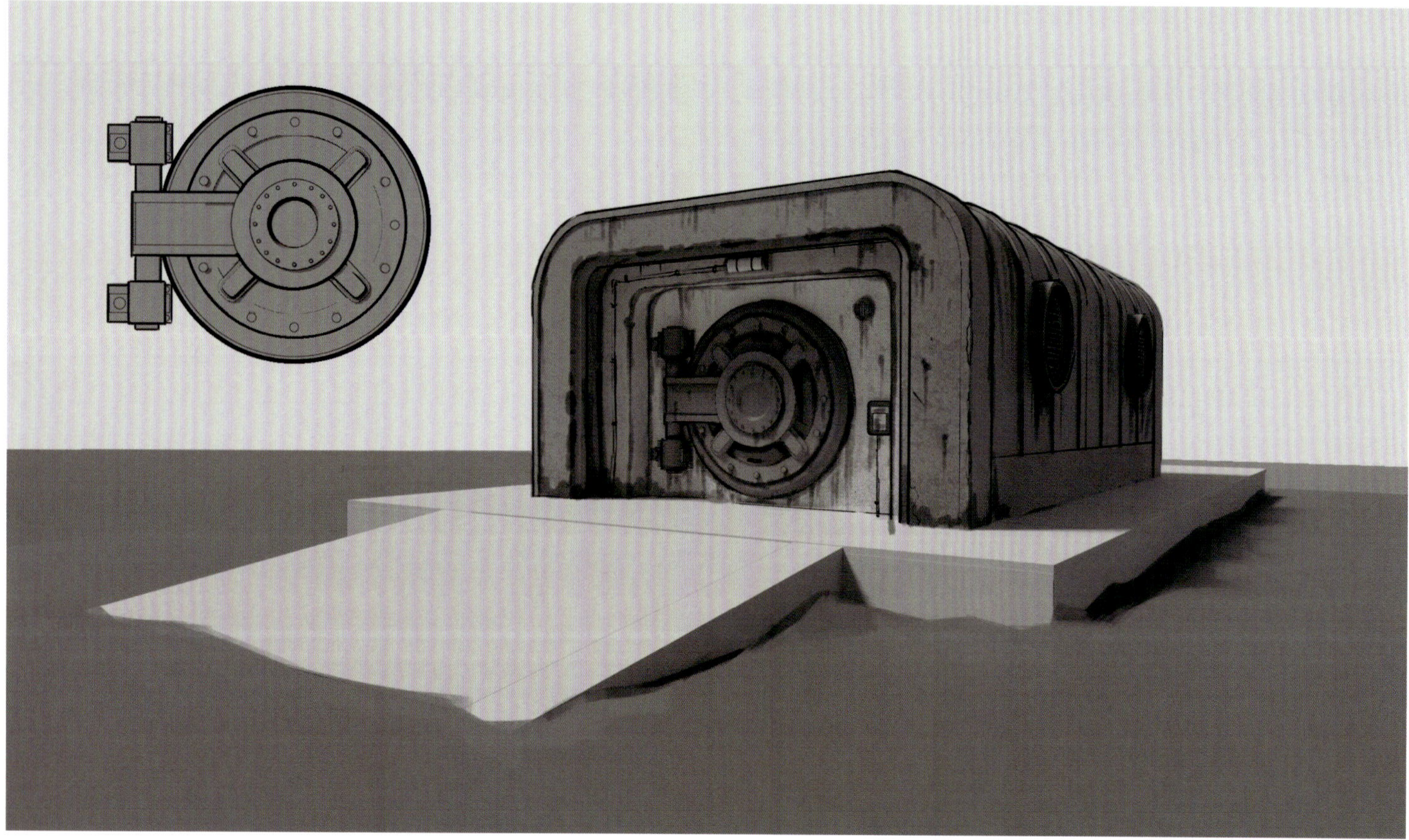

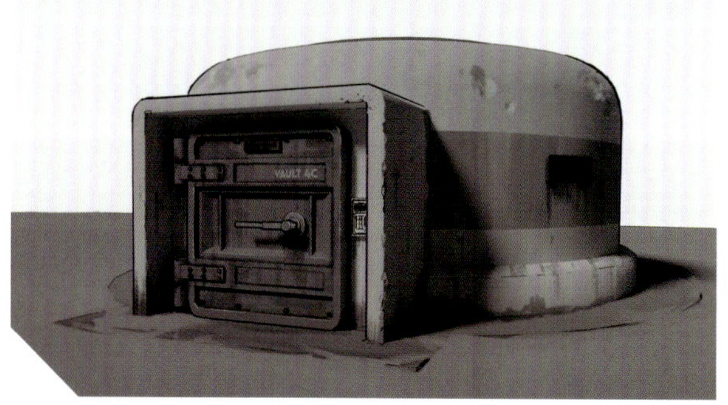

VAULT ENTRANCES

These unused Vault Entrance concepts draw inspiration from Cold War-era bunkers, military fallout shelters, and secure storage facilities. The fortified appearance is intended to create mystery and spark curiosity in players, as the structures are built to withstand catastrophes and protect high-value assets, suggesting something is being hidden from the surface.

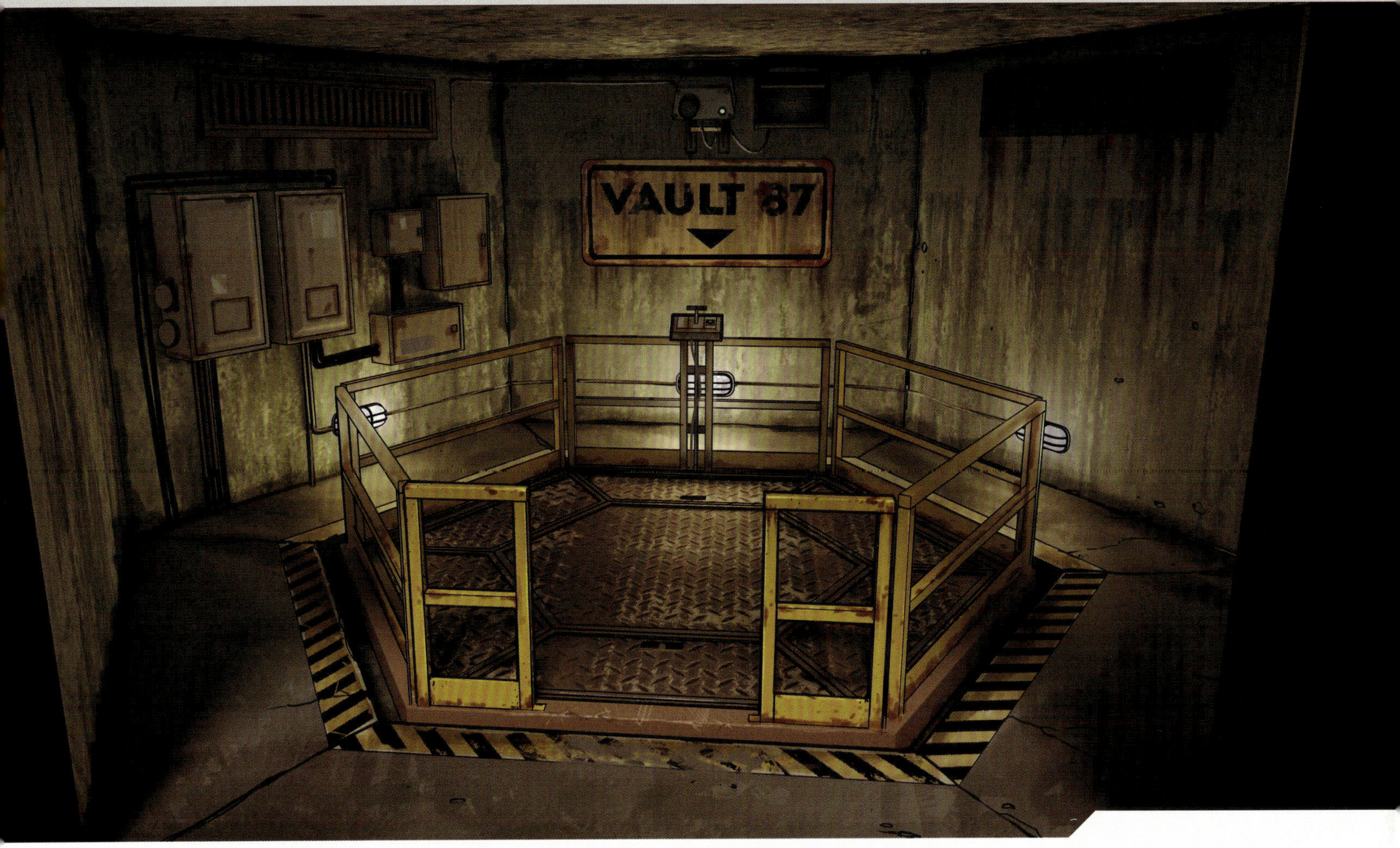

VAULT 87

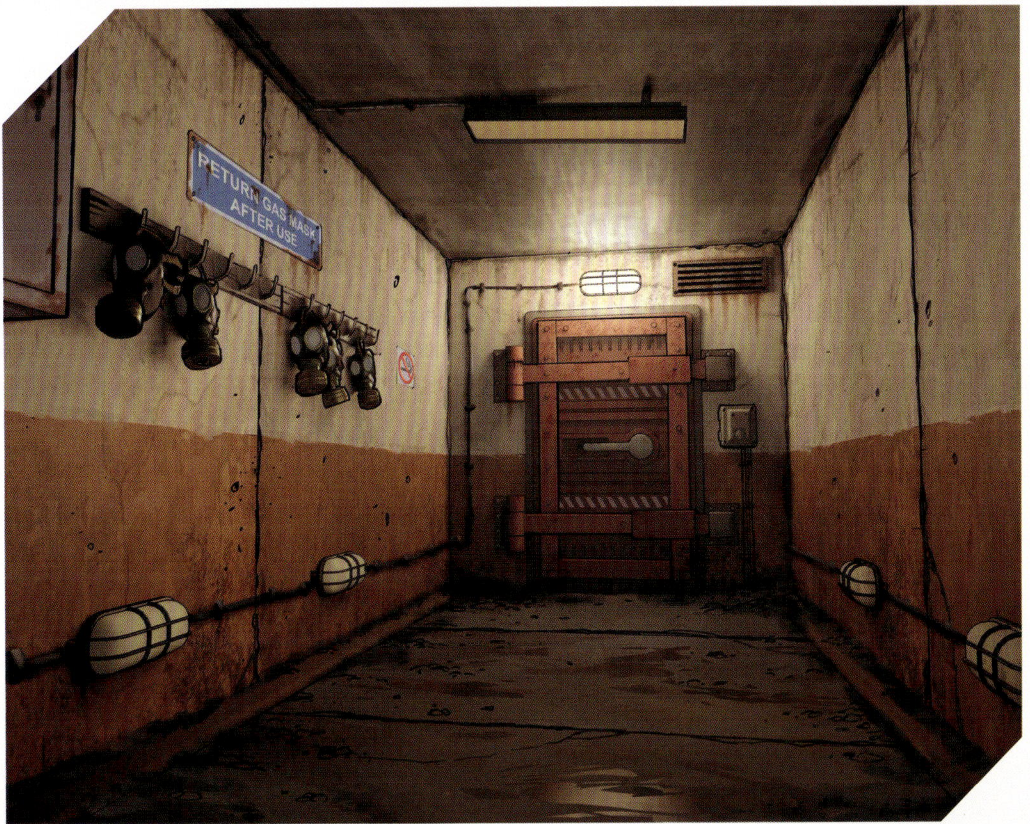
RETURN GAS MASK
AFTER USE

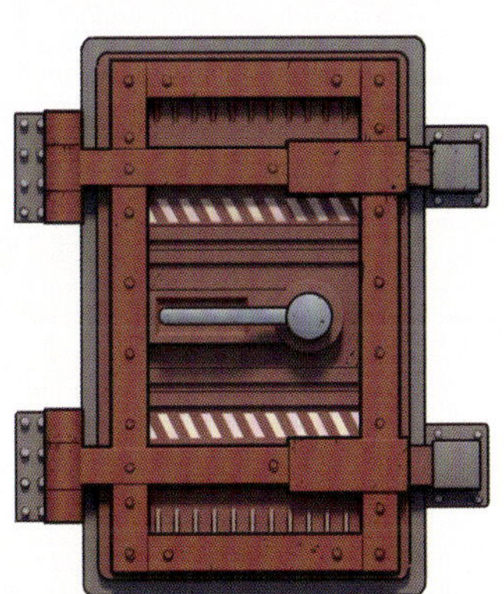

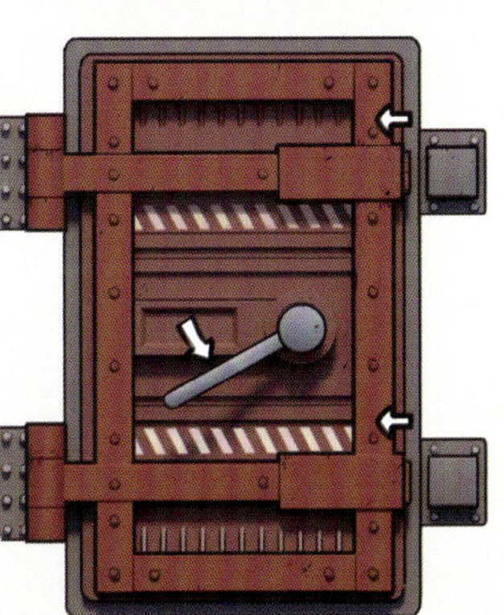

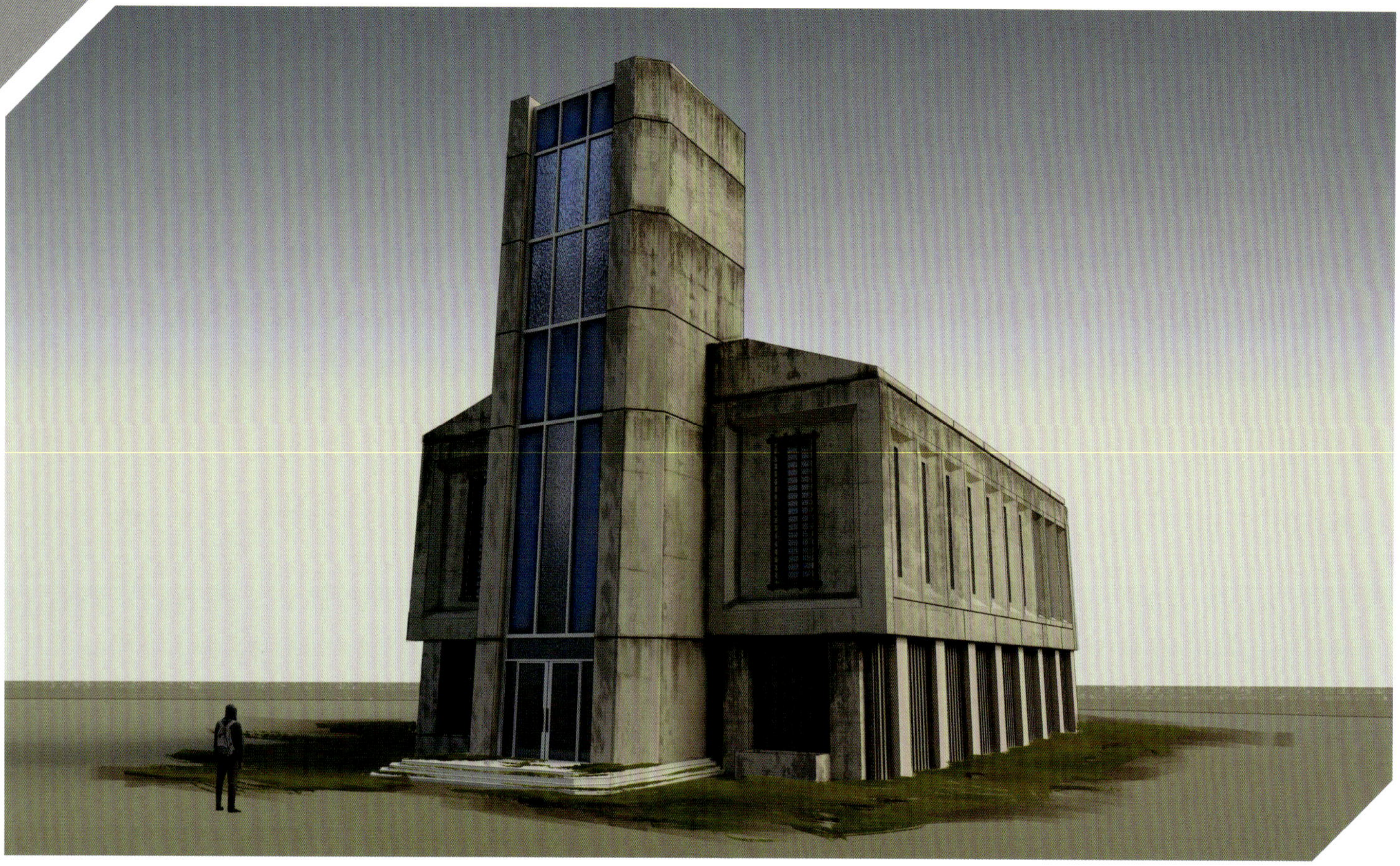

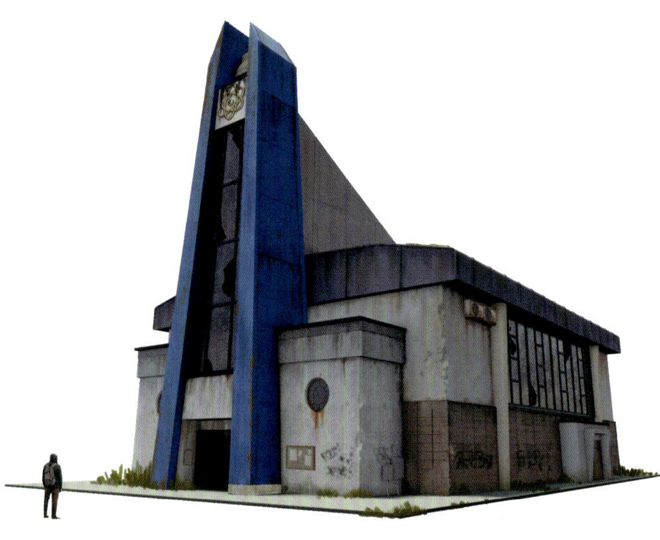

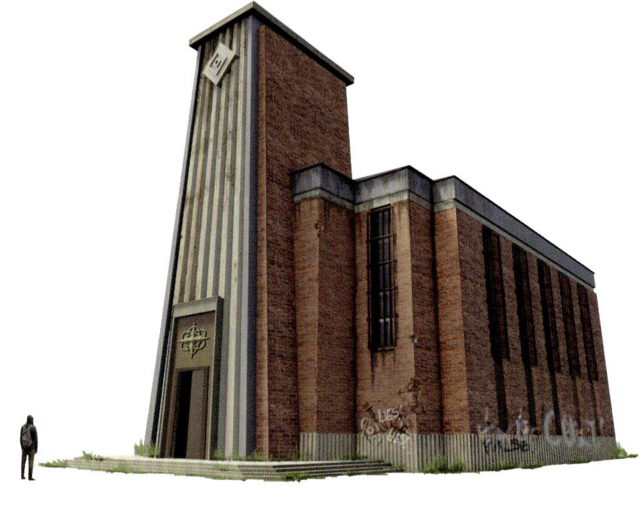

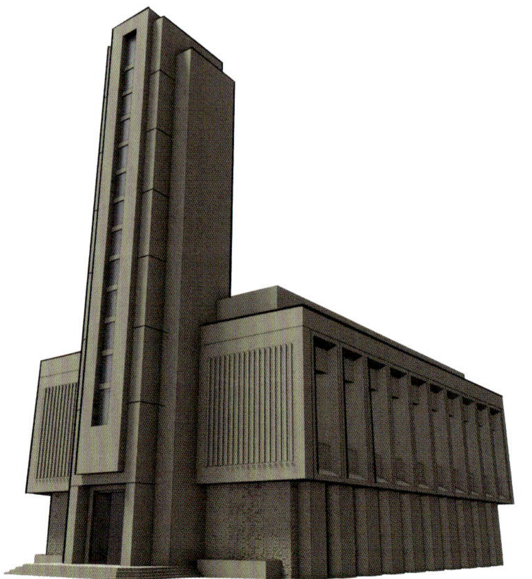

CHURCHES

Here are some early concepts of what Churches would have looked like in *Rust*. The sketches explore a stark architectural style, blending Brutalist design and a midcentury industrial feel with religious grandeur. Constructed primarily from raw concrete, steel, and aged brick, the Churches feature tall, narrow windows and imposing vertical lines.

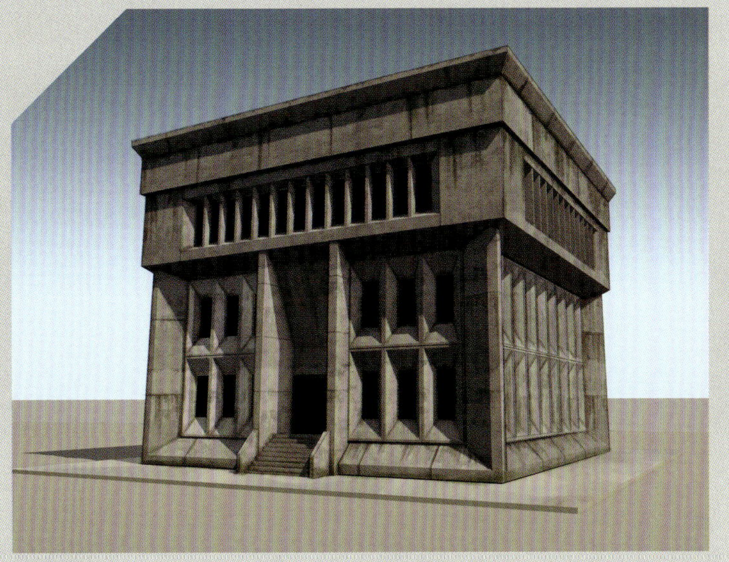

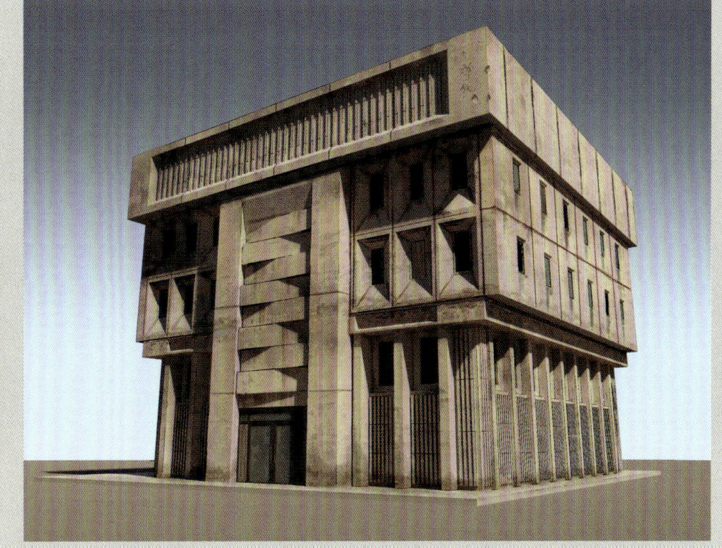

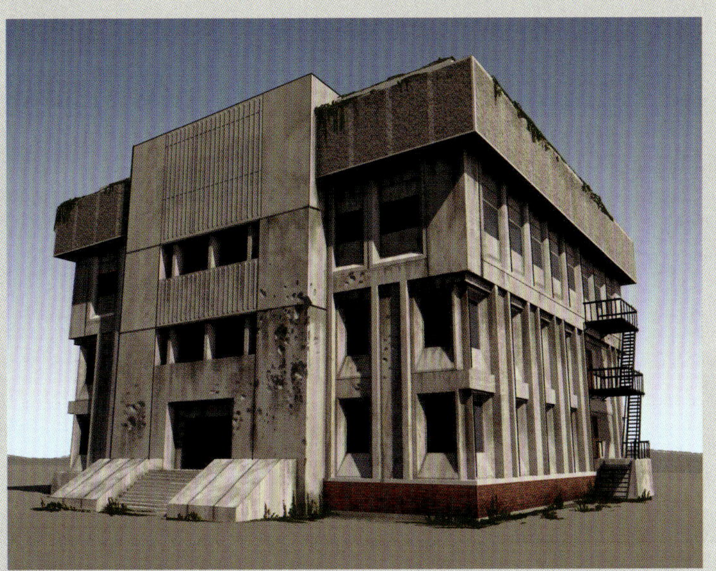

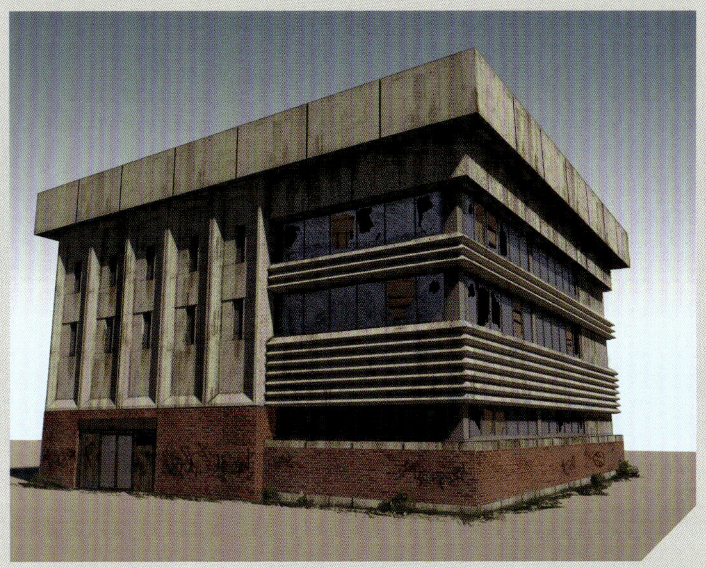

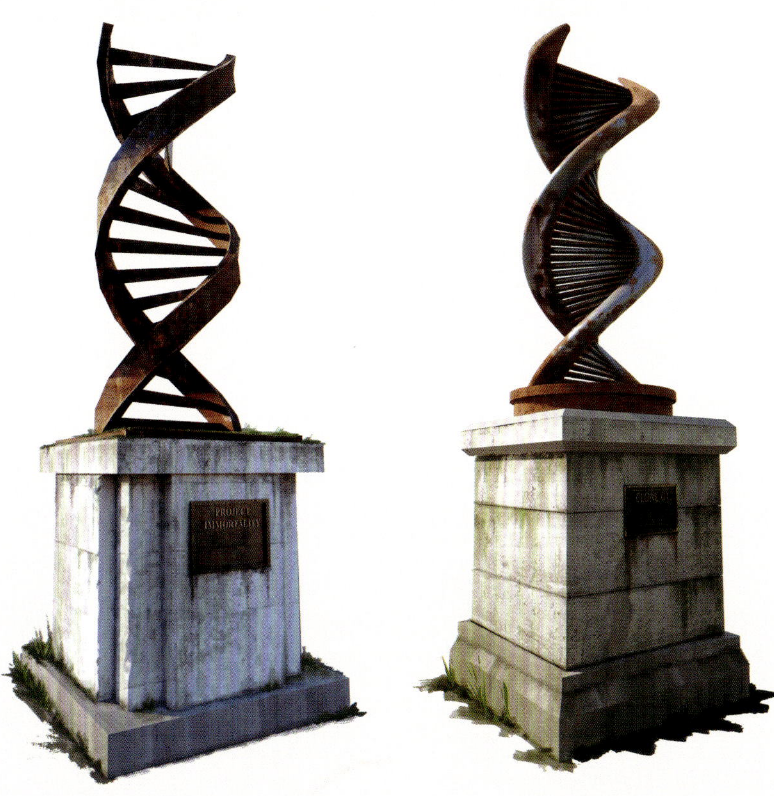

TOWN HALL

The Town Hall didn't make it into *Rust*, but its early concepts, inspired by a train terminal near the Facepunch office, draw heavily from Brutalist and civic architecture. These designs imply they were once administrative offices, possibly controlling city infrastructure or running Cobalt operations. Their bold, blocky shapes, recessed windows, and concrete surfaces were designed to mimic real-life government buildings.

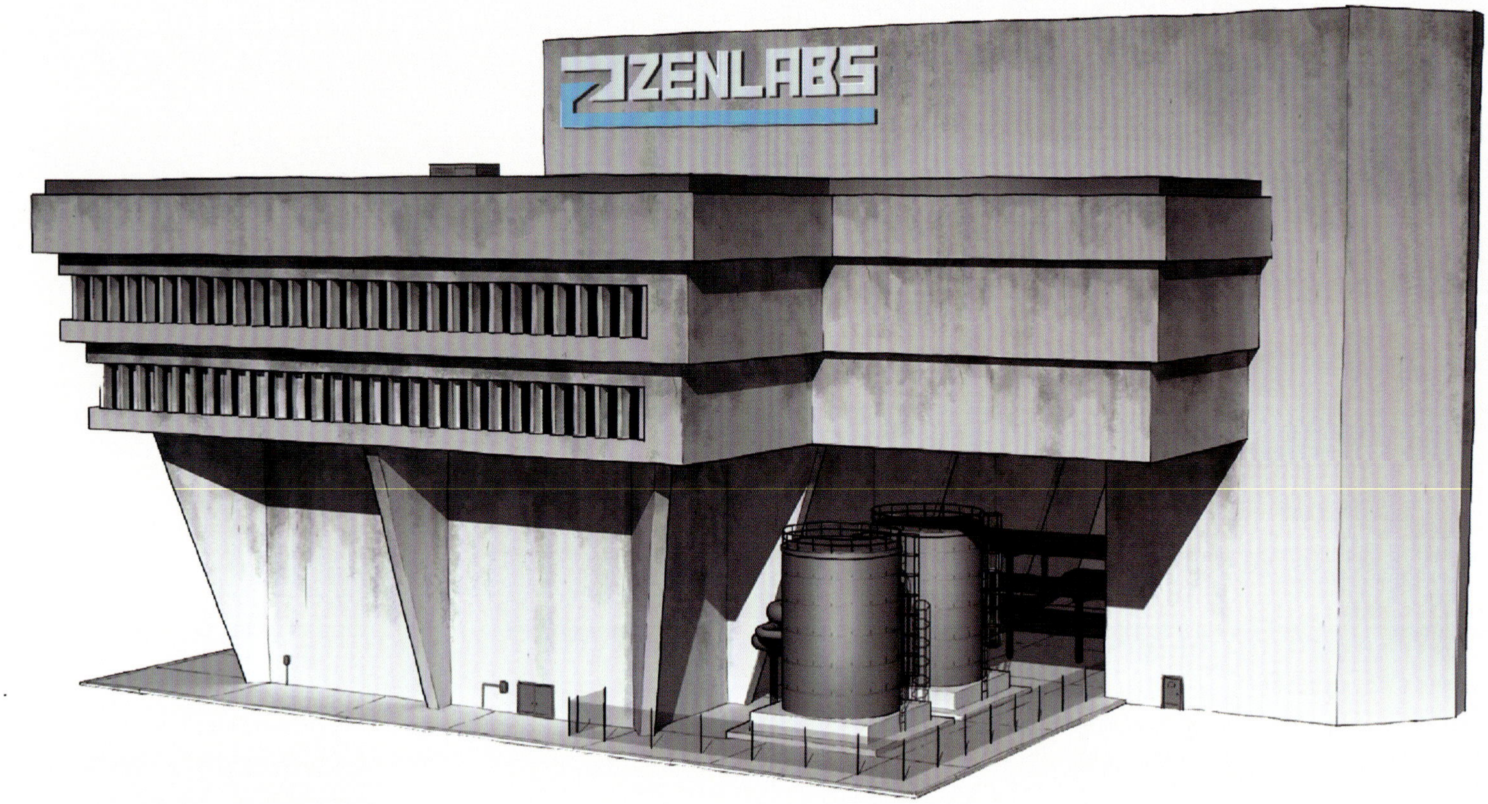

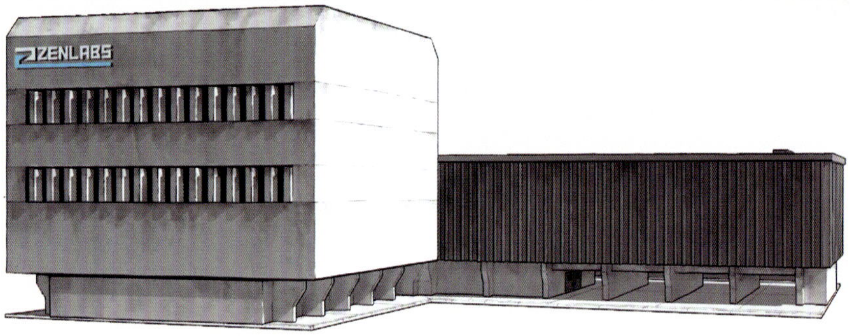

ZENLABS BUILDINGS

The Zenlabs buildings were created to deepen the lore surrounding the Scientists by hinting at their operations and motives. Drawing heavily from Brutalist architecture and monolithic industrial shapes, the design projects an air of control and authority.

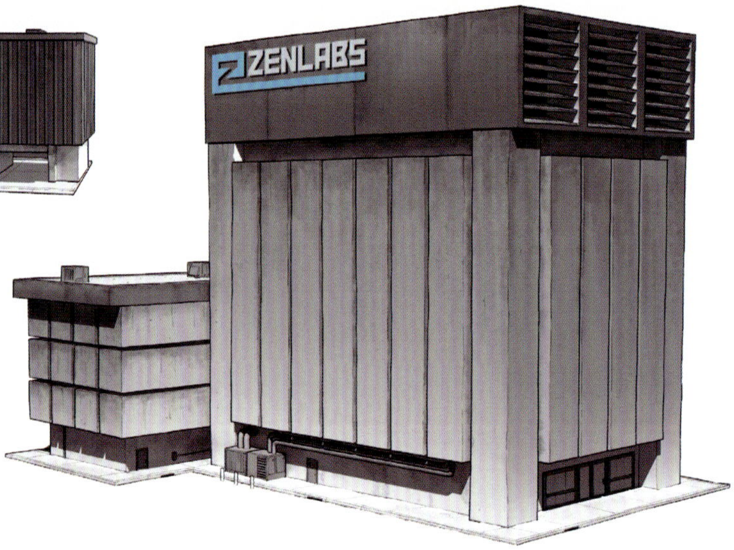

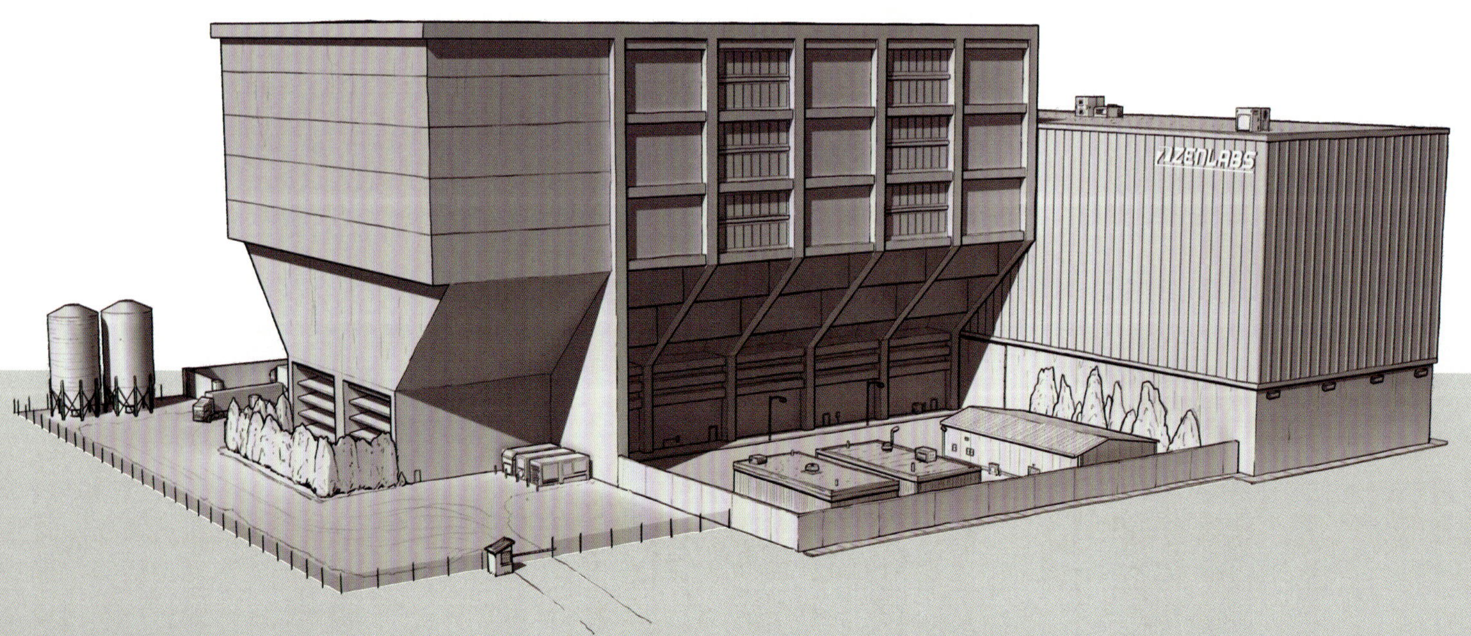

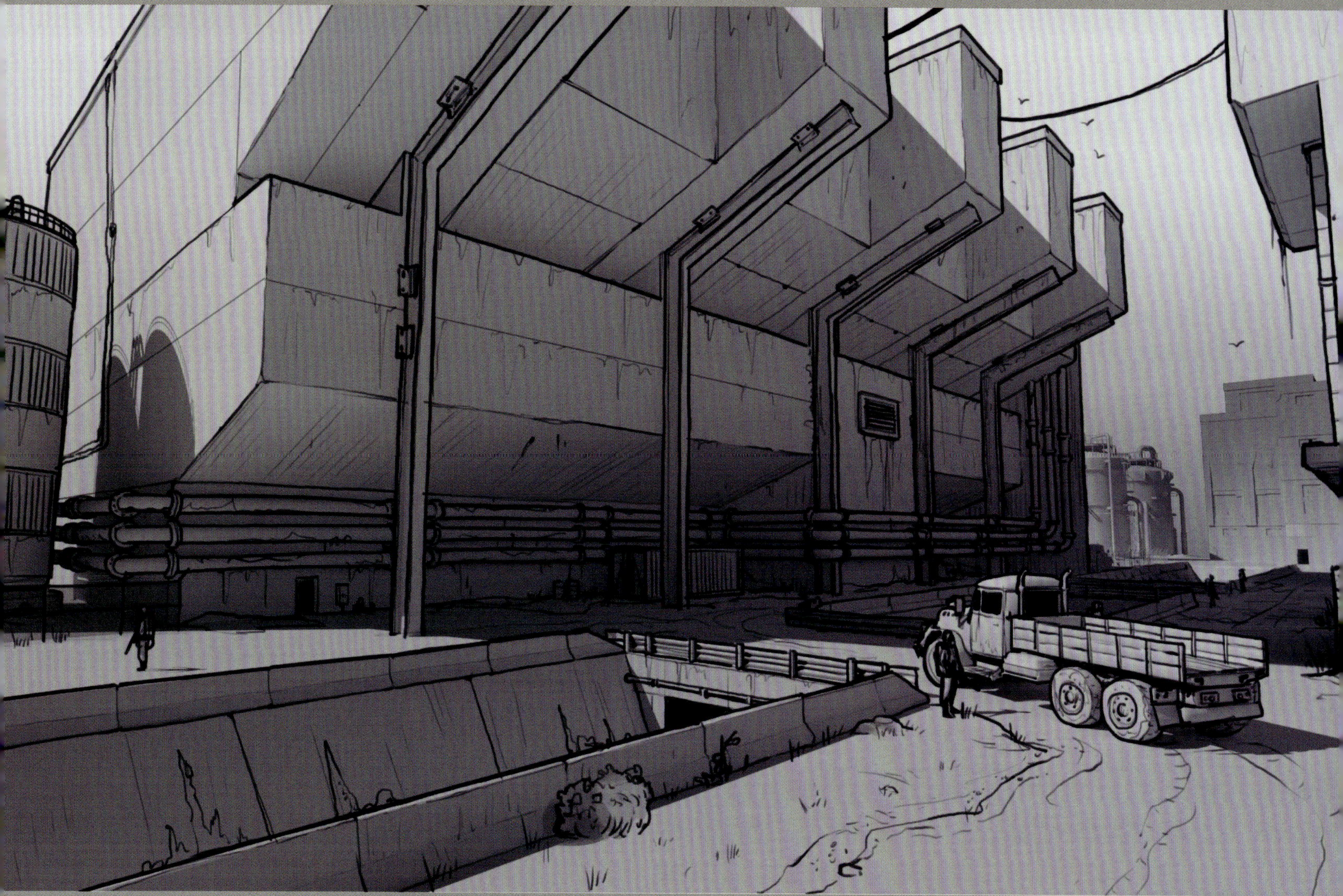

RESEARCH FACILITIES

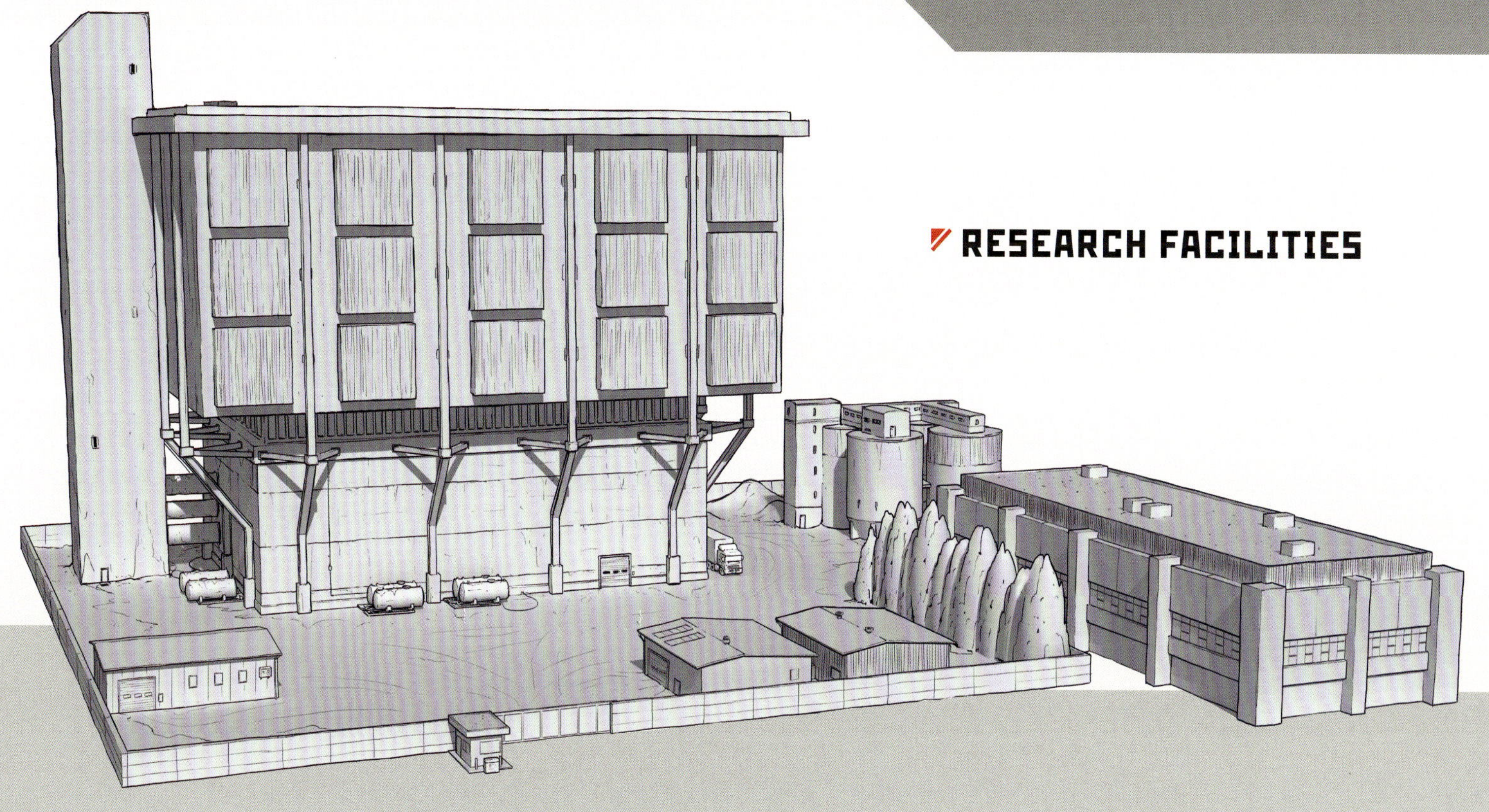

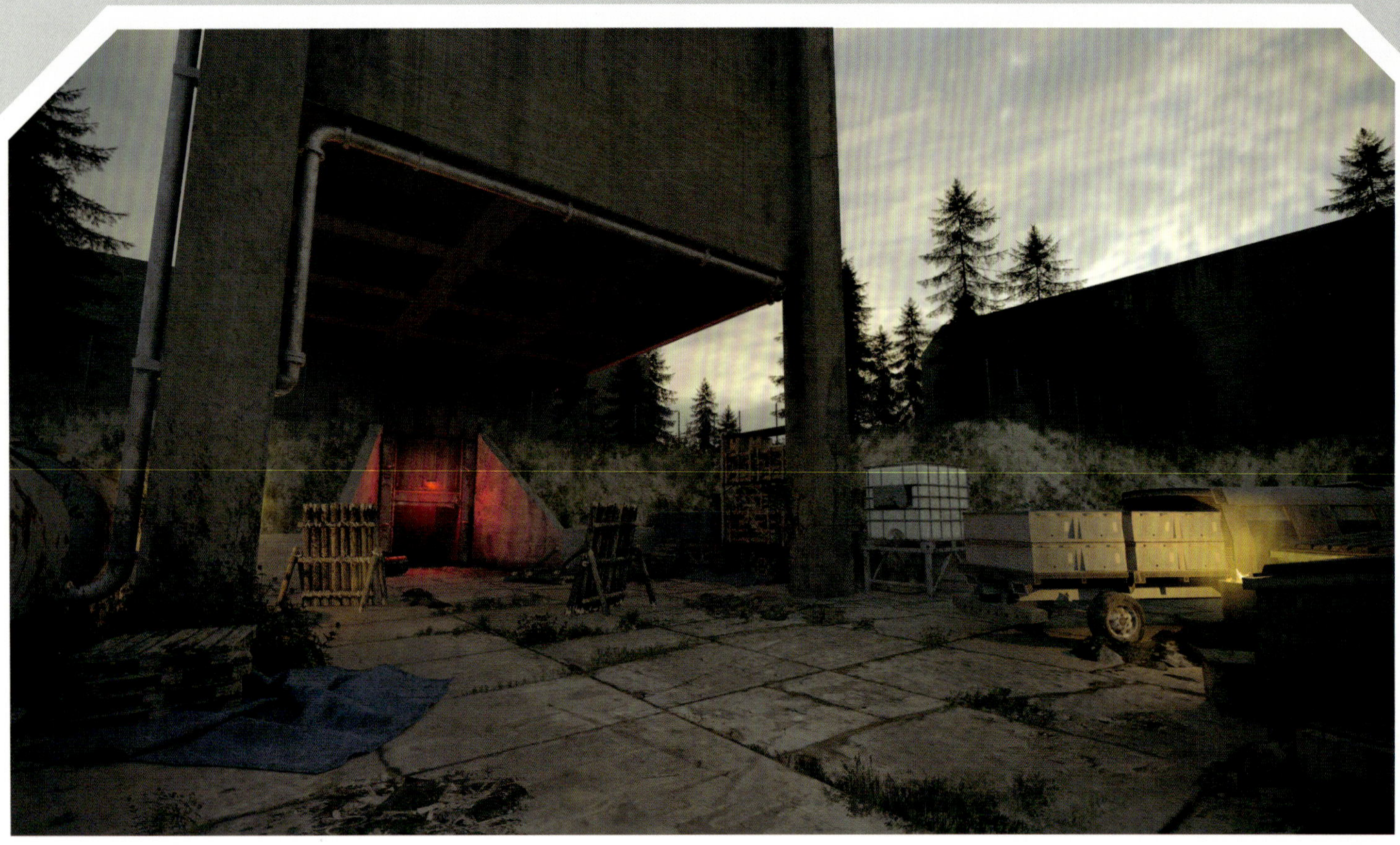

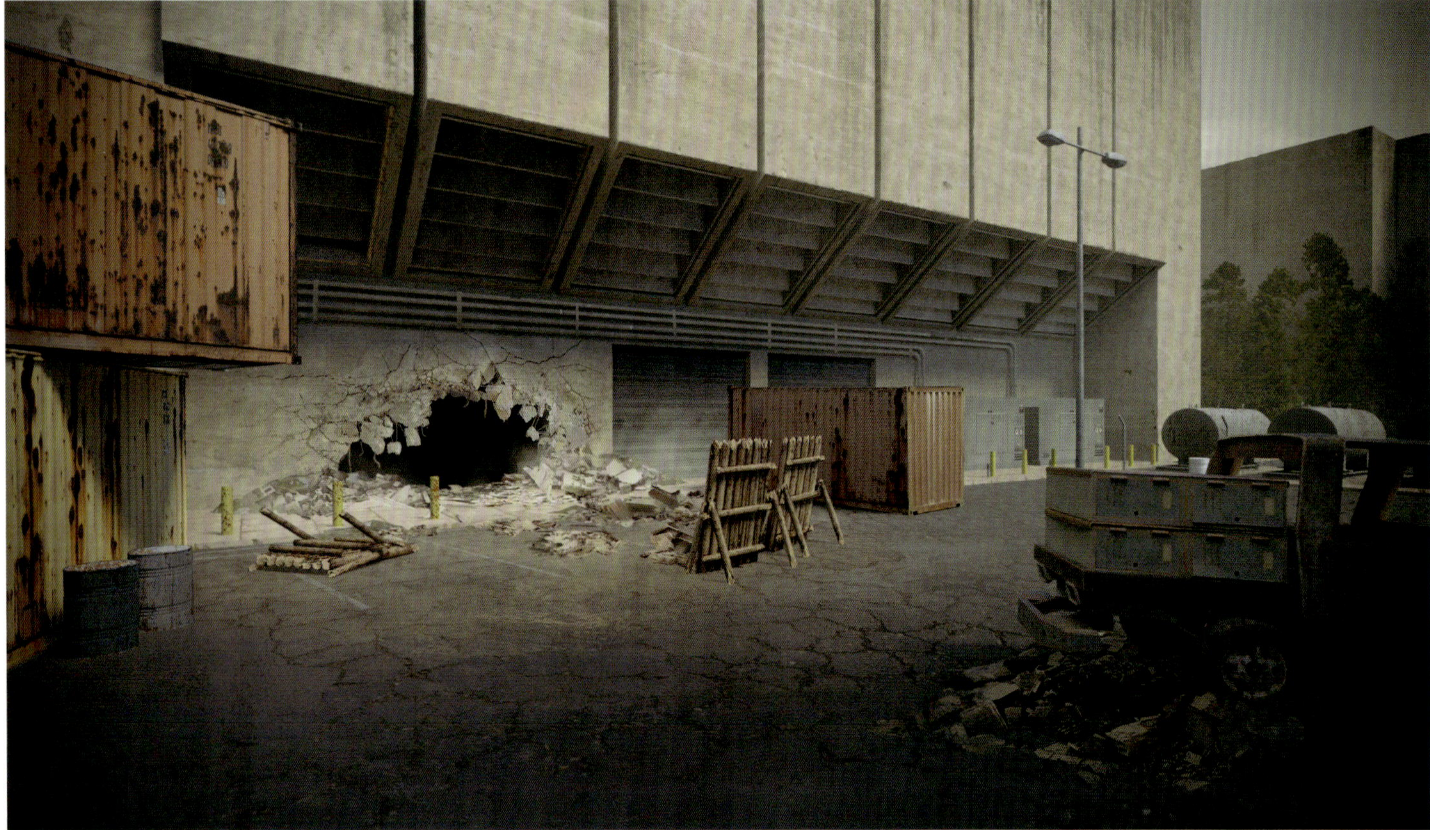

ZENLAB BUILDING ENTRANCES

These location sketches show a variety of potential entrances within the Zenlabs buildings, providing players with different options when entering Scientist-controlled buildings. Beside them are some early concepts of the lab interiors and how they could look after being abandoned.

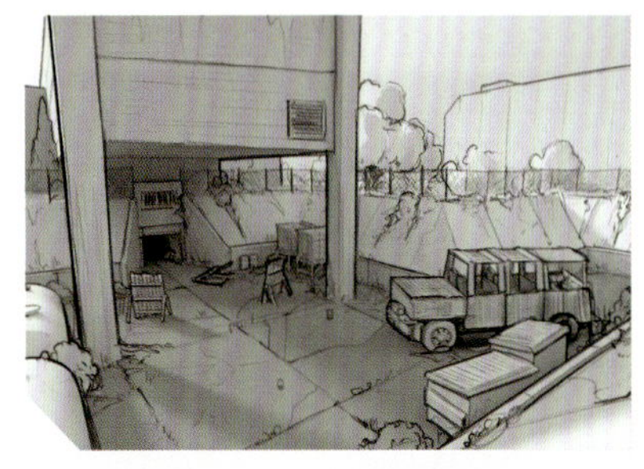

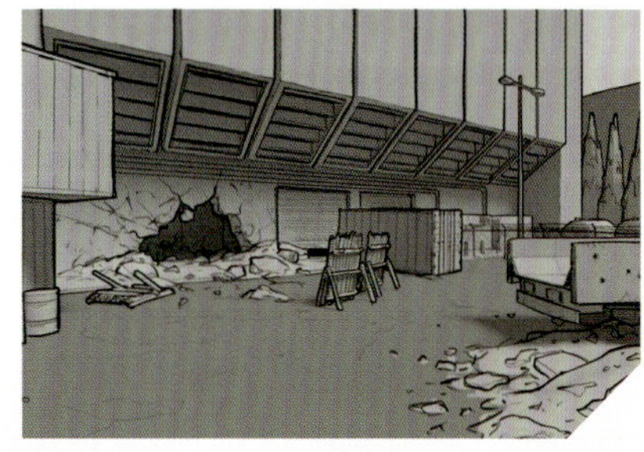

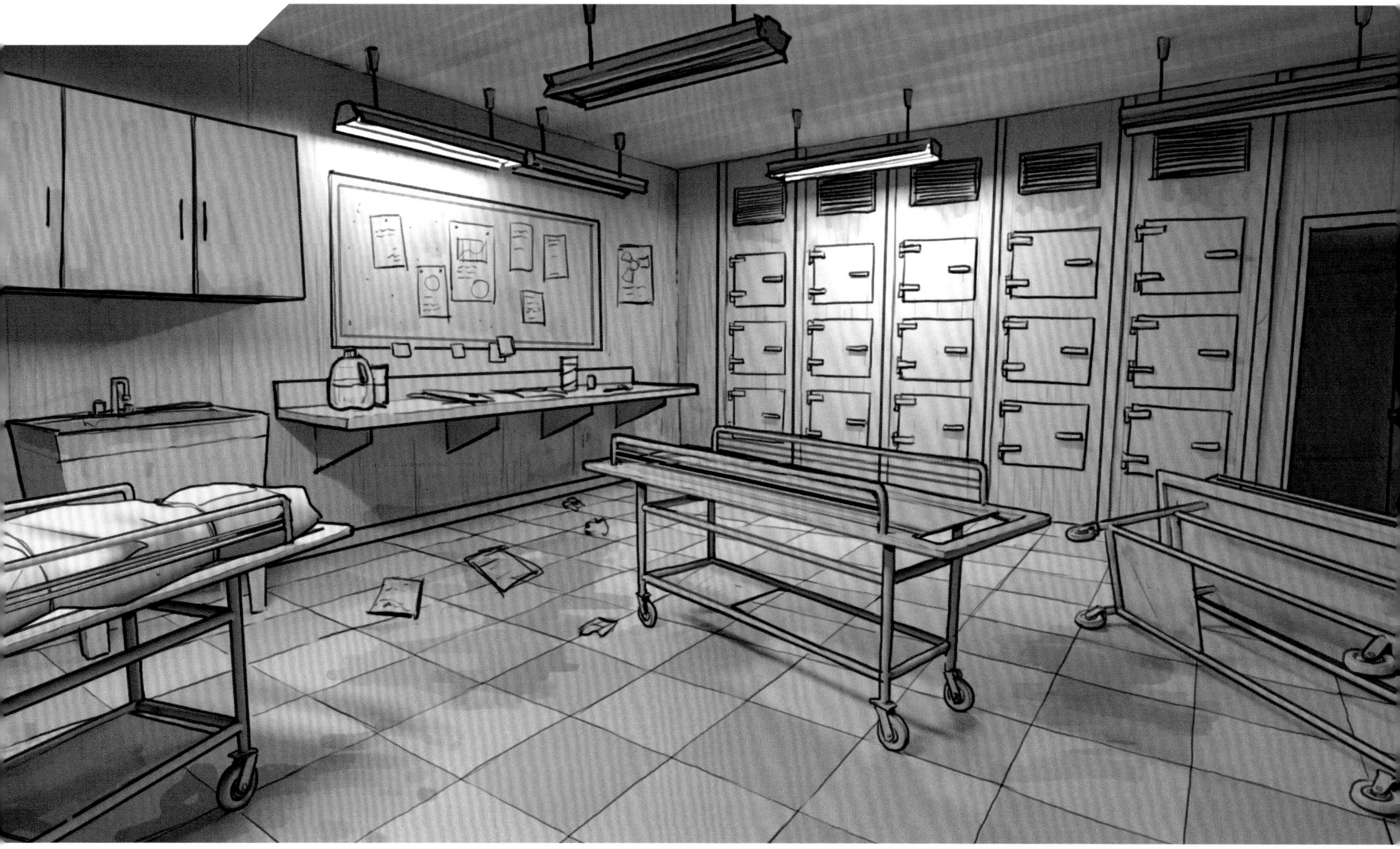

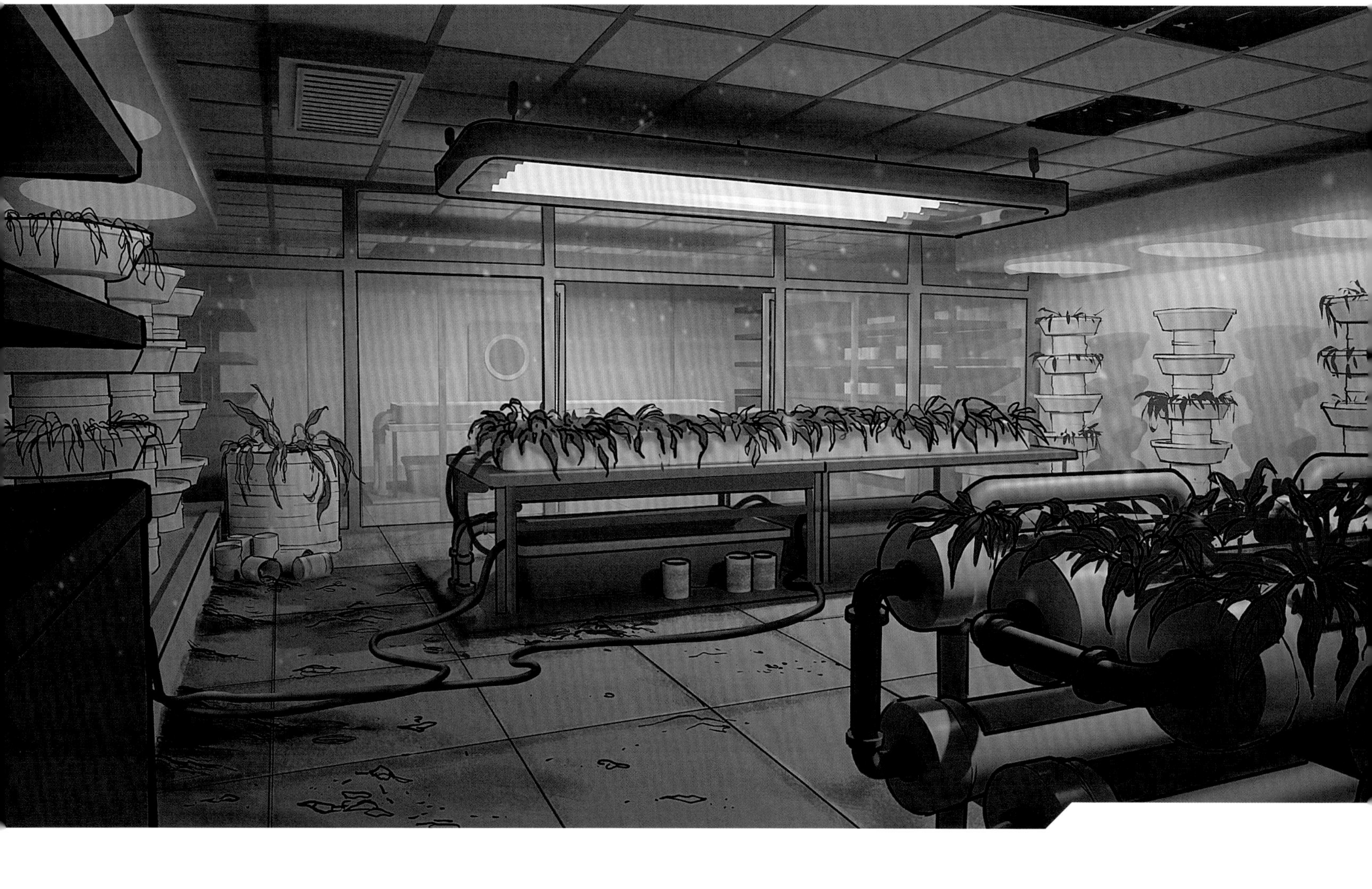

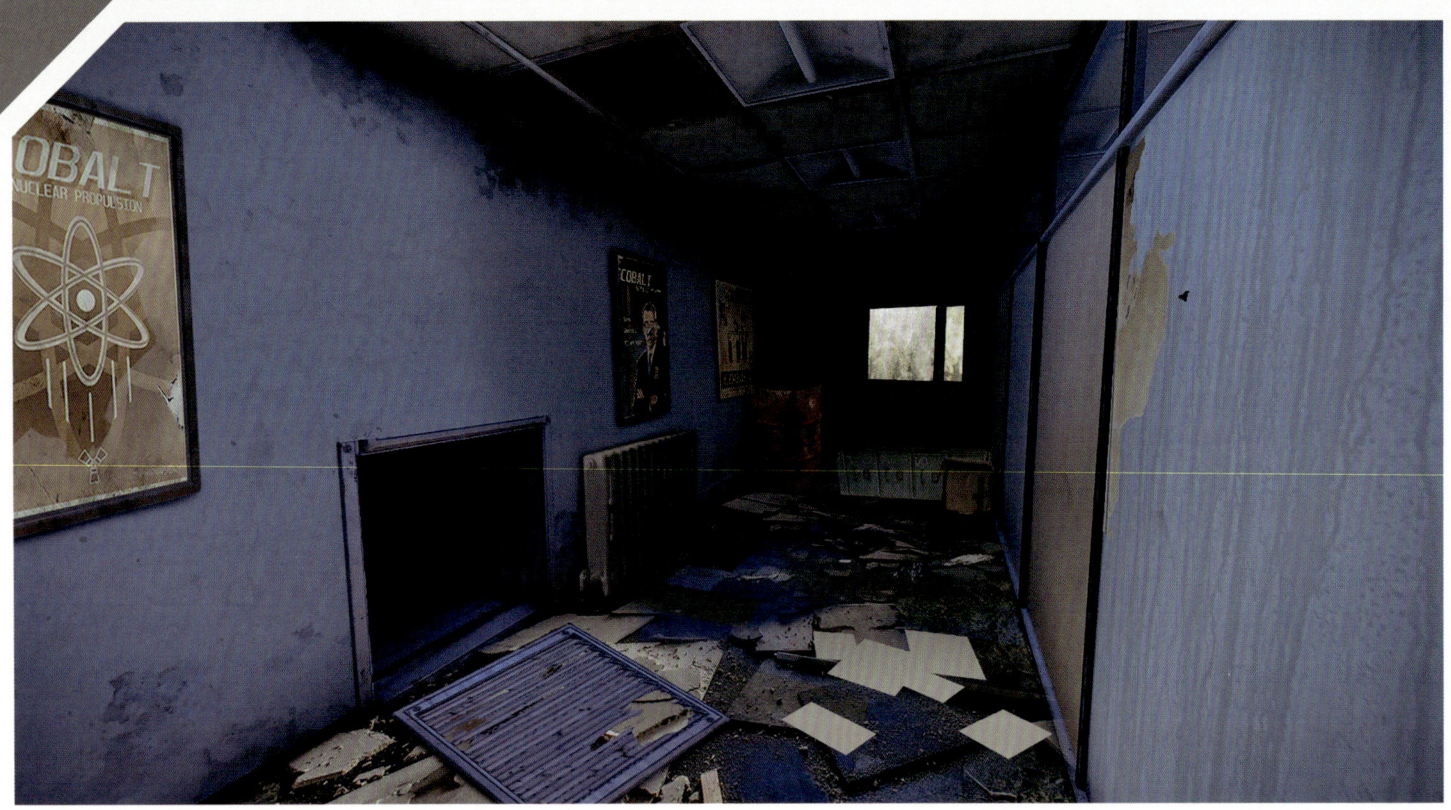

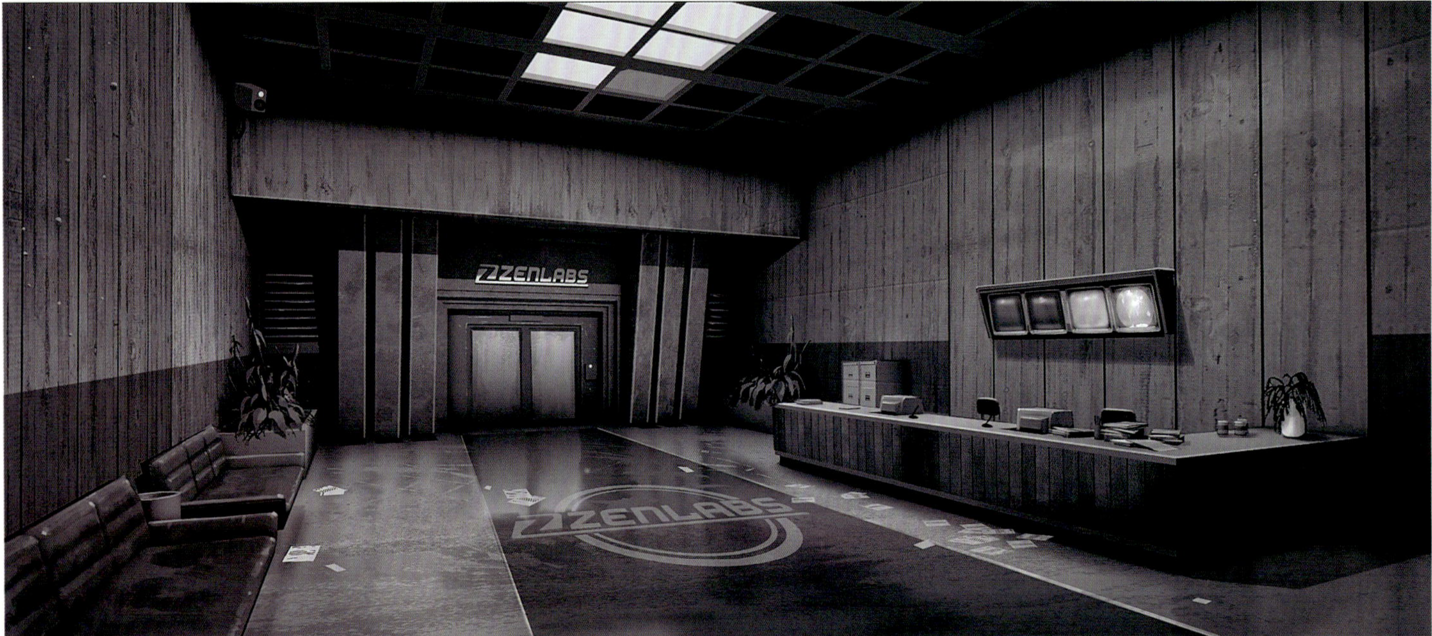

ZENLABS INTERIORS

The concept sketches for the interior of Zenlabs blend cold utility with clinical minimalism. Clean lines, harsh lighting, and deteriorating decor hint at an abandoned scientific facility. Brutalist influences surround scattered equipment and flickering monitors, implying that something went wrong and the facility was evacuated quickly. This space isn't designed for comfort but for purpose, reflecting the unsettling nature of the research that may have happened here.

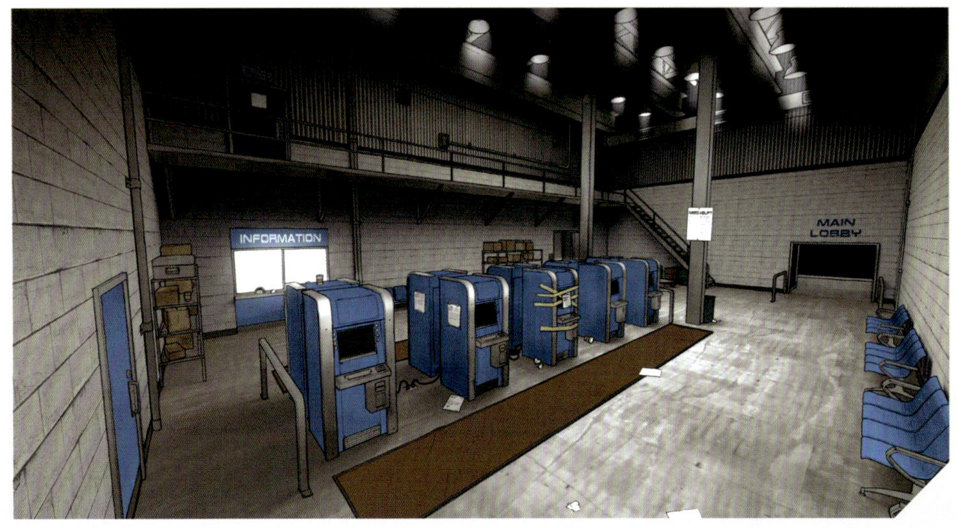

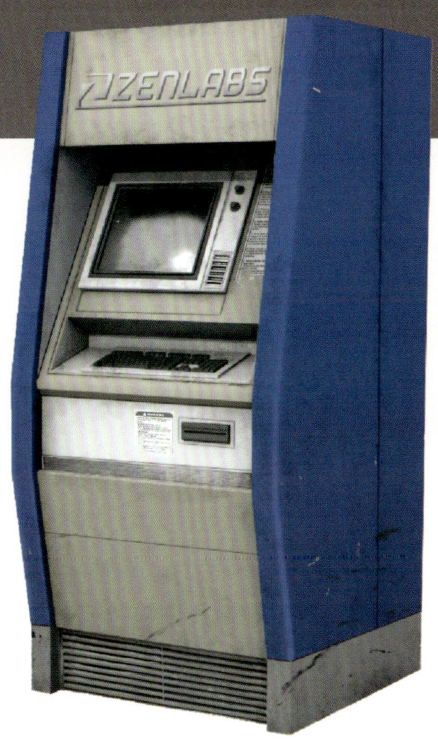

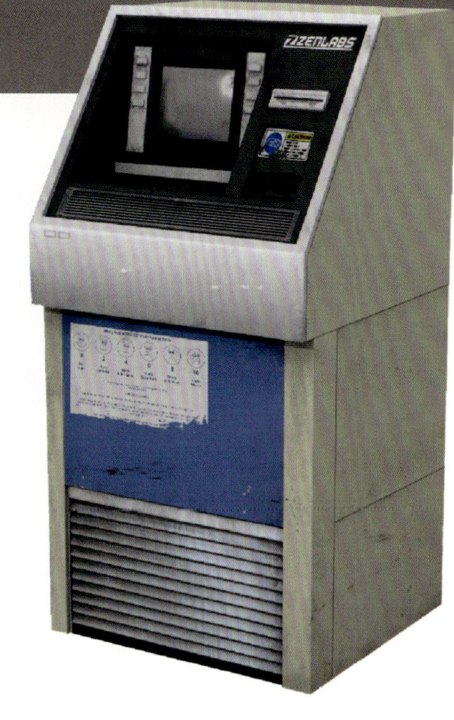

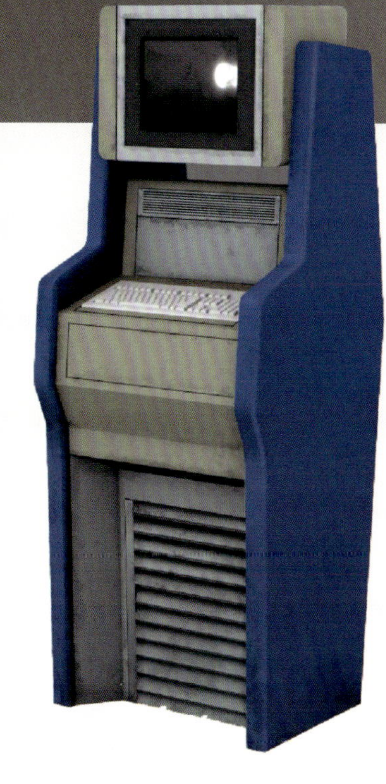

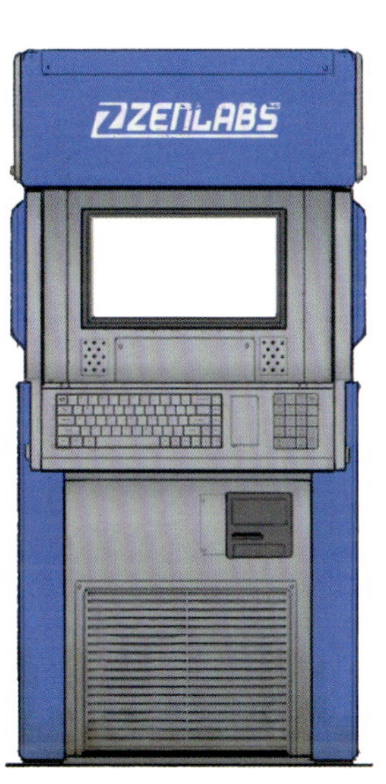

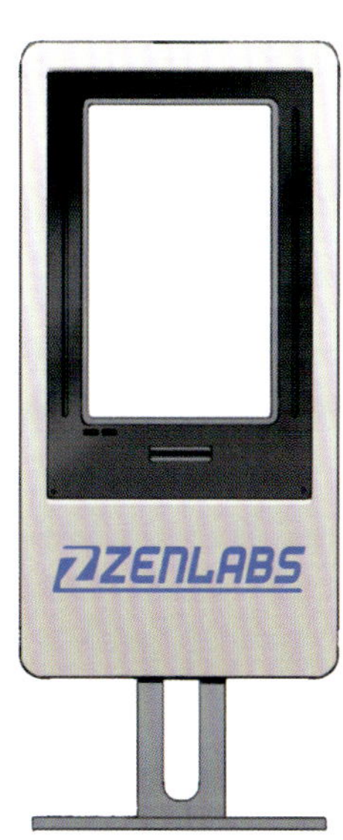

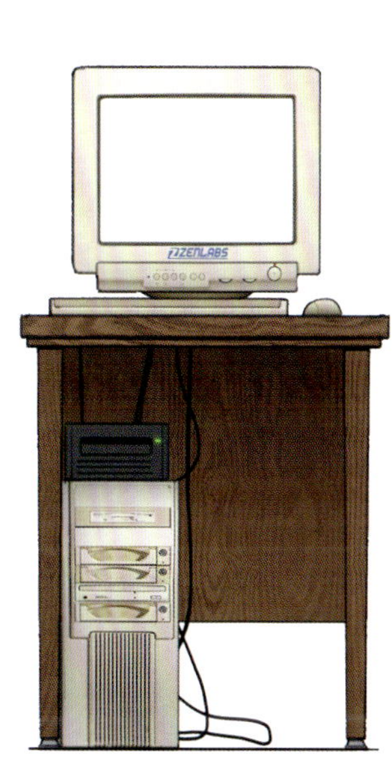

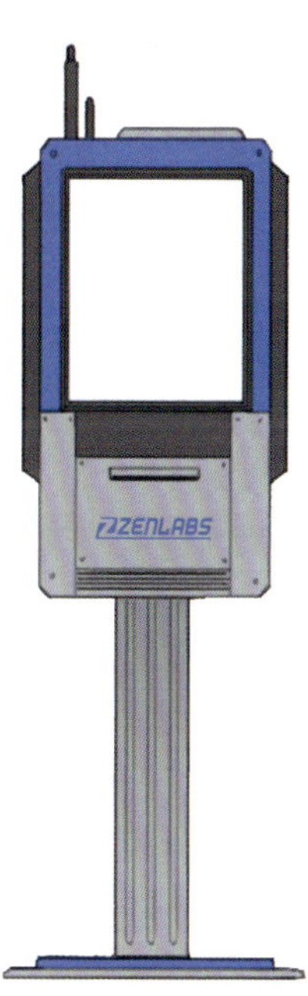

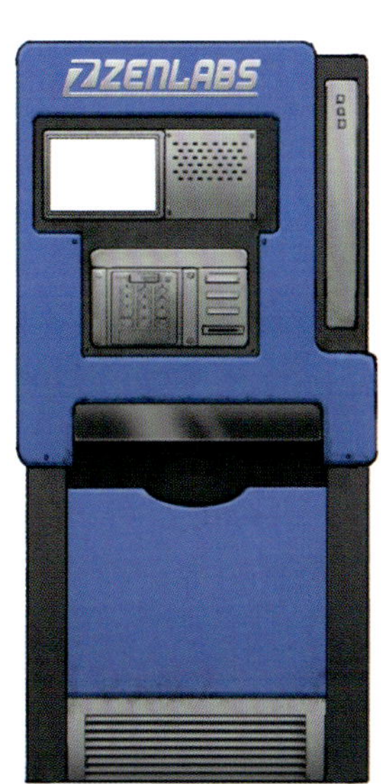

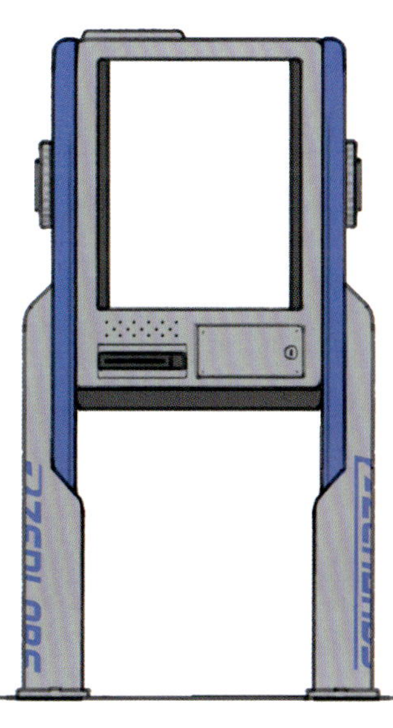

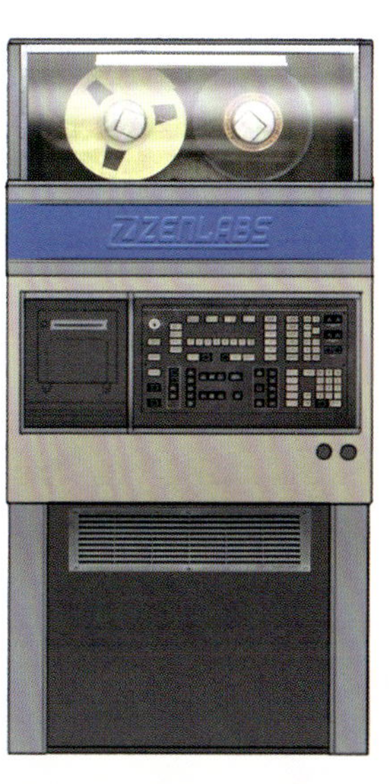

ZENLABS KIOSKS

The Zenlabs Kiosk concept was part of an early exploration into a potential quest system. Designed as interactive hubs, they would allow players to receive tasks from the Scientists in exchange for valuable resources.

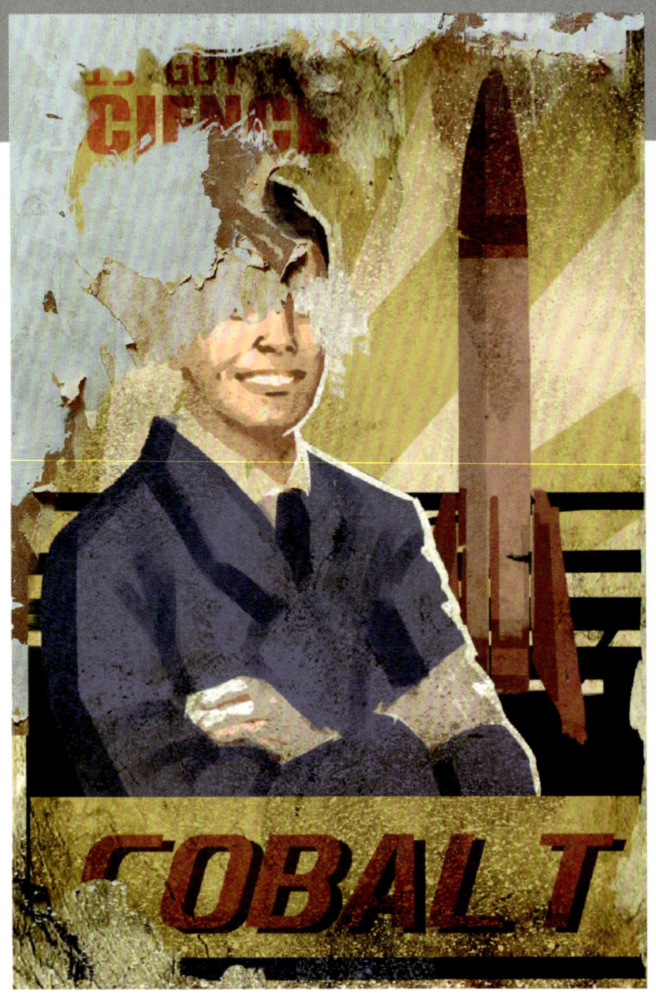
COBAL T

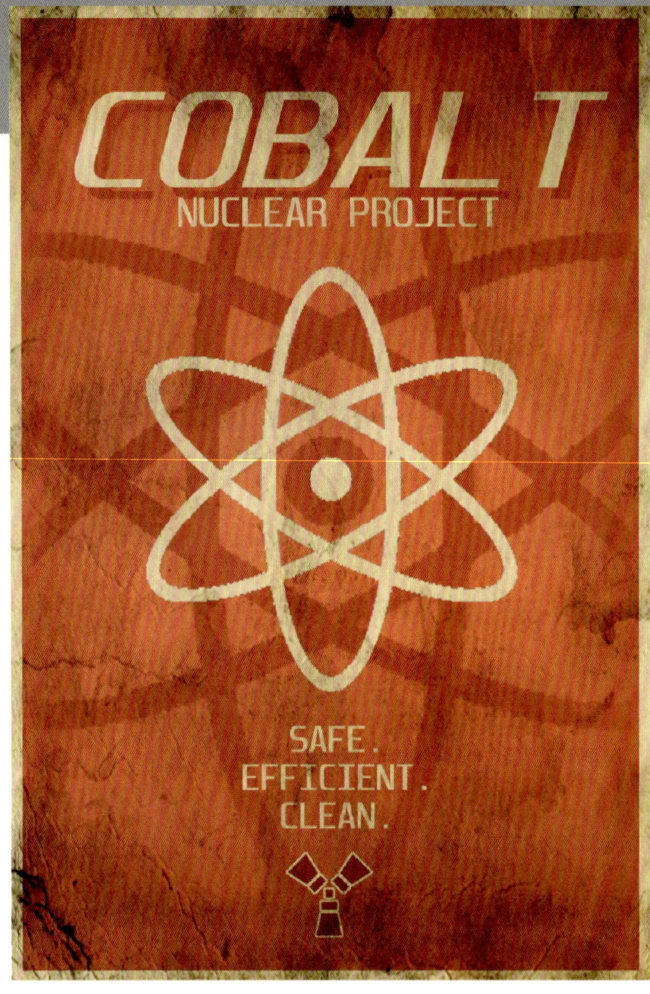
COBAL T
NUCLEAR PROJECT
SAFE.
EFFICIENT.
CLEAN.

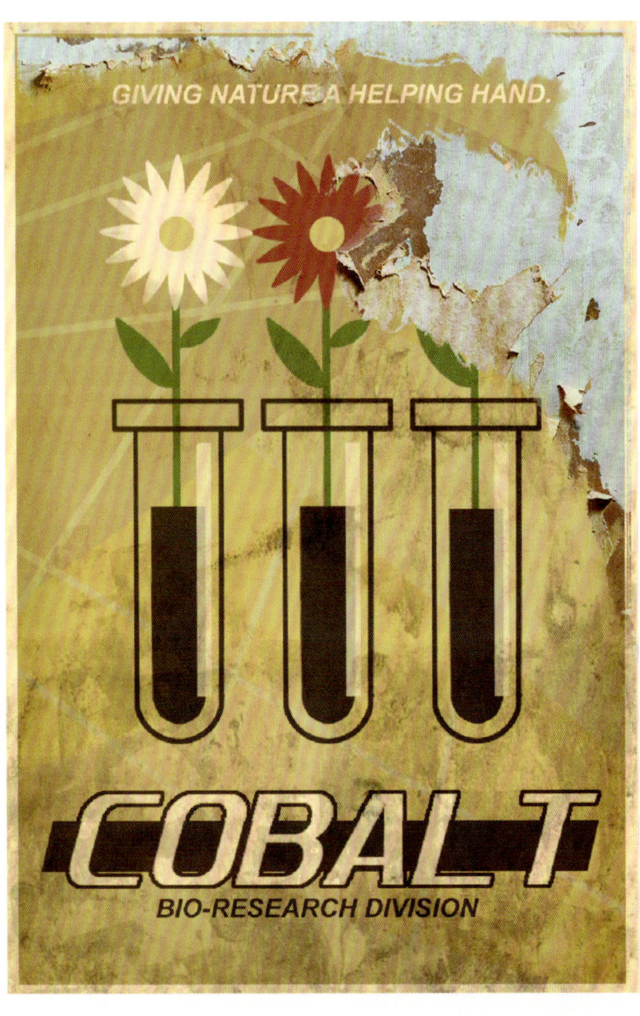
GIVING NATURE A HELPING HAND.
COBAL T
BIO-RESEARCH DIVISION

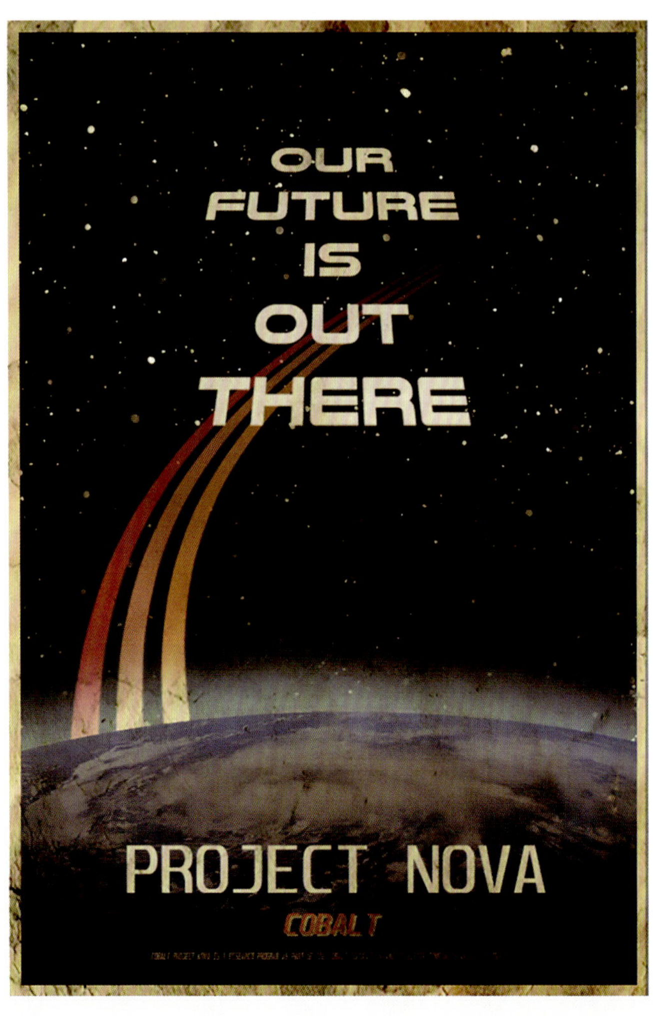
OUR
FUTURE
IS
OUT
THERE
PROJECT NOVA
COBAL T

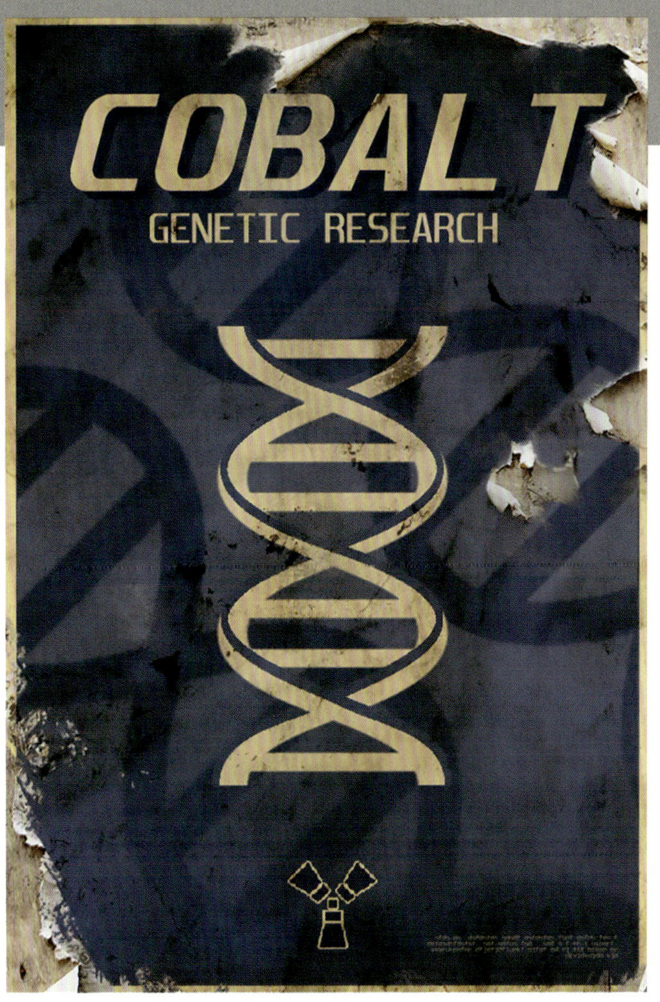
COBALT
GENETIC RESEARCH

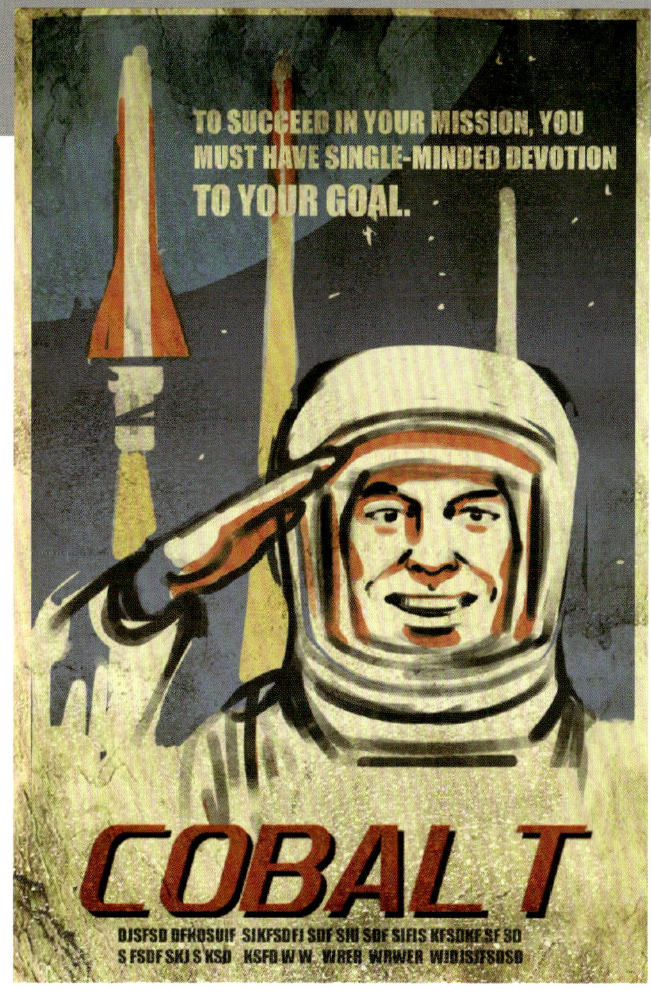
TO SUCCEED IN YOUR MISSION, YOU
MUST HAVE SINGLE-MINDED DEVOTION
TO YOUR GOAL.
COBALT

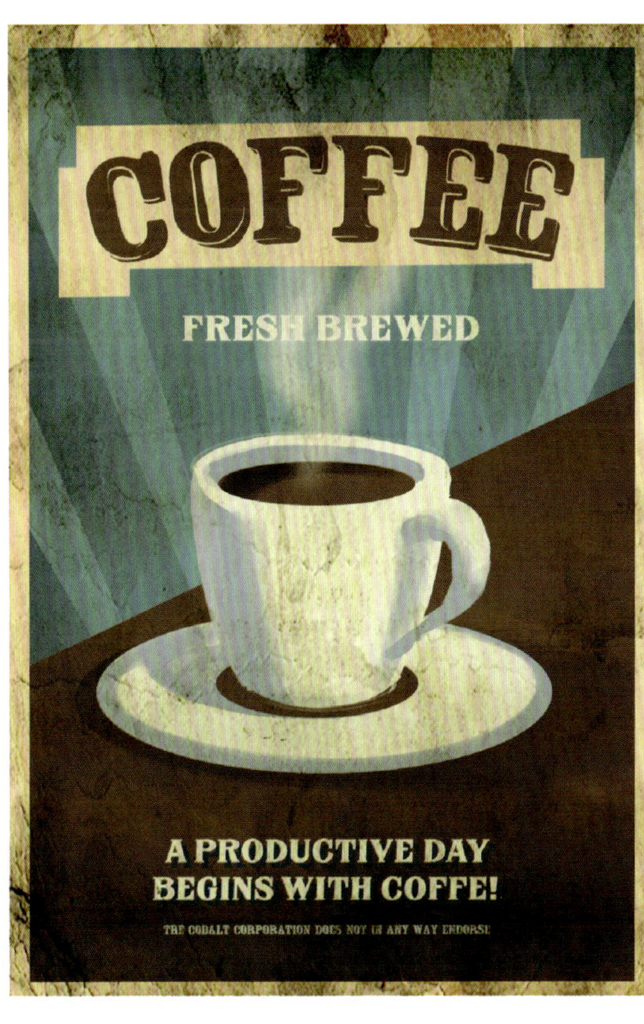
COFFEE
FRESH BREWED
A PRODUCTIVE DAY
BEGINS WITH COFFE!
THE COBALT CORPORATION DOES NOT IN ANY WAY ENDORSE

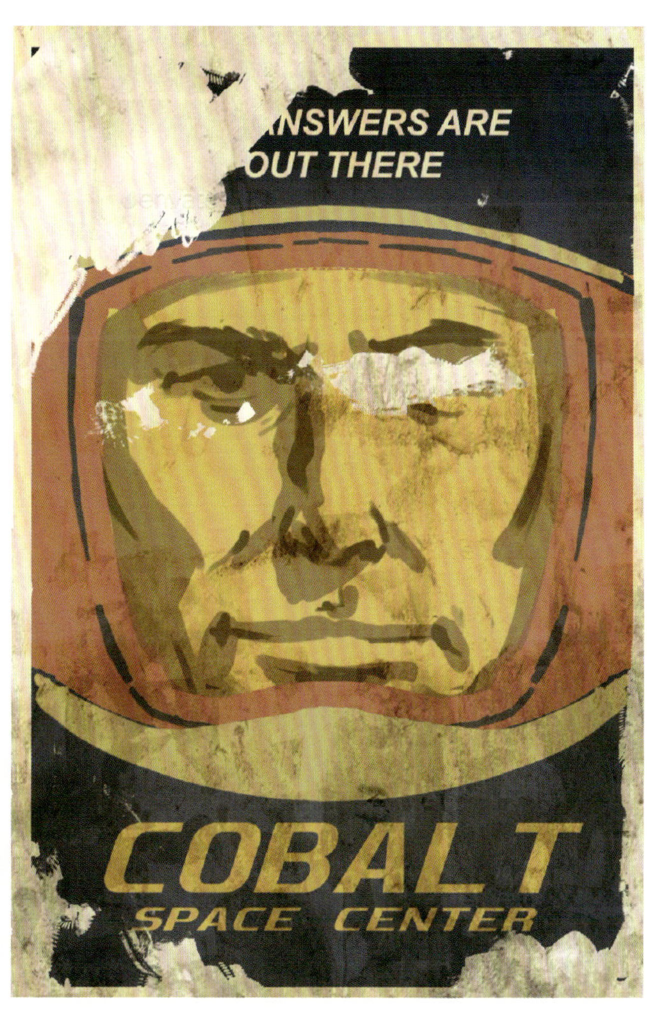
ANSWERS ARE
OUT THERE
COBALT
SPACE CENTER

BASE FOUNDATION PROCESS

These early sketches explore how base construction was designed. Early ideas included progressive material layering or brief animations triggered by each placed building block, adding speed and life to the building process.

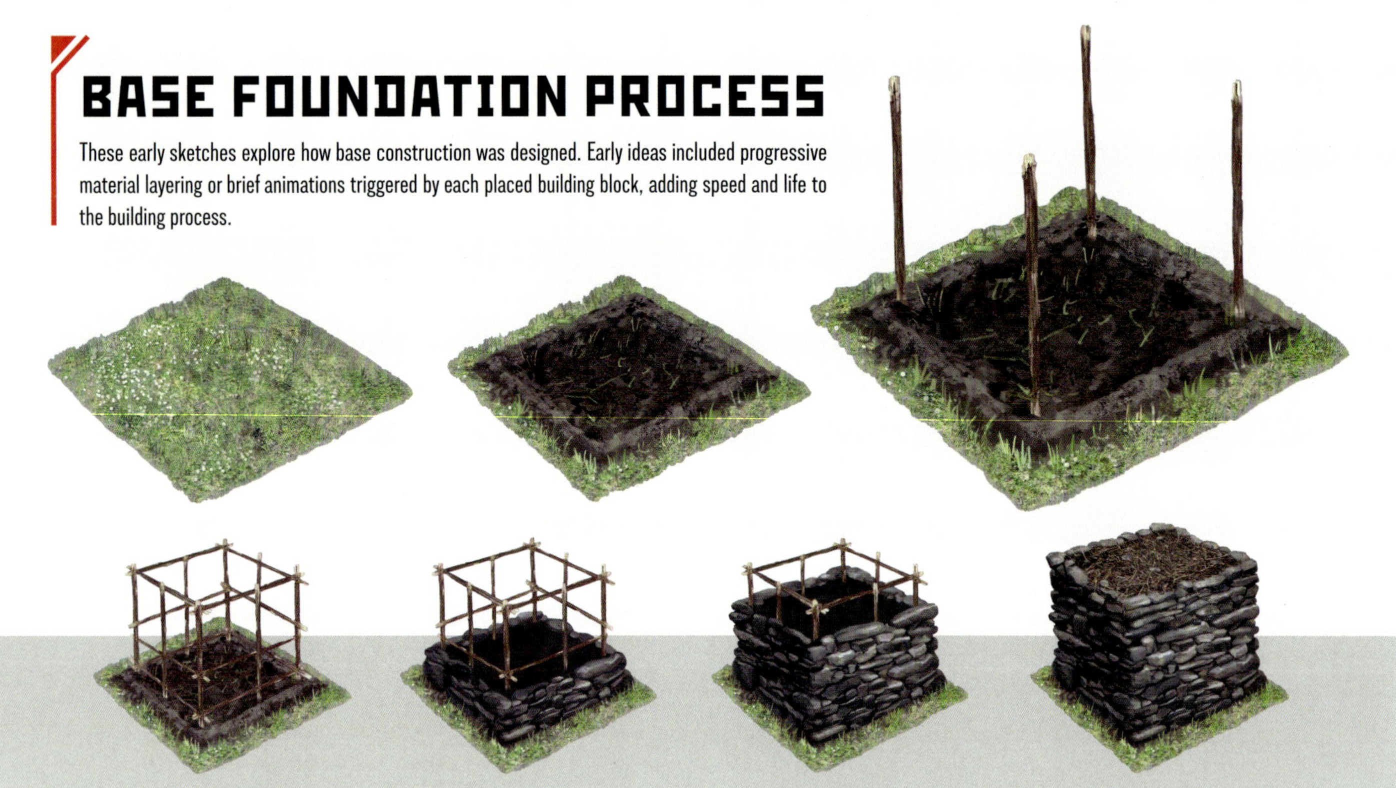

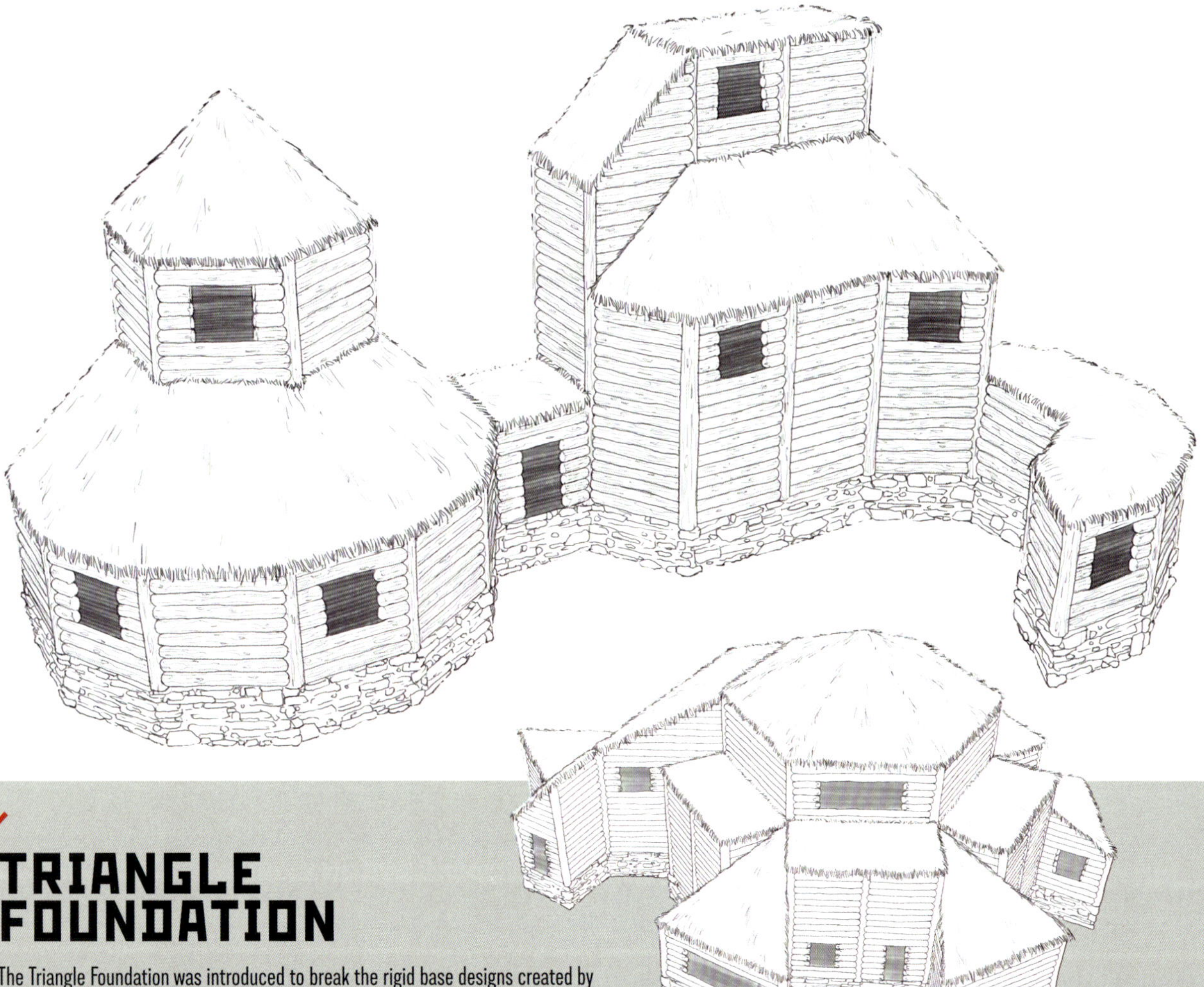

TRIANGLE FOUNDATION

The Triangle Foundation was introduced to break the rigid base designs created by Square Foundations. A triangular floor and roof piece dramatically expanded structural variety and unlocked more creative builds. Interestingly, this led to the unintentional discovery of honeycombing, a now-iconic defensive technique in base building.

TWIG BASE

Twig is the first building tier in *Rust*, designed to feel just secure enough for a night's shelter. Loose joints, gaps between sticks, and exposed framework show vulnerability, visually warning players that these structures offer little protection from curious or hostile eyes.

TWIG ROOF

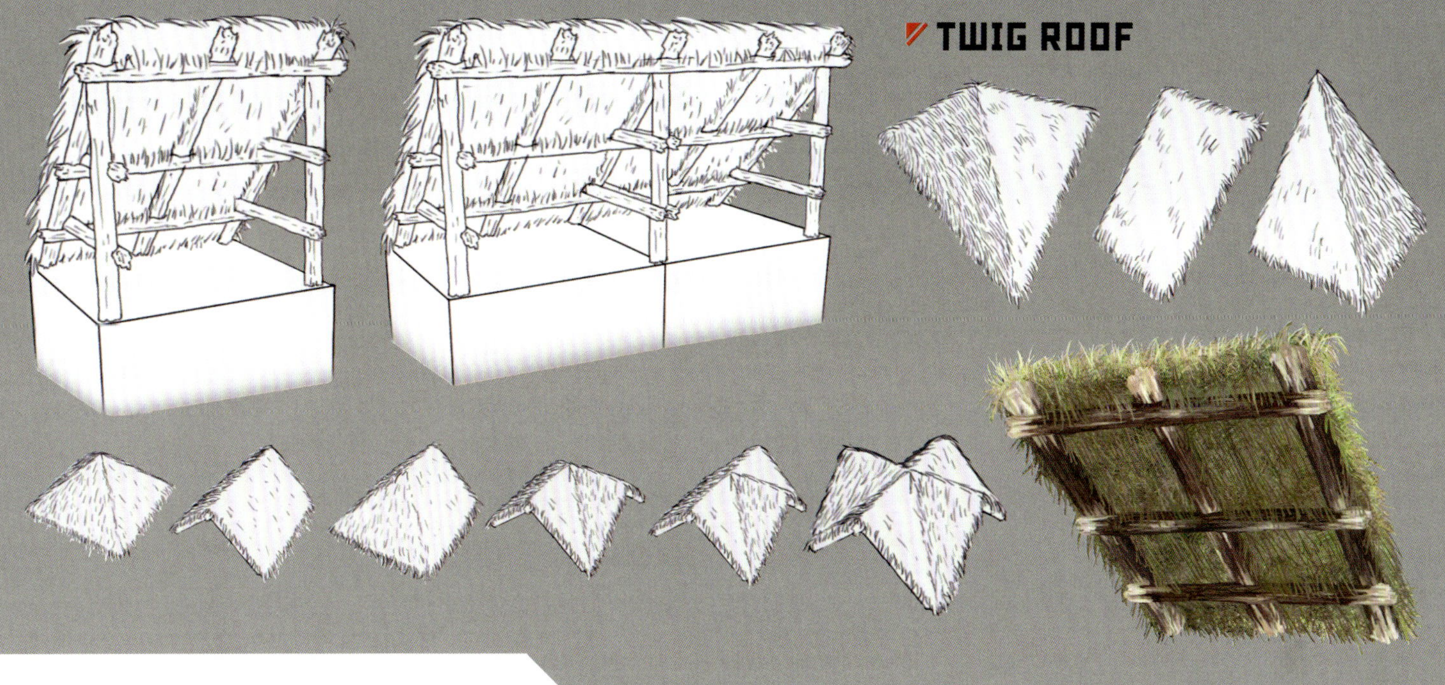

TWIG WALLS

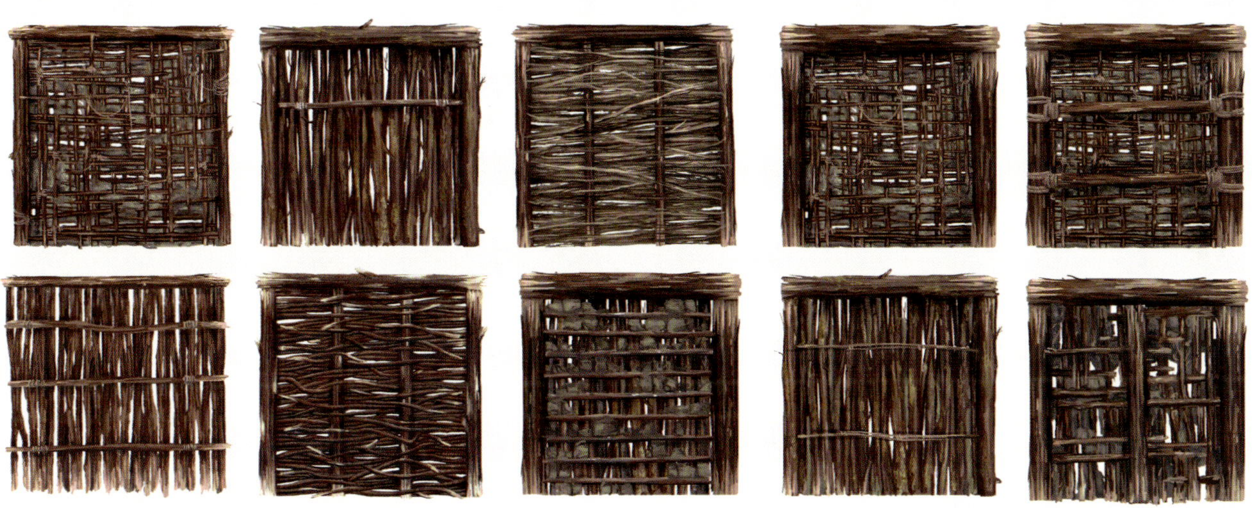

TWIG FLOORS

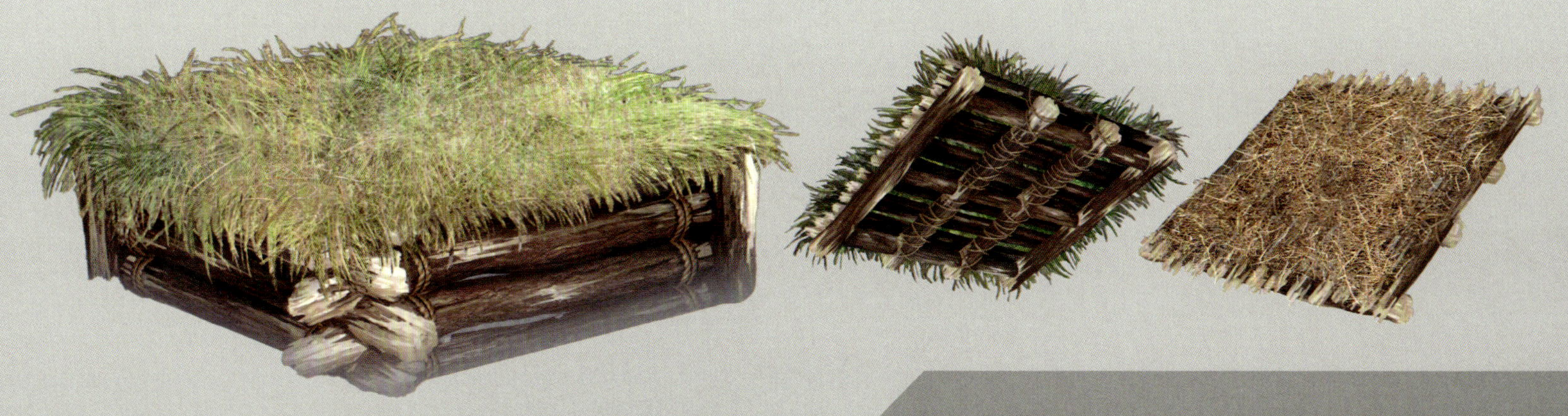

WOODEN BASE

Taking inspiration from primitive cabin architecture, early Wooden Base concepts feature notched log corners, sloped grass roofs, and basic structural framing. The design materials feel handcrafted and rough, creating a sense of vulnerability that contrasts with more fortified stone or metal tiers.

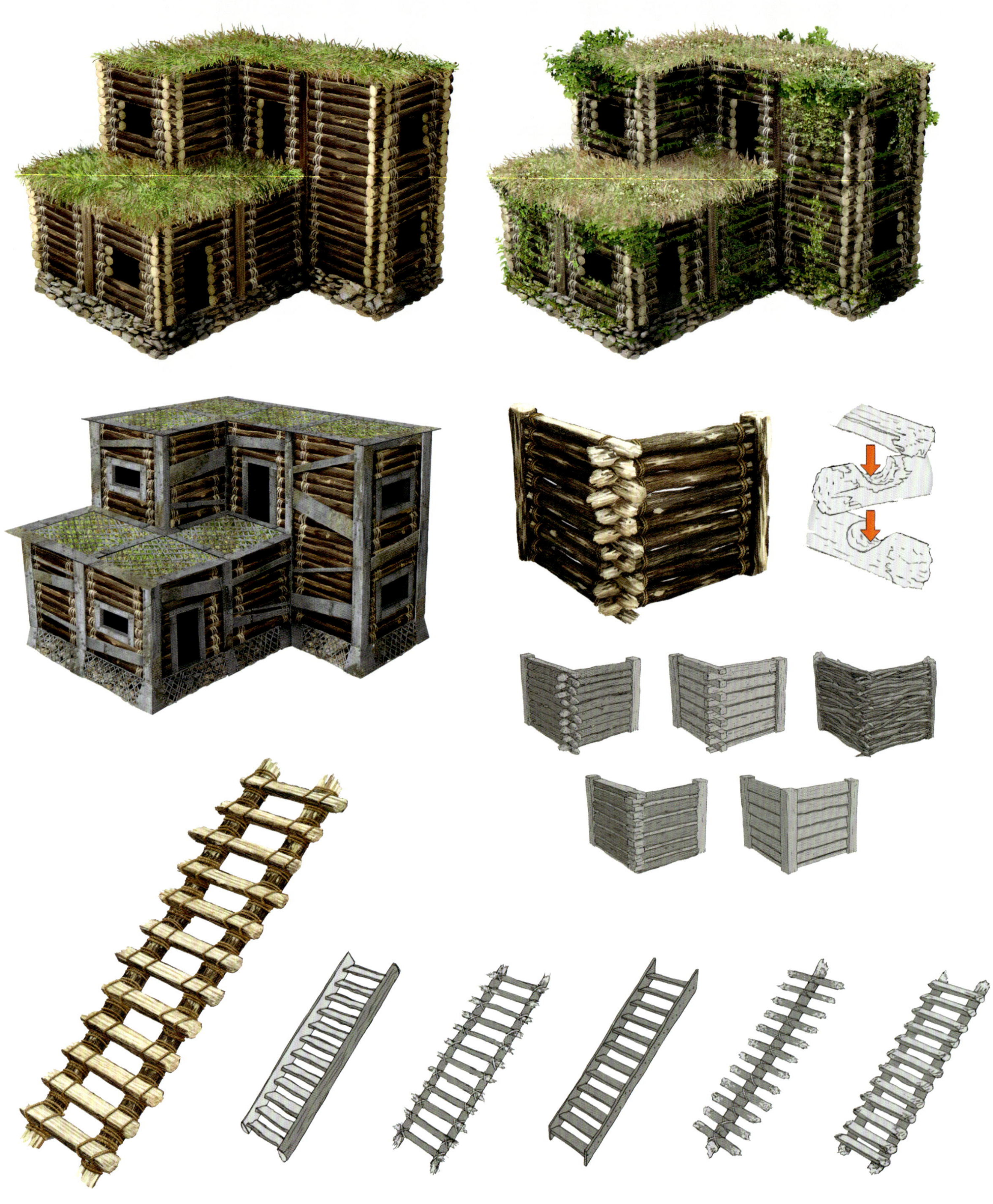

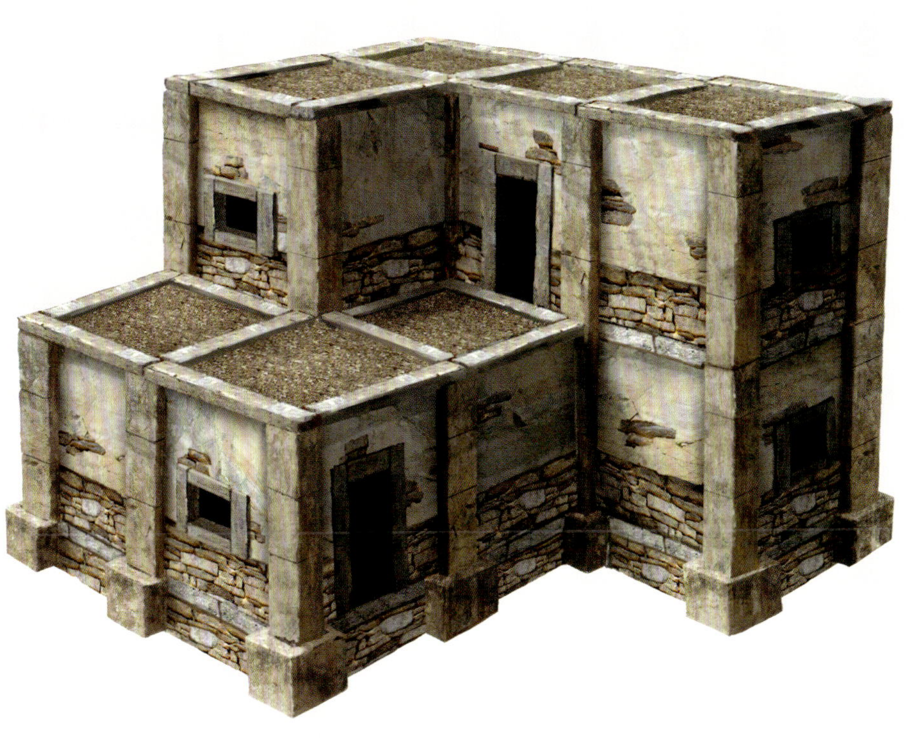
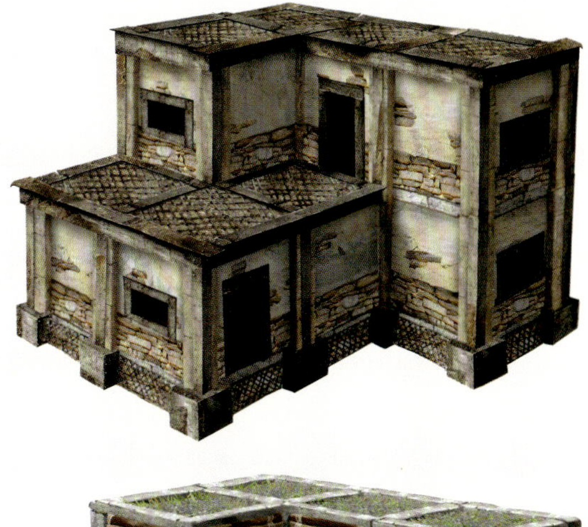
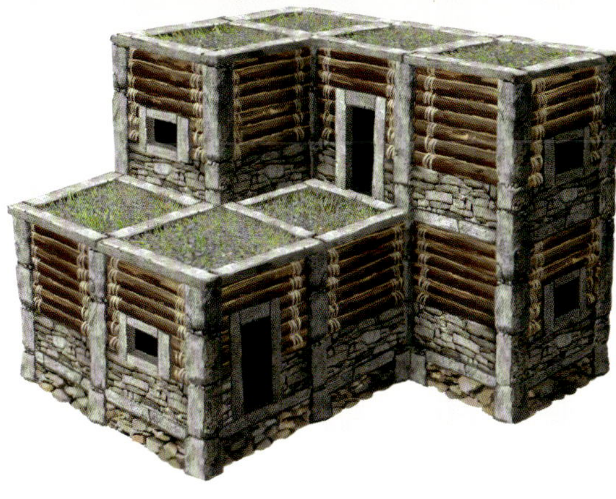
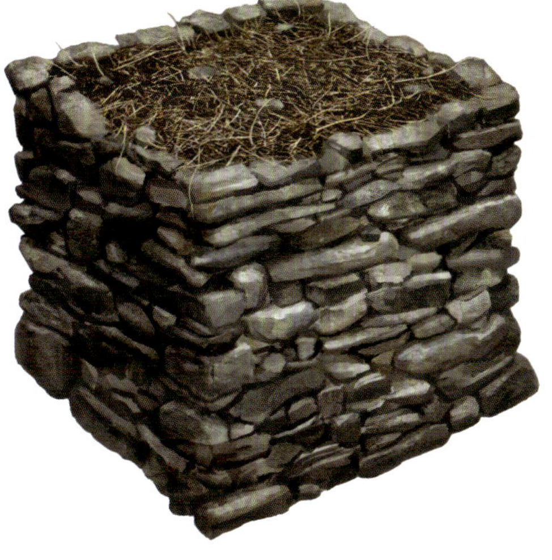

STONE BASE

The concept sketches of the early Stone Bases capture a rugged, hand-built aesthetic. The stonework-inspired design leans into a heavier natural feel, incorporating grass roofs, stone masonry with weathered textures, and blocky architecture.

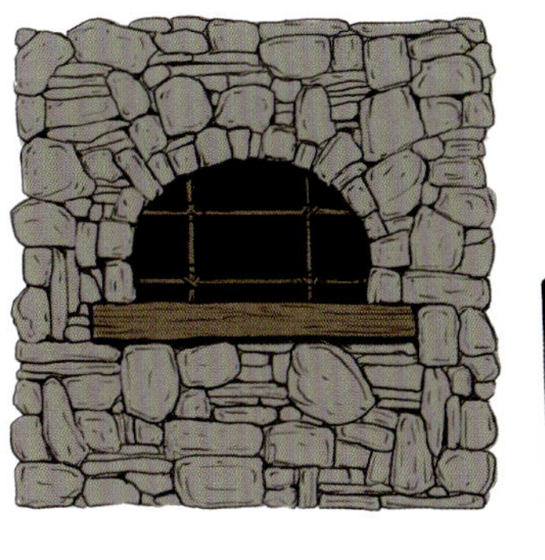
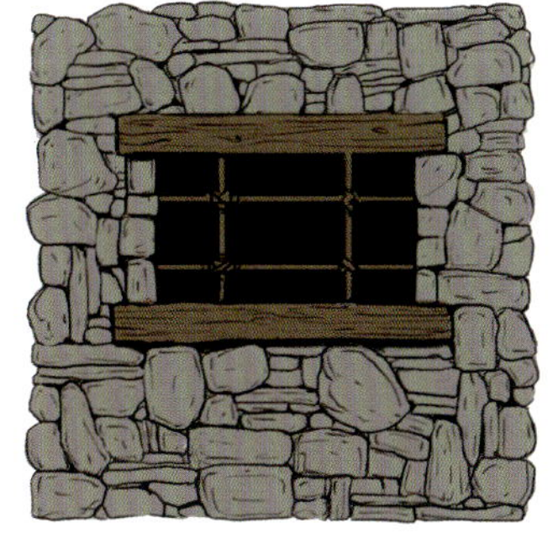
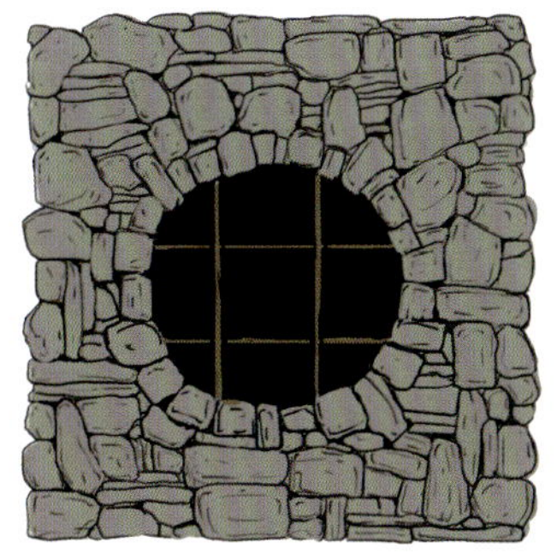
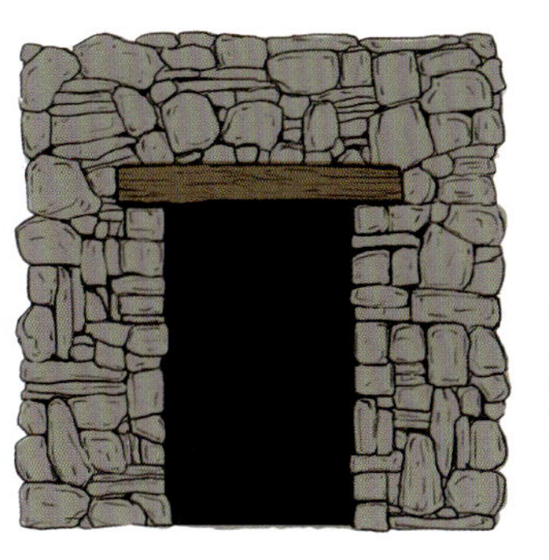
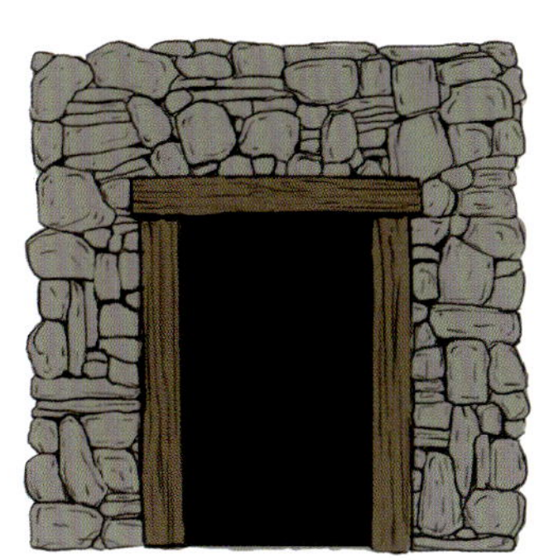
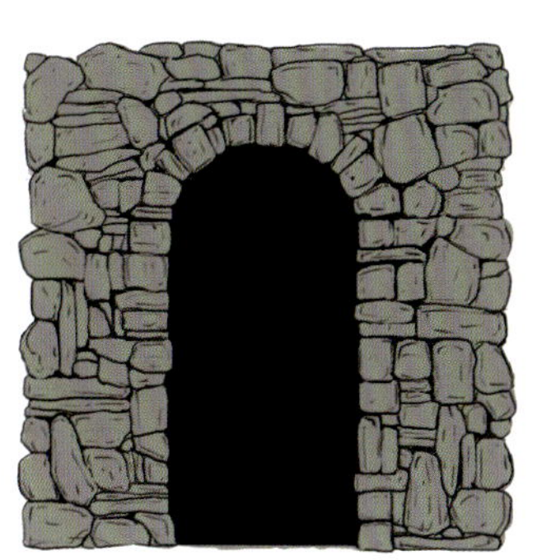

METAL BASE

Here are some early concepts exploring how upgraded bases could've looked. These first concepts all feature the same slightly exaggerated, blocky, and modular design. The Metal Base features exposed sheet metal, bolt fixtures, and rough patchwork construction.

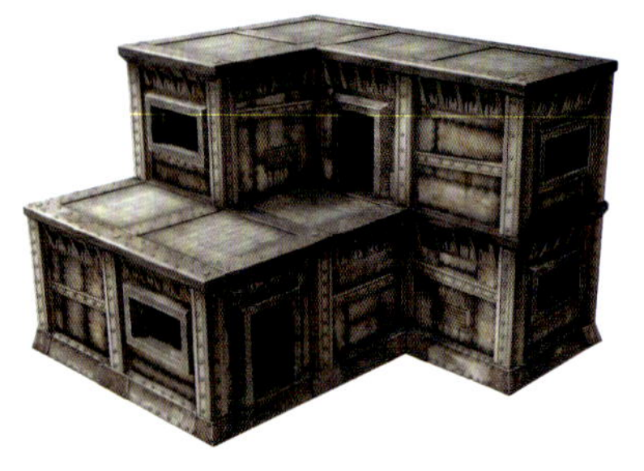
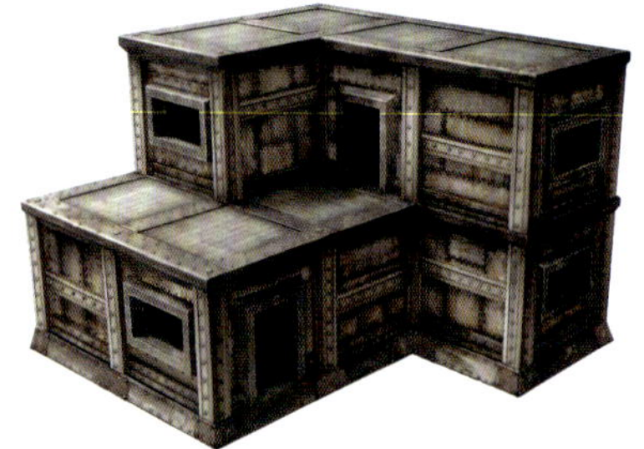
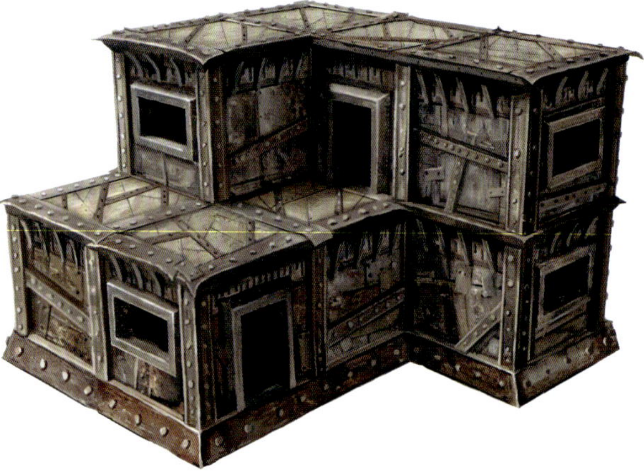
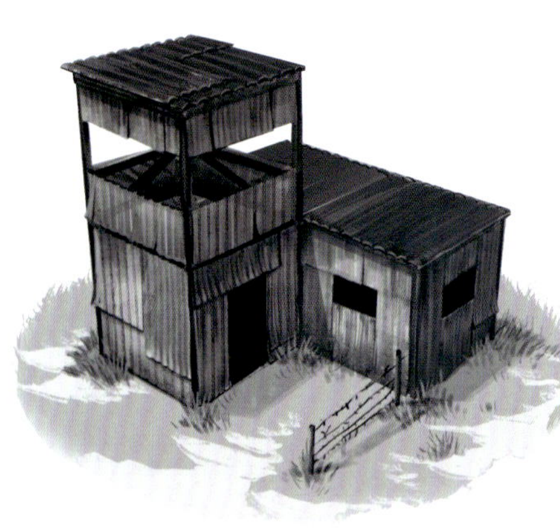
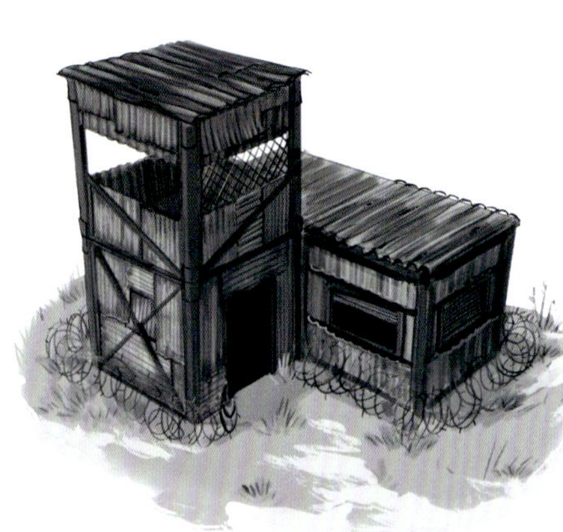
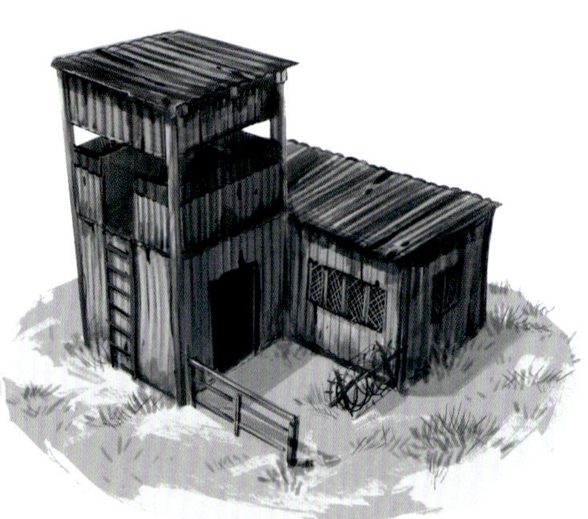
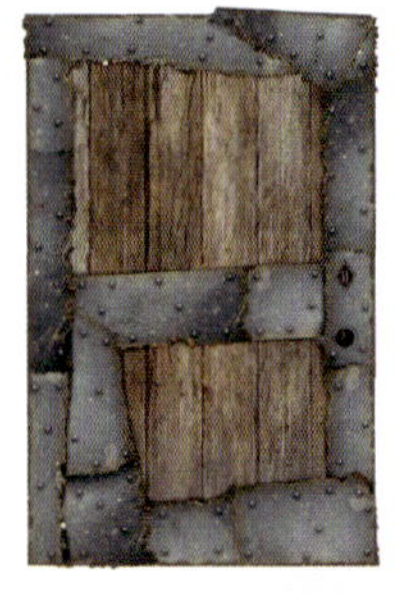
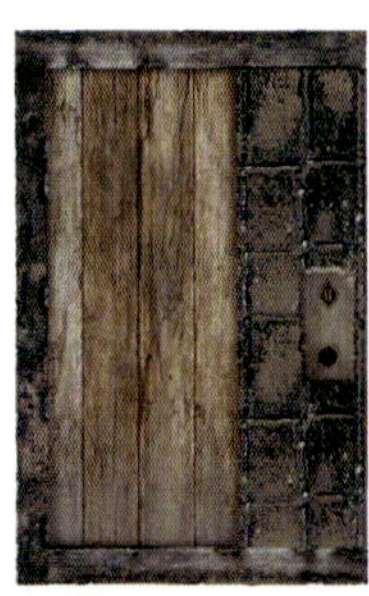
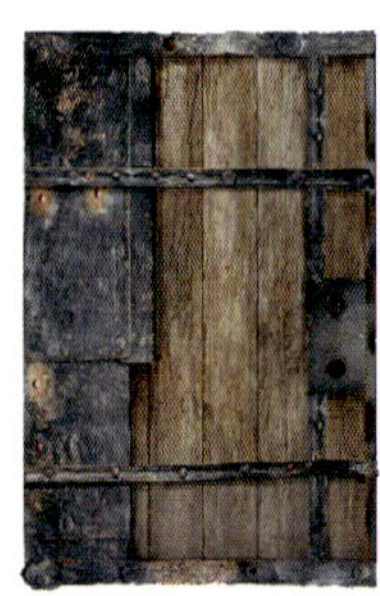
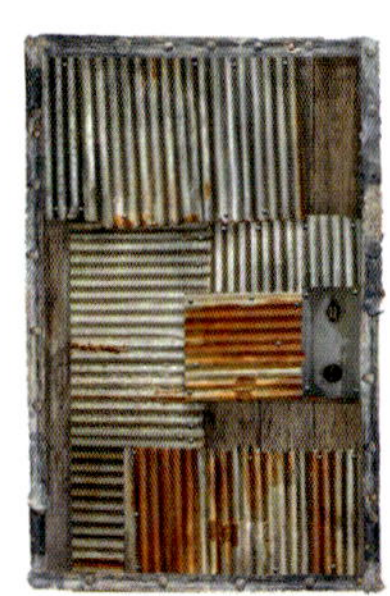
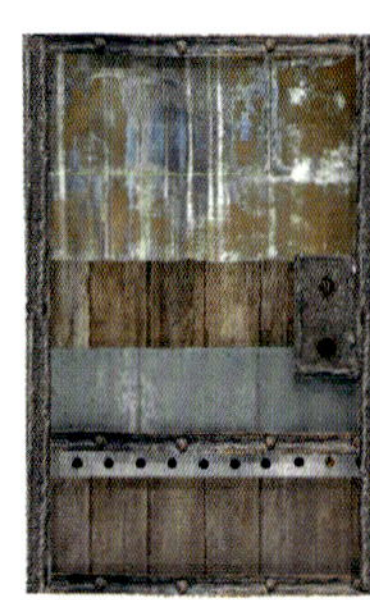
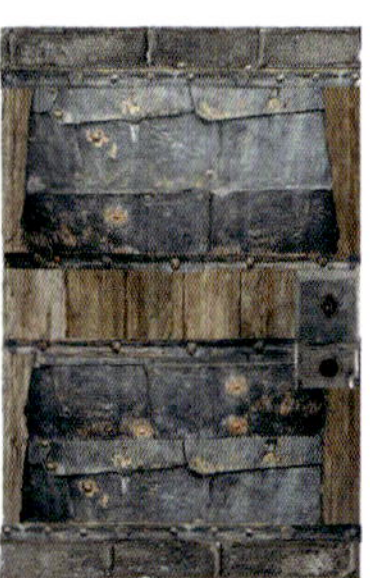
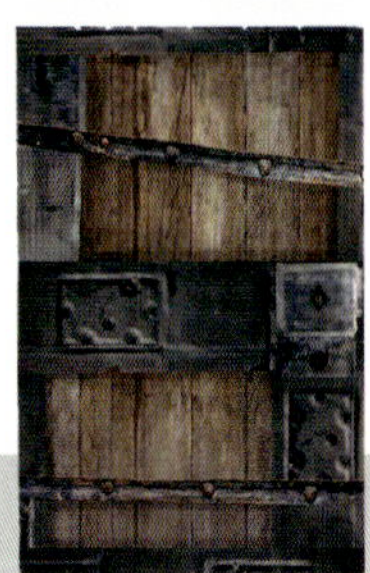
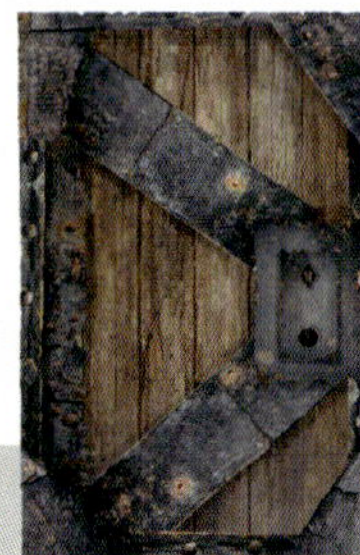
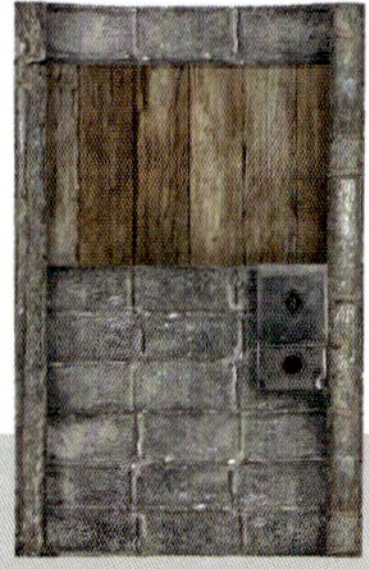
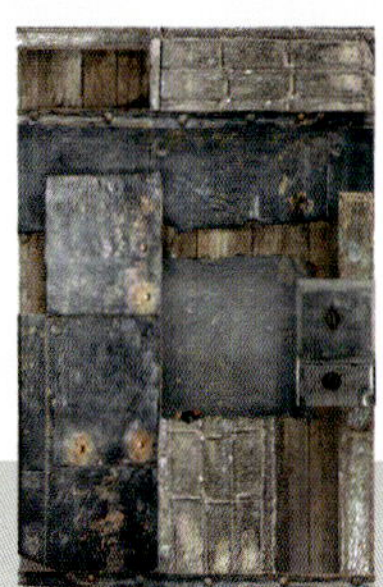
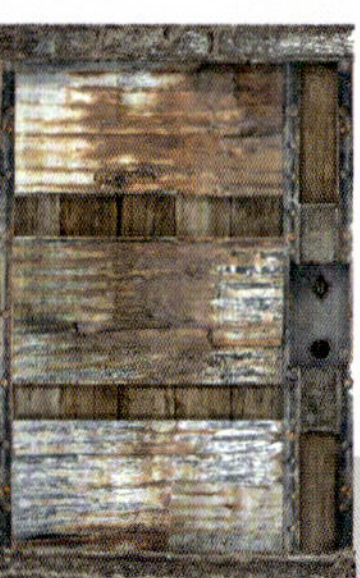

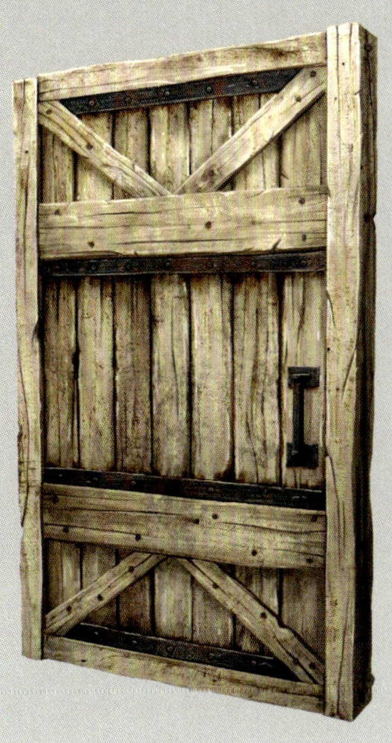
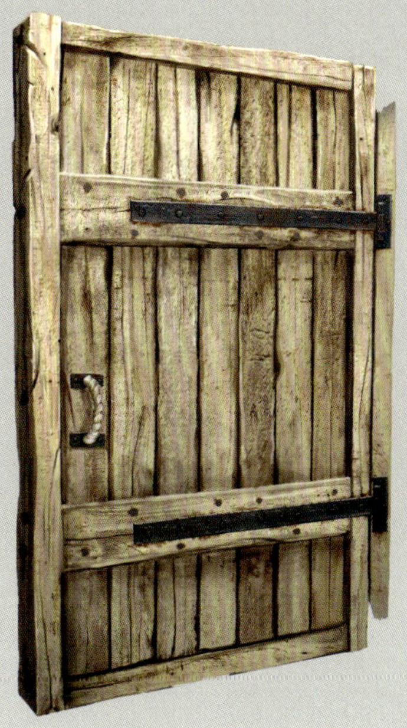
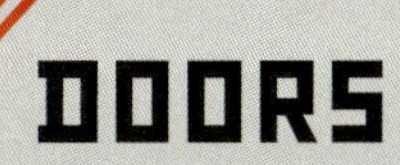

DOORS

Wooden Doors are an integral part of *Rust*. Crafted early in the game, they provide essential protection for starter bases. The simple barn-style design with large hinges, exposed nails, and roughly cut planks helps reinforce *Rust*'s handmade and scavenged aesthetic.

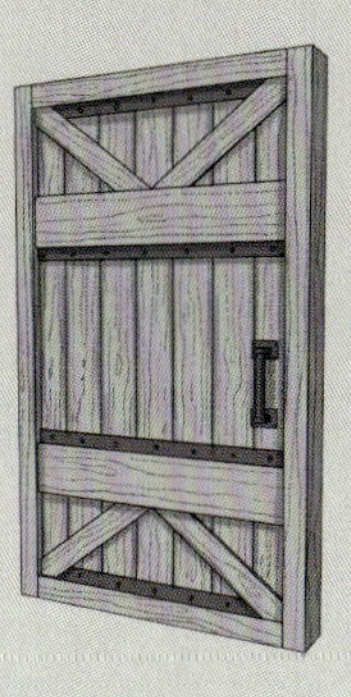
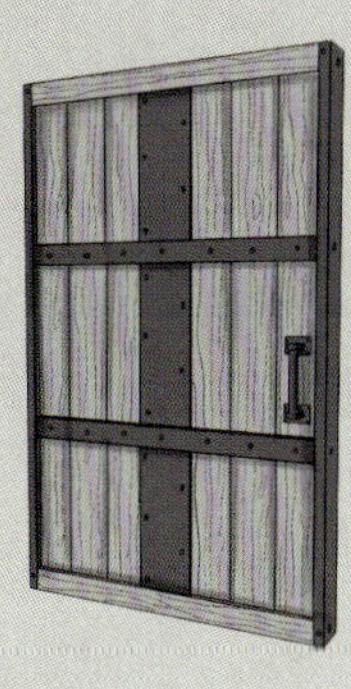
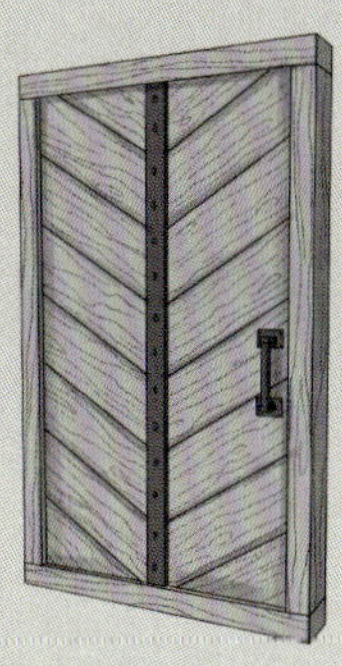
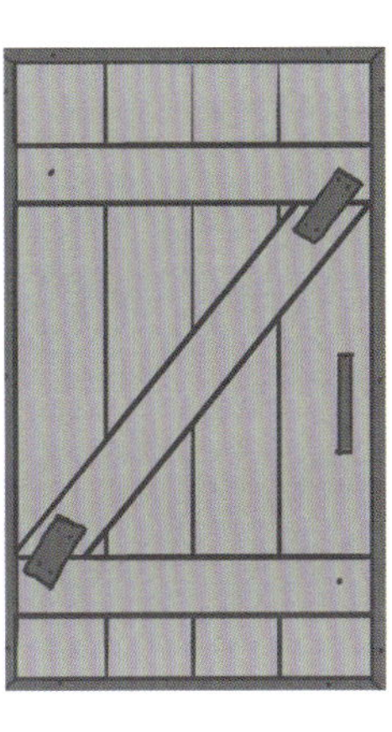
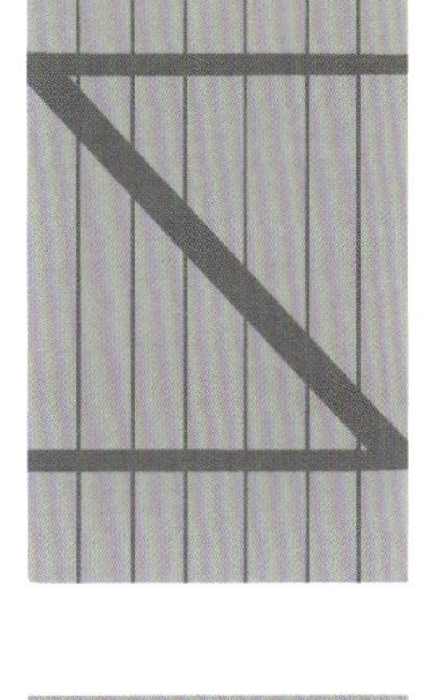
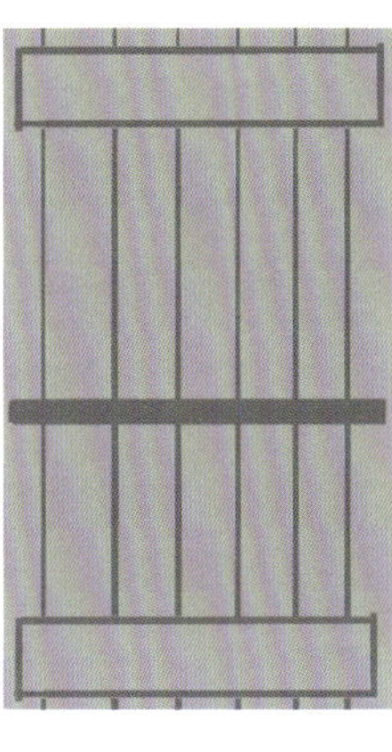
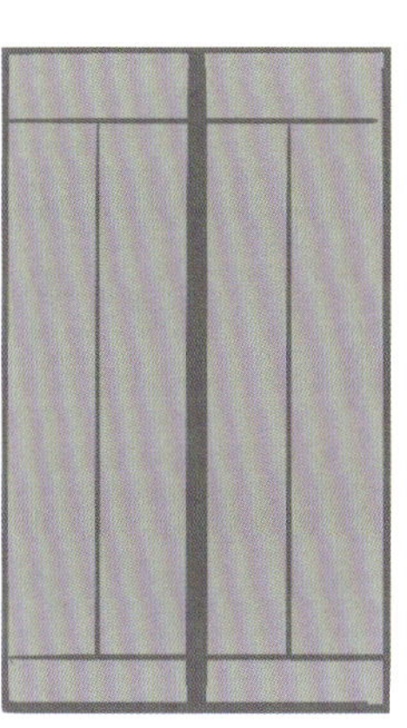
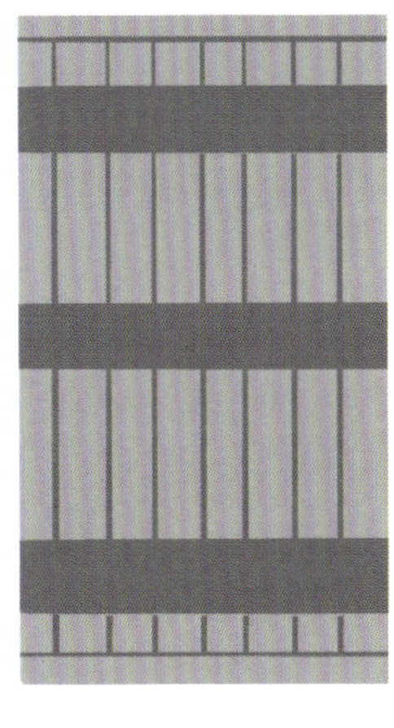
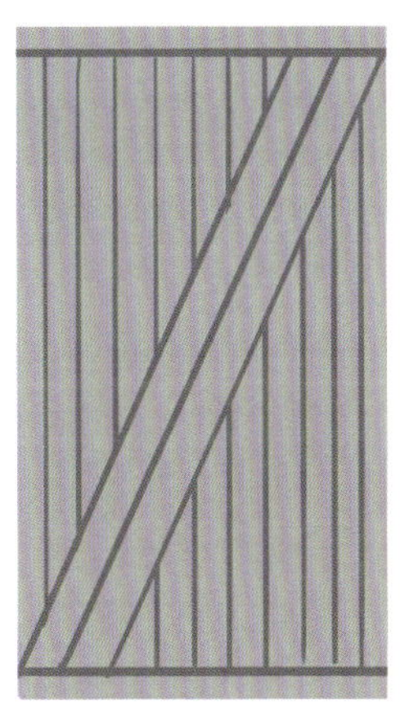
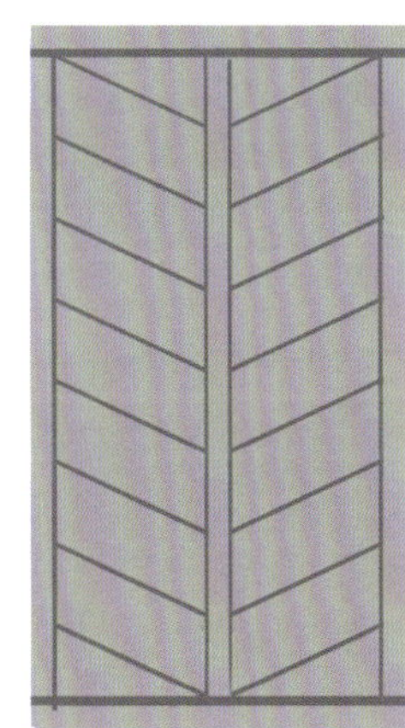
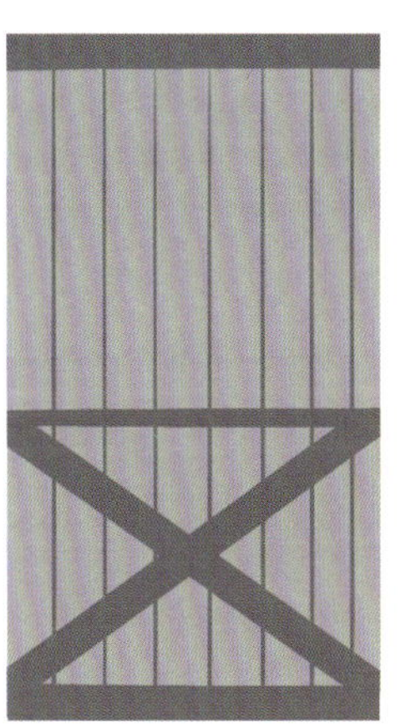
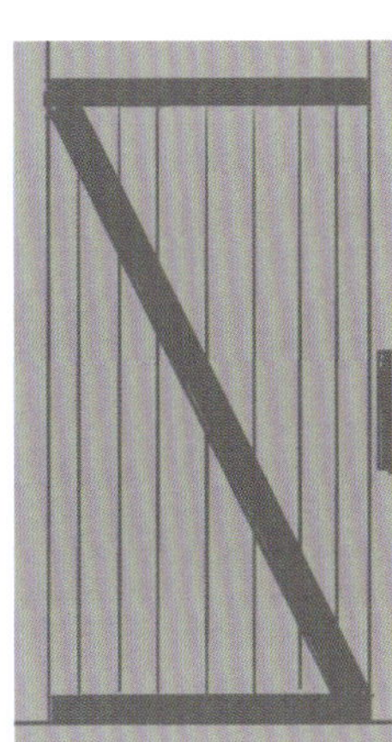
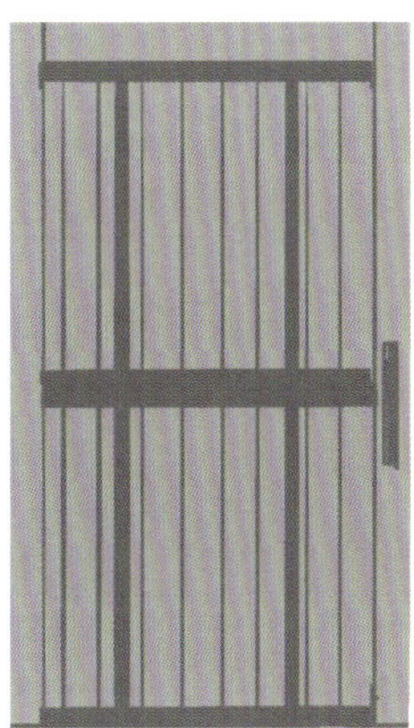
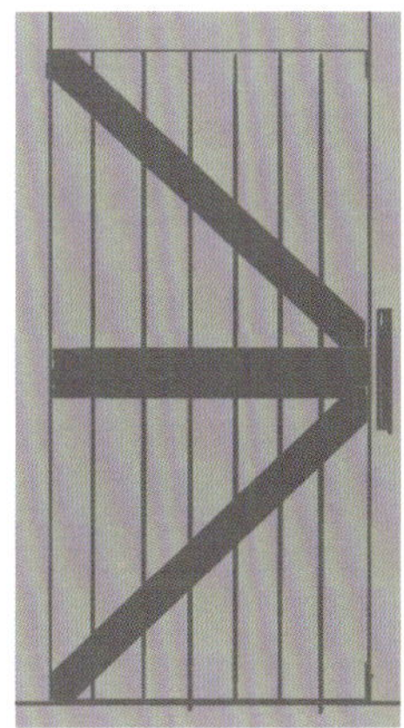
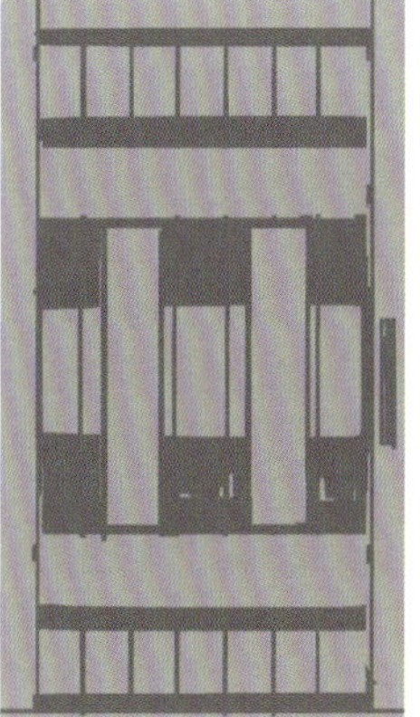

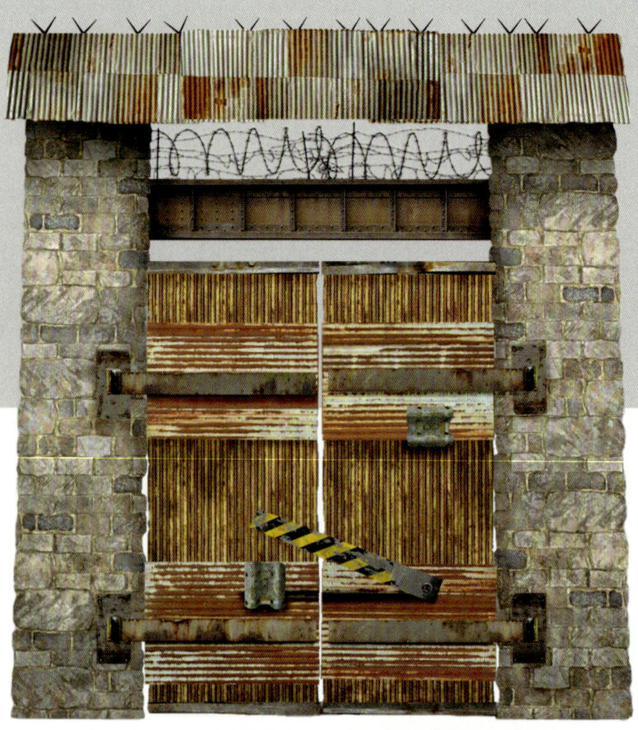

GATES

Gates are deployable defensive structures that range from crude wooden entrances to reinforced armored barriers. Each tier of gate follows the same progressions as a base: wood, stone, sheet metal, and armored. These early concepts show a variety of options throughout the progression. Gates tend to be paired with High External Walls to create compounds around bases.

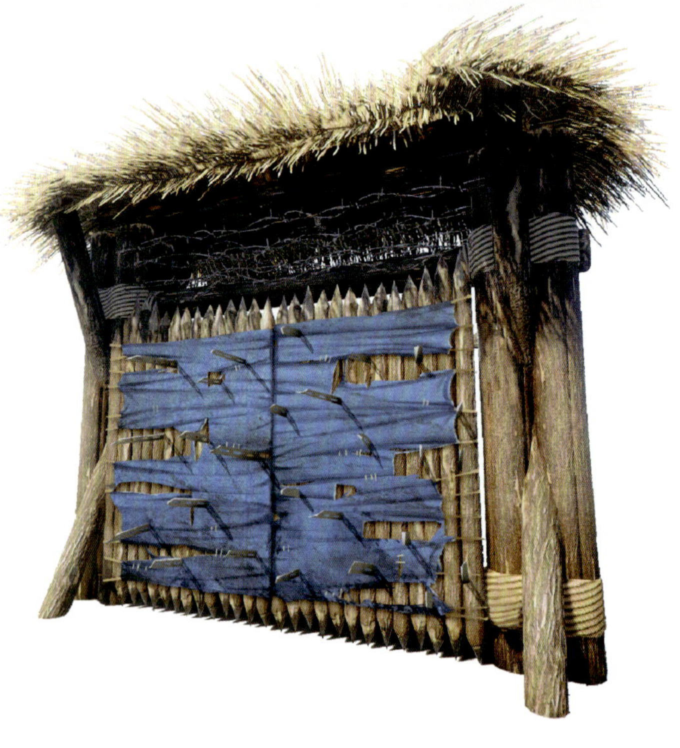

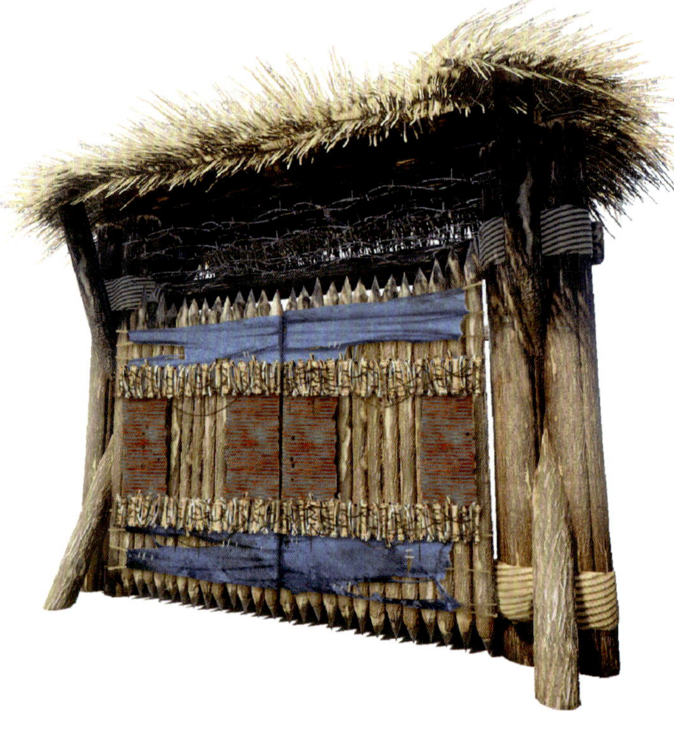

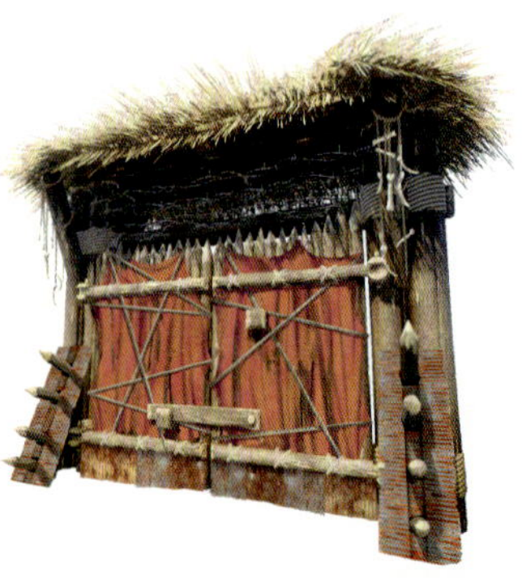

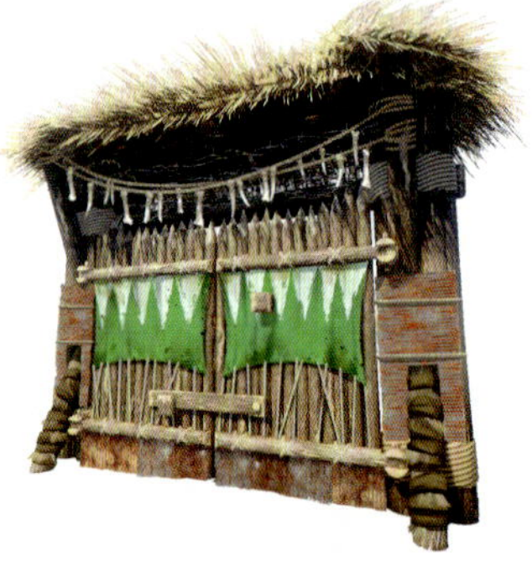

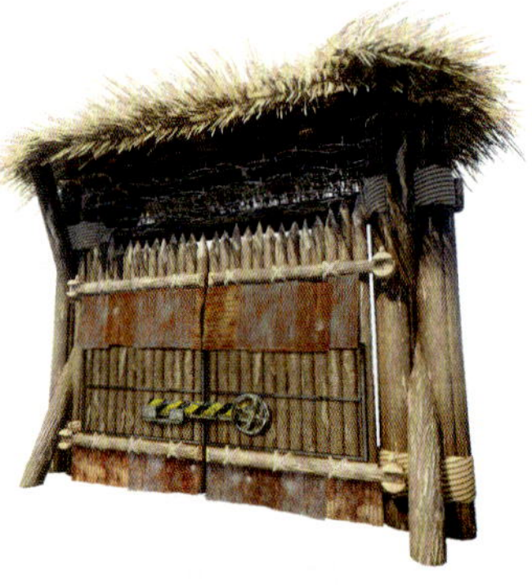

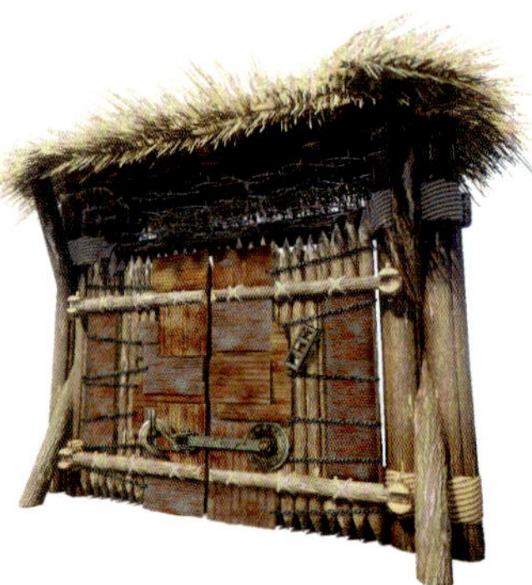

WOODEN GATES

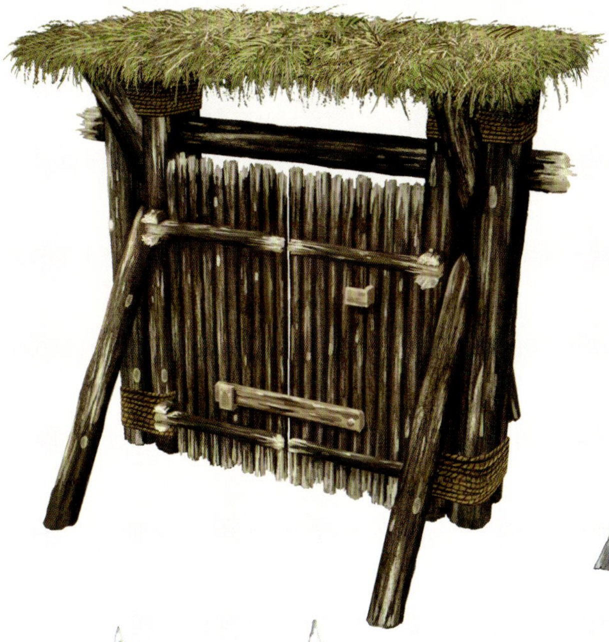

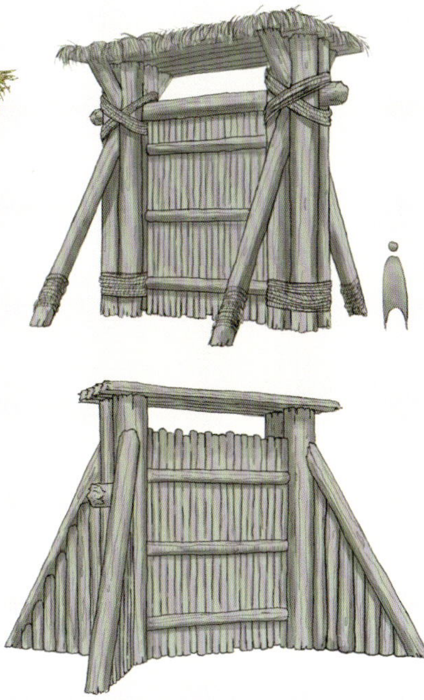

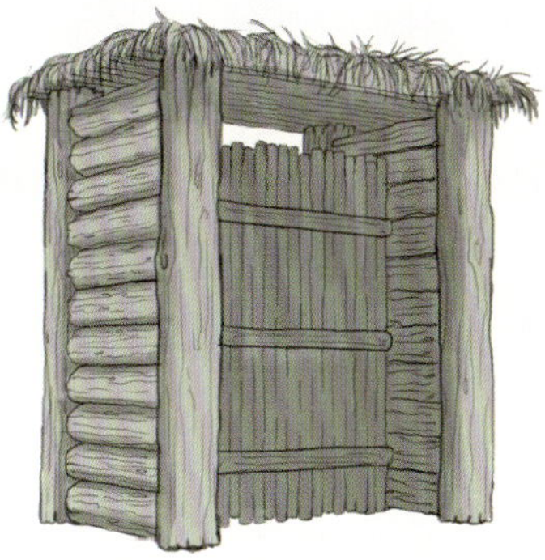

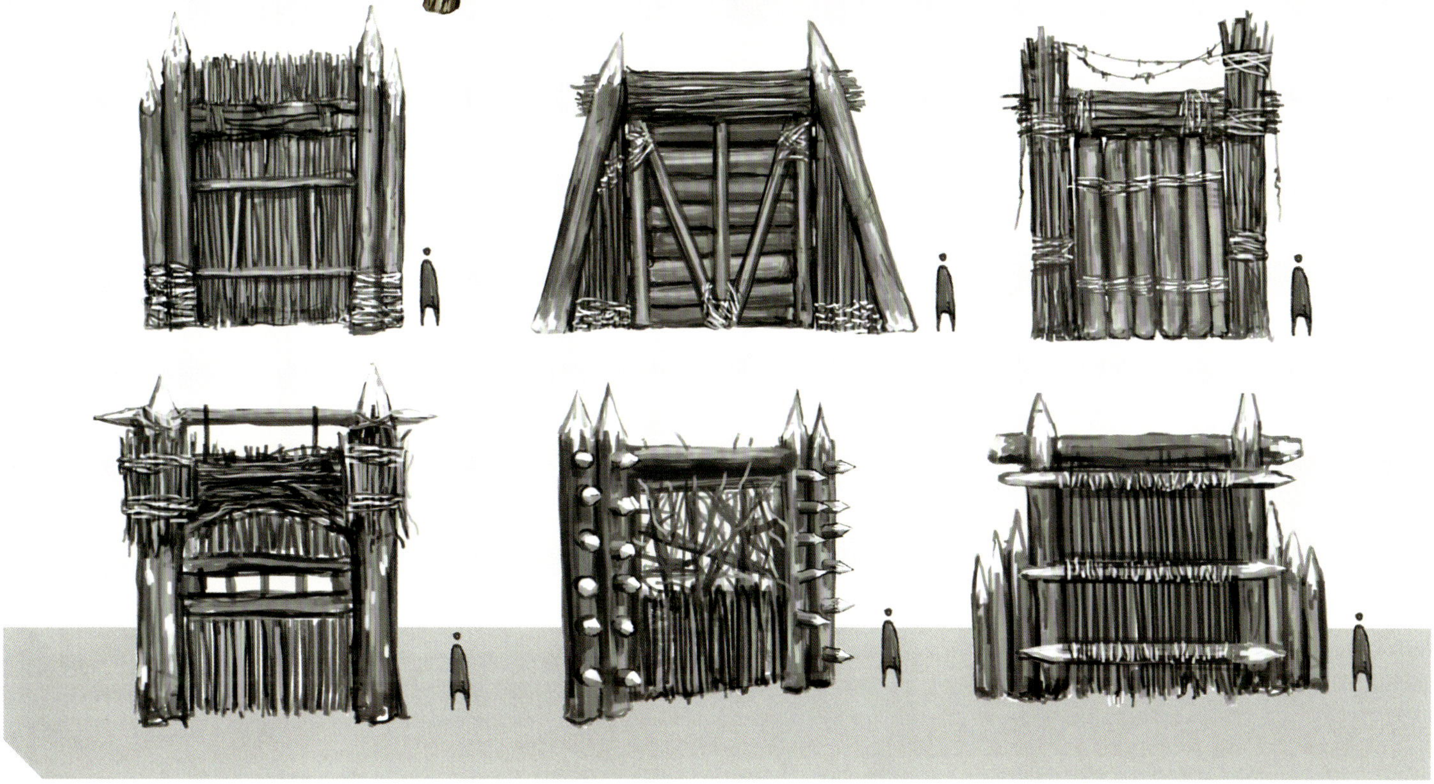

WOODEN GATE WALL

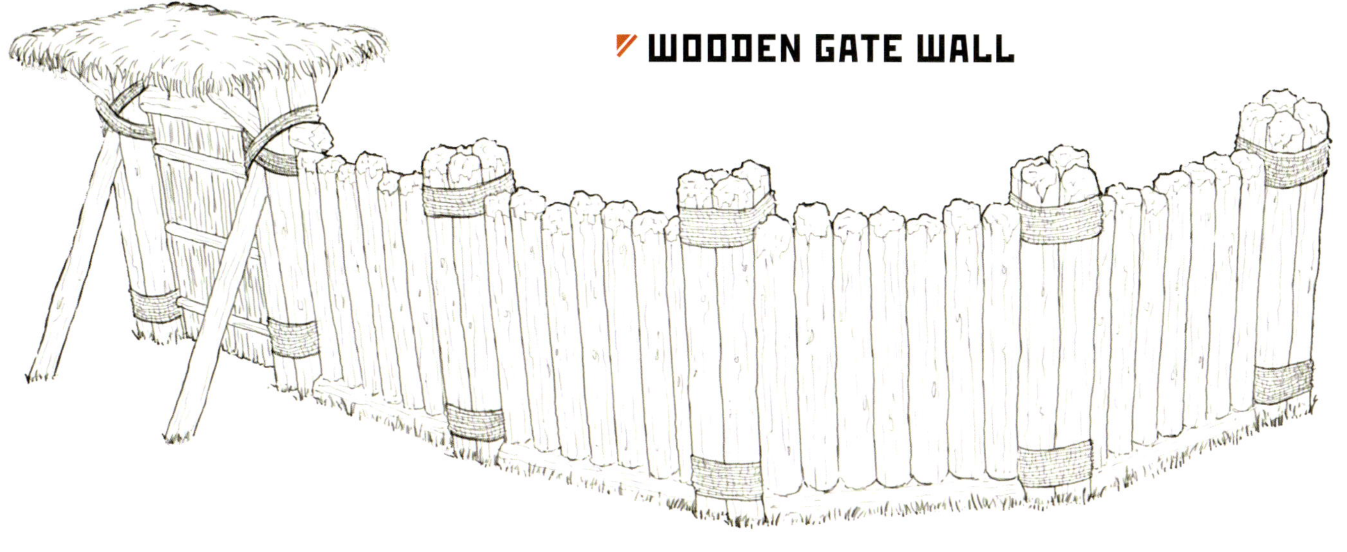

RESEARCH AND MIXING TABLES

The research and mixing table concepts were designed to reflect *Rust*'s scavenged and improvised aesthetic. The mixing table is assembled from battered sinks, brick ovens, and rusted chemistry apparatus, providing salvaged functionality. The research table, with mechanical cranks, worn frames, and repurposed engineering tools, offers a slightly more steampunk aesthetic.

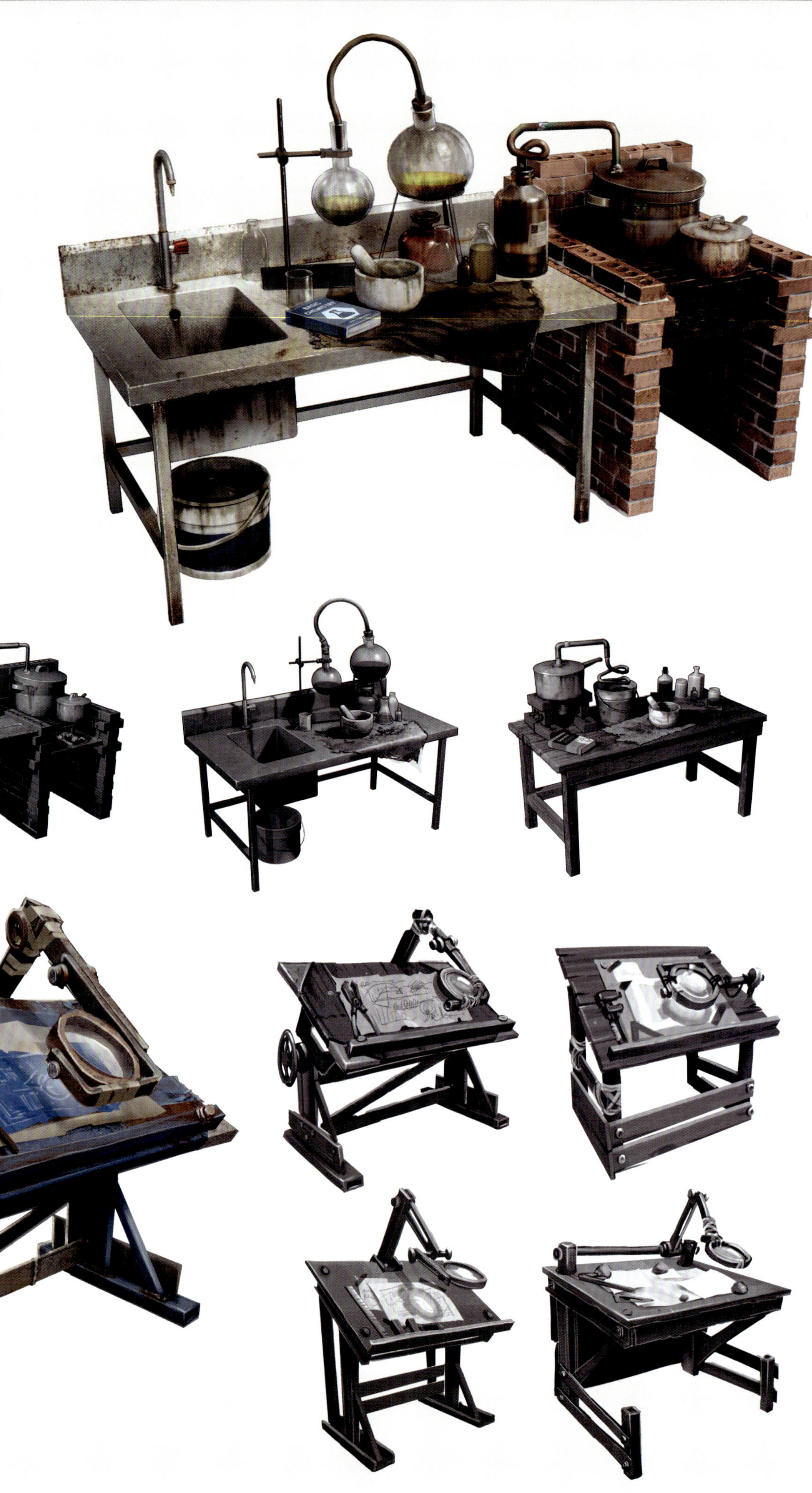

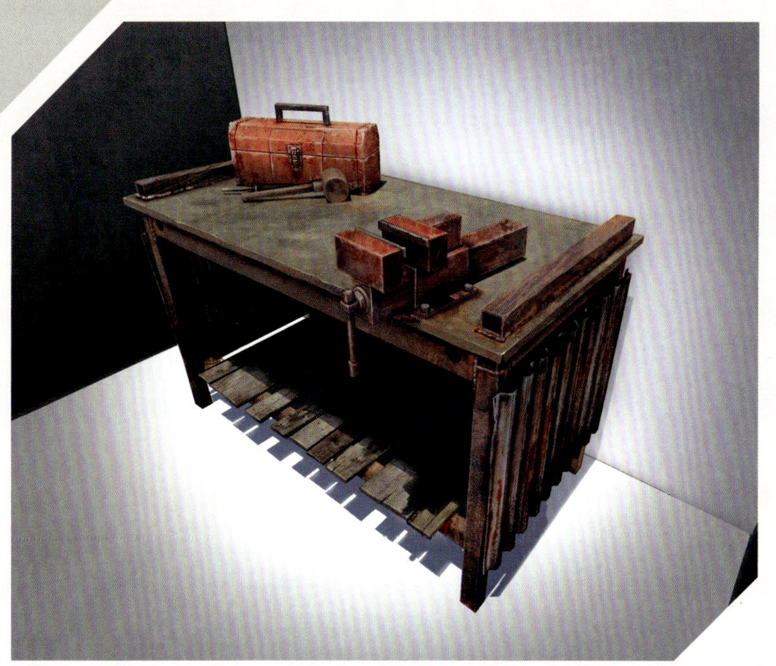

REPAIR BENCH

The Repair Bench is a great example of *Rust*'s grounded, scrappy aesthetic. The design leans heavily into the theme of resourcefulness. Constructed from salvaged materials, the bench feels sturdy but hand built, with mismatched elements suggesting it was assembled from whatever was available.

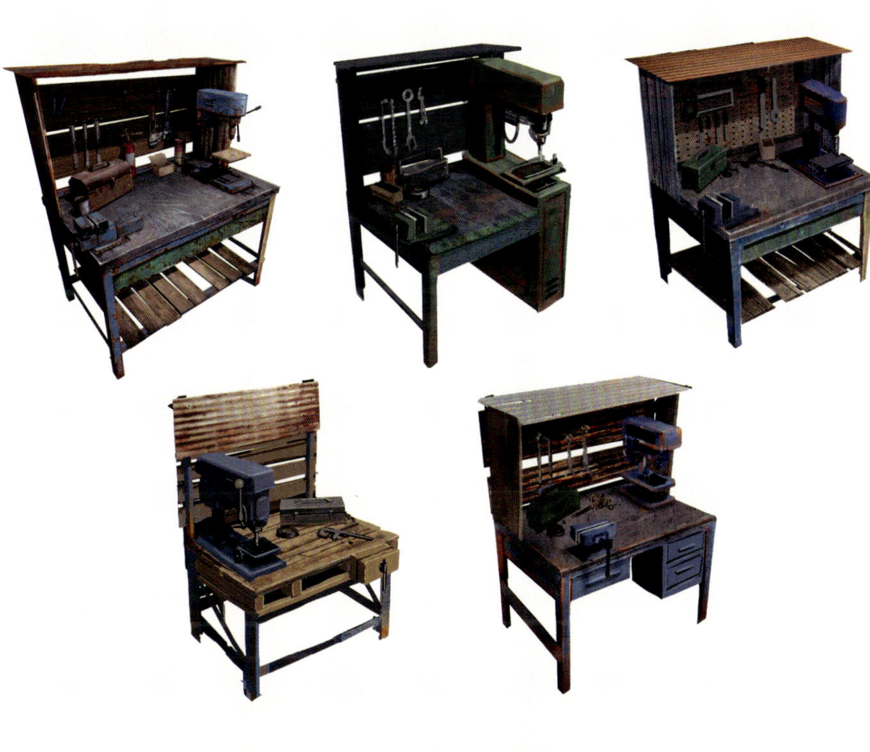

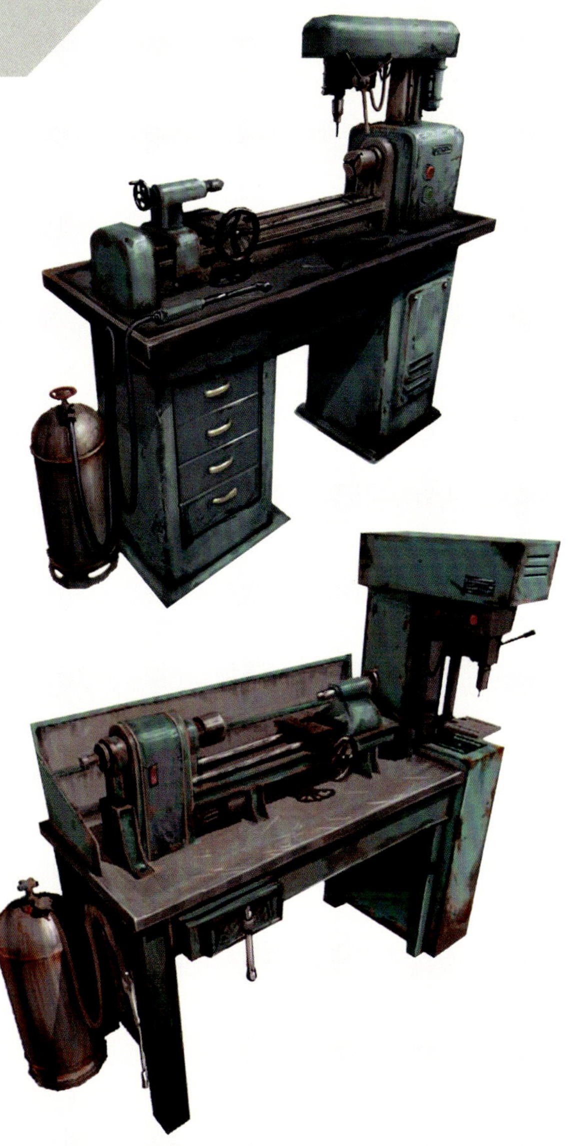

WORK BENCH

The Work Bench is an essential item for a player's progression throughout the game, as it has a three-tier tech-tree system to unlock the crafting recipe for items within each tier. These concepts show a variety of options for the bench as it progresses and needs more complicated equipment to support unlocking each tier.

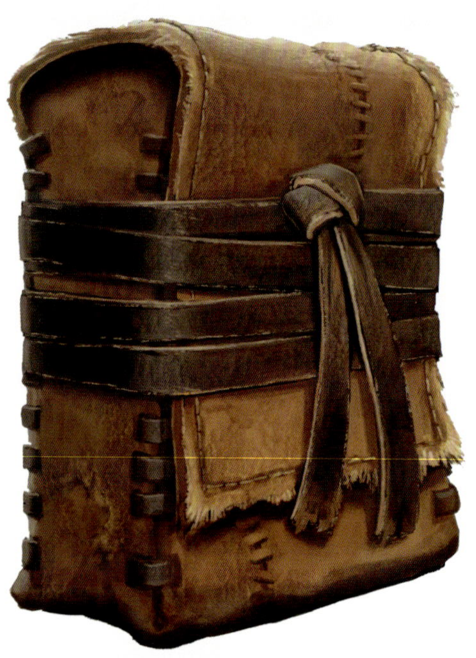

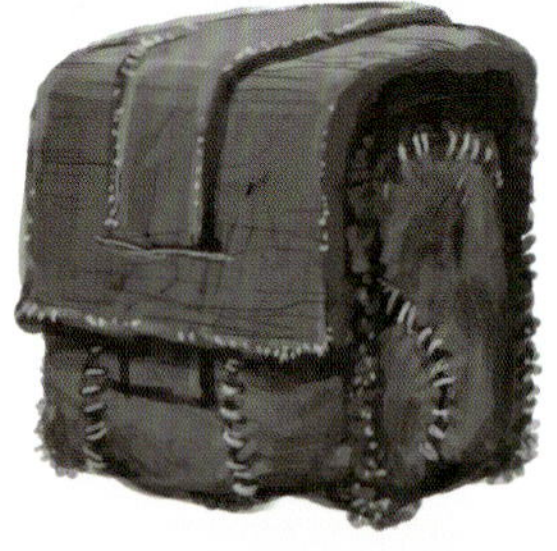

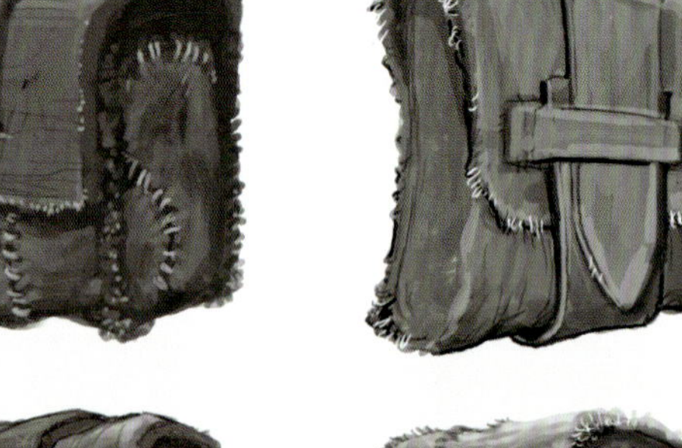

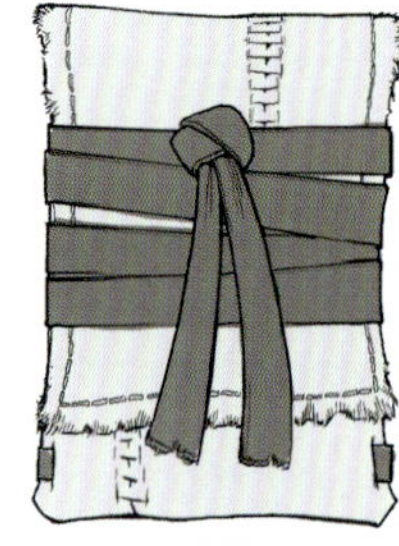

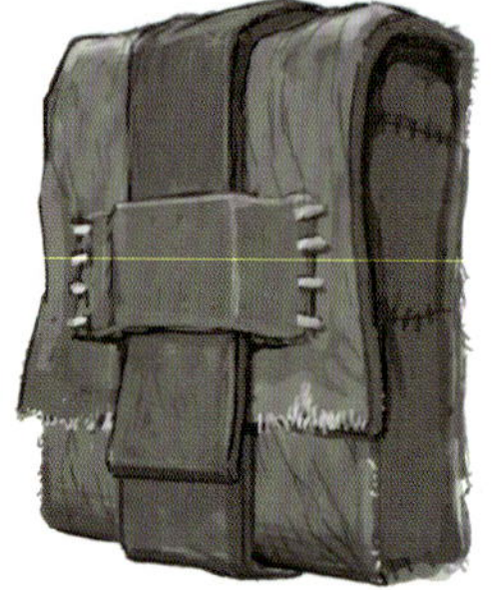

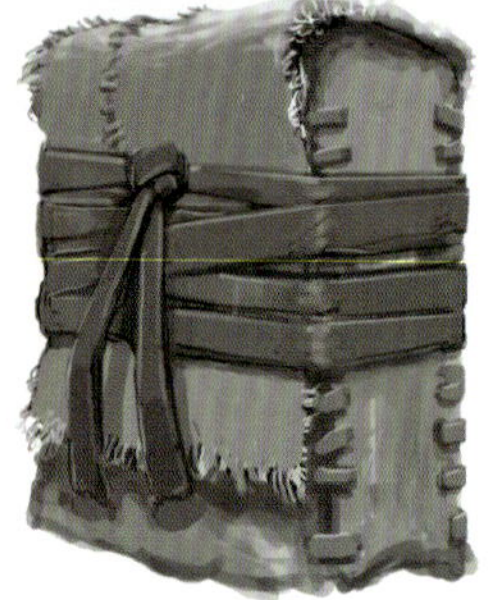

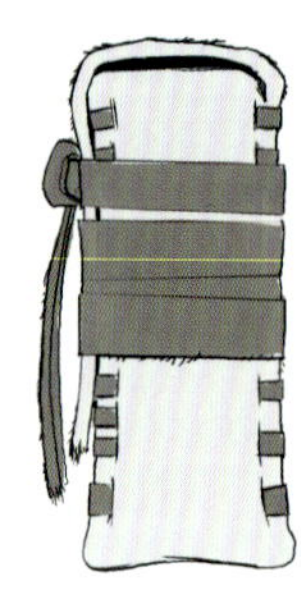

STASHES

Stashes are small, discreet storage containers used to hide valuable items underground. These concept sketches explore what eventually became the stash satchel and loot box. The sketches below show a variety of design ideas for food storage, ranging from makeshift oil drum coolers to a rusted icebox to food crates.

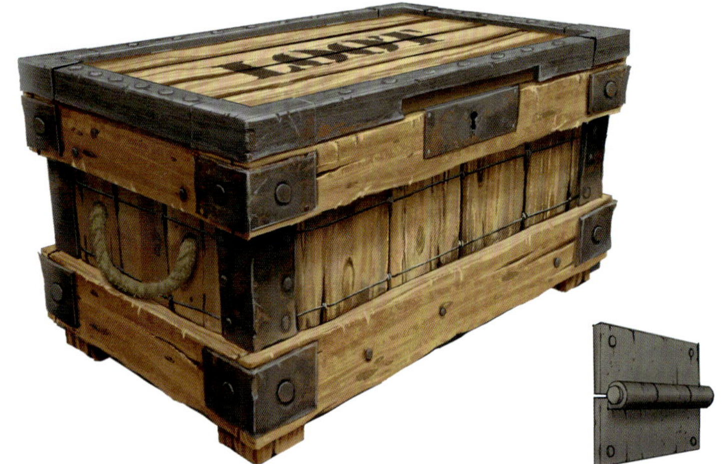

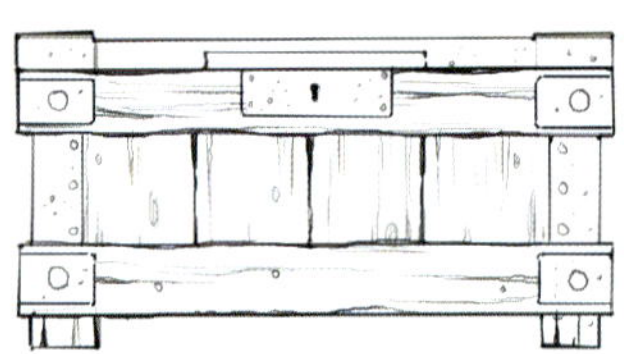

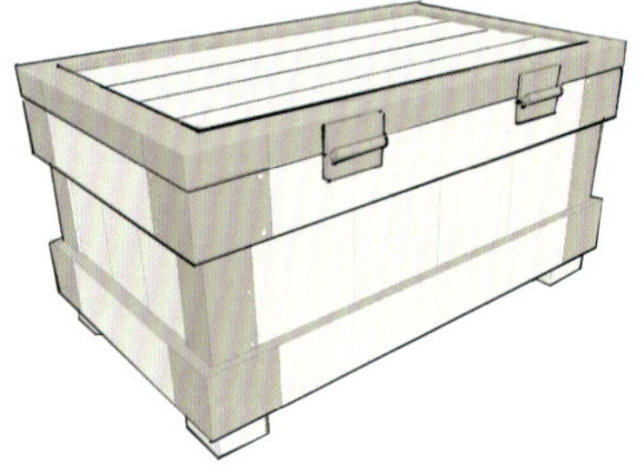

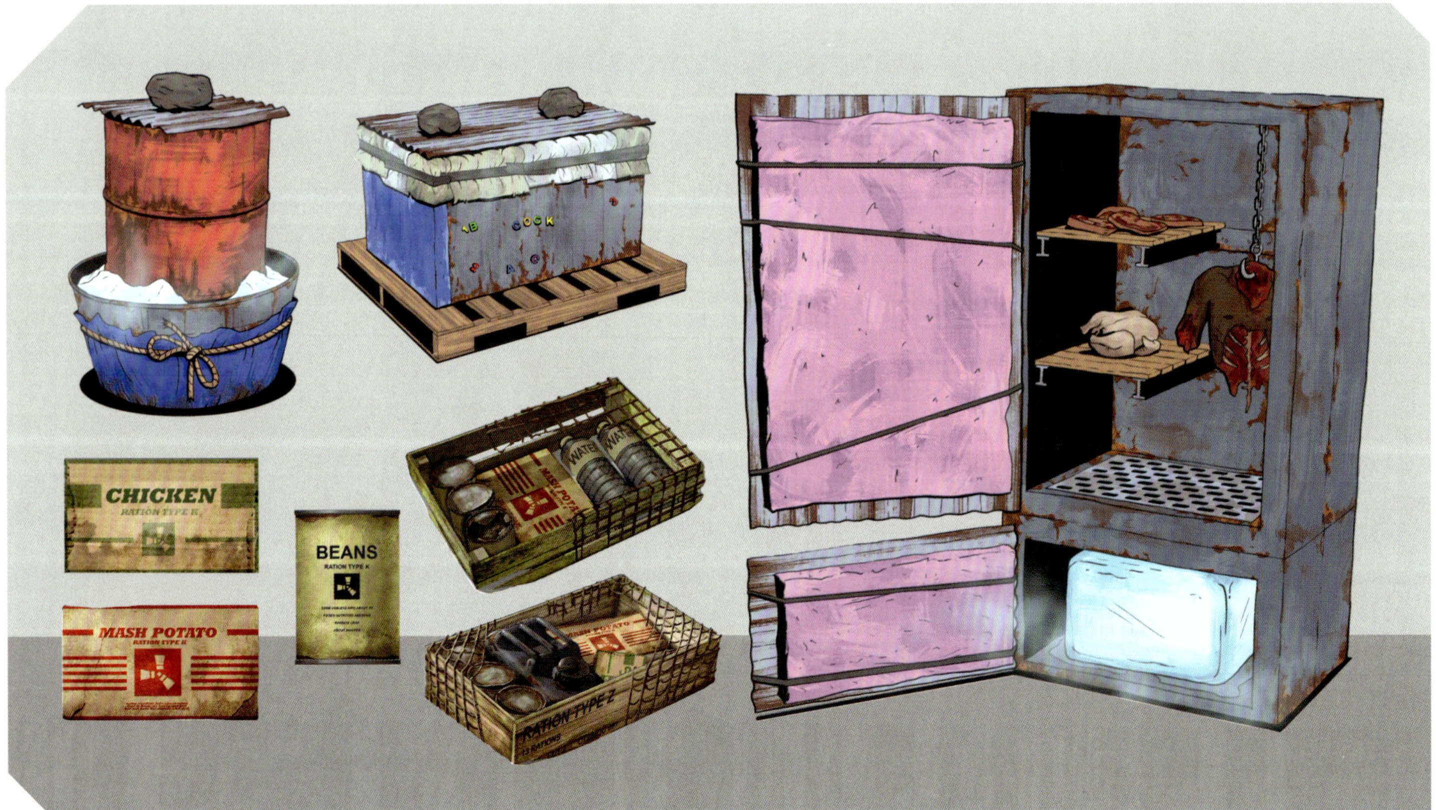

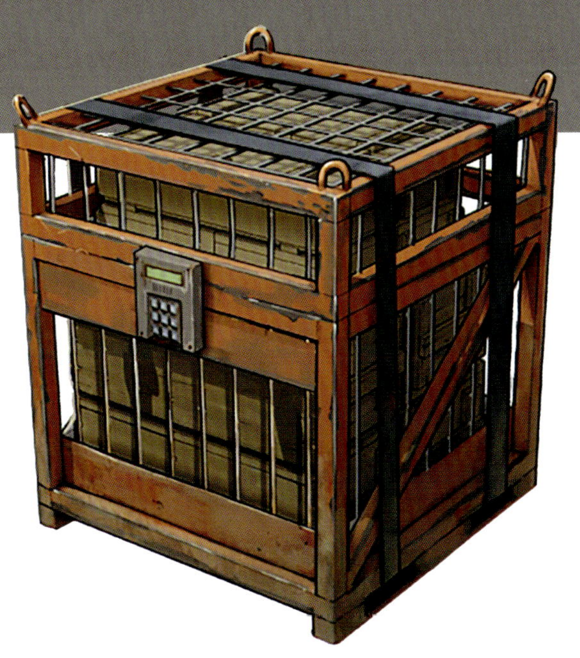

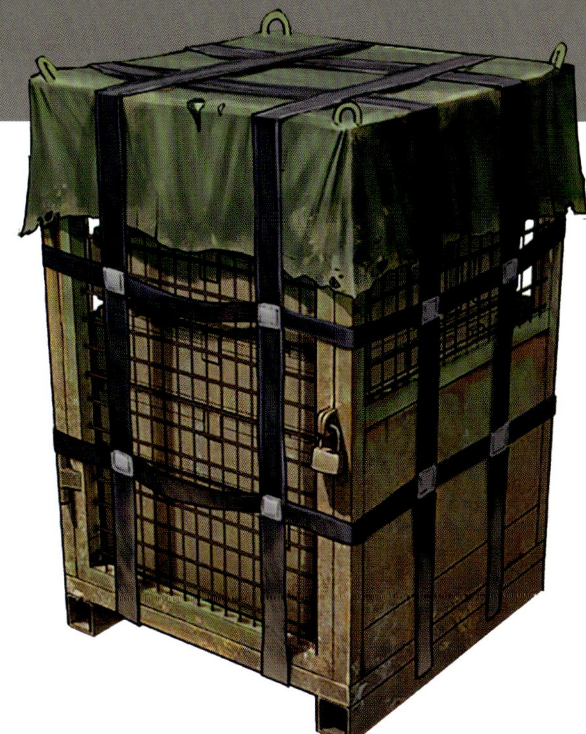

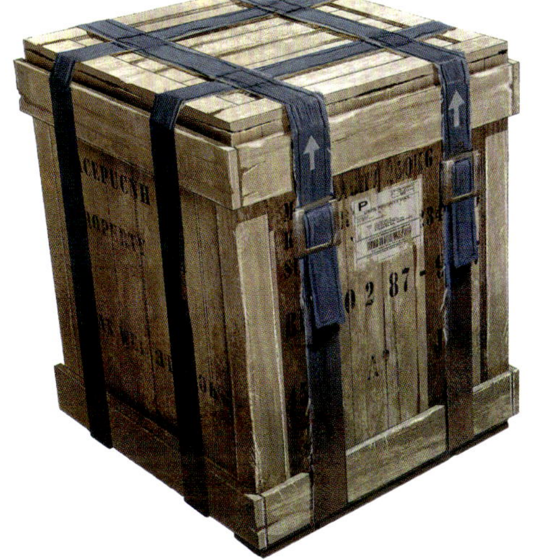

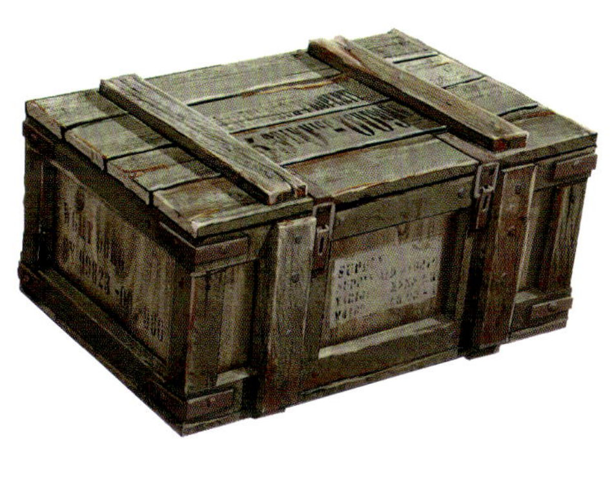

LOOT CRATES

There are a variety of Loot Crates in *Rust*, constructed from wood, netting, and metal caging. Their scarcity depends on location and the loot inside. Some are locked, holding valuable items like weapons or high-tech components; others are more common, spawning near monuments or alongside the road.

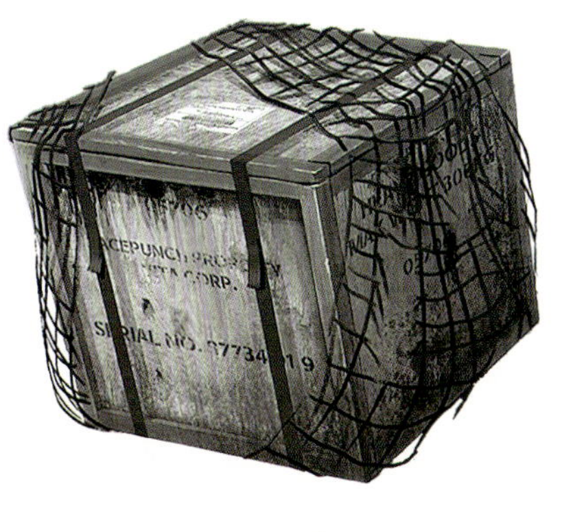

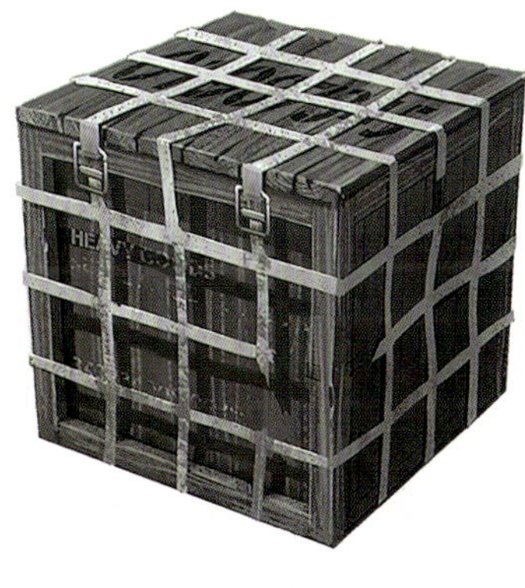

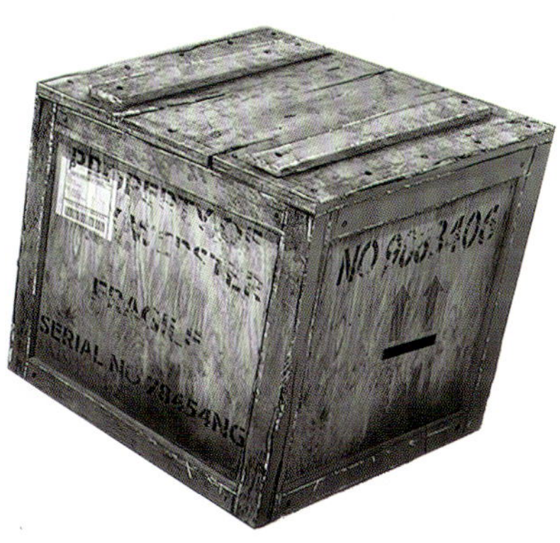

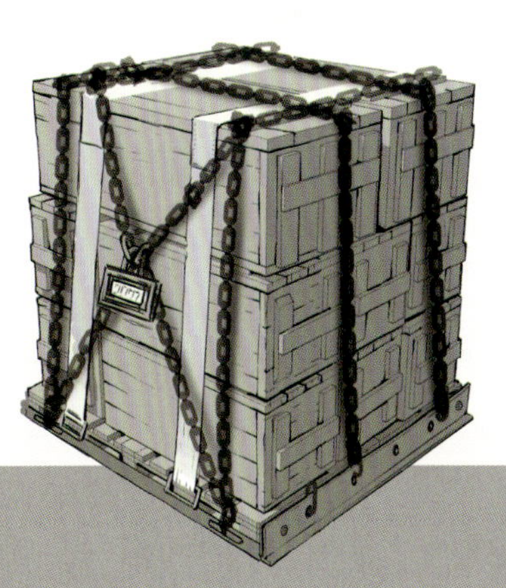

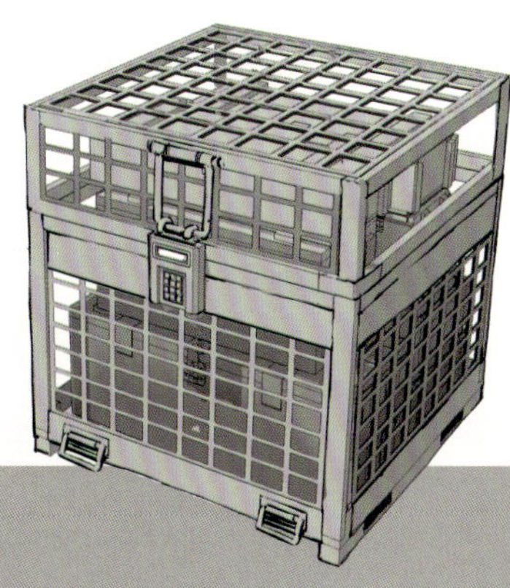

ELEVATORS

Based on an industrial warehouse elevator, these concepts show a few variations of how the structure, motor mechanism, and aesthetic could look and function. In the game, some Elevators can be found built into monuments, but they can also be crafted for advanced base builds.

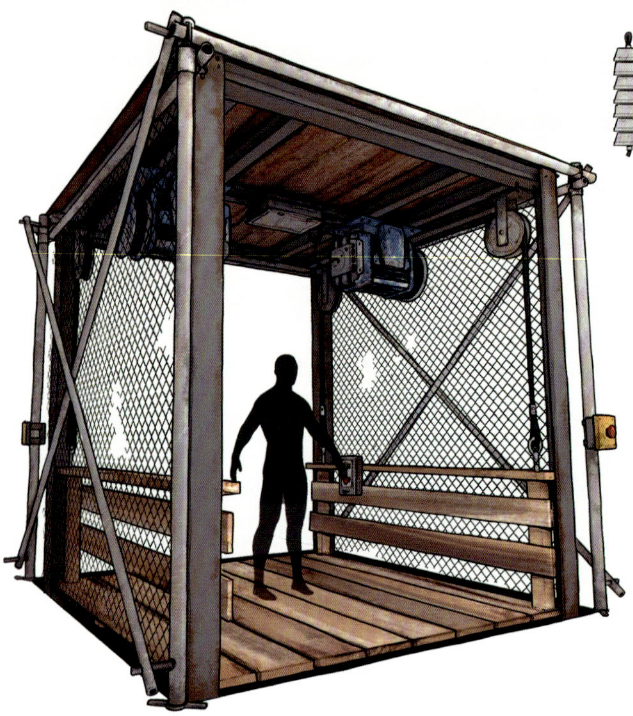

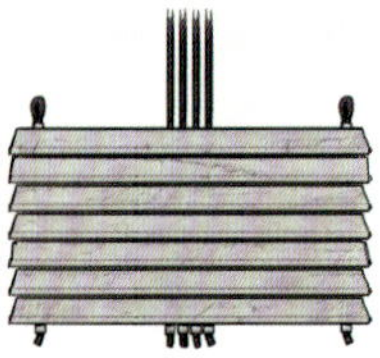

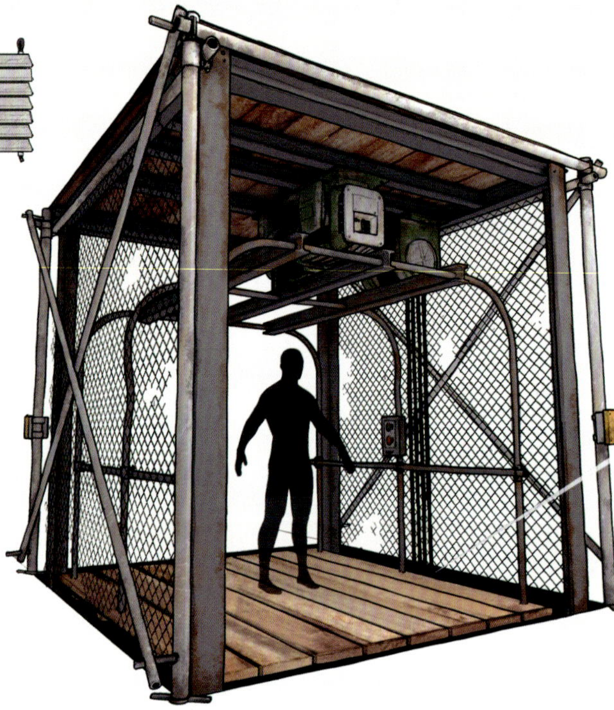

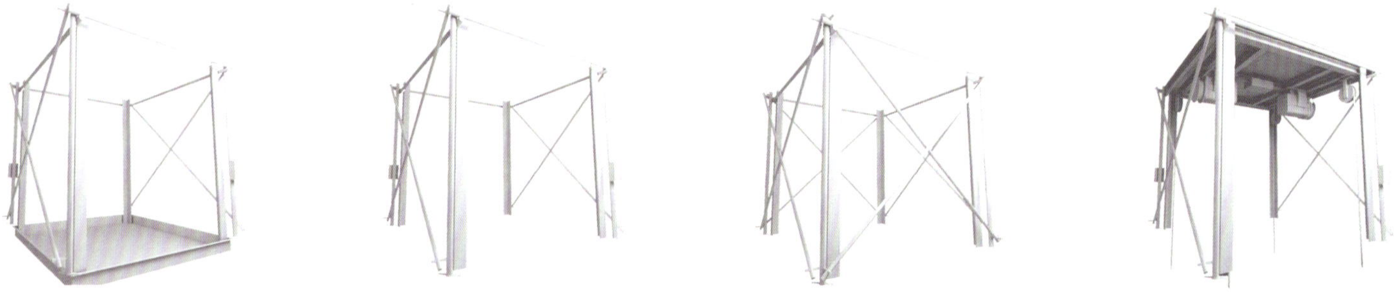

LOCKED DOORS

Locked Doors in *Rust* mainly feature in monuments and other points of interest. Their design is inspired by a naval-style or vault-like door with heavy-duty reinforced metal framing and a spinning locking mechanism.

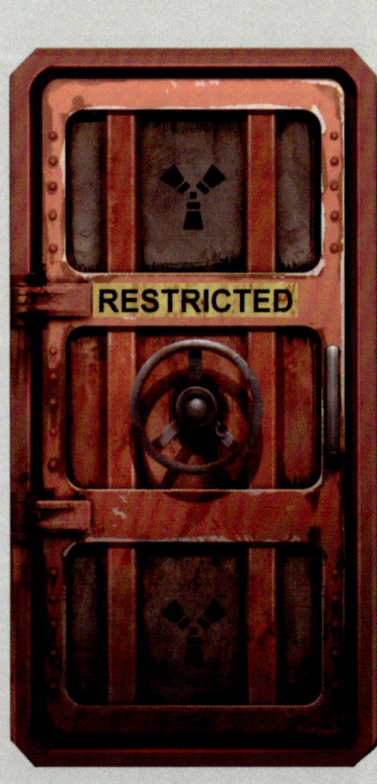

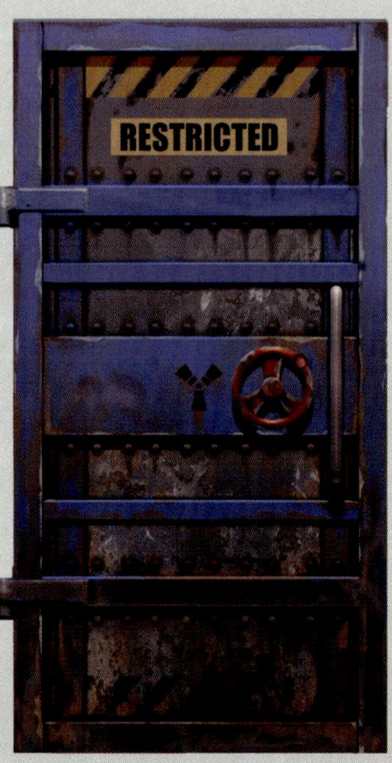

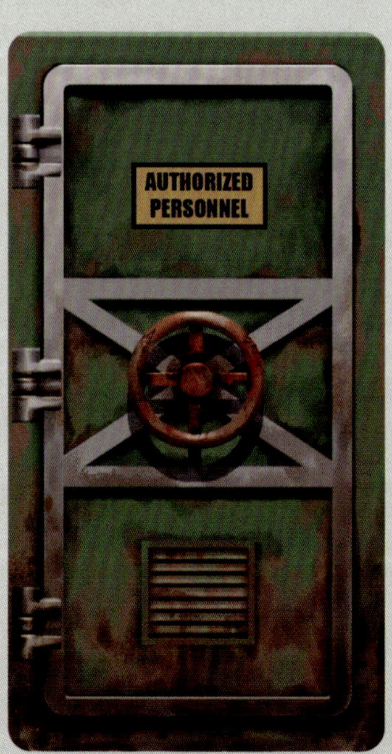

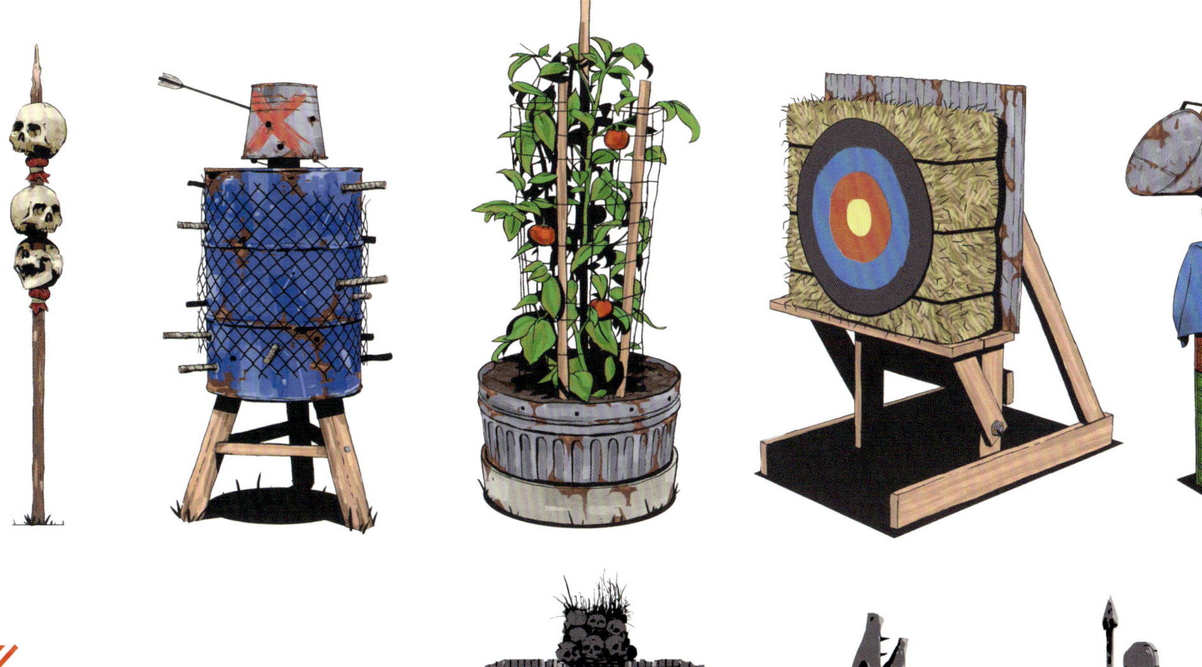

DECOR

Decor props were designed to offer players a way to personalize their bases while still serving a purpose. Whether it's a radio that plays music or a dummy for target practice, decorations are meant to feel useful, not just ornamental

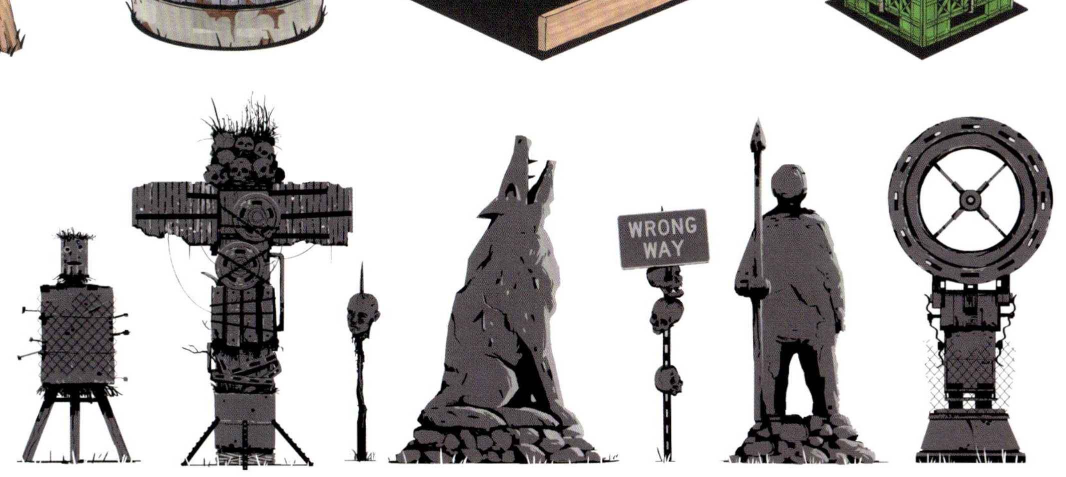

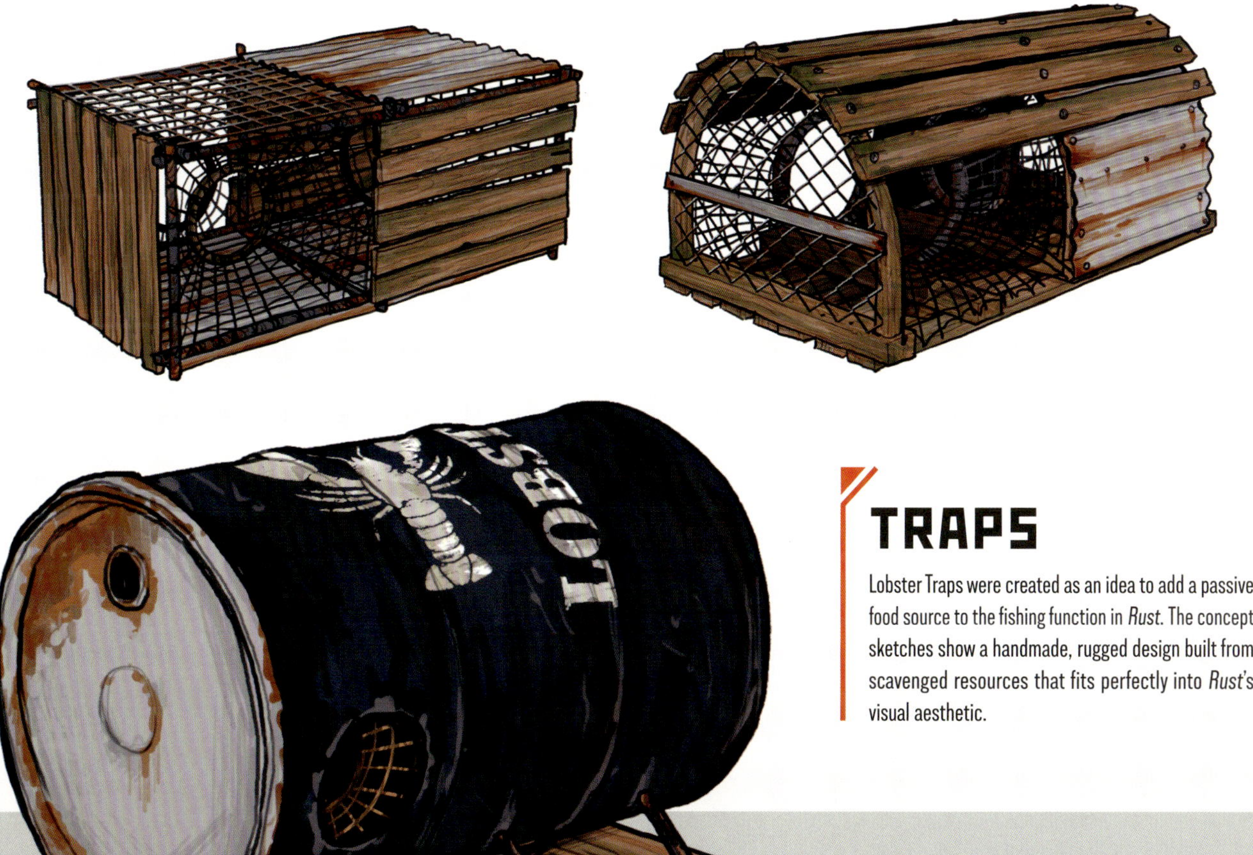

TRAPS

Lobster Traps were created as an idea to add a passive food source to the fishing function in *Rust*. The concept sketches show a handmade, rugged design built from scavenged resources that fits perfectly into *Rust*'s visual aesthetic.

FURNACE

The Furnace is a key crafting tool central to *Rust*'s gameplay. Players can craft different types of Furnace depending on their progression. The concepts below show the development of the standard Furnace and the Electric Furnace, alongside the BBQ and Water Treatment deployables.

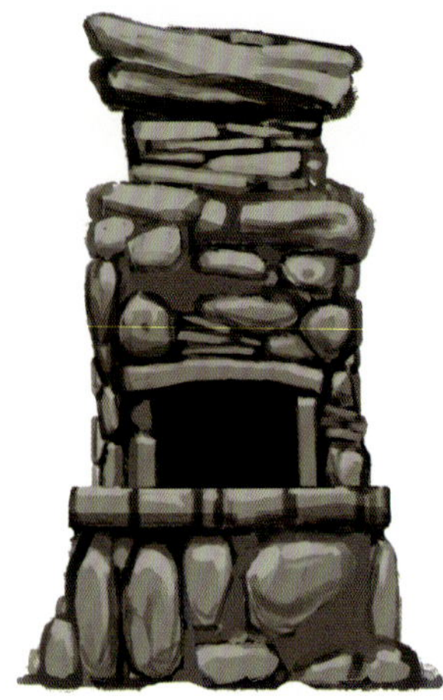
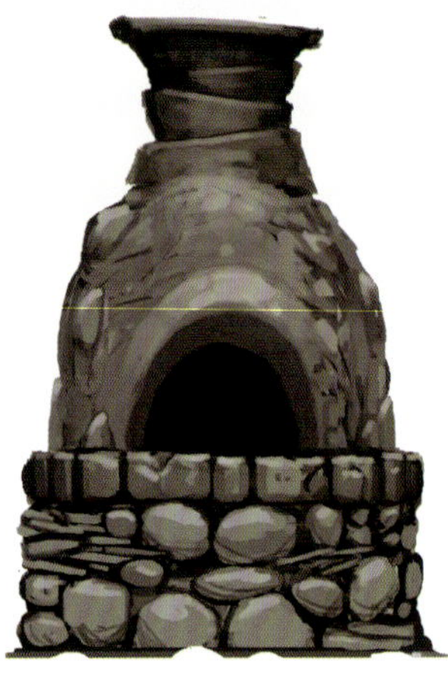
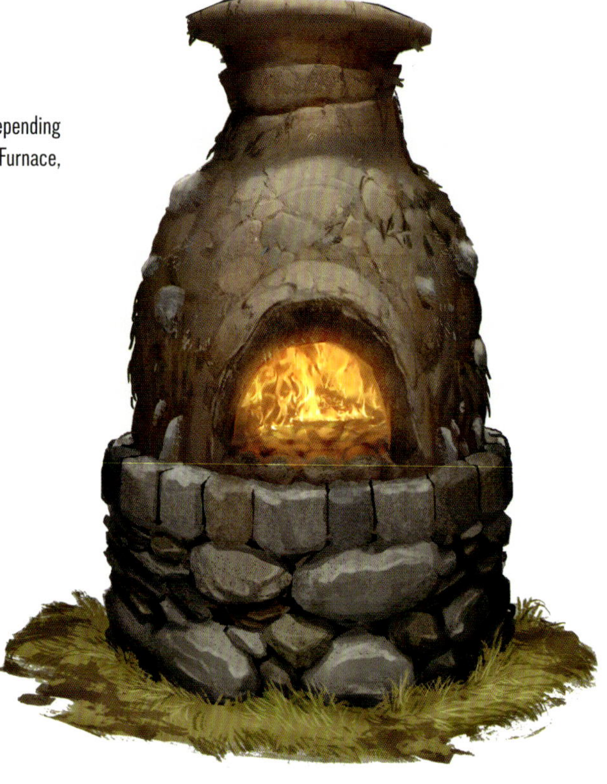
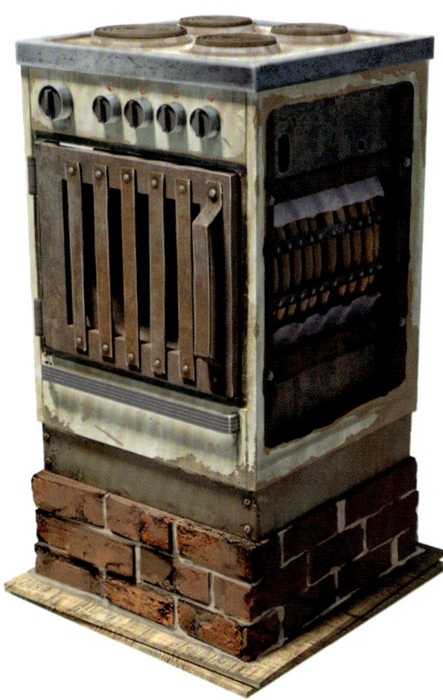
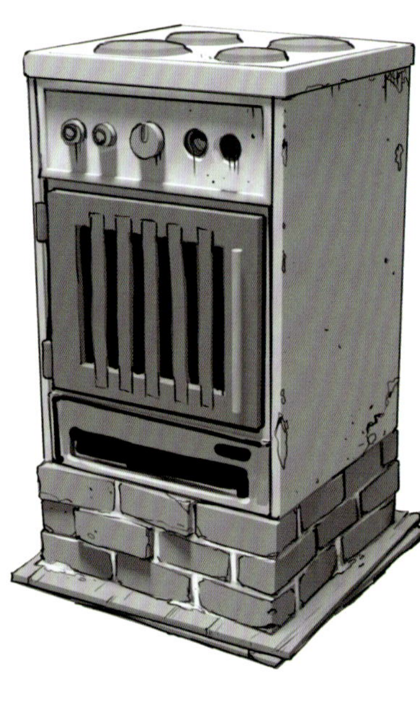
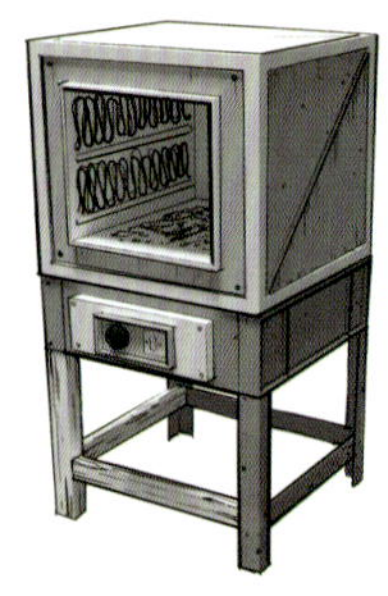
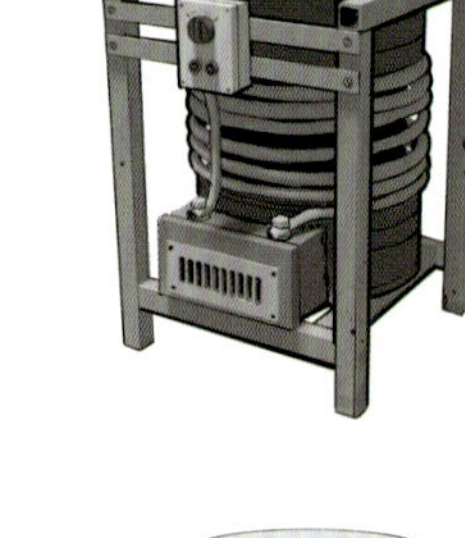
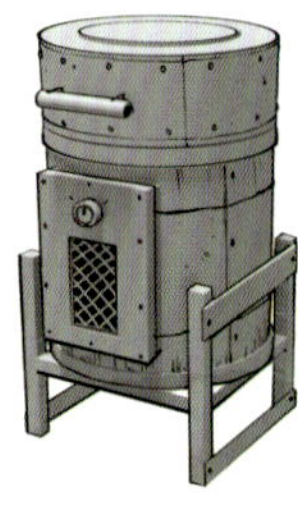
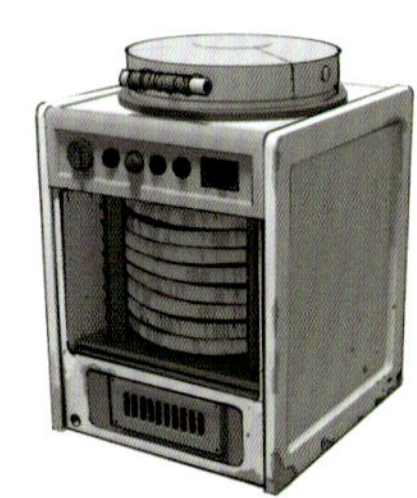
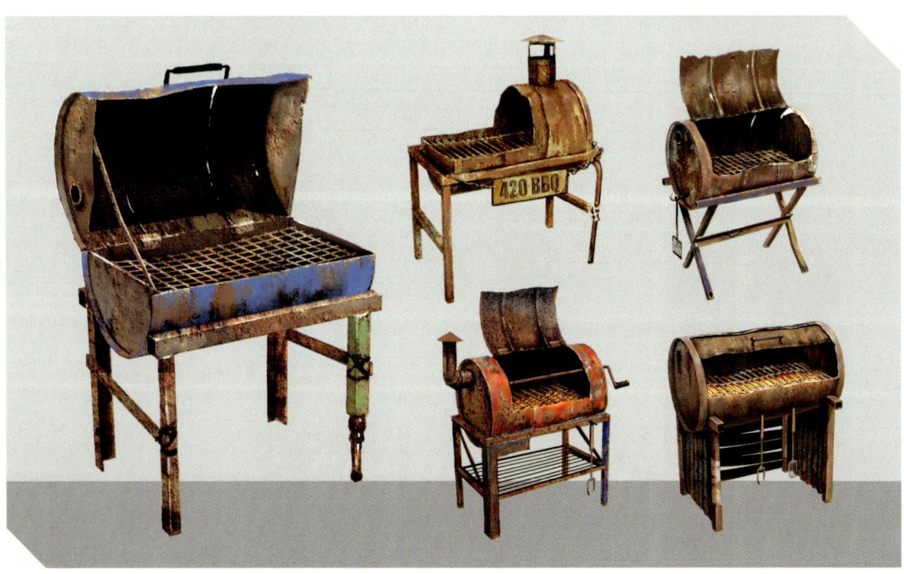

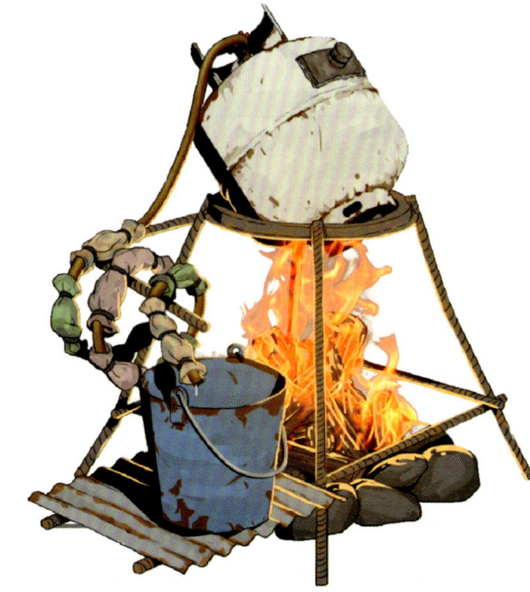

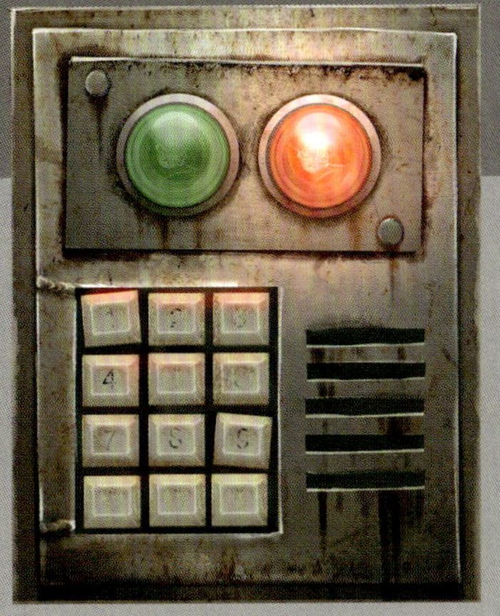

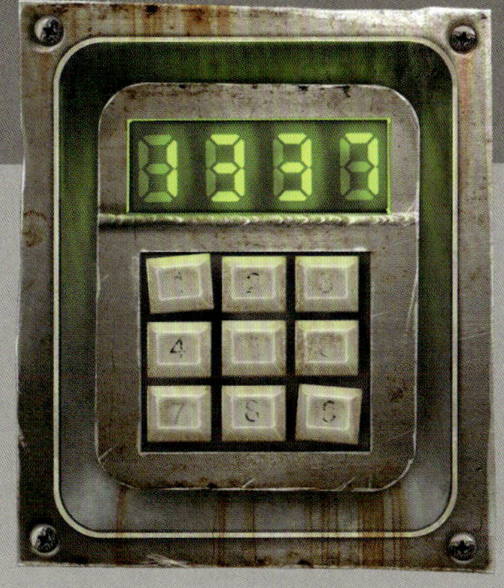

VENDING MACHINES AND CODE LOCKS

The Code Lock is the most secure way to protect a player's base. Secured by entering a four-digit PIN in a prompt, any player can attempt to enter a base. The below images also show some variants of the Coded Door Lock and Vending Machines.

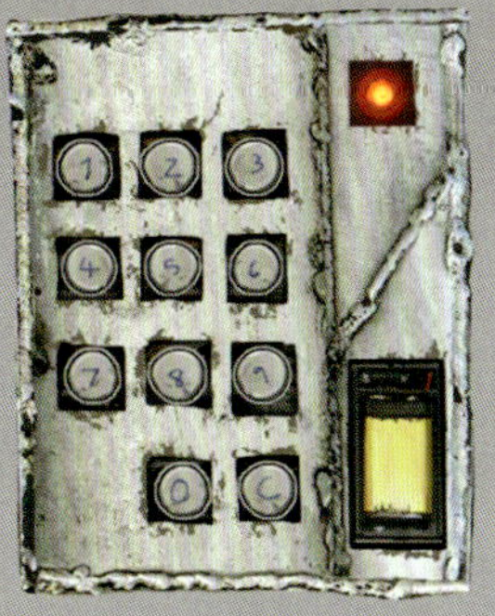

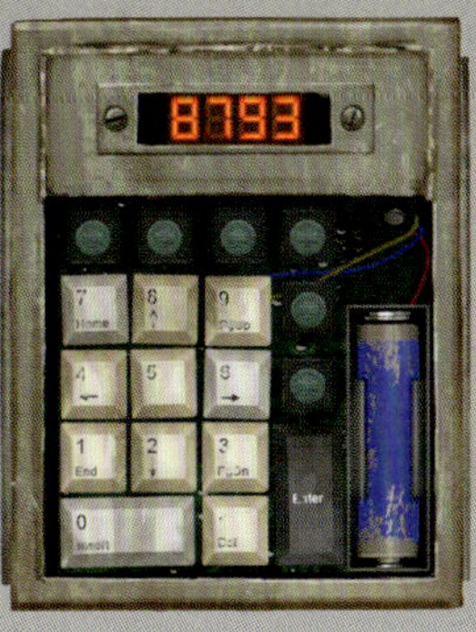

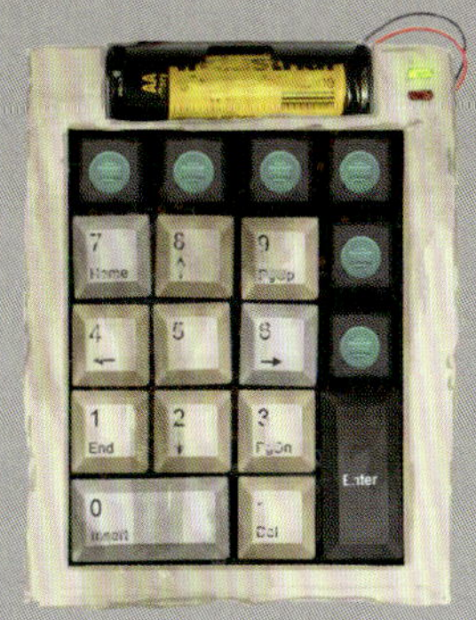

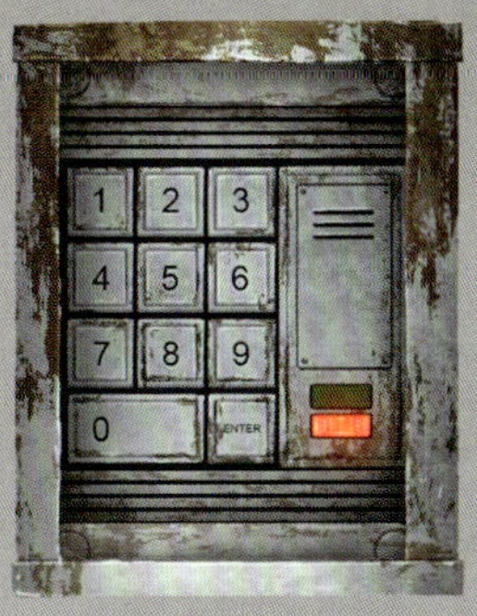

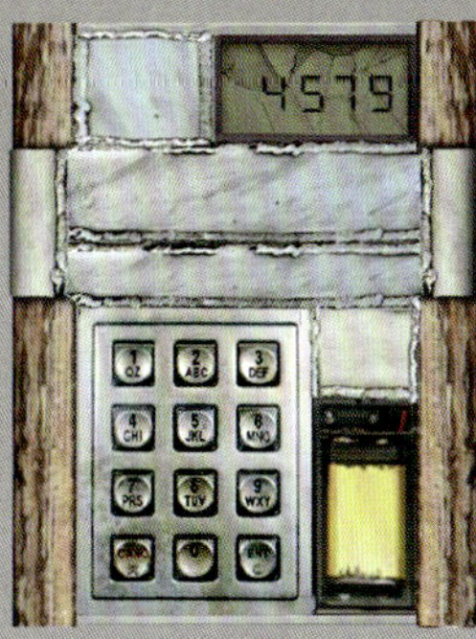

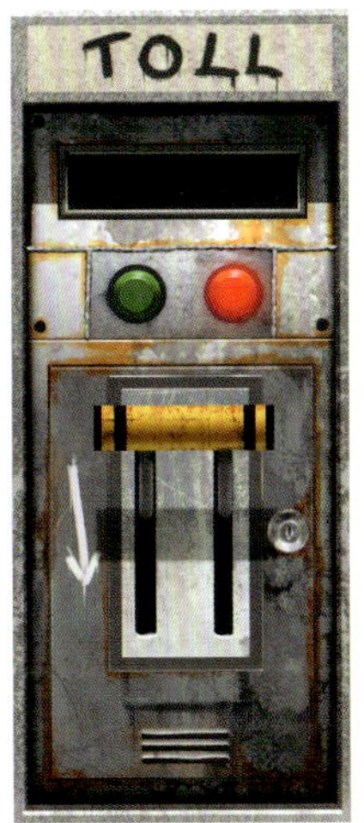

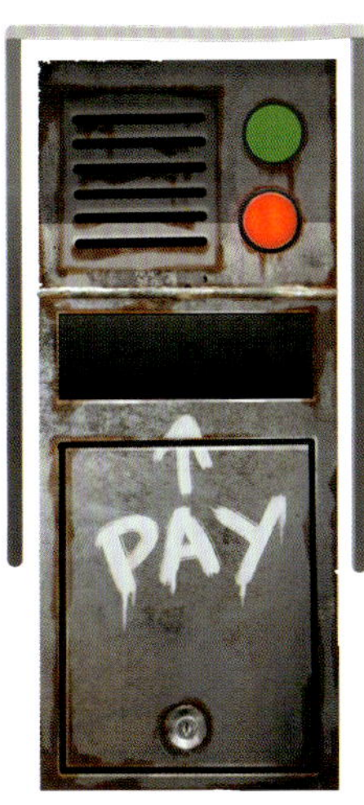

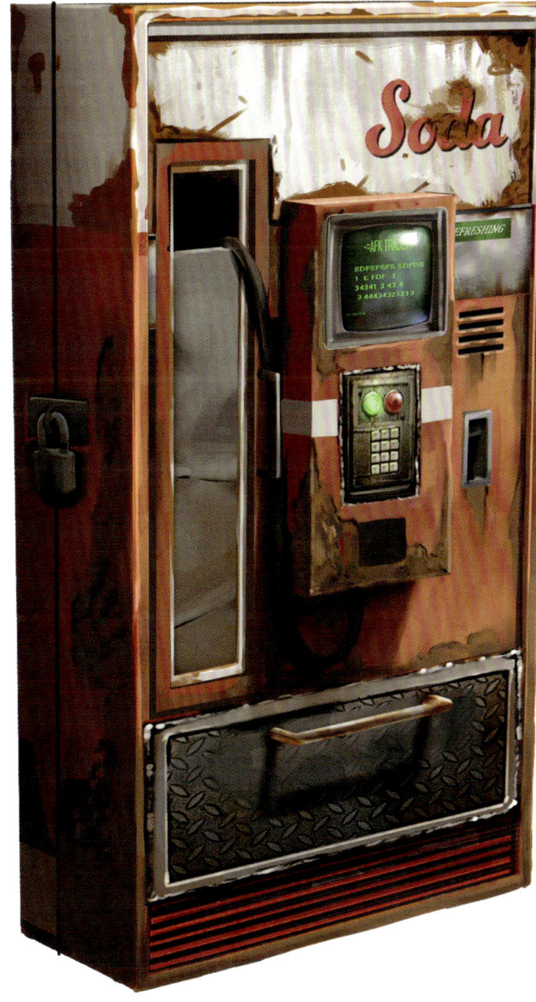

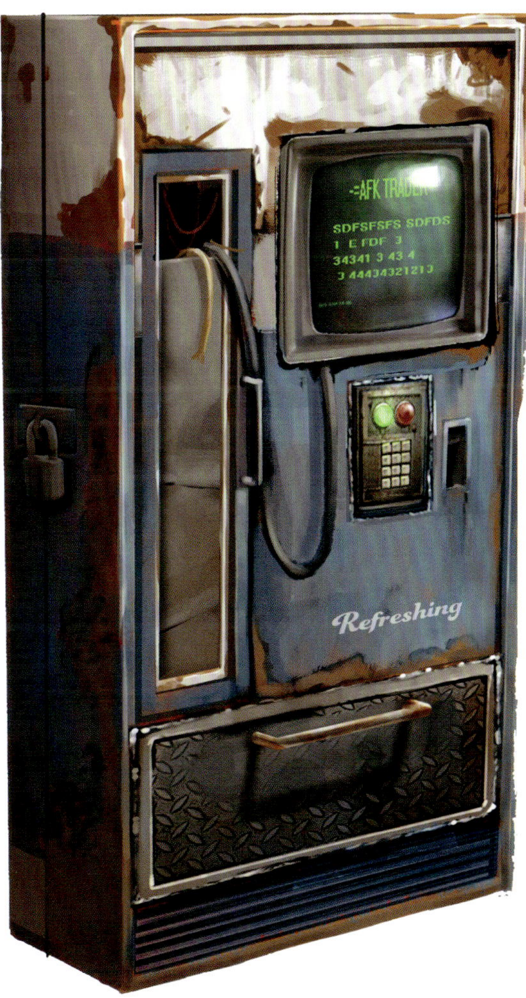

SORTING MACHINES

Farming resources and collecting loot are integral to *Rust*'s gameplay. This concept explores the idea of dropping all your loot into a large Sorting Machine, then having the machine organize it into boxes.

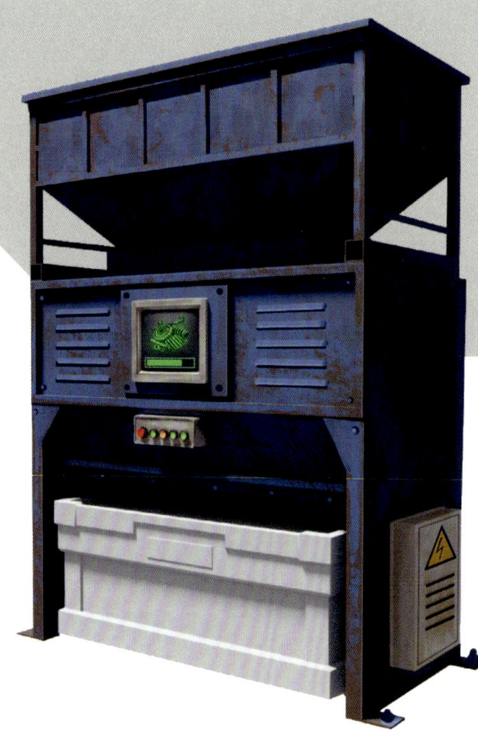

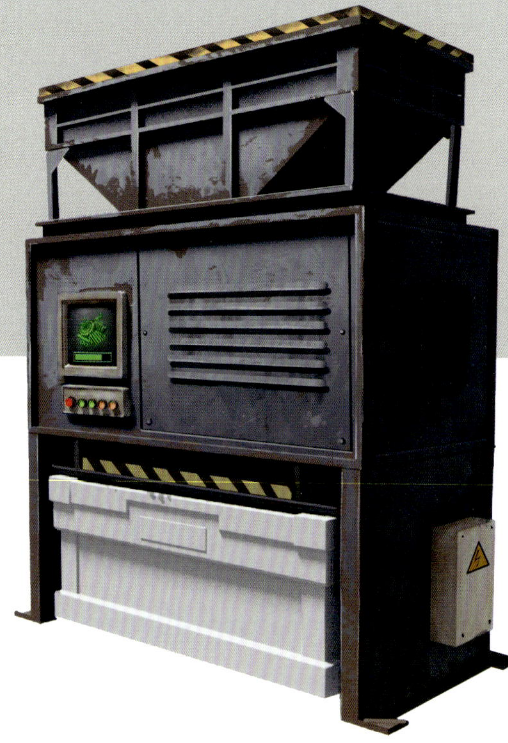

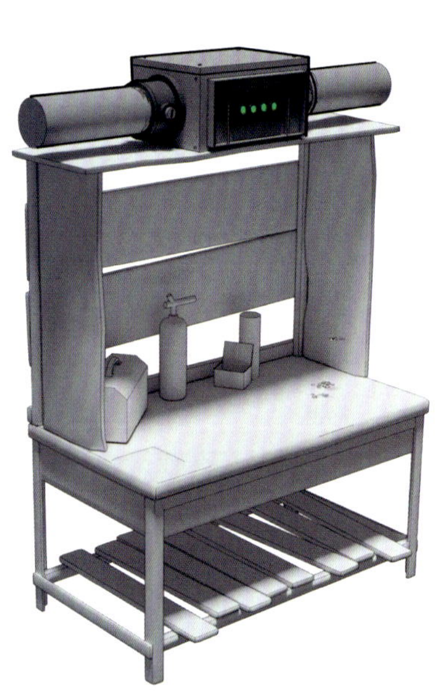

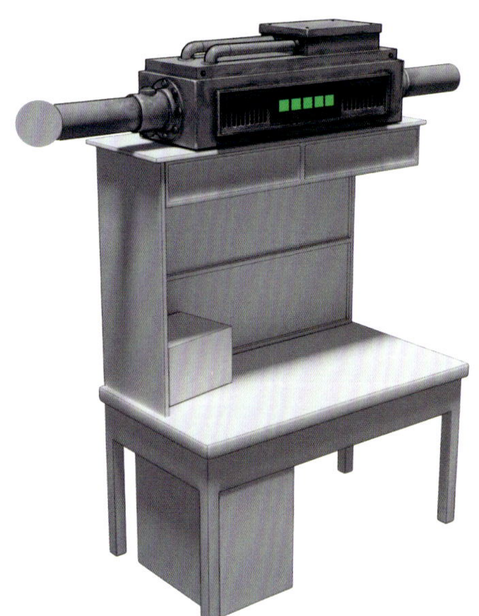

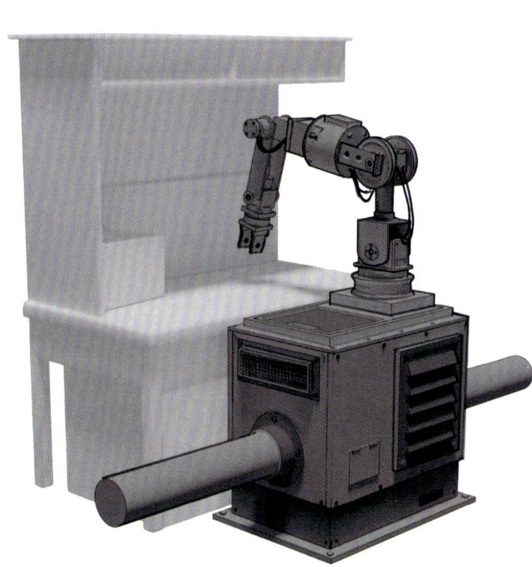

SORTING ADAPTOR

The Sorting Adaptor is the concept progression from the Sorting Machine, a much smaller and easier deployable to manage when automating your loot. The challenge with these concepts was visually making them easy to understand and use, even though the technology behind them is completely impossible in real life.

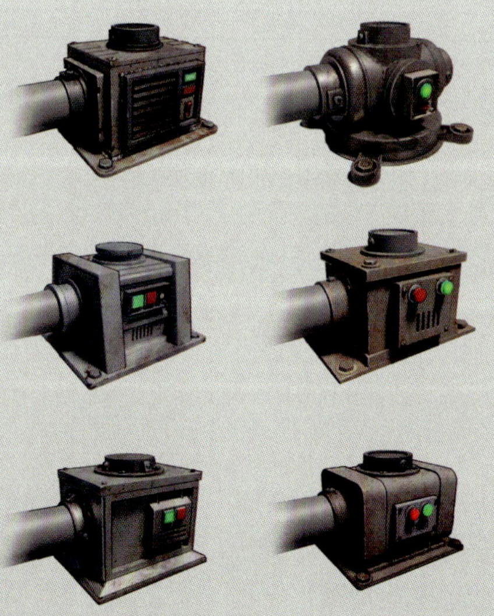

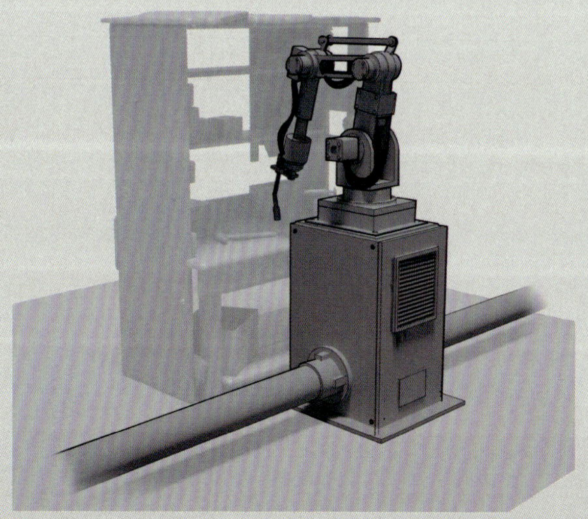

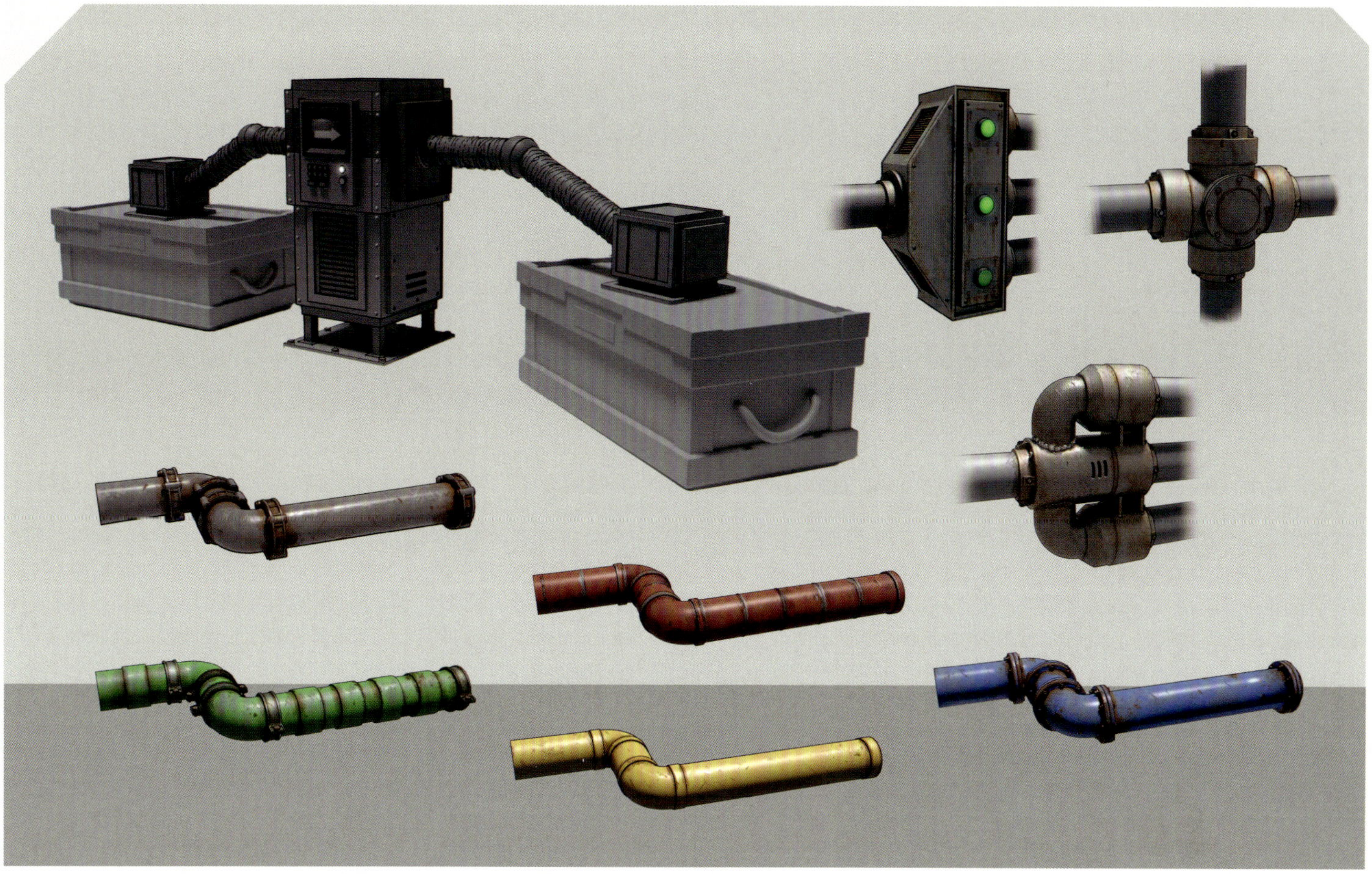

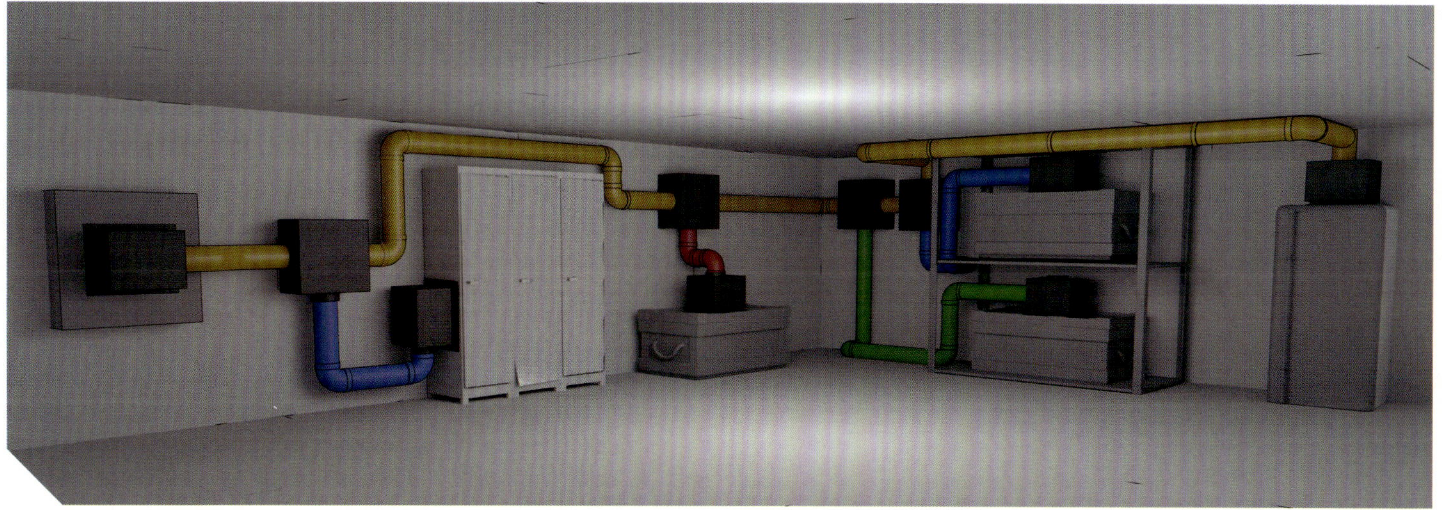

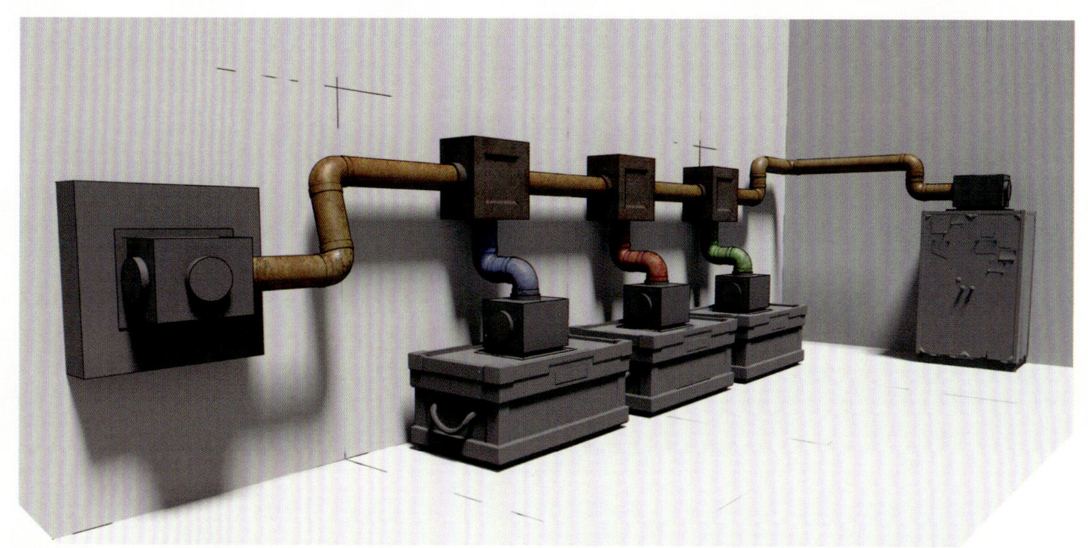

SORTING PIPES

The Sorting Pipes system helps move your loot around from box to box. The design had to be clear and understandable, as the system can get quite complicated. Colored pipes ended up being the perfect fix.

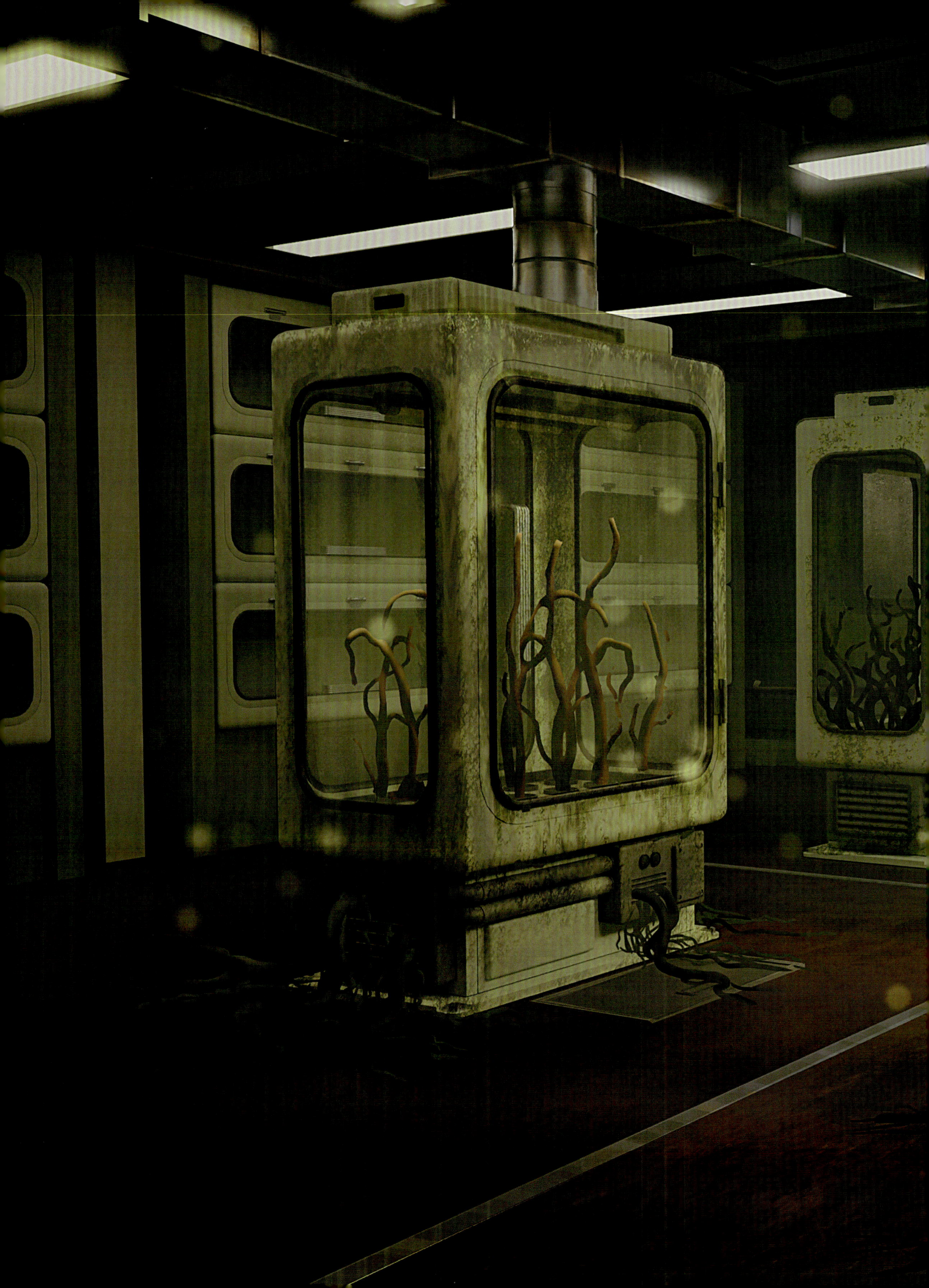

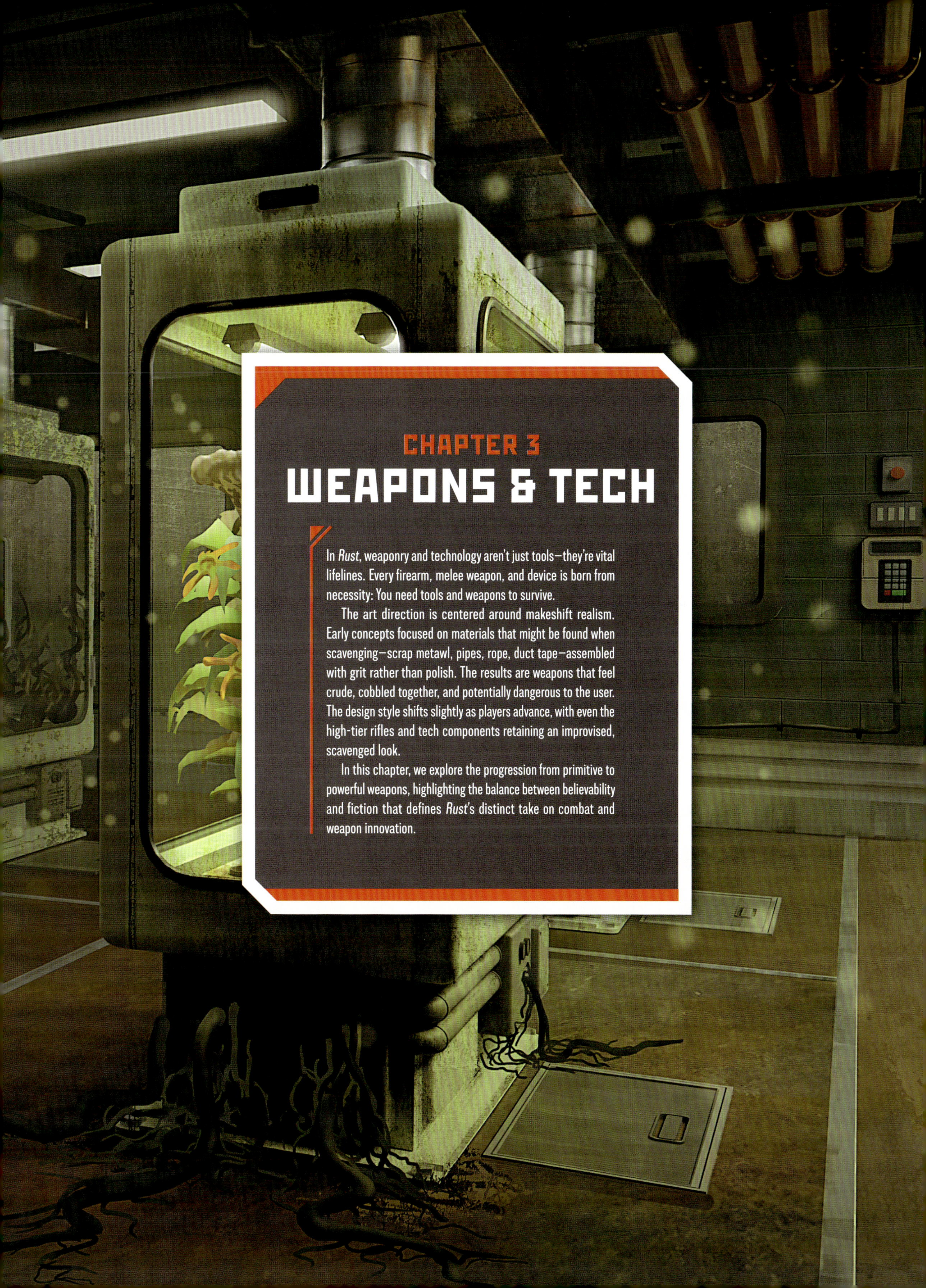

CHAPTER 3

WEAPONS & TECH

In *Rust*, weaponry and technology aren't just tools—they're vital lifelines. Every firearm, melee weapon, and device is born from necessity: You need tools and weapons to survive.

The art direction is centered around makeshift realism. Early concepts focused on materials that might be found when scavenging—scrap metawl, pipes, rope, duct tape—assembled with grit rather than polish. The results are weapons that feel crude, cobbled together, and potentially dangerous to the user. The design style shifts slightly as players advance, with even the high-tier rifles and tech components retaining an improvised, scavenged look.

In this chapter, we explore the progression from primitive to powerful weapons, highlighting the balance between believability and fiction that defines *Rust*'s distinct take on combat and weapon innovation.

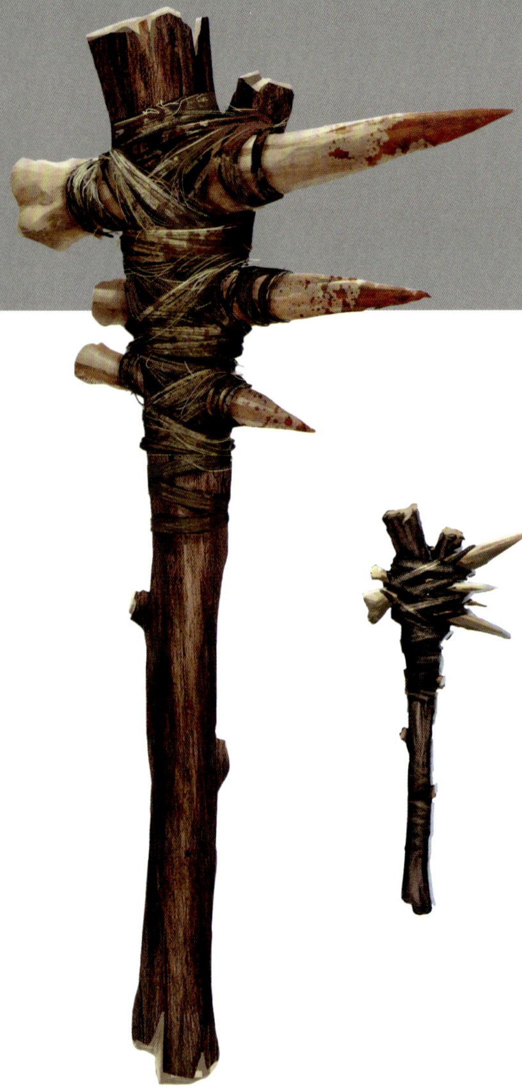

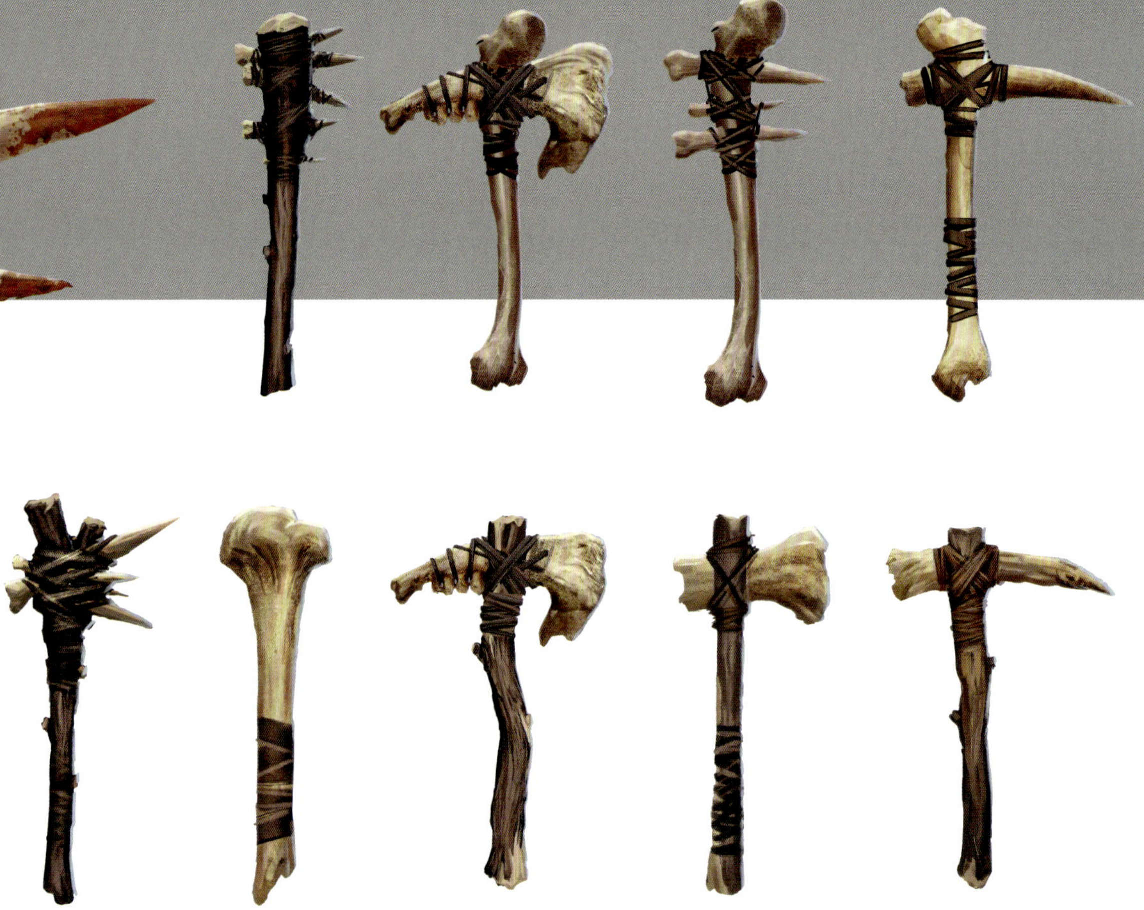

BONE TOOLS

These concept sketches explore *Rust*'s early-game melee weapons, crafted from bone, wood, and scrap and inspired by prehistoric tools. Embracing a raw, makeshift aesthetic, each piece is designed to feel desperate yet functional, perfectly grounded in the fictional realism of *Rust*.

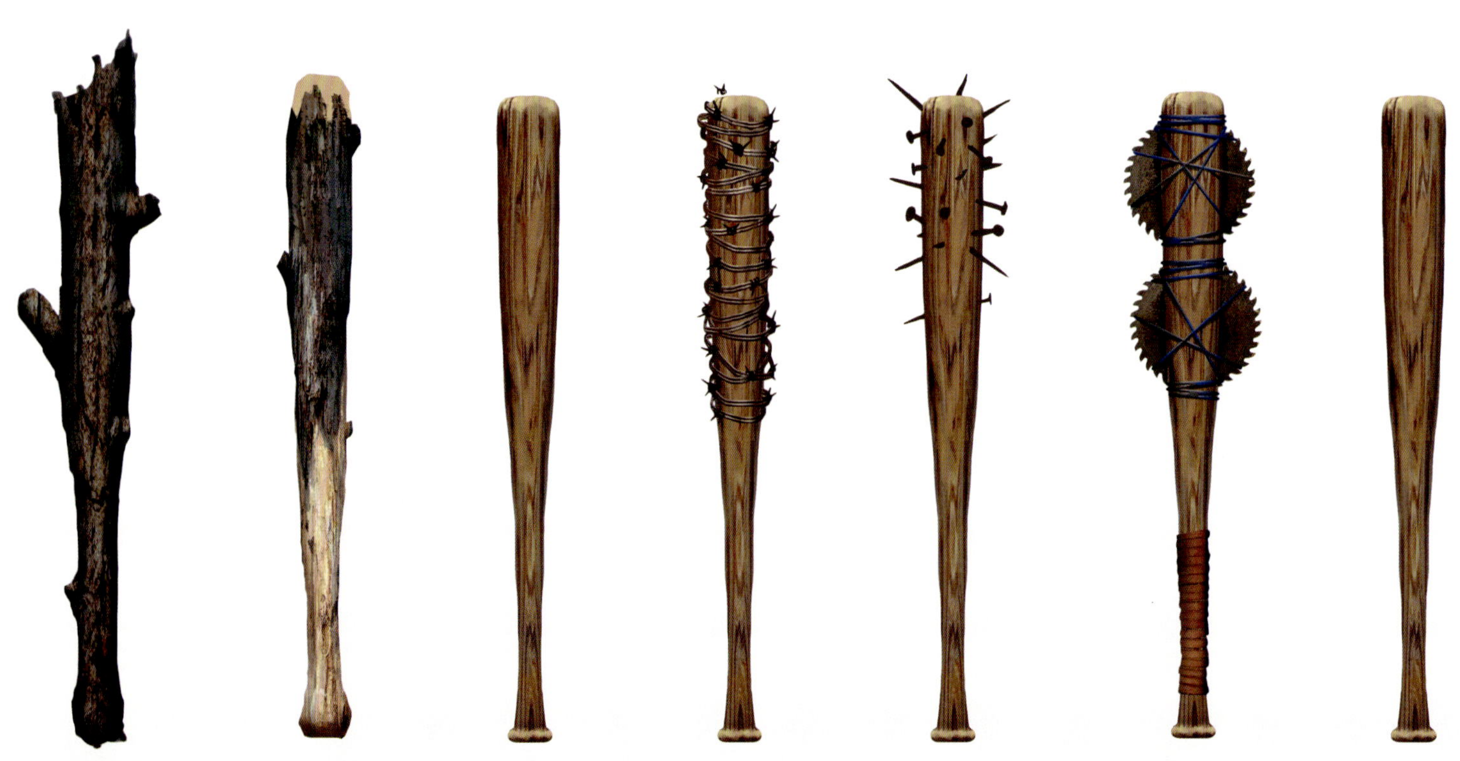

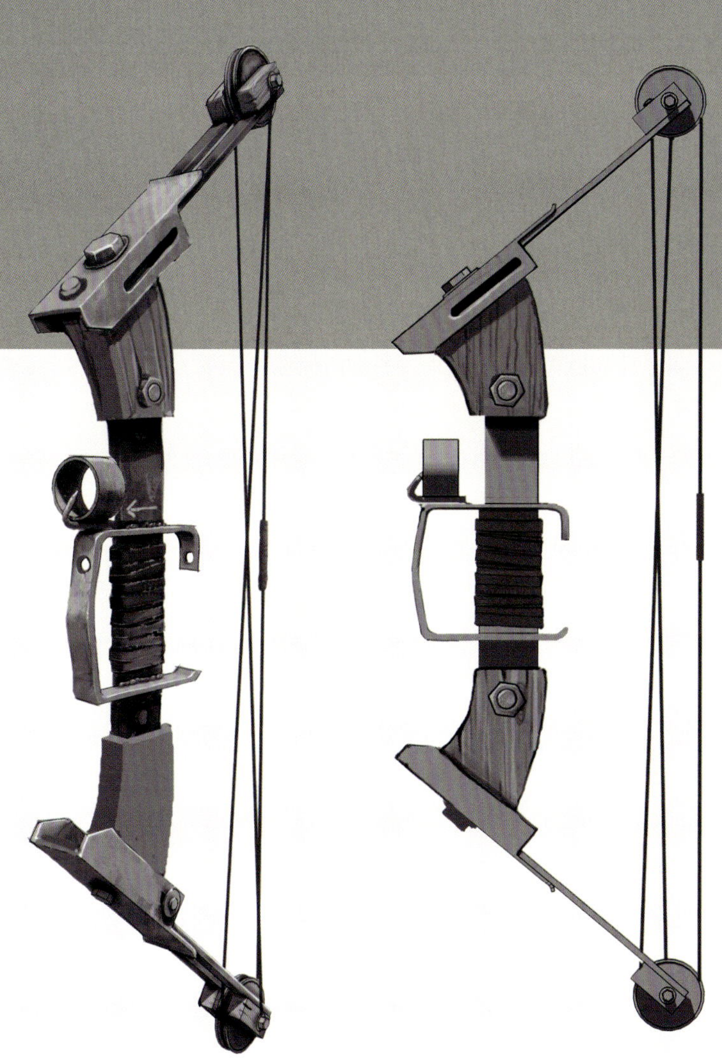

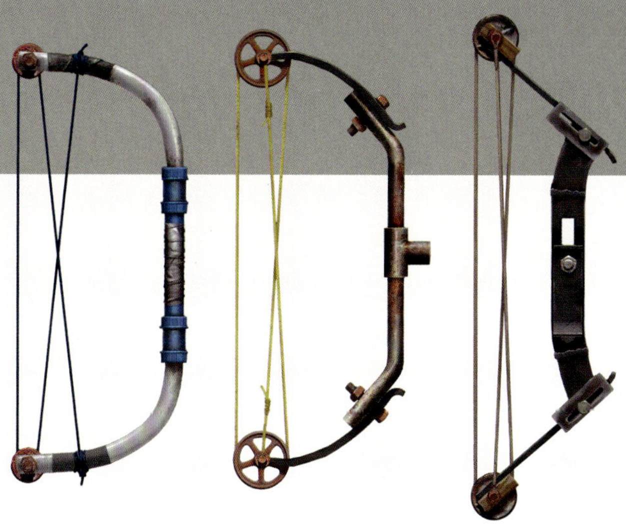

BOWS

Here are some concept sketches of Bows and Crossbows essential to the early game in *Rust*. The designs show a scrappy, DIY, and improvised look. Each item feels handcrafted and rough but functional, capturing the effect of weapons built from whatever materials are available.

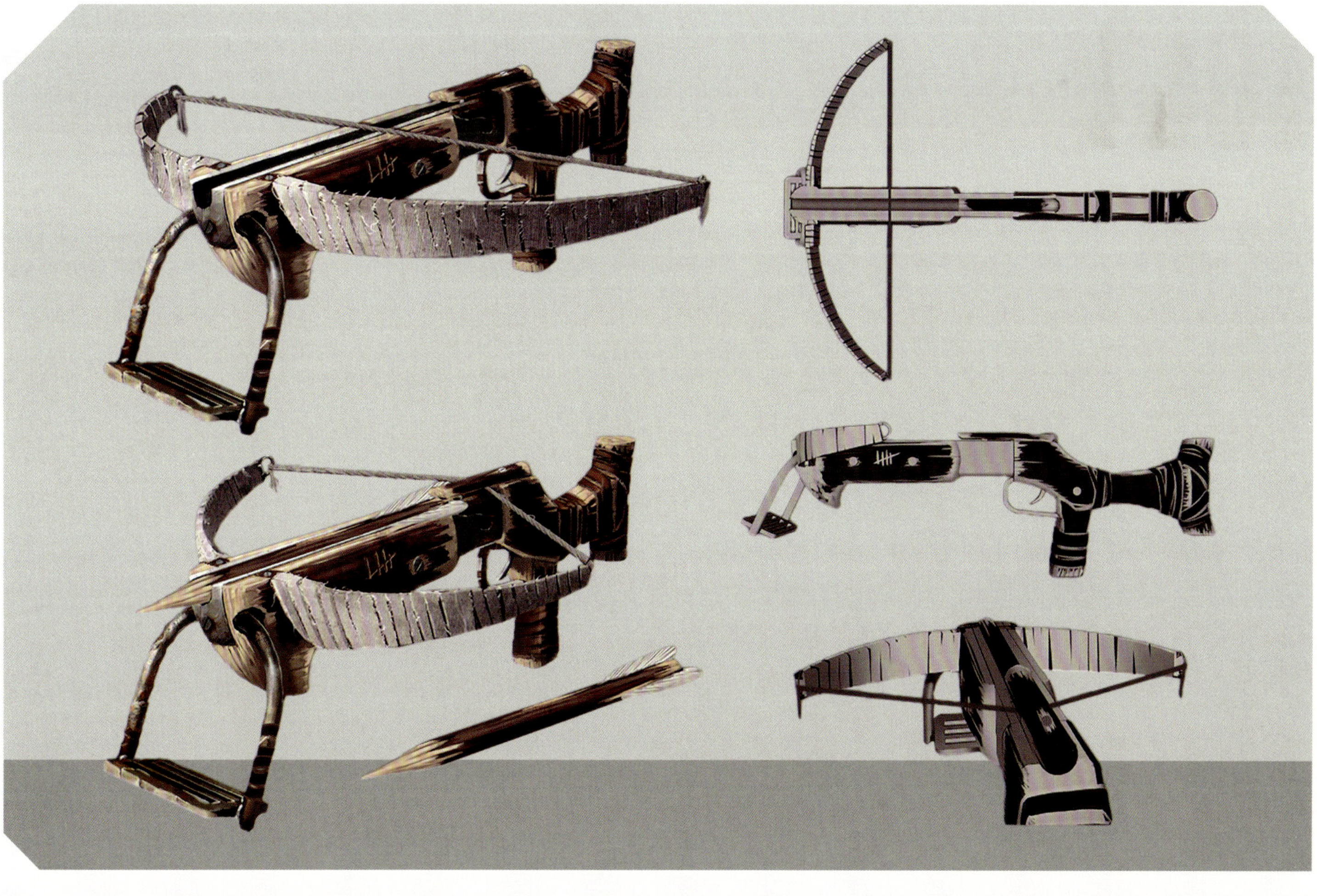

AXES, STONE HATCHETS, AND PICKAXES

Stone Hatchets, Axes, and Pickaxes are some of the first items players craft in *Rust*; they're essential for gathering wood and stone and for defense if needed. Each tool is made of raw materials, like sticks, stones, and cloth wraps, again inspired by prehistoric tools and weapons.

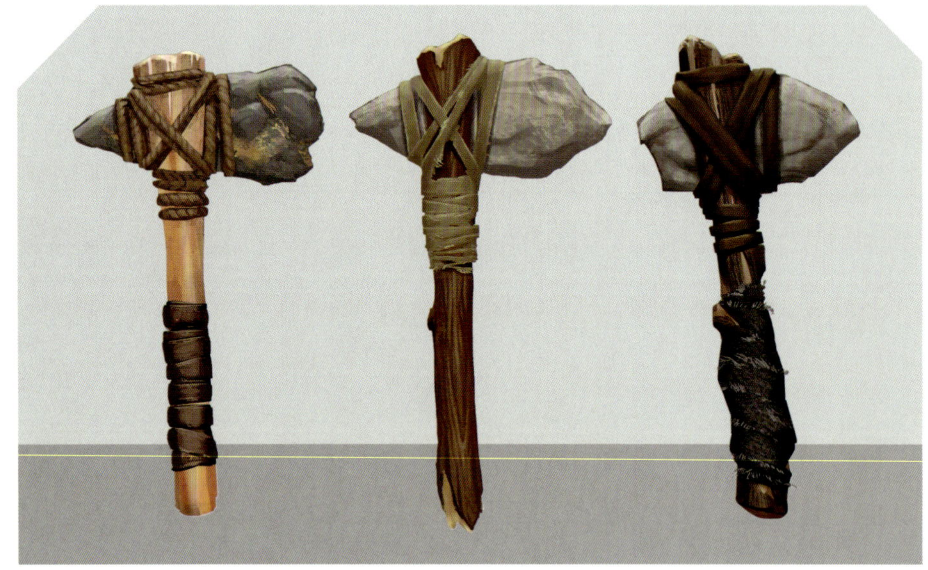

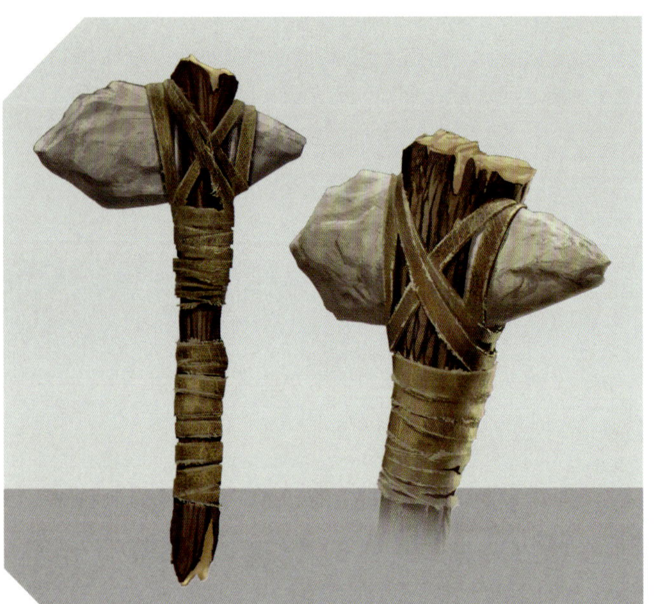

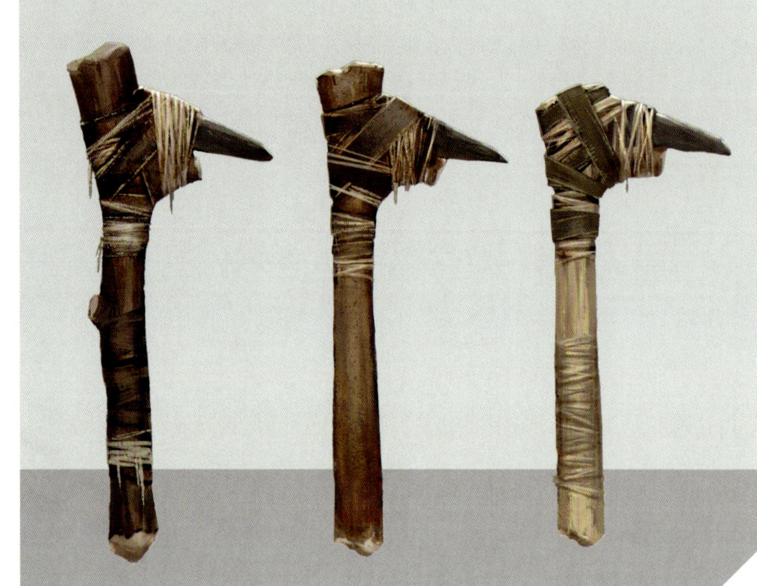

TORCH

The Torch is a starter item made from a stick wrapped with cloth and smeared with flammable tree resin. It allows players to see at night or light up their bases.

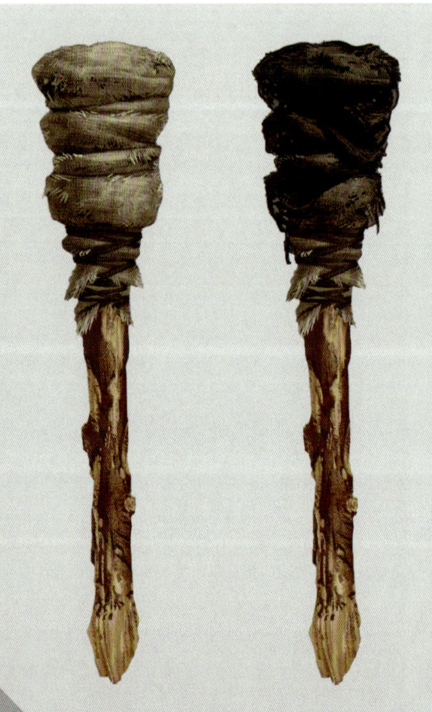

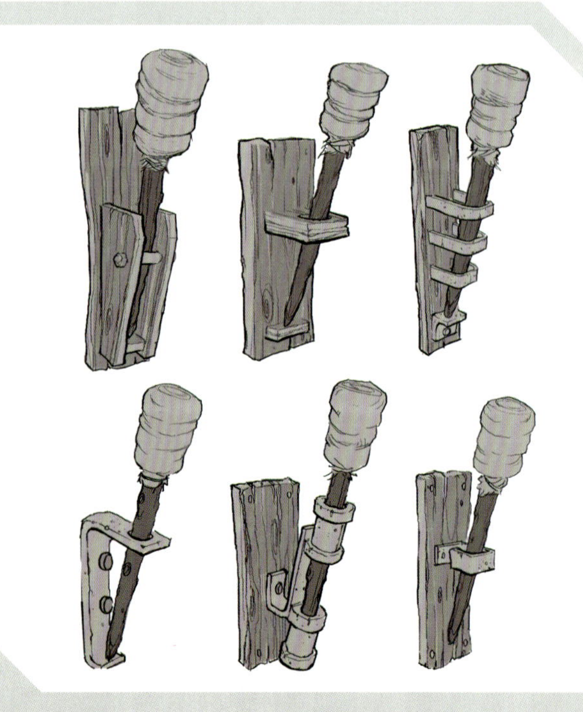

MELEE WEAPONS

Melee Weapons were inspired by medieval close-combat weapons but with a modern scavenged twist. The designs are kept simple and practical, with a handmade and improvised look, as if they were quickly assembled to serve a purpose.

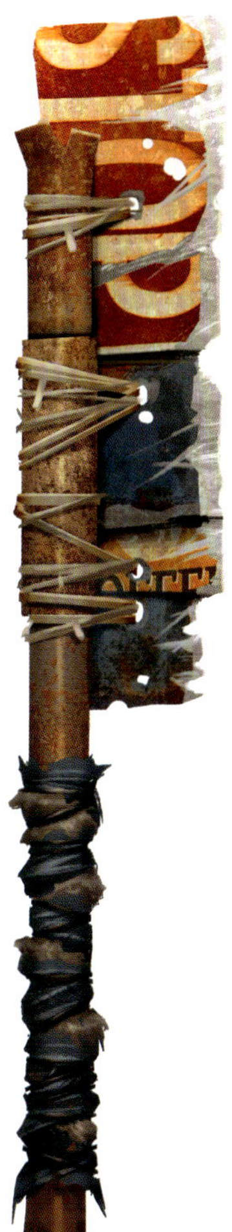

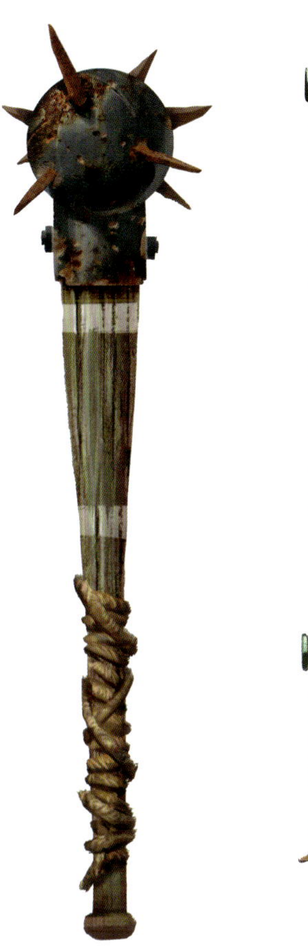

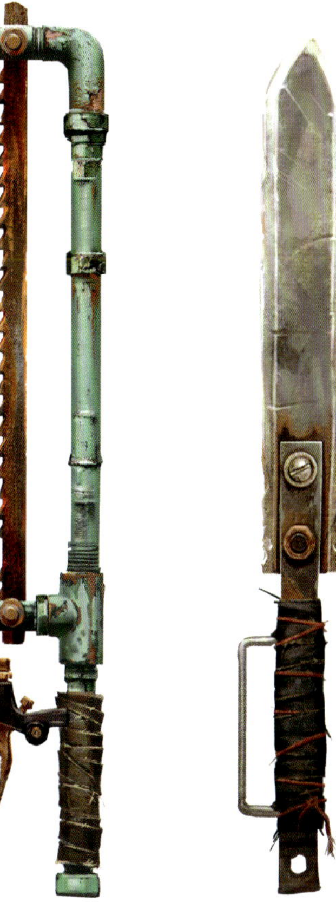

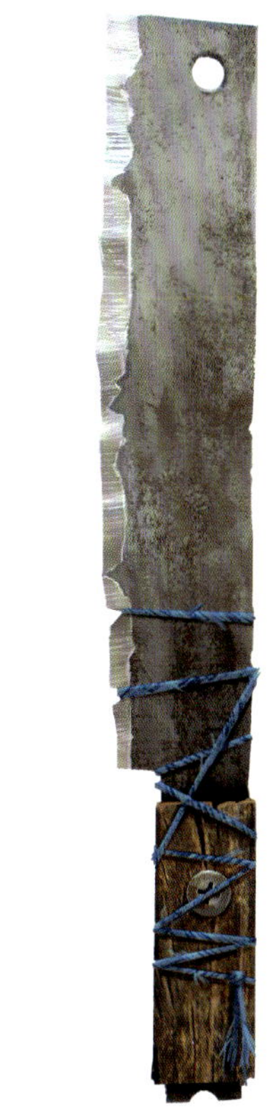

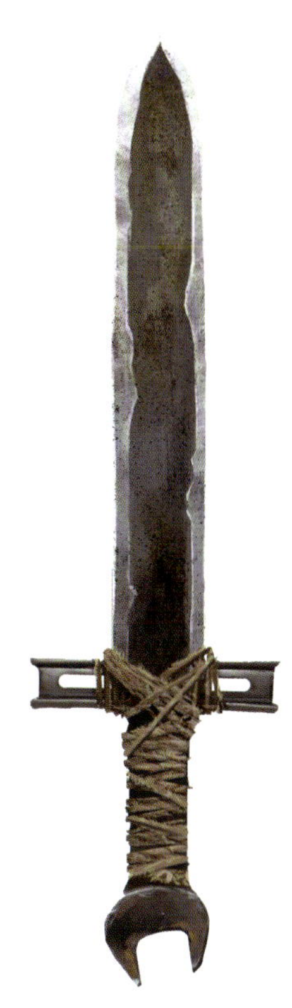

SCAVENGED TOOLS

Each scavenged tool was created from mismatched modern salvaged parts, like scrap metal heads, piping, or wheel hubs with bolts or bindings holding everything together. Their designs focus on practicality, showing clear wear and makeshift repairs that suggest they've been used and fixed many times.

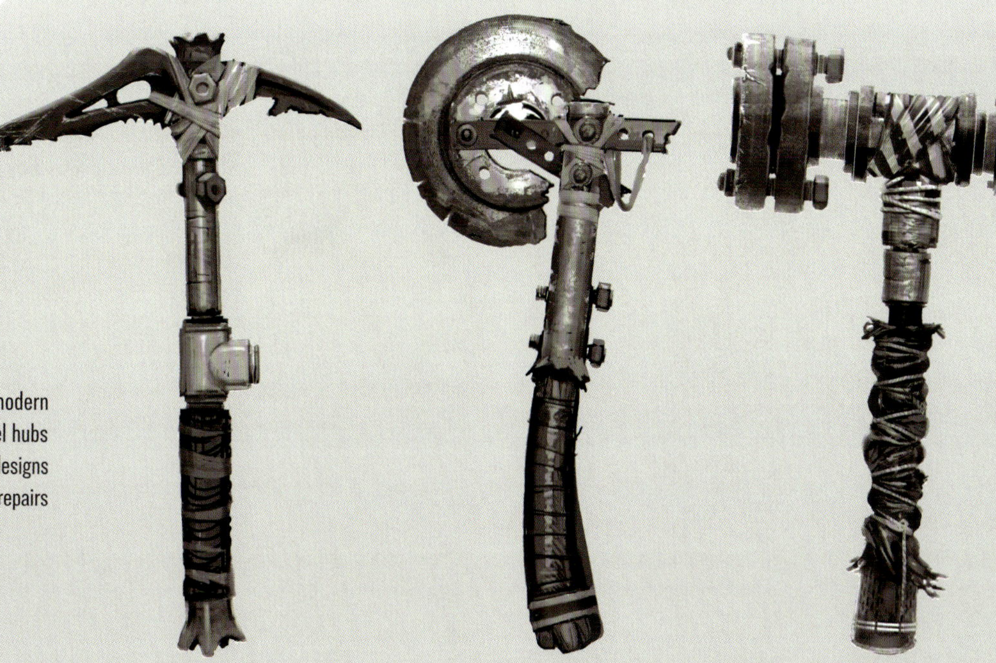

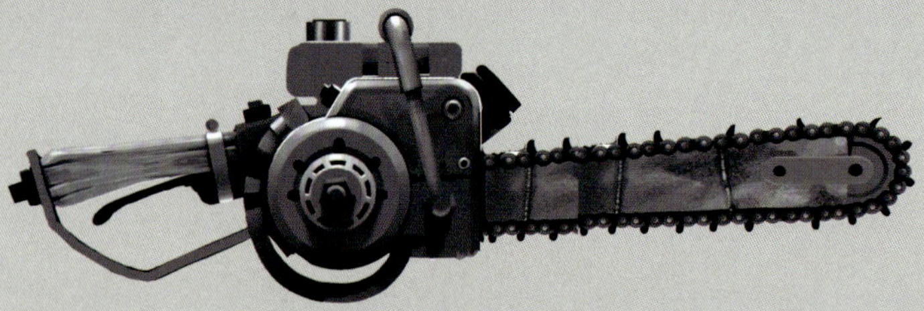

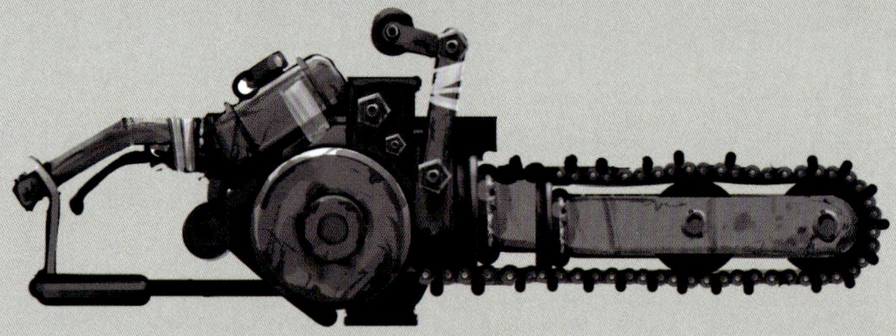

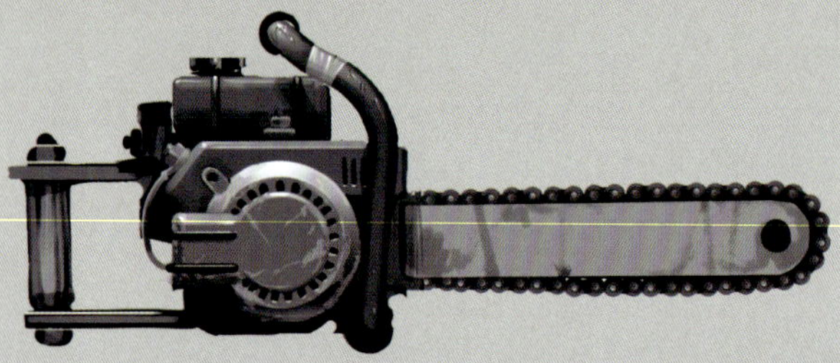

CHAINSAWS

The Chainsaw stands out as a more advanced tool, but its aesthetic is still barely functional and crude. These concepts show a variety of designs based on the same idea, including a rugged chain and improvised handles, all patched together with some scavenged old machinery parts.

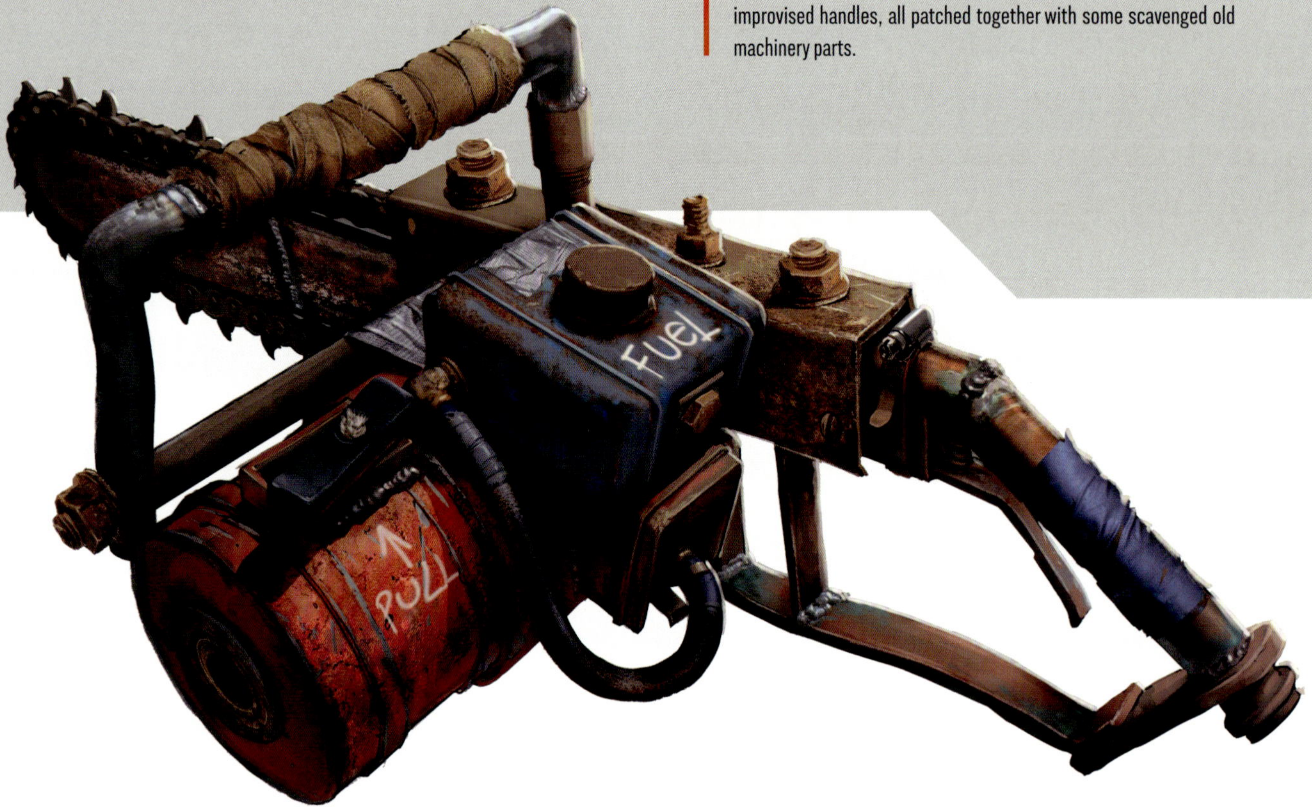

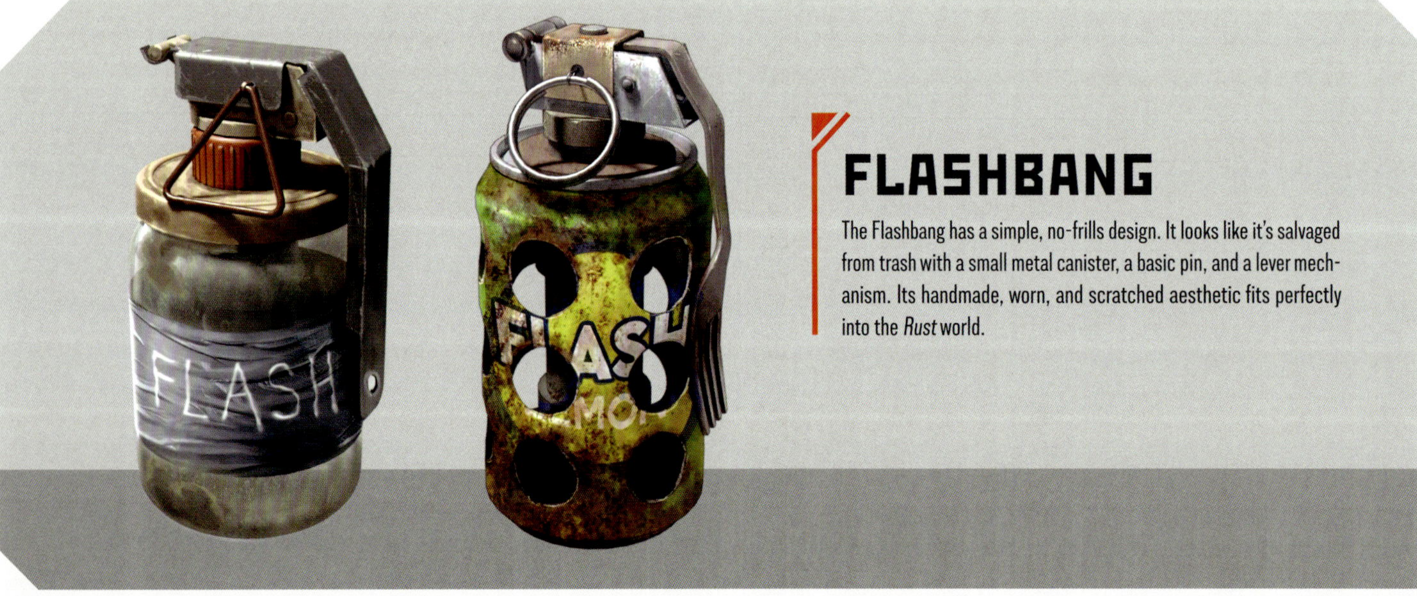

FLASHBANG

The Flashbang has a simple, no-frills design. It looks like it's salvaged from trash with a small metal canister, a basic pin, and a lever mechanism. Its handmade, worn, and scratched aesthetic fits perfectly into the *Rust* world.

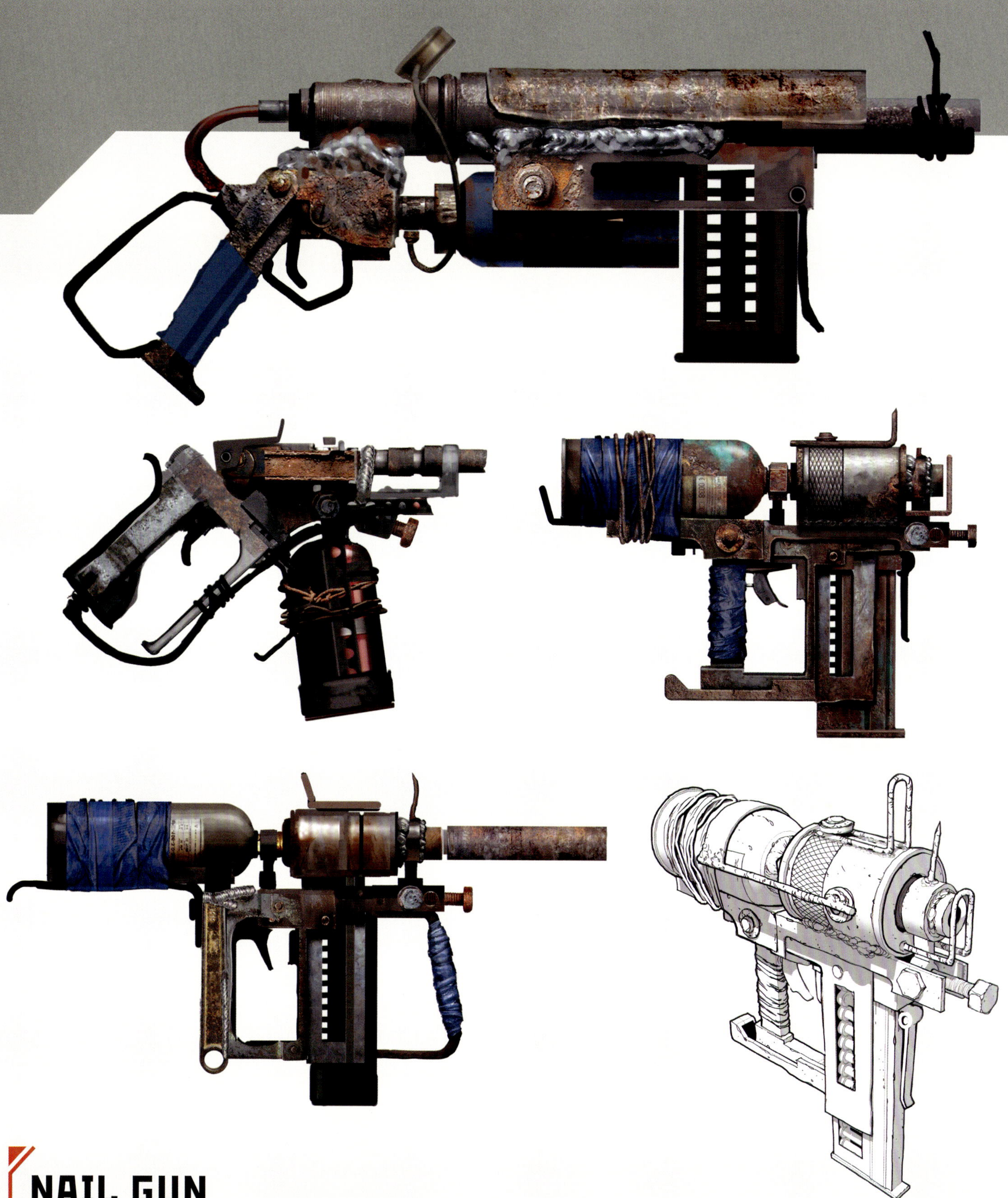

NAIL GUN

The Nail Gun's design reinforces *Rust*'s focus on resourcefulness by turning everyday tools into weapons. These concepts show a few builds, with a mix of metal and plastic materials linked to a gas canister. Its used and worn appearance suggests it's been scavenged from a construction site.

BOLT-ACTION RIFLE

The Bolt-Action Rifle is a high-powered rifle capable of making accurate shots from long distances. It has a handcrafted, battle-scarred design with a long barrel, wooden stock, and simple iron sights.

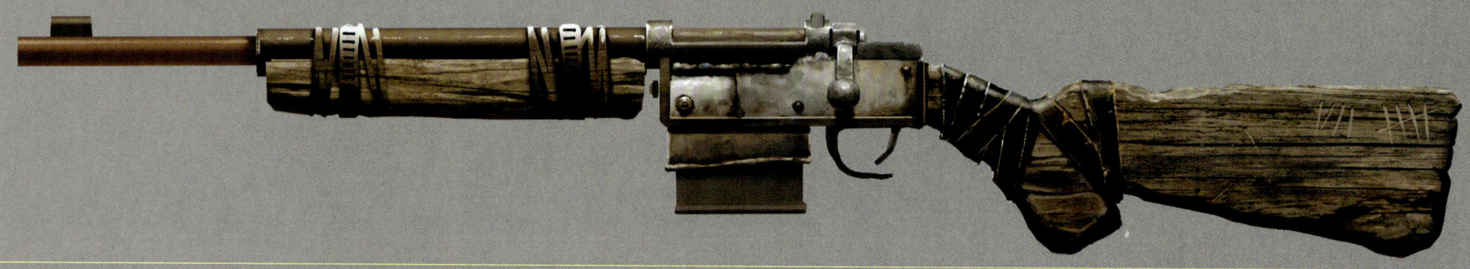

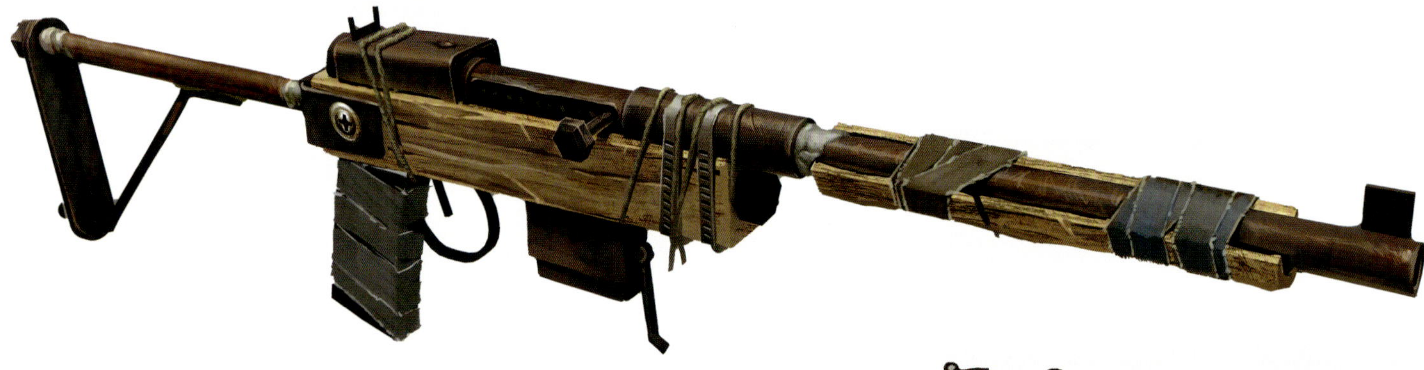

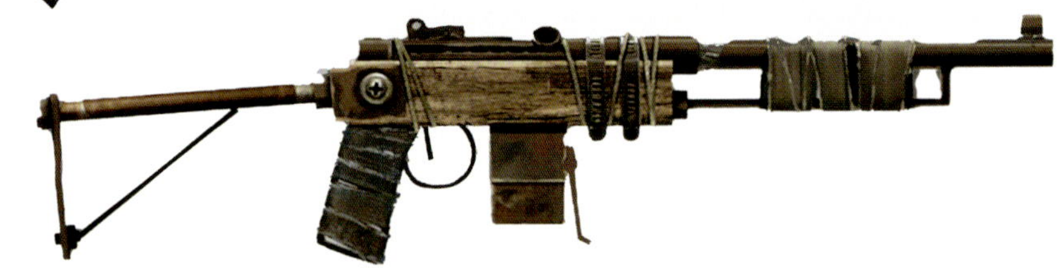

SEMI-AUTOMATIC RIFLE

The Semi-Automatic Rifle (SAR) features a practical, no-nonsense design. It combines a metal body with a basic wooden stock and grip, all showing wear, scratches, dents, and patched parts, suggesting it's been used and maintained in tough conditions.

REVOLVERS

The Revolver has a rough, patched-together look. It combines a basic metal frame with a simple worn wooden grip. The metal is scratched and slightly rusted, giving it a handmade and scavenged feel.

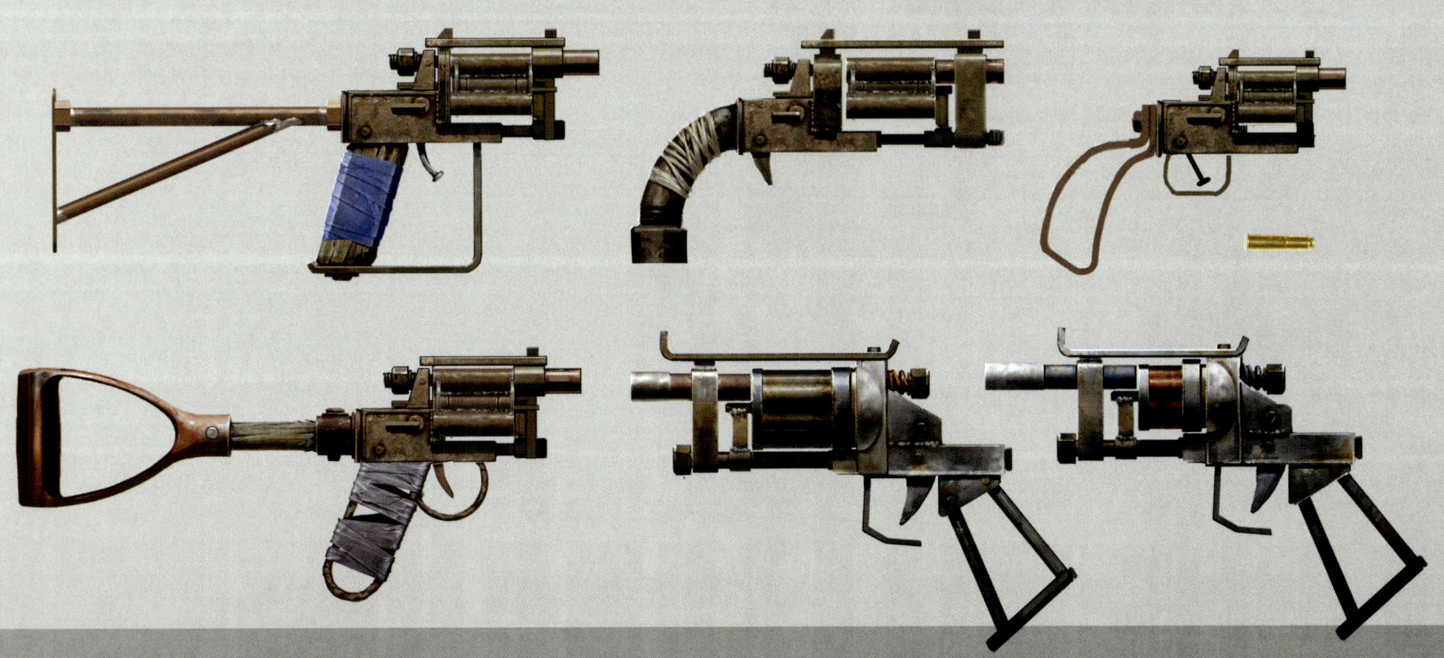

AUTOMATIC PISTOLS

These early concepts of the Semi-Automatic Pistol show a straightforward, compact pistol design but with a clunky, homemade aesthetic. Its metal body and wrapped grip are simple, with scratches, minor bits of rust, and a well-used look that suggests it's just about being kept operational.

SILENCERS

Silencers in *Rust* are simple, functional weapon attachments designed to suppress gunfire noise and muzzle flash. These first concepts explore a range of designs with modern improvised household and salvaged items.

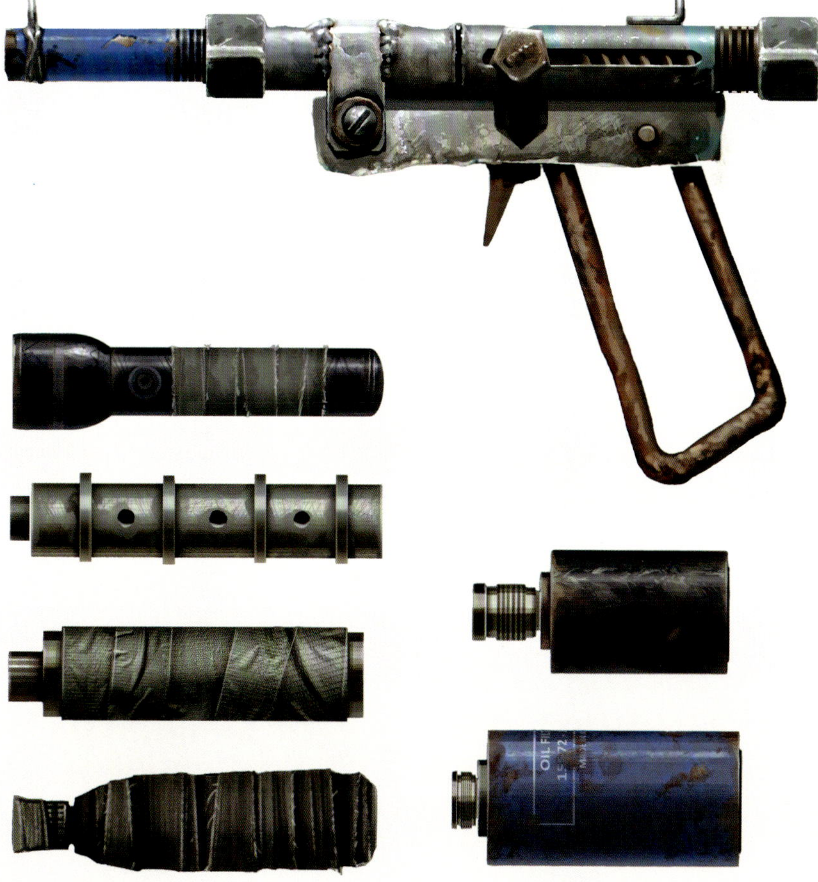

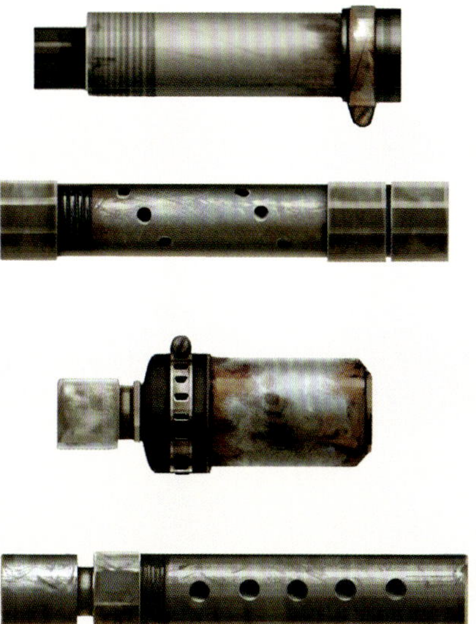

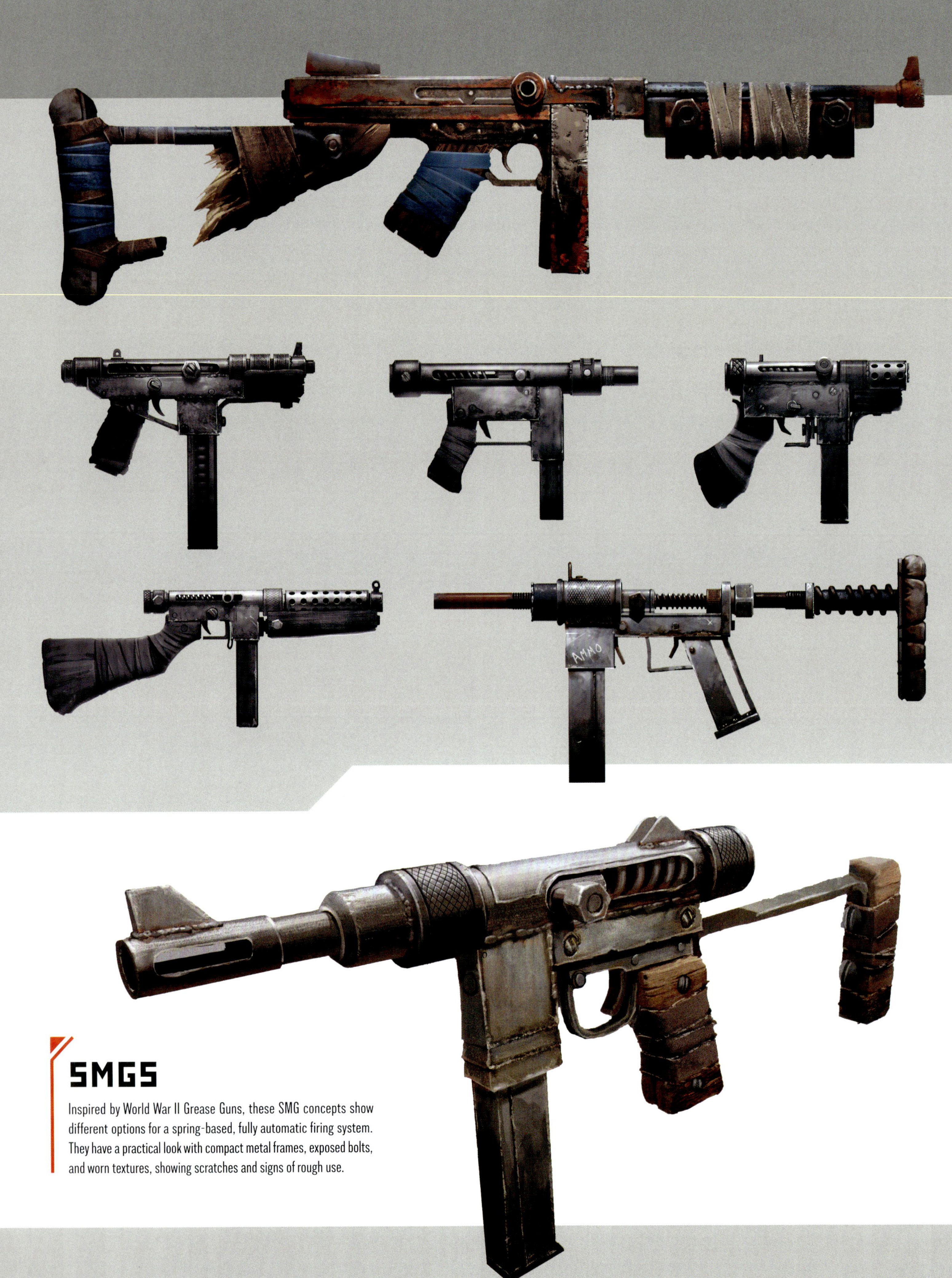

SMGS

Inspired by World War II Grease Guns, these SMG concepts show different options for a spring-based, fully automatic firing system. They have a practical look with compact metal frames, exposed bolts, and worn textures, showing scratches and signs of rough use.

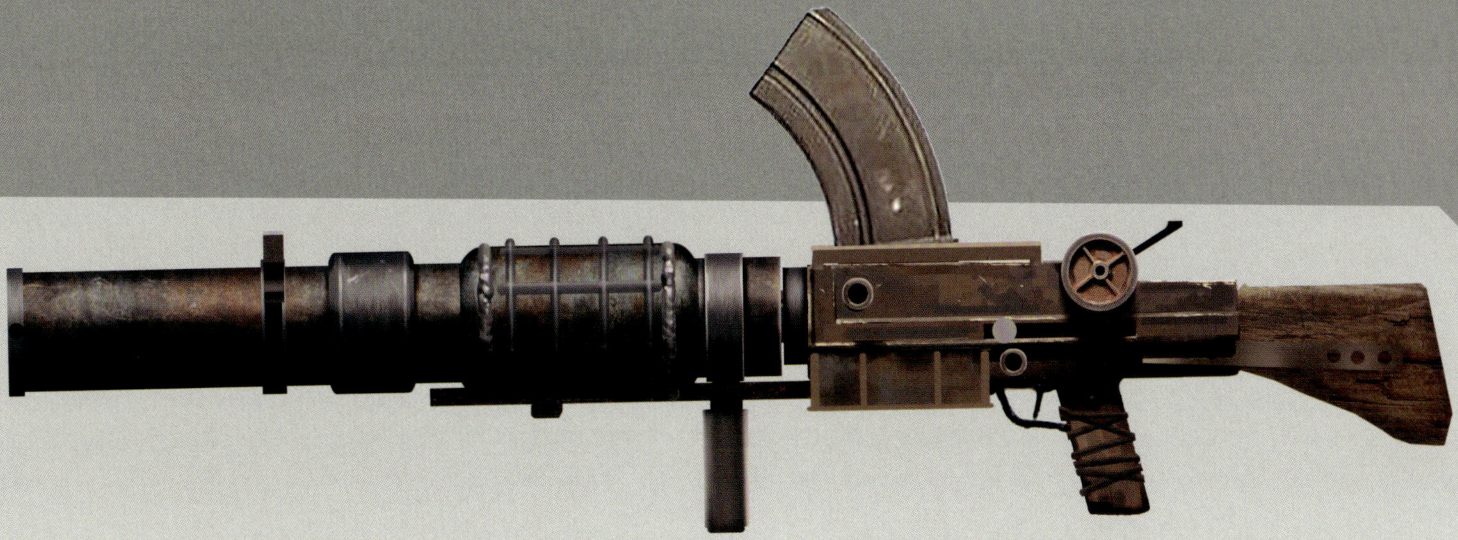

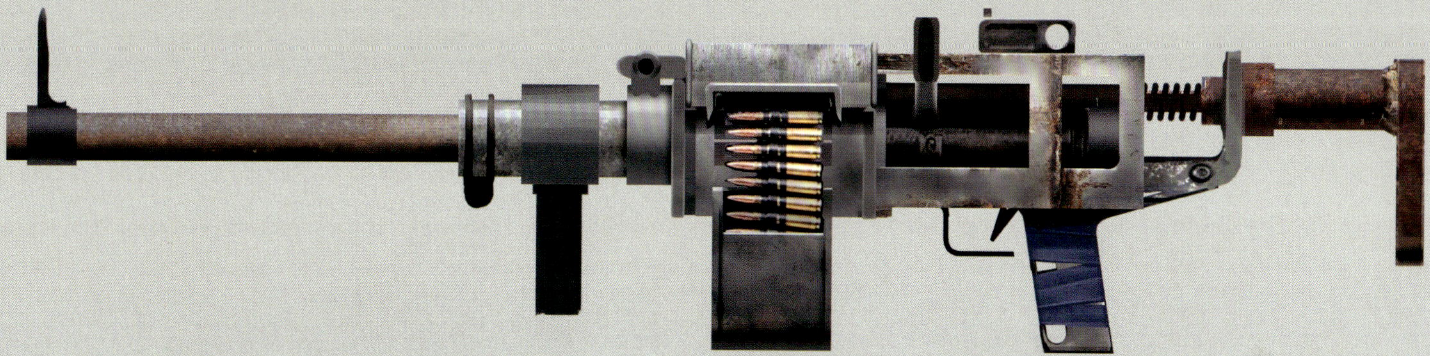

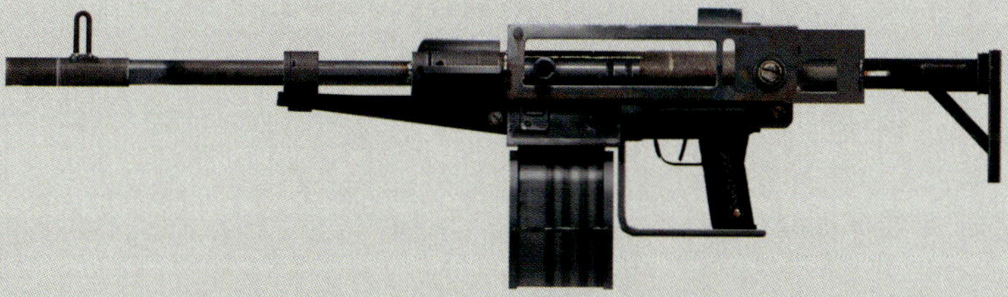

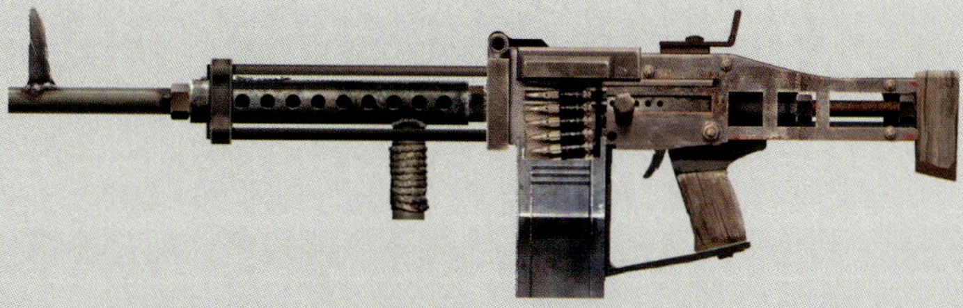

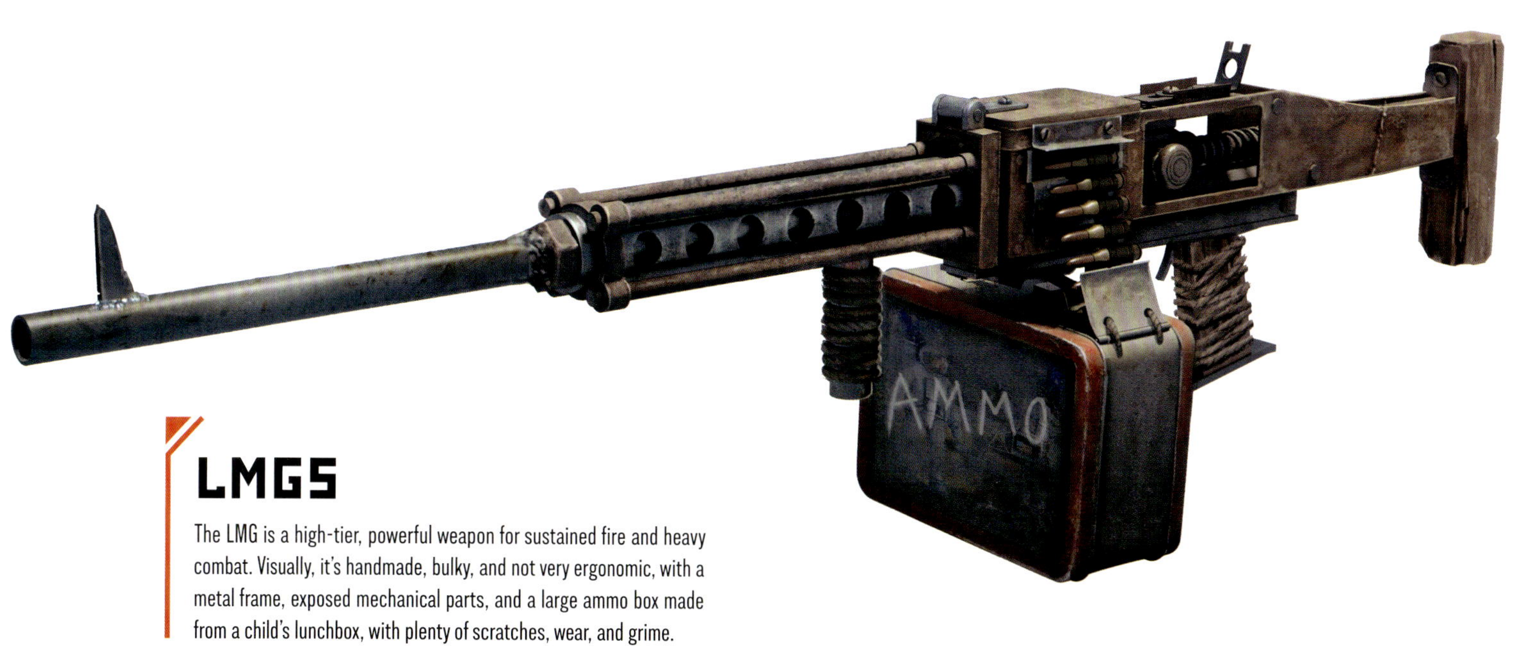

LMGS

The LMG is a high-tier, powerful weapon for sustained fire and heavy combat. Visually, it's handmade, bulky, and not very ergonomic, with a metal frame, exposed mechanical parts, and a large ammo box made from a child's lunchbox, with plenty of scratches, wear, and grime.

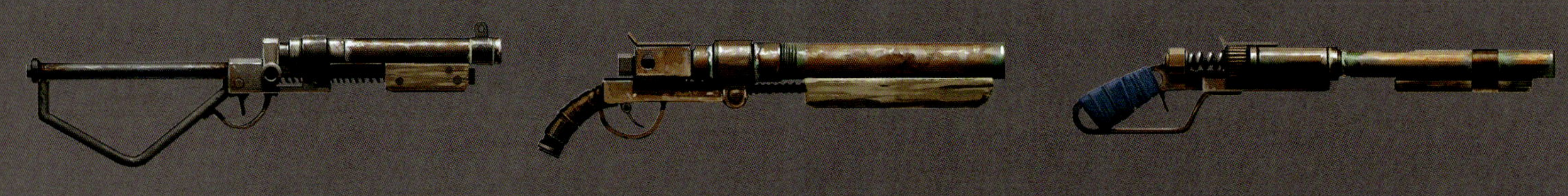

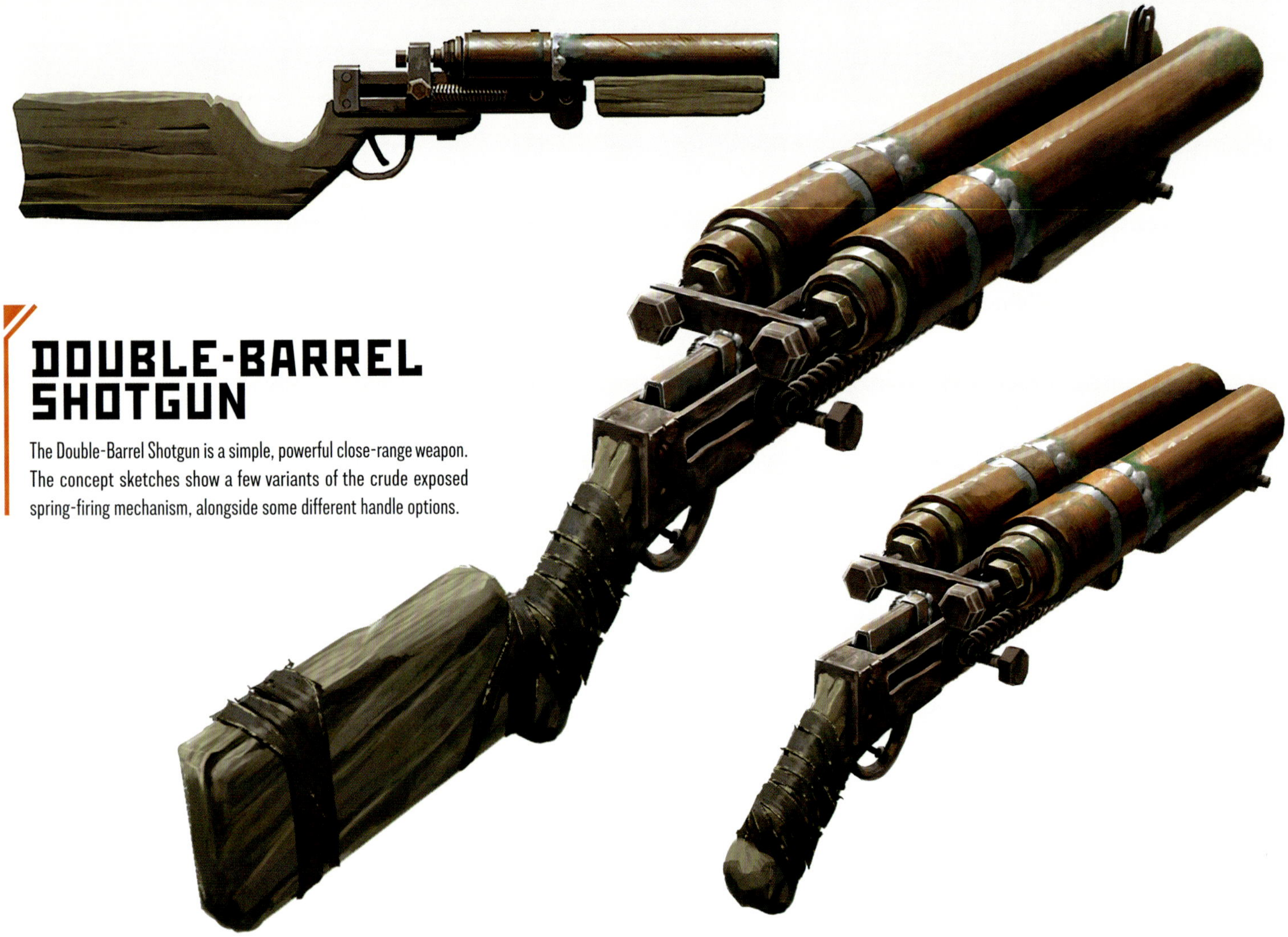

DOUBLE-BARREL SHOTGUN

The Double-Barrel Shotgun is a simple, powerful close-range weapon. The concept sketches show a few variants of the crude exposed spring-firing mechanism, alongside some different handle options.

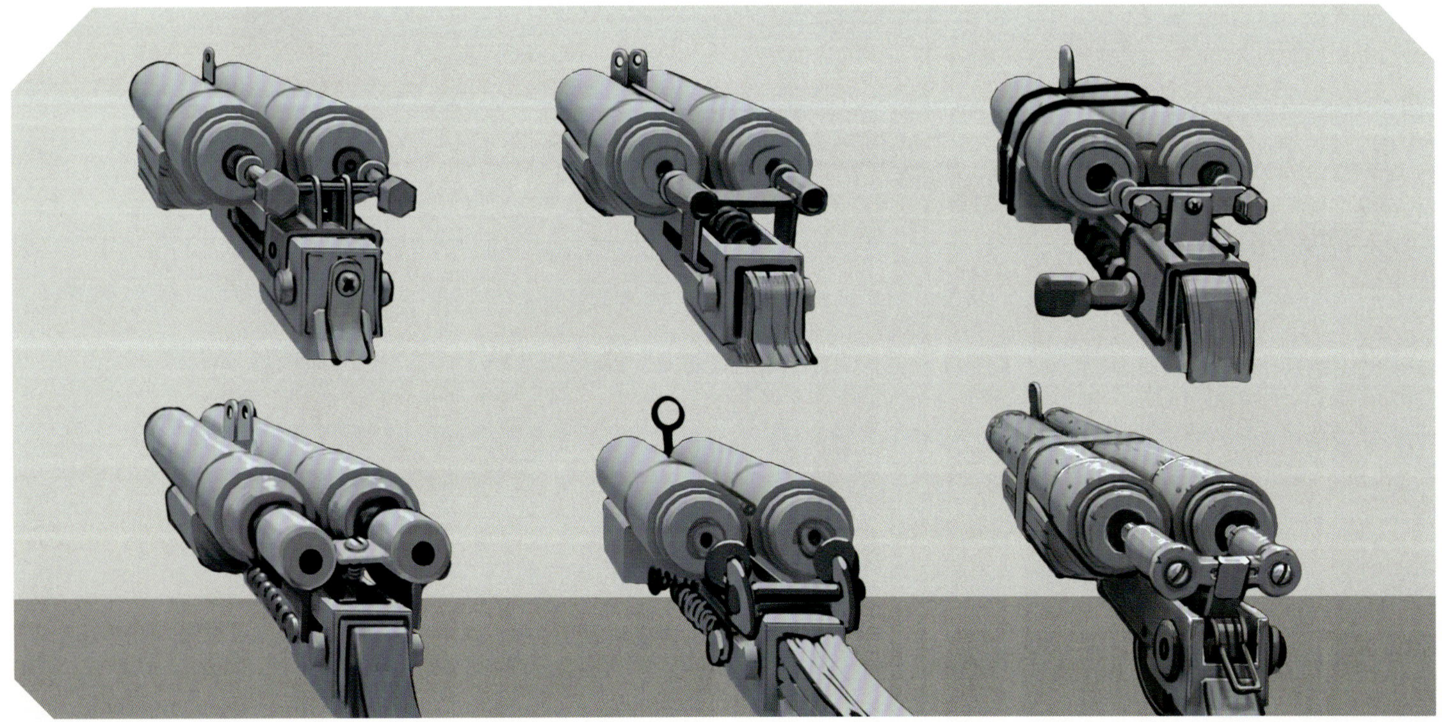

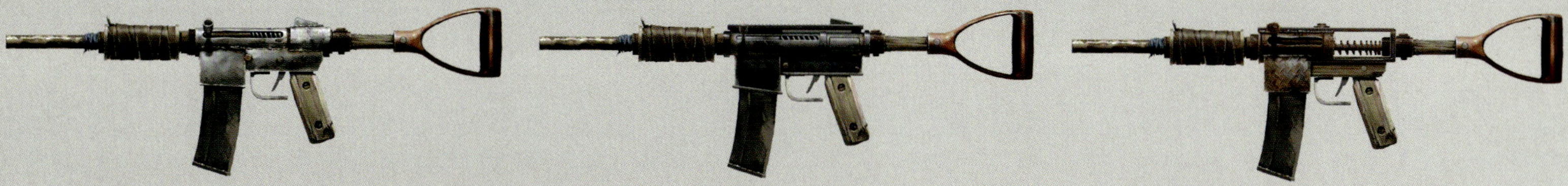

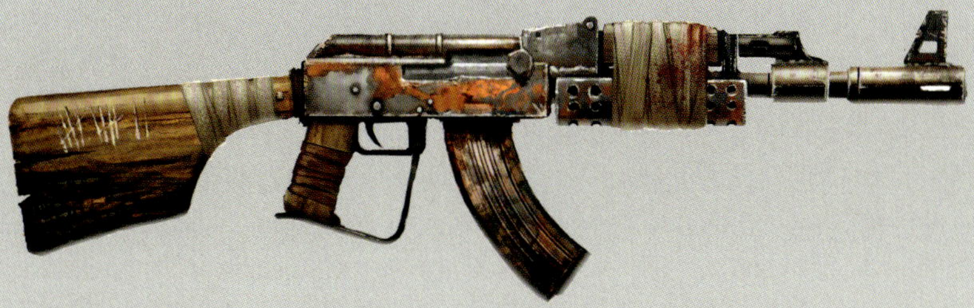

ASSAULT RIFLE

The Assault Rifle (AK) is the most iconic weapon in *Rust*. These early sketches take a familiar rifle form based on the AK-47 and reimagine it through the lens of scavenging, improvisation, and wear.

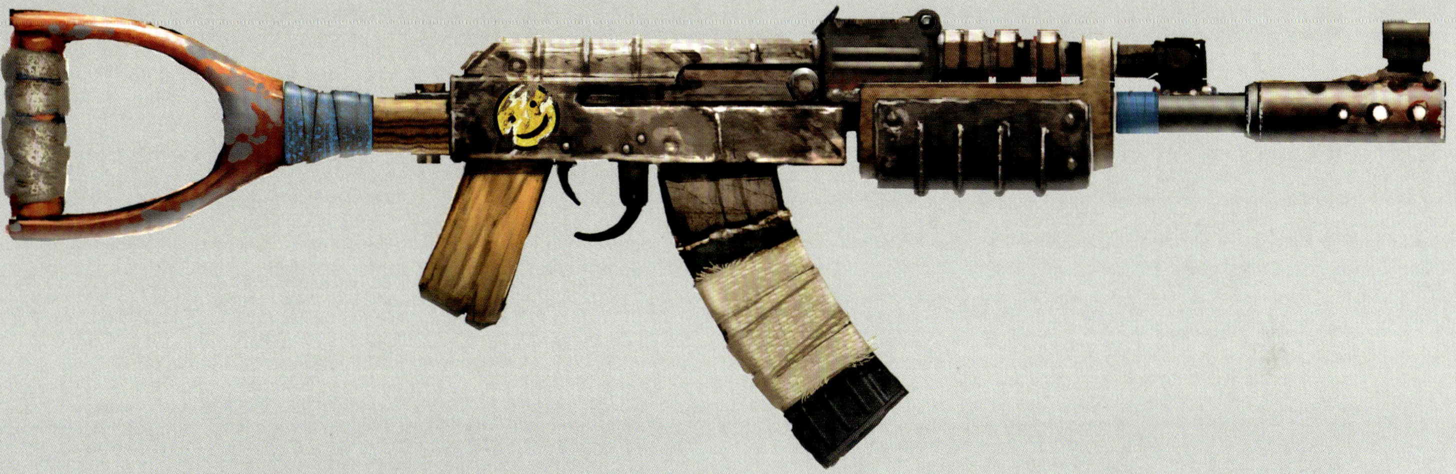

IMPROVISED SCOPES

Visually, Improvised Scopes look cobbled together and barely functional. Made from scrap, pipes, lenses, and bolts, they are often duct-taped or welded together. They are very low tech but provide enough magnification to be beneficial. These early concepts show a few design variations.

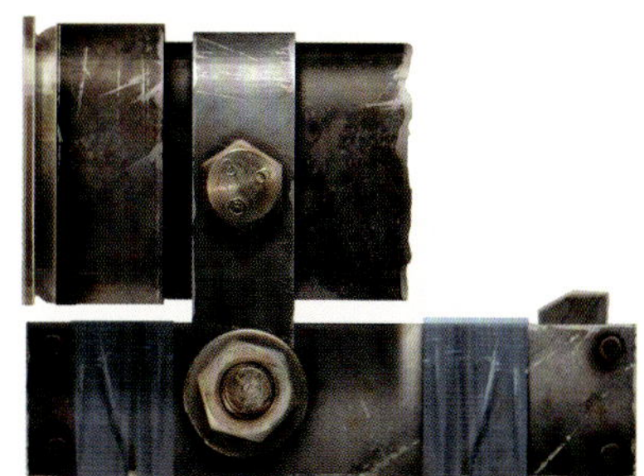

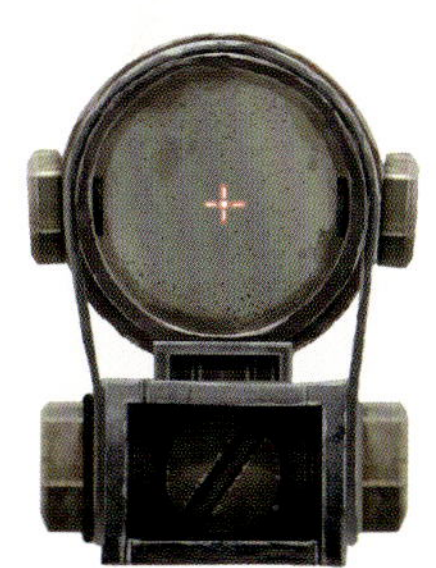

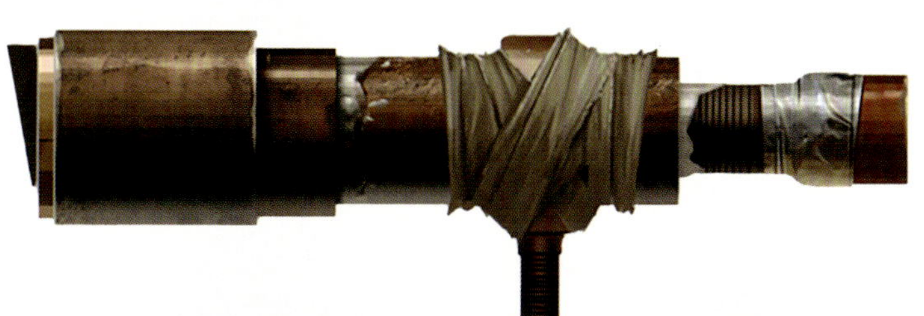

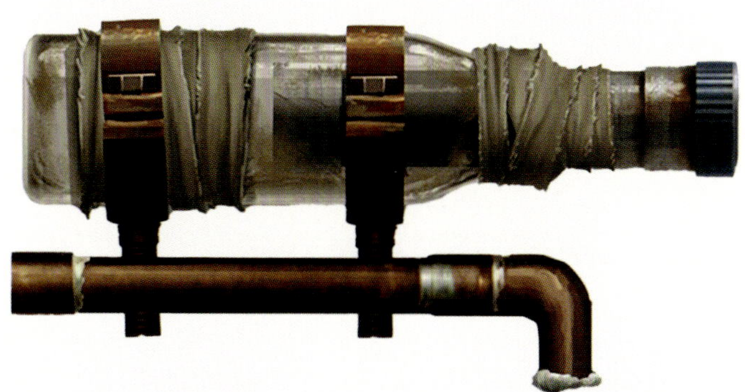

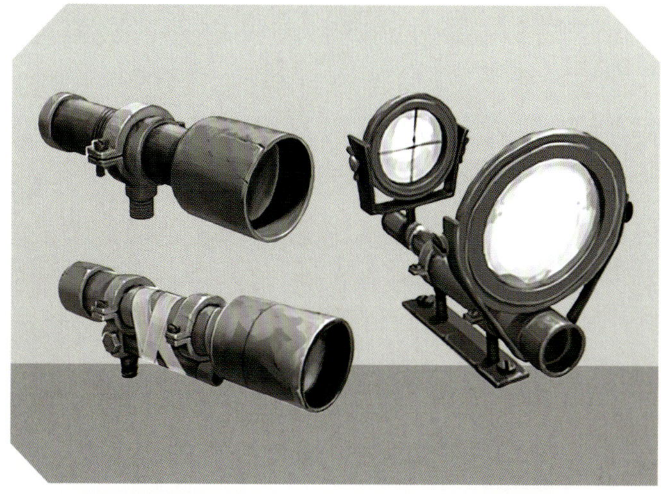

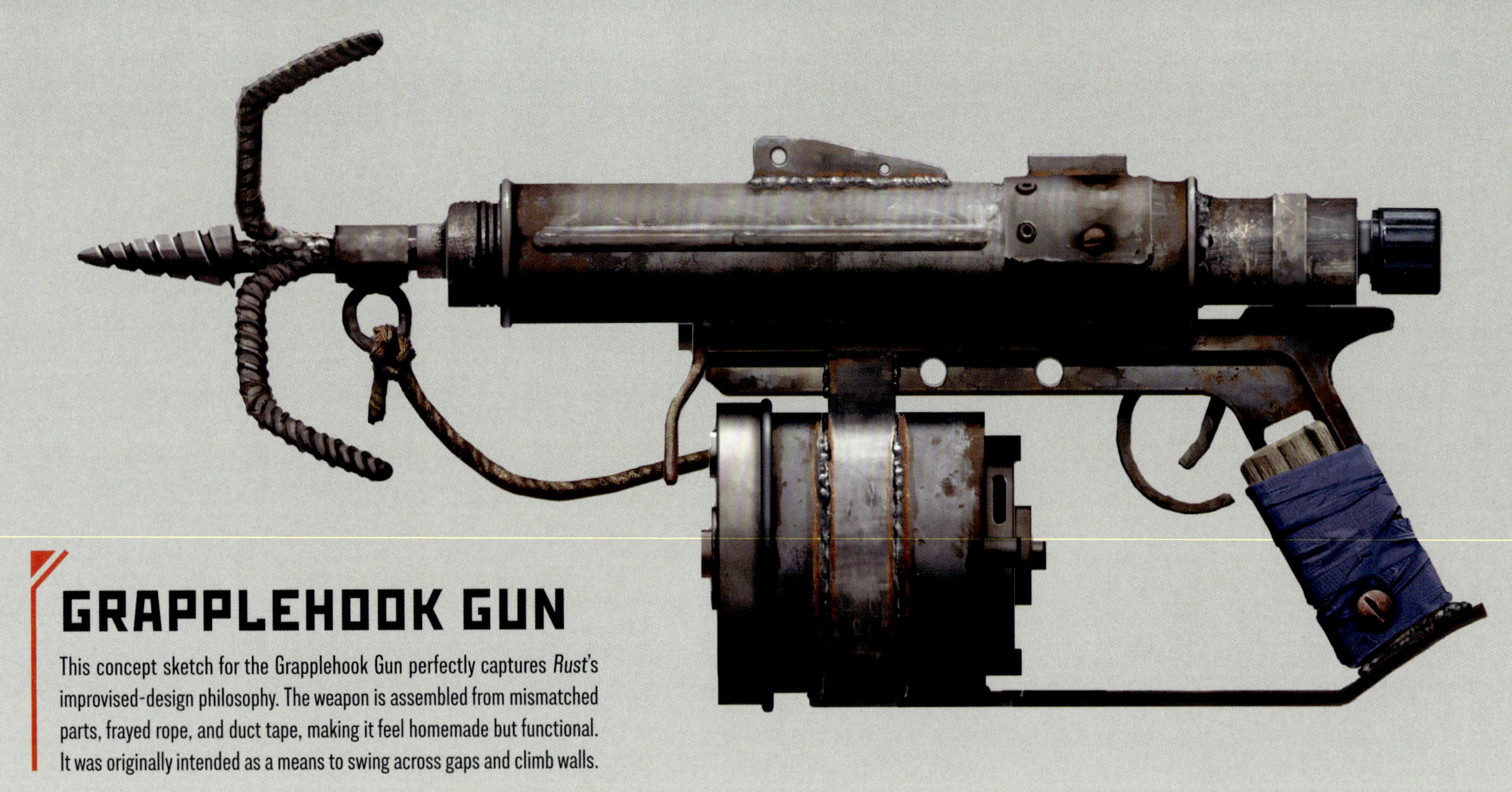

GRAPPLEHOOK GUN

This concept sketch for the Grapplehook Gun perfectly captures *Rust*'s improvised-design philosophy. The weapon is assembled from mismatched parts, frayed rope, and duct tape, making it feel homemade but functional. It was originally intended as a means to swing across gaps and climb walls.

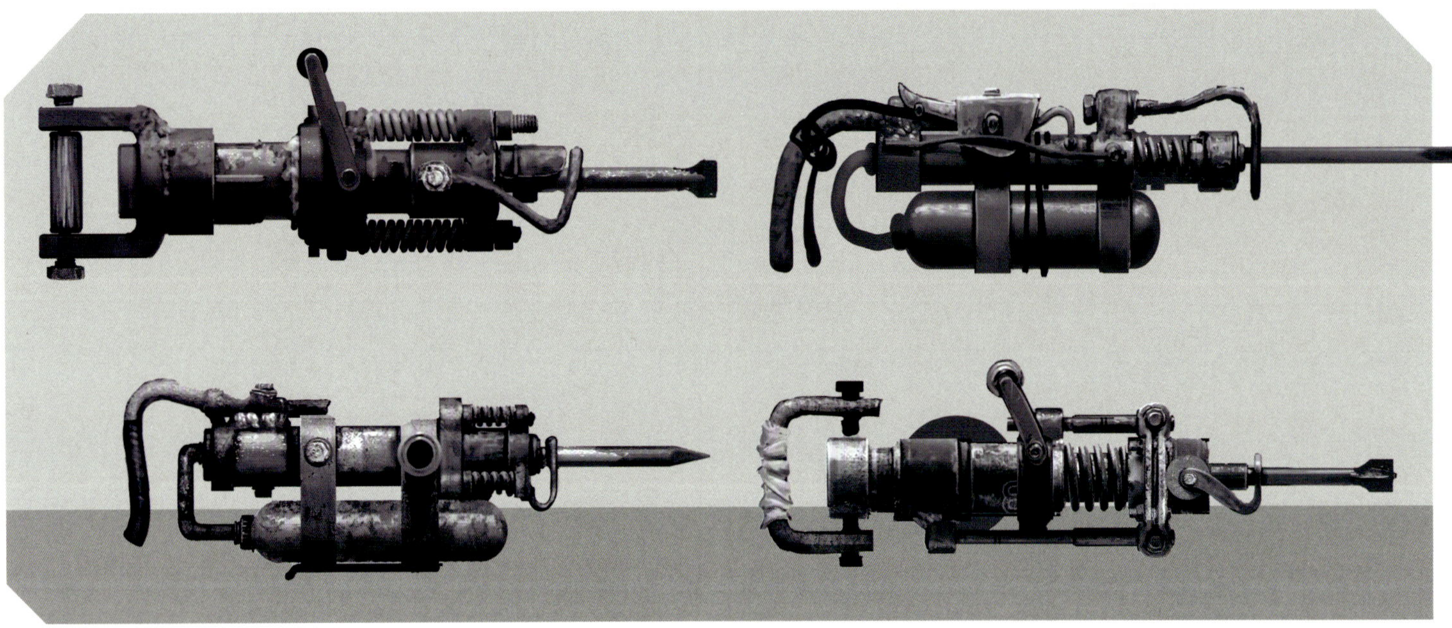

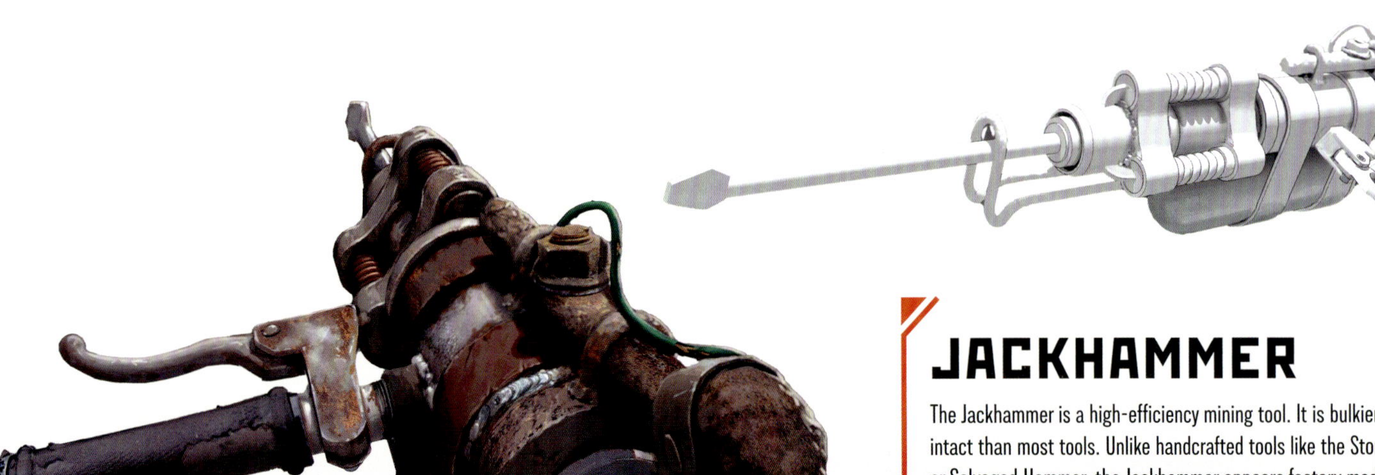

JACKHAMMER

The Jackhammer is a high-efficiency mining tool. It is bulkier and more intact than most tools. Unlike handcrafted tools like the Stone Pickaxe or Salvaged Hammer, the Jackhammer appears factory made but well aged, suggesting it's a rare find—something that's been looted, not built.

HOMING MISSILE LAUNCHER

The Homing Missile Launcher is built from repurposed industrial parts with a mounted sight that resembles a hacked-together projector or camera. The frame includes a taped-up pillow for padding and makeshift iron sights fashioned from scrap. It is a crude yet functional weapon.

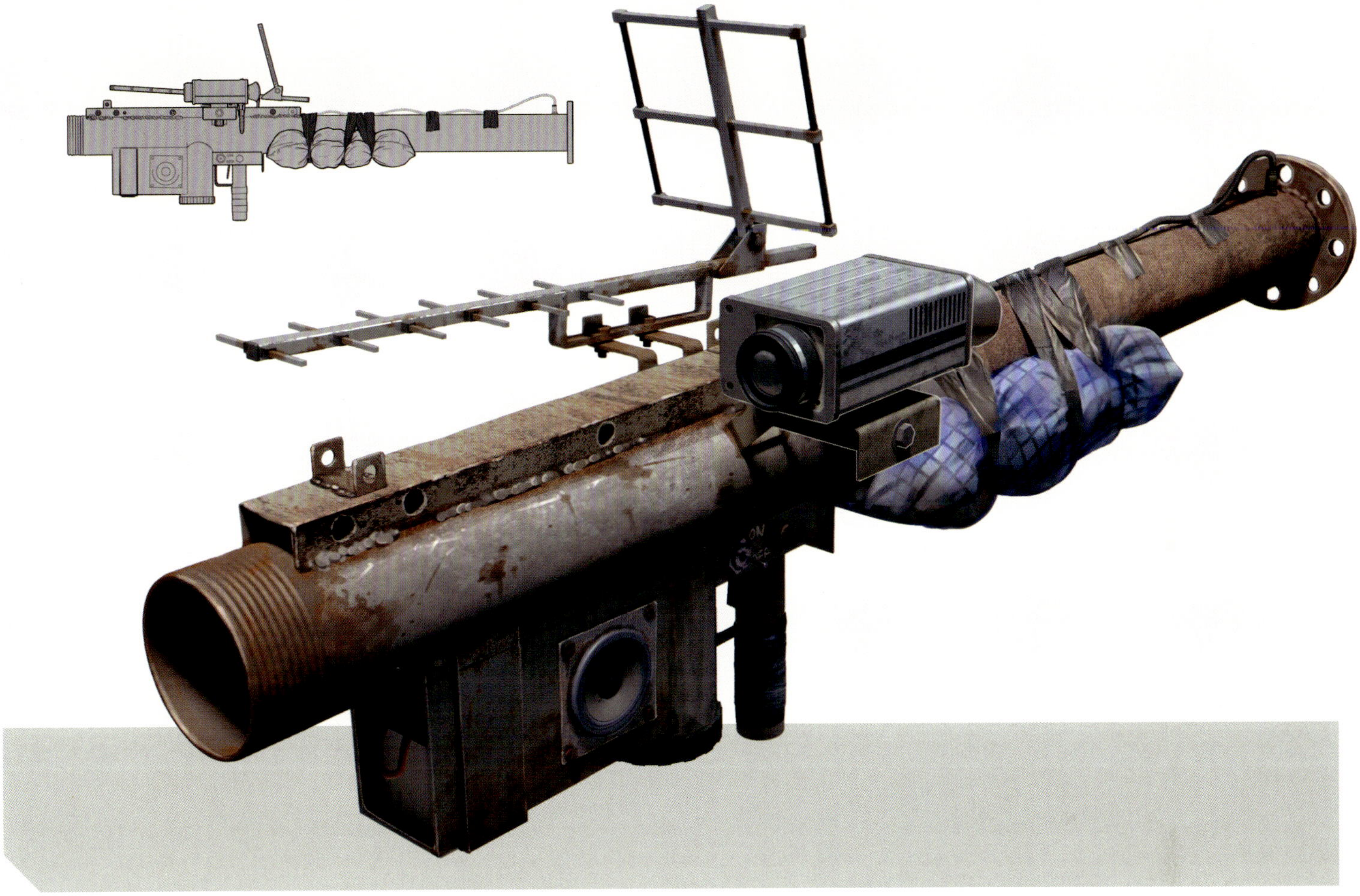

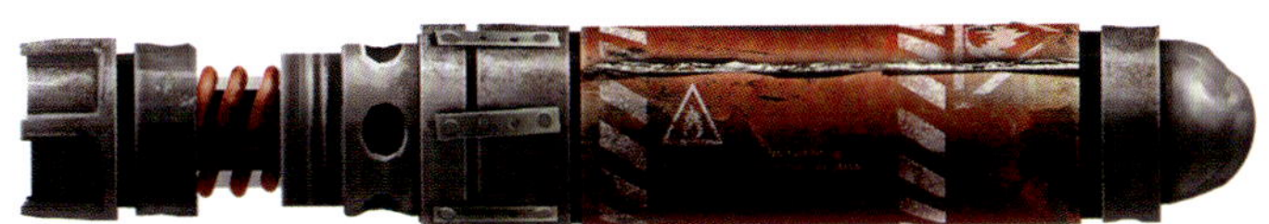

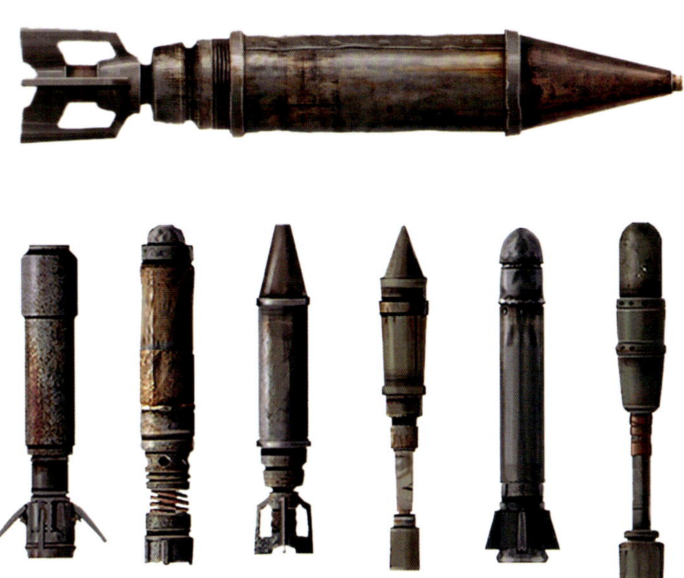

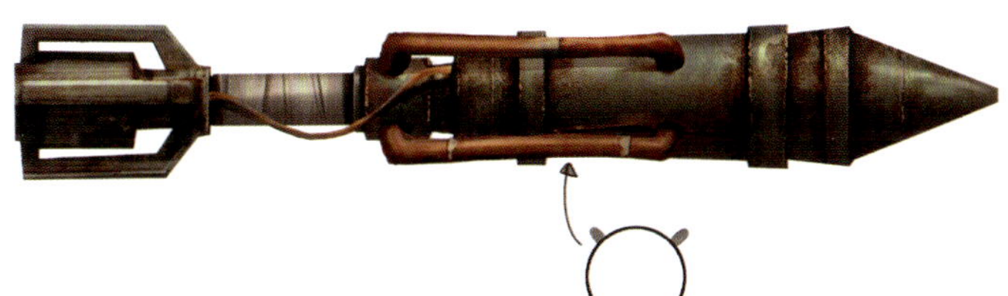

ROCKET LAUNCHER AMMO

In these concept sketches of the RPG Ammo, each projectile is slightly varied, exploring different ways to help distinguish ammo types. Some are sleek but old and scratched; others look completely custom, as if they were fabricated in a workshop with spare metal and leftover explosives.

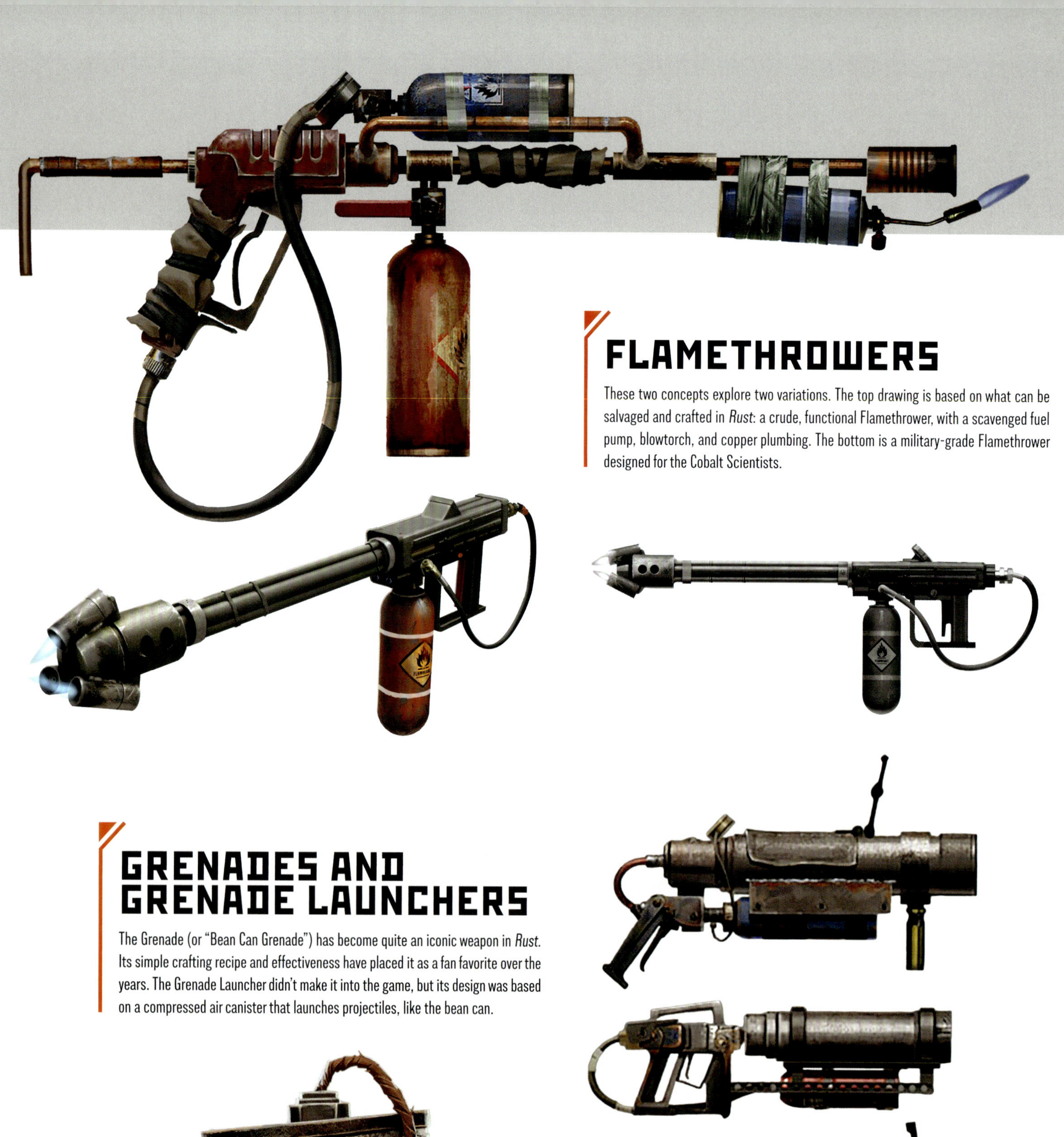

FLAMETHROWERS

These two concepts explore two variations. The top drawing is based on what can be salvaged and crafted in *Rust*: a crude, functional Flamethrower, with a scavenged fuel pump, blowtorch, and copper plumbing. The bottom is a military-grade Flamethrower designed for the Cobalt Scientists.

GRENADES AND GRENADE LAUNCHERS

The Grenade (or "Bean Can Grenade") has become quite an iconic weapon in *Rust*. Its simple crafting recipe and effectiveness have placed it as a fan favorite over the years. The Grenade Launcher didn't make it into the game, but its design was based on a compressed air canister that launches projectiles, like the bean can.

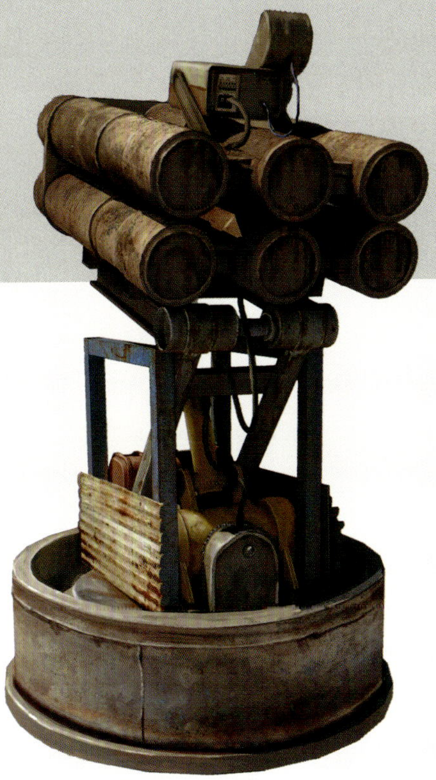

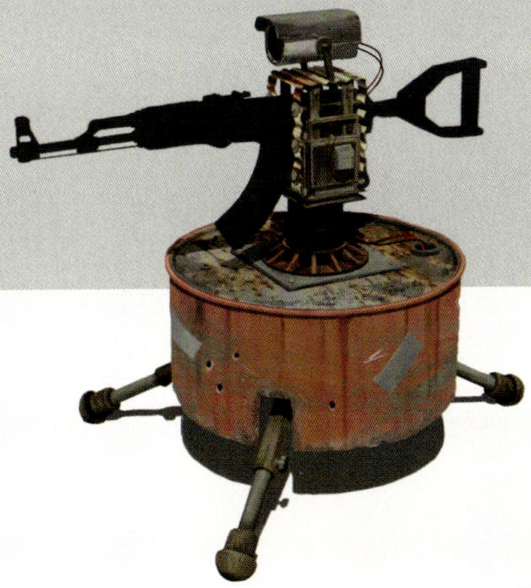

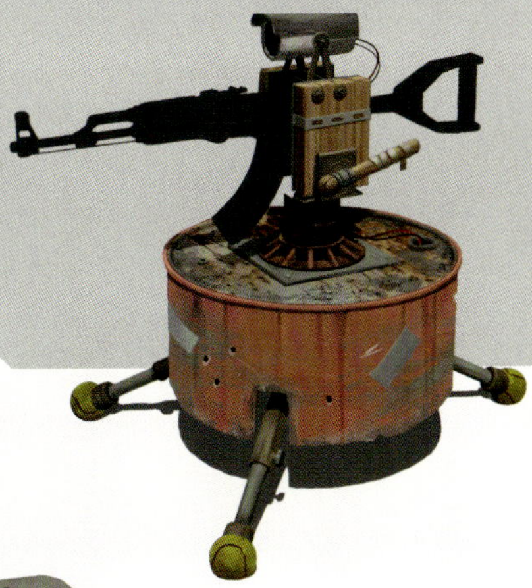

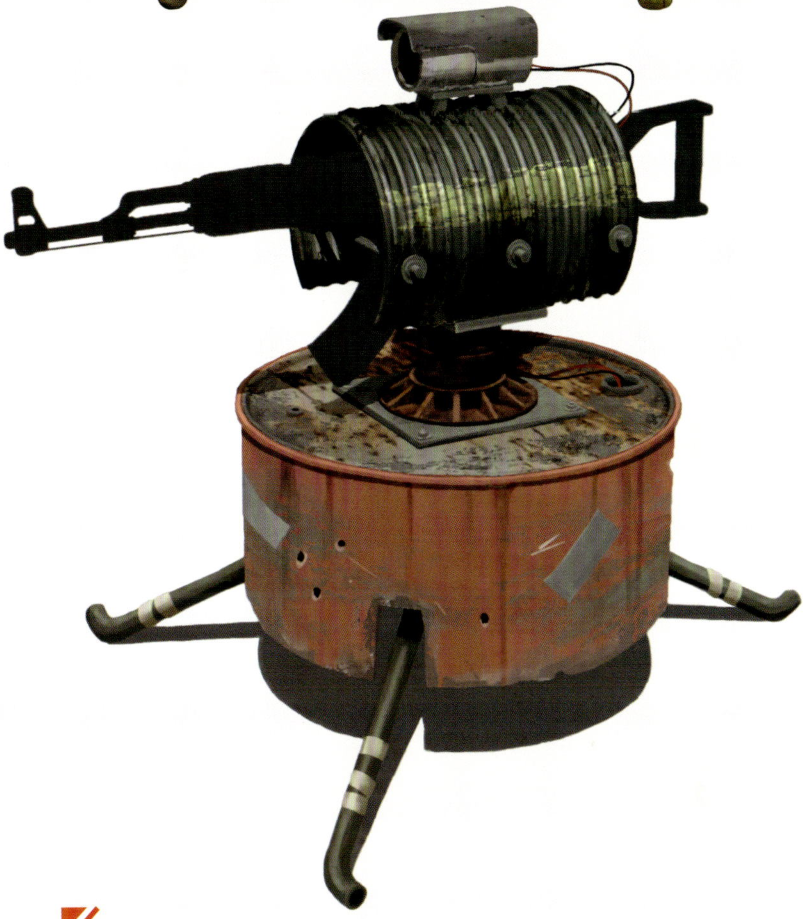

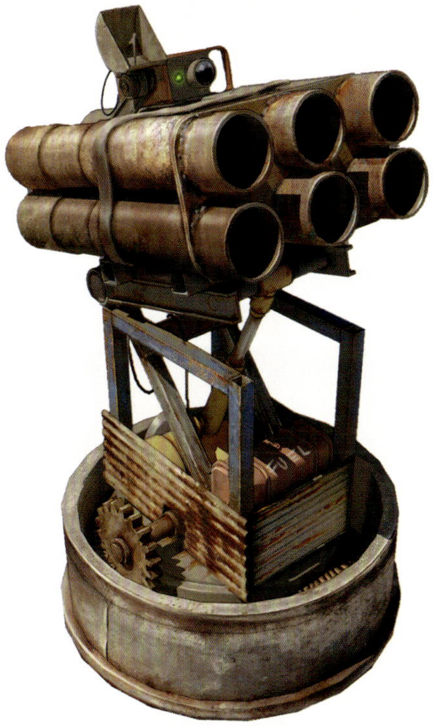

TURRETS

Turrets are automated defensive systems used to protect player bases from intruders. They can be loaded with different weapons or ammunition types and require power to operate. These concepts show a few variants of Turrets that fire weapons from LMGs to Assault Rifles to missile launchers.

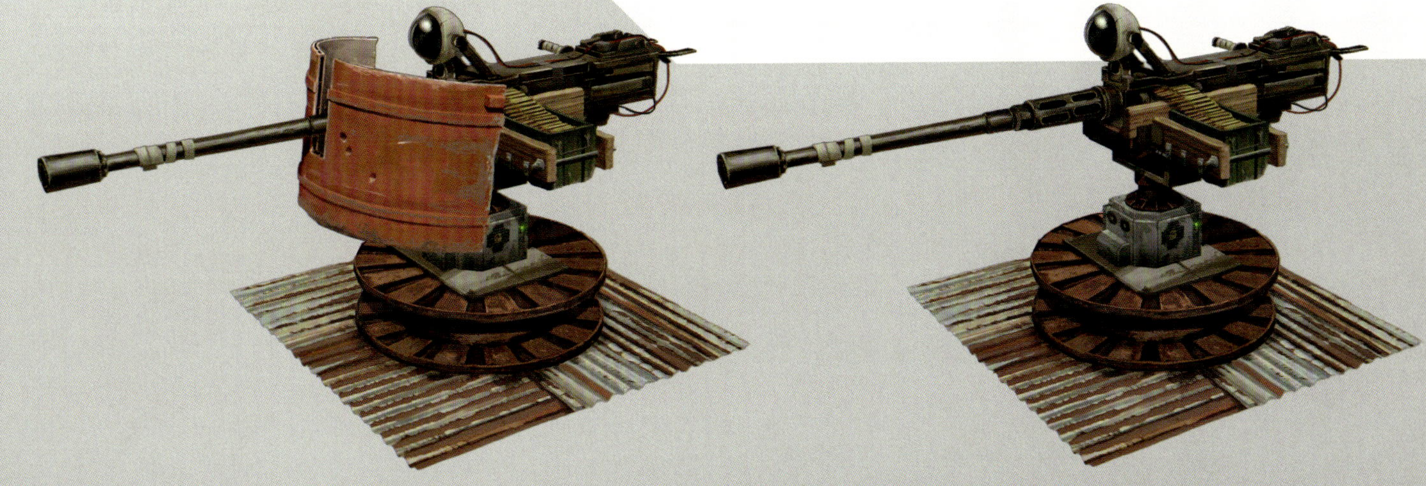

CAML

The CAML didn't make it into *Rust*, but these concepts show a few variations of the potential design. Inspired by military quadruped drones, it looks more like a reclaimed agricultural or mining robot than a high-tech war machine.

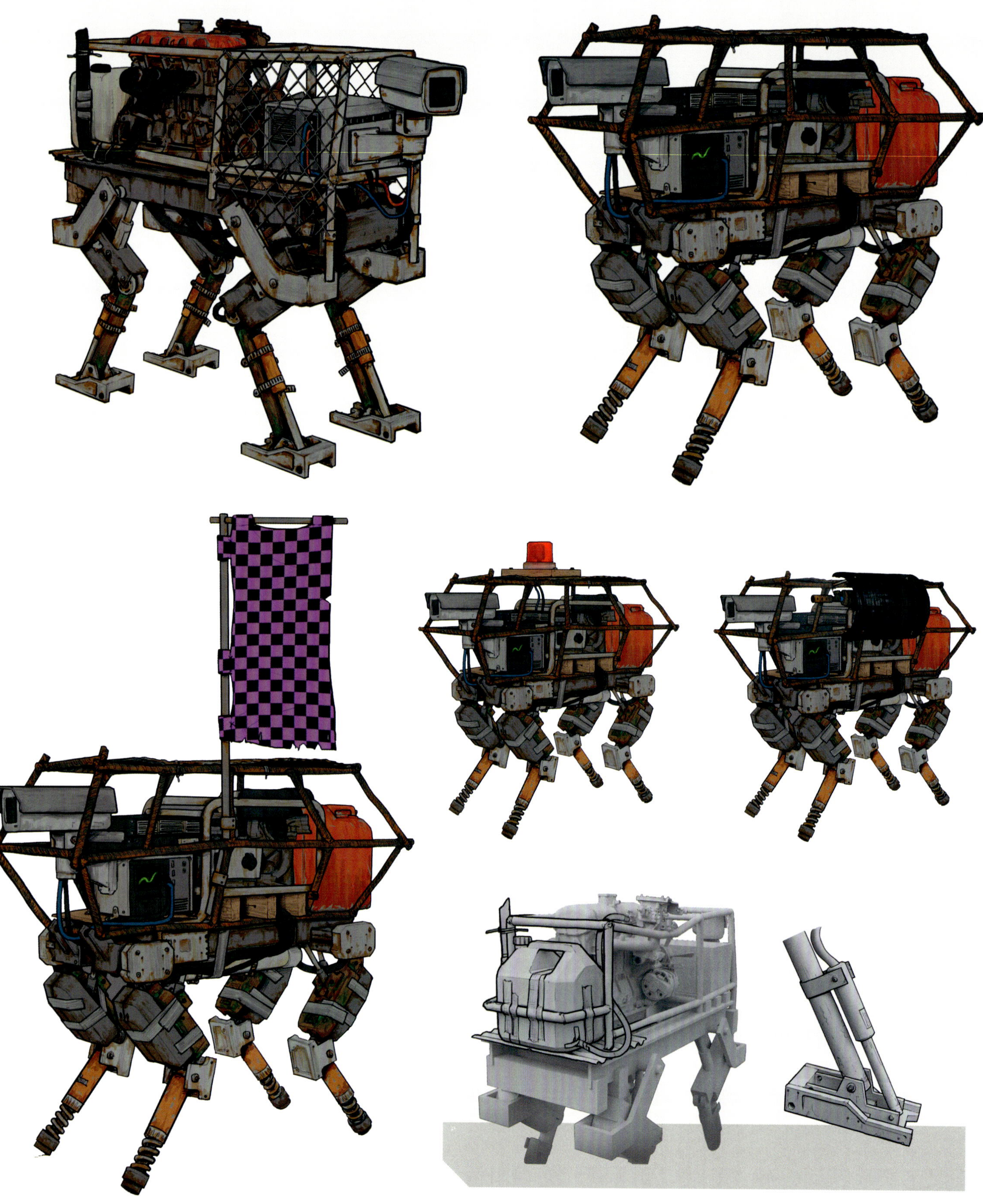

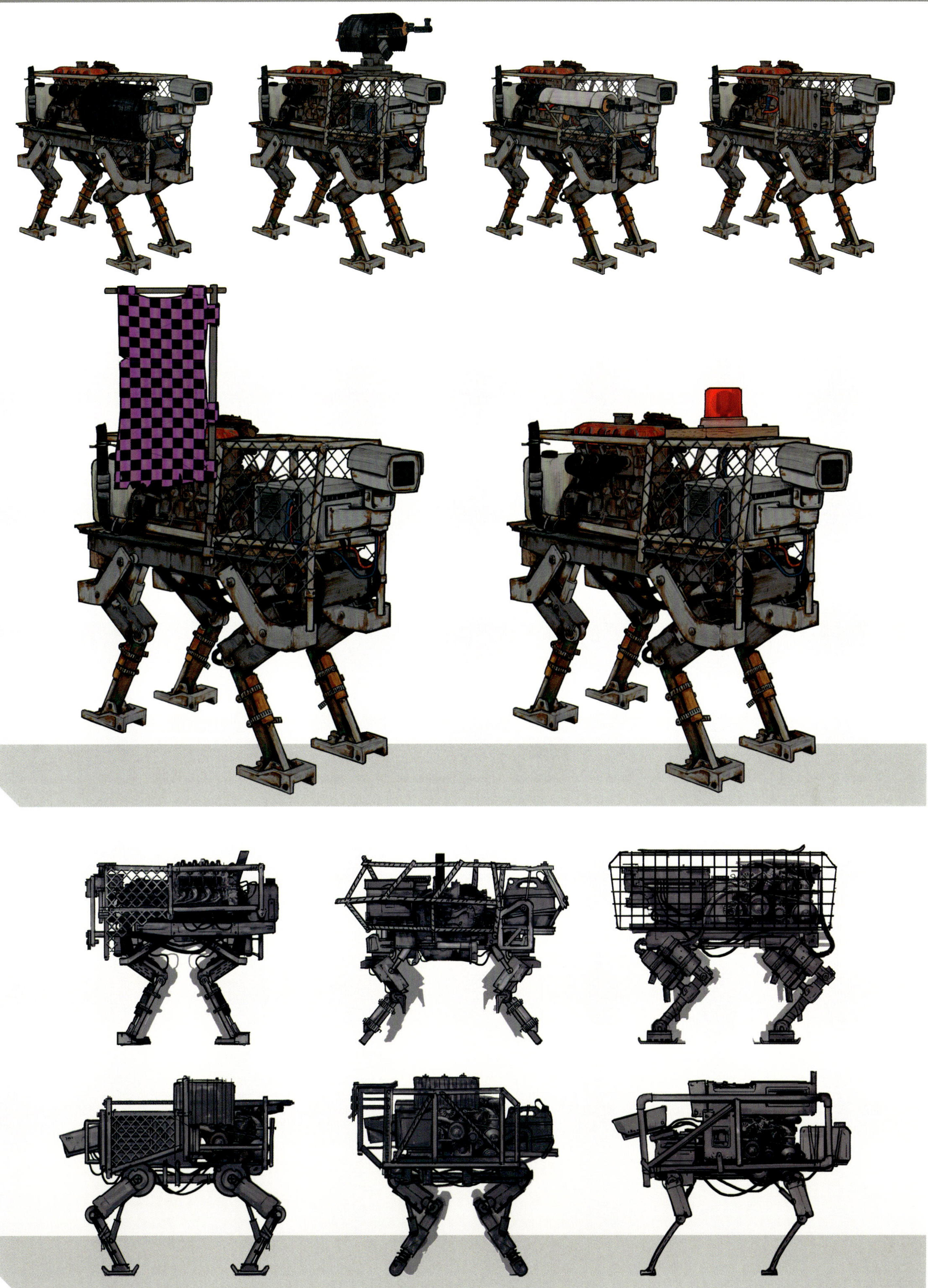

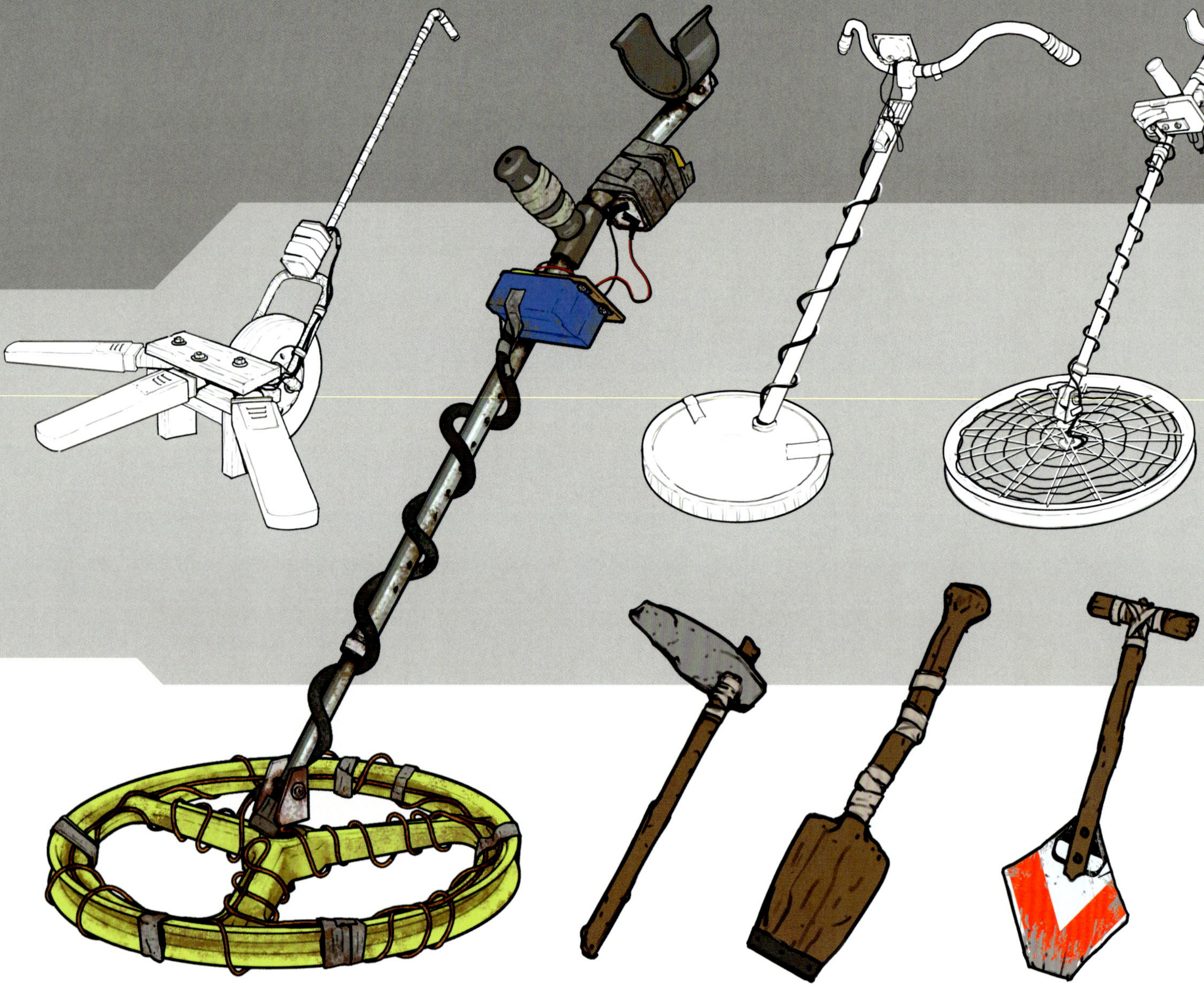

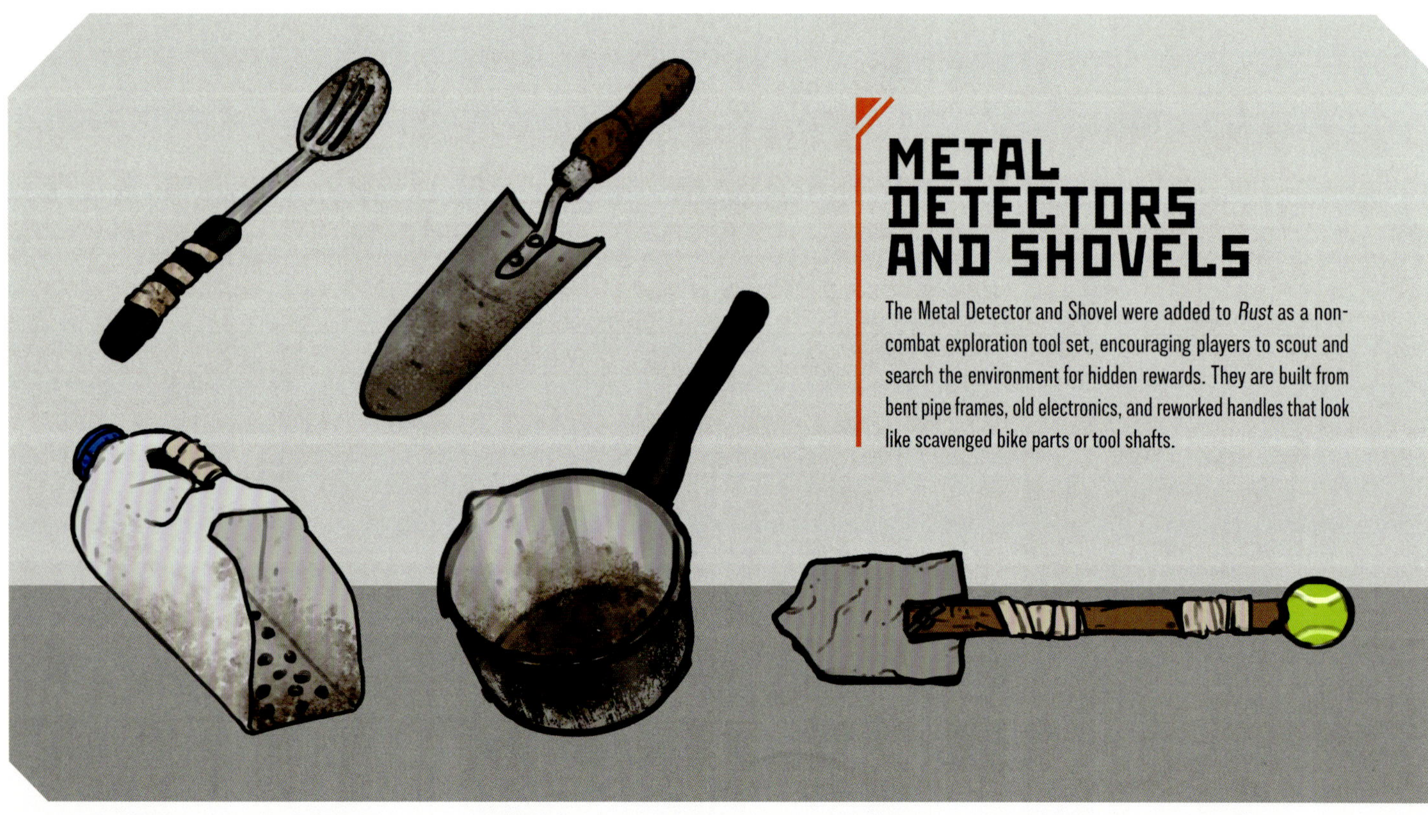

METAL DETECTORS AND SHOVELS

The Metal Detector and Shovel were added to *Rust* as a non-combat exploration tool set, encouraging players to scout and search the environment for hidden rewards. They are built from bent pipe frames, old electronics, and reworked handles that look like scavenged bike parts or tool shafts.

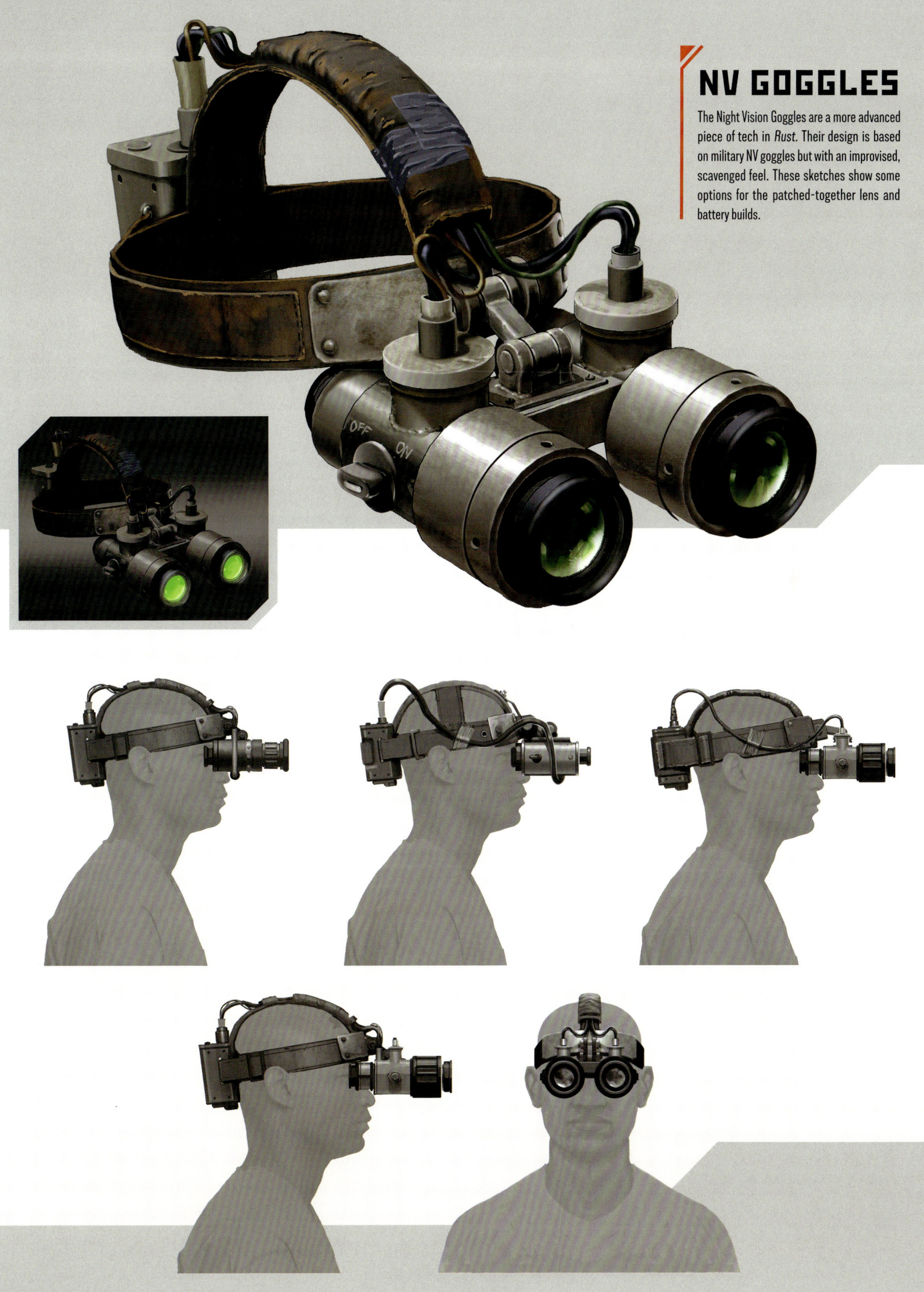

NV GOGGLES

The Night Vision Goggles are a more advanced piece of tech in *Rust*. Their design is based on military NV goggles but with an improvised, scavenged feel. These sketches show some options for the patched-together lens and battery builds.

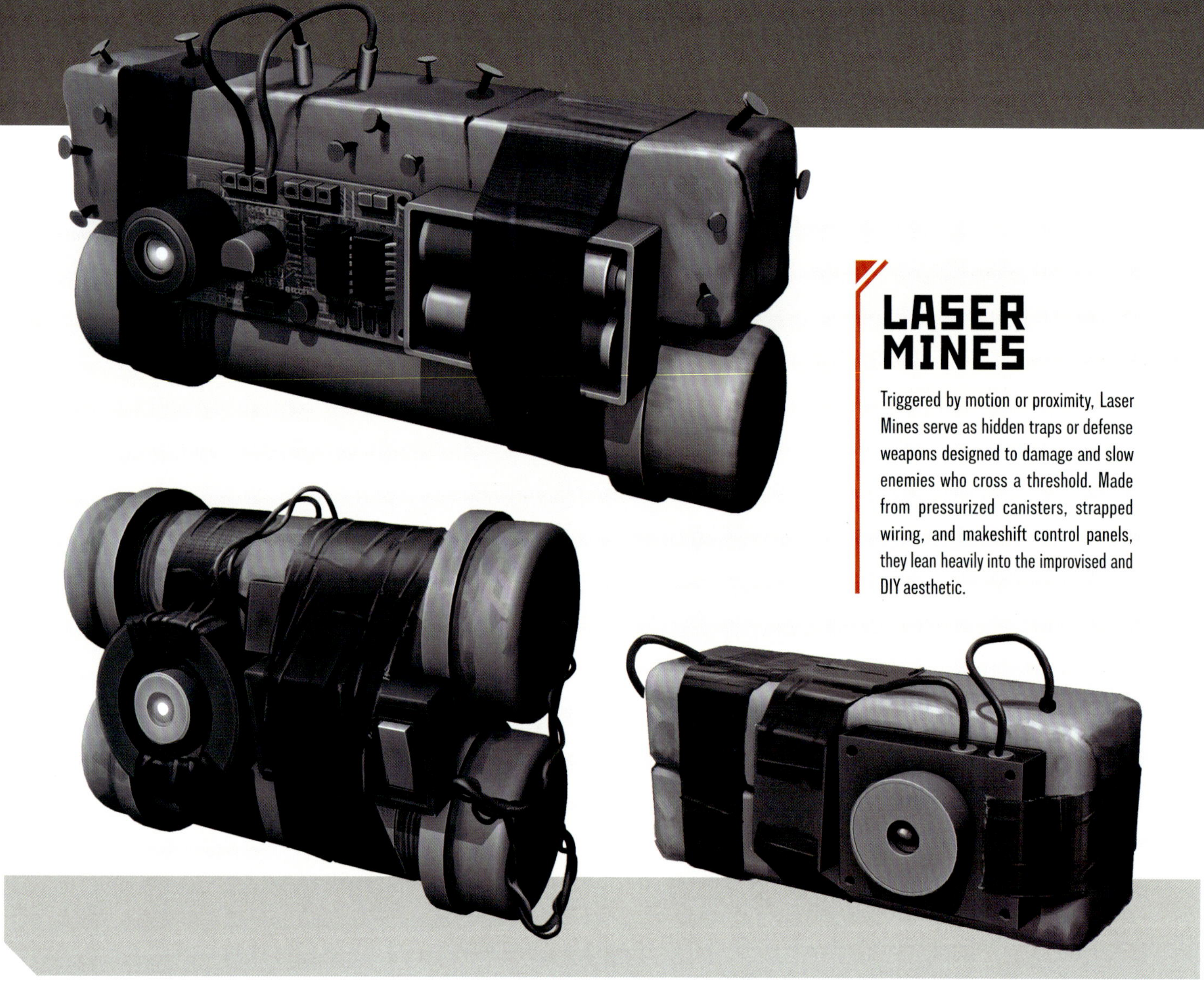

LASER MINES

Triggered by motion or proximity, Laser Mines serve as hidden traps or defense weapons designed to damage and slow enemies who cross a threshold. Made from pressurized canisters, strapped wiring, and makeshift control panels, they lean heavily into the improvised and DIY aesthetic.

SENSORS

Seismic Sensors are small, practical devices that detect motion, presence, or light. These concepts explore different designs and mounts. The sensors are basic, with metal casings, duct tape, and plastic housings. They are used as part of automated security systems within *Rust*'s electrical building systems.

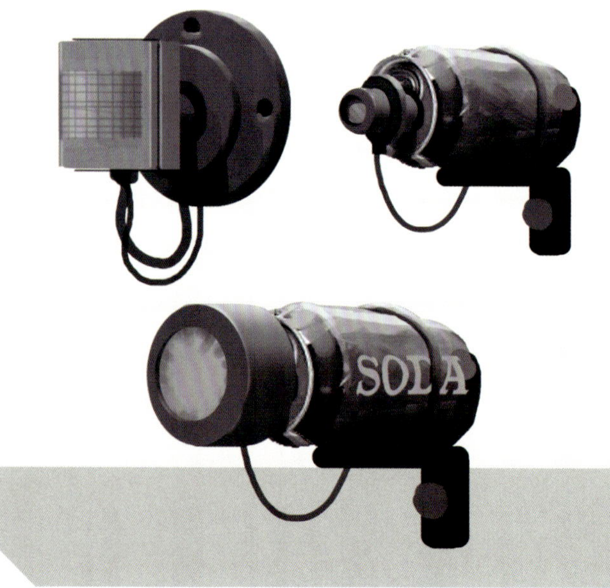

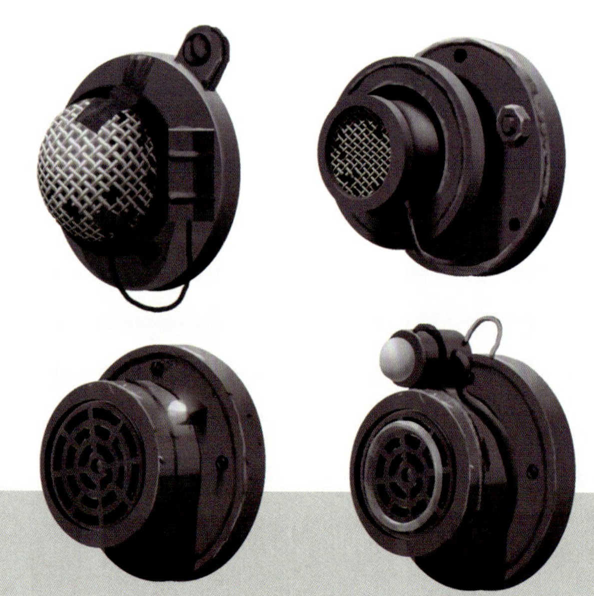

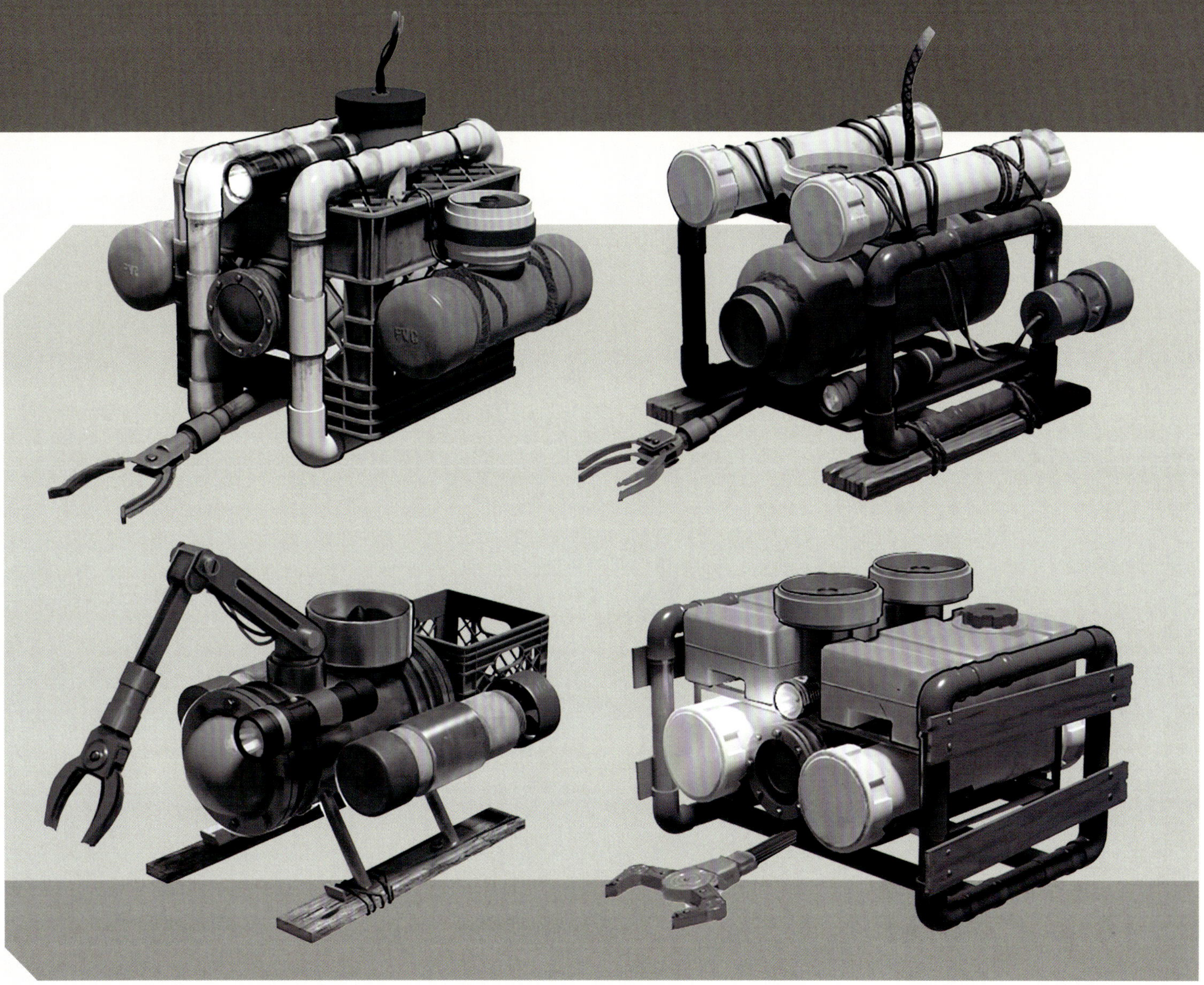

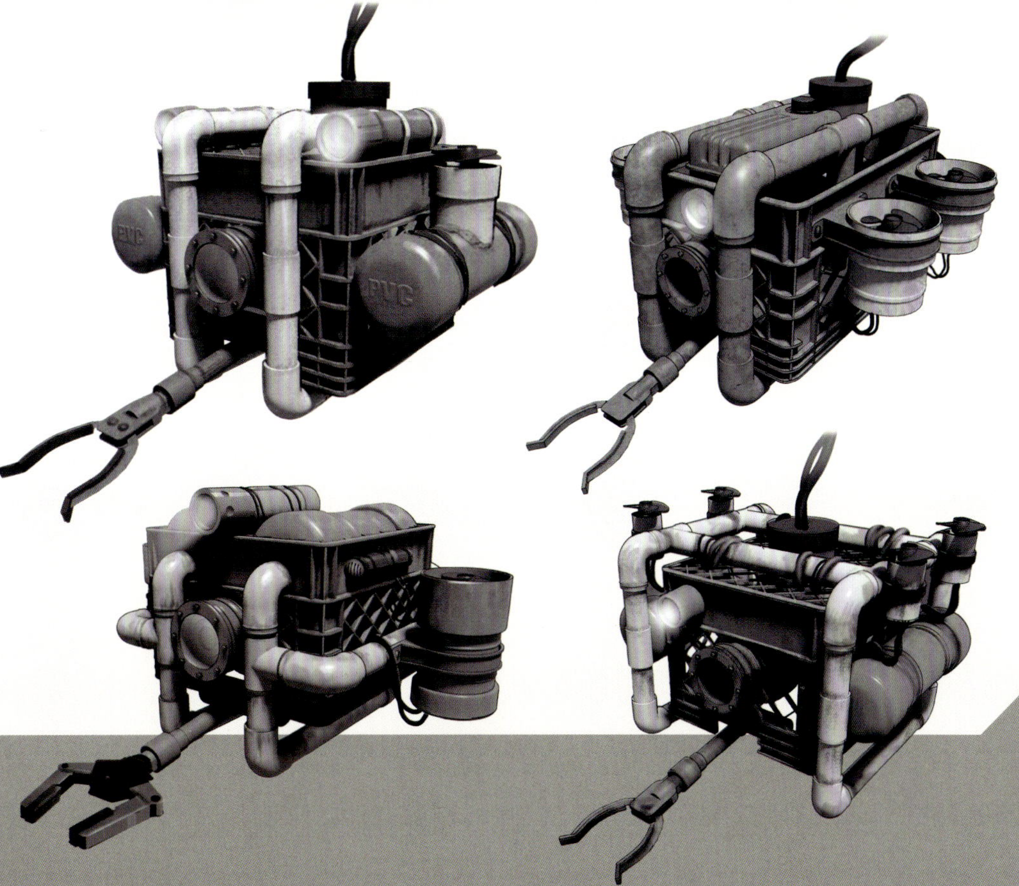

UNDERWATER DRONE

The Underwater Drone didn't make it into *Rust*, but these concepts explore the idea of a homemade, remote-controlled submersible. The designs are bulky, with a DIY propulsion system, a milk crate for storage, a flashlight, and a grabber arm to interact with items underwater.

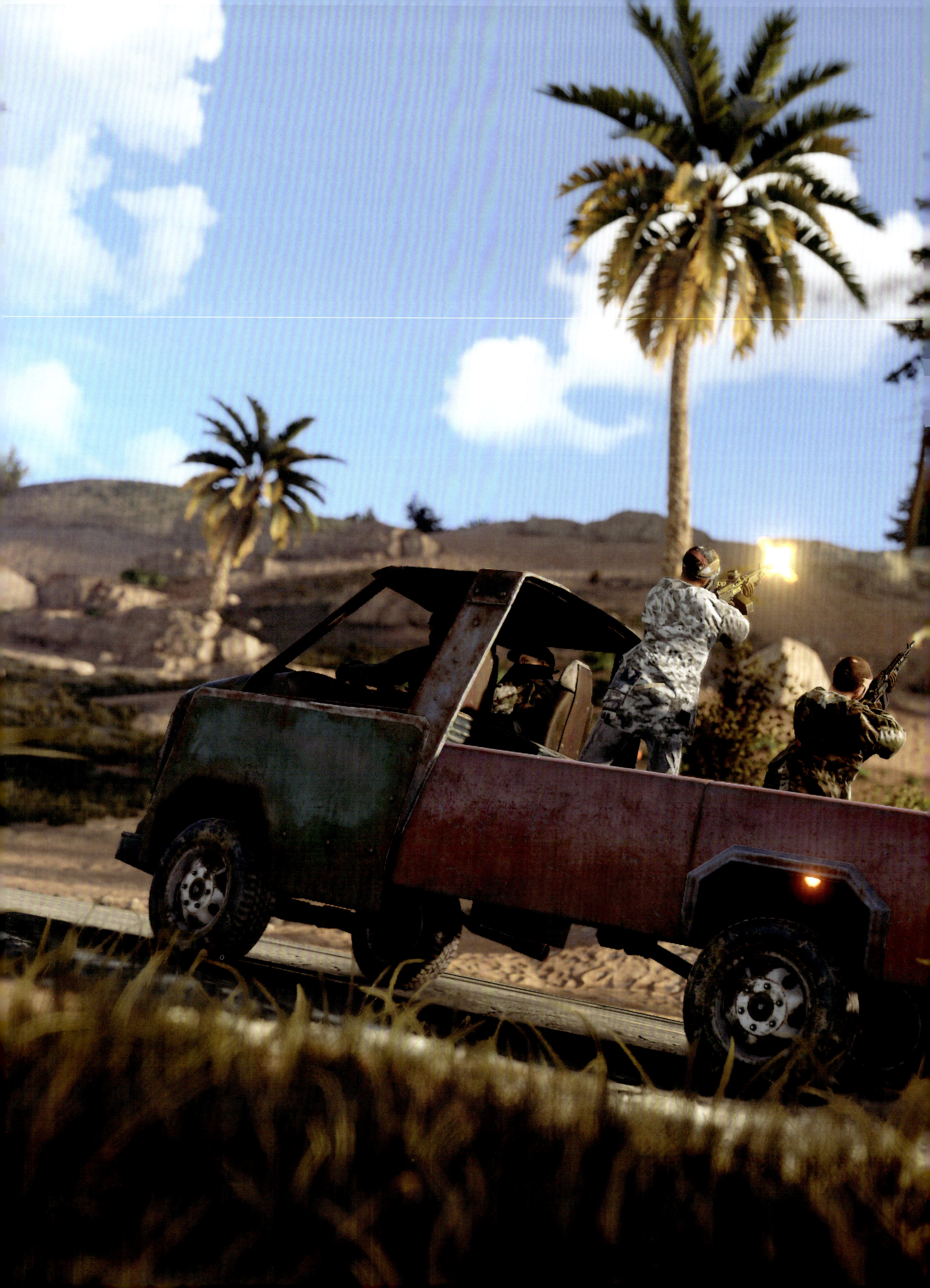

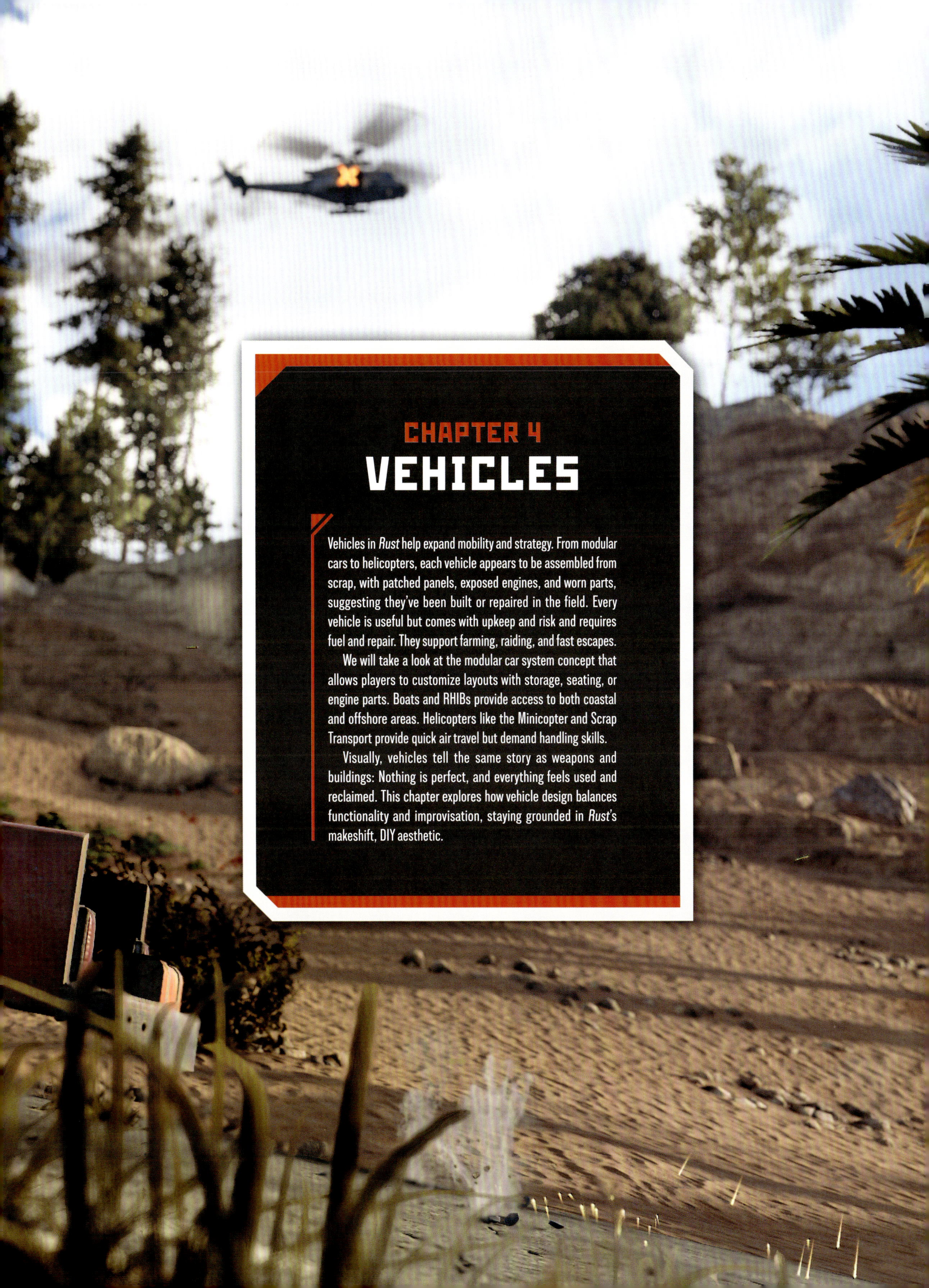

CHAPTER 4
VEHICLES

Vehicles in *Rust* help expand mobility and strategy. From modular cars to helicopters, each vehicle appears to be assembled from scrap, with patched panels, exposed engines, and worn parts, suggesting they've been built or repaired in the field. Every vehicle is useful but comes with upkeep and risk and requires fuel and repair. They support farming, raiding, and fast escapes.

We will take a look at the modular car system concept that allows players to customize layouts with storage, seating, or engine parts. Boats and RHIBs provide access to both coastal and offshore areas. Helicopters like the Minicopter and Scrap Transport provide quick air travel but demand handling skills.

Visually, vehicles tell the same story as weapons and buildings: Nothing is perfect, and everything feels used and reclaimed. This chapter explores how vehicle design balances functionality and improvisation, staying grounded in *Rust*'s makeshift, DIY aesthetic.

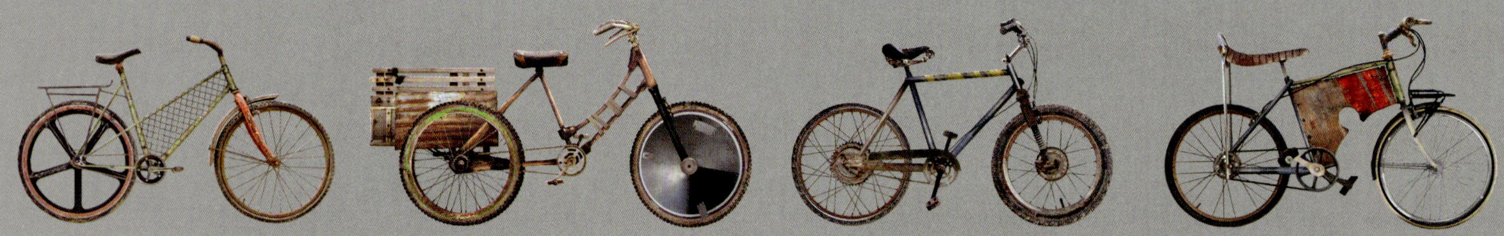

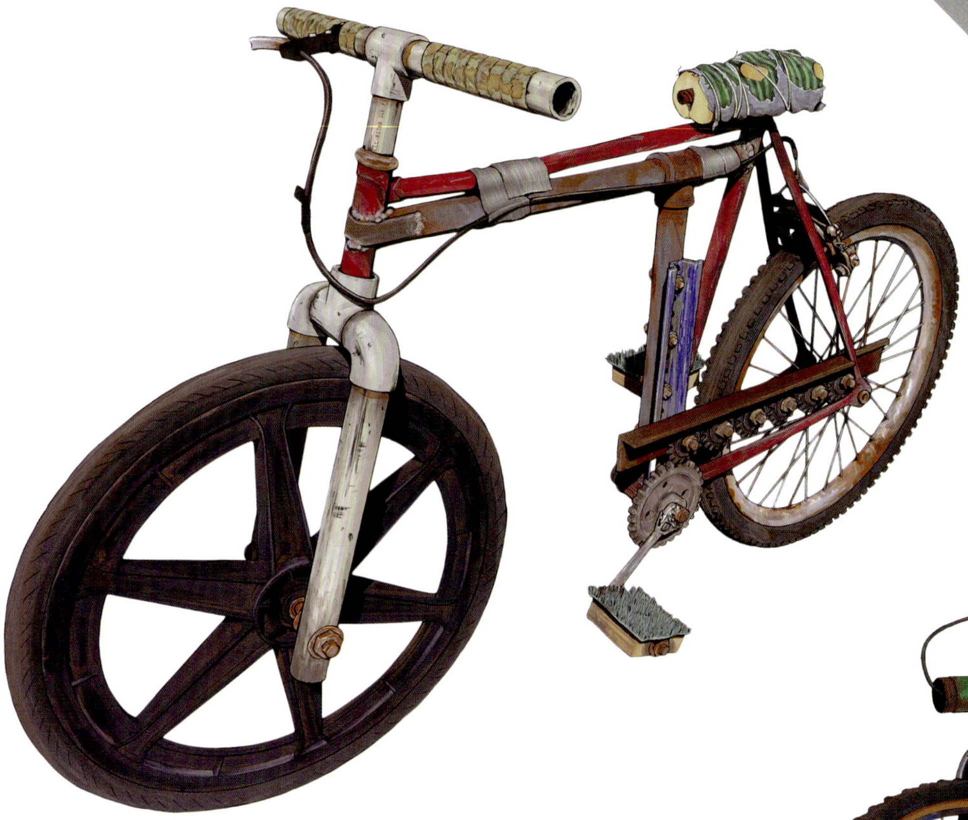

BIKES

These Bike concepts range from BMX-style builds to utility trikes. The initial sketches had the aim of finding a unique silhouette for the Bikes, with welded-on cargo baskets, mismatched frames, salvaged wheels, and hand-wrapped grips. Nothing is new; each Bike feels built from a scrapyard, held together with bolts and duct tape.

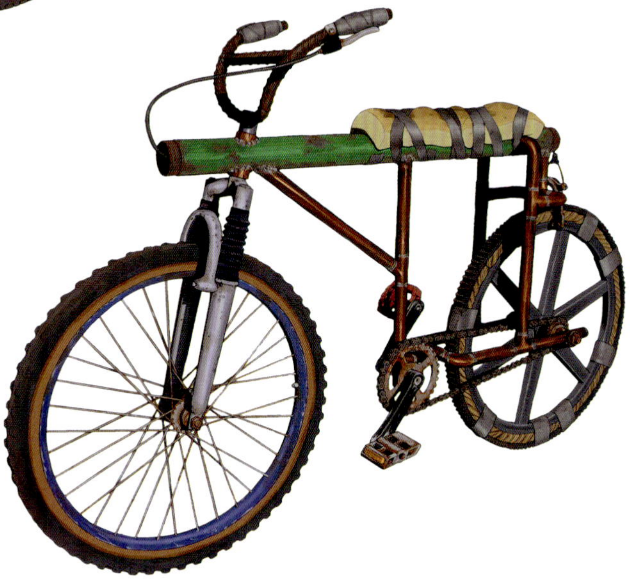

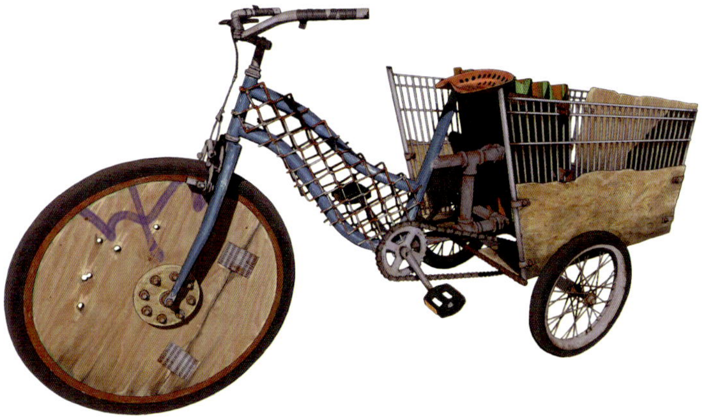

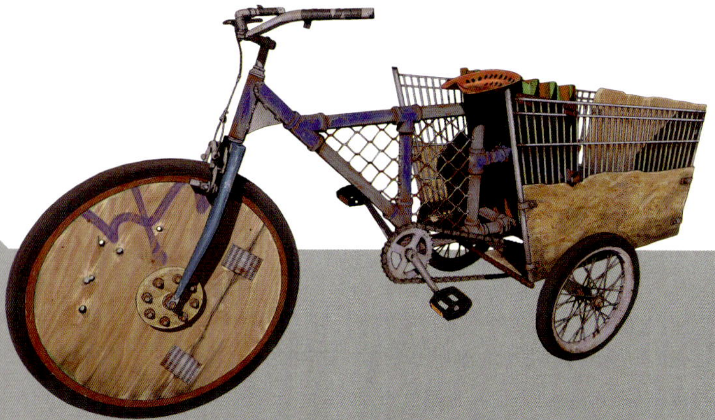

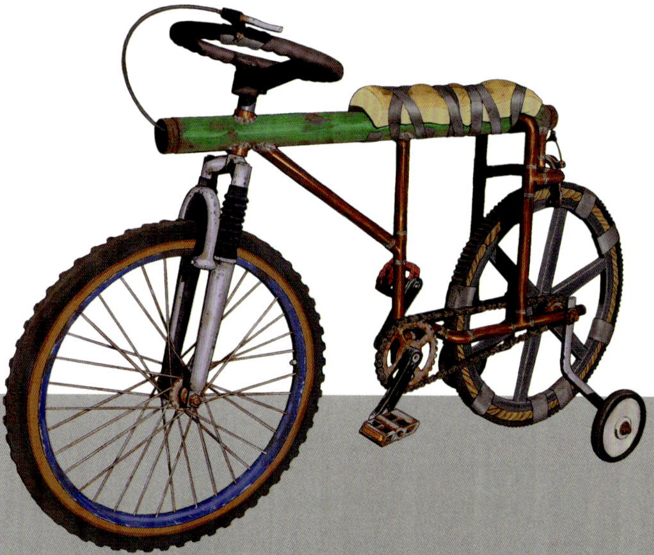

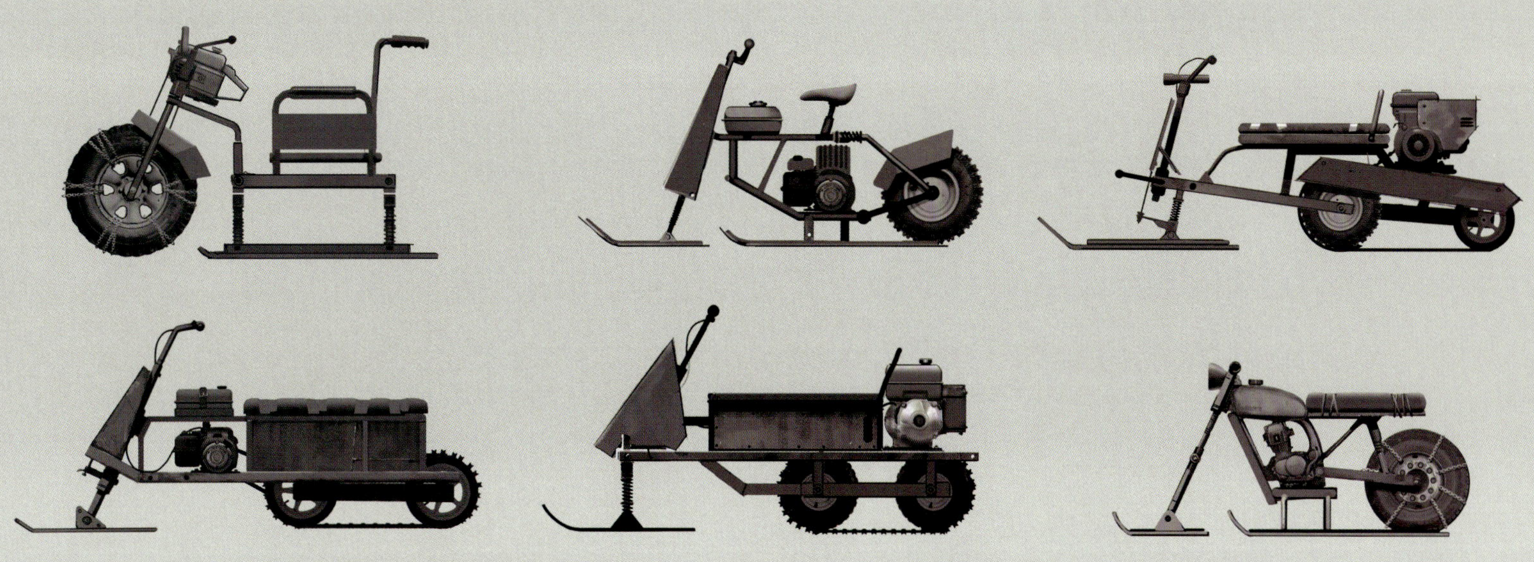

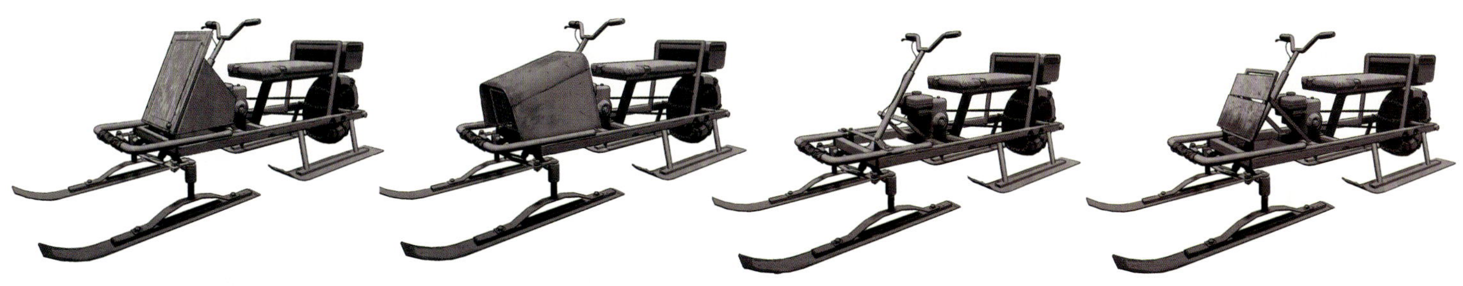

SNOWMOBILE

Here are a variety of Snowmobile designs, constructed from salvaged tanks, sawed-off skis, and exposed engine parts. The inspiration is rooted in a retro 1970–'80s homemade feel. It looks fast, loud, and just stable enough to be useful, whether hauling gear or escaping across the tundra.

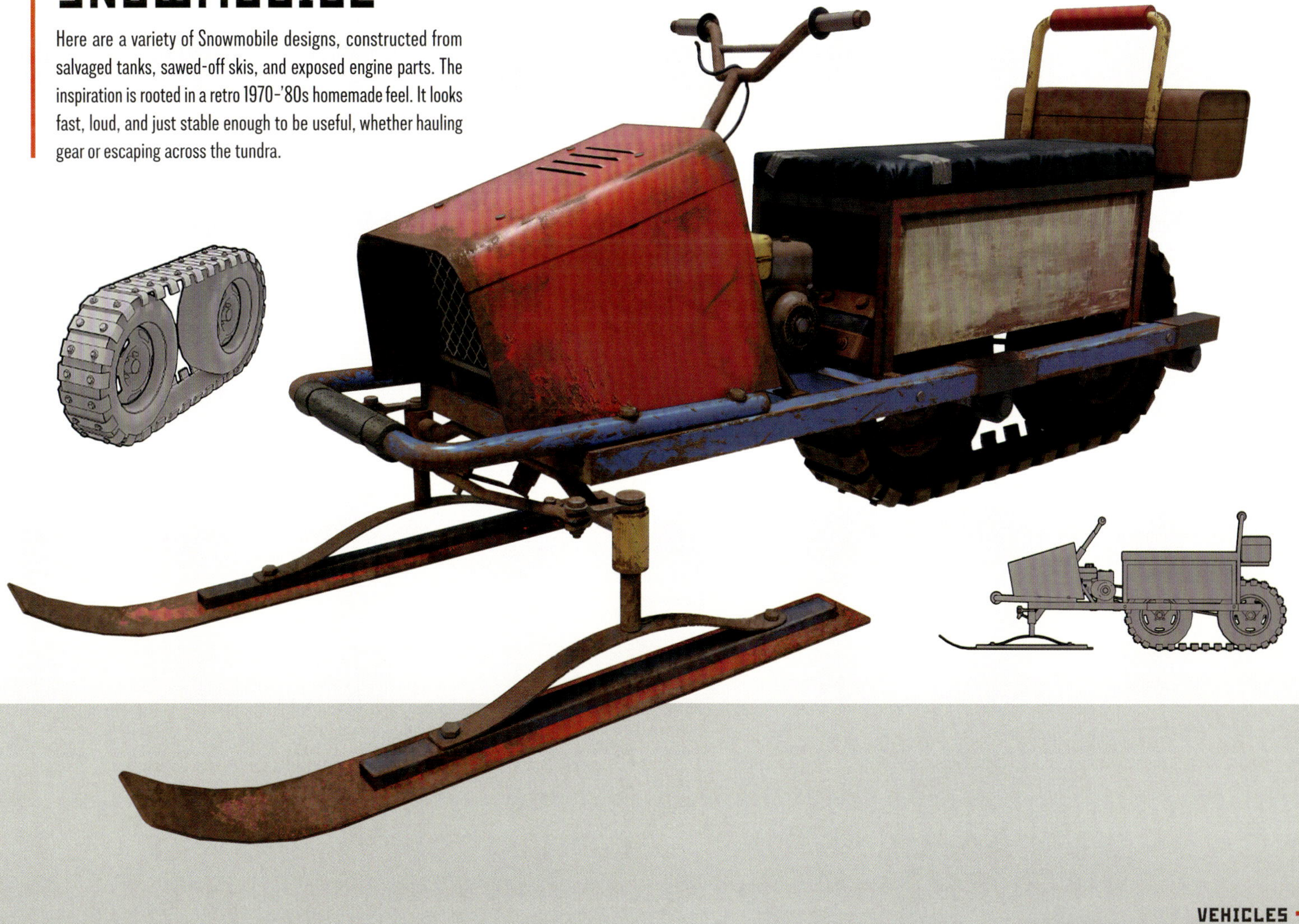

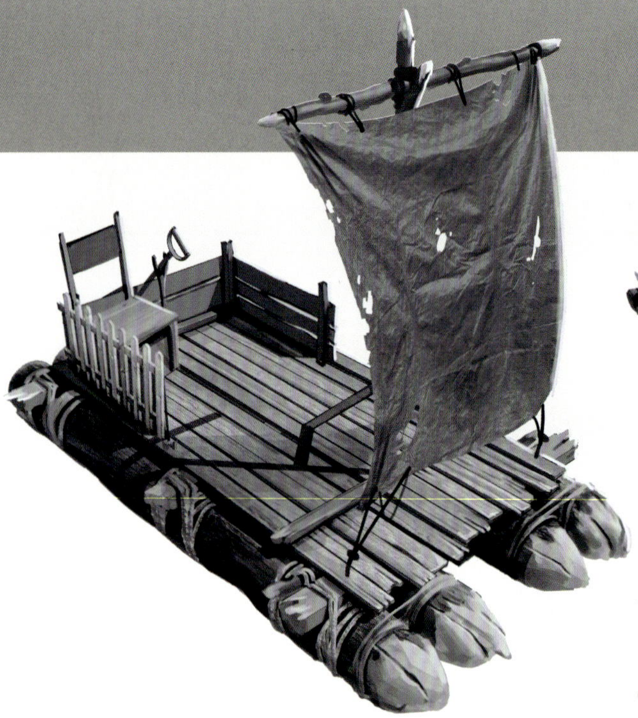

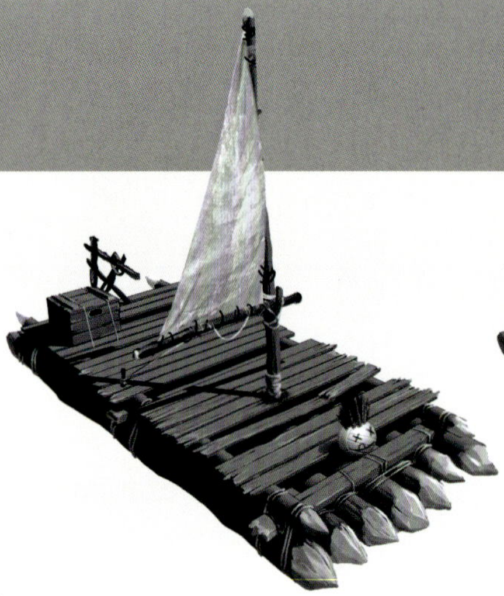

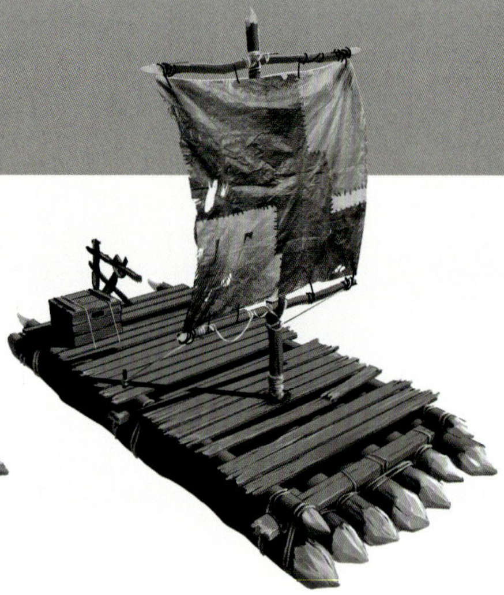

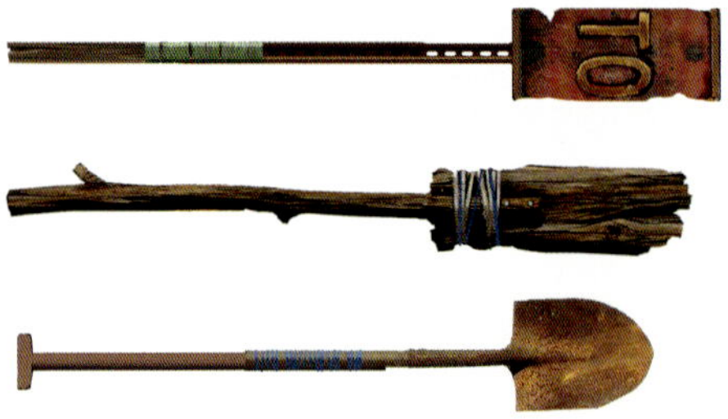

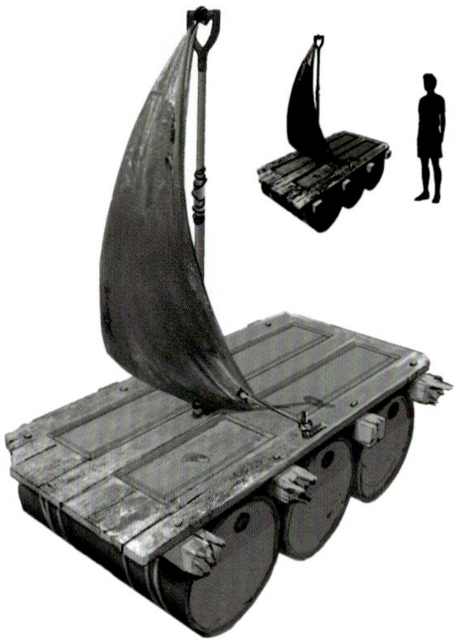

RAFTS

Early concepts for Rafts explored a modular build style which ultimately proved too ambitious at the time, so it was unfortunately shelved. The Rafts that made it into the game lean into the handmade aesthetic with mismatched planks, patched sails, and rudimentary steering tools like brooms or shovels.

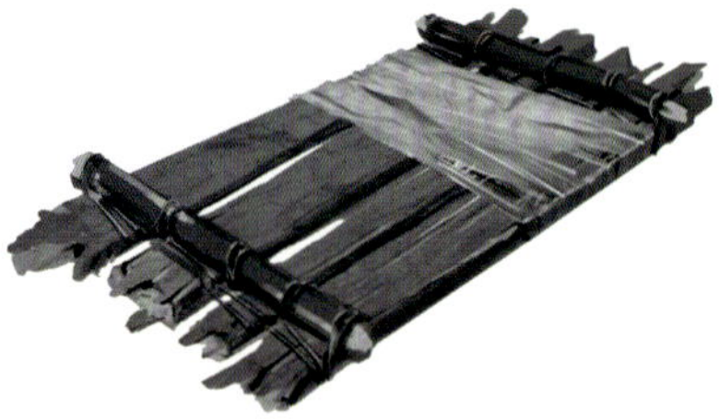

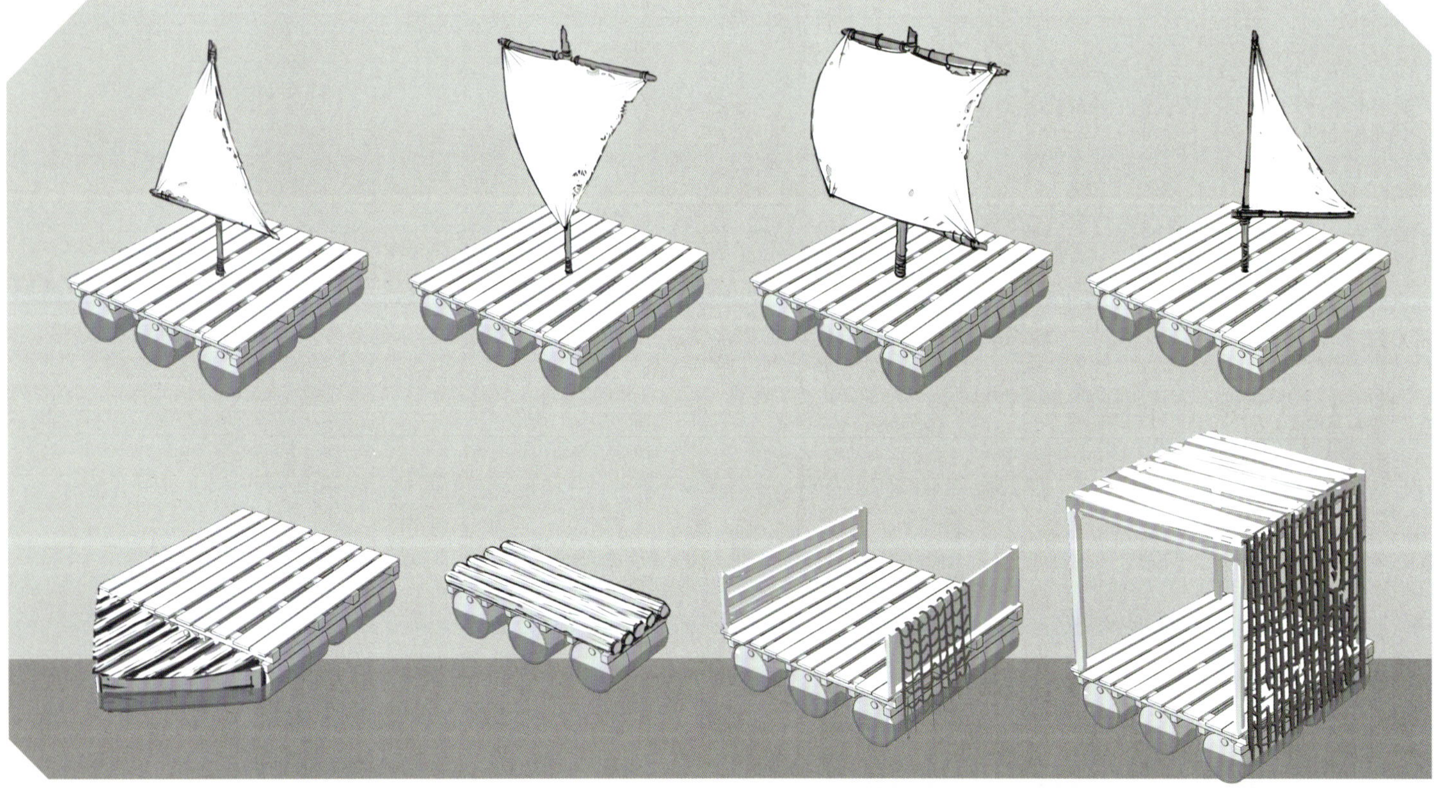

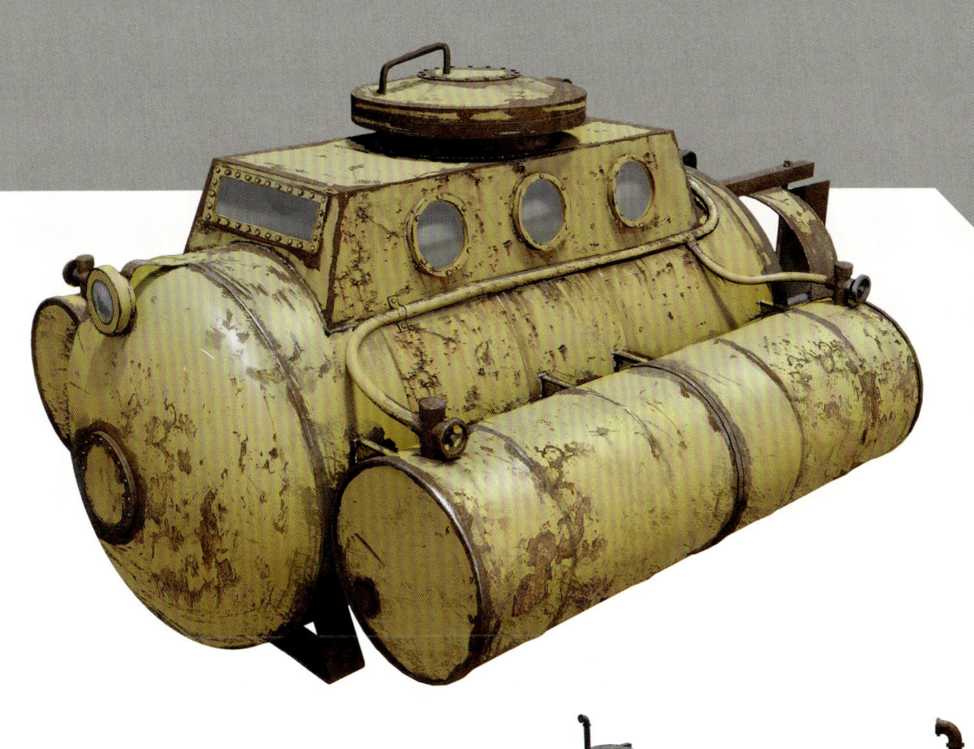

SUBMARINES

Constructed from old storage tanks, rusted valves, and welded pressure seals, the Submarines in *Rust* are inspired by the WWII X-class submarine. The concept designs are crude but functional. They focus on making the subs feel both dangerous and essential to survival, perfect for stealthy travel or underwater raids.

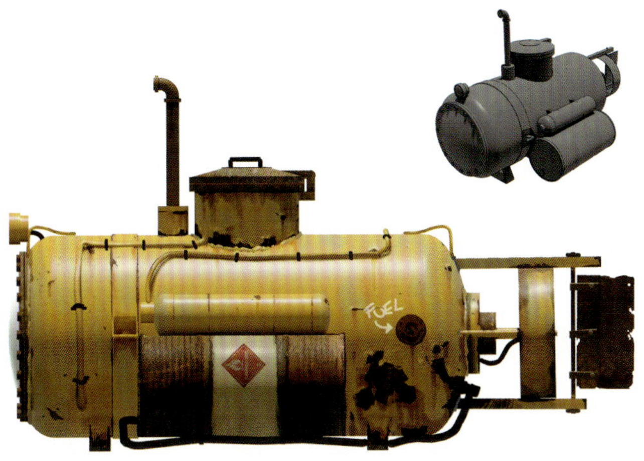

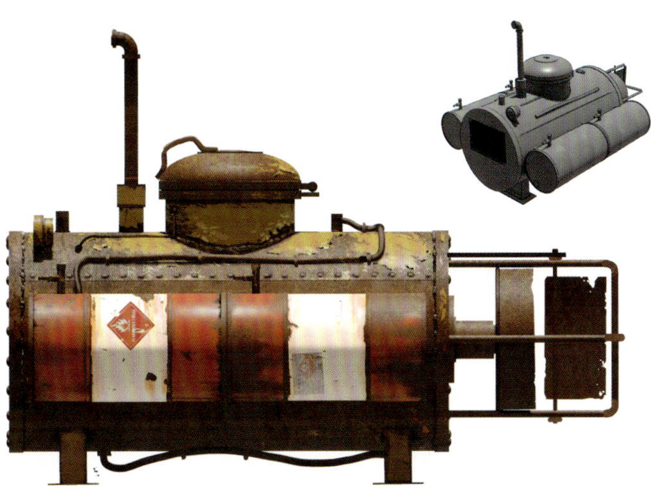

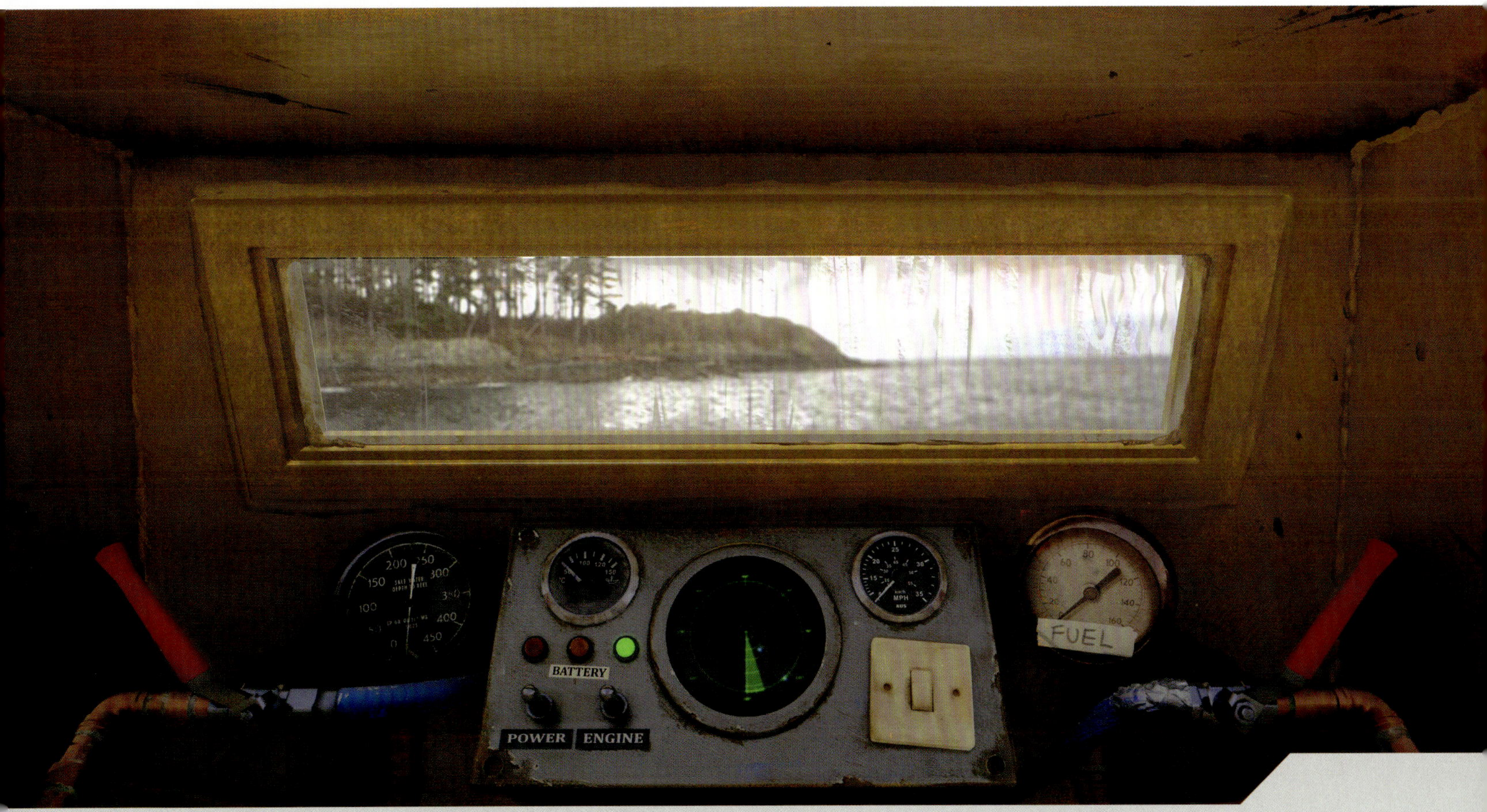

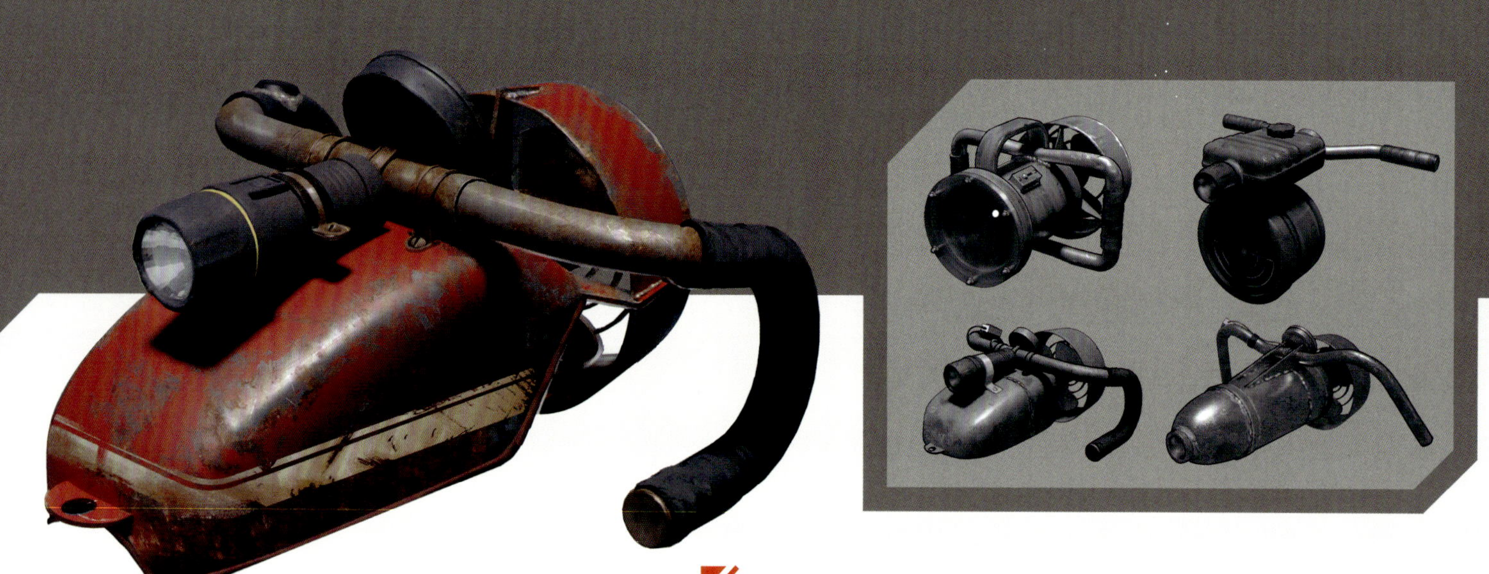

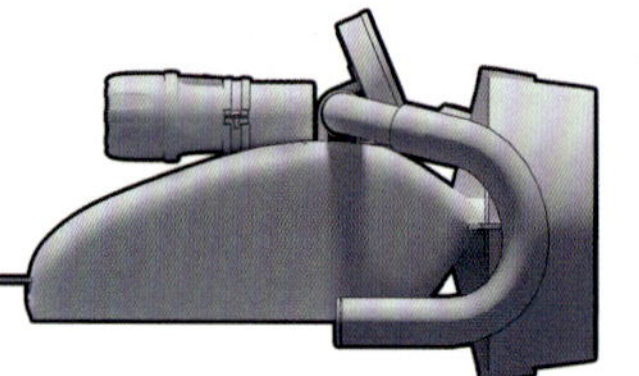

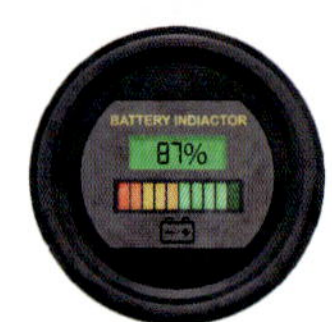

DIVER PROPULSION VEHICLE

The Diver Propulsion Vehicle (DPV) is a compact underwater mobility tool made from salvaged motorbike parts. Its concept leans heavily on visible mechanics, exhaust, battery, and pressure gauges. Built for quick underwater traversal or stealthy coastal entries, it's the perfect way for players to outswim danger.

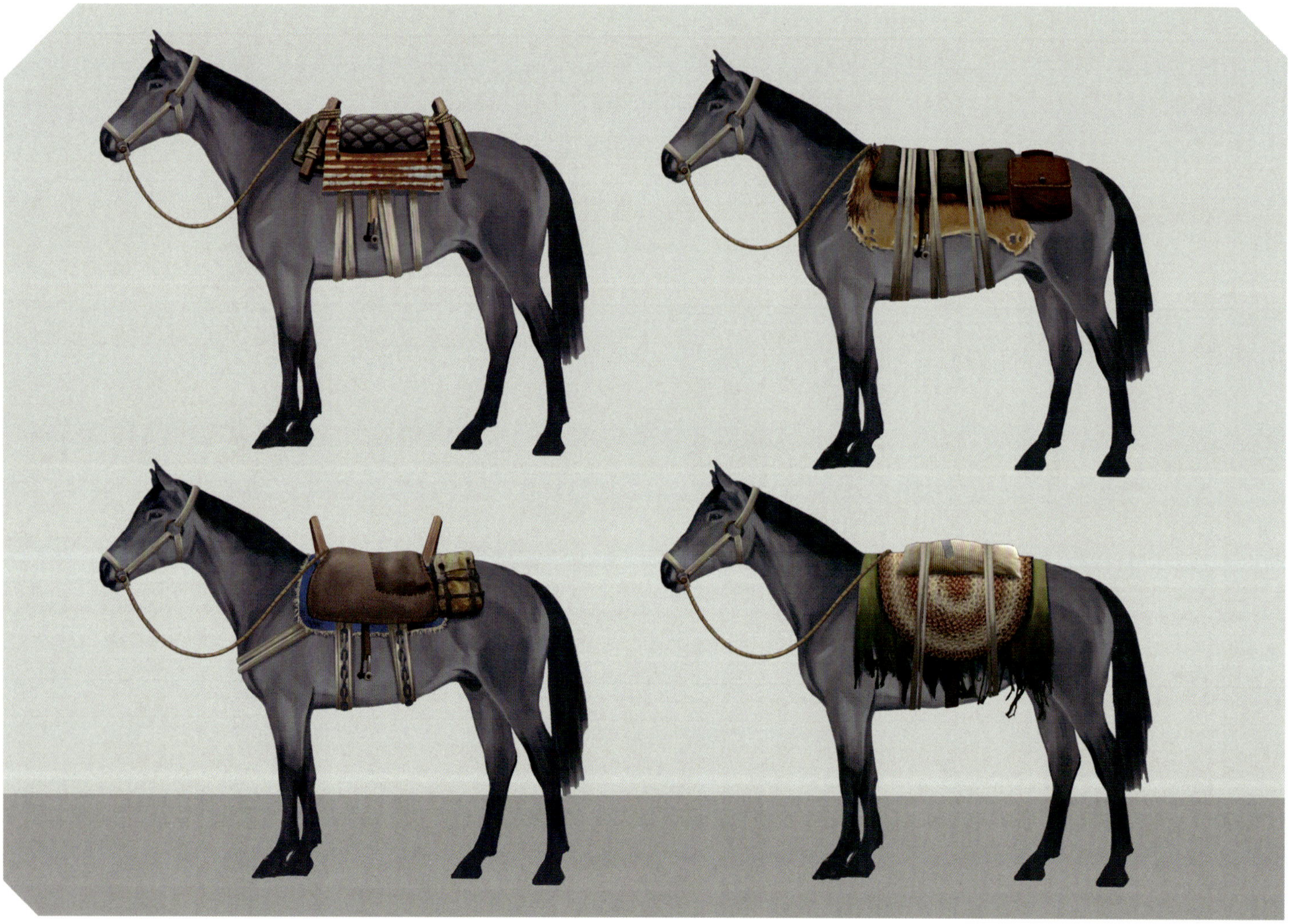

HORSE SADDLES

These concepts explored a variety of saddle setups for horses, from crude wooden frames to cloth-wrapped bags, pillows, and rugs. Nothing is ornamental; every strap and bundle is practical, stitched together from found materials. Some offer storage pouches, while some have a more basic approach.

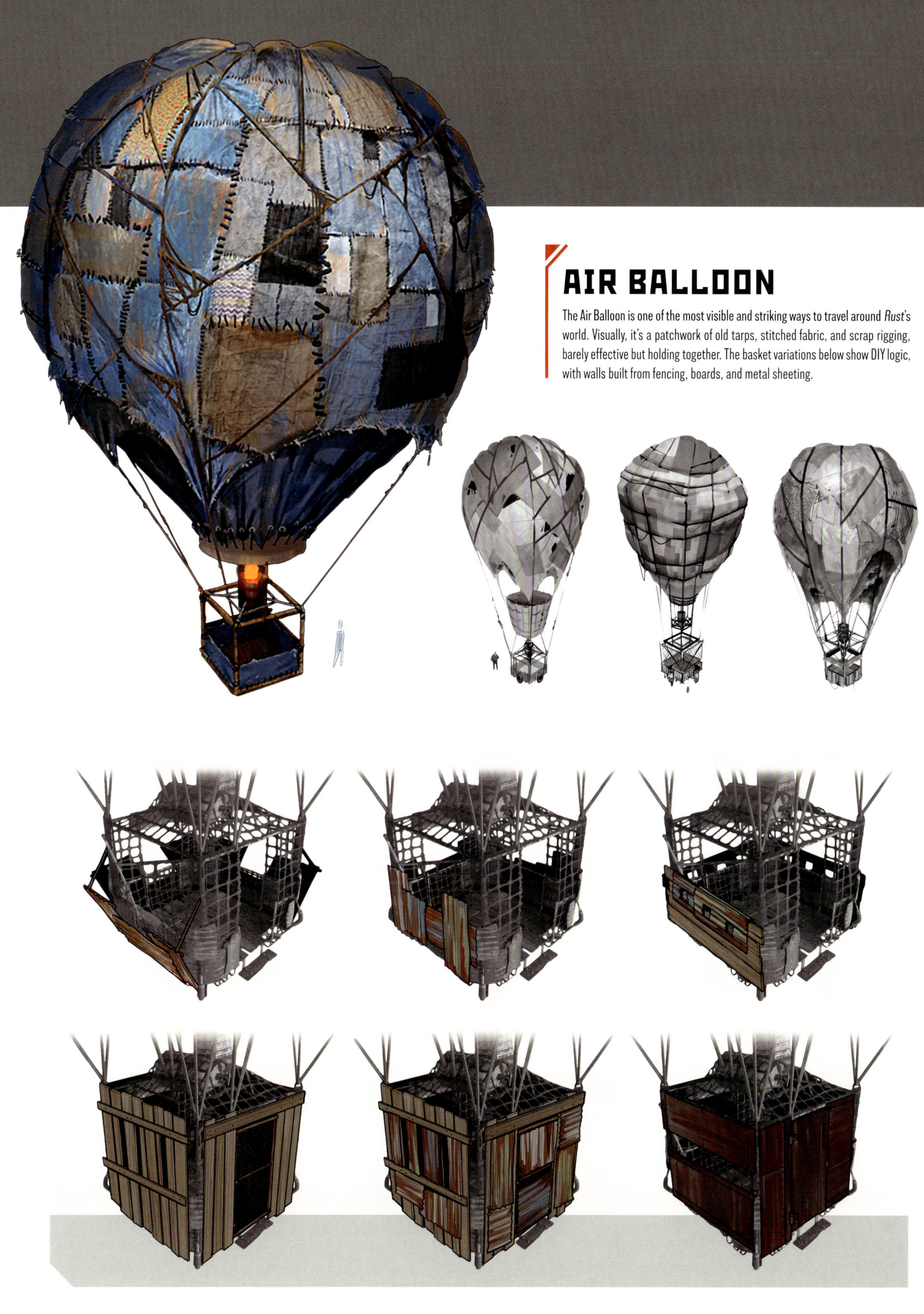

AIR BALLOON

The Air Balloon is one of the most visible and striking ways to travel around *Rust*'s world. Visually, it's a patchwork of old tarps, stitched fabric, and scrap rigging, barely effective but holding together. The basket variations below show DIY logic, with walls built from fencing, boards, and metal sheeting.

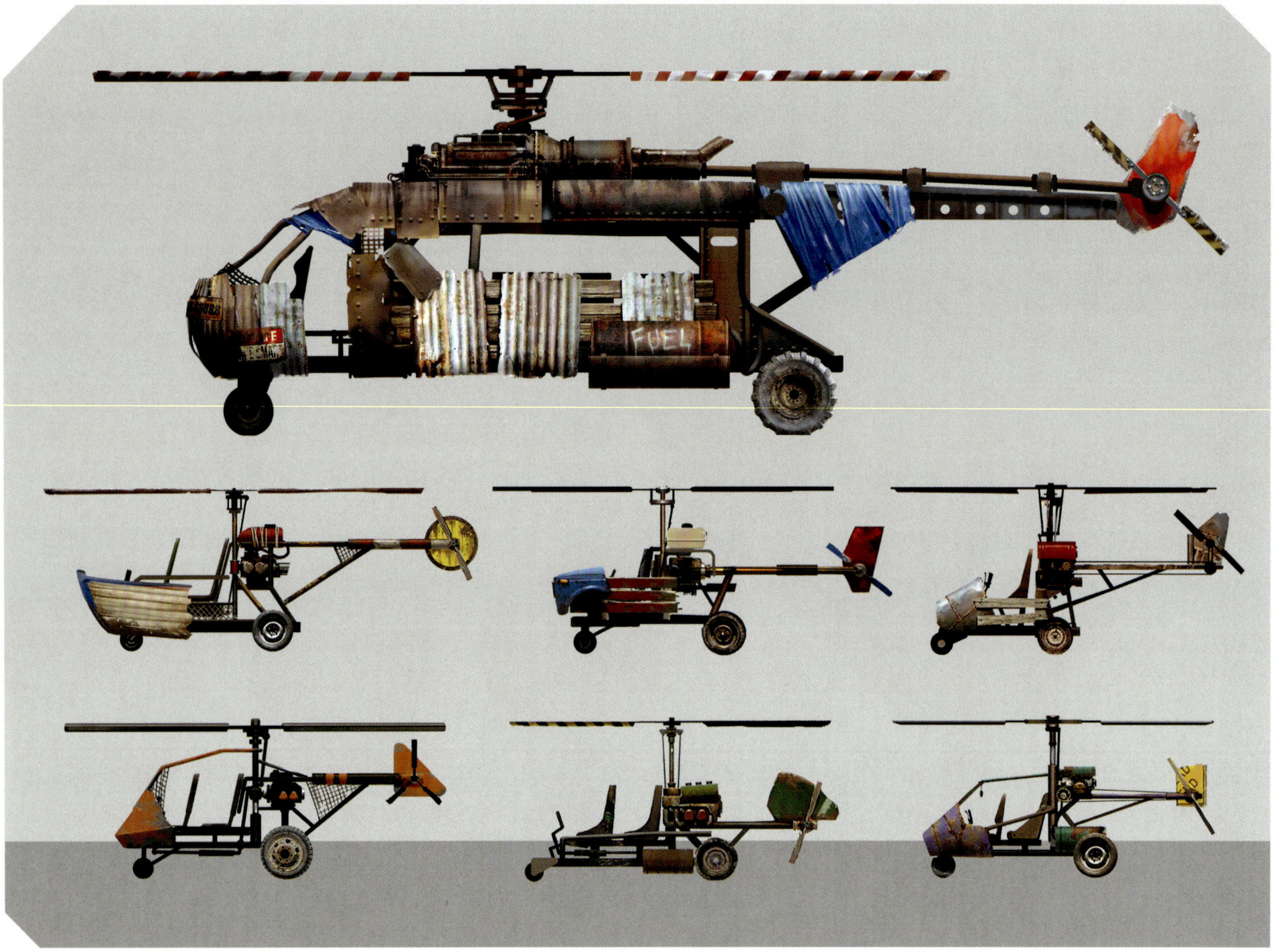

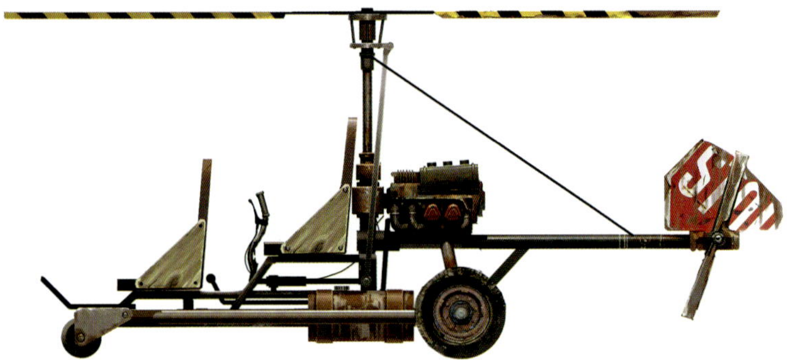

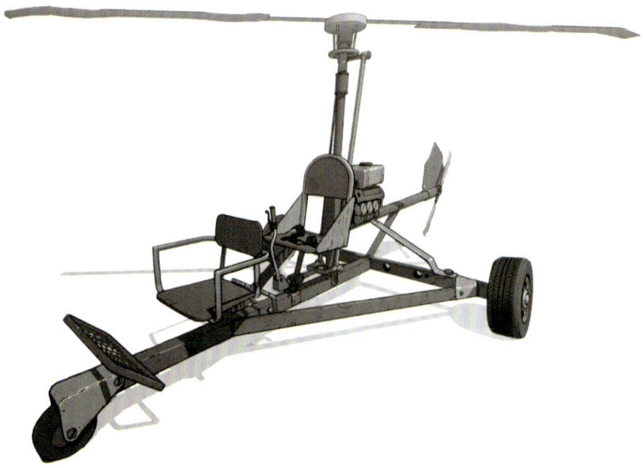

HELICOPTERS

These Helicopter concepts show a range of designs with stripped-down, salvaged tech, exposed engines, misshapen frames, and parts that look borrowed from everything but aircraft. Whether it's a single-seat Minicopter or a Transport Helicopter, each model was designed with a distinguishable silhouette. They feel more like flying machines than fully fledged helicopters.

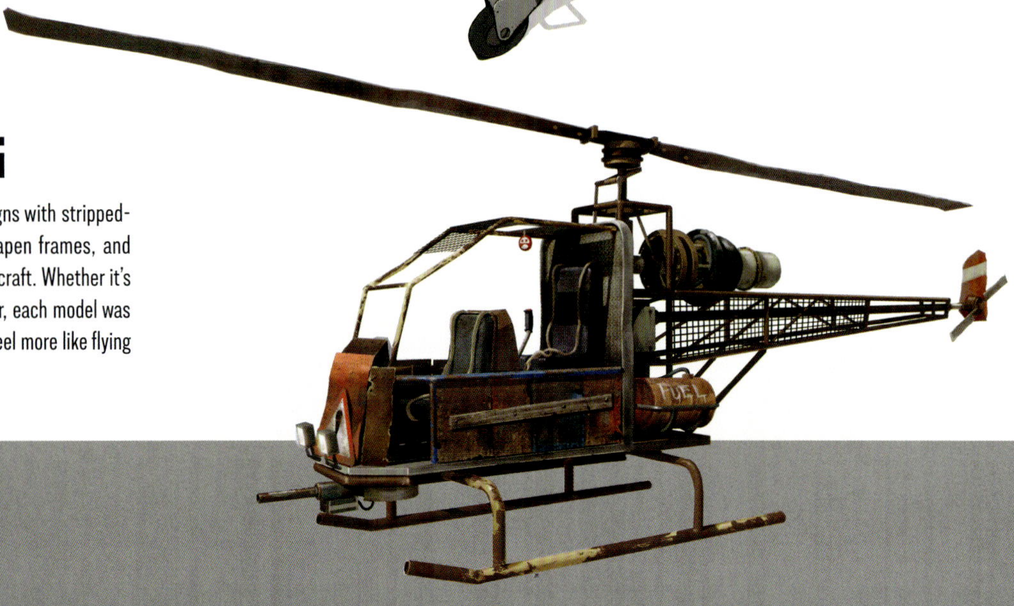

HELIPAD

The concept sketches for the Helipad explore how landing zones might have looked. Some are compounds, fenced in with DIY setups; others are more formal with flight towers and concrete pads. Their design prioritizes quick identification, giving players a visual landmark from the sky, whether it's part of a monument or a player base.

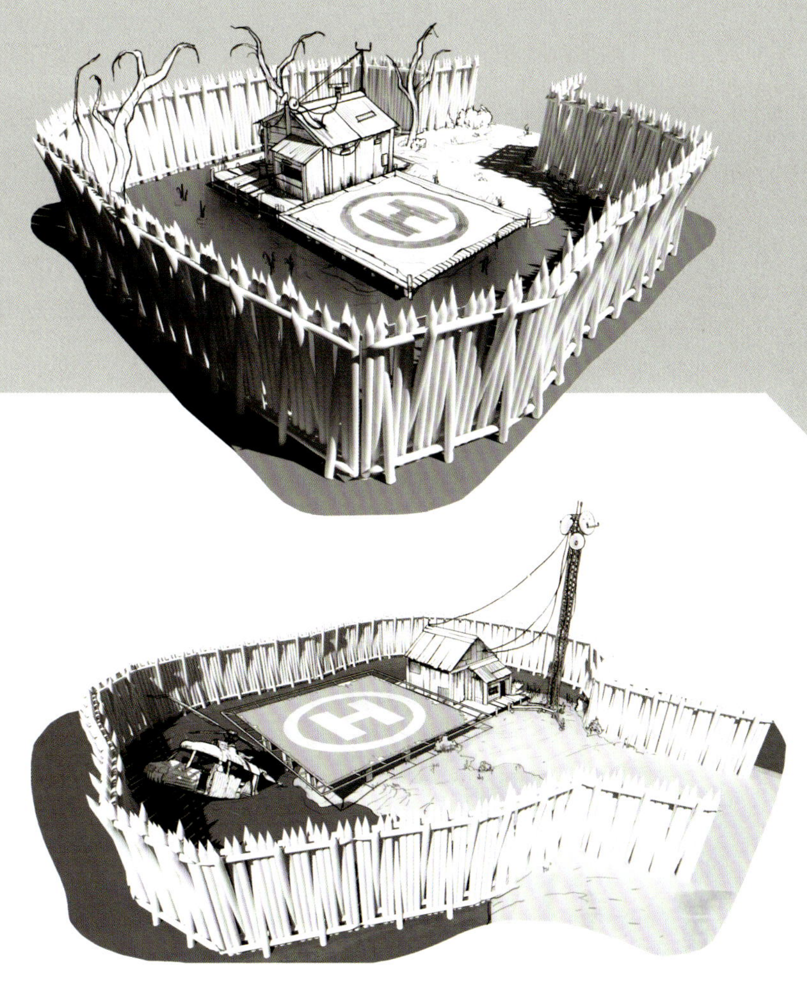

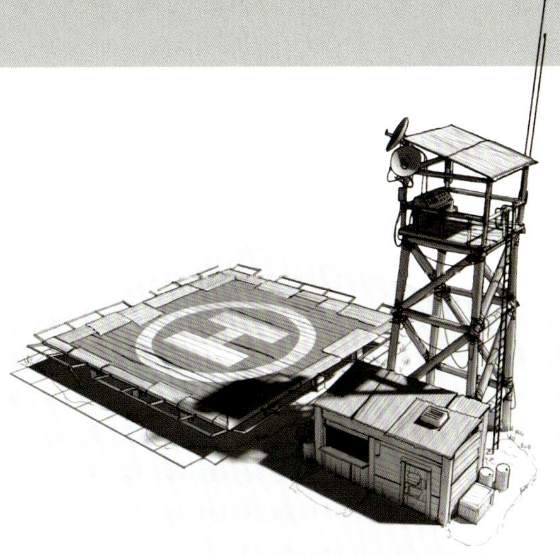

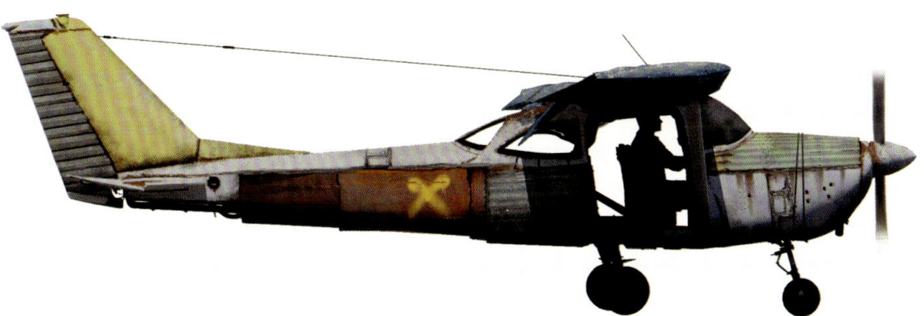

AIRPLANES

These airplane designs were inspired by the vintage Cessna plane. They lean heavily into the salvage aspect of *Rust* with weathered fuselages, sun-bleached panels, and improvised repair jobs that define their look. These concepts didn't make it into the game, but they would have offered long-distance mobility and speed.

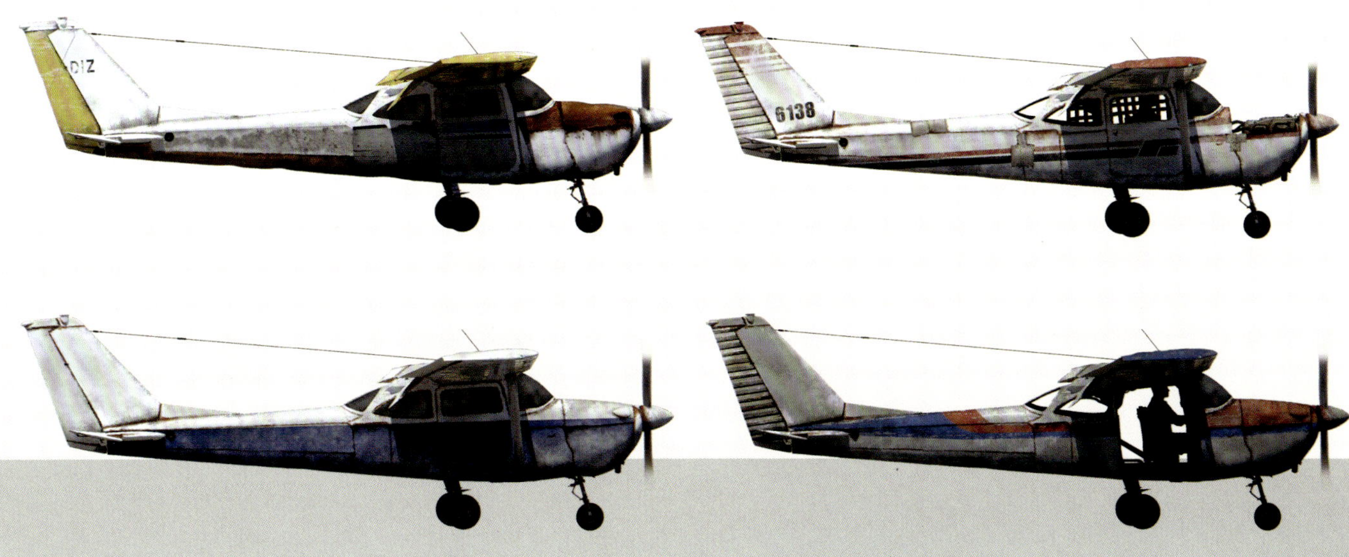

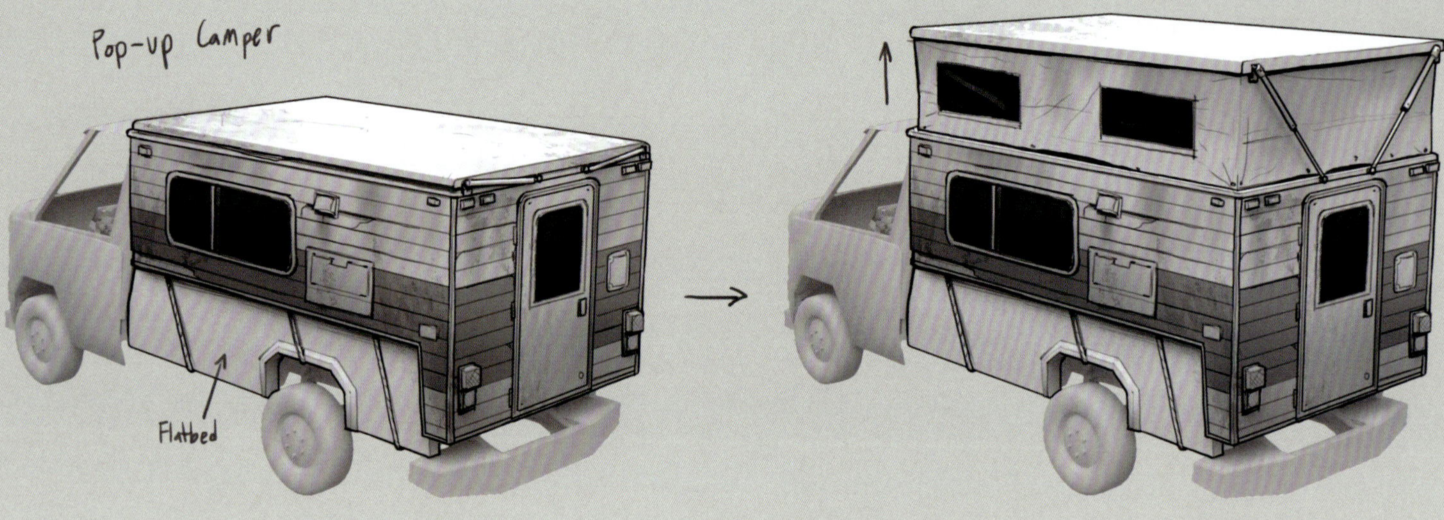

CAMPER

The Camper was envisioned as a mobile base extension, part transport, part shelter. Designs focused on how players might repurpose abandoned vehicles into livable spaces, complete with storage and sleeping space. The pop-up-roof concept was inspired by real-life camper vans and added a lot visually but ultimately was scrapped.

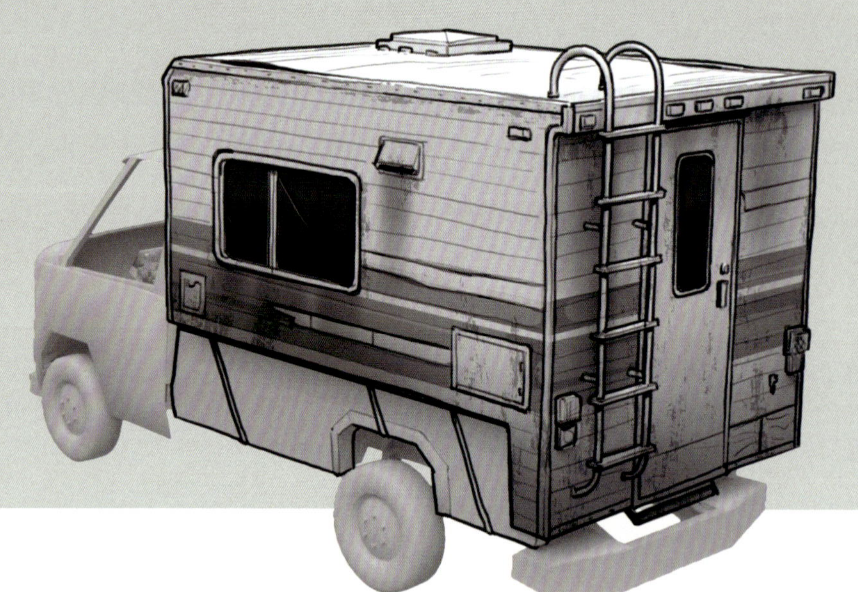

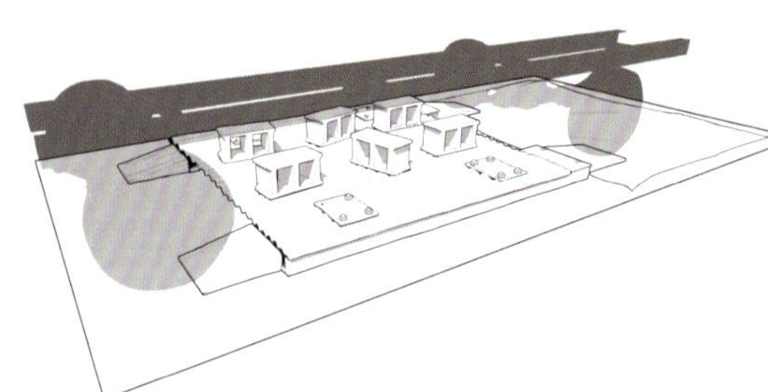

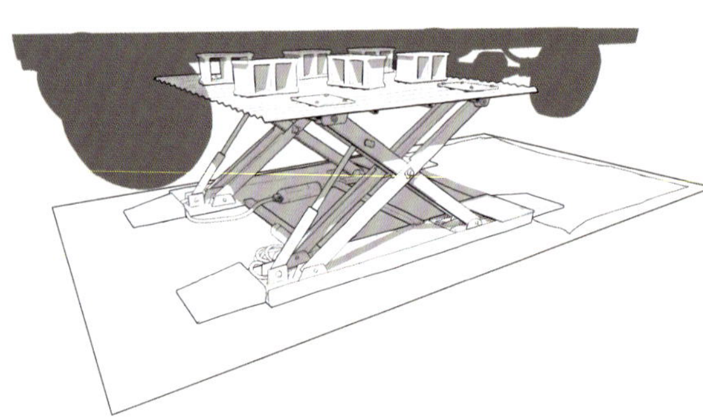

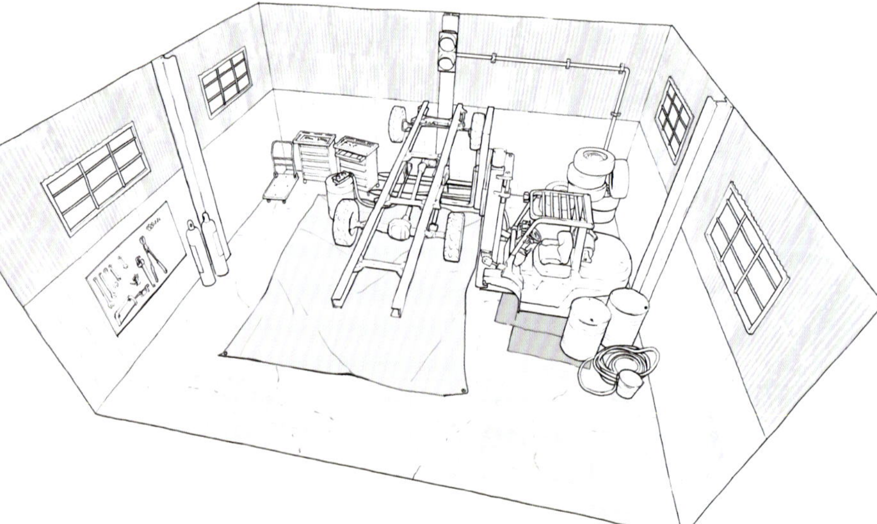

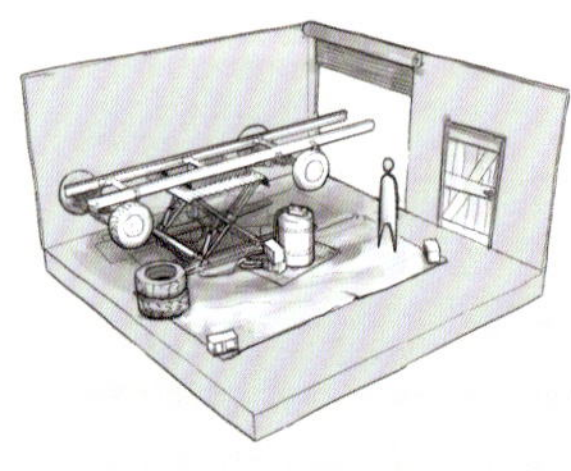

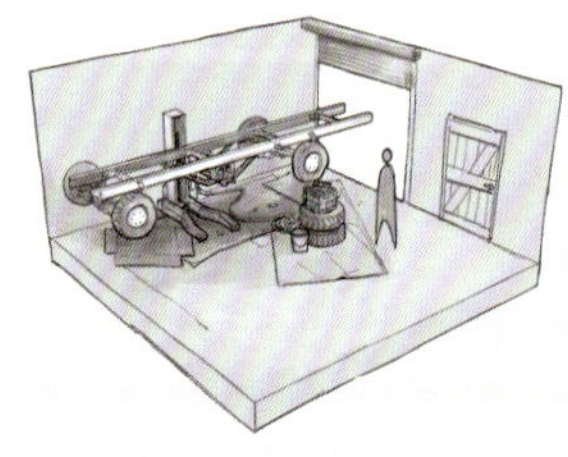

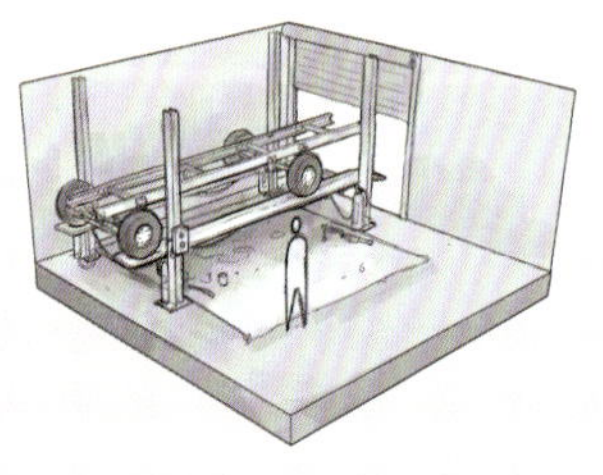

GARAGE

Garages are key for safe vehicle storage and repair. These concepts are centered around a standard working garage, with elevated work bays, storage, and lifting machinery. The design is a stripped-back workspace, with just enough room and tools to get the job done.

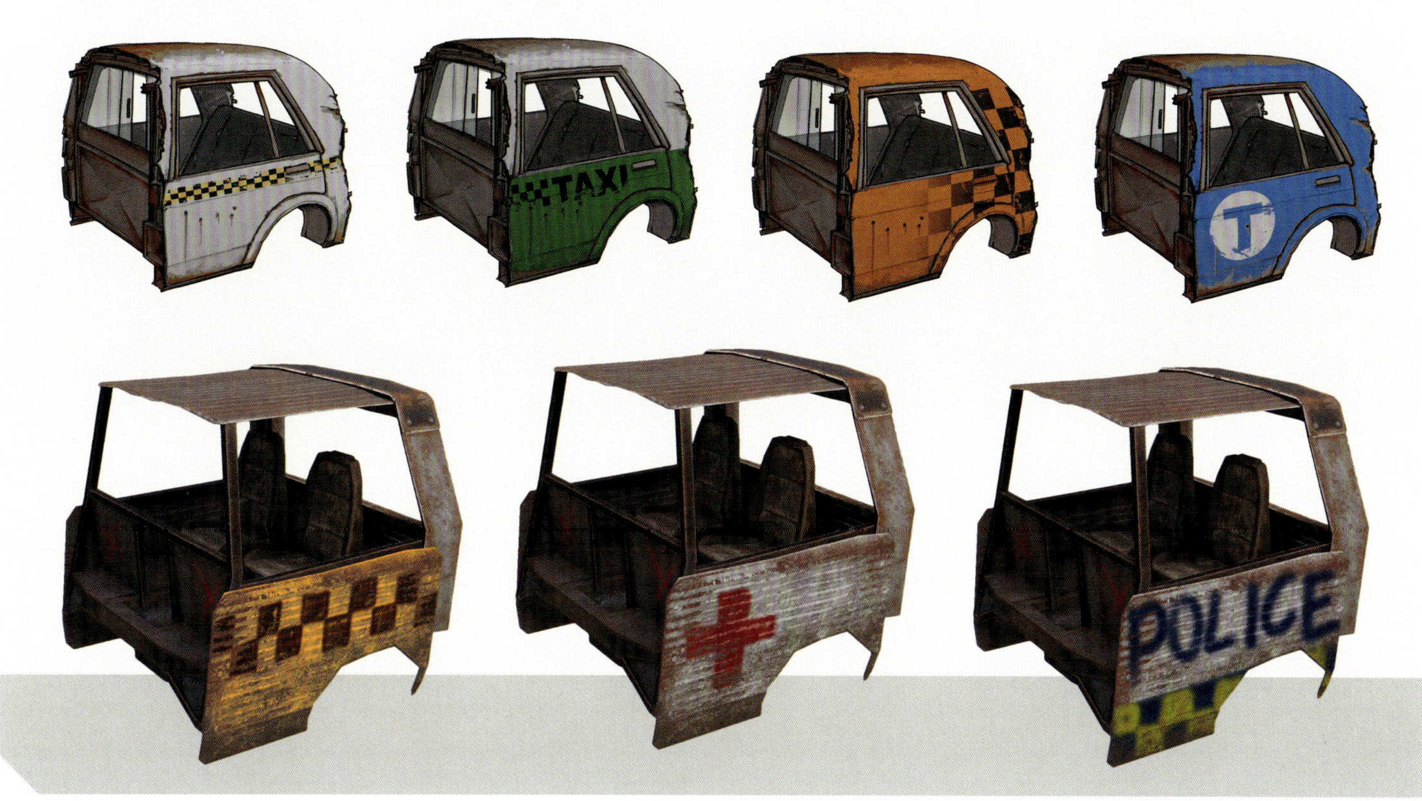

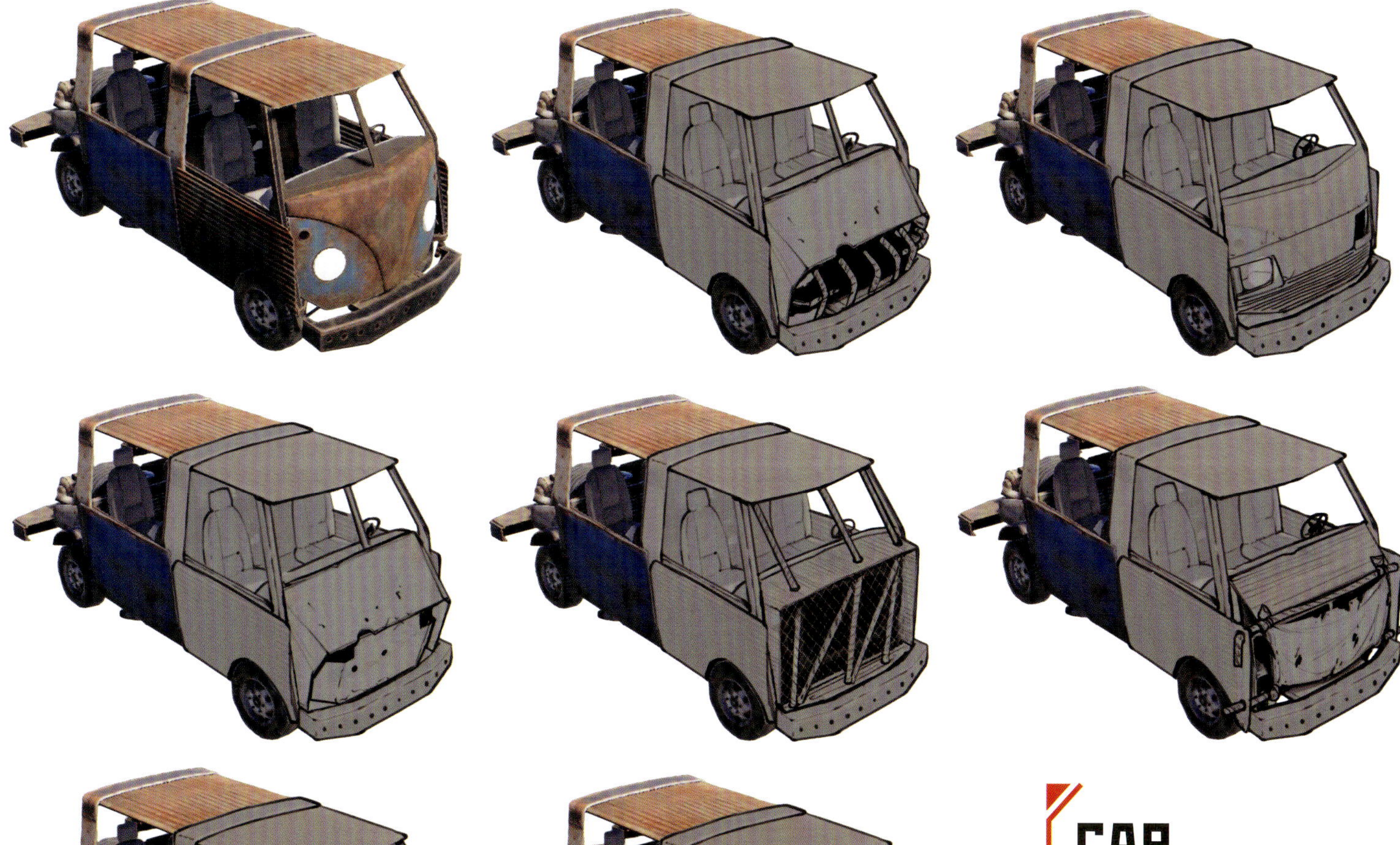

CAR MODULES 1

The modular vehicle system was designed to be interchangeable across vehicles. From stripped-down frames to reskinned variants with markings like "Police" or "Taxi," each modular body design enables a wide variety of vehicle combinations.

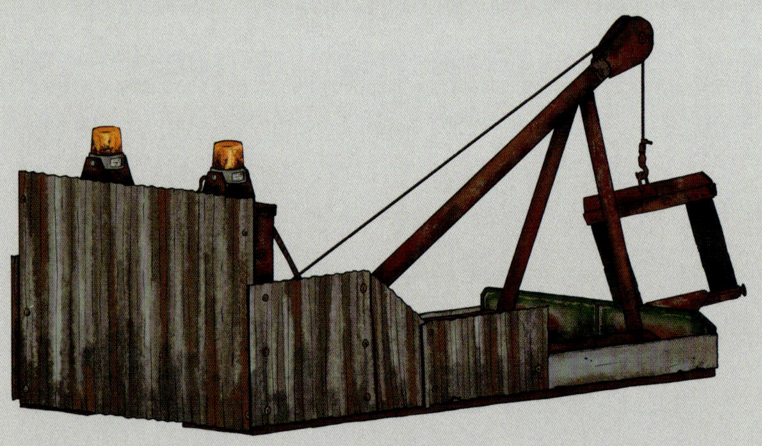

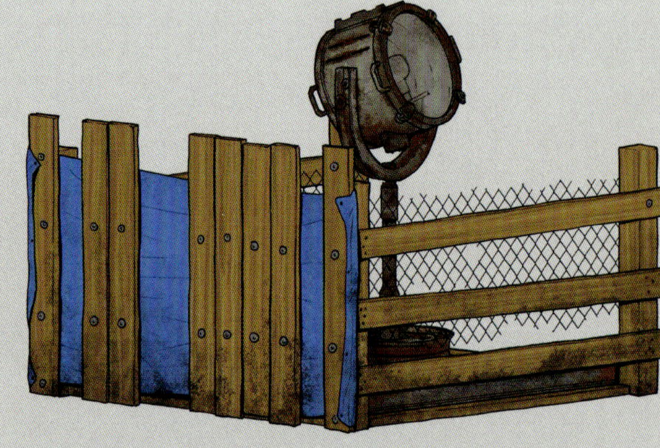

CAR MODULES 2

The system was designed to give players a high level of customization that affects the vehicles not only cosmetically but also functionally. The system mechanics are simple: The module you choose dramatically changes what the vehicle is used for.

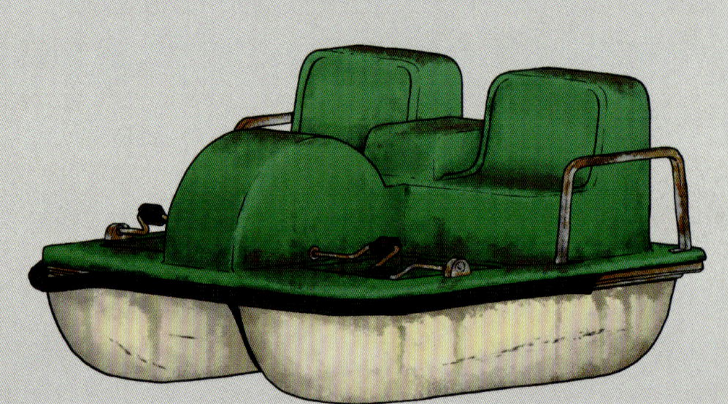

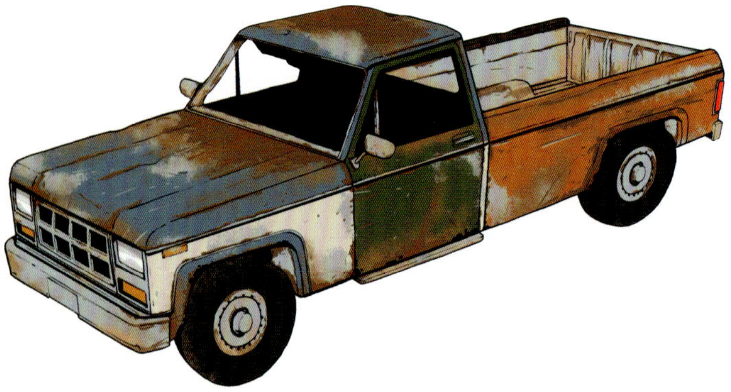

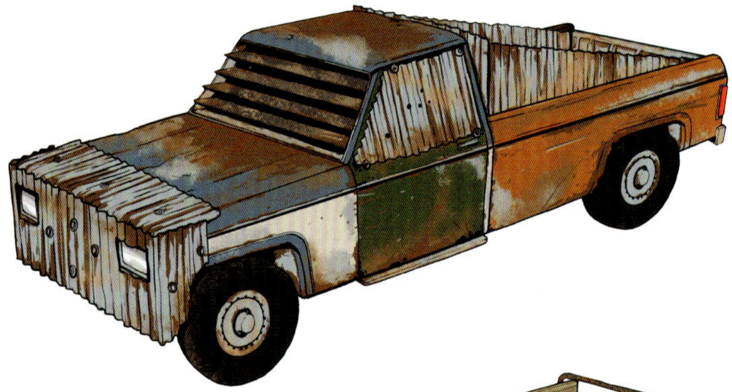

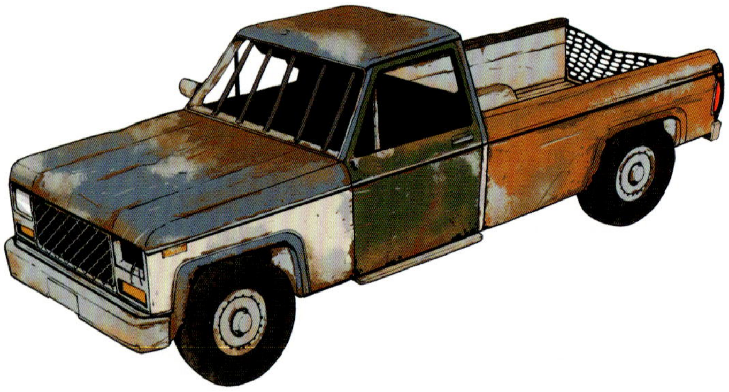

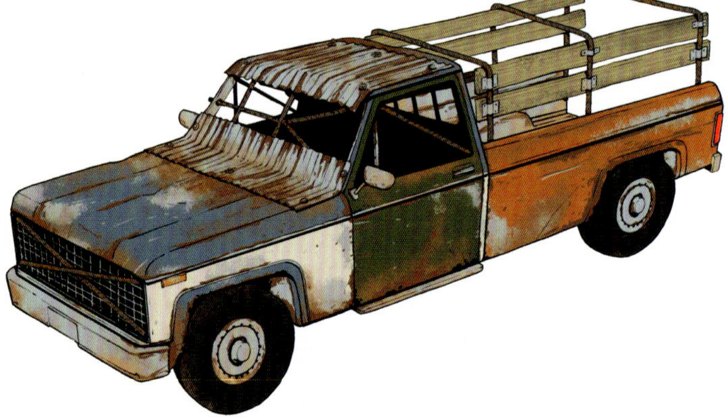

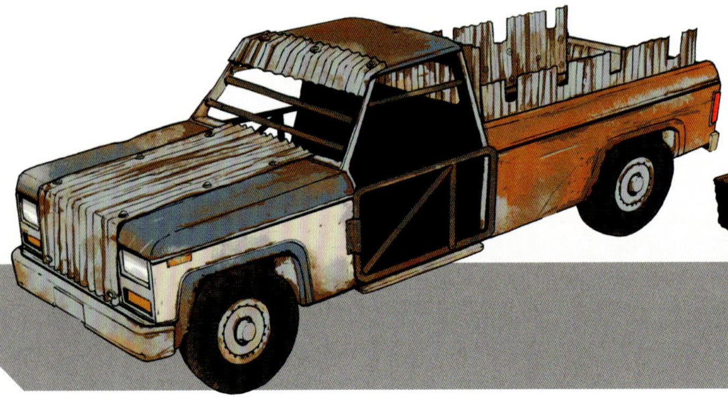

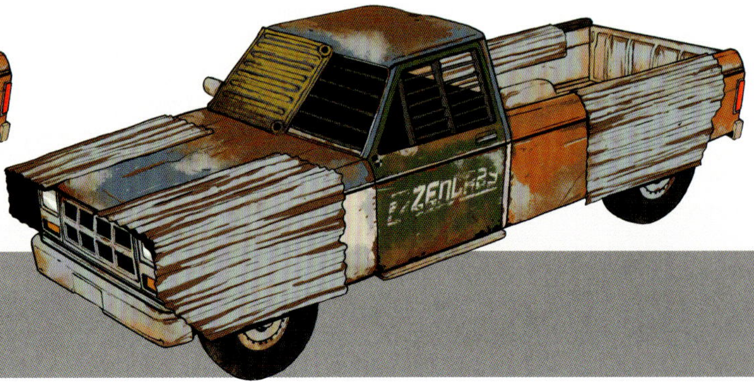

CAR MODULES 3

These module concepts cover seating, storage, and steering. Seating modules are cut from old vehicle shells, with salvaged metal and wooden boards added for support. Storage modules come in all forms: rusty tanks, open crates, and makeshift beds. Steering modules explore the bare minimum needed to control a vehicle.

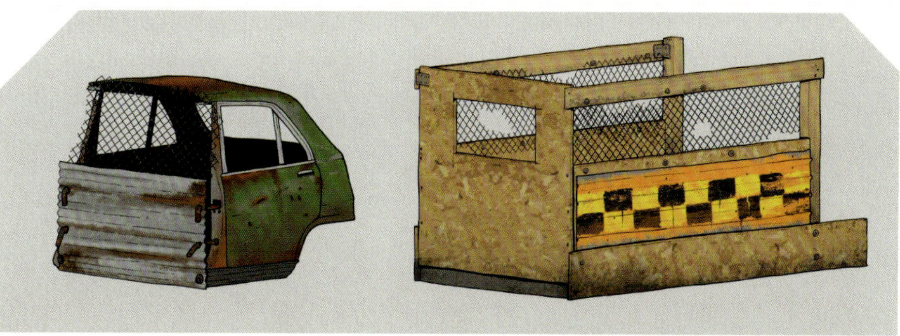

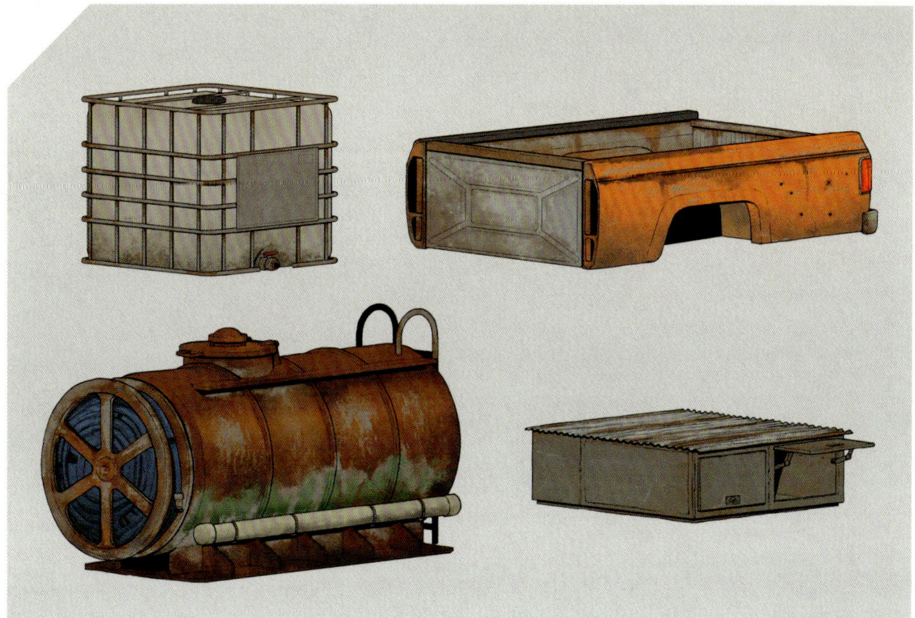

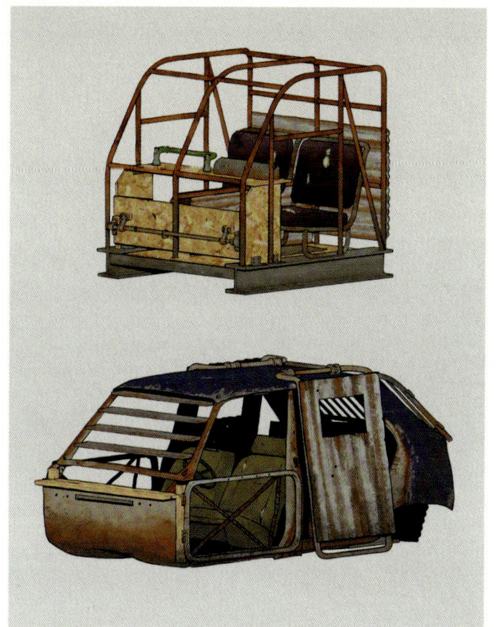

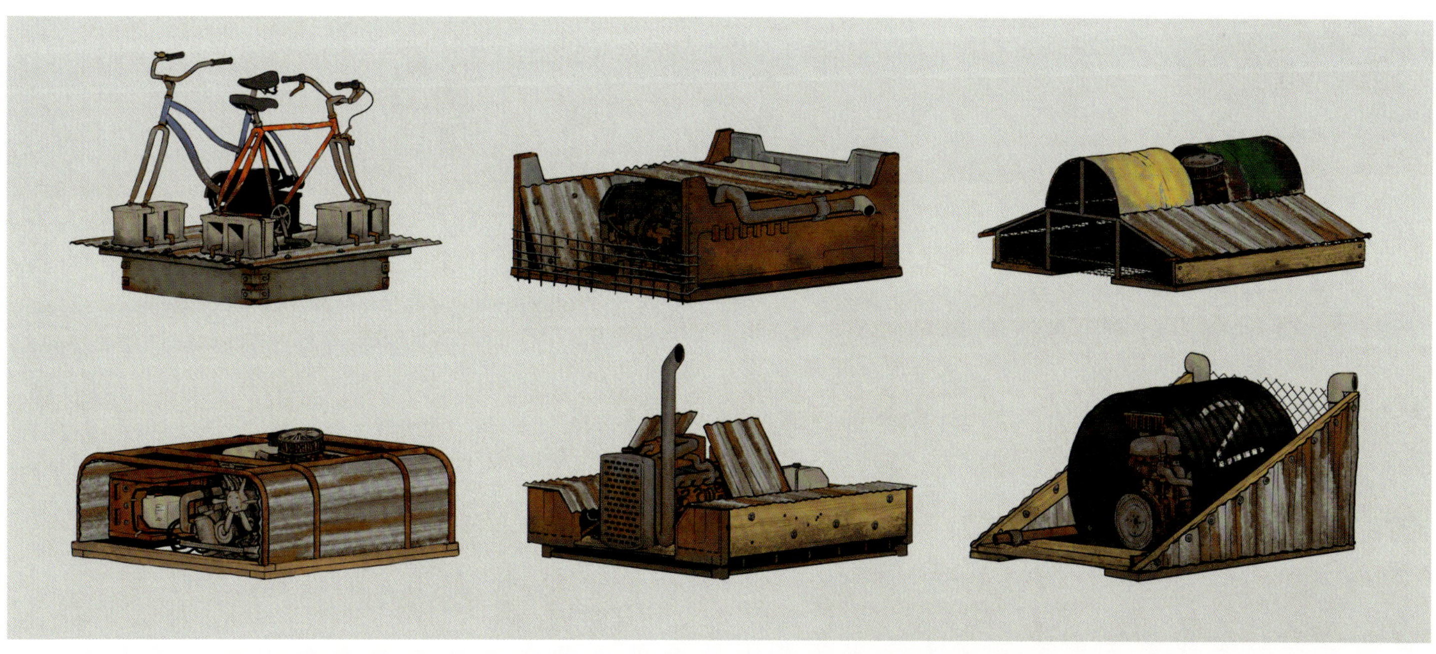

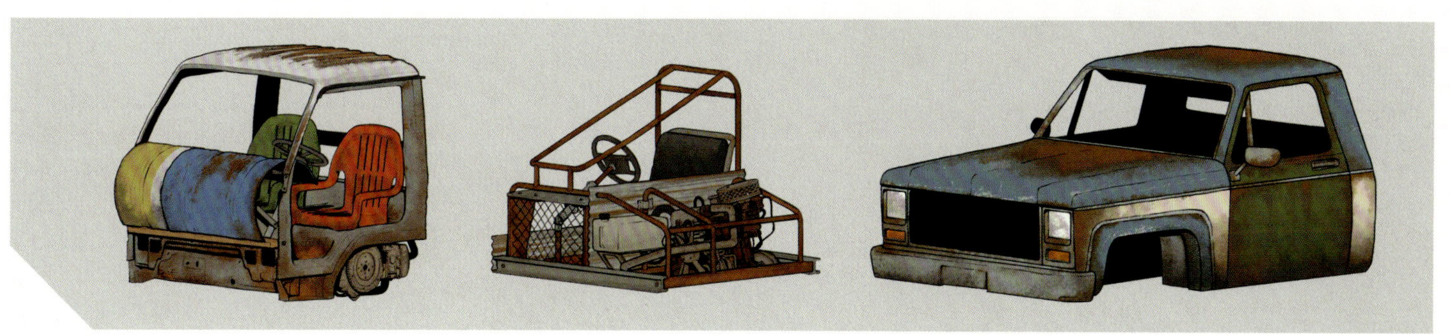

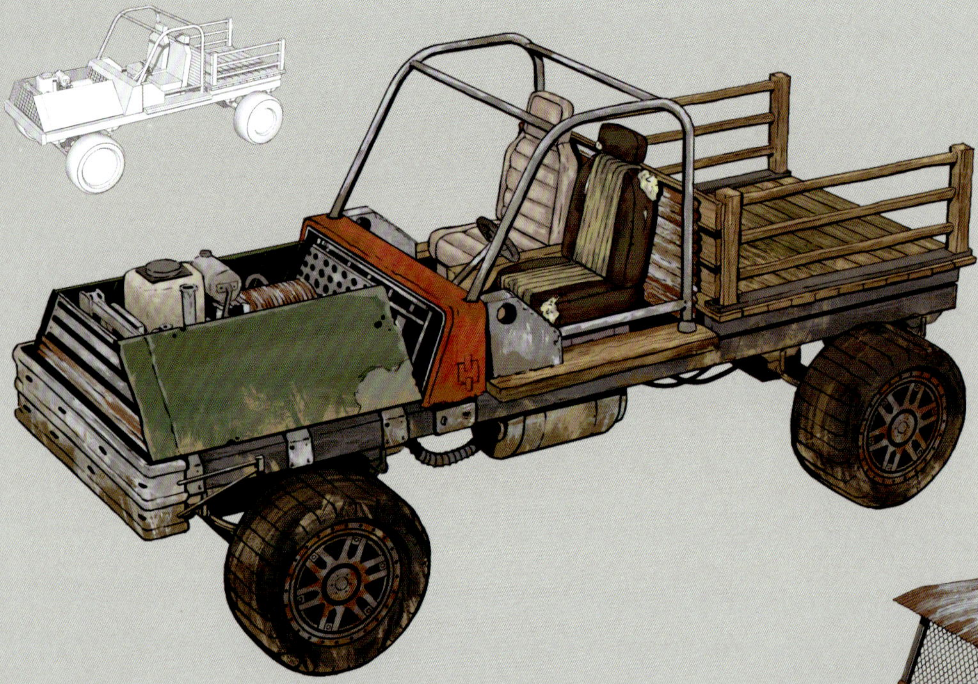

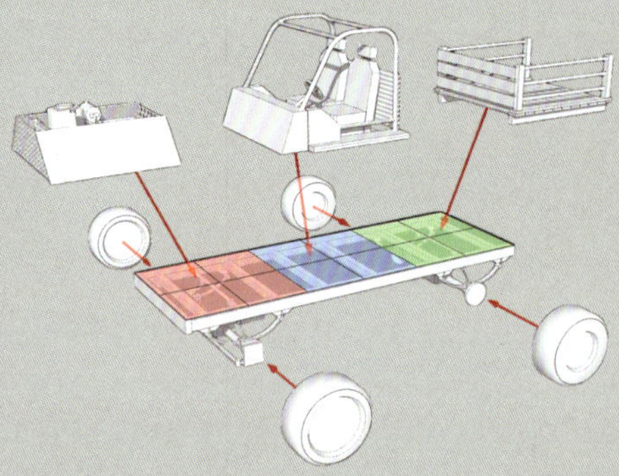

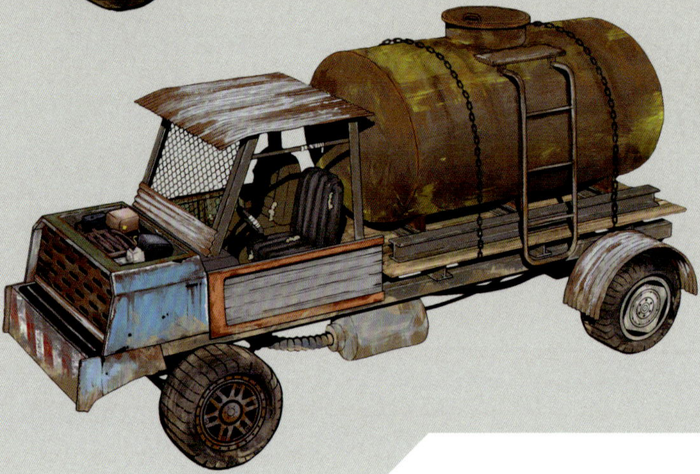

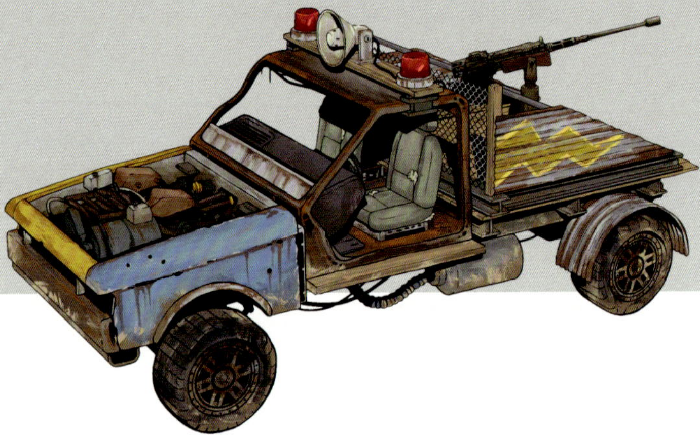

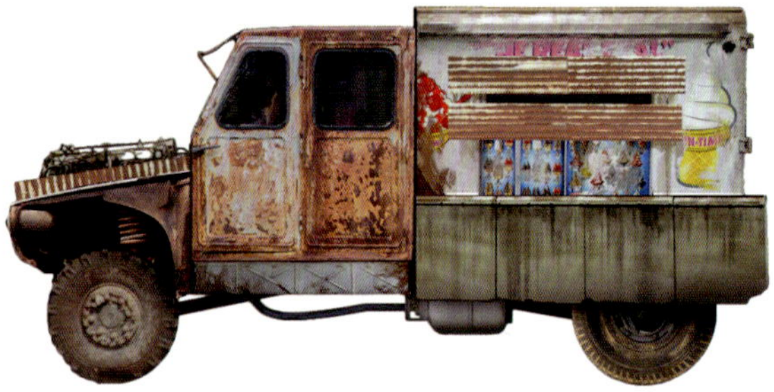

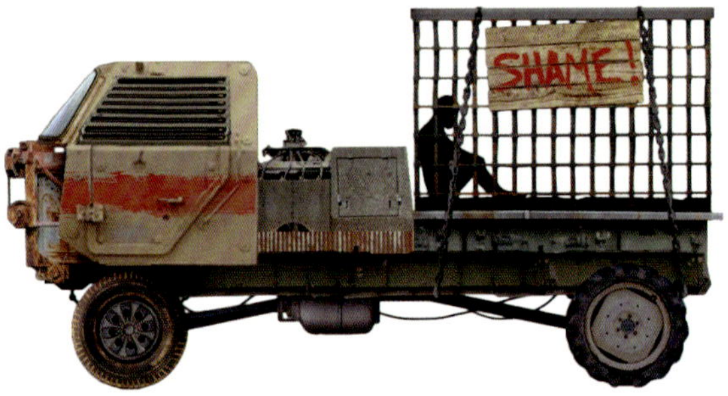

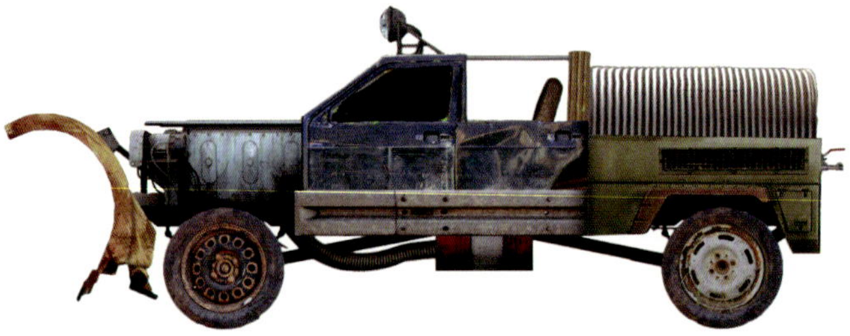

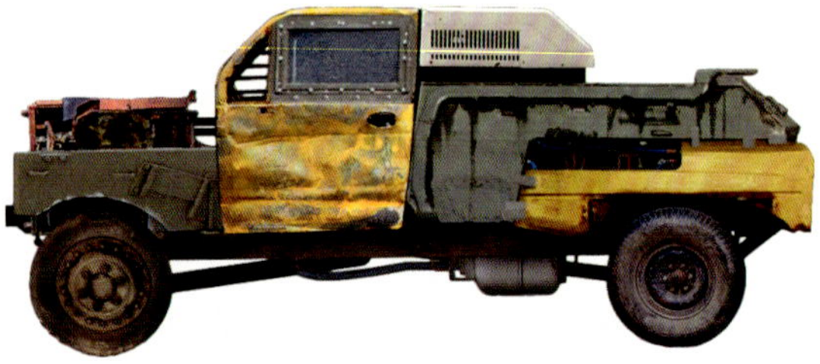

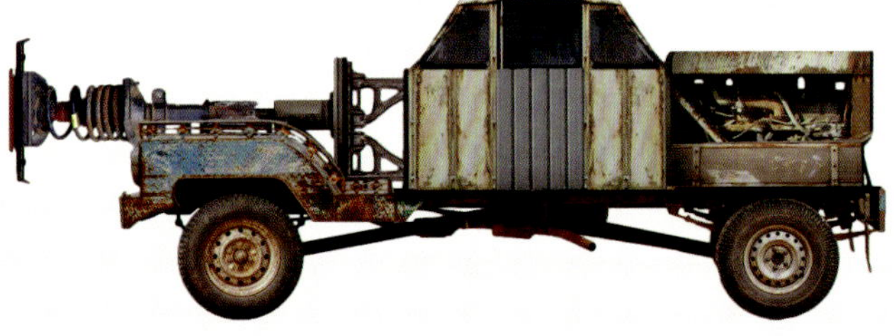

TRUCKS

Here are some Truck concept variations that didn't make it into the game. Each Truck variant is tailored to a different utility: transport, water hauling, cargo, or defense. They have exposed engines, makeshift gun mounts, or steel cage beds.

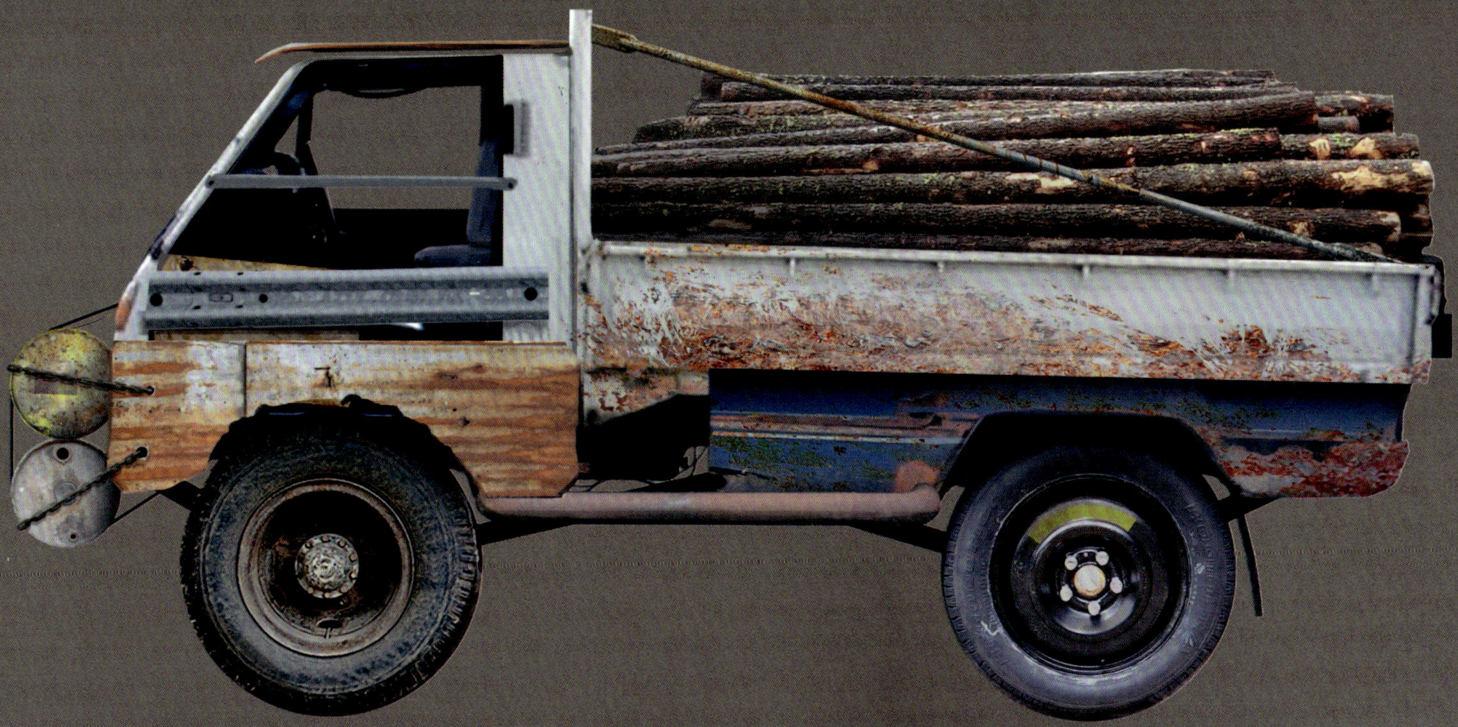

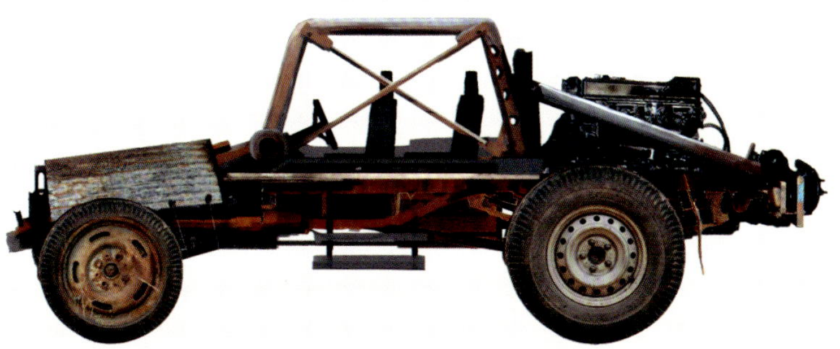

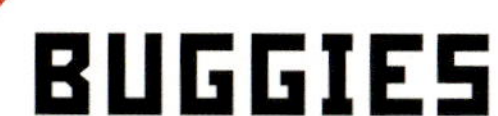

BUGGIES

These Buggy concepts show a few build varieties with welded frames, oversized tires, and cutaway panels that expose their raw mechanics. They lean heavily into a scavenged feel, using wooden cargo rails, rebar roll cages, or fenders made from old signage.

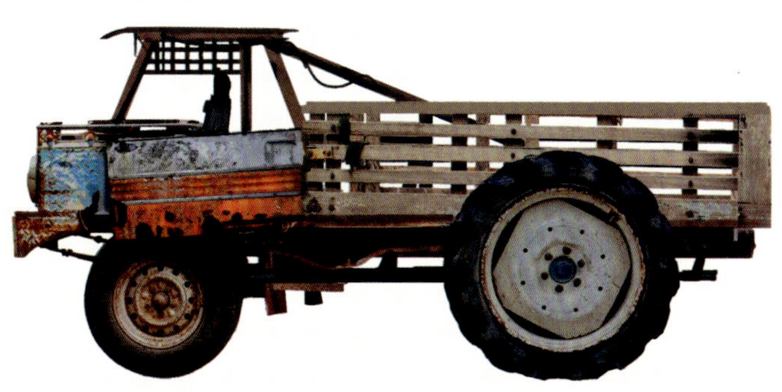

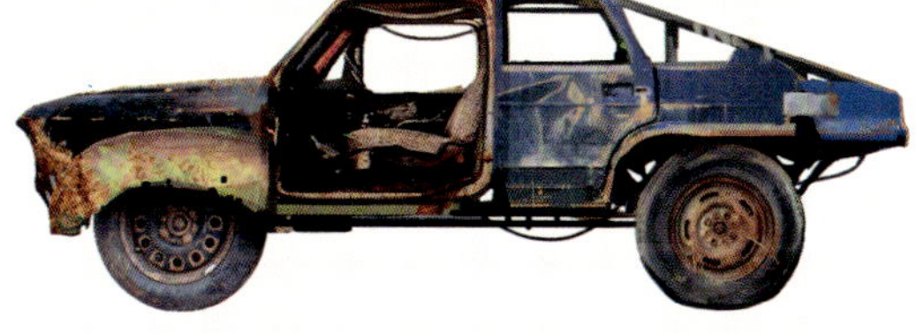

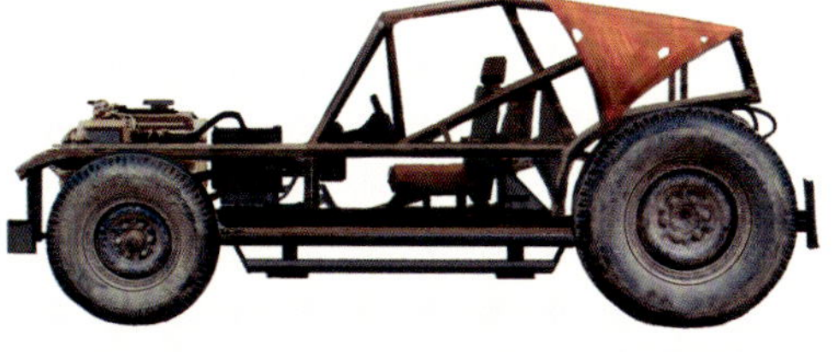

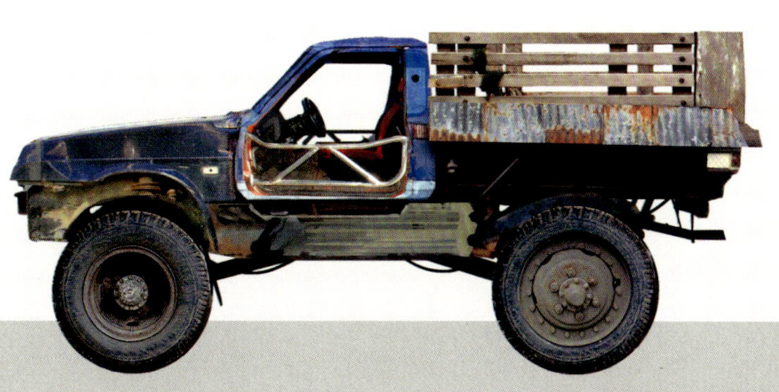

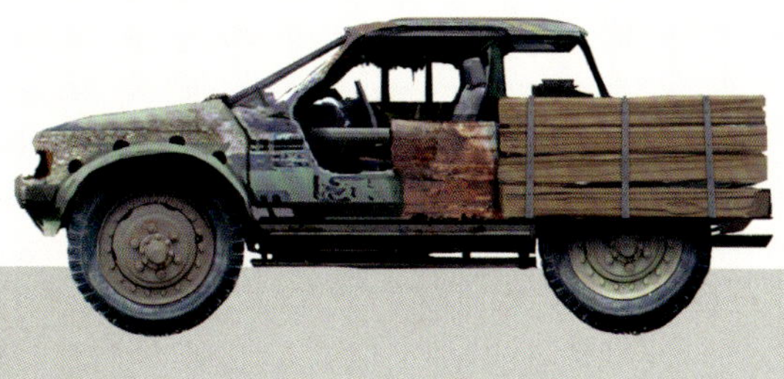

ARMORED TRUCKS

These sketches explore a heavier class of vehicle, designed for convoy protection and area control. The Trucks are bulky and reinforced but not overengineered. The builds show what defensive upgrades could've looked like, with plated panels, mesh grilles, and barricade-style shielding.

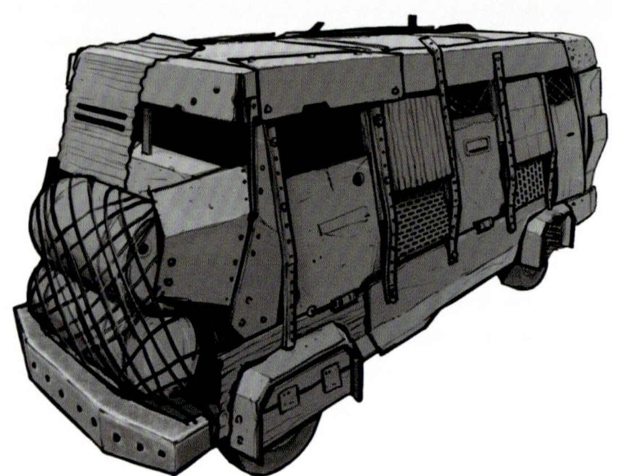

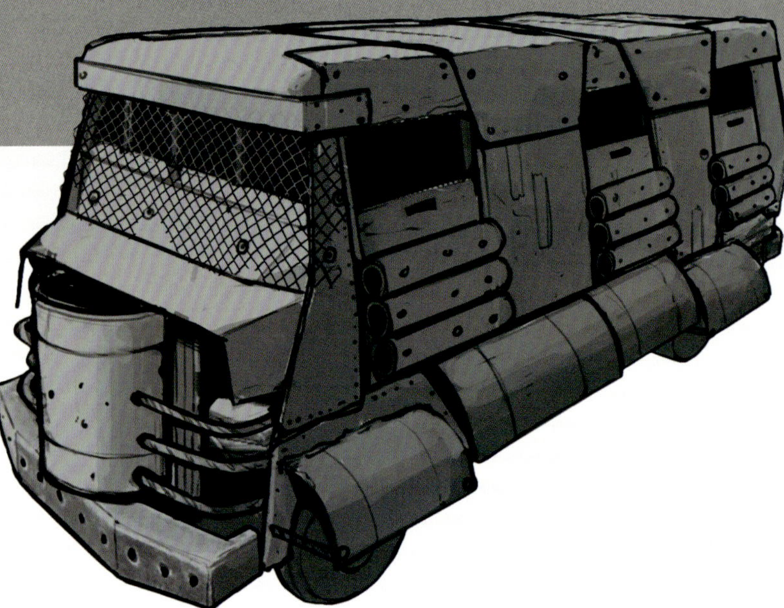

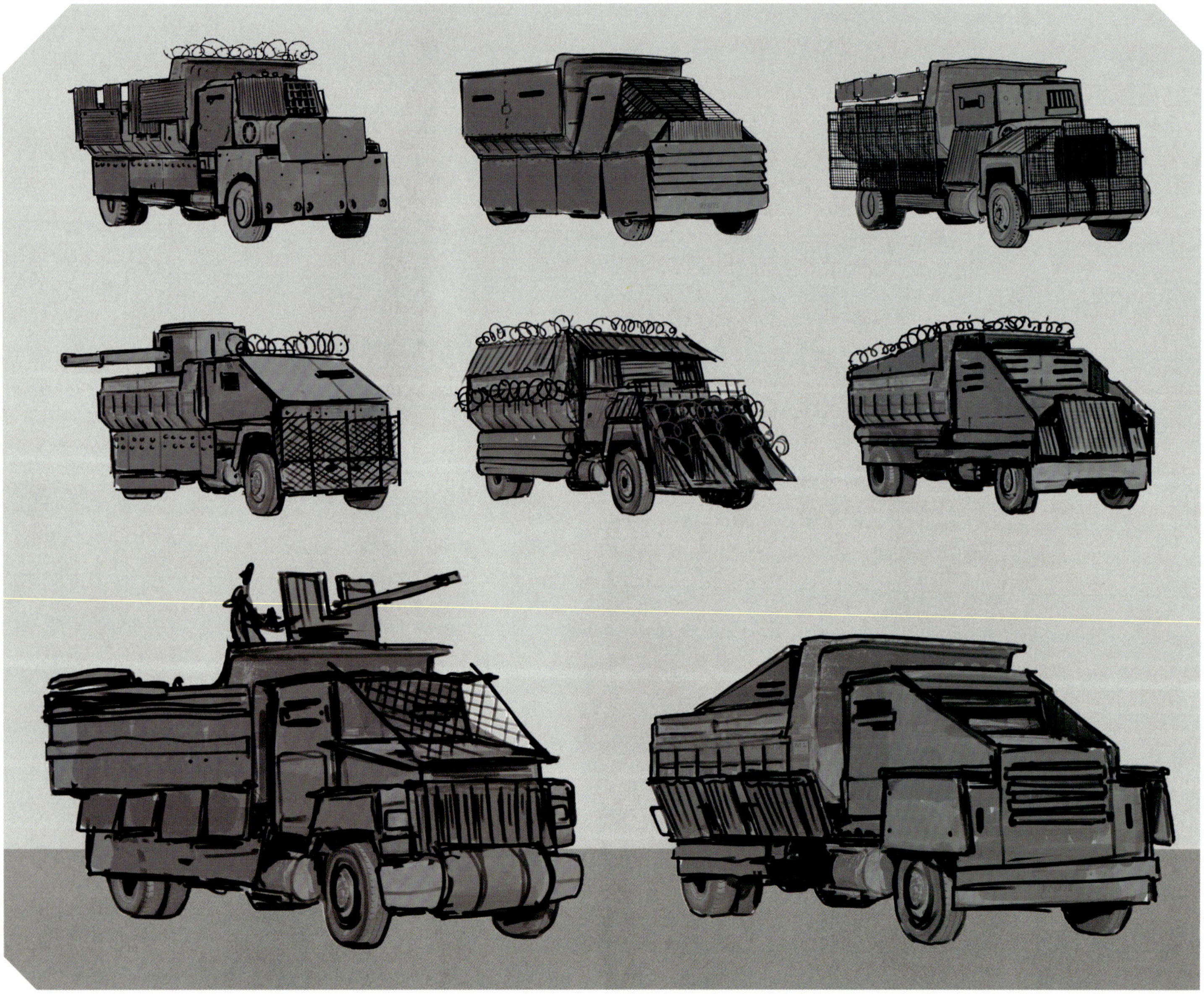

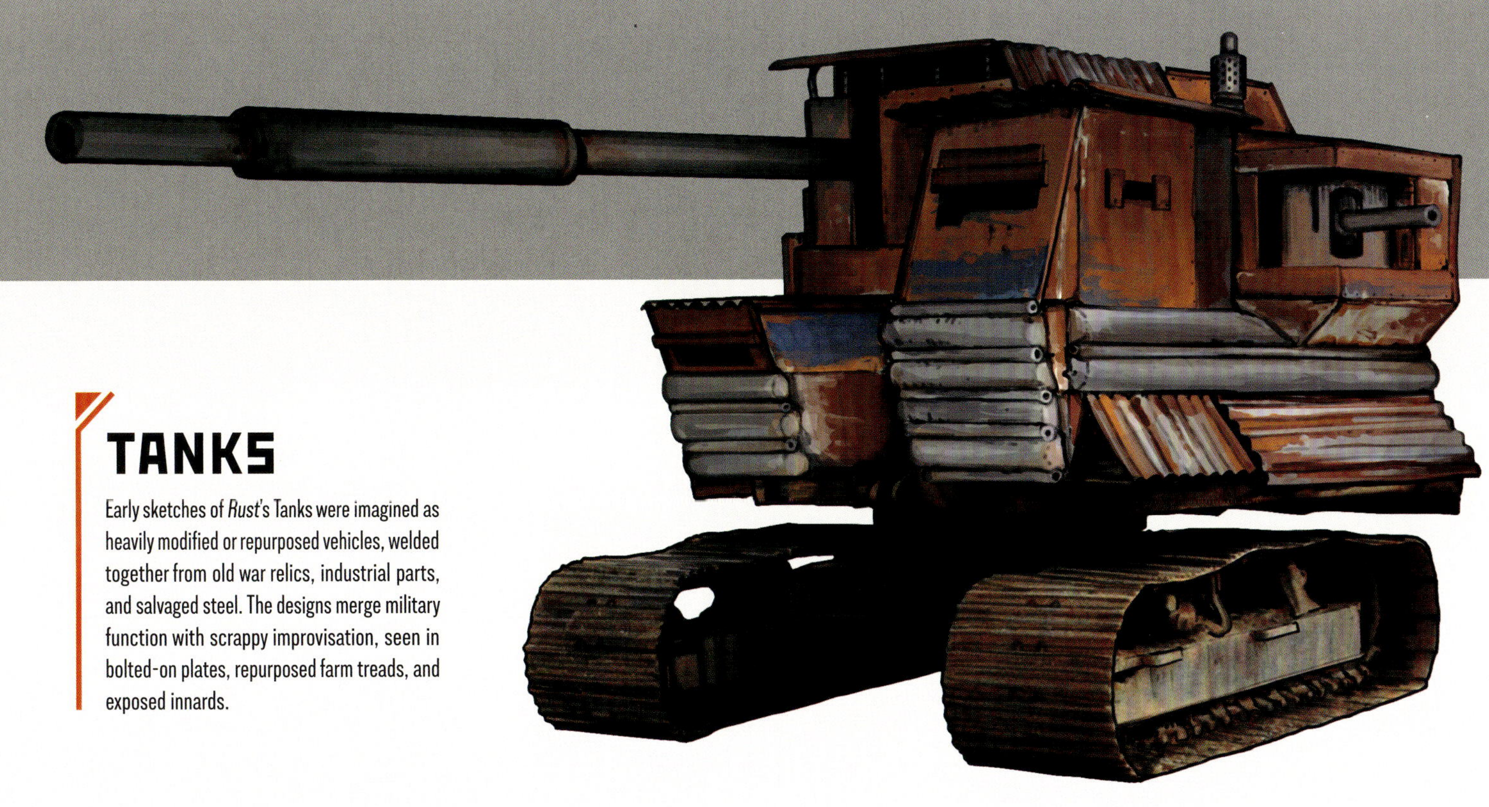

TANKS

Early sketches of *Rust*'s Tanks were imagined as heavily modified or repurposed vehicles, welded together from old war relics, industrial parts, and salvaged steel. The designs merge military function with scrappy improvisation, seen in bolted-on plates, repurposed farm treads, and exposed innards.

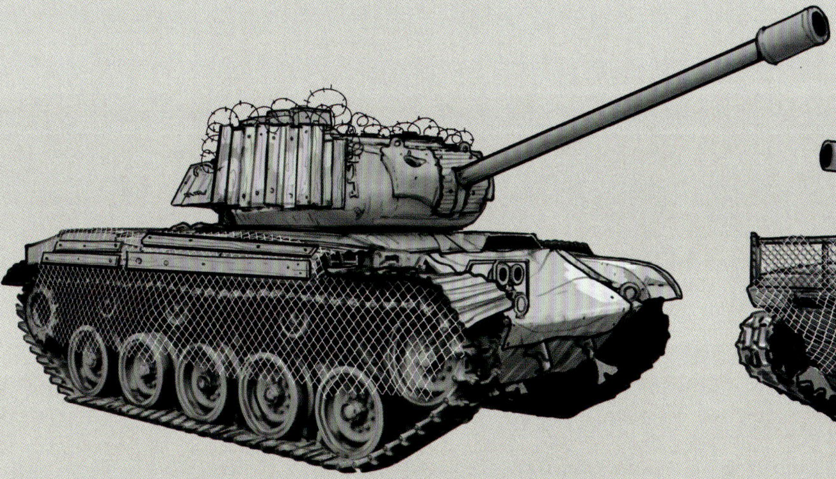

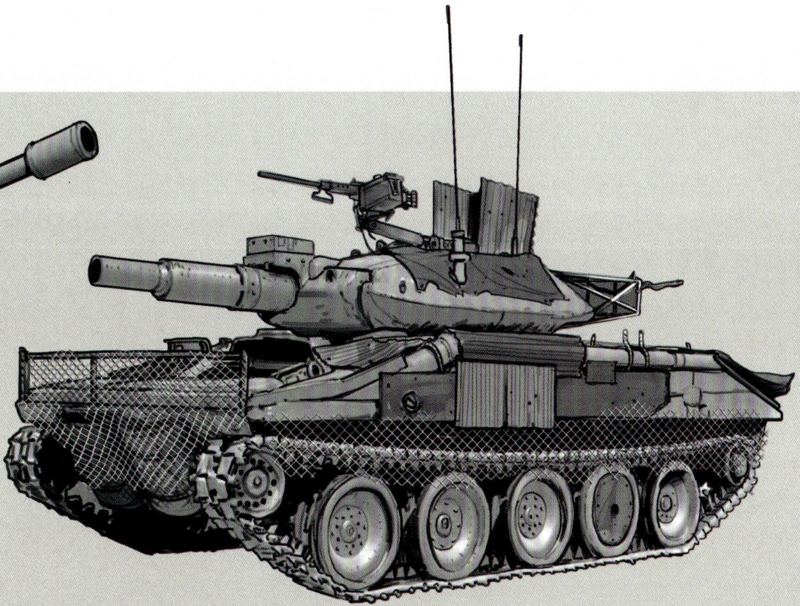

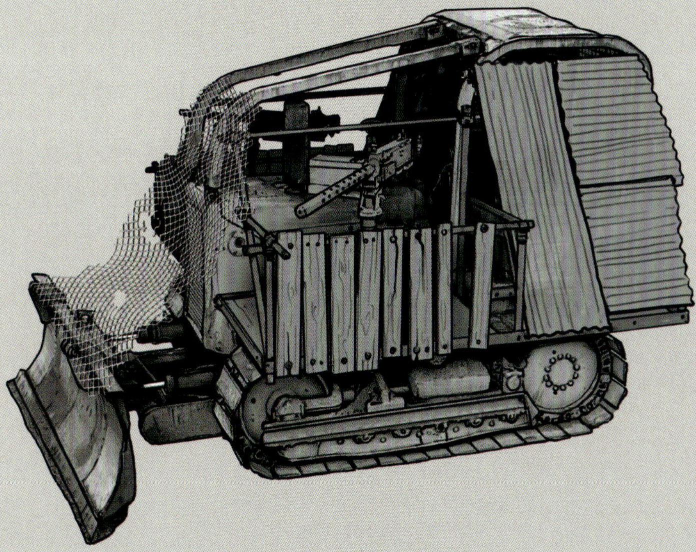

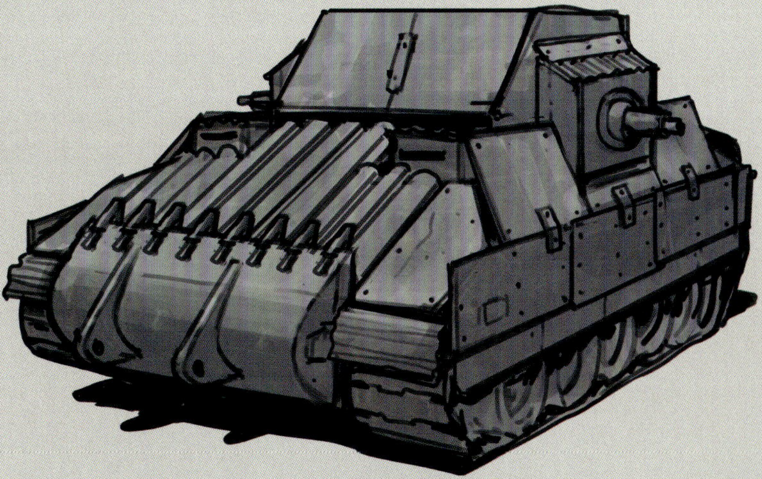

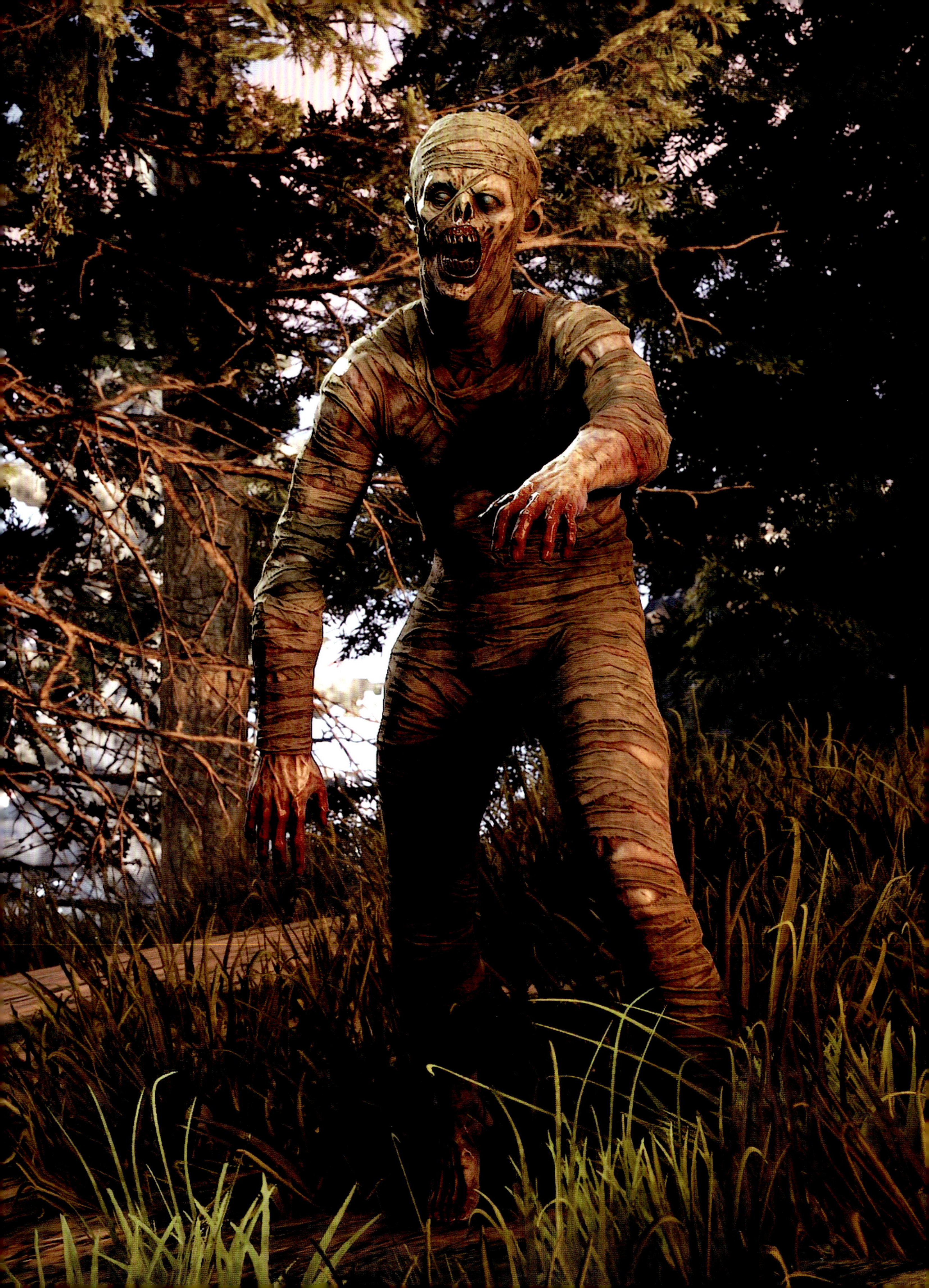

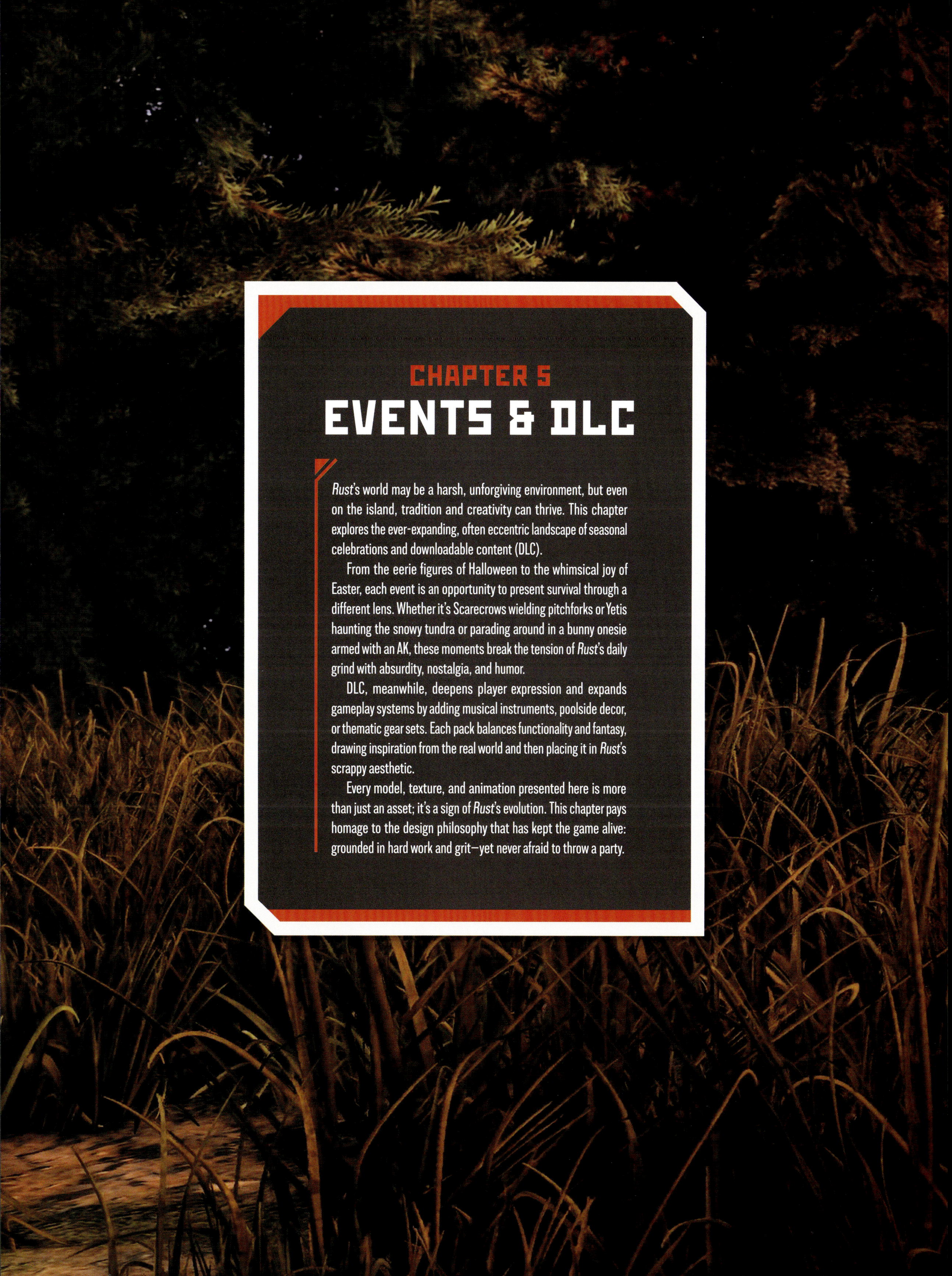

CHAPTER 5

EVENTS & DLC

Rust's world may be a harsh, unforgiving environment, but even on the island, tradition and creativity can thrive. This chapter explores the ever-expanding, often eccentric landscape of seasonal celebrations and downloadable content (DLC).

From the eerie figures of Halloween to the whimsical joy of Easter, each event is an opportunity to present survival through a different lens. Whether it's Scarecrows wielding pitchforks or Yetis haunting the snowy tundra or parading around in a bunny onesie armed with an AK, these moments break the tension of *Rust*'s daily grind with absurdity, nostalgia, and humor.

DLC, meanwhile, deepens player expression and expands gameplay systems by adding musical instruments, poolside decor, or thematic gear sets. Each pack balances functionality and fantasy, drawing inspiration from the real world and then placing it in *Rust*'s scrappy aesthetic.

Every model, texture, and animation presented here is more than just an asset; it's a sign of *Rust*'s evolution. This chapter pays homage to the design philosophy that has kept the game alive: grounded in hard work and grit—yet never afraid to throw a party.

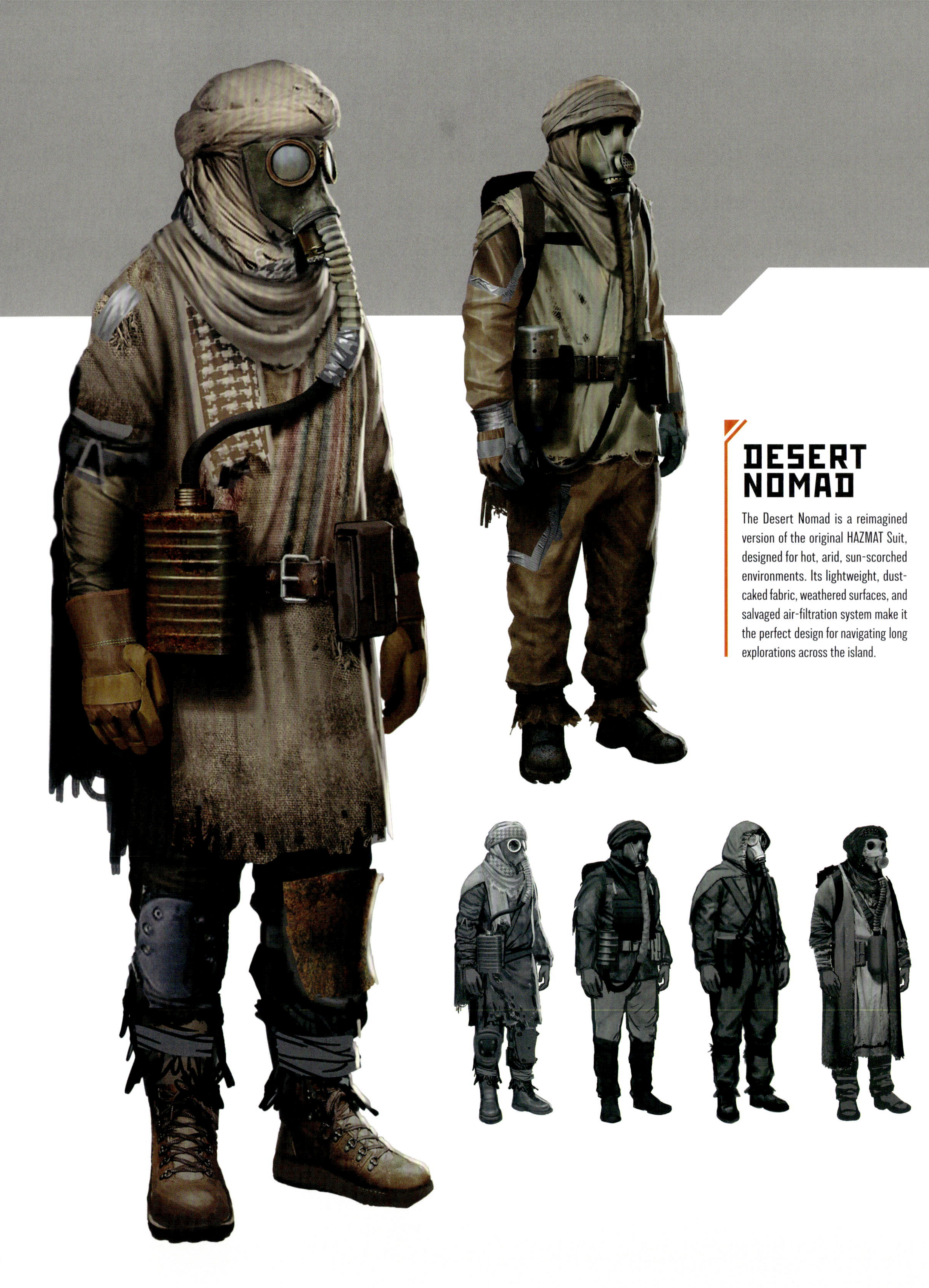

DESERT NOMAD

The Desert Nomad is a reimagined version of the original HAZMAT Suit, designed for hot, arid, sun-scorched environments. Its lightweight, dust-caked fabric, weathered surfaces, and salvaged air-filtration system make it the perfect design for navigating long explorations across the island.

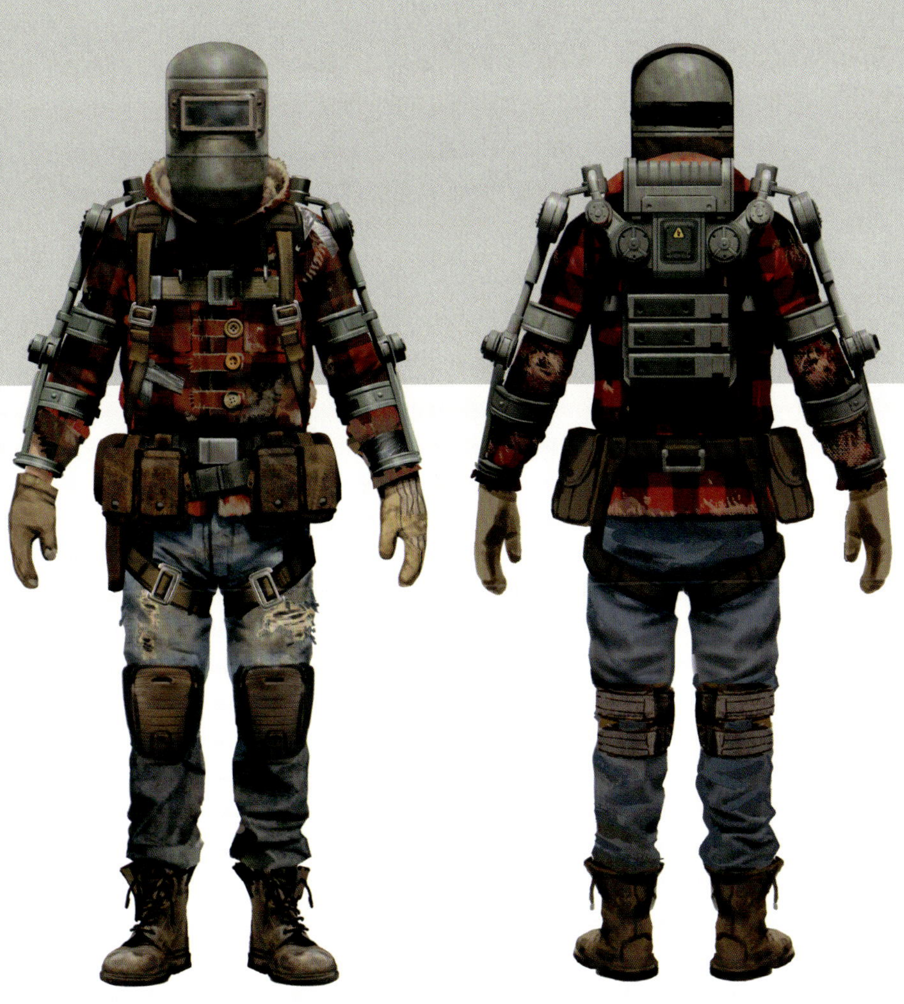

LUMBERJACK

Military exoskeletons and retro '80s tech inspired these concepts for the Lumberjack HAZMAT. The suit channels a homemade, Tony Stark-style aesthetic, with exposed wiring, clunky plating, and an improvised exorig built from salvaged components and cobbled-together tech.

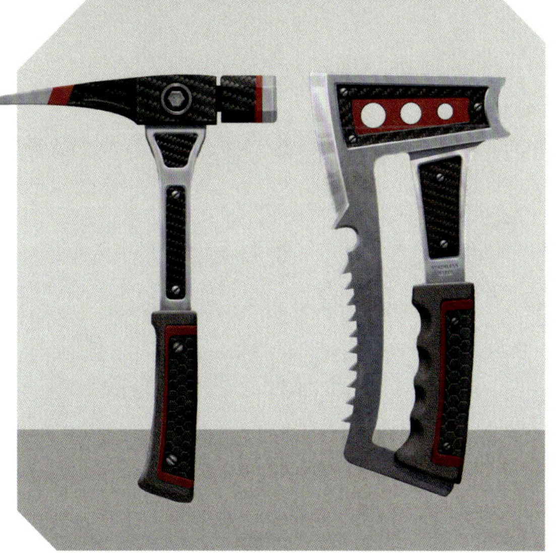

HATCHETS AND PICKAXES

These concepts for Hatchets and Pickaxes reflect the different stages of progression in *Rust* from stones tied to wood to sleek carbon-fiber tools. The more primitive designs are clunky, with the use of concrete and rebar to create a handmade feel, while the higher-end tools look straight off the shelf.

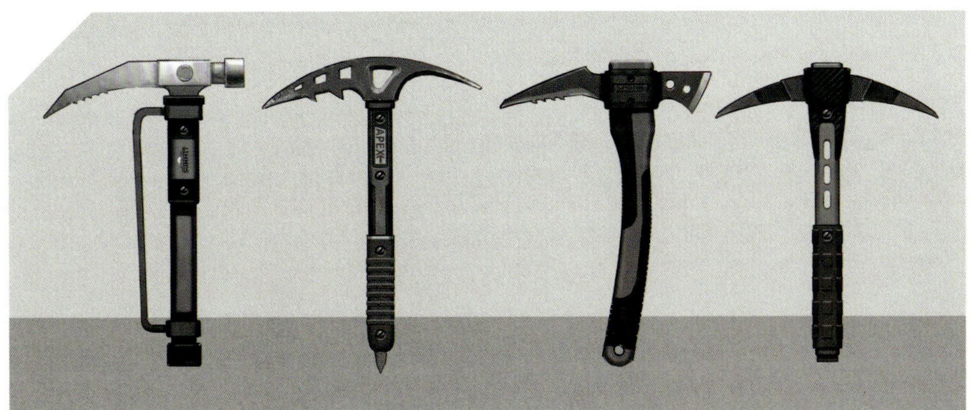

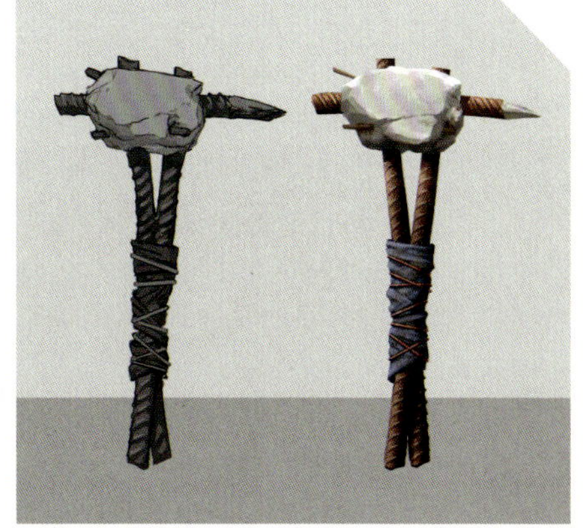

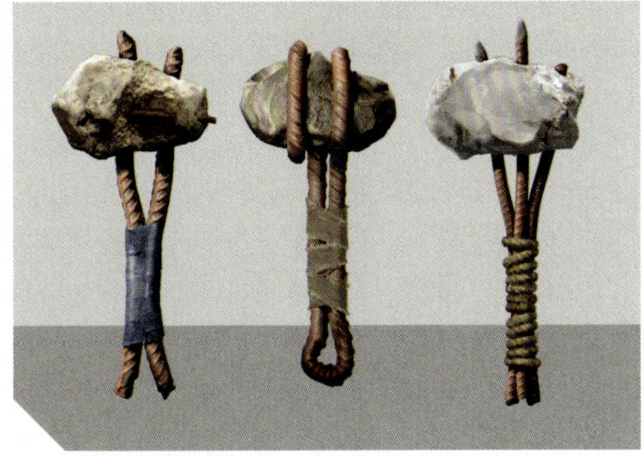

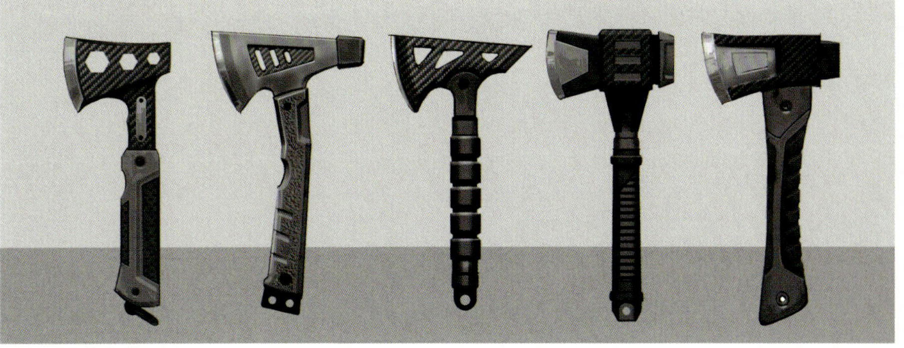

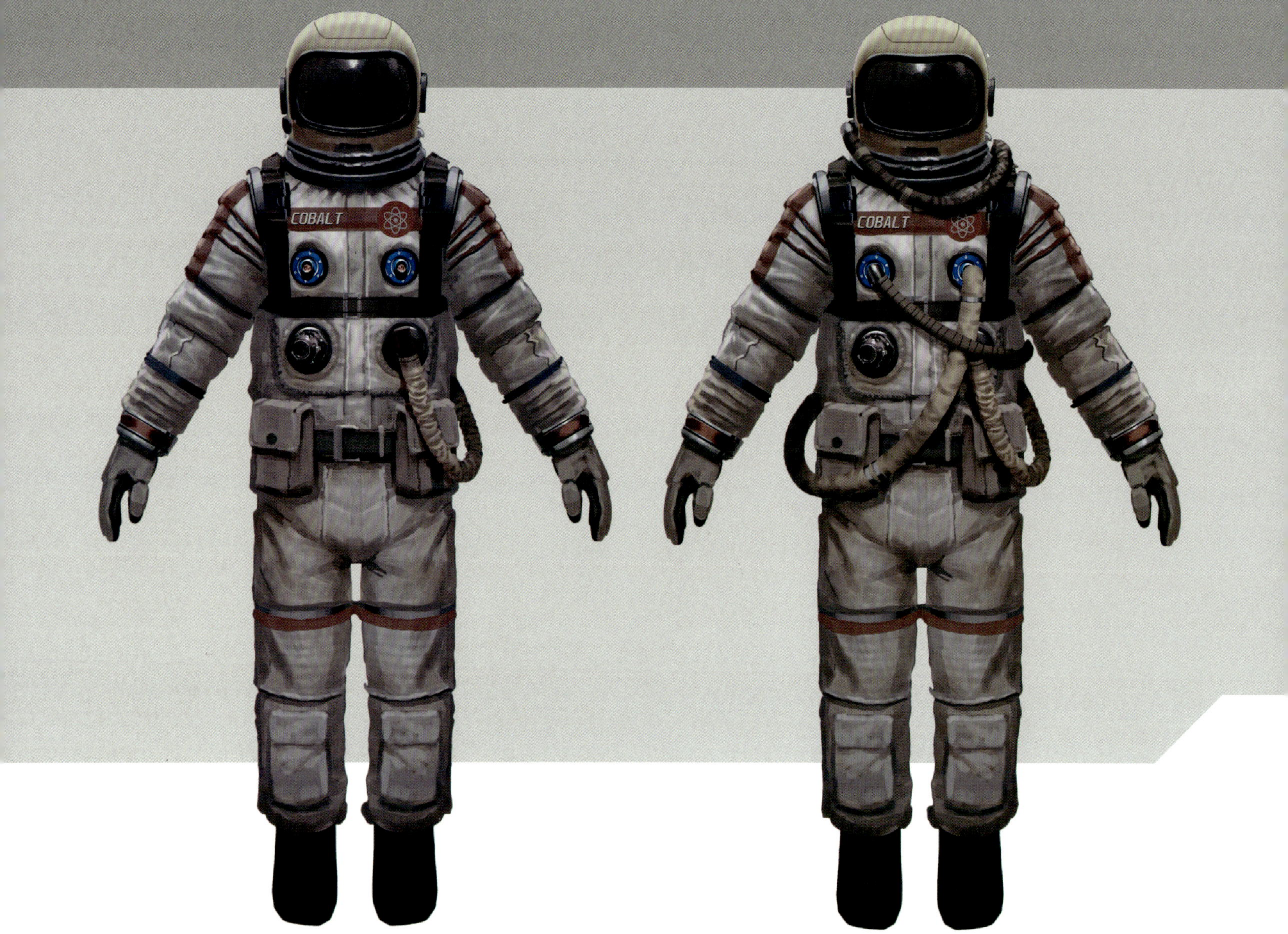

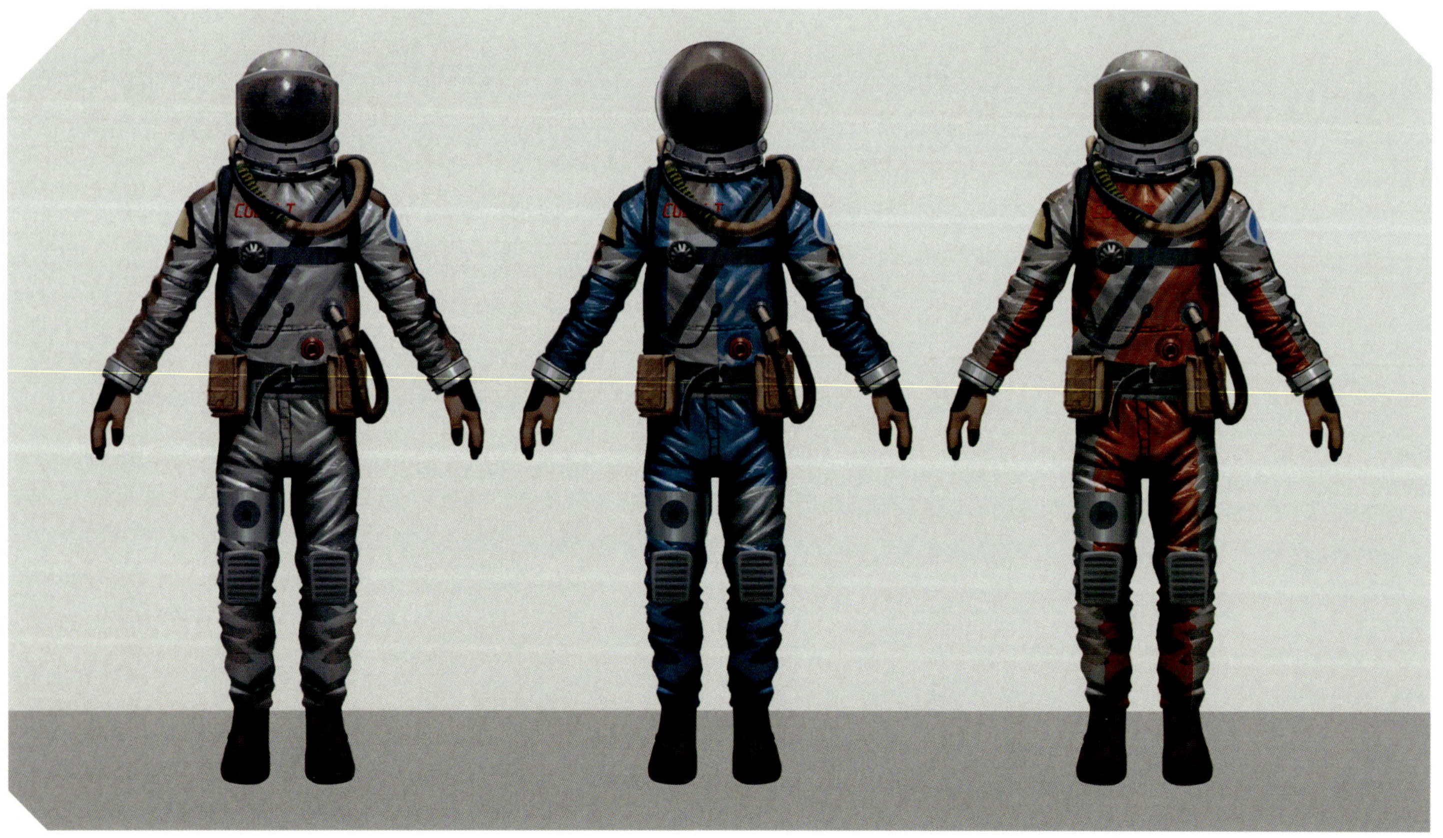

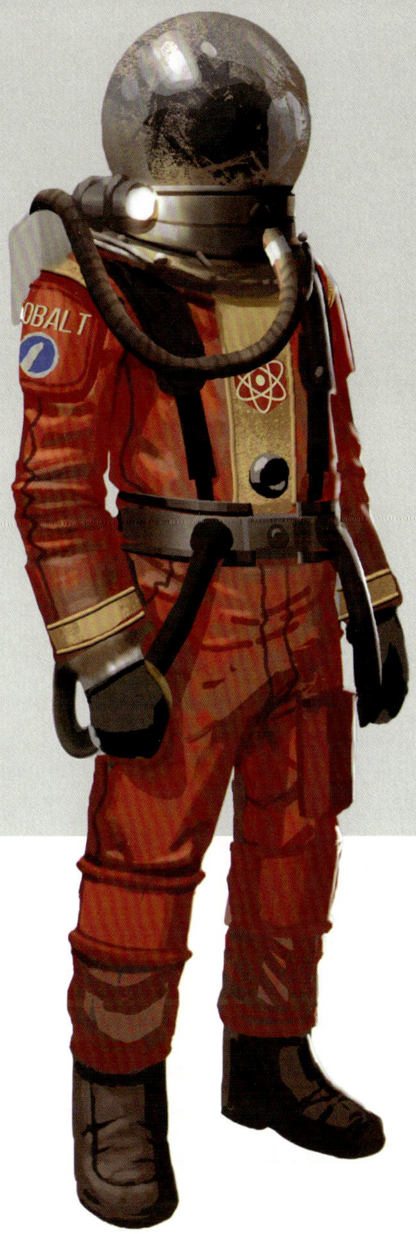

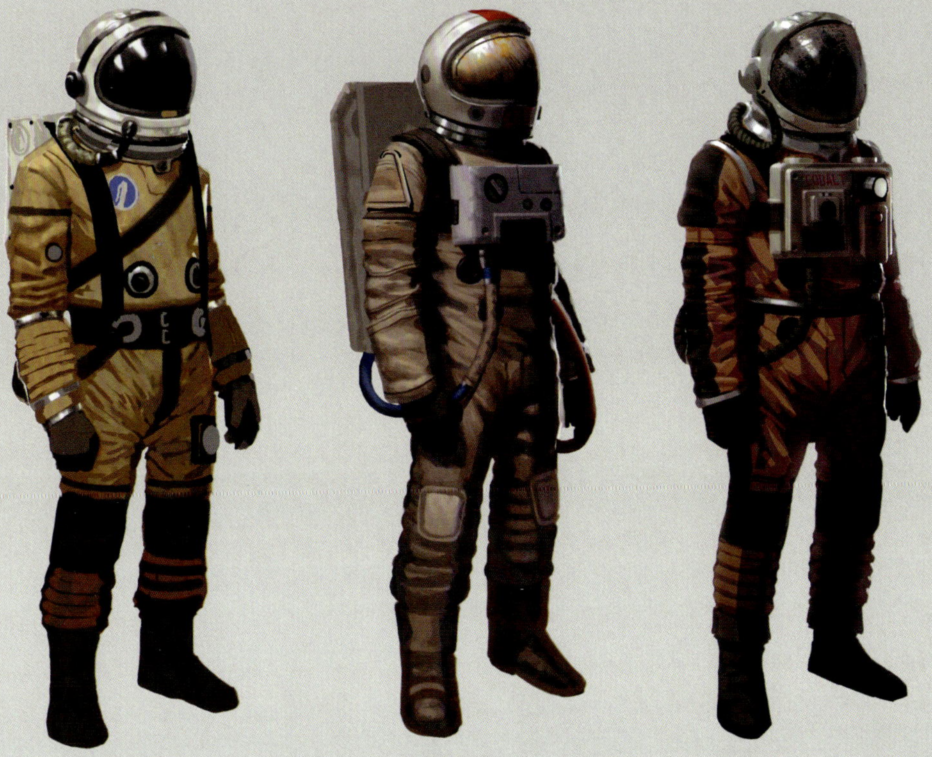

SPACESUITS

This concept was the first experiment with alternate looks for the HAZMAT. As *Rust*'s lore evolved and Cobalt became a defined presence, it made sense to lean into the Cold War-era aesthetic. The idea of a corporation exploring high-tech ventures made a spacesuit an exciting direction to explore. Visually distinct yet grounded in reality, the spacesuit reimagines radiation protection with a retrofuturistic edge.

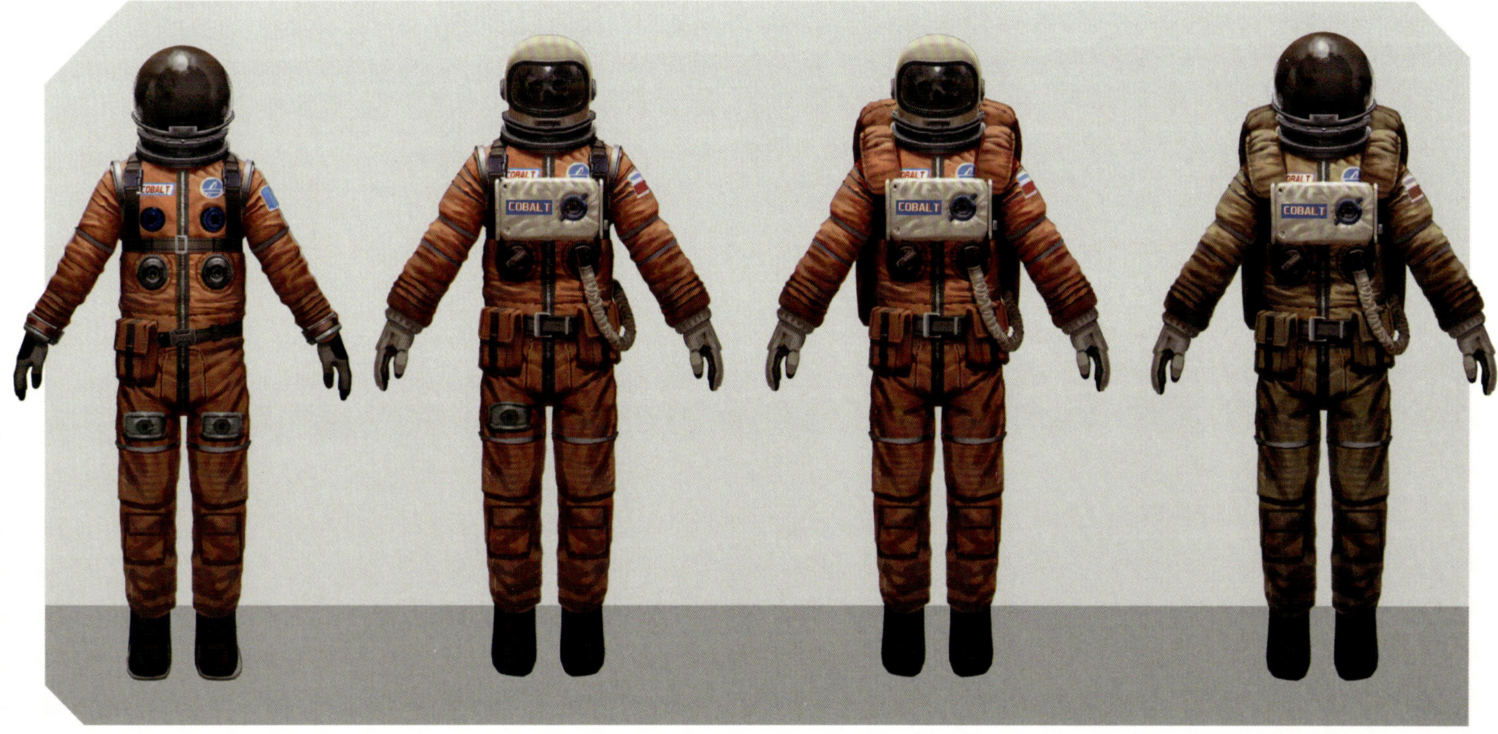

HAZMAT DIVER

These designs evolved from classic deep-sea diving suits, imagined through the lens of *Rust*. The suits are bulky and claustrophobic by design, drawing from mid-twentieth century naval gear, vintage salvage, and a steampunk aesthetic. Each silhouette leans into exaggerated features: oversized helmets, rugged packs, and articulated joints, which create a slightly haunting feel to each design.

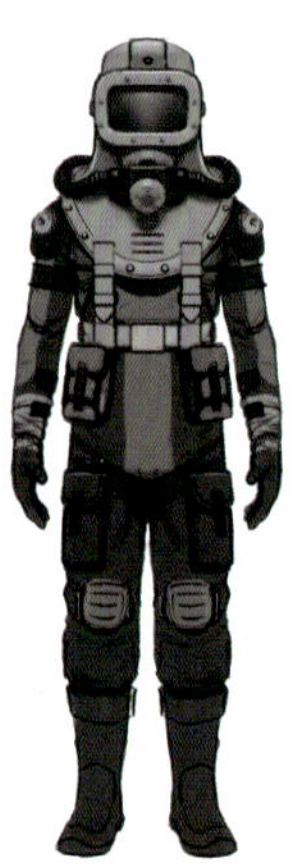
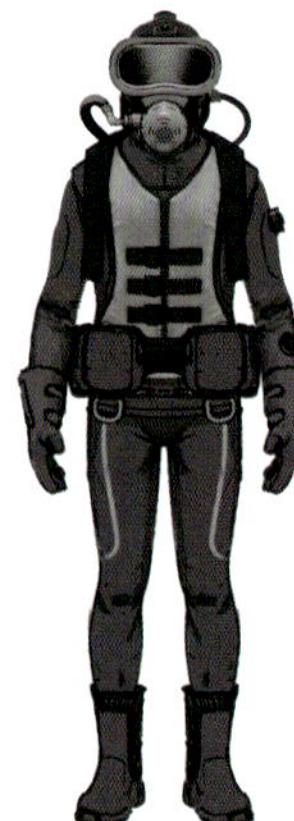
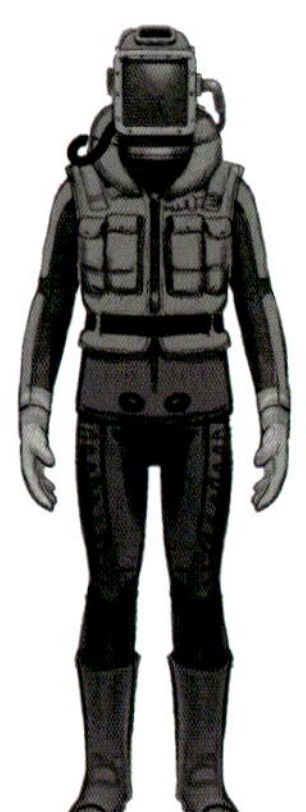
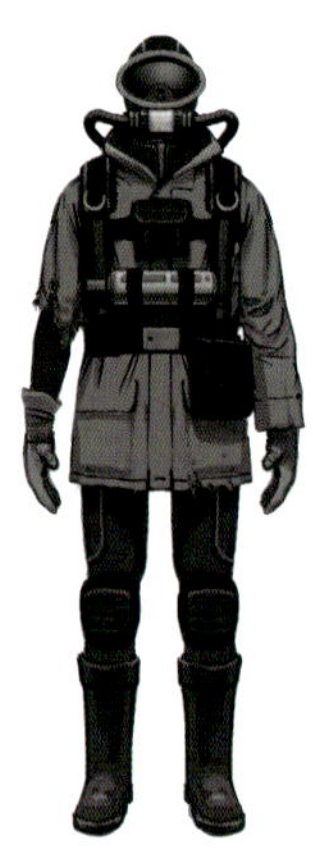
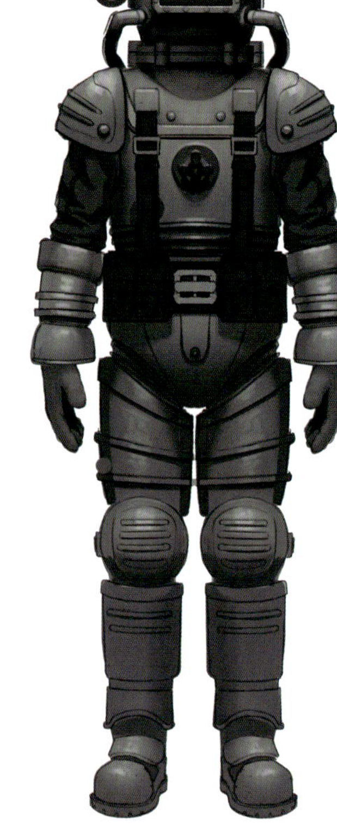
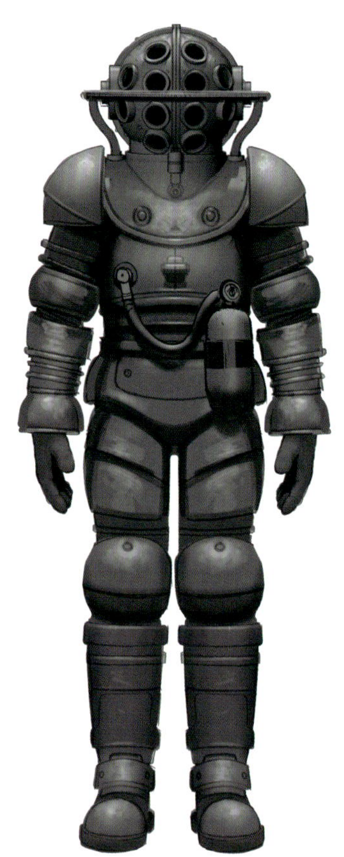
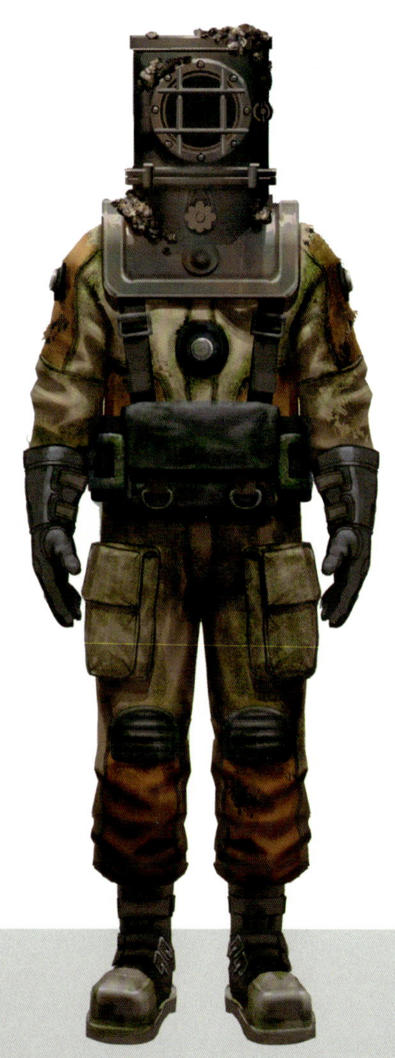
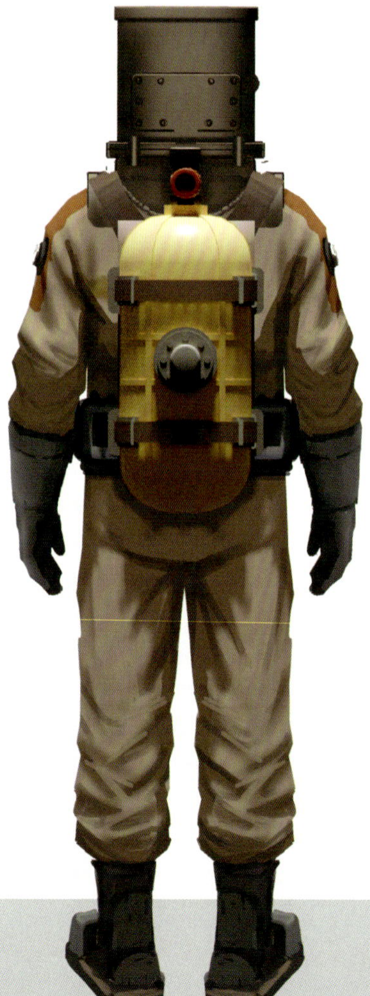
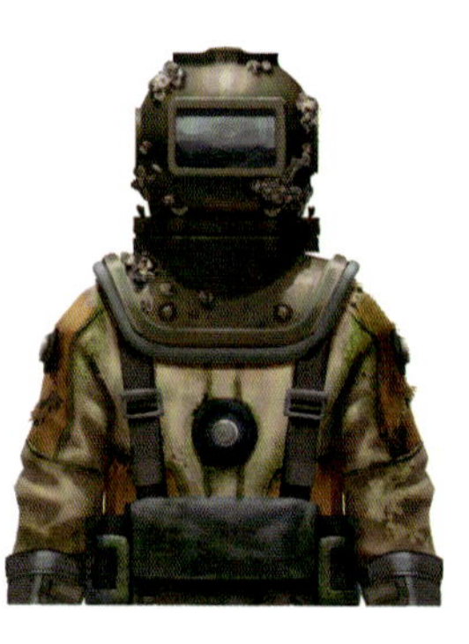
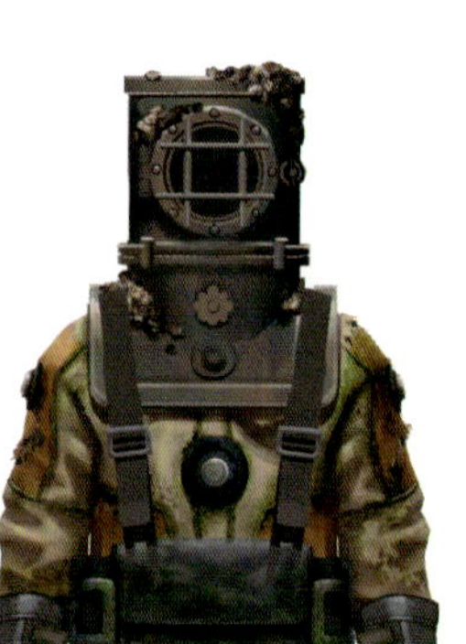
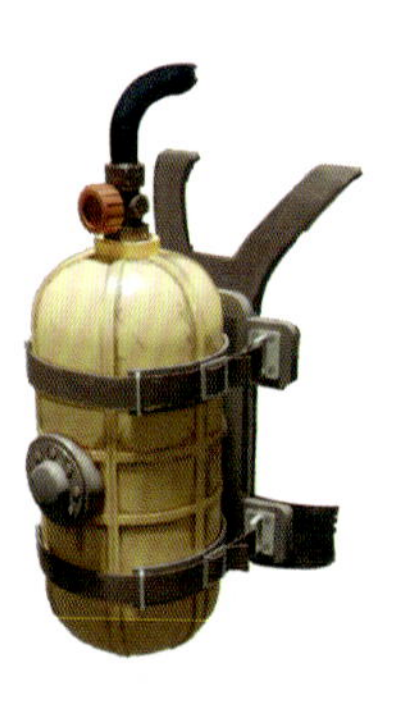
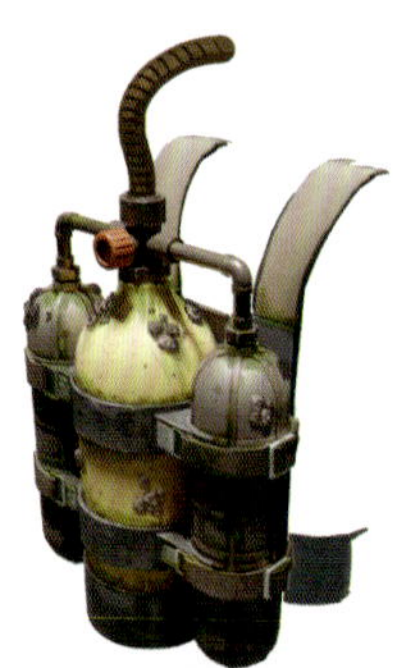
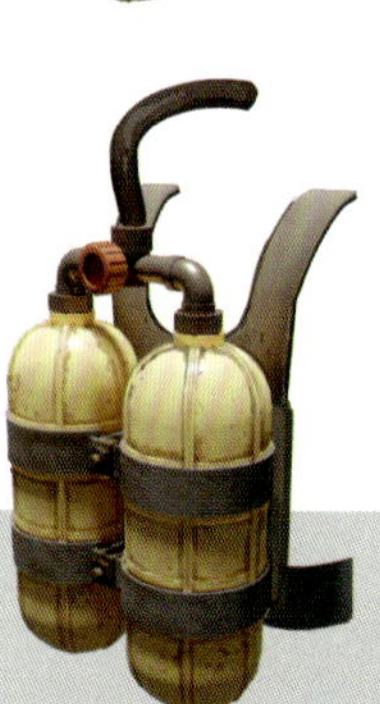
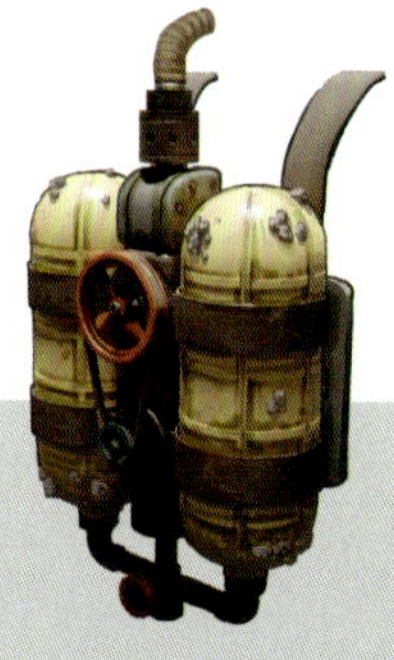

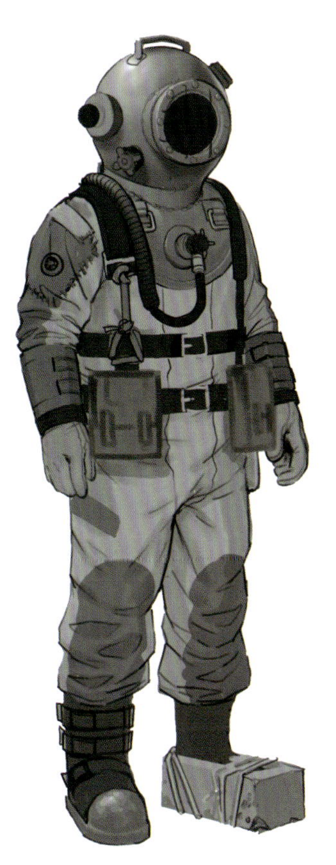

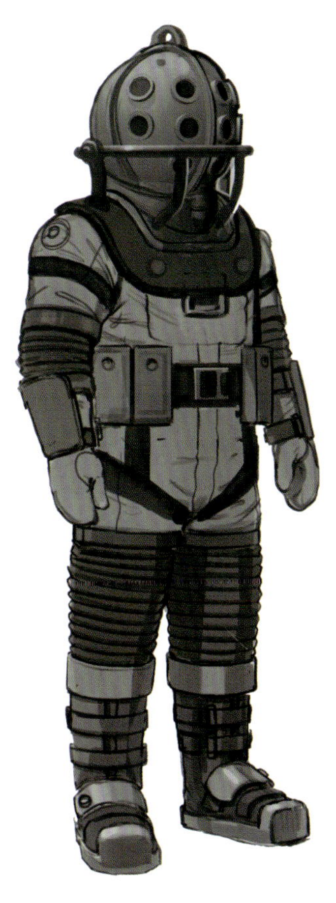

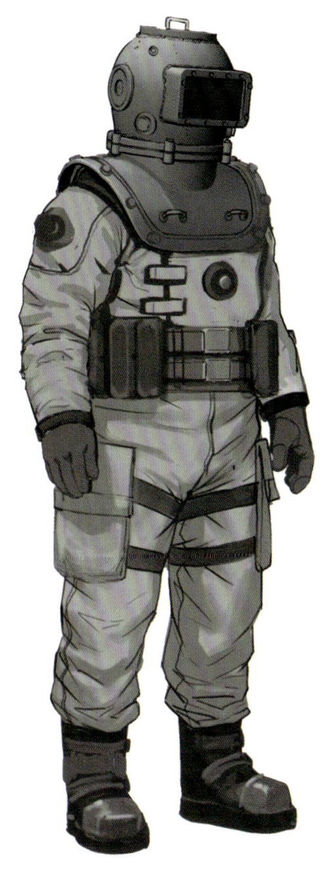

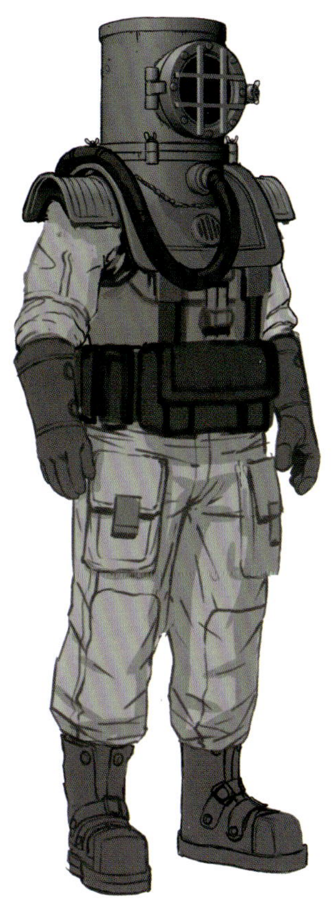

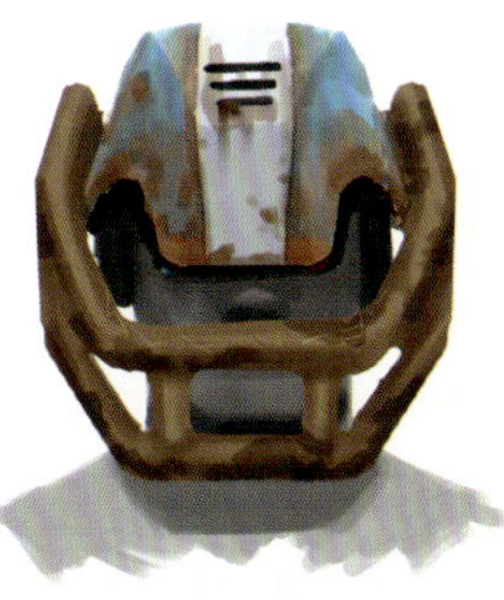

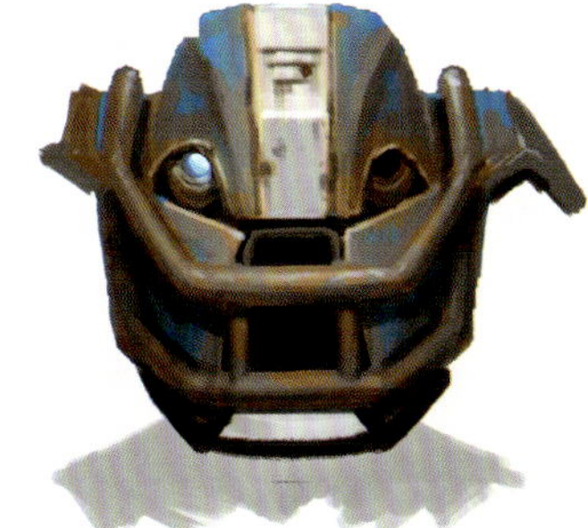

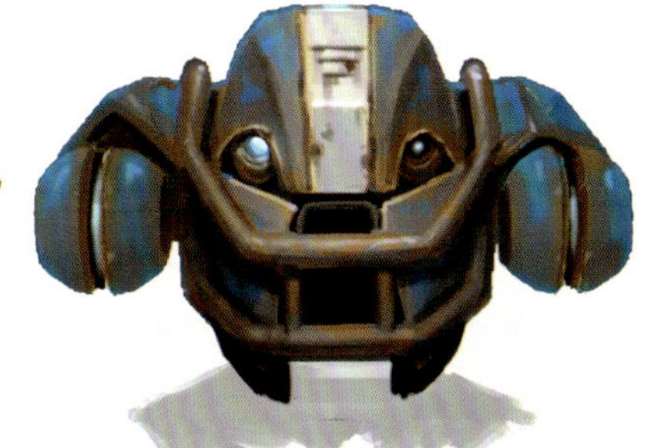

CLATTER HAT

This quirky design was part of a DLC pack to promote a new game release from Facepunch called *Clatter*, a game where you command customizable squads of fighting robots. These concepts are taken from the various *Clatter* characters, and despite their playful look, they still embody *Rust*'s cobbled-together, scrappy feel.

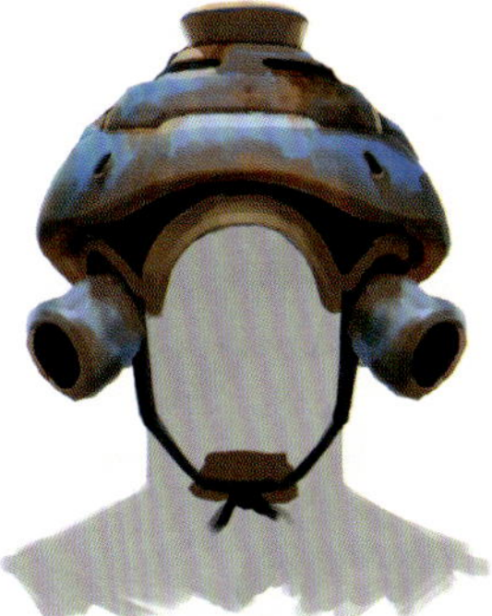

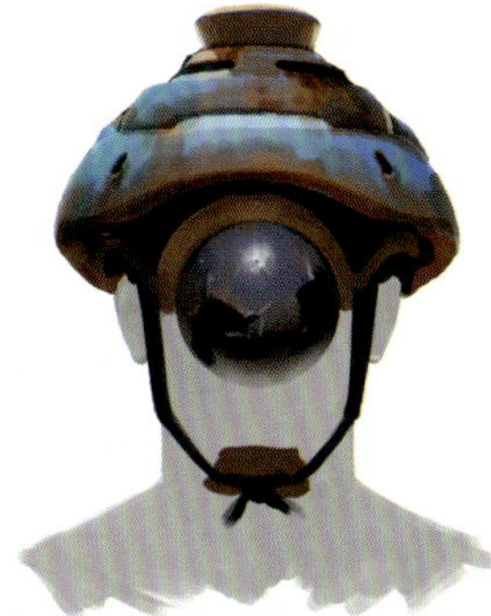

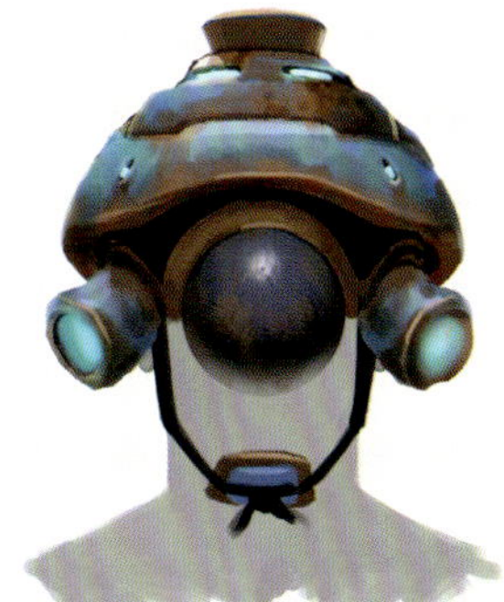

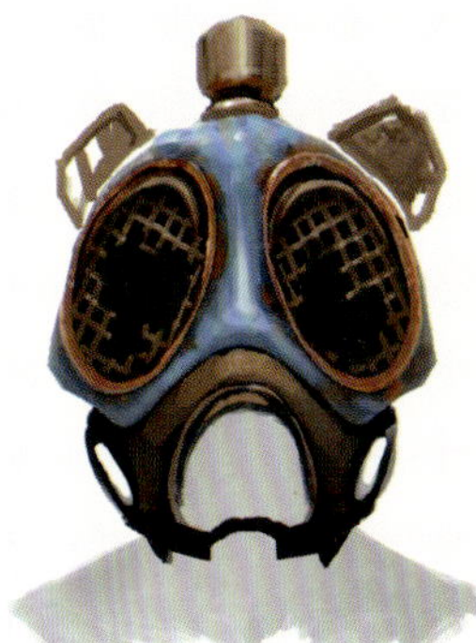

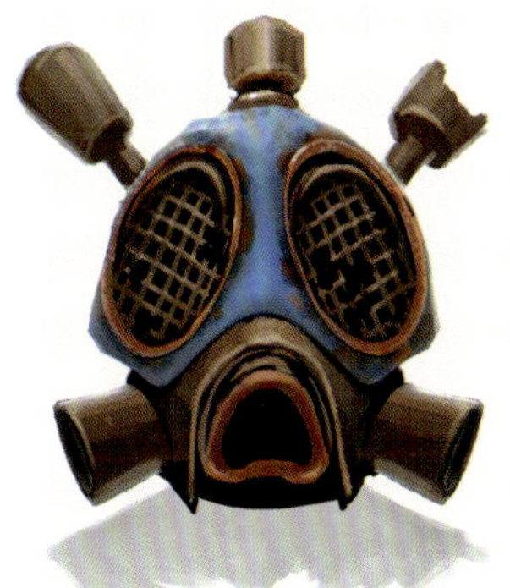

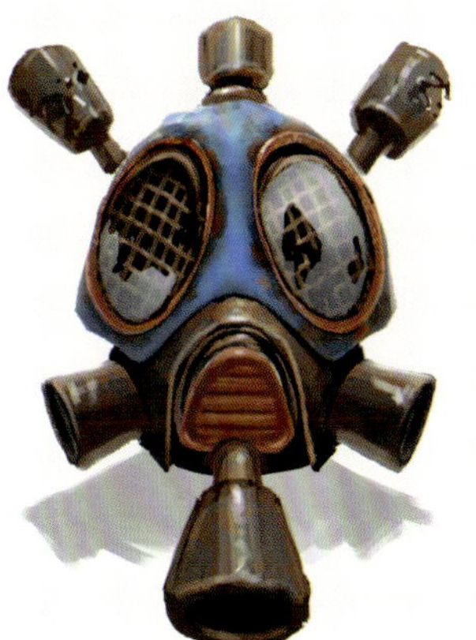

ABYSS WEAPONS

The Abyss DLC pack was one of the first DLCs to experiment with environmental weapon dressing. These concepts show the Speargun, the Abyss Assault Rifle, and the unused Octopus Rifle, all dressed to fit a sunken, underwater feel.

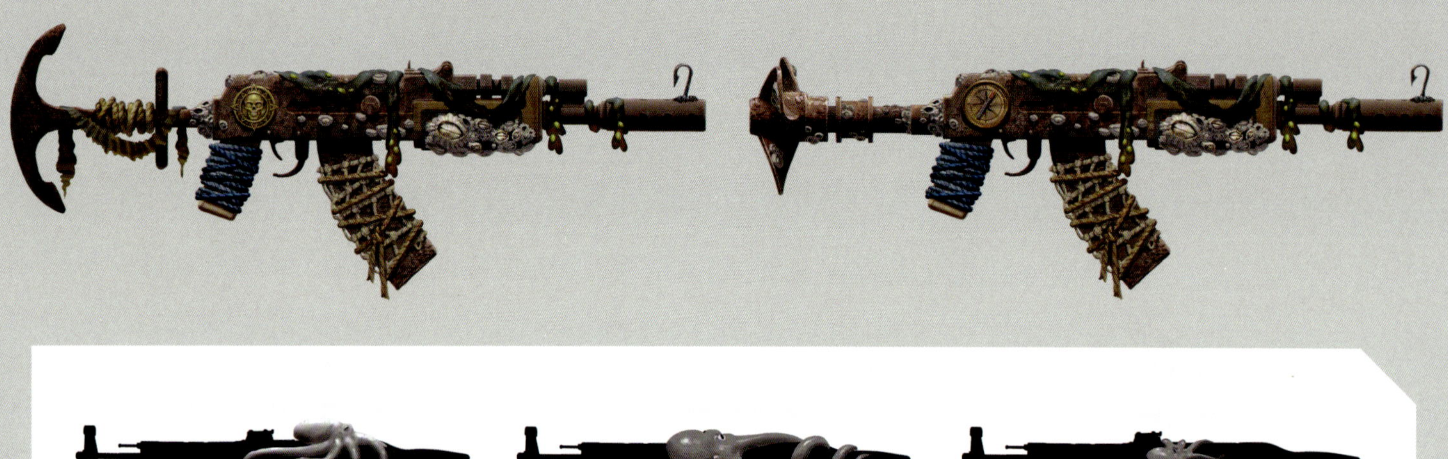

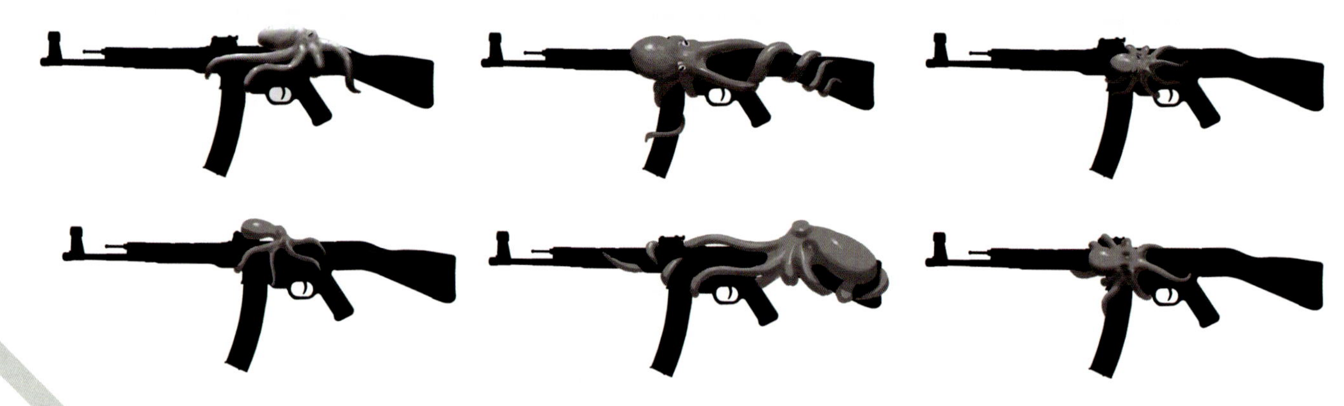

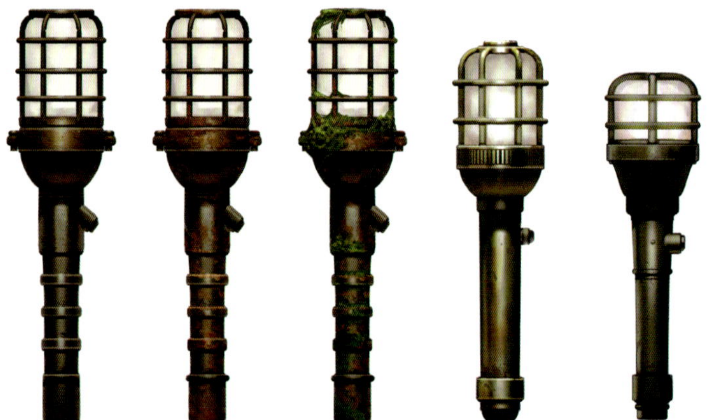

ABYSS TOOLS

These concepts are also part of the Abyss pack and follow the same design theme. The Abyss Torch was inspired by antique brass diver lamps, and the unused Abyss Hatchet is made from a salvaged boat rudder. These new underwater tools are grounded in reality and remain consistent with the original concept.

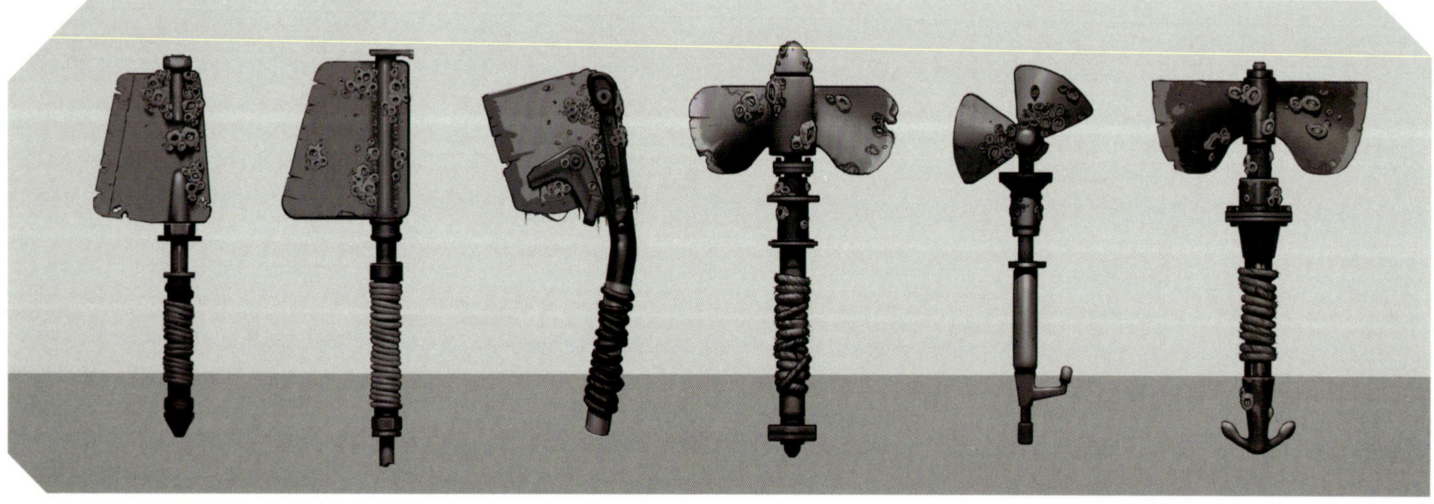

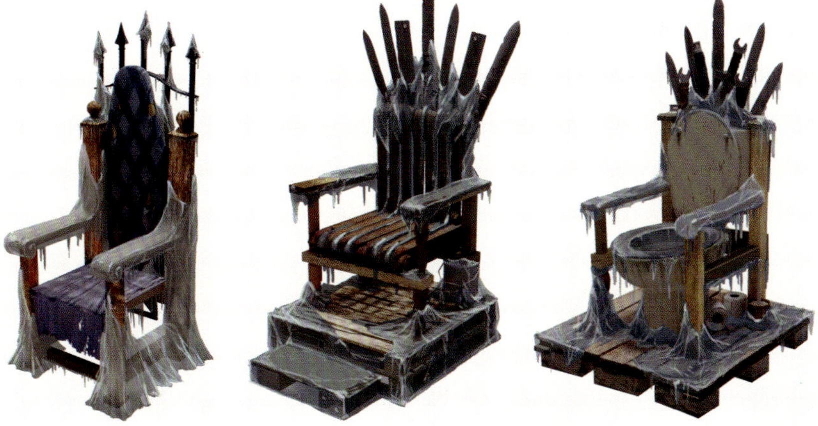

THE ICE THRONE

The Ice Throne, part of the Ice King DLC pack, is a decorative item inspired by various works of fantasy in recent times. These concepts show a few variants of the throne, modeled from chairs, pallets, salvaged blades, weapons, and ice. Below are the concept sketches for the Yeti, which was going to be part of an event but didn't make it into the game.

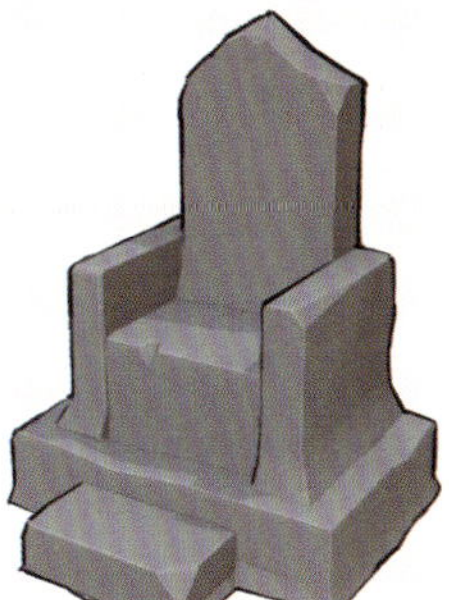

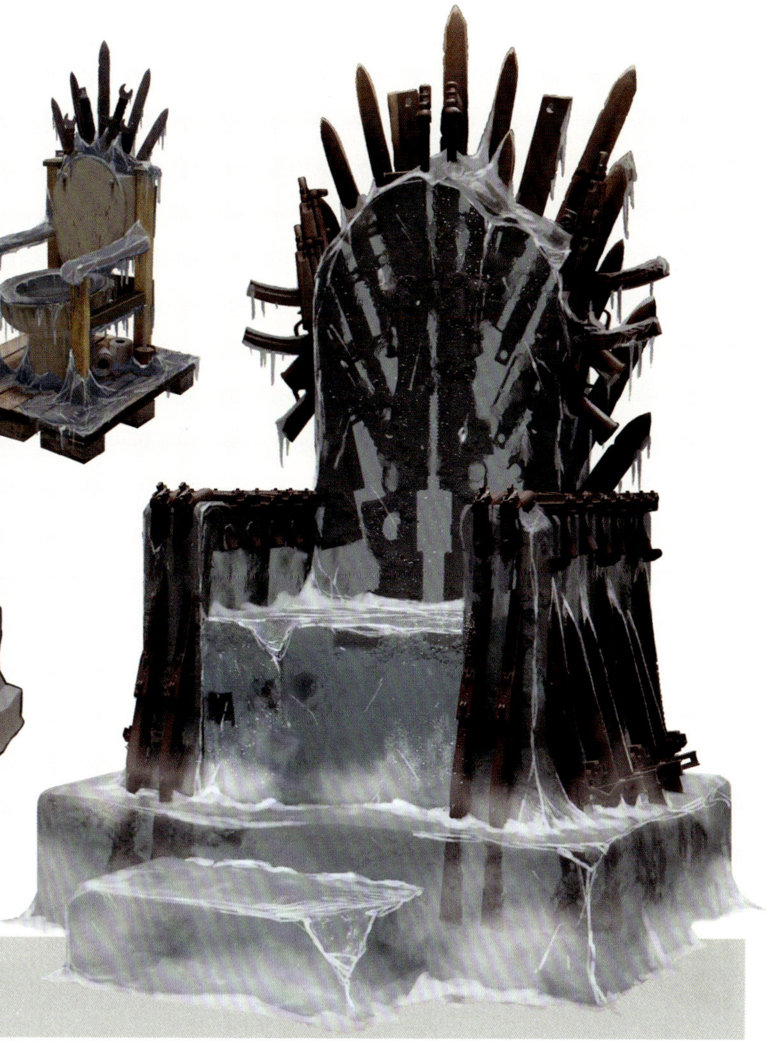

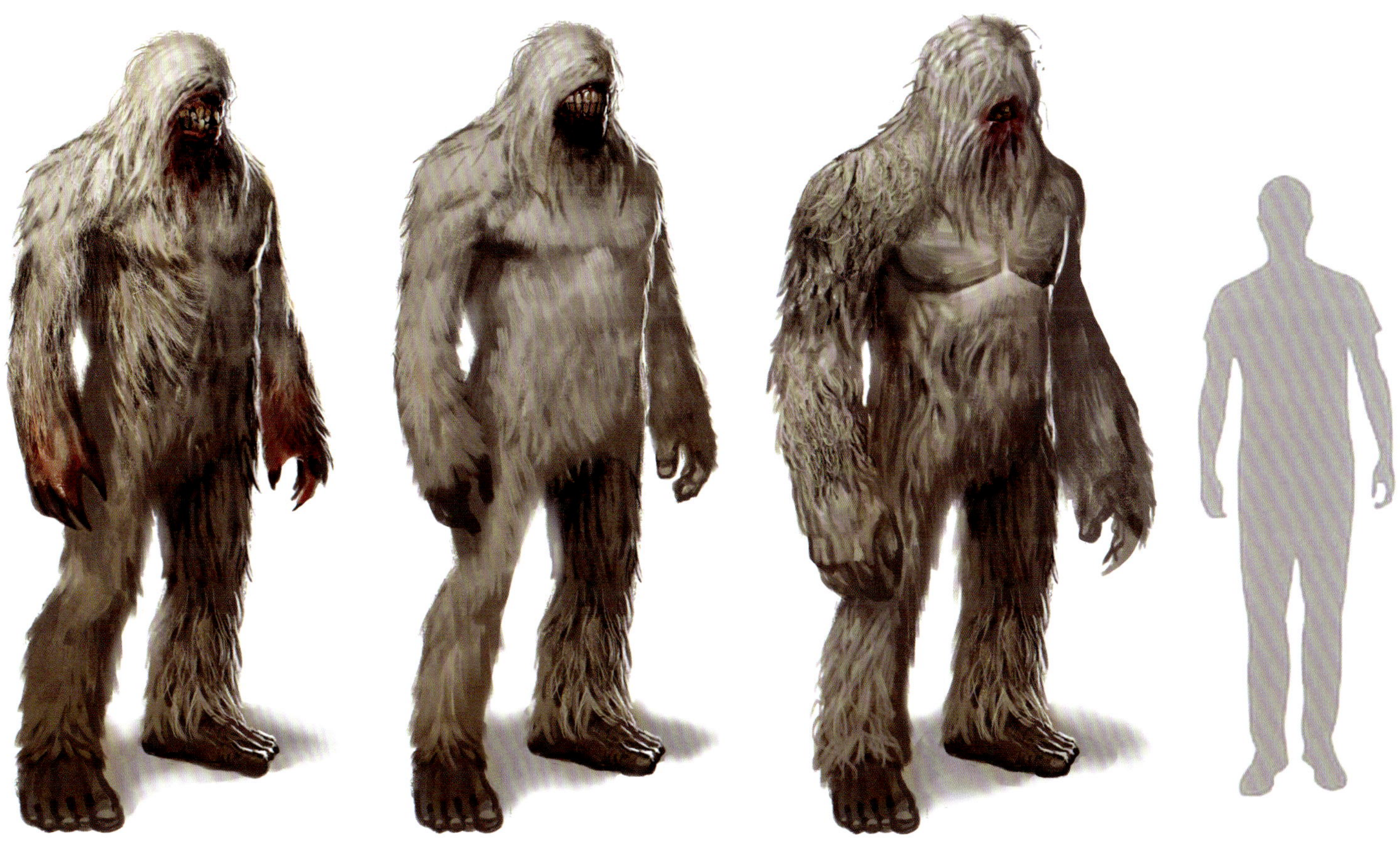

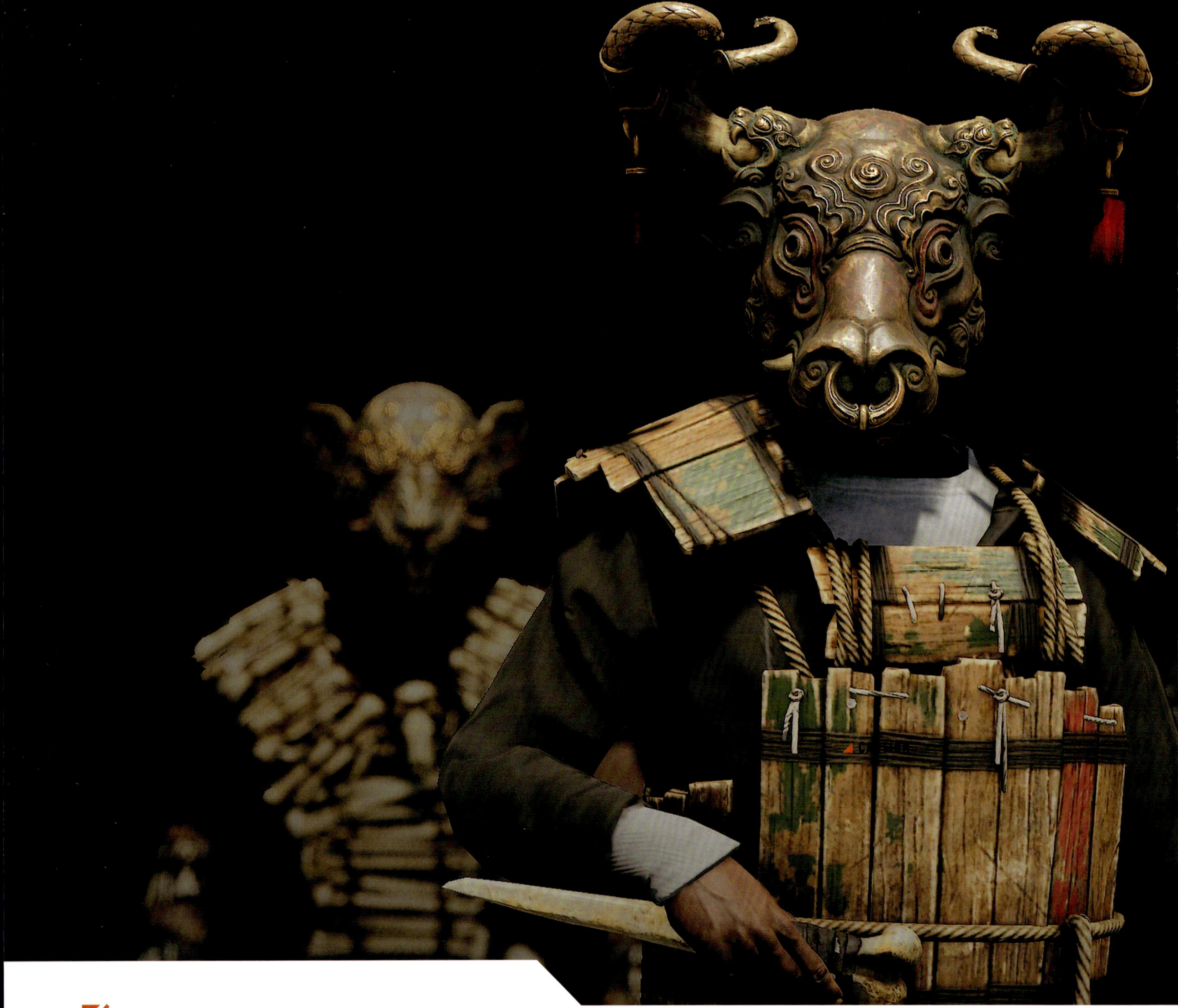

CHINESE NEW YEAR

The Lunar New Year events bring a bright, celebratory contrast to the game's otherwise bleak world. These events introduce thematic items and decor, like firecrackers, dragon masks, and red lanterns that draw from traditional Chinese New Year celebrations. Rather than pristine cultural replicas, the items reflect *Rust*'s hallmark handmade aesthetic: slightly battered and assembled from salvage.

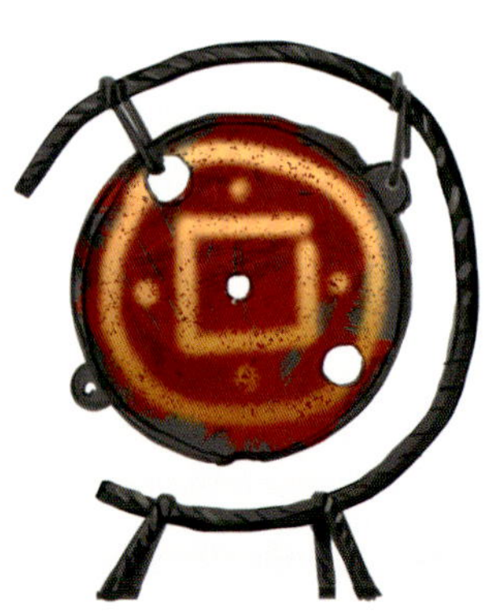

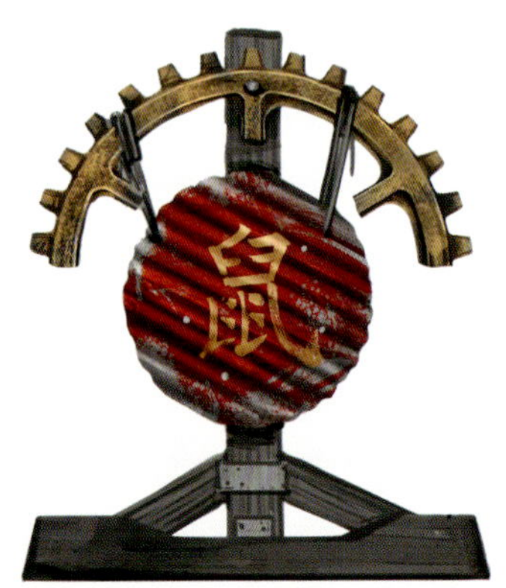

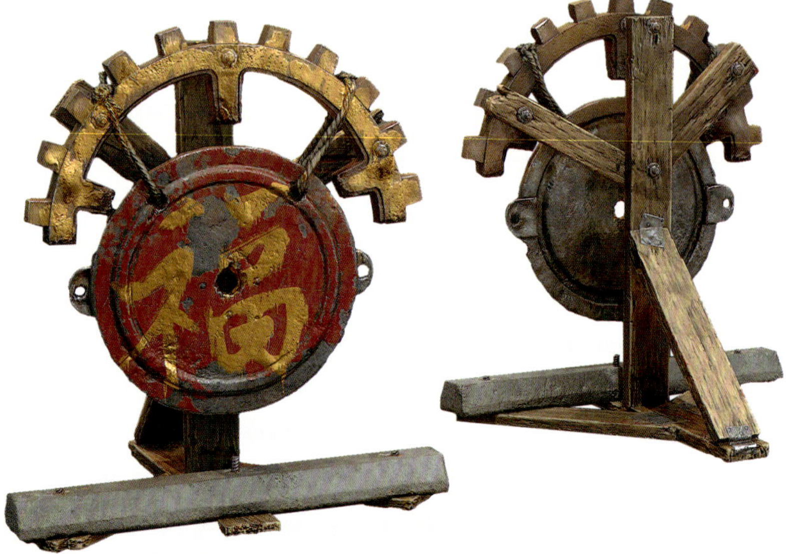

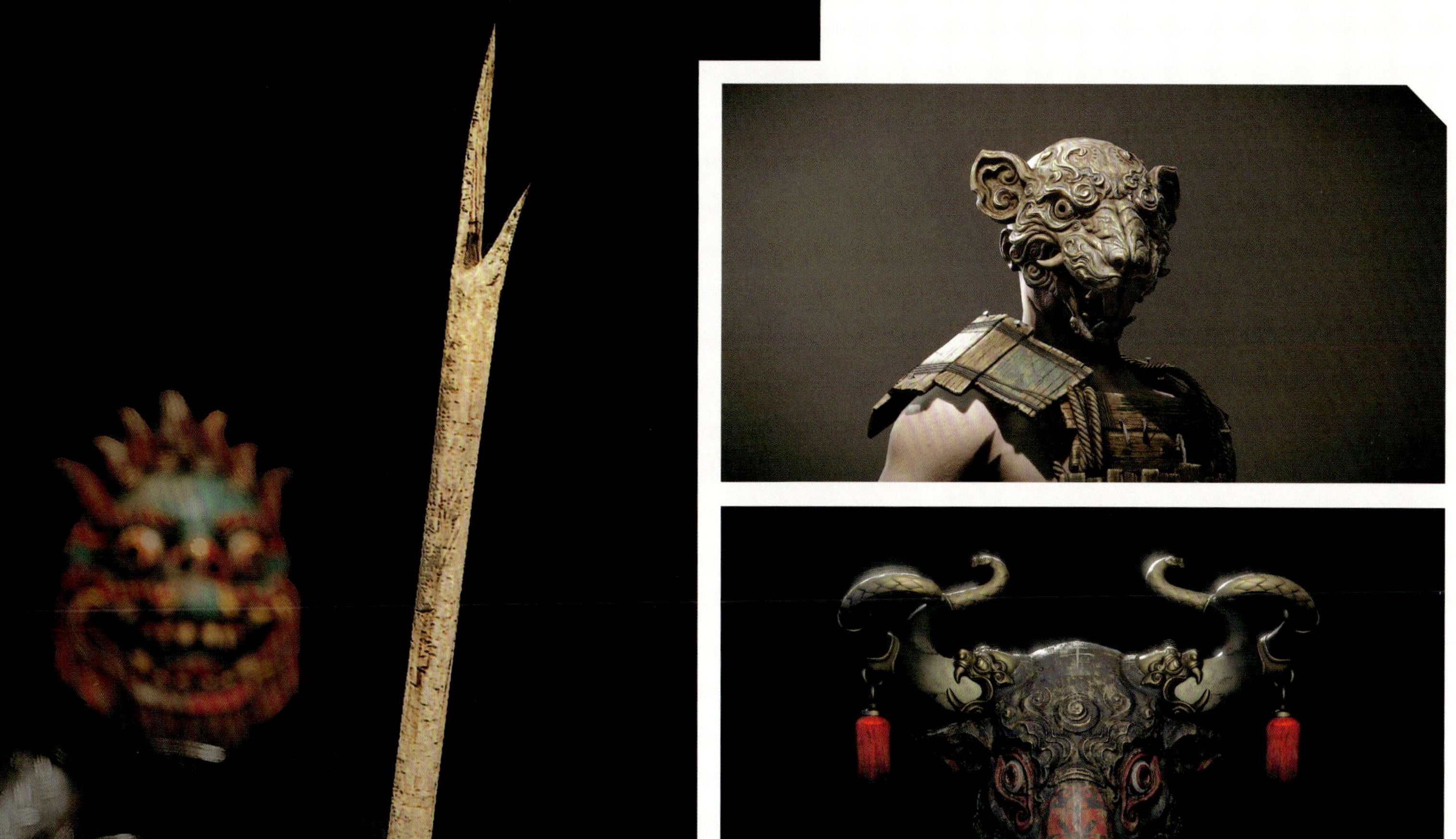

GONG

Inspired by ceremonial instruments, the Gong props were a chance to add flair and ceremony to the player experience. The early sketches below explored construction from sheet metal, bike gears, and salvaged signs.

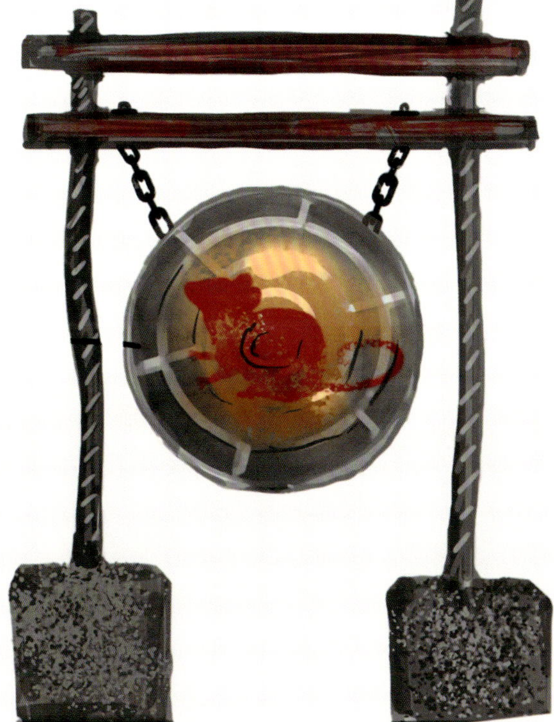

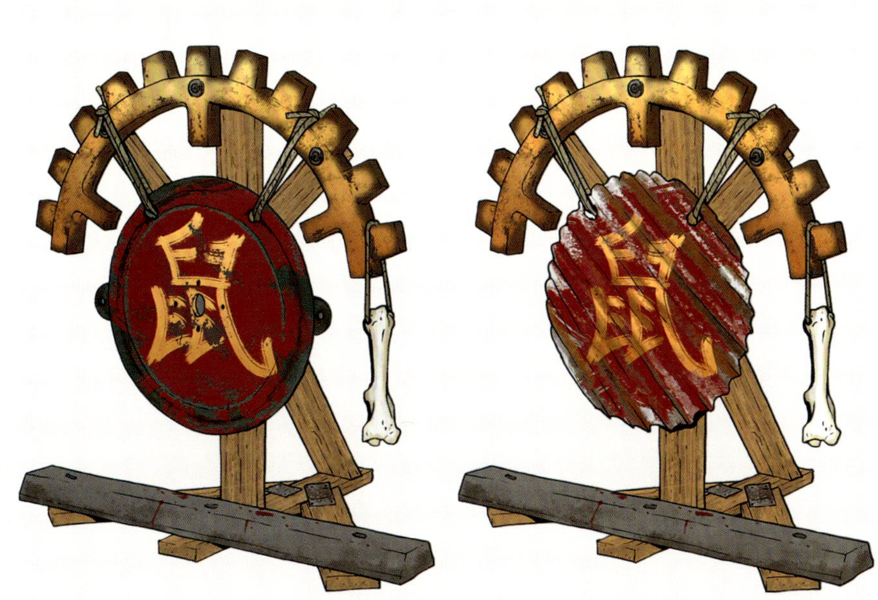

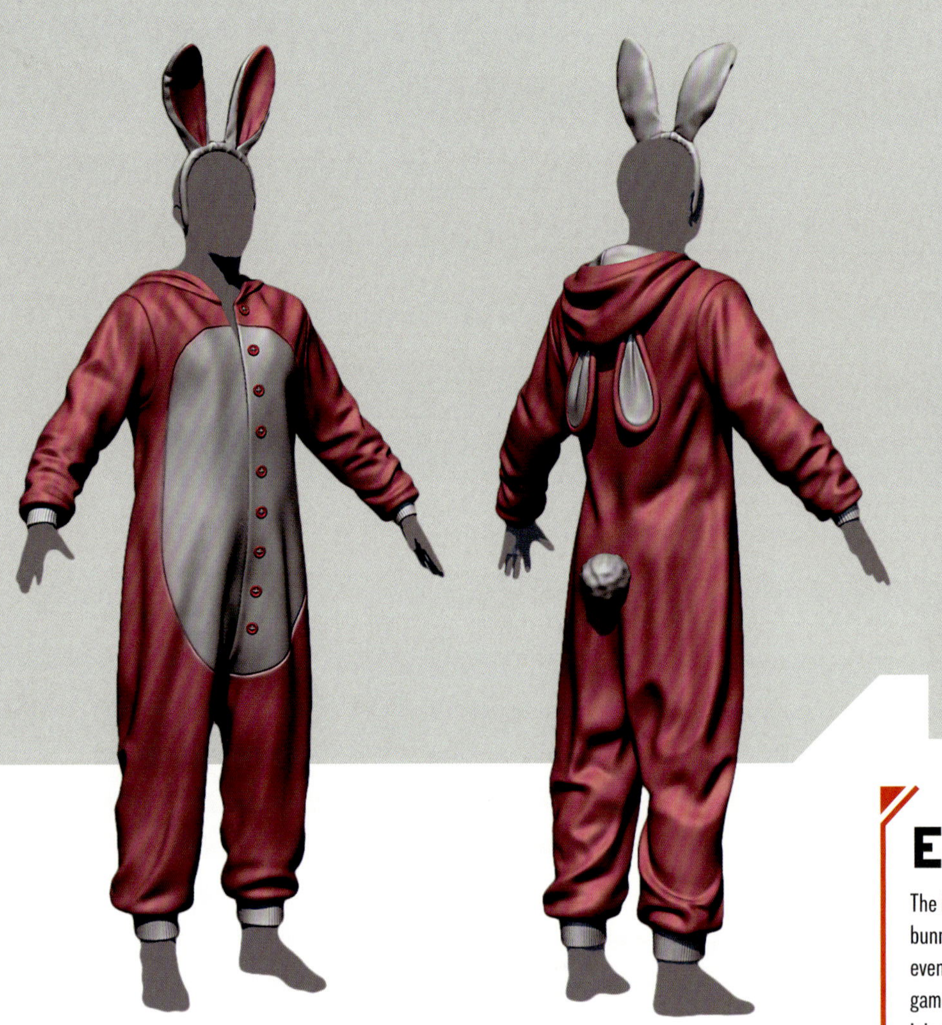

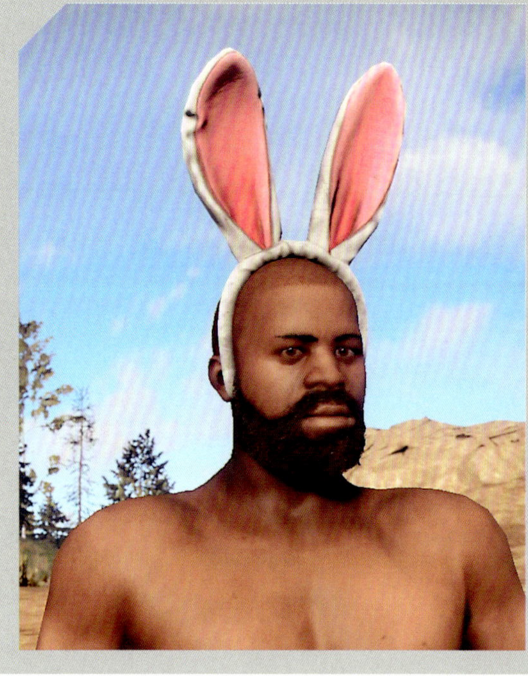

EASTER

The Easter seasonal events tend to lean into absurdity in the best way, with bunny onesies, chicken helmets, and *Rust*-themed Imperial eggs. These events let players break from the tension of survival and engage with the game in a more humorous, social way. The art direction embraces this shift, injecting seasonal fun without fully stepping outside *Rust*'s identity.

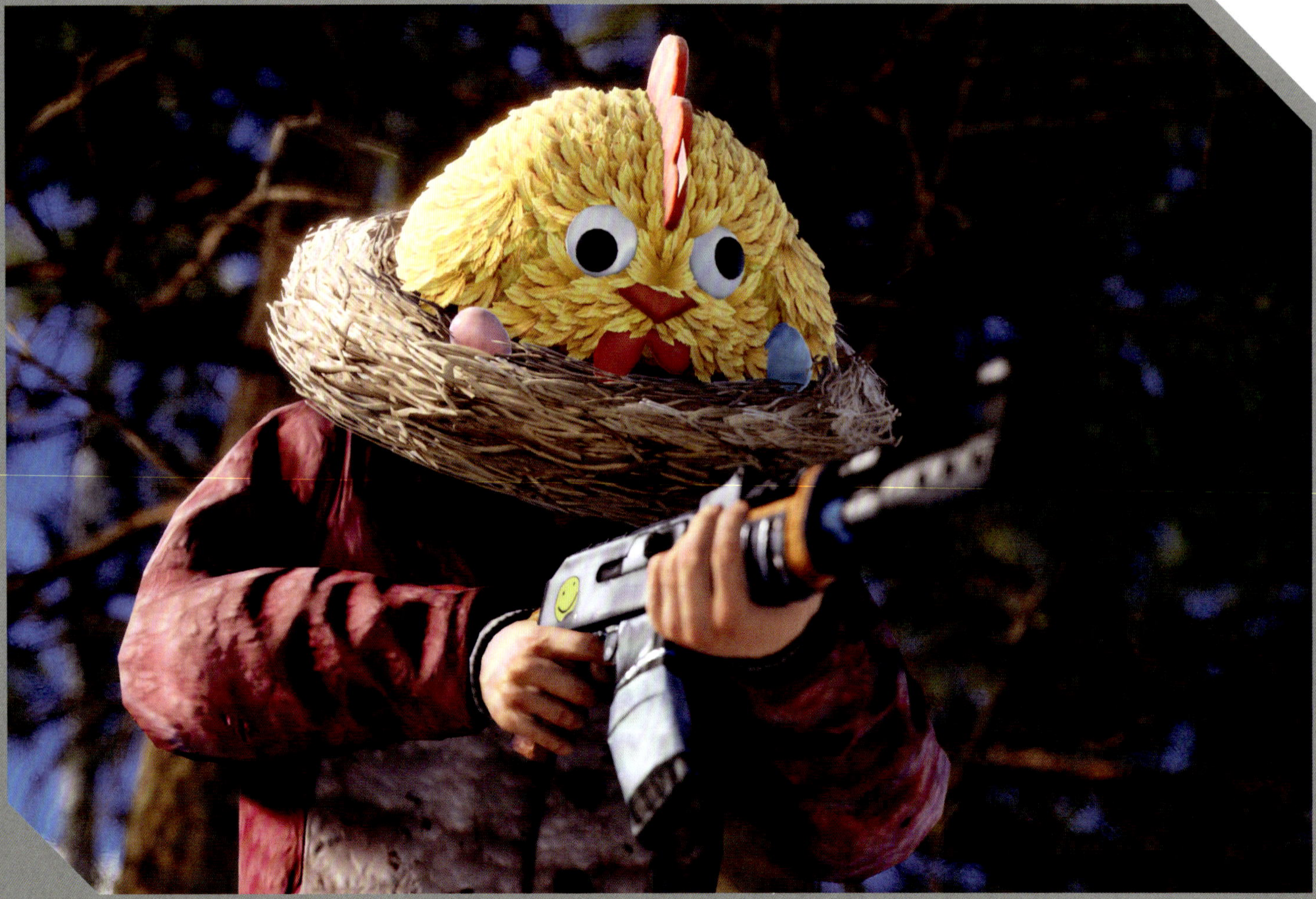

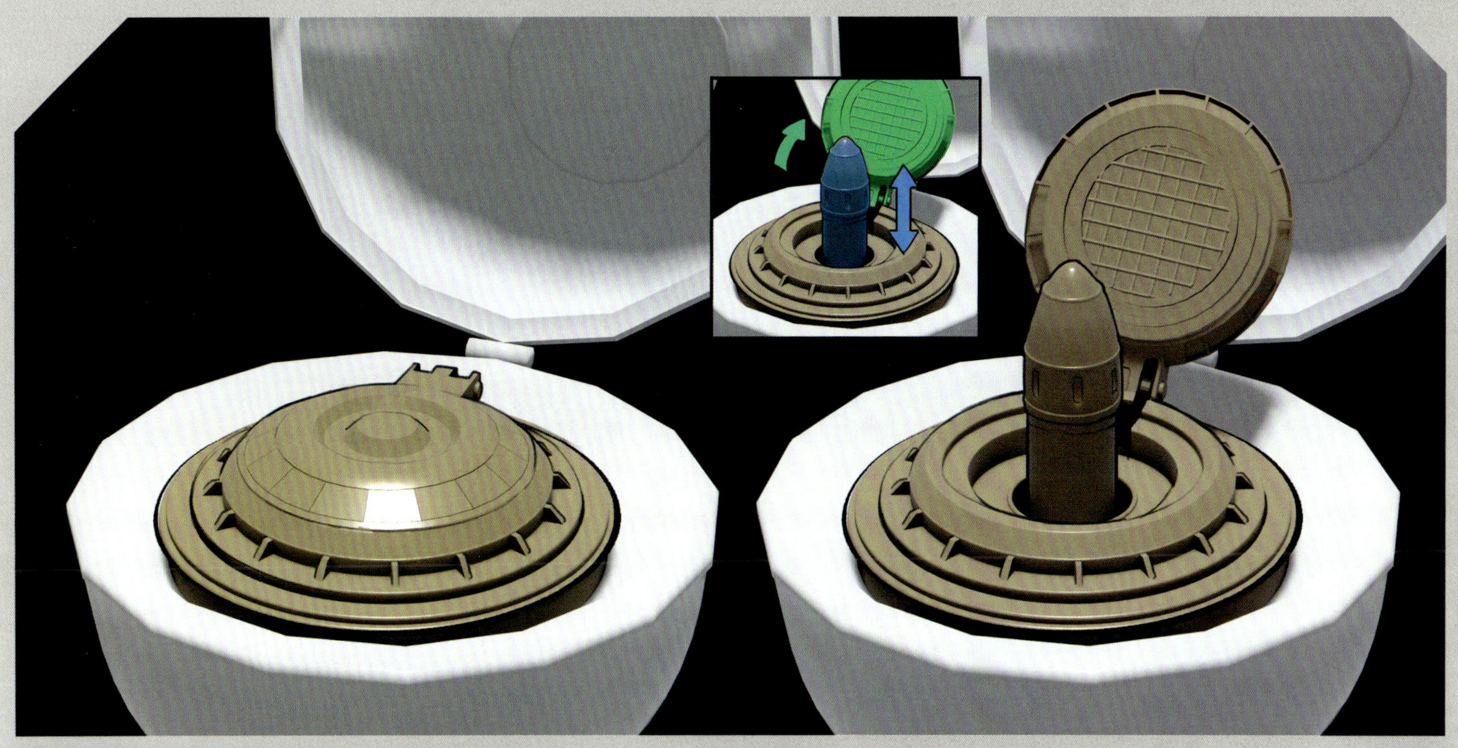
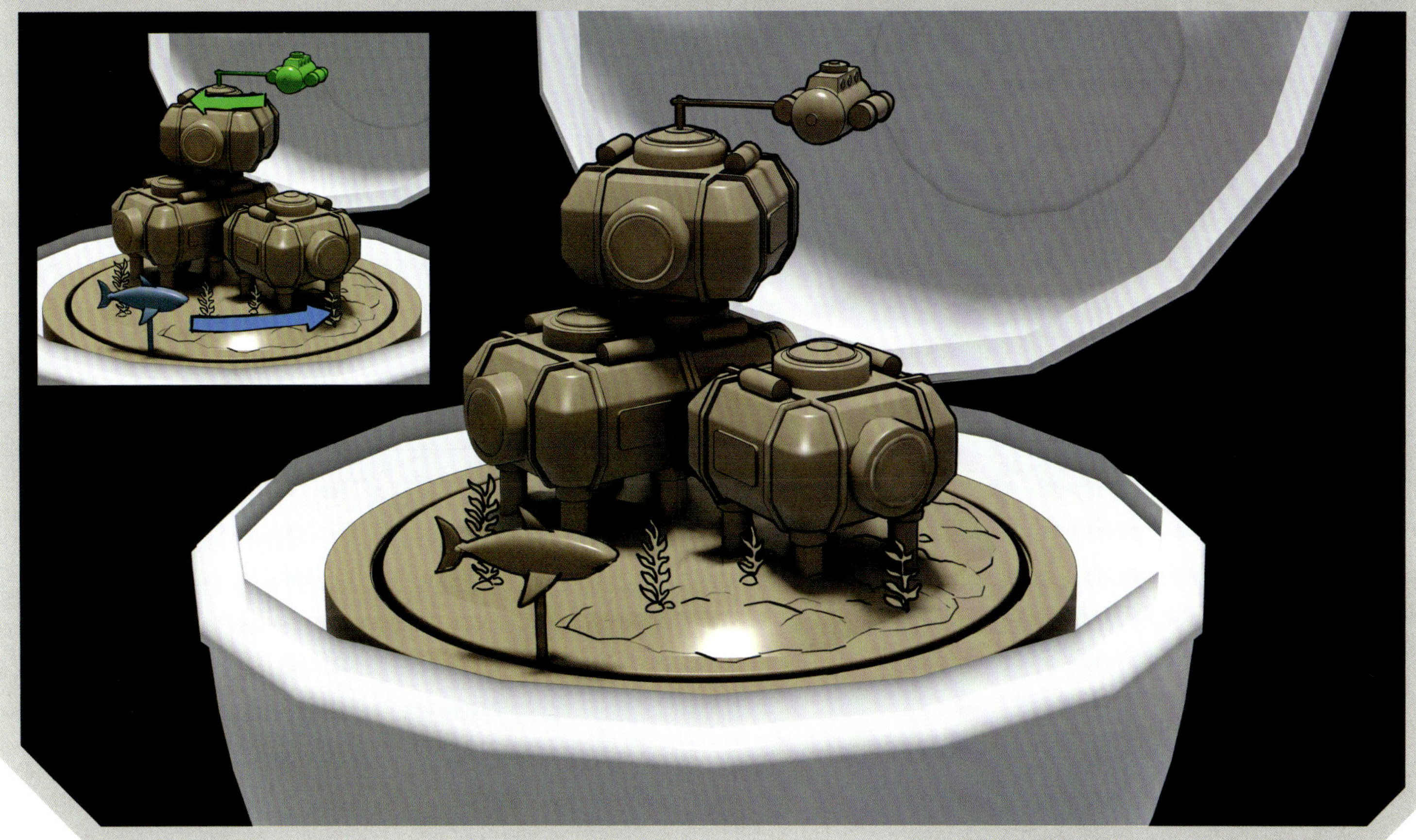
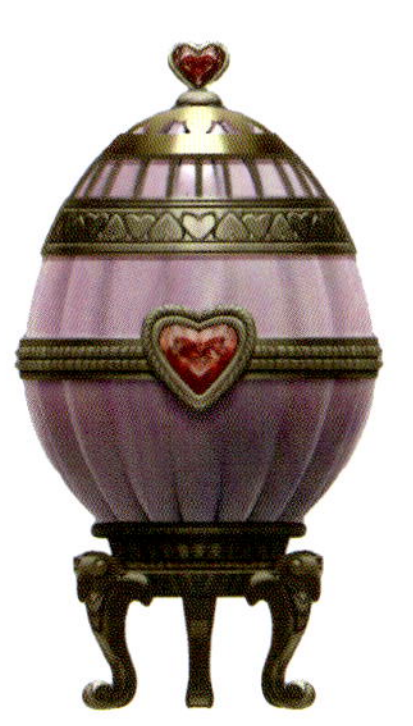
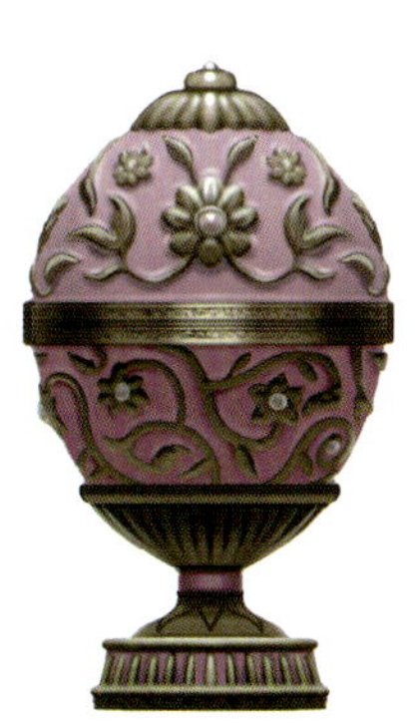
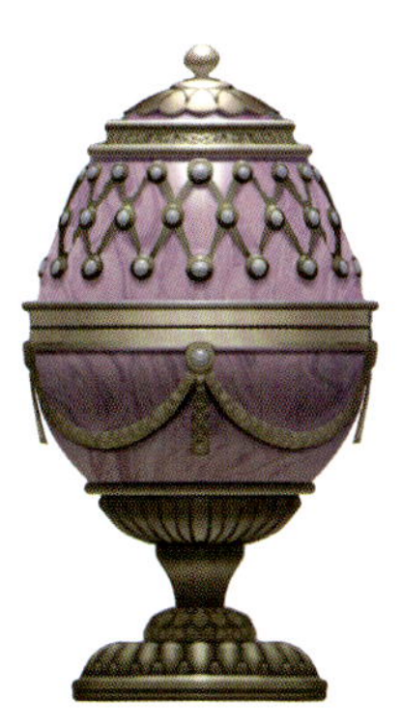
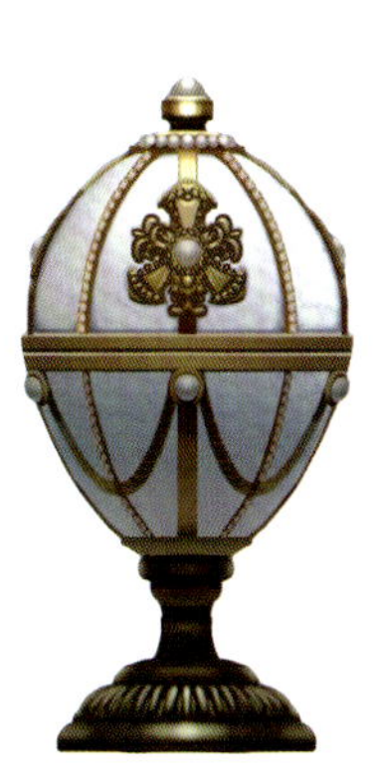
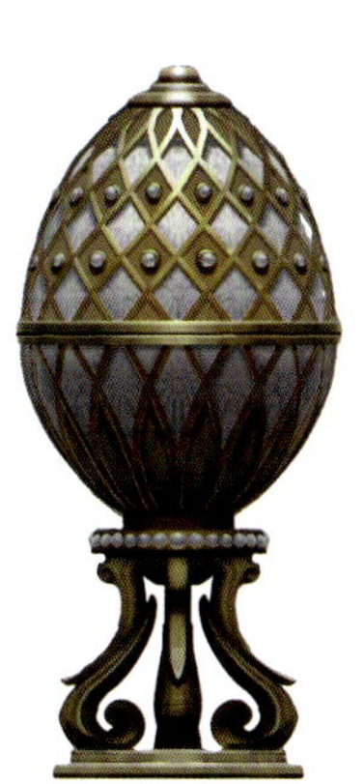
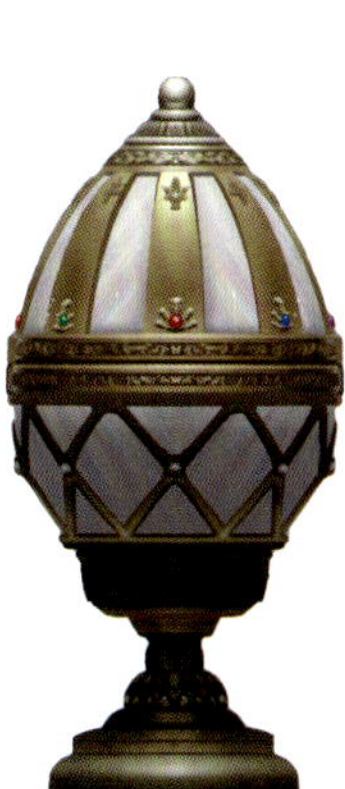

HALLOWEEN

The Halloween events embrace a darker, more theatrical tone, amplifying the game's brutality with eerie atmosphere and horror-inspired visuals. These limited-time events introduce themed items, enemies, and decor that lean into folklore, the grotesque, and the simply ridiculous.

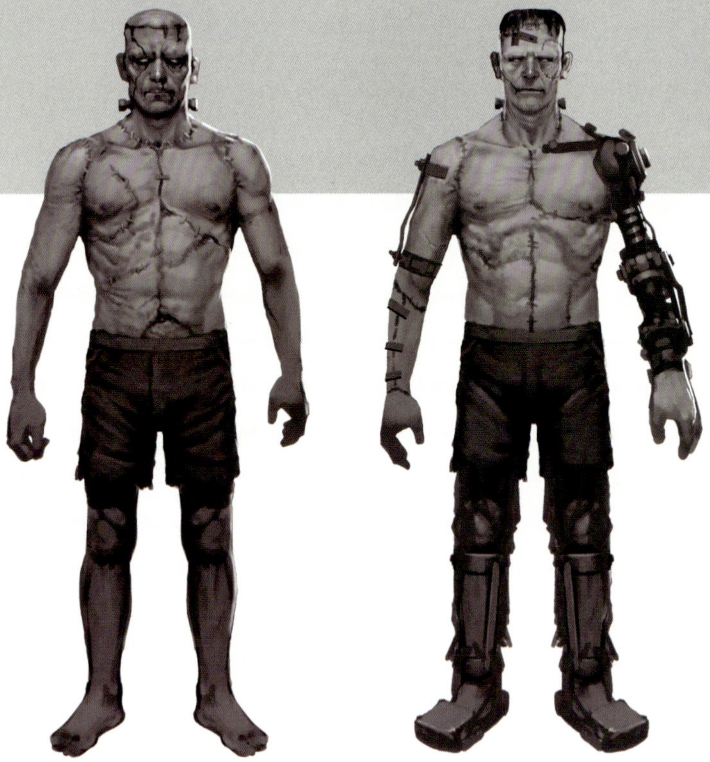

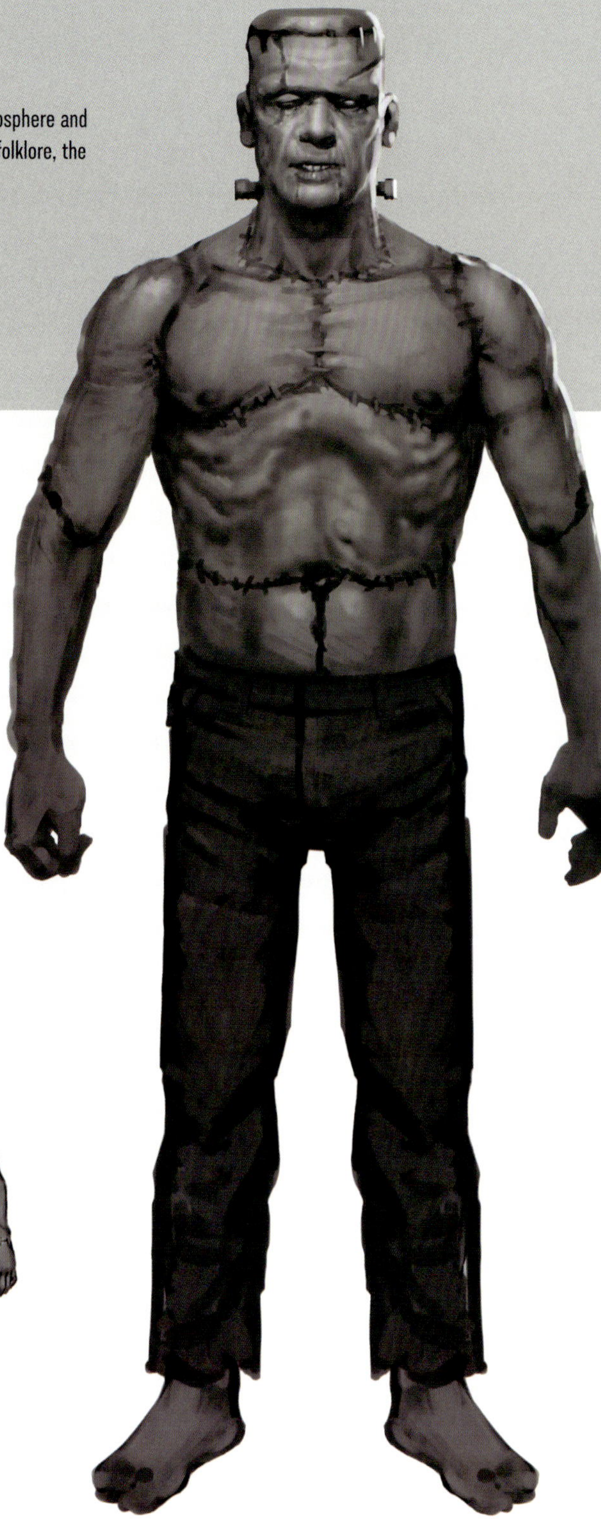

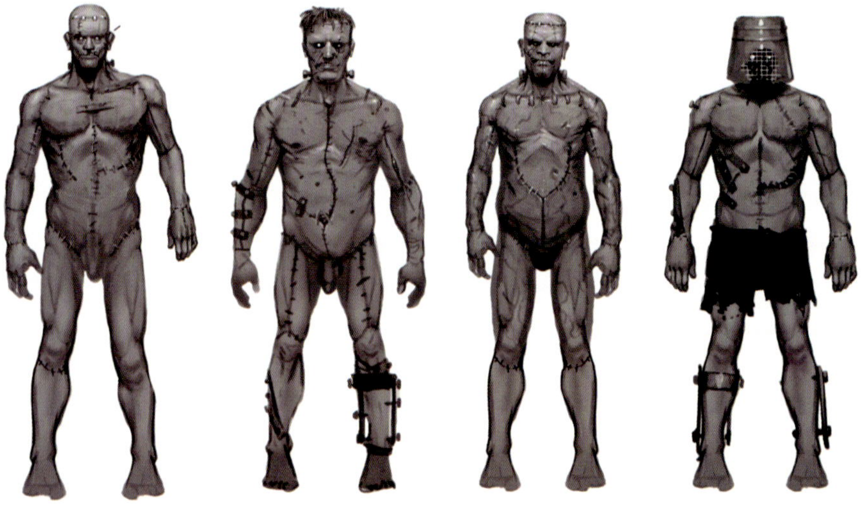

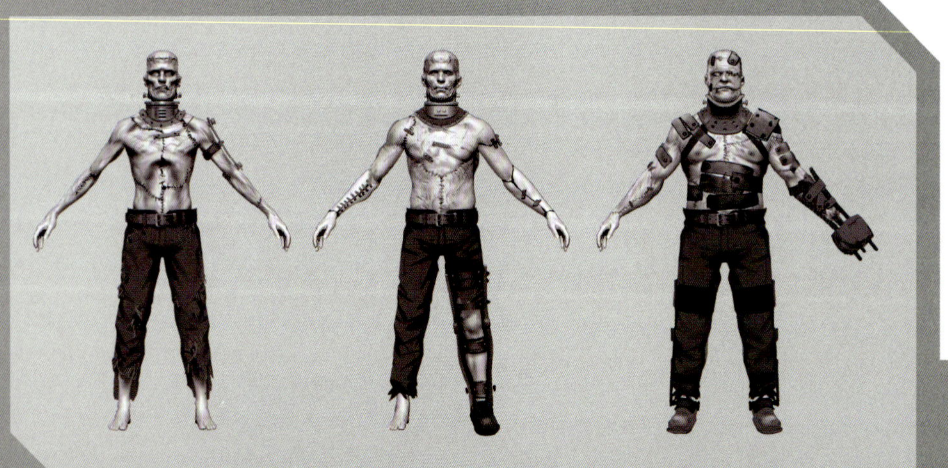

FRANKENSTEIN

Here are the initial concepts for *Rust*'s very own Frankenstein. He was introduced as part of the first Halloween in-game event.

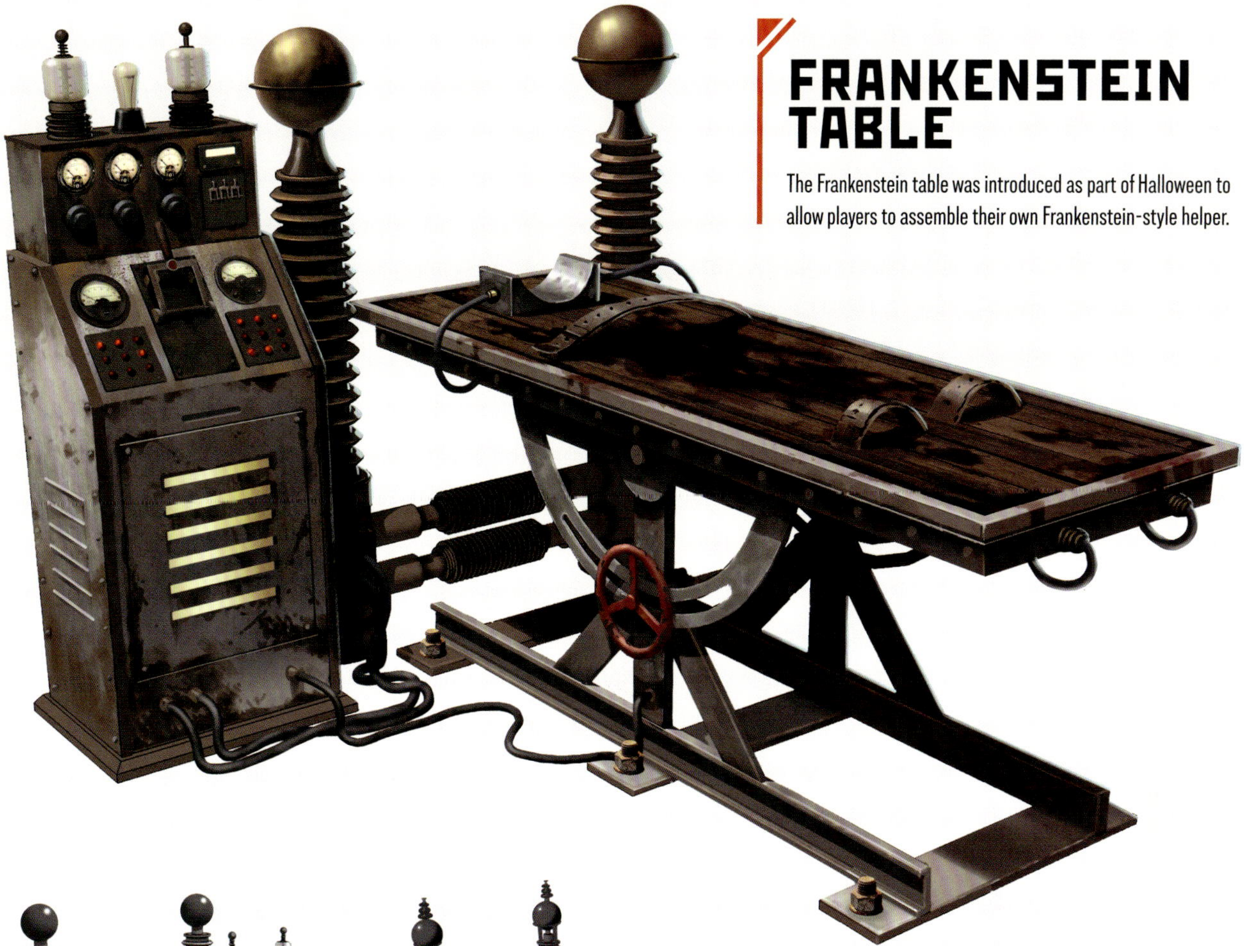

FRANKENSTEIN TABLE

The Frankenstein table was introduced as part of Halloween to allow players to assemble their own Frankenstein-style helper.

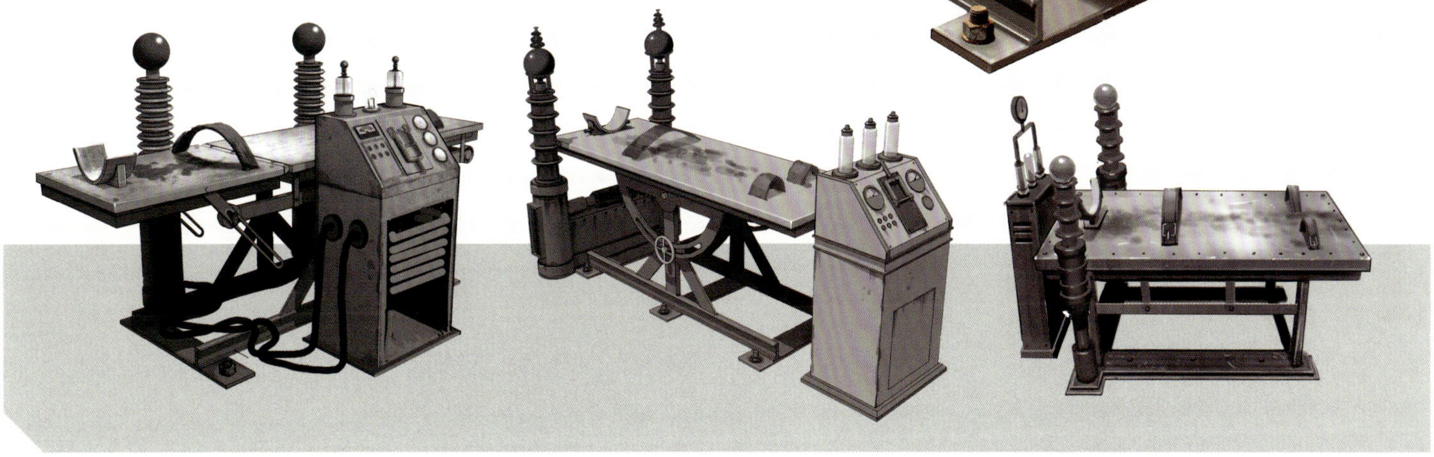

SURGEONS

Here are some early concepts for some horror-based surgical skins for Halloween.

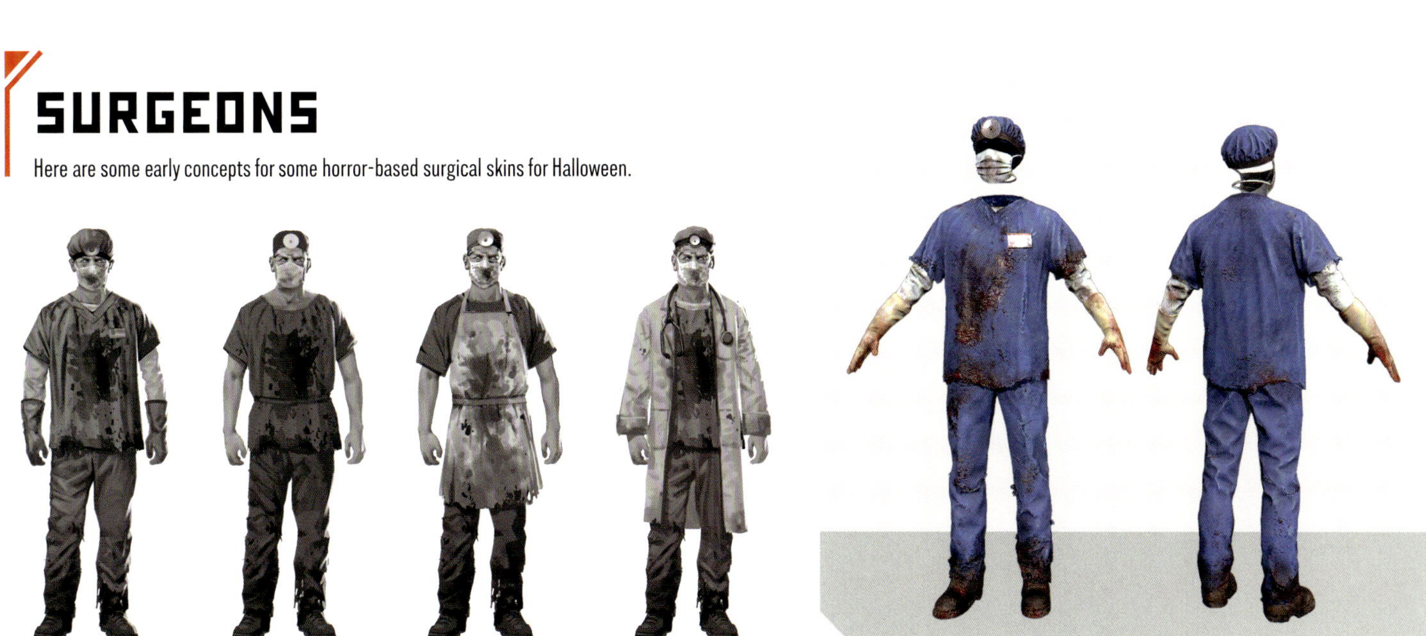

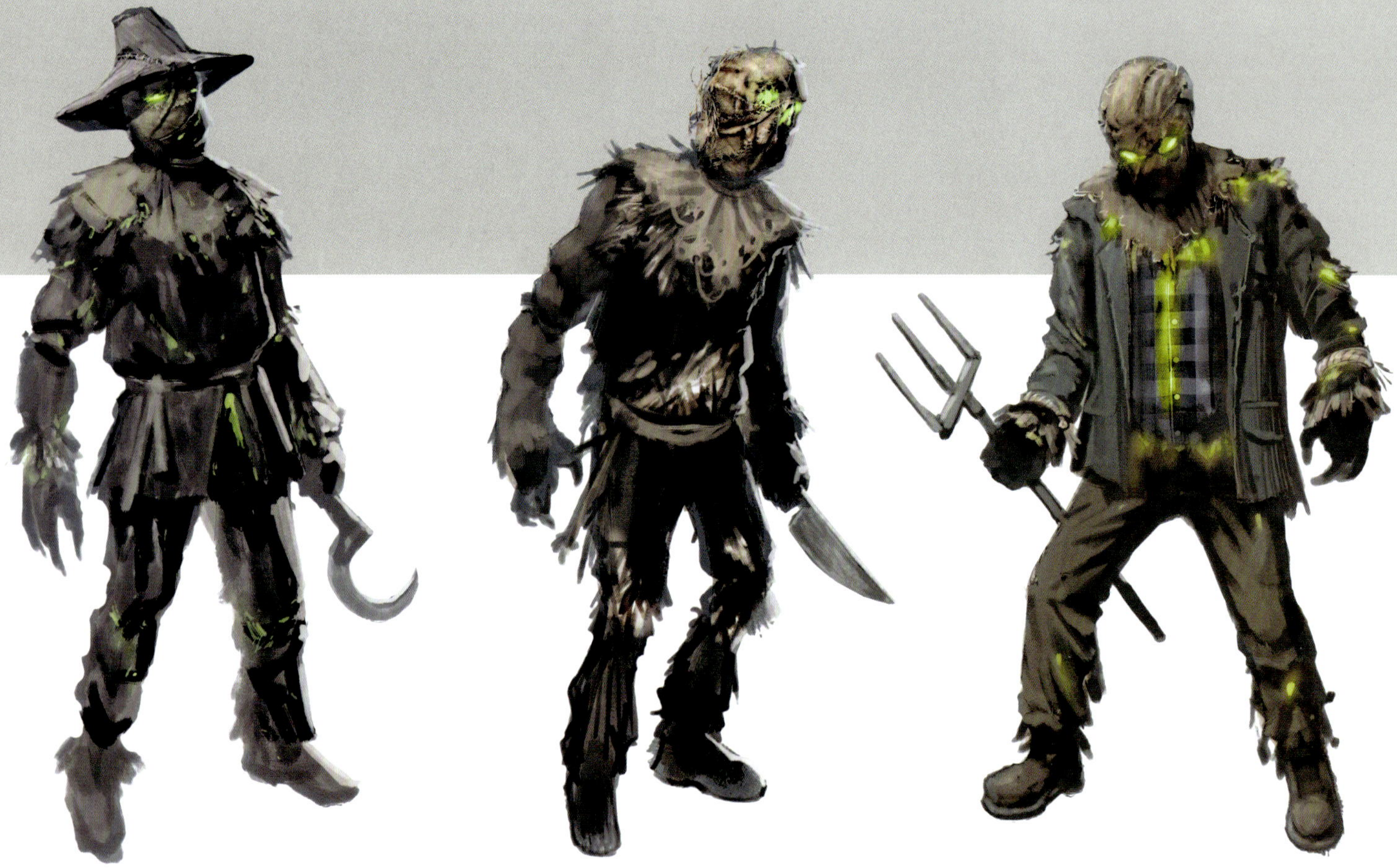

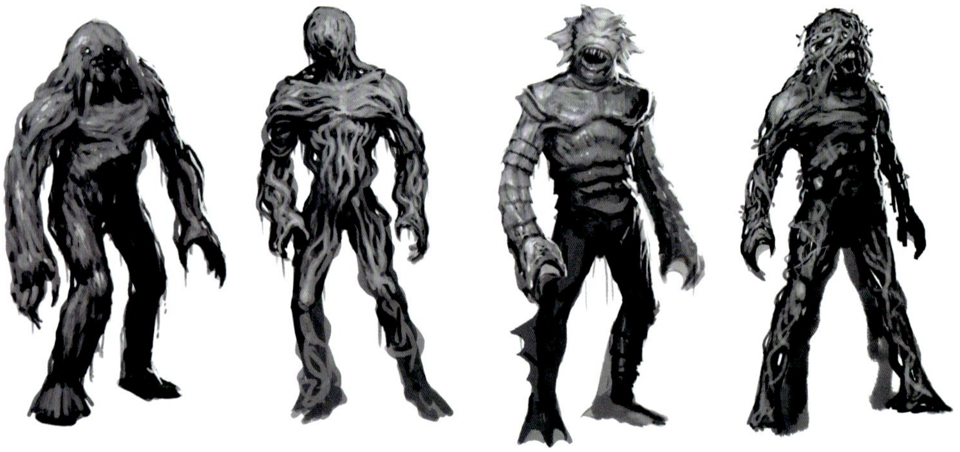

SCARECROWS

The Scarecrow is a seasonal NPC enemy introduced during Halloween events. These early concepts draw inspiration from a few places: One comes from folk horror and has scrappy silhouettes, tattered fabrics, and glowing eyes. The others derive from mythical beasts and creatures that could torment players during the events.

SHAMAN TORCH

Designed to look like something dragged from a dark ritual, the Shaman Torch combines bones, feathers, and the original Torch to create a ceremonial tool.

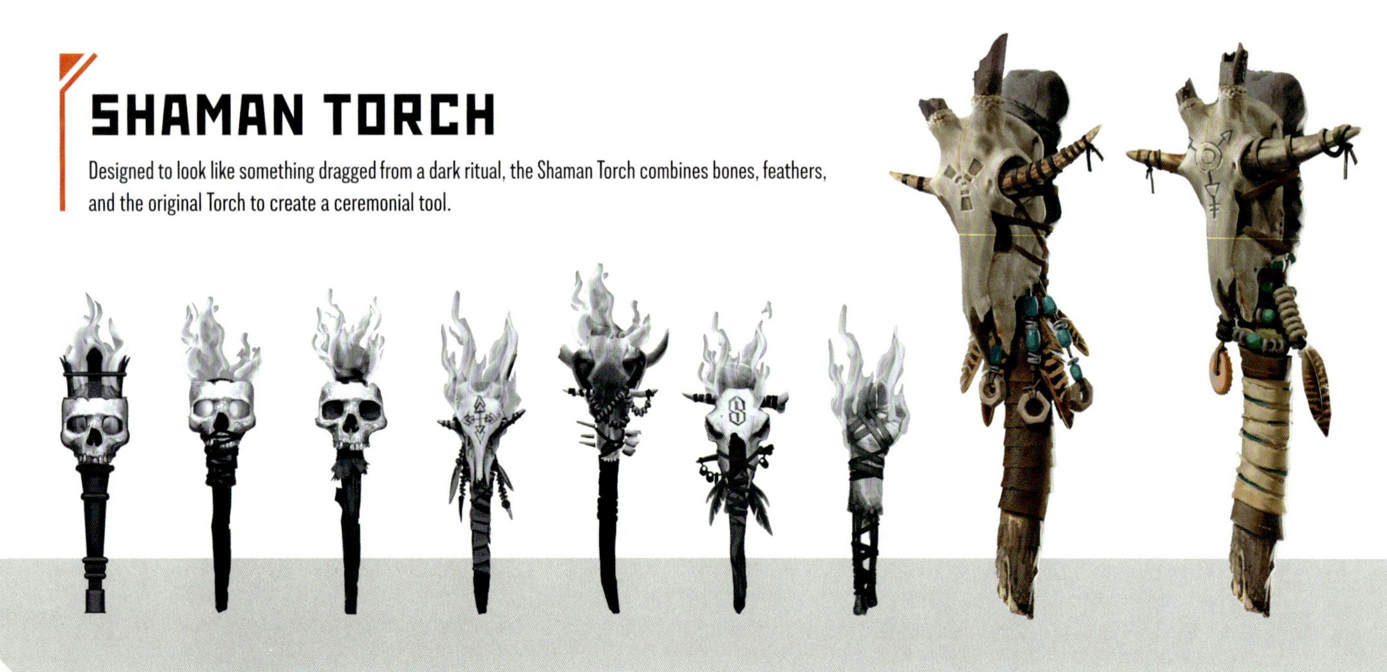

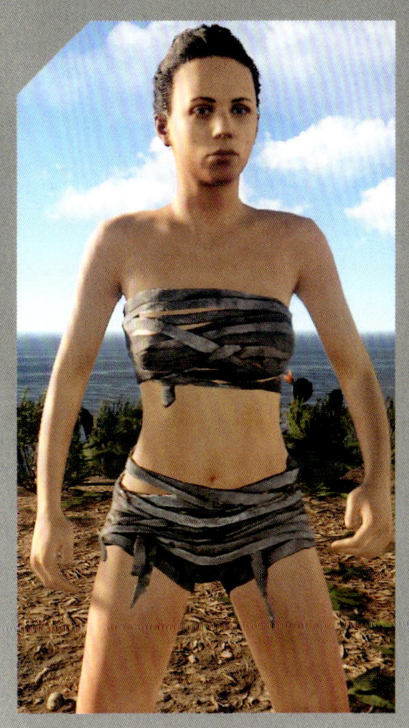
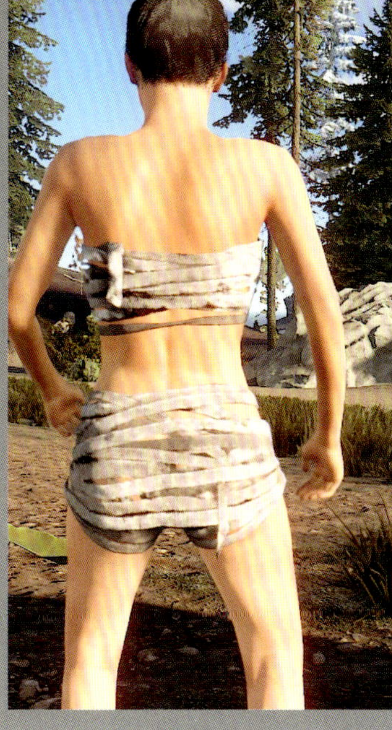
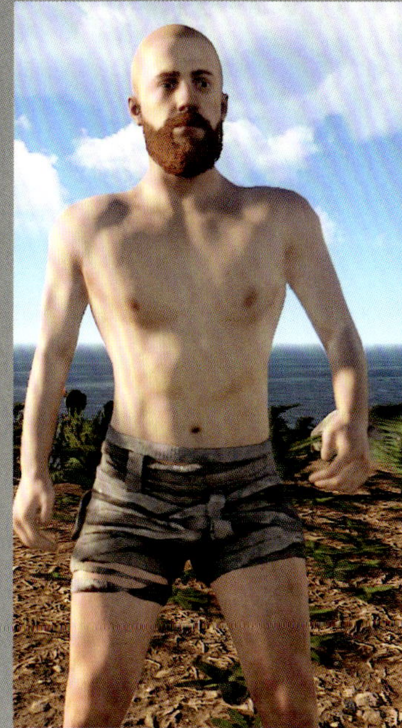
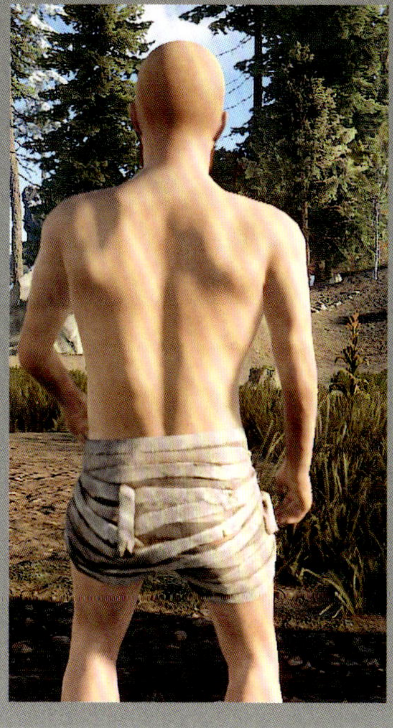
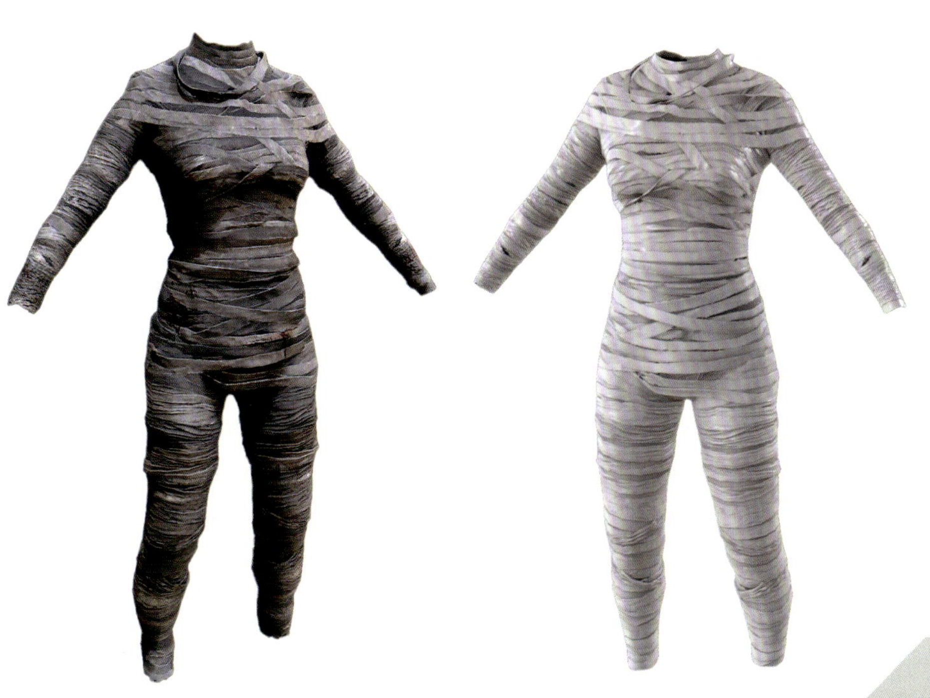

MUMMY WRAPS

The Mummy Wraps are a cosmetic clothing item during Halloween events, aligning with the game's seasonal tradition of introducing themed content that blends humor and horror with the overall scrappy aesthetic. Made of aged linen with just enough gaps to feel eerie, the design plays off classic horror tropes.

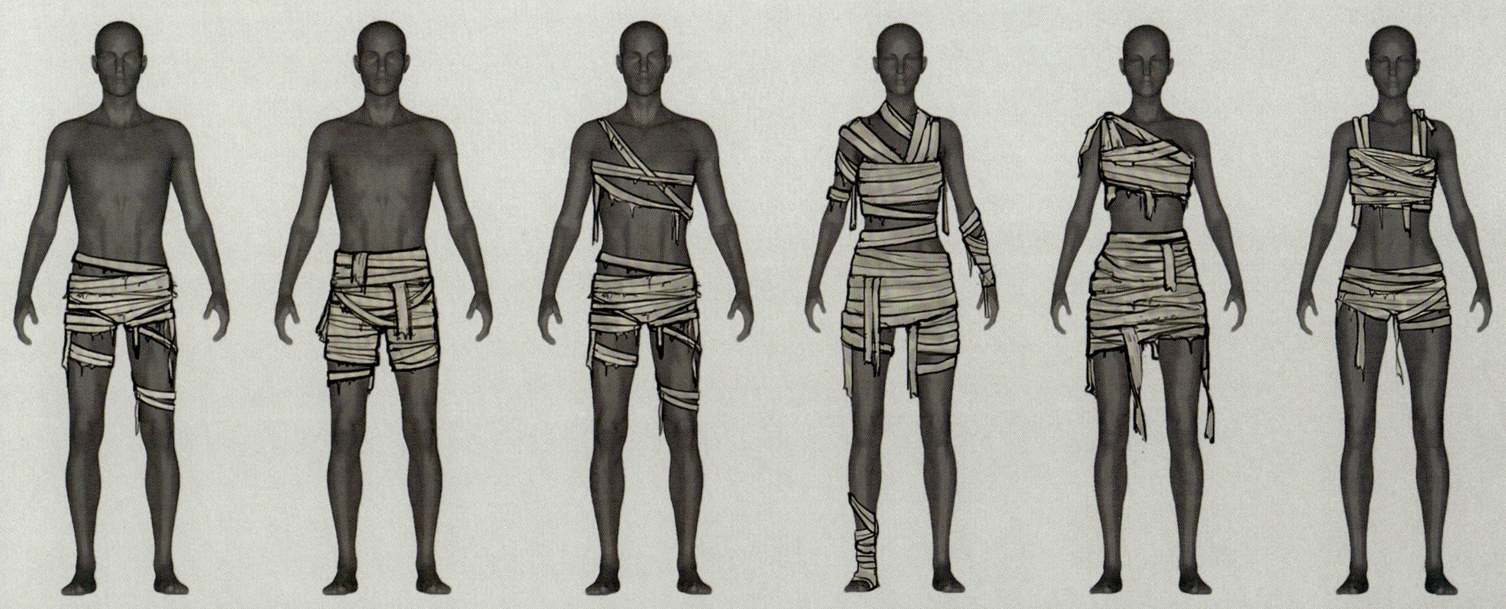

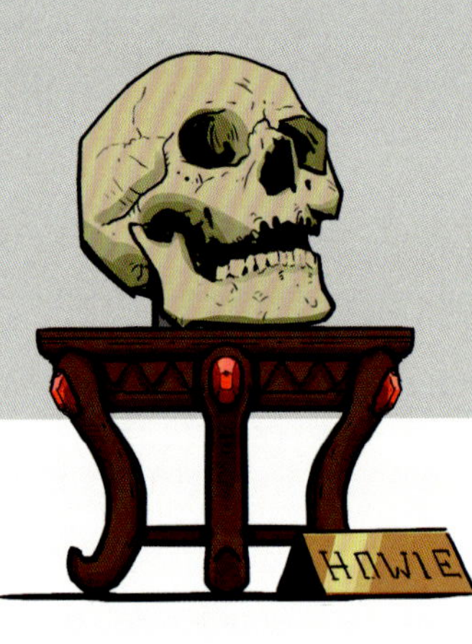

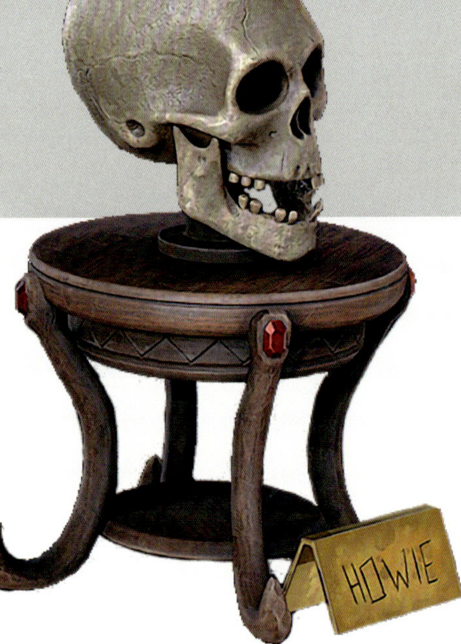

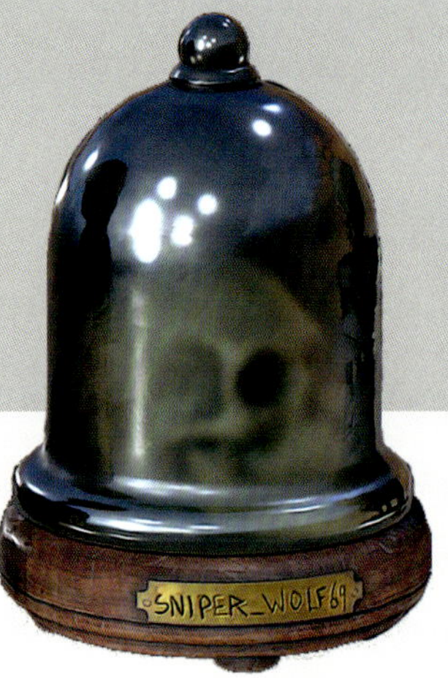

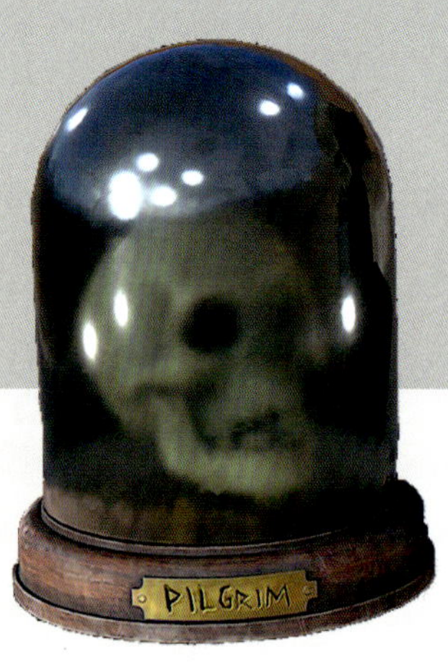

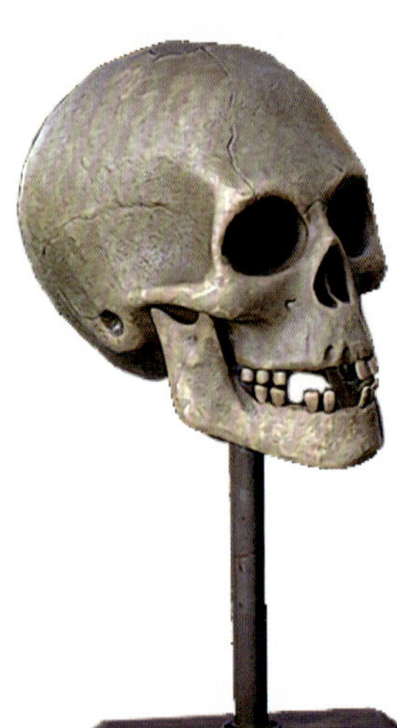

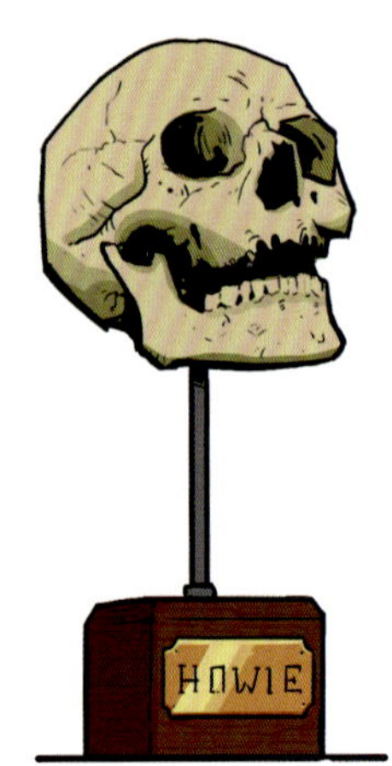

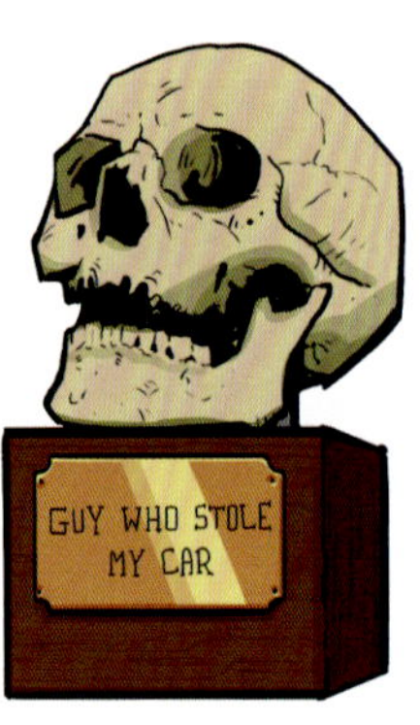

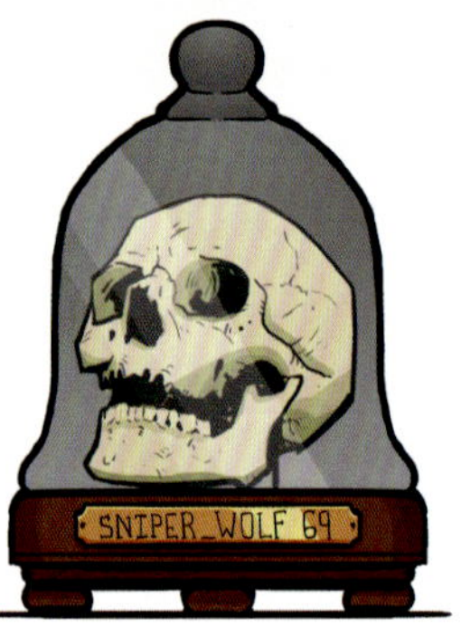

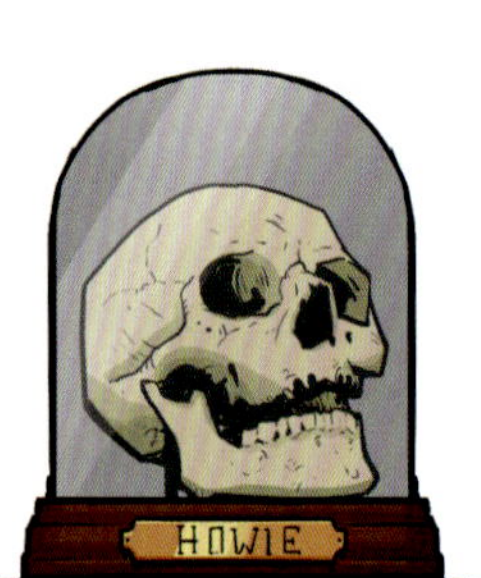

SKULL TROPHIES

Skull Trophies were a fun way to add more collectibles to the game. Each design mixes aged materials with playful engravings to keep things light.

DOLLS

Uncanny and unsettling, these were designed to hit that uneasy horror sweet spot.

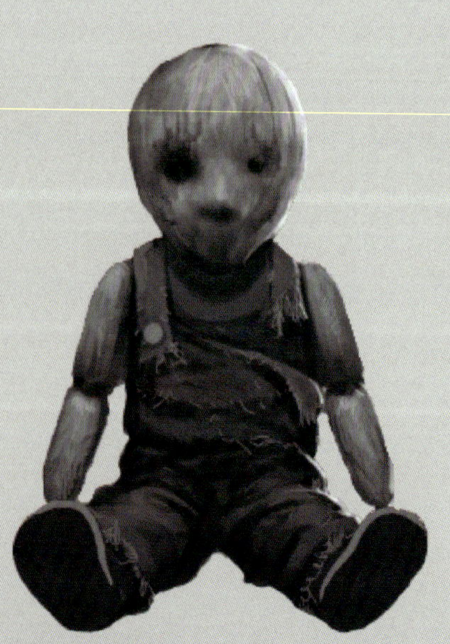

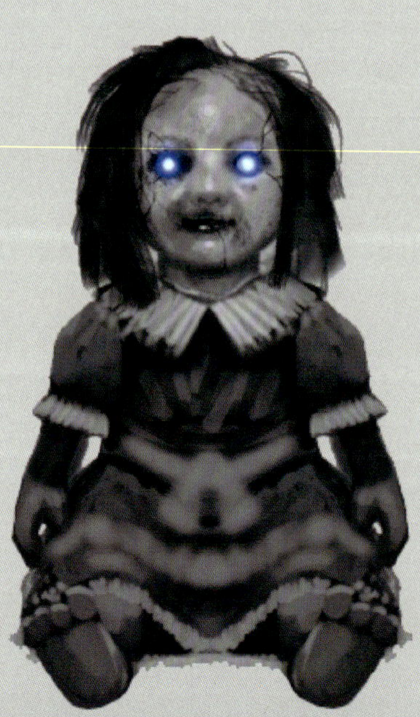

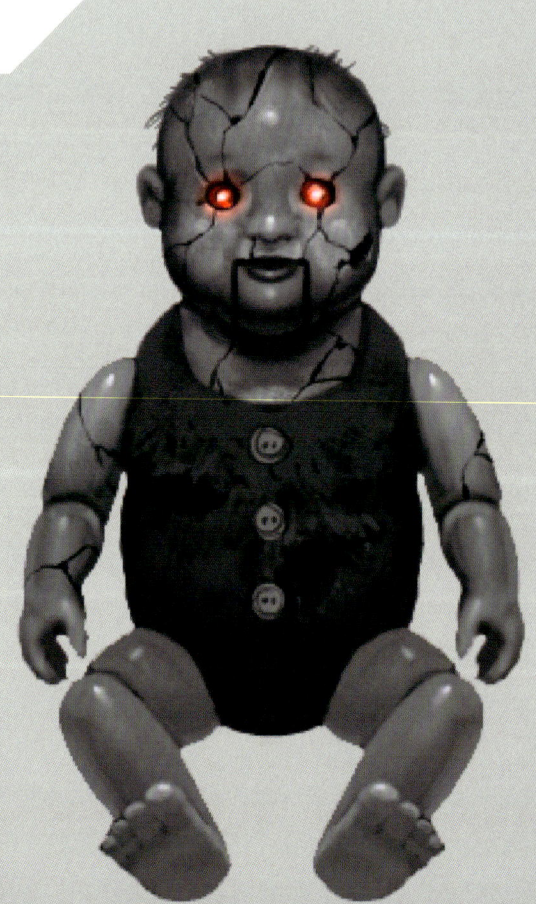

SKULL PIKES

Halloween wouldn't feel complete without something menacing on a stick. These evolved from classic horror iconography, with exaggerated silhouettes and a bit of twisted fun.

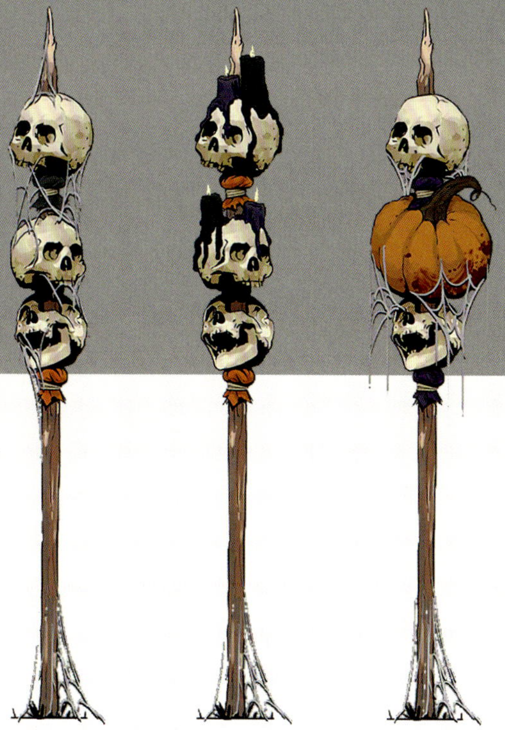

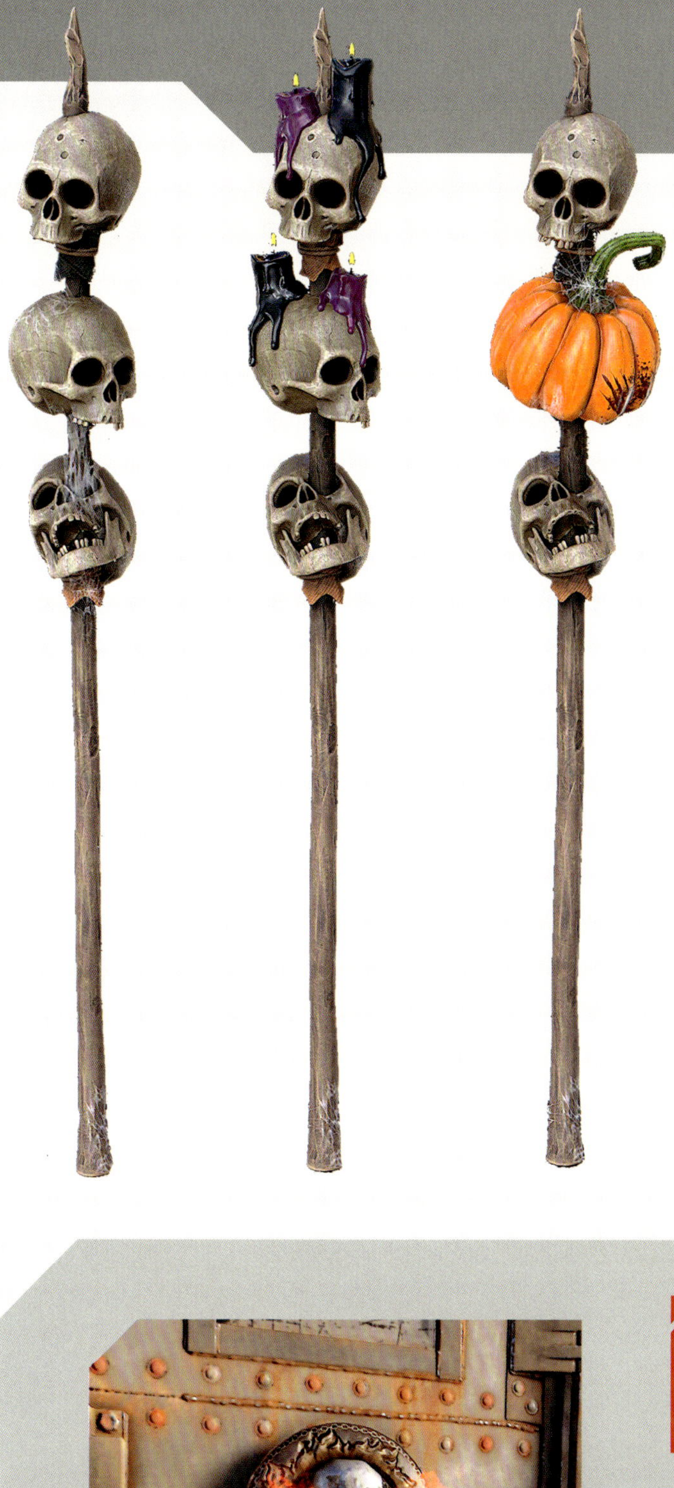

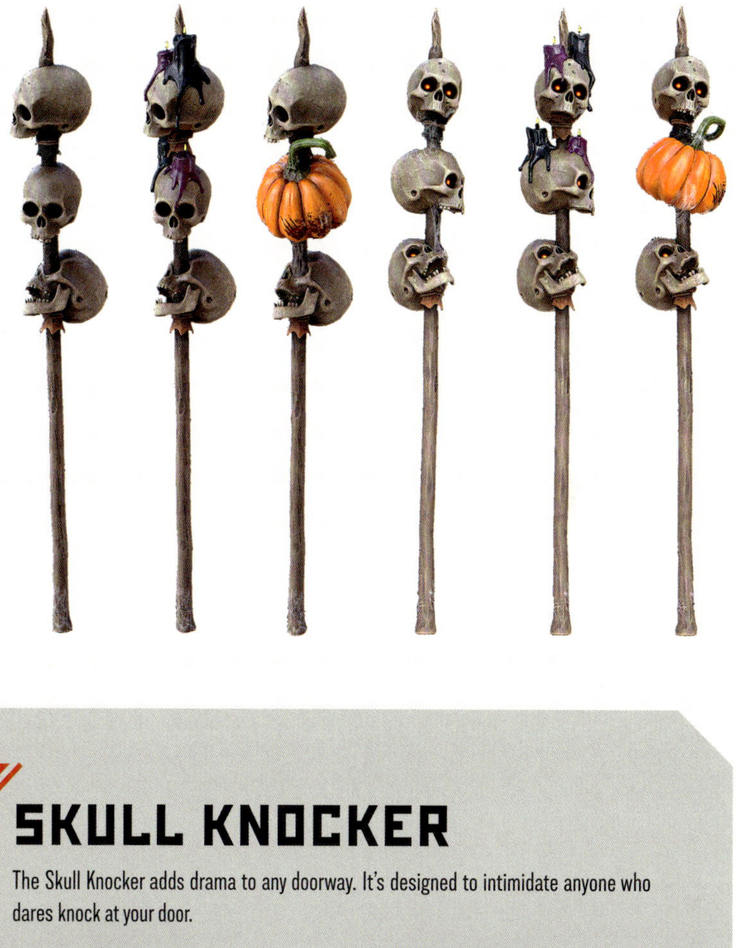

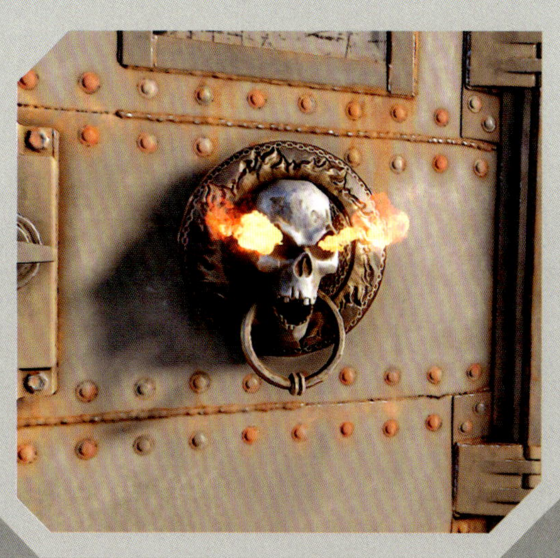

SKULL KNOCKER

The Skull Knocker adds drama to any doorway. It's designed to intimidate anyone who dares knock at your door.

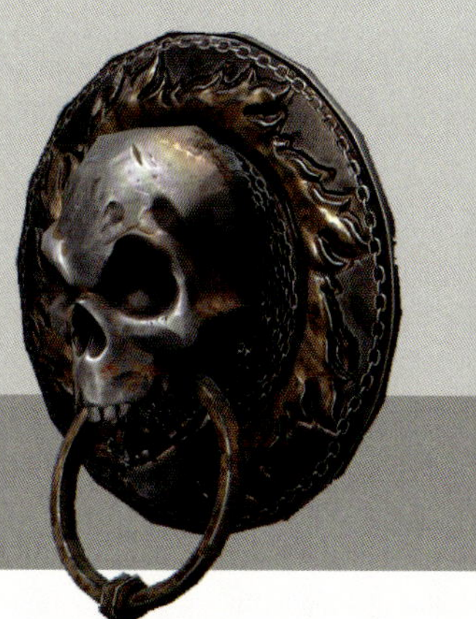

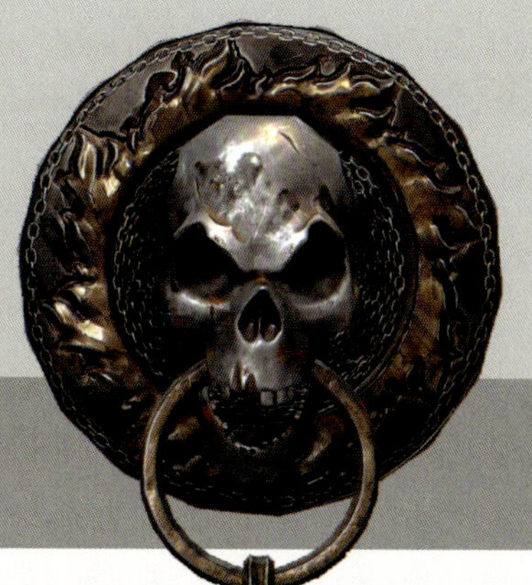

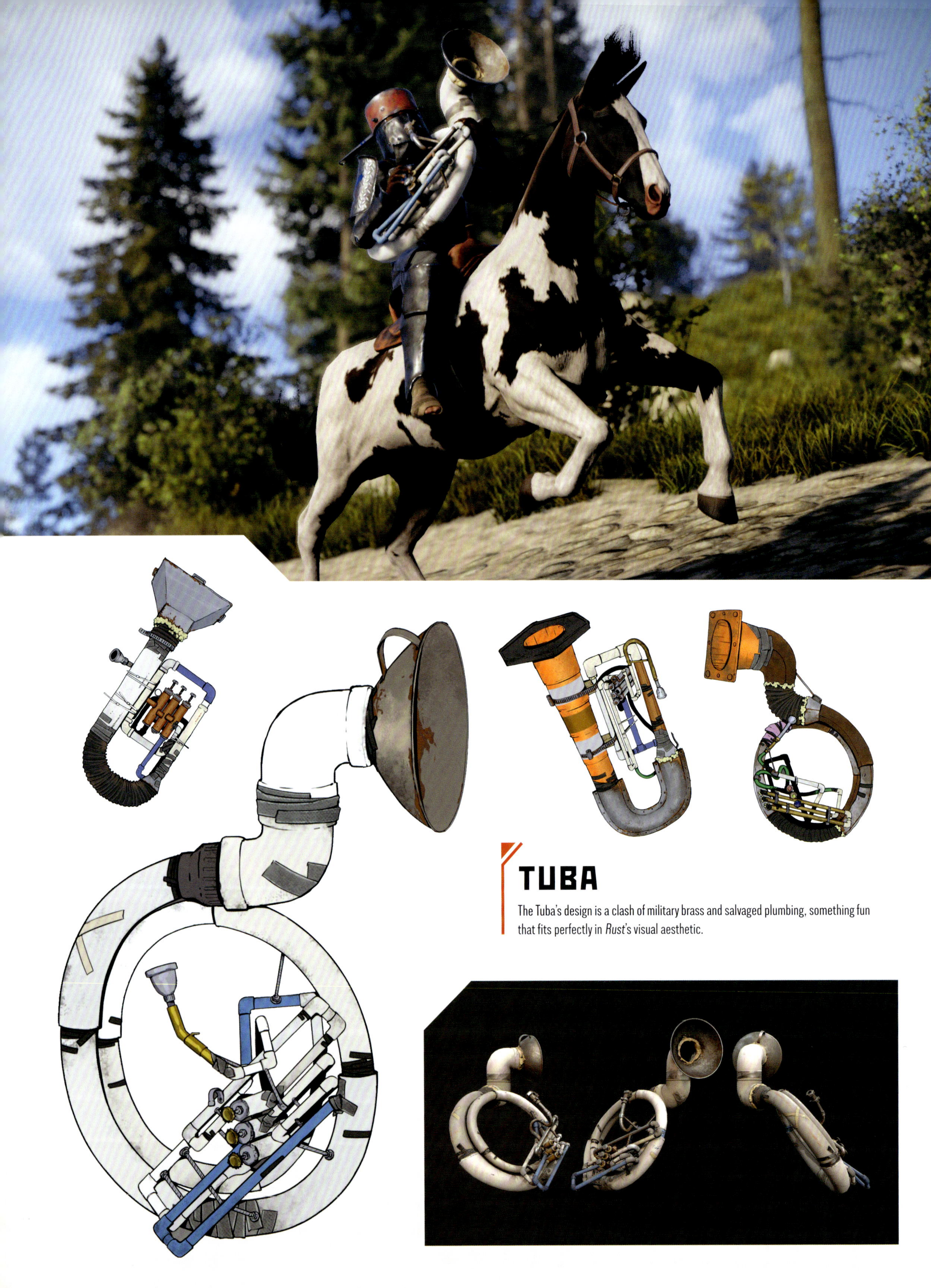

TUBA

The Tuba's design is a clash of military brass and salvaged plumbing, something fun that fits perfectly in *Rust*'s visual aesthetic.

STRINGED INSTRUMENTS

These concepts explore what musical instruments built from scratch might look like in *Rust*.

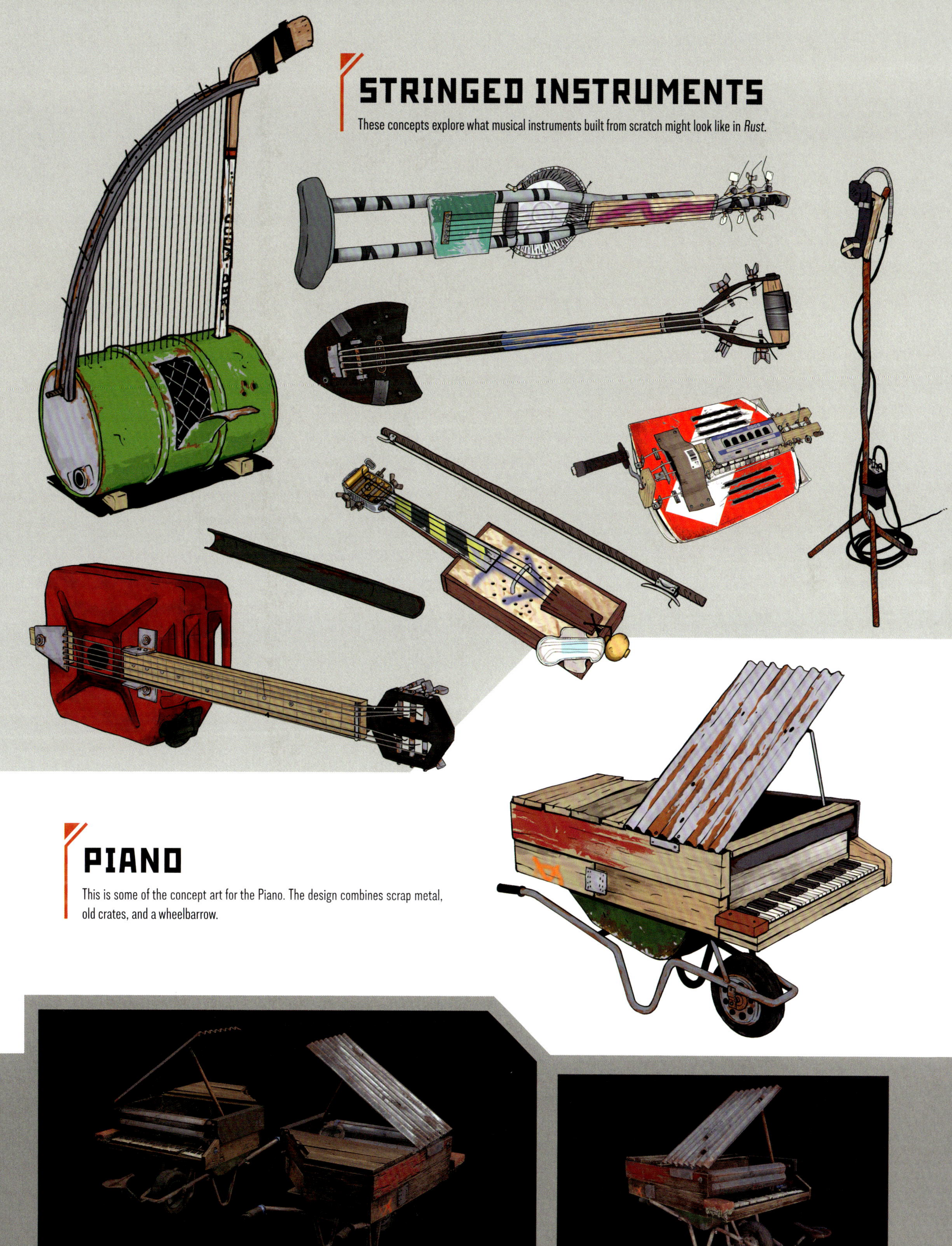

PIANO

This is some of the concept art for the Piano. The design combines scrap metal, old crates, and a wheelbarrow.

INSTRUMENTS

The small handheld Instruments were designed from practical objects, believable enough to play while adding a sense of humor and fun.

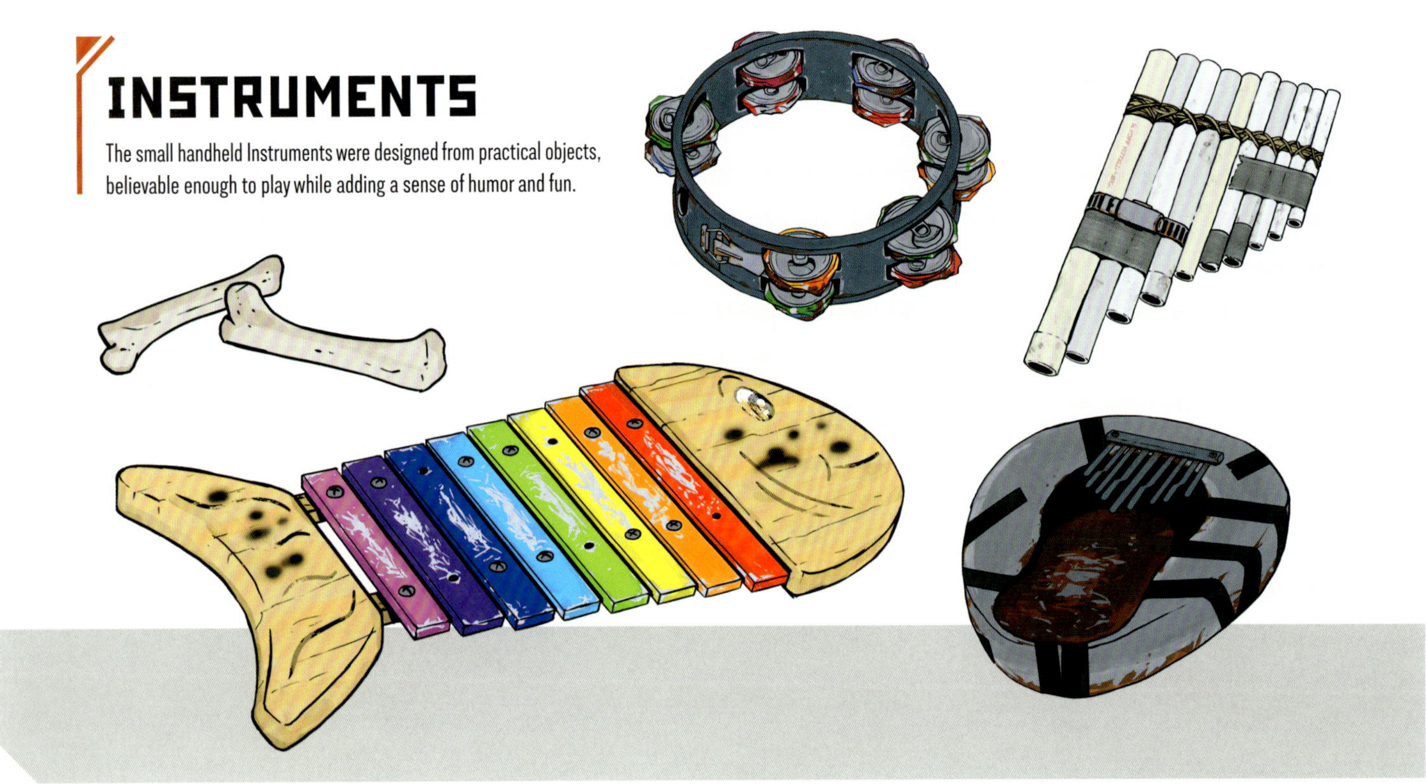

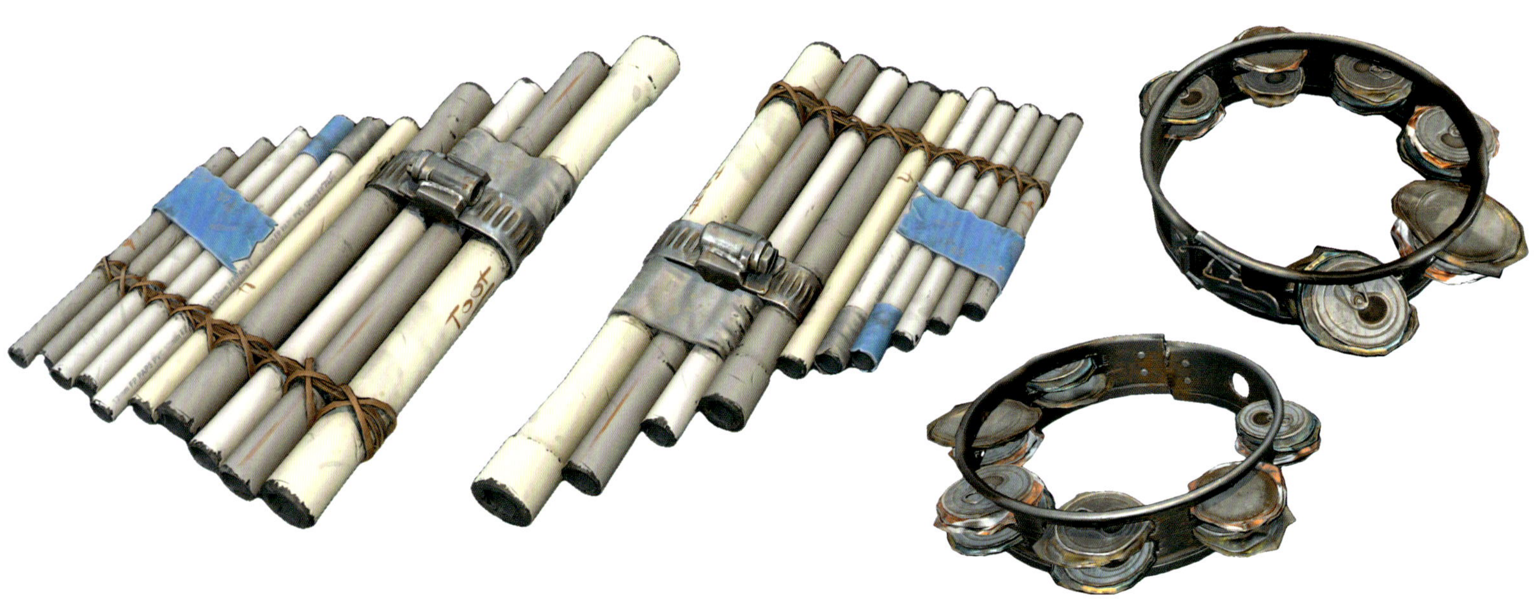

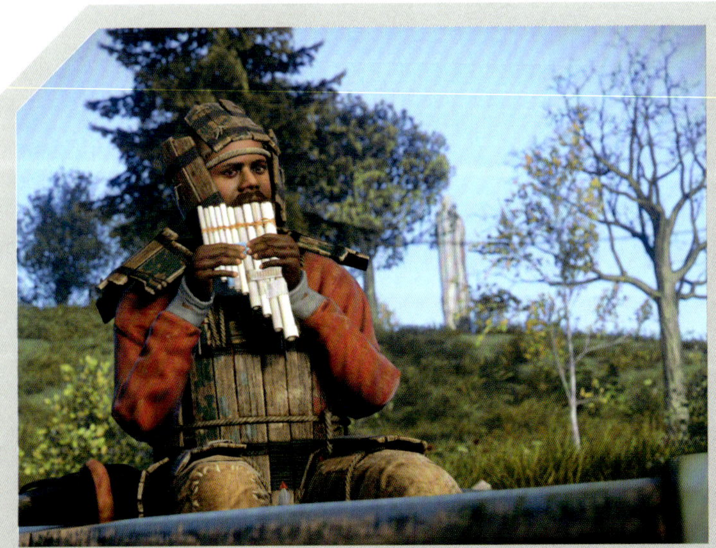

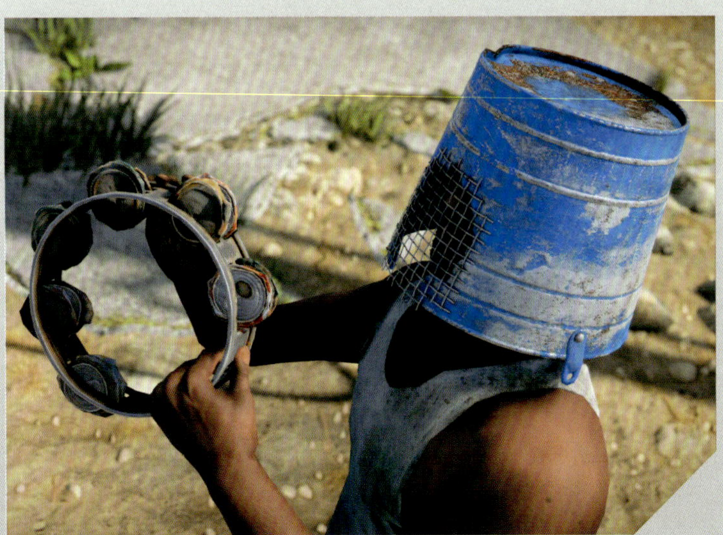

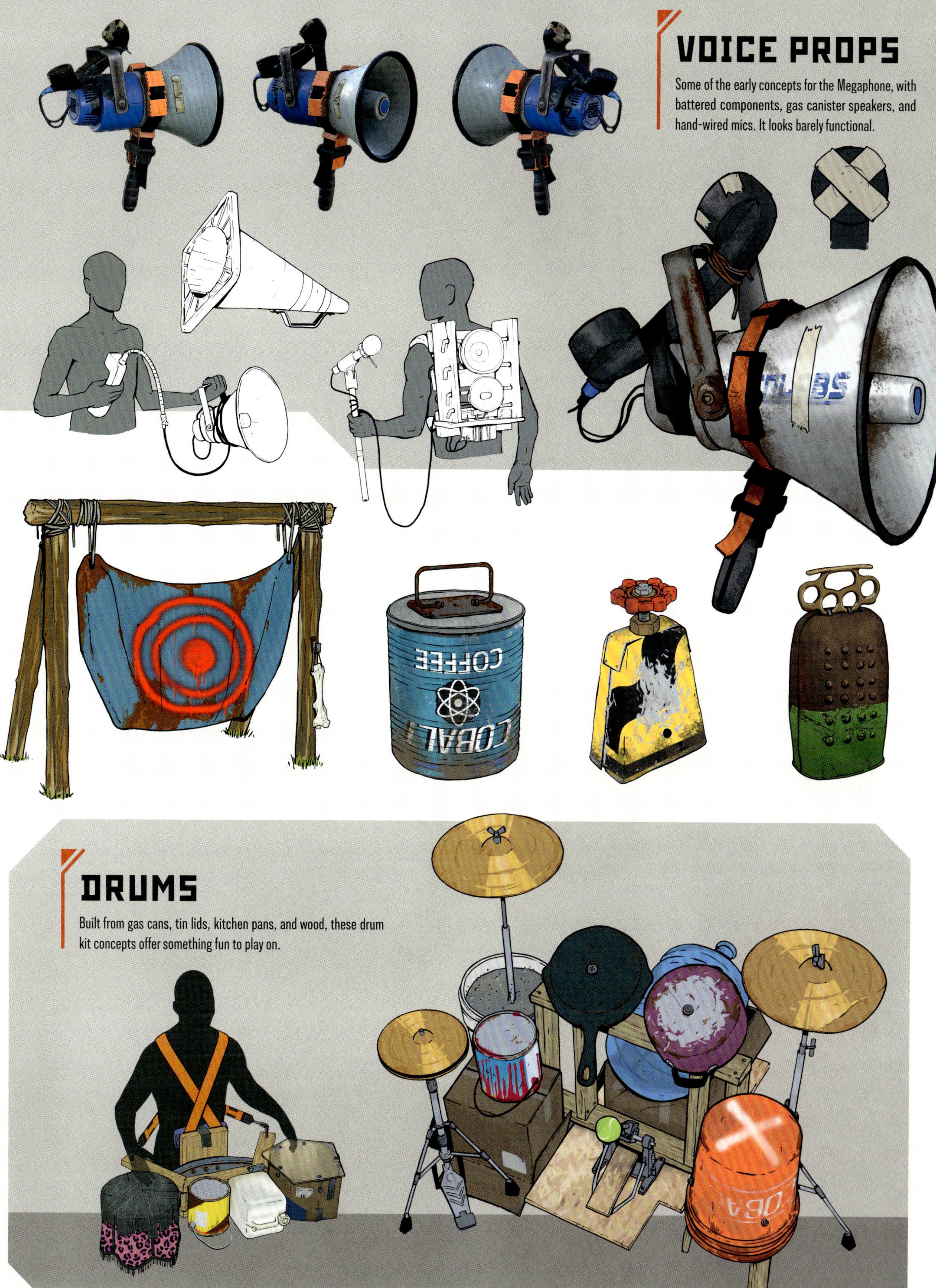

VOICE PROPS

Some of the early concepts for the Megaphone, with battered components, gas canister speakers, and hand-wired mics. It looks barely functional.

DRUMS

Built from gas cans, tin lids, kitchen pans, and wood, these drum kit concepts offer something fun to play on.

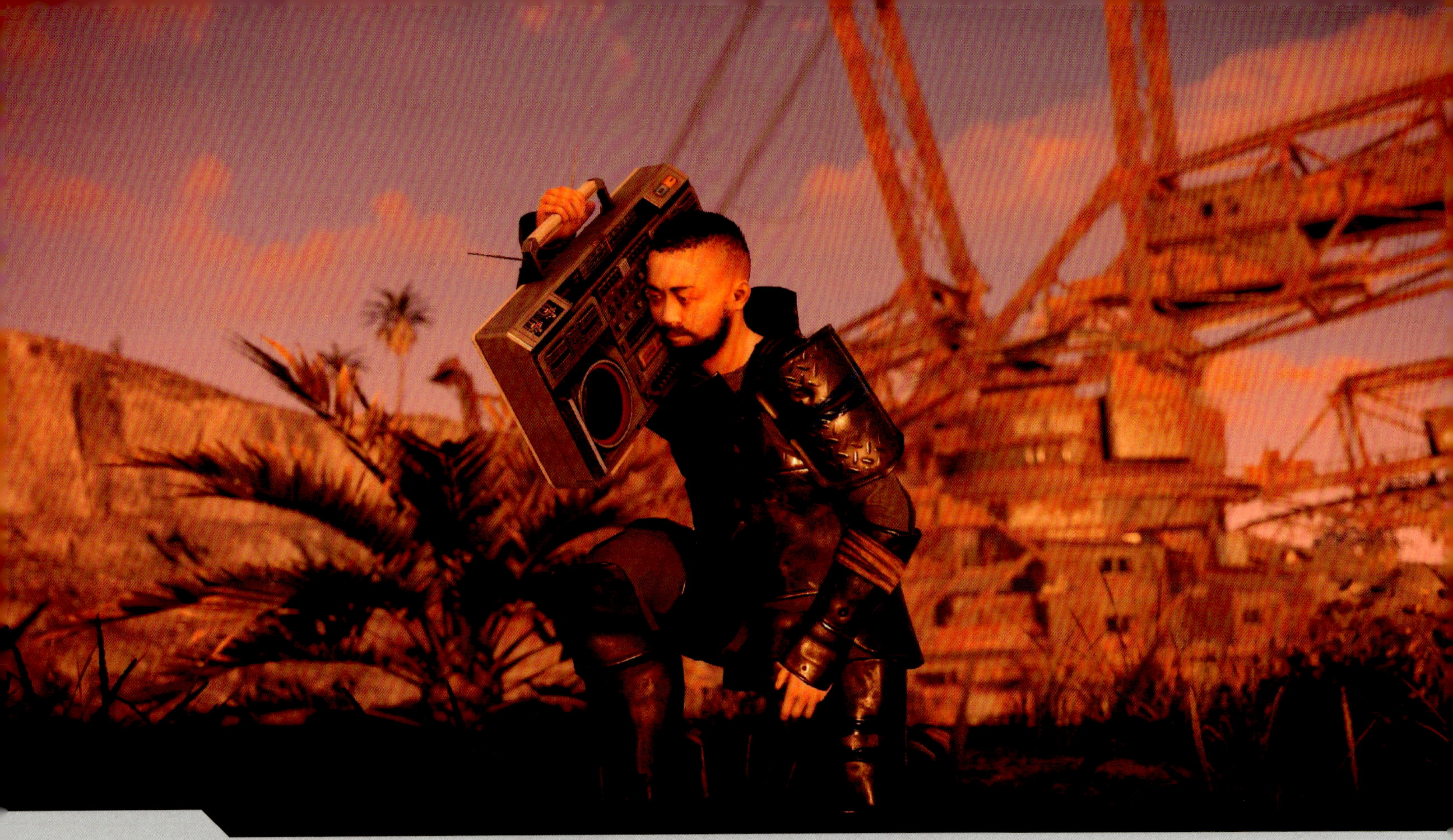

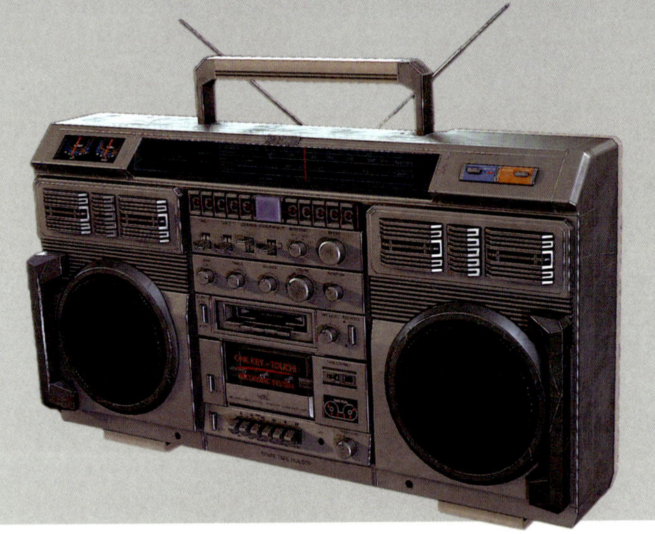

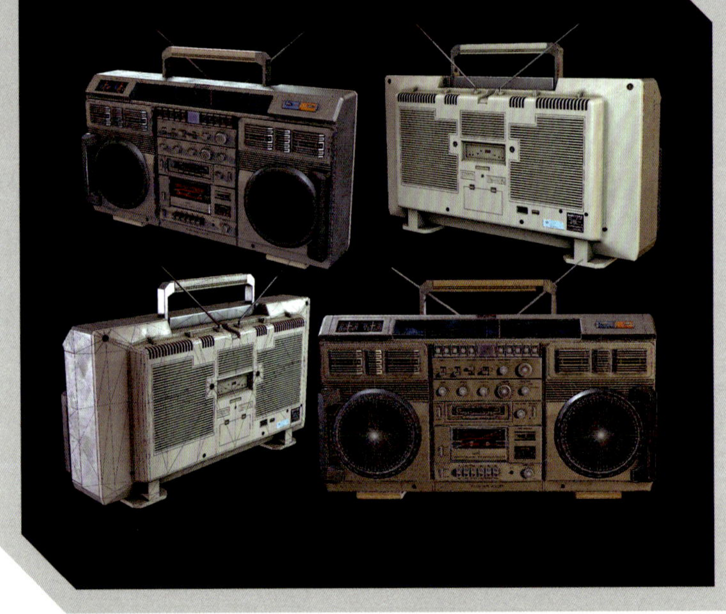

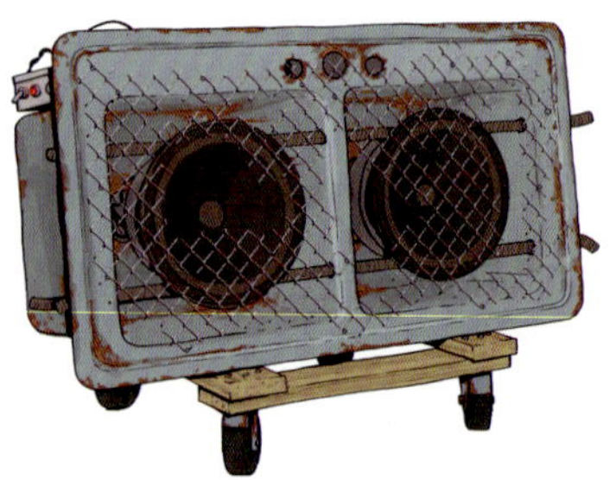

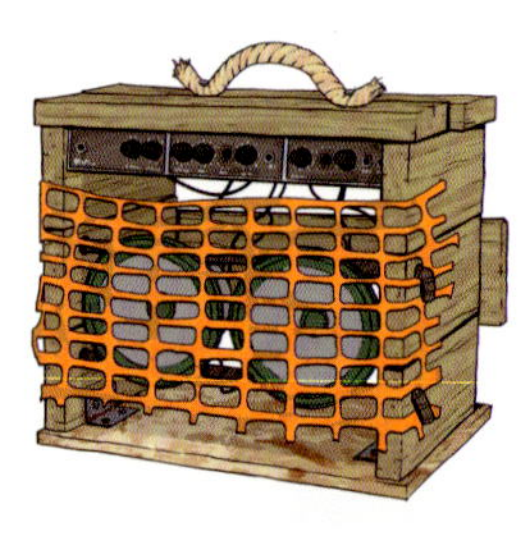

BOOM BOX

Boom Boxes were introduced to *Rust* as part of a DLC set, allowing players to play music in-game via either preloaded tracks or custom streaming audio. The designs range from classic silver '80s-style radios to makeshift speakers crafted from oil drums and scrap.

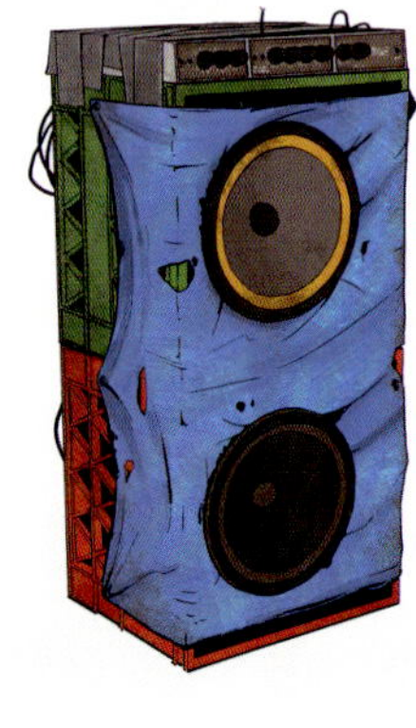

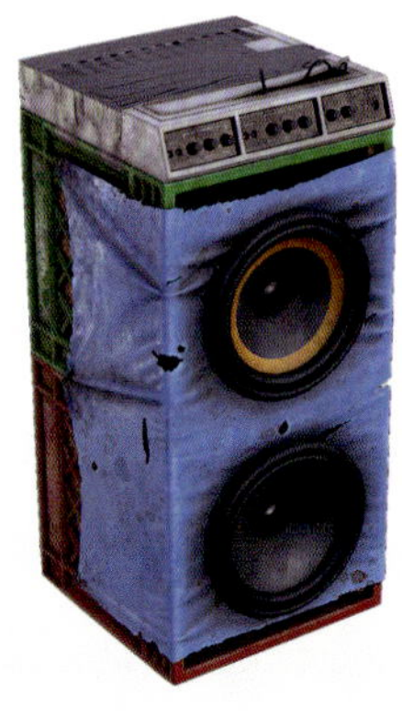

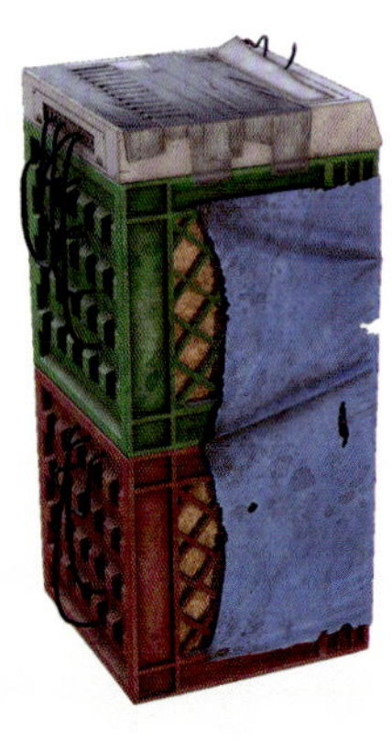

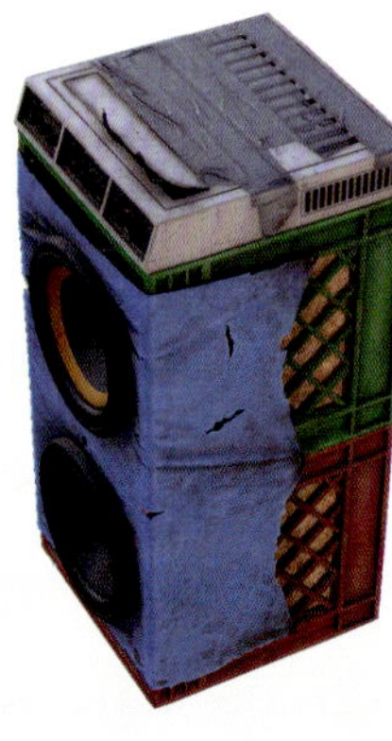

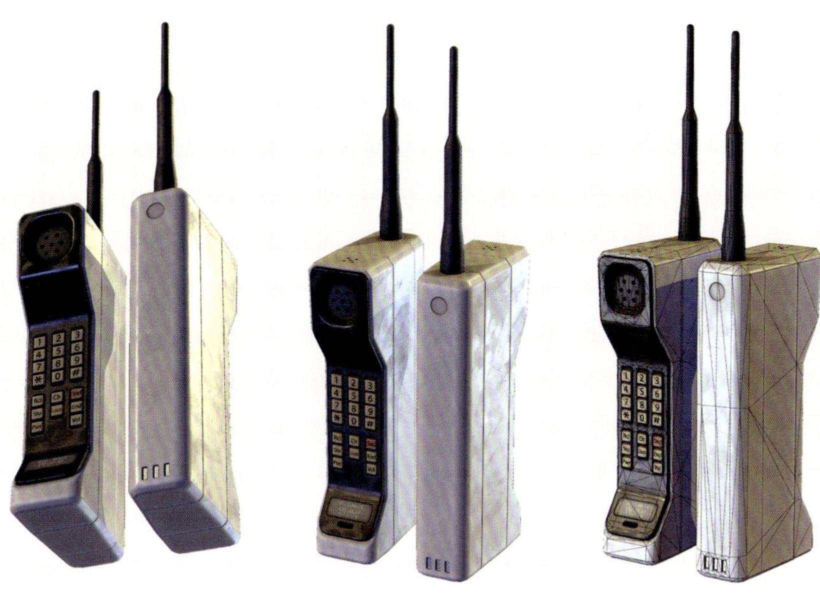

MOBILE PHONE

Mobile Phones are part of the Voice Props DLC, and while they don't play a critical role in a player's survival, they serve as a fun, immersive prop that aids in social interactions with other players. Unmistakably retro, these mobile phones look more like bricks than communication tools.

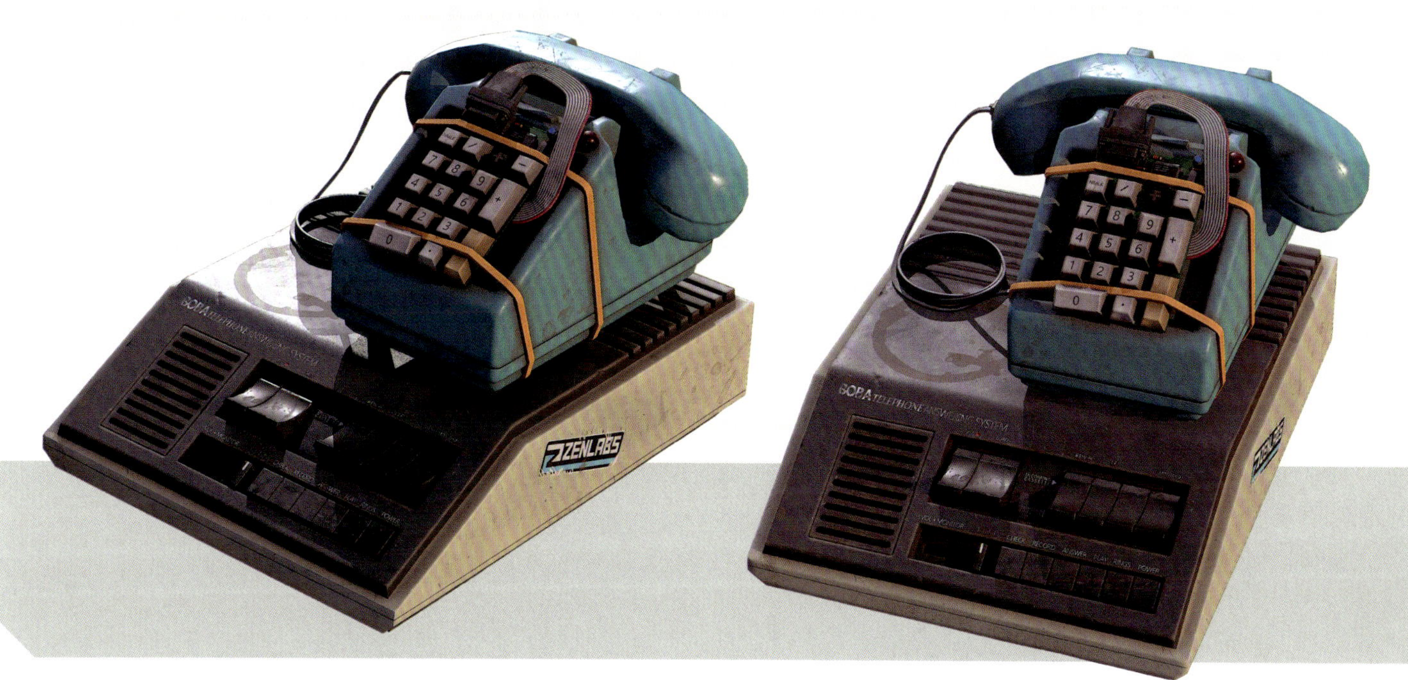

CASSETTE RECORDER

Another item from the Voice Props DLC is the Cassette Recorder, which allows players to record and play custom audio through either the standalone player or tapes inserted into certain vehicles, like the modular car. Rough around the edges but still functional, it looks like something pulled from an abandoned bunker or garage.

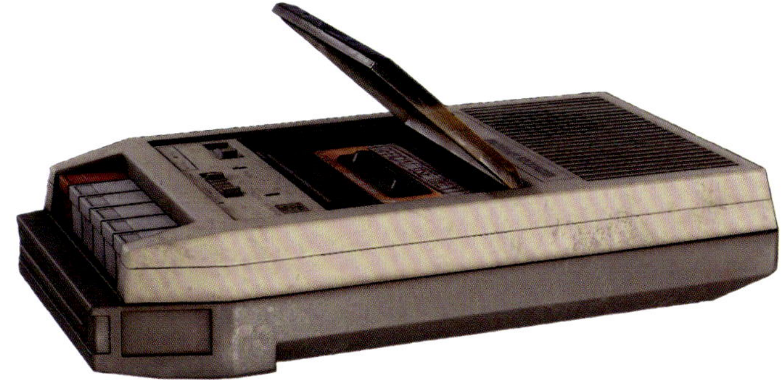

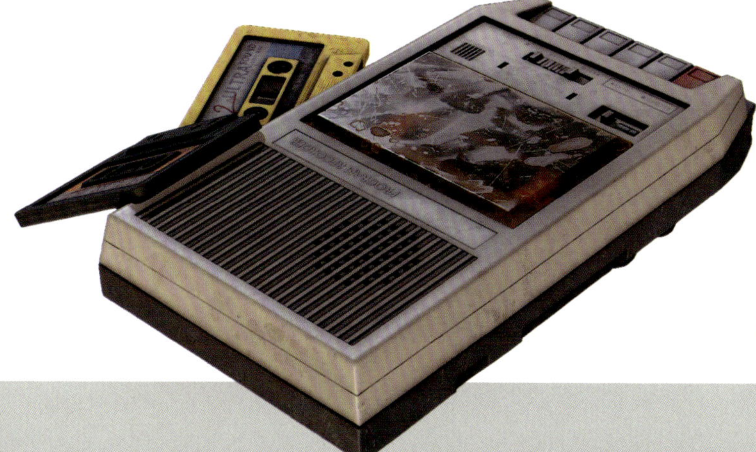

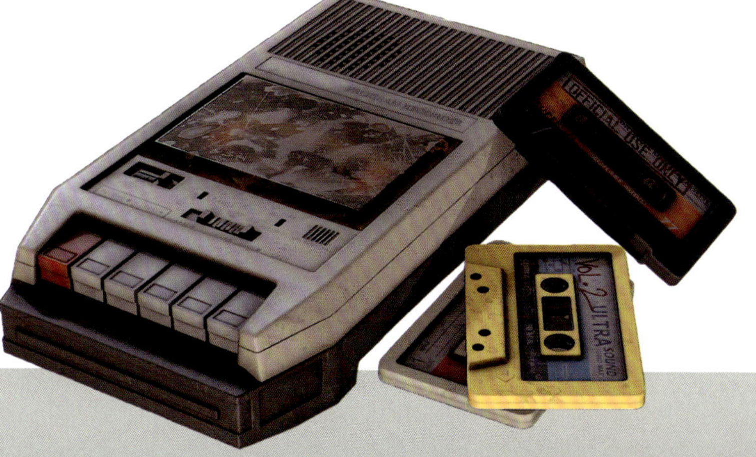

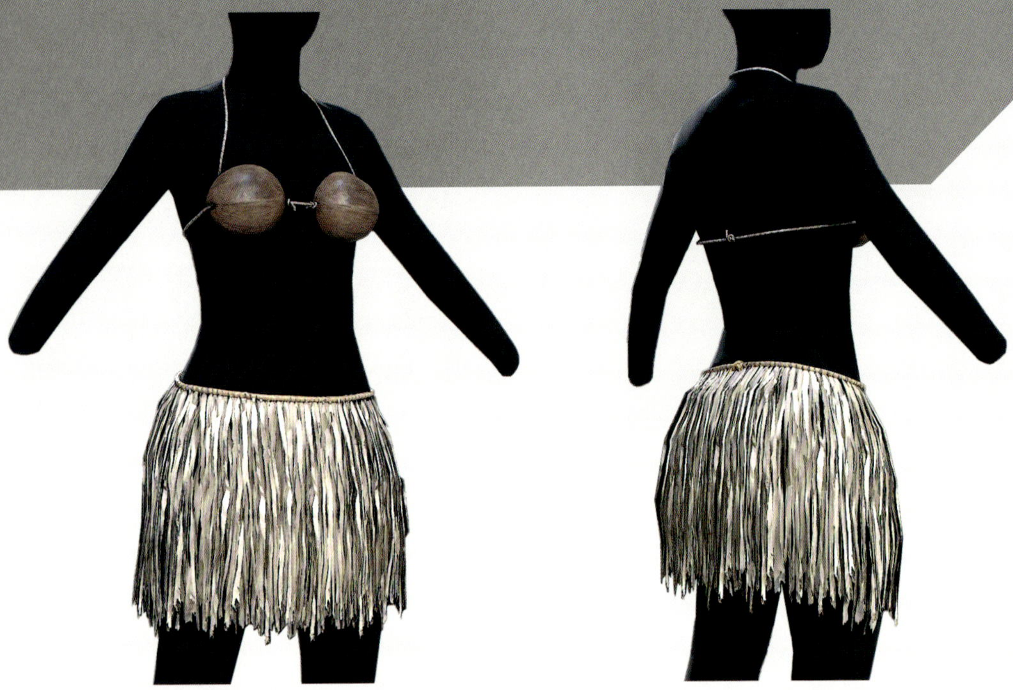

SUNBURN

This summer DLC collection leans heavily into the lighthearted absurdity of *Rust*, from grass skirts and retro shades to cartoonish swimsuits and themed trunks. The Sunburn Pack embraces a casual beachside aesthetic, with items that look like they've been thrifted, scavenged, or handmade.

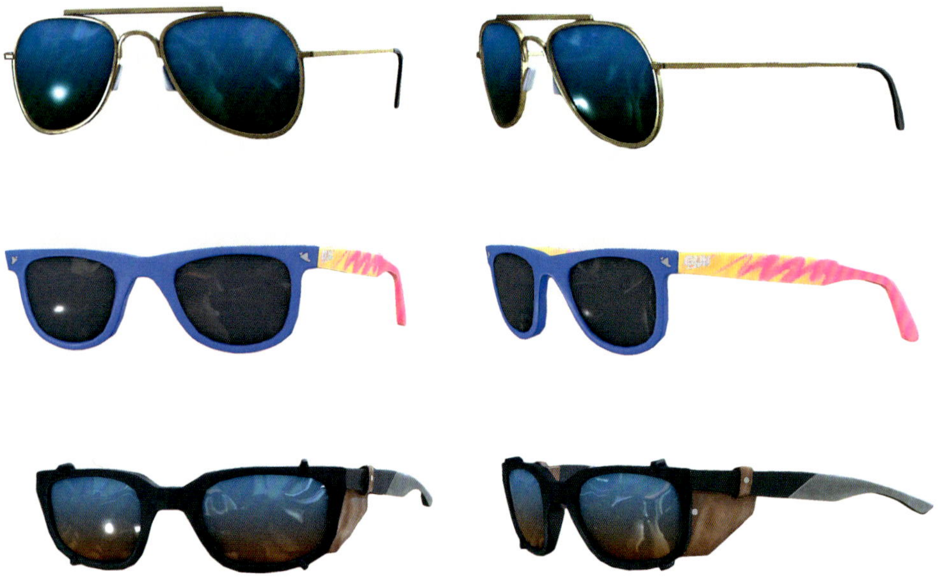

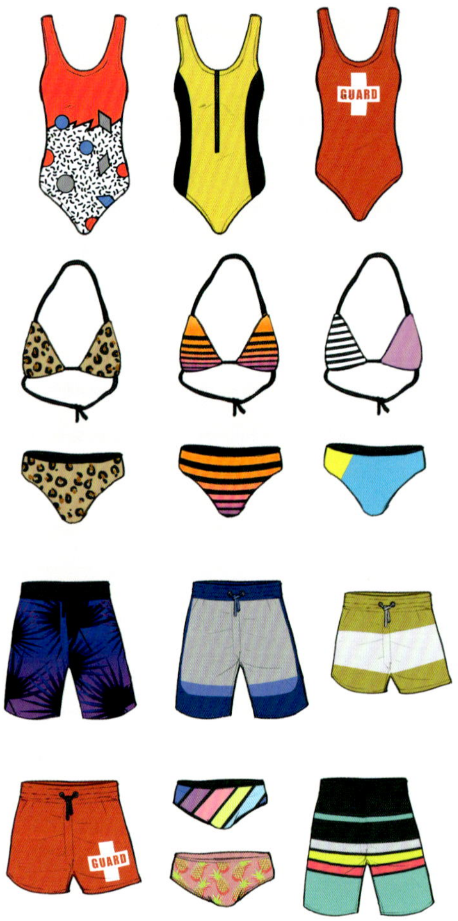

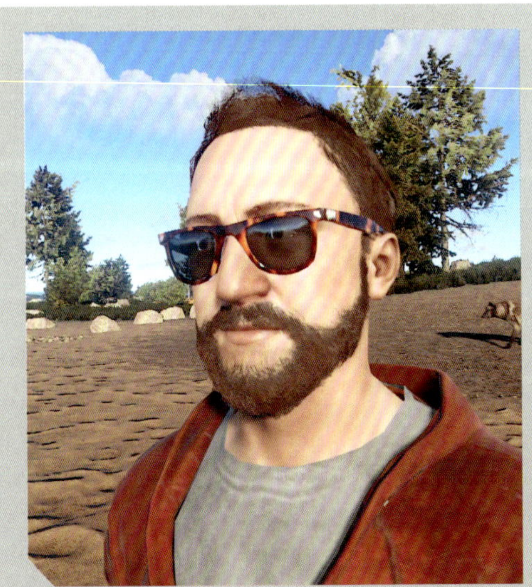

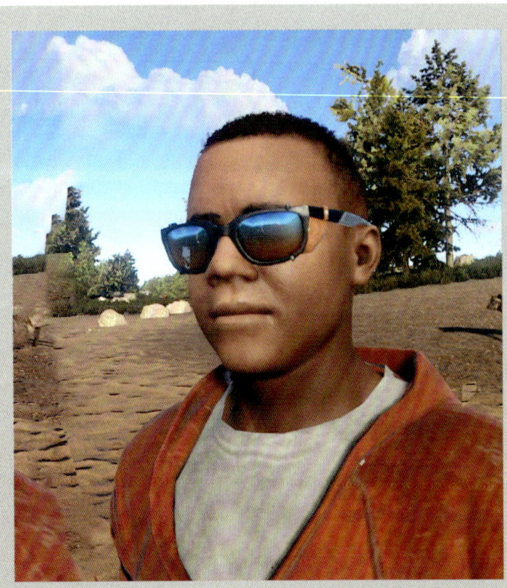

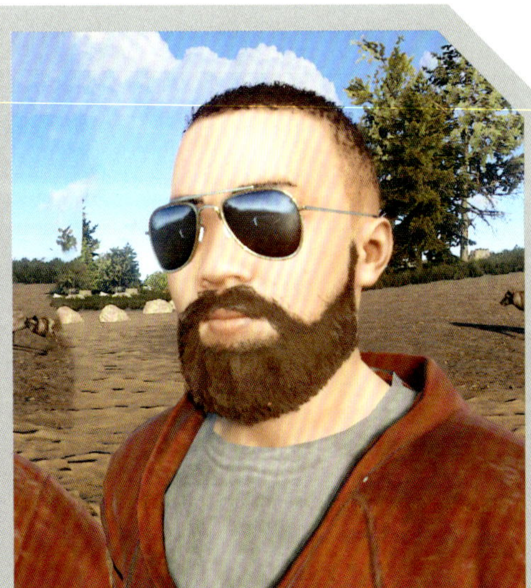

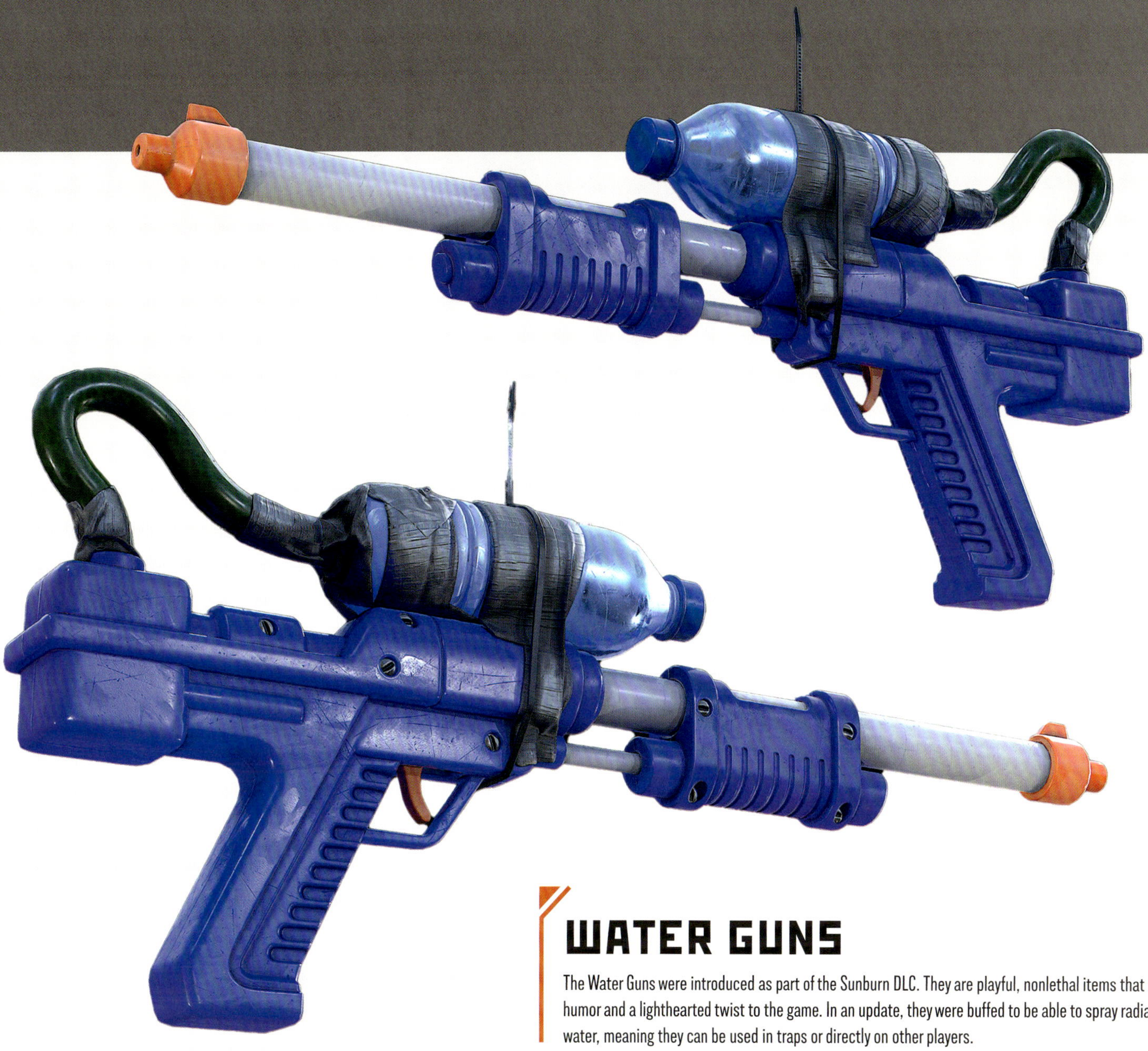

WATER GUNS

The Water Guns were introduced as part of the Sunburn DLC. They are playful, nonlethal items that add humor and a lighthearted twist to the game. In an update, they were buffed to be able to spray radiated water, meaning they can be used in traps or directly on other players.

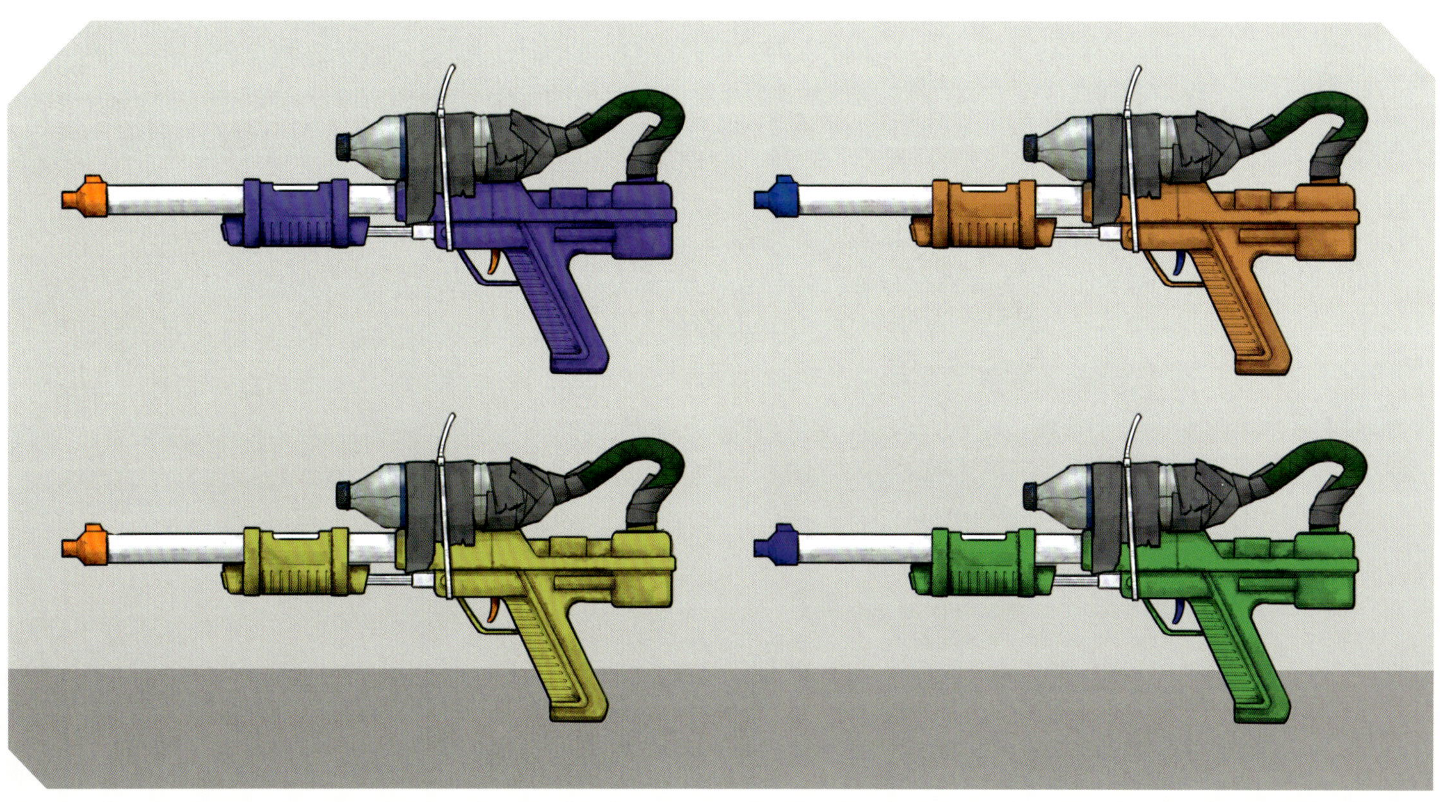

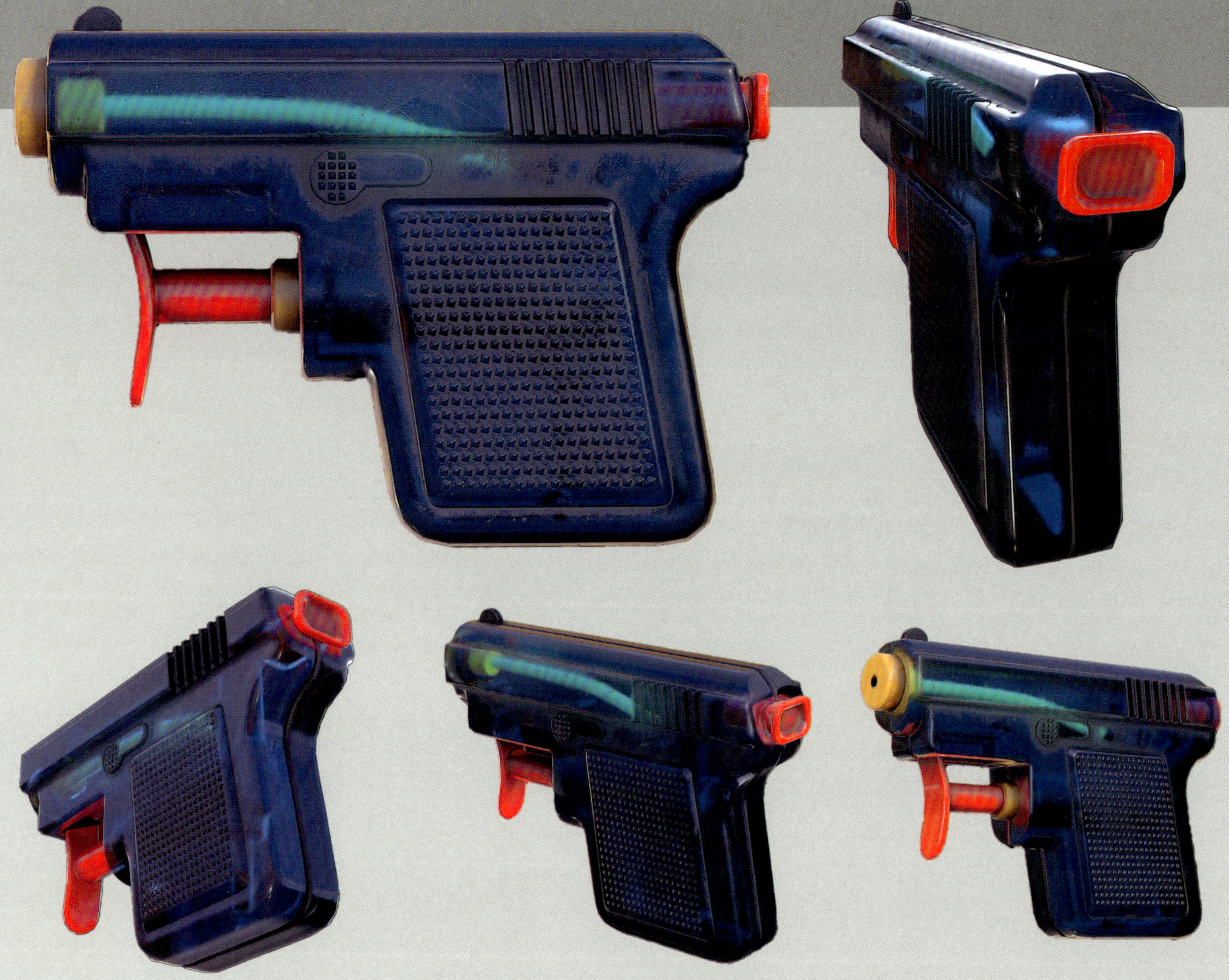

WATER PISTOLS

Alongside the Water Guns, Water Pistols were introduced to *Rust* as another playful toy-like addition with translucent plastic, neon colors, oversized nozzles, and exaggerated shapes. Despite their playful appearance, they can also be used with radiated water to inflict damage and deter attackers.

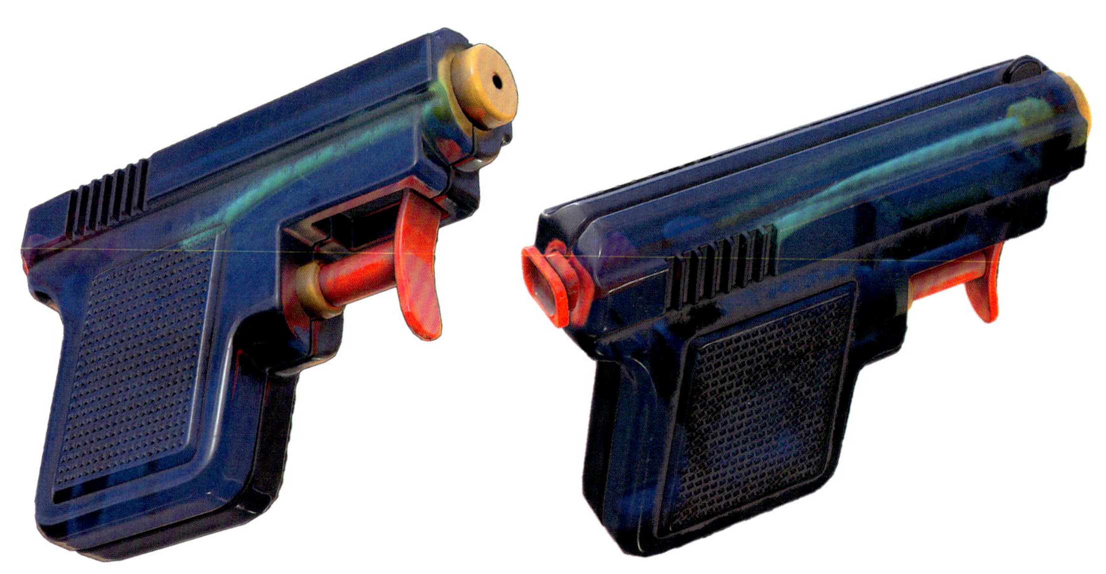

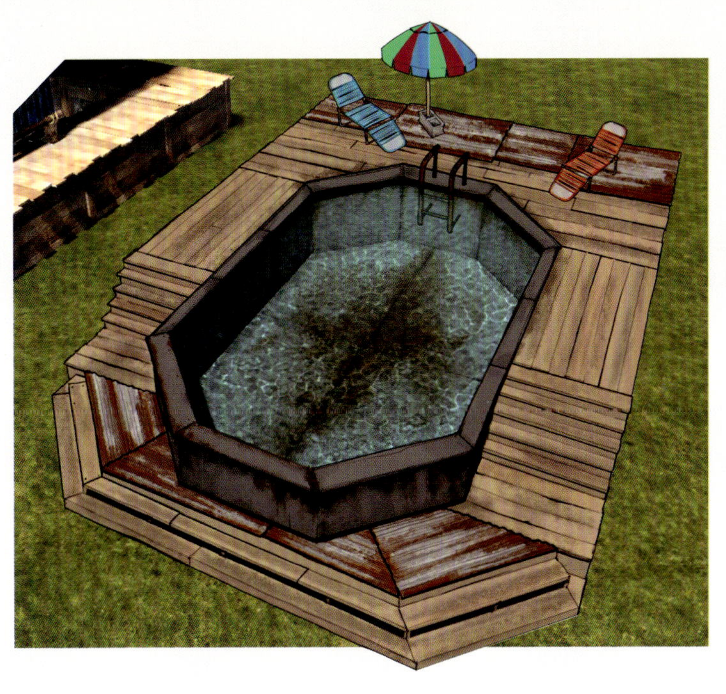

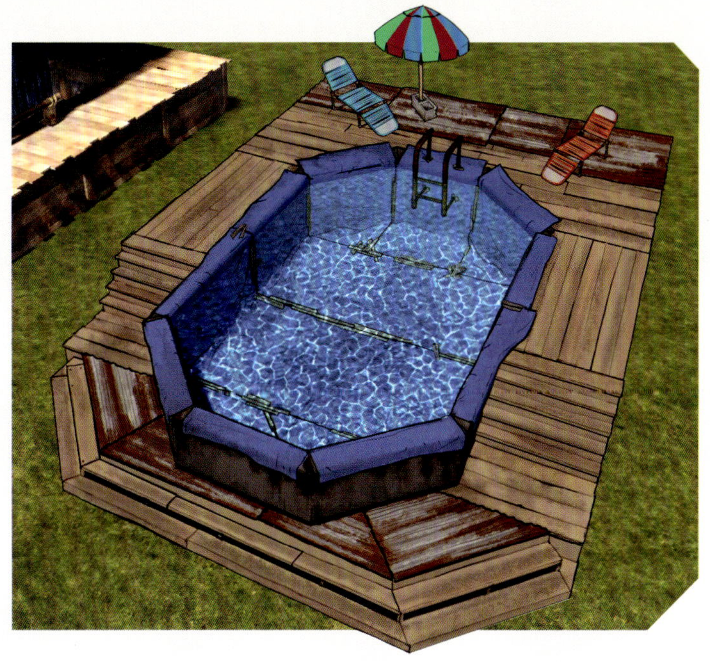

POOLS

Pools are a decorative summer item. Complete with weathered decking and parasols, Pools can be filled with water and entered by players, functioning as a prop for social spaces or role-play.

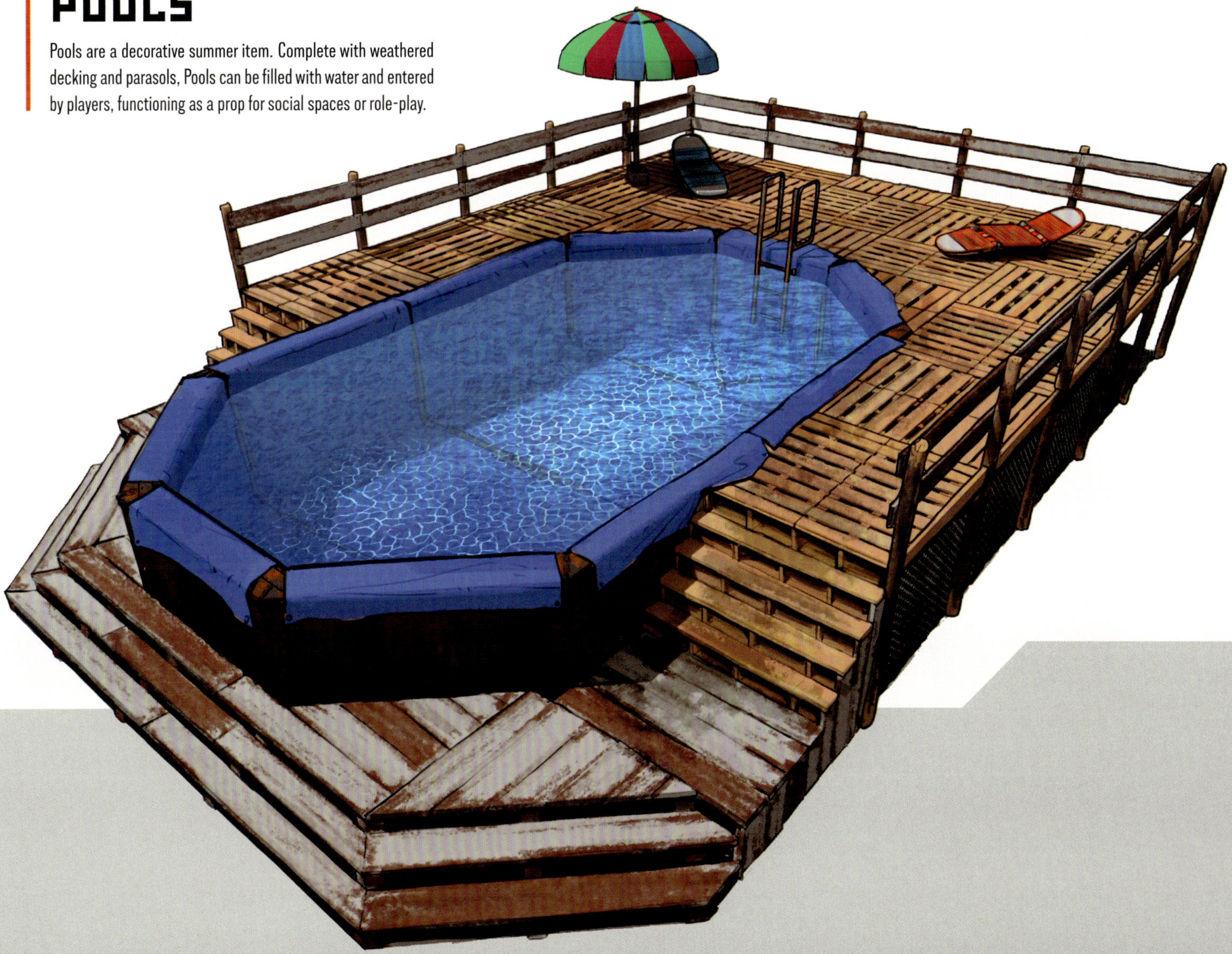

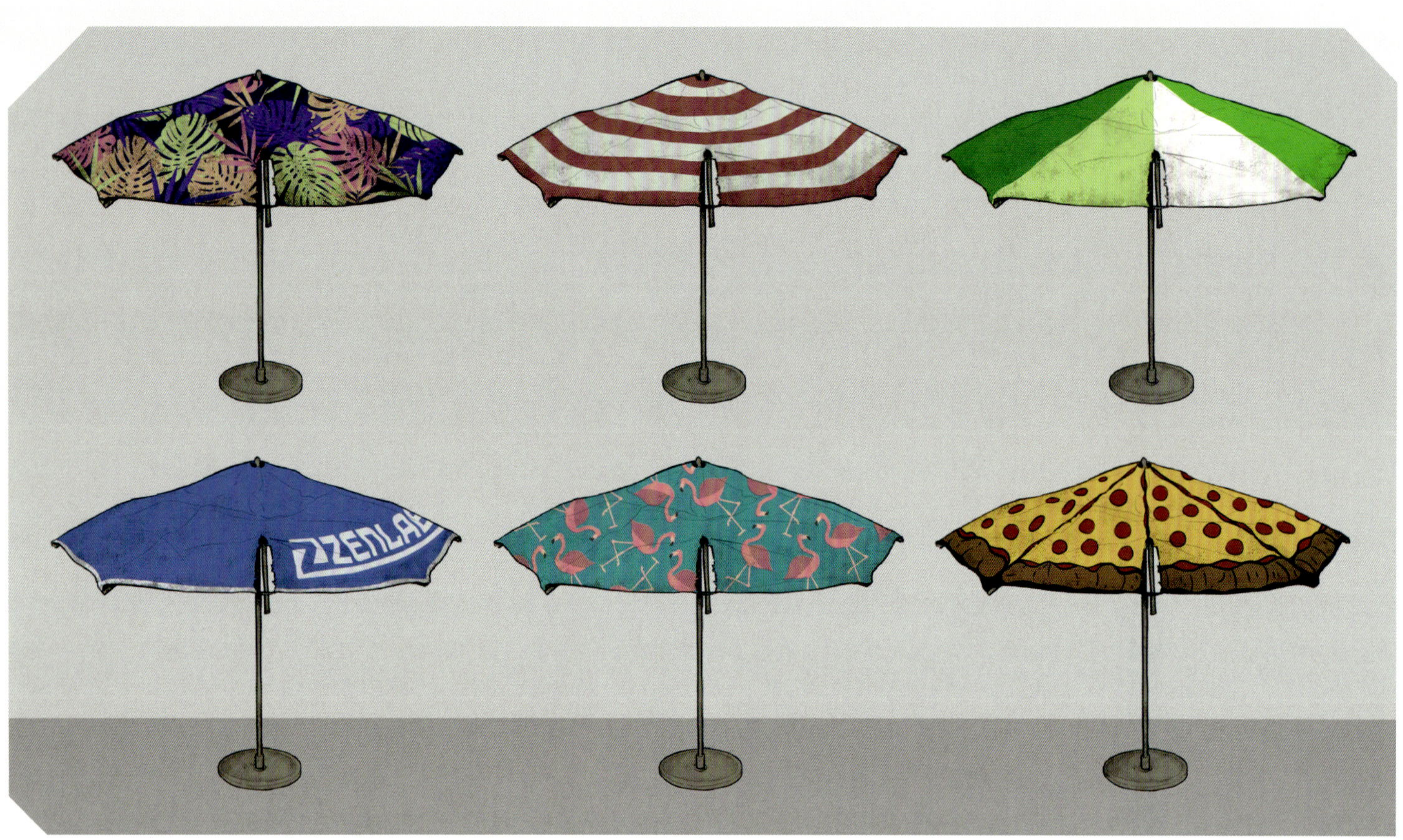

POOL DECOR

Pool Decor brings an element of summer comfort to *Rust*. These weathered loungers and parasols can add humor and personality to a base. Faded fabrics and rusted frames set the stage for a brief moment of relaxation.

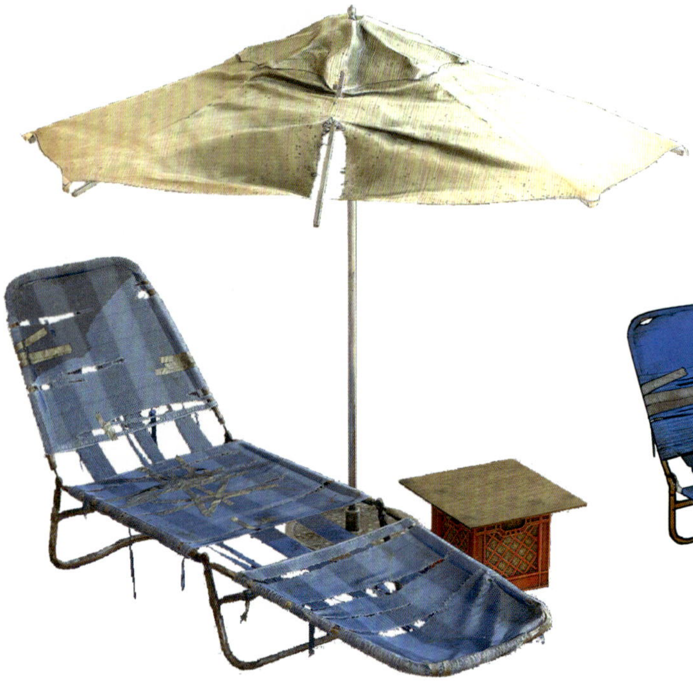

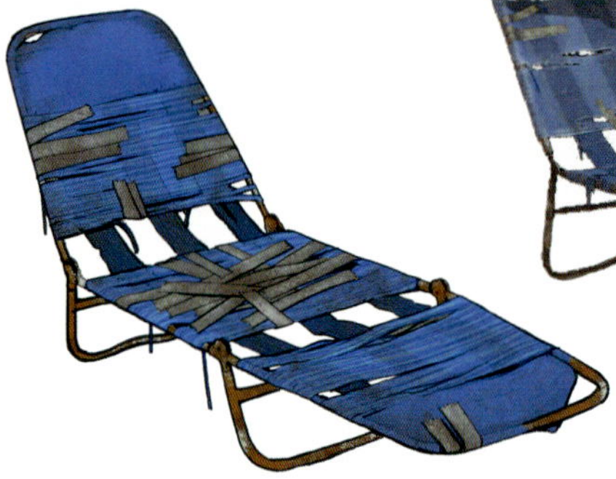

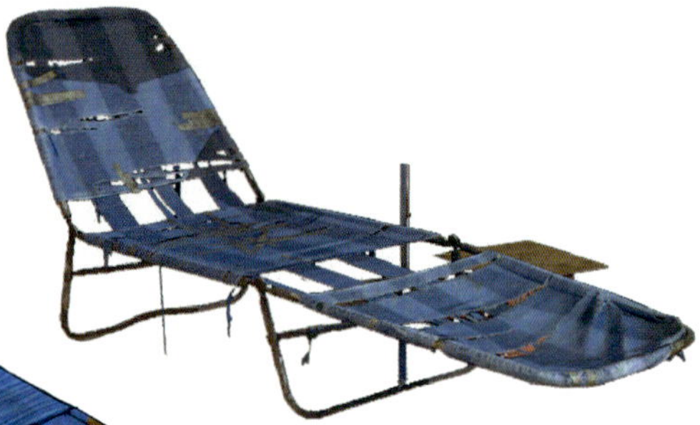

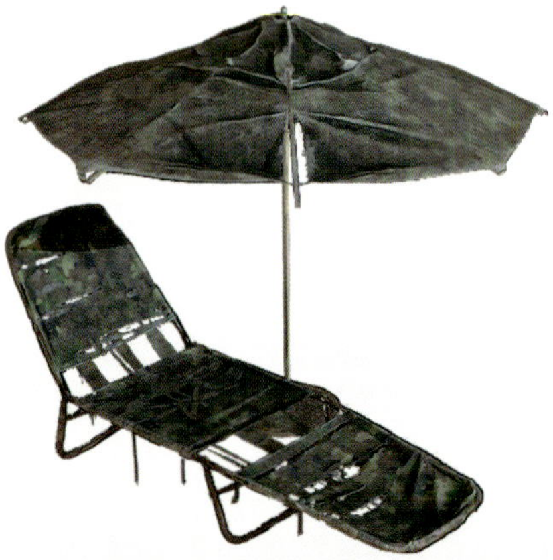

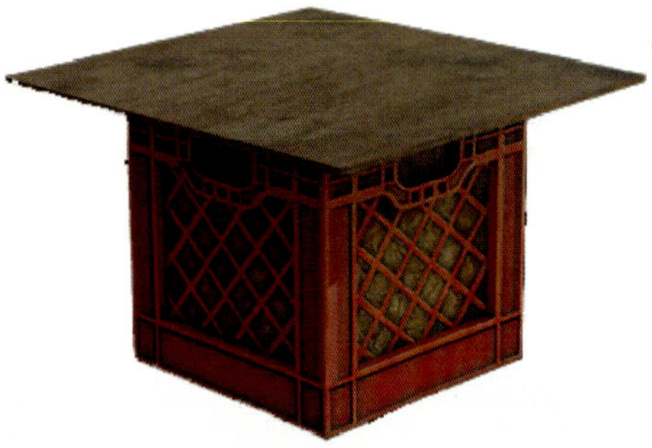

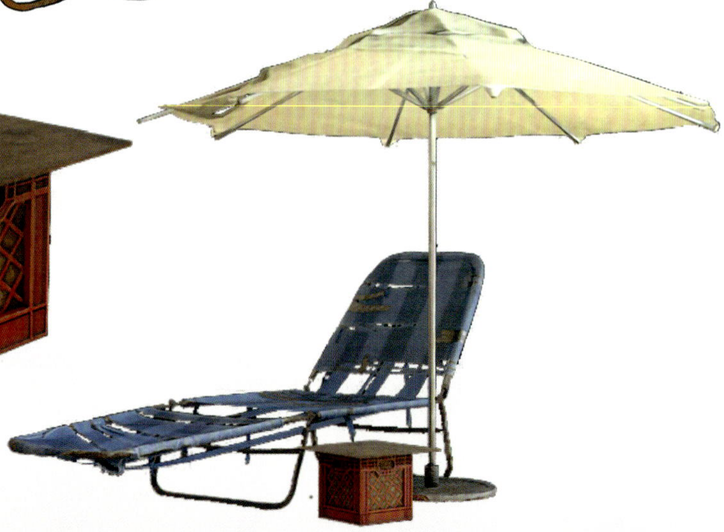

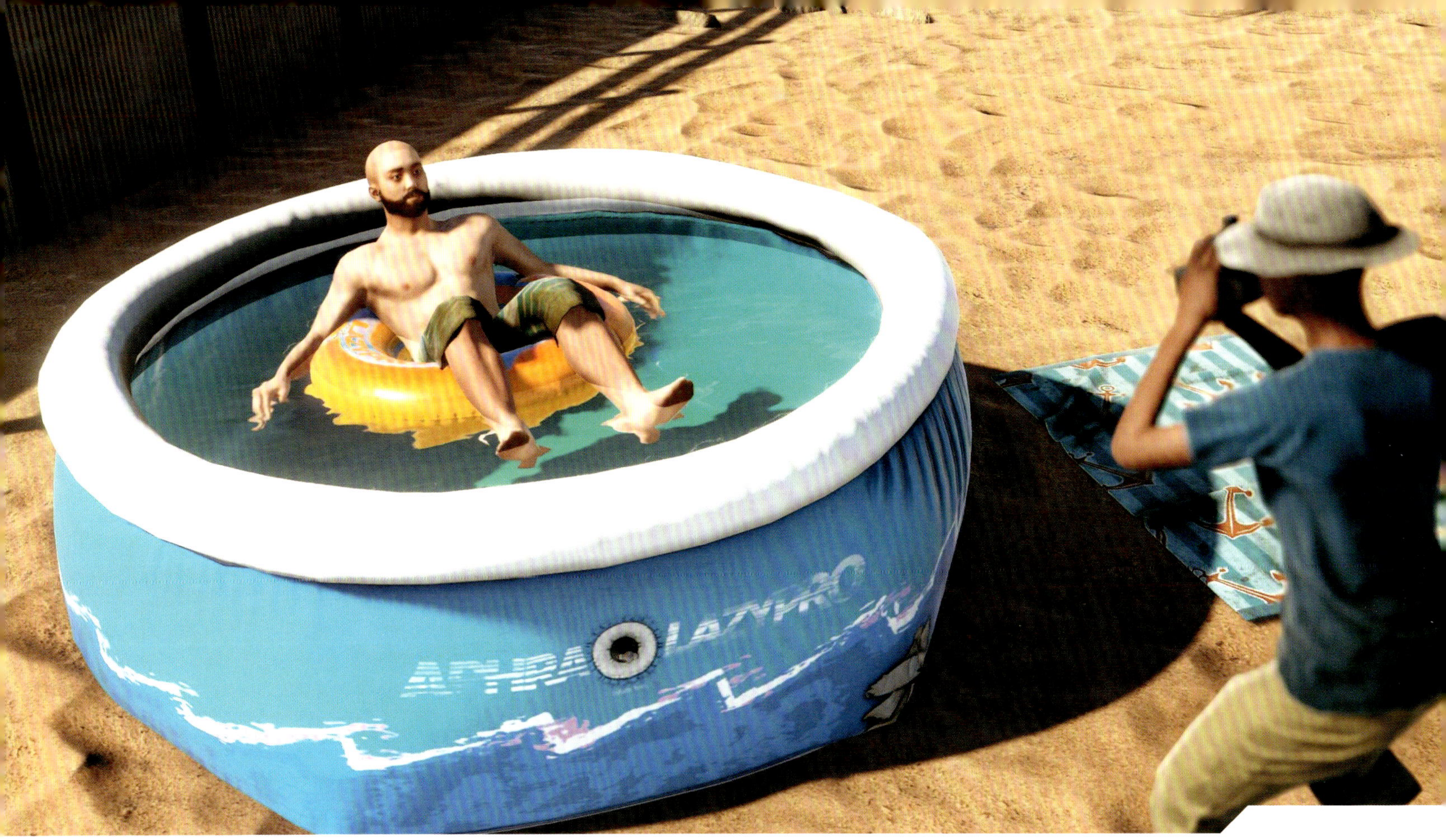

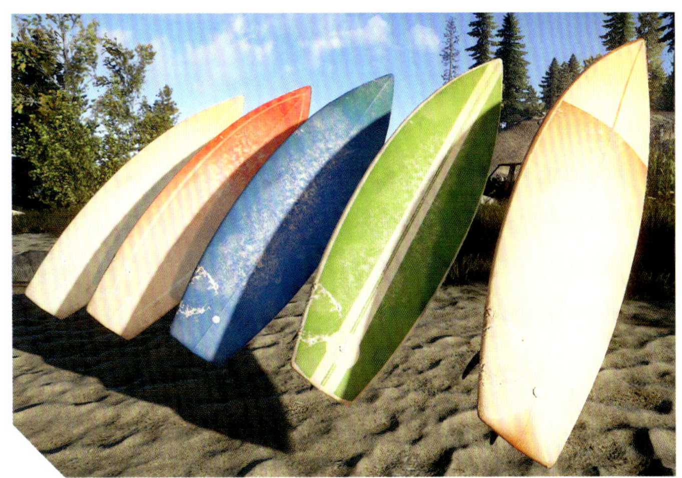

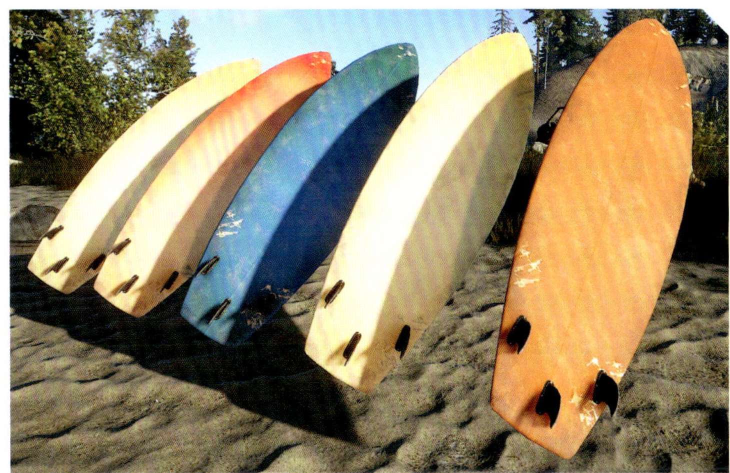

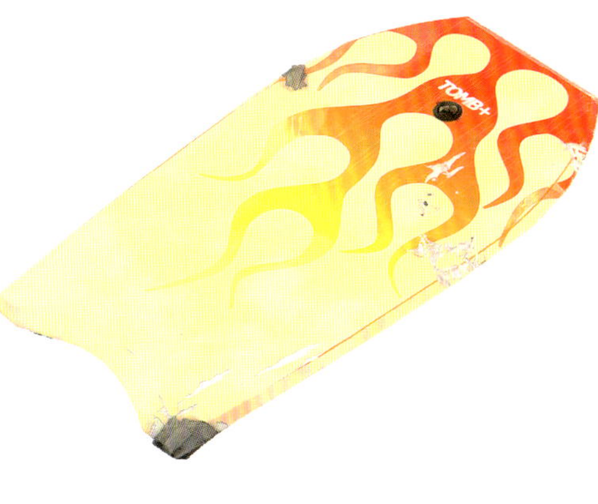

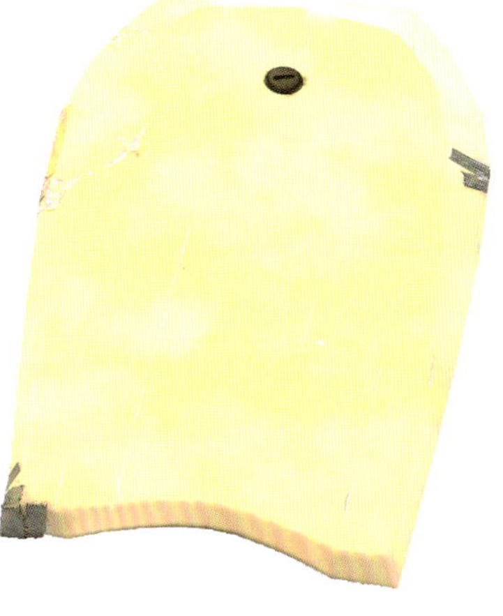

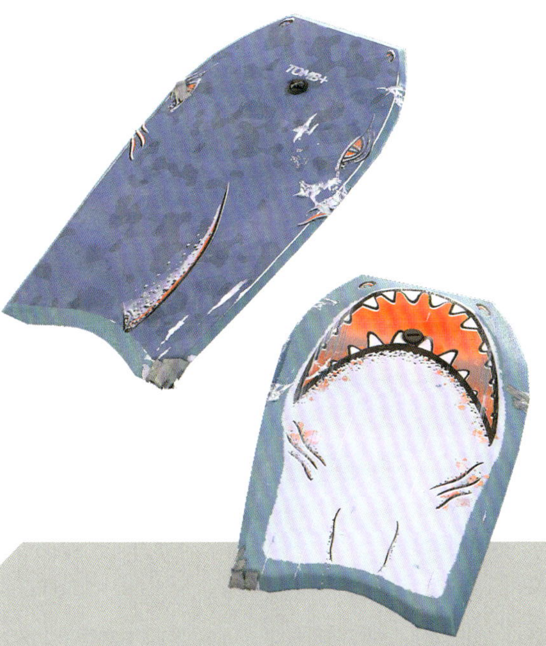

BOOGIE BOARDS

The Boogie Board was introduced as a fun cosmetic item that allows players to float and paddle across water. It's not fast or efficient, but it provides a simple and cheap way to cross bodies of water.

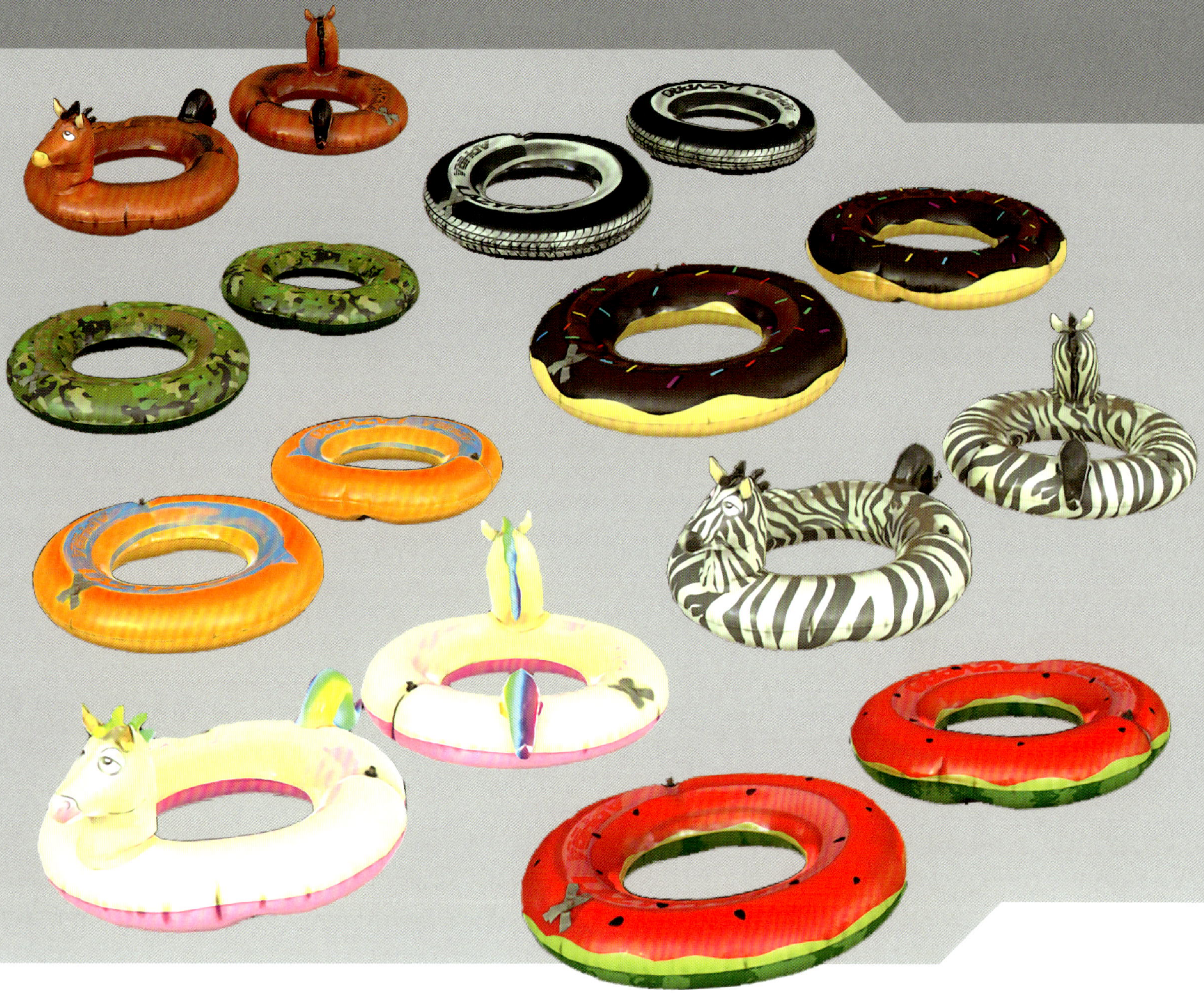

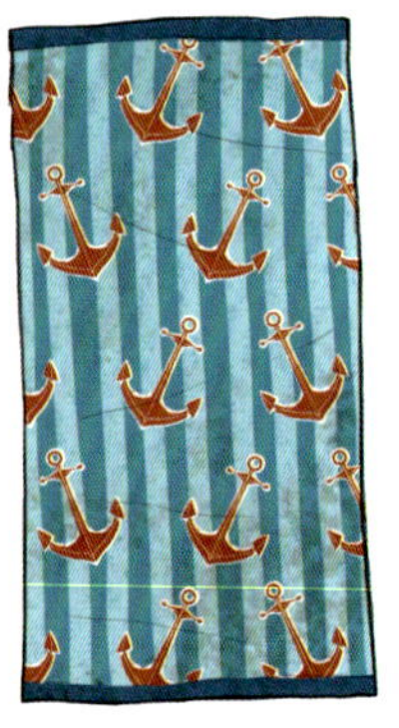
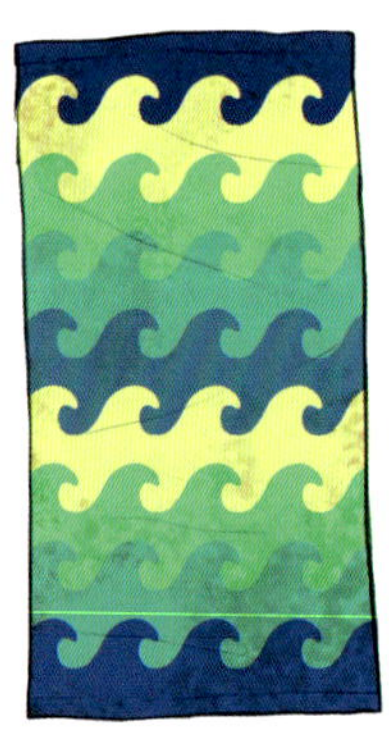
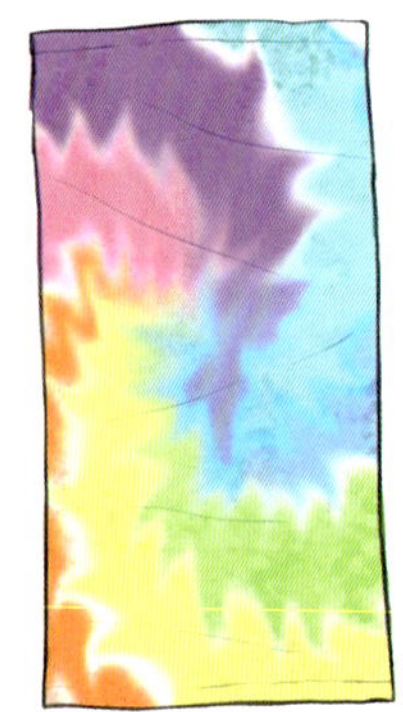
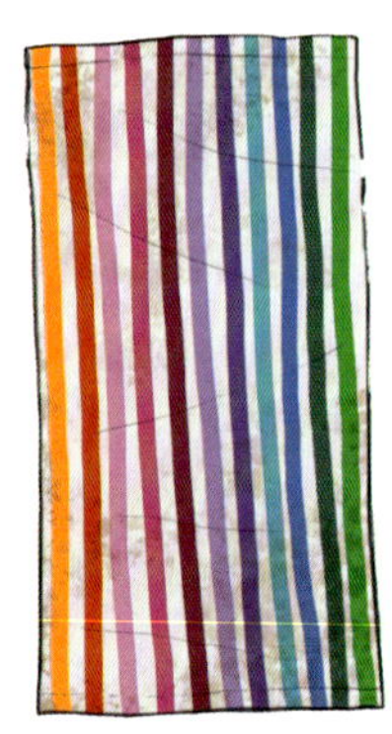
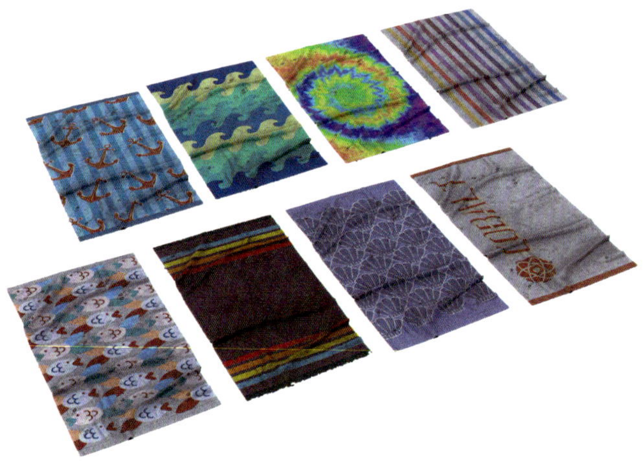
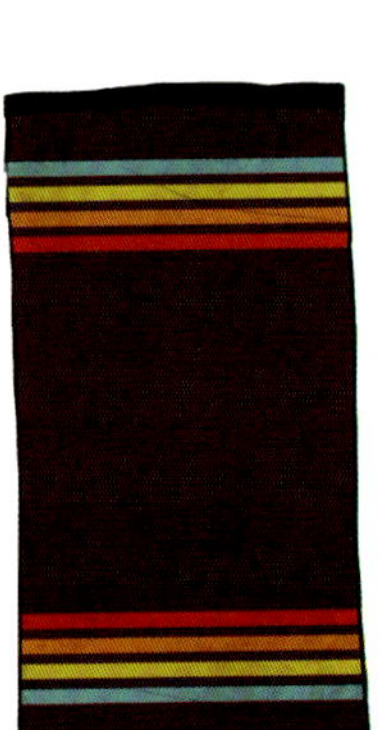
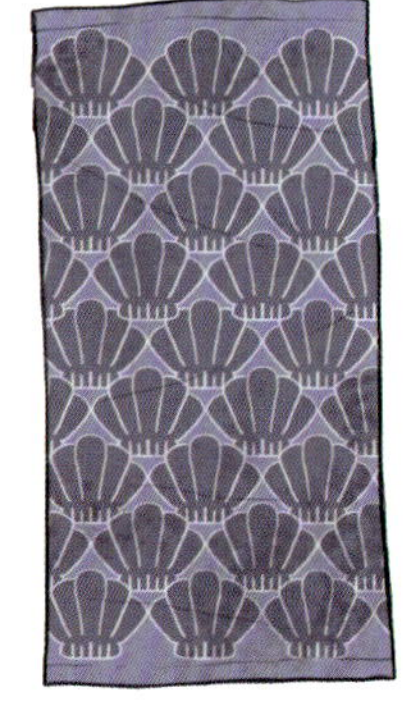
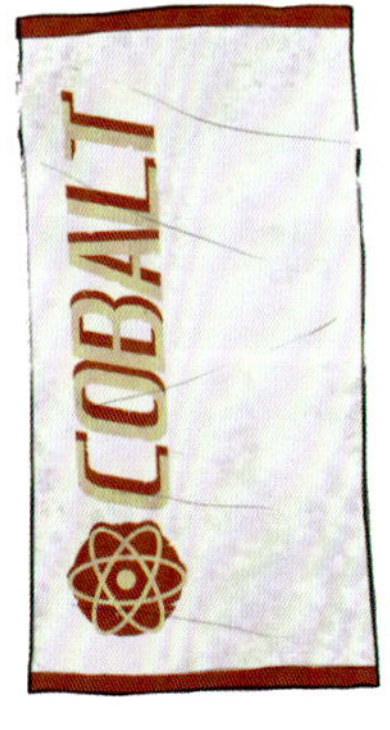

POOL PROPS

Pool Props are purely cosmetic additions to *Rust*. They include items like inflatable rings and beach towels. Players can interact with many of them, sitting, lounging, or floating in pools or across bodies of water.

TOOL CUPBOARDS

The Tool Cupboard (TC) is one of the most vital in-game items, central to both gameplay mechanics and base ownership. A vital component of territorial control, the TC is the beating heart of any base. While it serves a crucial back-end function, its art style and design were carefully constructed to feel believable. These concept sketches are for the Retro TC, made from an old filing cabinet, retro monitors, and scavenged electronics.

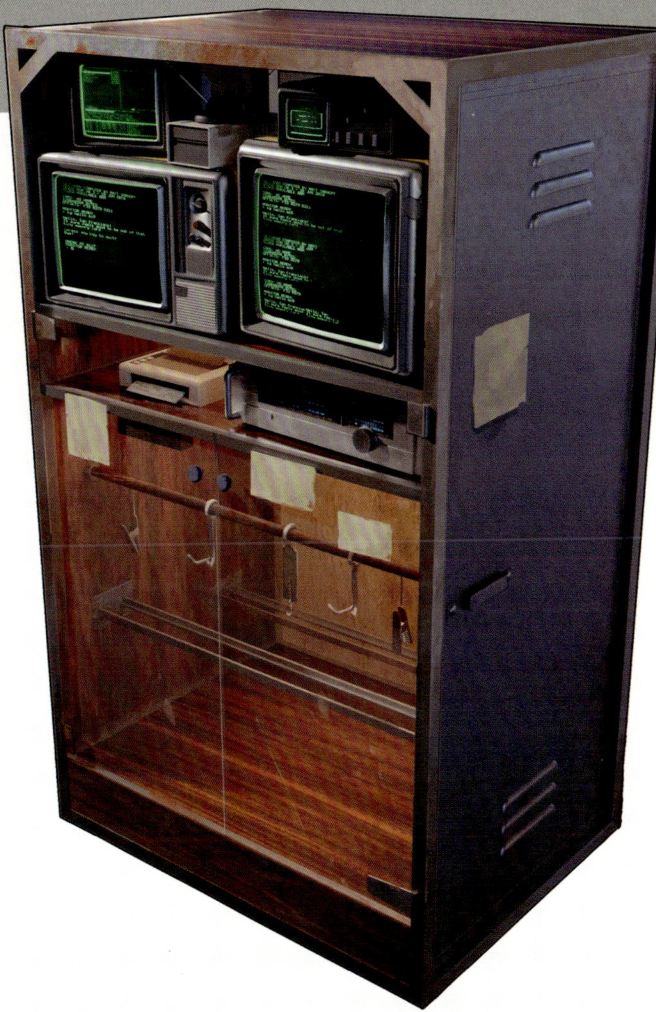

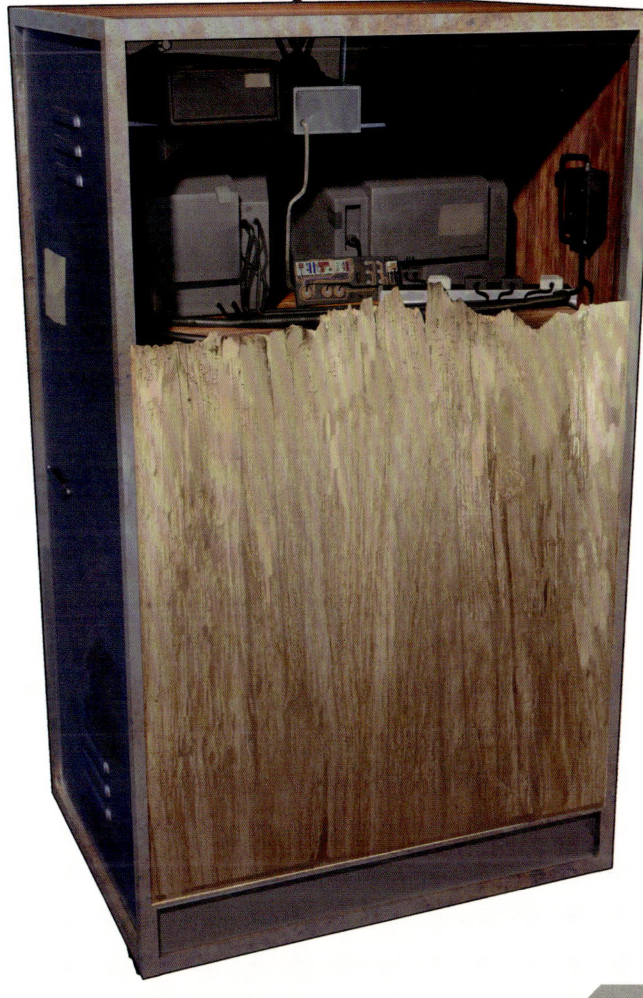

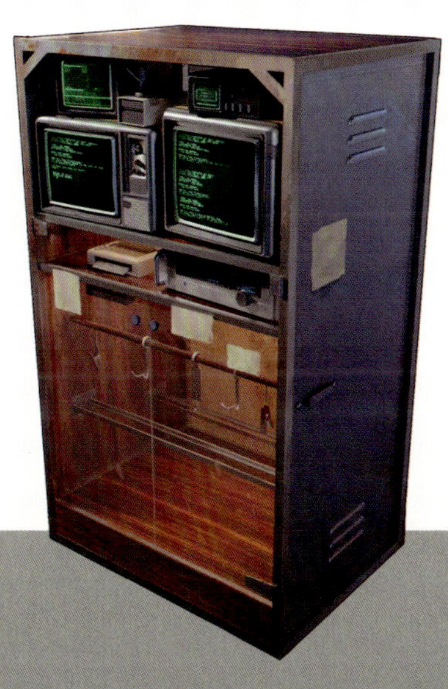

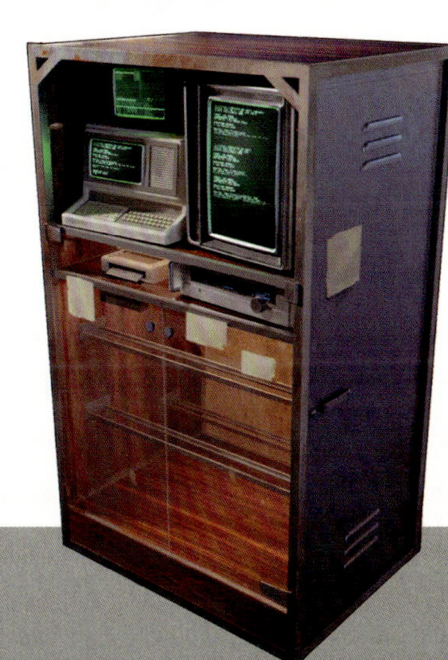

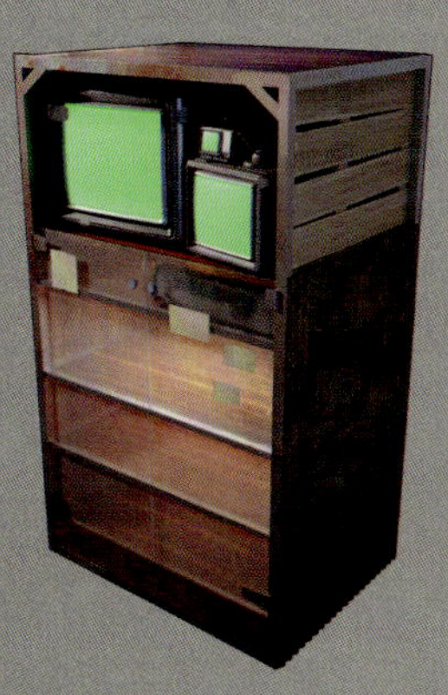

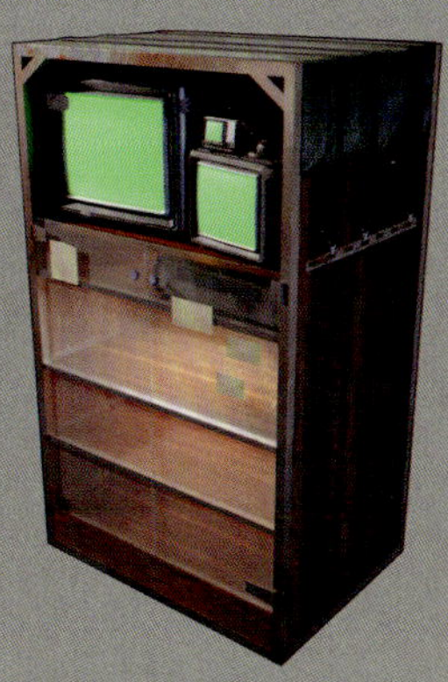

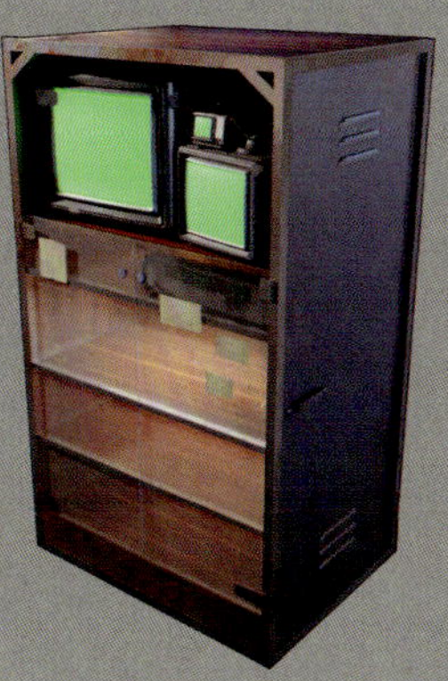

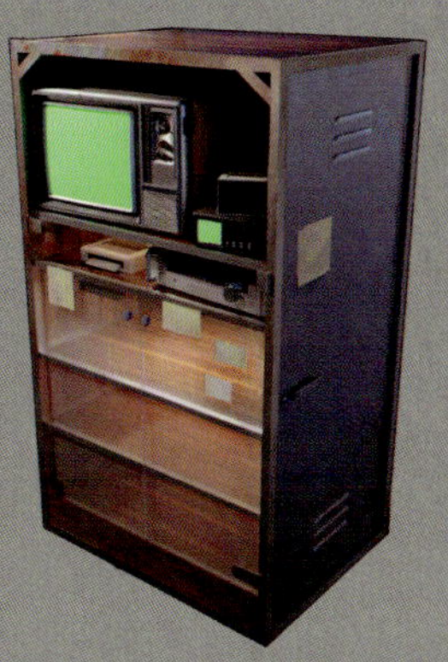

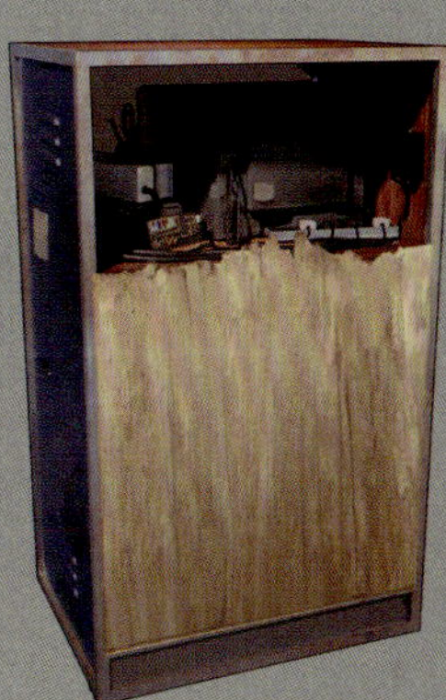

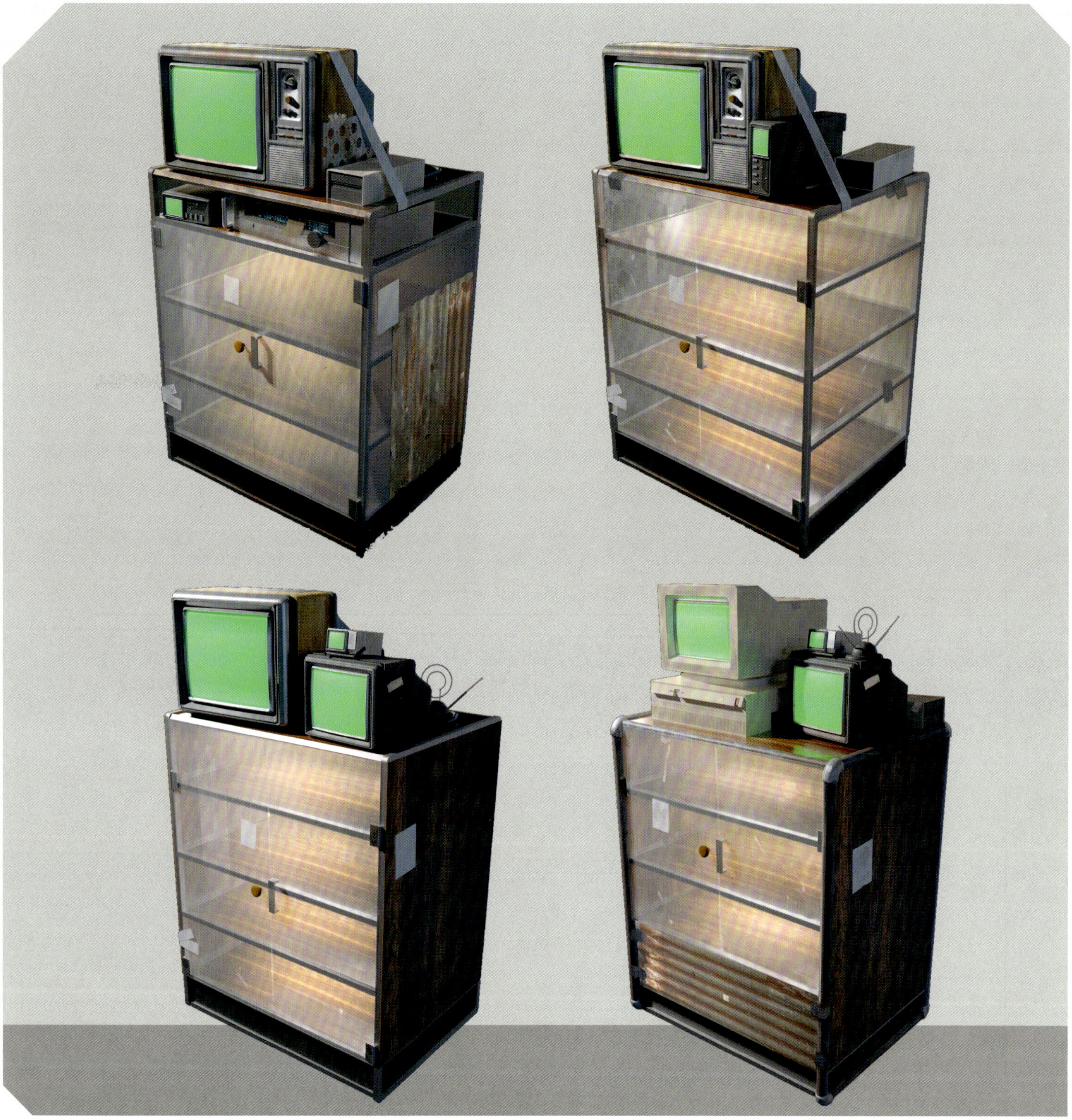

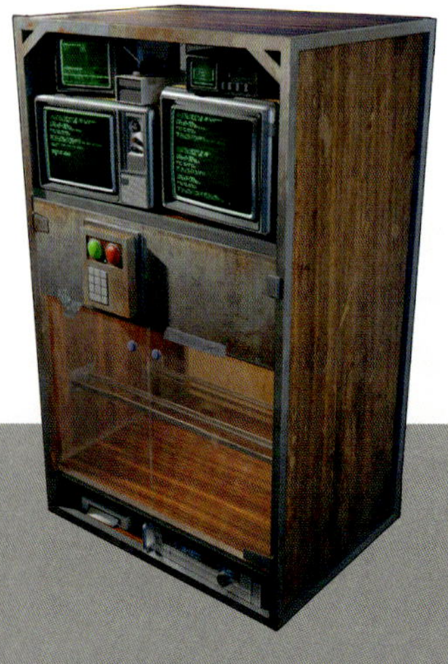
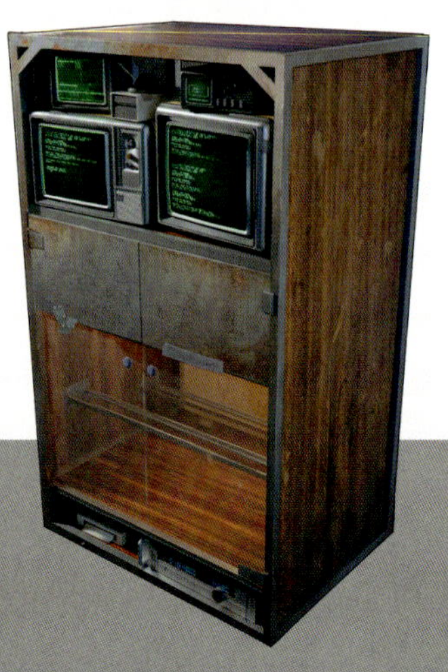
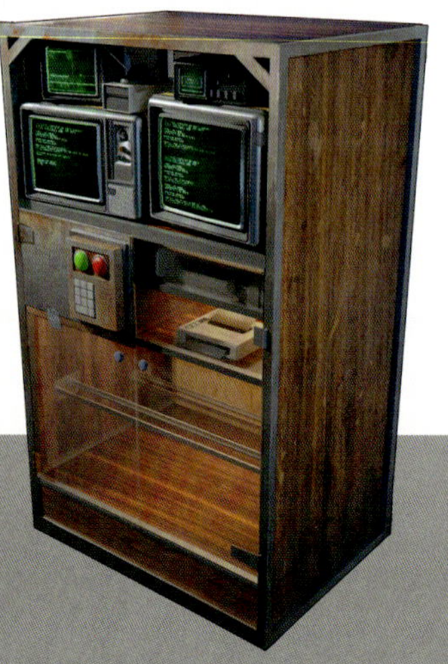
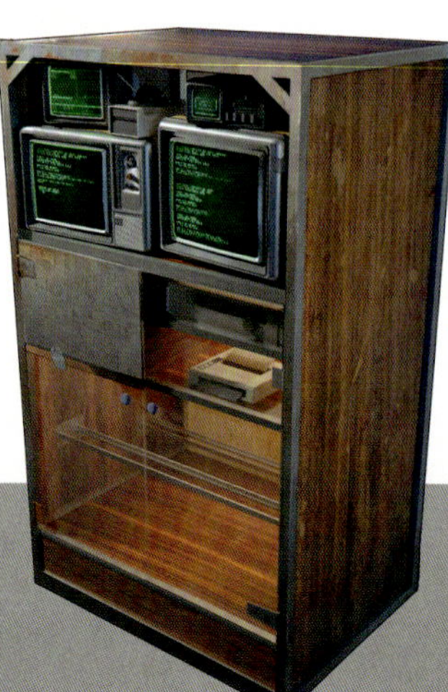

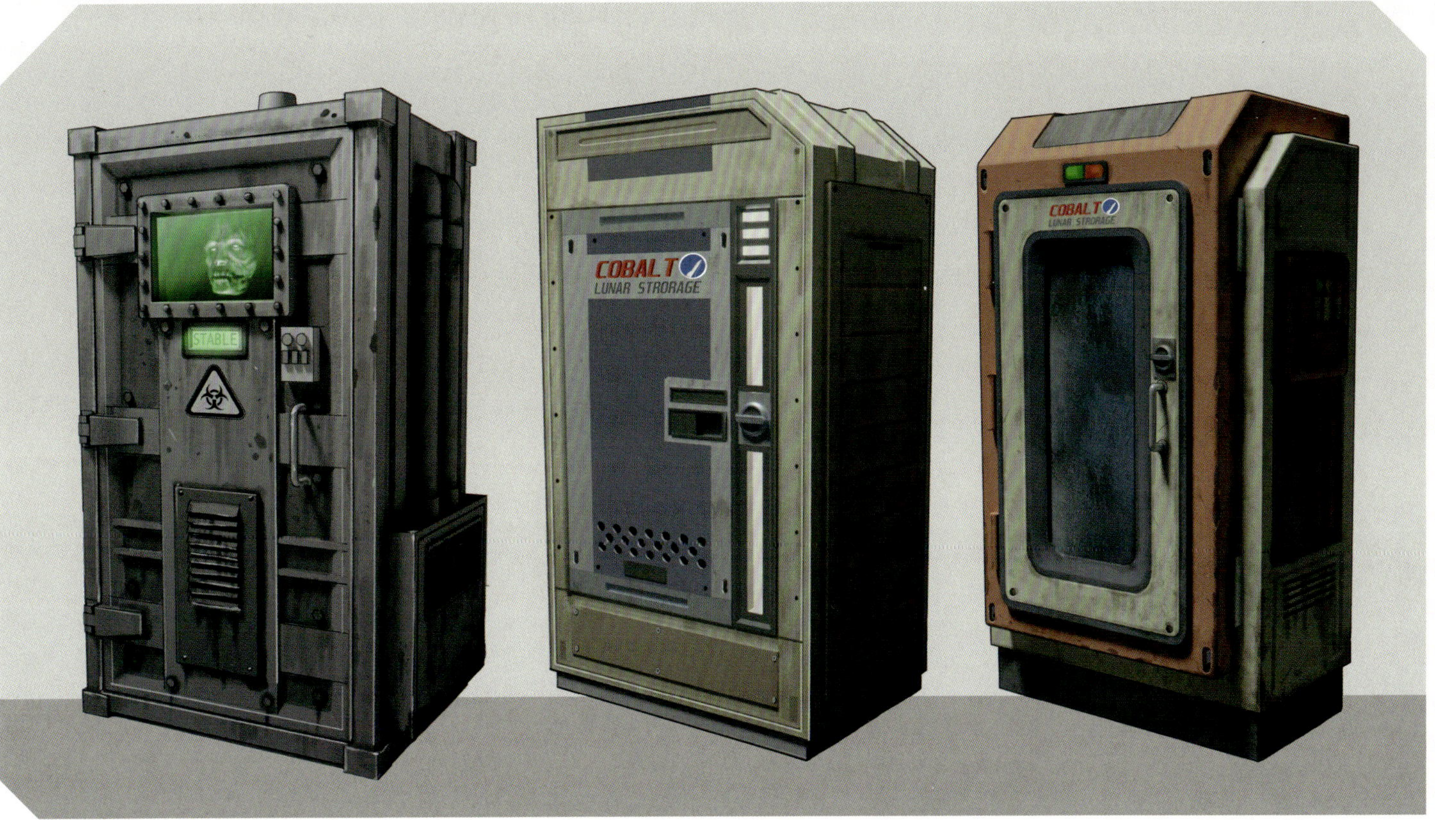

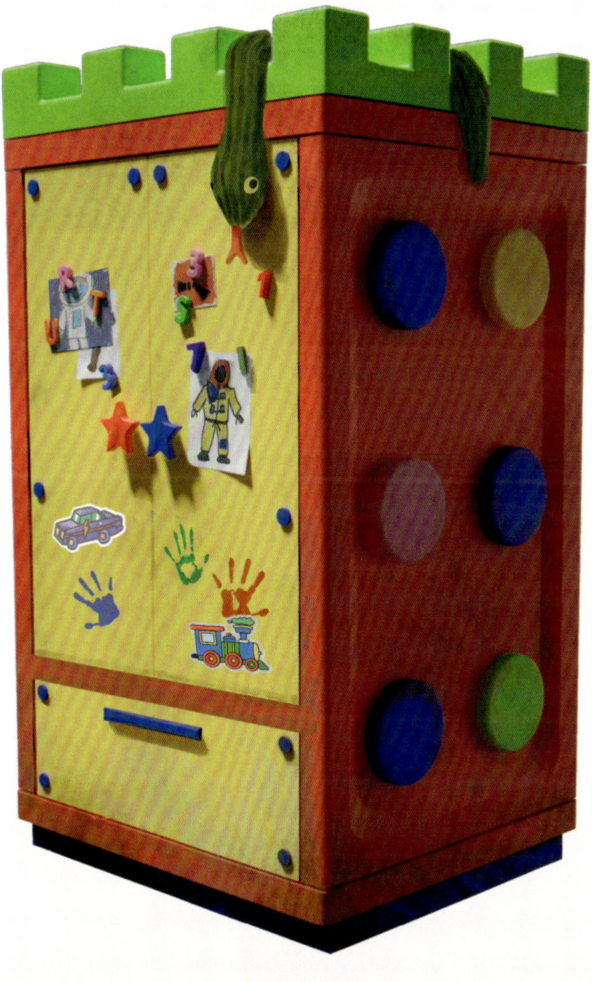

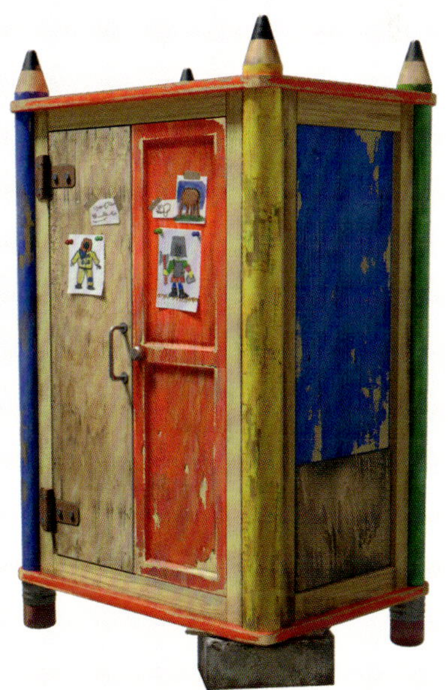

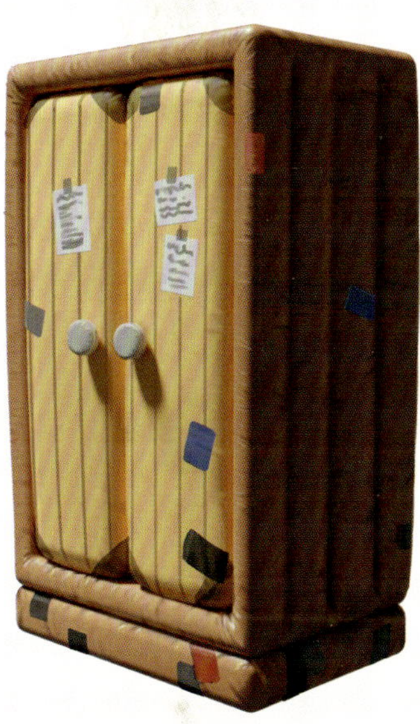

TOOL CUPBOARD VARIATIONS

While the default TC has a consistent appearance, skins and DLC variations have introduced alternate visual styles. These variations might include different exterior finishes, interior configurations, or small thematic changes. However, the core silhouette and function remain unchanged. Here are some concepts of some variations that were explored but didn't make it into the game.

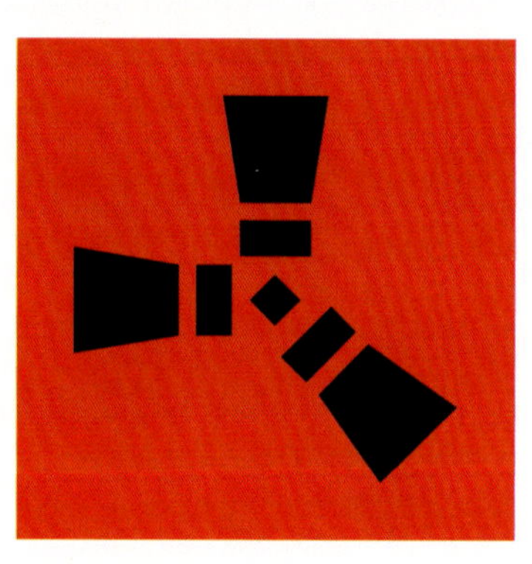